THE NORTHERN GOSHAWK: A TECHNICAL ASSESSMENT OF ITS STATUS, ECOLOGY, AND MANAGEMENT

Michael L. Morrison, Editor

Studies in Avian Biology No. 31

A PUBLICATION OF THE COOPER ORNITHOLOGICAL SOCIETY

Cover drawing by Joyce V. VanDeWater

STUDIES IN AVIAN BIOLOGY

Edited by

Carl D. Marti
Raptor Research Center
Boise State University
Boise, ID 83725

Studies in Avian Biology is a series of works too long for *The Condor*, published at irregular intervals by the Cooper Ornithological Society. Manuscripts for consideration should be submitted to the editor. Style and format should follow those of previous issues.

Price $23.00 including postage and handling. All orders cash in advance; make checks payable to Cooper Ornithological Society. Send orders to Cooper Ornithological Society, *c/o* Western Foundation of Vertebrate Zoology, 439 Calle San Pablo, Camarillo, CA 93010.

ISBN: 0-943610-68-0

Library of Congress Control Number: 2006924902
Printed at Cadmus Professional Communications, Ephrata, Pennsylvania 17522
Issued: 14 June 2006

DEDICATION

This volume is dedicated to the memory of Suzanne Meredith Joy whose passion for life was exemplified in her outstanding contributions to our understanding of the ecology, demography, and habitats of the Northern Goshawk on the Kaibab Plateau in Arizona.

CONTENTS

LIST OF AUTHORS

David E. Andersen
USGS Minnesota Cooperative Fish and Wildlife
Research Unit
Department of Fisheries, Wildlife, and Conservation Biology
University of Minnesota
St. Paul, MN 55108

Marc J. Bechard
Department of Biology
Boise State University
Boise, ID 83725

Trevor E. Becker
Biology Department
Southern Connecticut State University
New Haven, CT 06515
(Current address: 1481 Georges Hill Road, Southbury, CT
06488)

Clint W. Boal
U.S. Geological Survey
Texas Cooperative Fish and Wildlife Research Unit
Department of Range, Wildlife, and Fisheries Management
Texas Tech University
Lubbock, TX 79409-2120

Thomas Bosakowski
24 Third Street
Worcester, MA 01602

Douglas A. Boyce, Jr.
USDA Forest Service
Pacific Northwest Research Station
2770 Sherwood Lane, Suite 2A
Juneau, AK 99801-8545

Rob G. Bijlsma
Doldersummerweg 1
7983 LD Wapse
The Netherlands

Patrik Byholm
Bird Ecology Unit
Department of Ecology and Systematics
Division of Population Biology
University of Helsinki, P.O.Box 65
FIN-00014, Helsinki, Finland

Carlos Carroll
Klamath Center for Conservation Research
P. O. Box 104
Orleans, CA 95556

Sonya K. Daw
Southeast Utah Group
National Park Service
2282 SW Resource Boulevard
Moab, UT 84532

Steven M. Desimone
Washington Department of Fish and Wildlife
Forest Wildlife Unit, Wildlife Program
600 Capitol Way North
Olympia, WA 98501

Stephen DeStefano
USGS Massachusetts Cooperative Fish and Wildlife
Research Unit
Holdsworth Natural Resource Center
University of Massachusetts
Amherst, MA 01003

Frank I. Doyle
Wildlife Dynamics Consulting
Box 129
Telkwa, BC, V0J 2X0, Canada

Joseph E. Drennan
479 Bartlett Street
San Francisco, CA 94110

Graham D. Fairhurst
Department of Biology
Boise State University
Boise, ID 83725
(Current address: gdfair@gmail.com)

D. Michael Fry
Department of Animal Sciences
University of California
Davis, CA 95616

Russell T. Graham
USDA Forest Service
Rocky Mountain Research Station
1221 South Main Street
Moscow, ID 83843

Christina Hargis
USDA Forest Service
2500 S. Pine Knoll
Flagstaff, AZ 86001
(Present name: Christina Vojta)

Michael F. Ingraldi
Research Branch
Arizona Game and Fish Department
2221 West Greenway Road
Phoenix, AZ 85023

Suzanne M. Joy
deceased

Gregory S. Kaltenecker
Idaho Bird Observatory
Department of Biology
Boise State University
Boise, ID 83725

John J. Keane
Graduate Group in Ecology and Department of
Animal Sciences,
University of California
Davis, CA 95616
(Current address: Sierra Nevada Research Center, Pacific
Southwest Research Station, USDA Forest Service, 2121
Second Street, Suite A101, Davis, CA 95616)

PATRICIA L. KENNEDY
Eastern Oregon Agricultural Research Center and
Department of Fisheries and Wildlife
Oregon State University
P.O. Box E, 372 South 10th Street
Union, OR 97883

ROBERT E. KENWARD
Natural Environment Research Council Centre for
Ecology and Hydrology,
Winfrith Technology Centre,
Dorchester DT2 8ZD, United Kingdom

ERKKI KORPIMÄKI
Section of Ecology
Department of Biology
University of Turku
FIN-20014 Turku, Finland

MICK MARQUISS
Centre for Ecology and Hydrology
Banchory
Kincardineshire AB31 4BY, UK

CLINTON MCCARTHY
USDA Forest Service
Intermountain Region
Ogden, UT 84401

MICHAEL T. MCGRATH
Montana Department of Natural Resources and
Conservation
Southwestern Land Office
1401 27th Avenue
Missoula, MT 59804

MICHAEL L. MORRISON
Great Basin Institute
University of Nevada
Reno, NV 89557
(Current address: Department of Wildlife and Fisheries
Sciences, Texas A&M University, College Station, TX
77843-2258)

KATHLEEN M. PAULIN
USDA Forest Service
Ashley National Forest
Vernal, UT 84078

RICHARD T. REYNOLDS
USDA Forest Service
Rocky Mountain Research Station
2150 Centre Avenue, Suite 350, Building A
Fort Collins, CO 80526-1891

AIMEE M. ROBERSON
USDI Fish and Wildlife Service
New Mexico Ecological Services Field Office
2105 Osuna Road NE
Albuquerque, NM 87113-1001

RONALD L. RODRIGUEZ
USDA Forest Service
Dixie and Fish Lake National Forests
Cedar City, UT 84720

ANDI S. ROGERS
Arizona Game and Fish Department, Region II
3500 South Lake Mary Road
Flagstaff, AZ 86001

CHRISTIAN RUTZ
Department of Zoology
University of Oxford
South Parks Road
Oxford OX1 3PS, UK

SUSAN R. SALAFSKY
USDA Forest Service
Rocky Mountain Research Station
2150 Centre Avenue, Suite 350, Building A
Fort Collins, CO 80526-1891

DWIGHT G. SMITH
Biology Department
Southern Connecticut State University
New Haven, CT 06515

JOHN R. SQUIRES
USDA Forest Service
Rocky Mountain Research Station
Forestry Sciences Laboratory
P.O. Box 8089
Missoula, MT 59807

SARAH A. SONSTHAGEN
Department of Integrative Biology
Brigham Young University
Provo, UT 84602
(Current address: Department of Biology and Wildlife,
Institute of Arctic Biology, University of Alaska
Fairbanks, Alaska 99775)

RISTO TORNBERG
Department of Biology
University of Oulu, P.O.Box 3000
FIN-90014 Oulu, Finland

JARED UNDERWOOD
Department of Integrative Biology
Brigham Young University
Provo, UT 84602
(Current address: School of Life Sciences, Arizona State
University, Tempe AZ,
85287)

CLAYTON M. WHITE
Department of Integrative Biology
Brigham Young University
Provo, UT 84602

J. DAVID WIENS
USDA Forest Service
Rocky Mountain Research Station
2150 Centre Avenue, Suite 350, Building A
Fort Collins, CO 80526-1891

BRIAN WOODBRIDGE
USDI Fish and Wildlife Service
1829 South Oregon Street
Yreka, CA 96097

PUTTING STUDIES OF NORTH AMERICAN GOSHAWKS IN CONTEXT

ROBERT E. KENWARD

Writing the foreword for this collection of papers provides an opportunity to take stock of how research on the Northern Goshawk (*Accipiter gentilis*) has developed on both sides of the Atlantic Ocean. The first period of international overview of the Northern Goshawk was in 1980–1981. An early monograph on goshawks (Fischer 1980) was not easily accessible to western biologists, because it came from what was then East Germany. Moreover, the only English language text was in 60 of its 250 references. Most of the early quantitative studies of this species were published in German and Scandinavian languages (Hagen 1942, Holstein 1942, Brüll 1964; Höglund 1964a, b; Sulkava 1964).

However, by the late 1970s quantitative studies also originated from Britain and North America (McGowan 1975), including the first radio tracking of free-living hawks (Bendock 1975, Kenward 1976). These studies, and a need to make European material accessible in English, stimulated the collection of 21 papers for a symposium in Oxford titled *Understanding the Goshawk* (Kenward and Lindsay 1981a). The main topics were population trends (four papers), wild and domestic breeding (six), hunting behavior and predation (seven). Not one paper focused on features of the habitat.

Around 1980, rather little knowledge of Goshawks was crossing the Atlantic in either direction. In 1982, a remarkable raptor enthusiast, the late Richard Olendorff, provided search findings from a pioneering raptor management information system that he had just established. Among 139 references that mentioned goshawks in the text, including 23 that Olendorff considered substantially about goshawks, only six were also among the 250 in Fischer (1980).

Since about 1990, great interest in habitat requirements has developed in North America, as a result of attempts to use the Northern Goshawk as a flagship species for preserving old-growth forest. Useful reviews of the politics and resulting work were published by Reynolds et al. (1992), Squires and Reynolds (1997), Bosakowski (1999), Kennedy (2003) and in the proceedings of a goshawk symposium (Block et al. 1994). So is most work on Northern Goshawks now done west of the Atlantic?

This question can be best answered by examining publications in scientific journals, because books,

reports, and conference proceedings tend to be biased towards work in particular geographic areas. I searched the Raptor Information System (RIS) (<http://ris.wr.usgs.gov/> [24 February 2005]) for papers in scientific journals with Northern Goshawk in the title or keywords. Results were filtered for work in the wild (either in Europe or North America), to exclude conference proceedings and into two 15-yr periods to seek trends. In the 15 yr of forest interest since 1990, 147 journal papers included 85 (58%) from Europe, compared with 74 publications including 41 (55%) from Europe in the 1975–1989 period (Fig. 1a). Papers on goshawks doubled both in Europe and North America.

A new database of goshawk demography and feeding habits (Rutz et al., *this volume*) that traced citations from recent publications without using the RIS, suggests that the RIS may slightly underestimate European publications. In August 2004, the database included 174 references from 1975 onward with 108 (62%) from Europe. For North American work, 49 of 66 references (74%) were also in the RIS, compared with 36 of 108 (33%) for Europe (Fig. 1b).

So, research on goshawks remains very healthy east of the Atlantic, and it is good for the research in Europe to continue informing researchers in America, as Mike Morrison understood when he sought two review papers from Europe for this volume. It is also worth noting that the 972 citations for Northern Goshawk (title + keyword) in the RIS in July 2004 were not greatly exceeded by the 1,082 for Golden Eagle (*Aquila chrysaetos*), which was beaten only by Bald Eagle (*Haliaeetus leucocephalus*) (2,563) and Peregrine Falcon (*Falco peregrinus*) (1,442). A perfect bibliography might well give a citation bronze medal to studies of the Northern Goshawk.

In the 22 papers of this volume, the focus of research is more holistic than a decade earlier. Among 23 papers in Block et al. (1994), 10 had habitat issues in the title and were extensively concerned with where goshawks nest. Research now tends to emphasize how goshawks are performing in different situations rather than where they nest. In this volume, only four of the 22 papers have habitat in the title, and one of the four actually concentrates on habitats of goshawk prey. Joseph Drennan uses

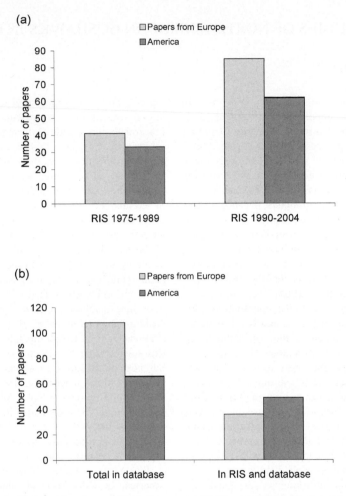

FIGURE. 1. The Raptor Information System (RIS) shows a parallel increase in goshawk publications in Europe and America (a) with European papers represented less than in a new database on demography and diet (b).

the diet of goshawks in the southwestern US and elsewhere to illustrate the converging requirements of predator and prey species. His prey-based approach illustrates why habitat use remains an important theme throughout this volume.

Two papers, one by Sarah Sonsthagen and the other by Jared Underwood, in each case with Ronald Rodriguez and Clayton White as co-authors, give data on habitats used by 42 adult female goshawks that were tracked by satellite in Utah between 2000 and 2003. Another paper by Carlos Carroll, Ronald Rodriguez, Clinton McCarthy, and Kathleen Paulin, is linked to these two by location (Utah) and use of remote sensing. These authors model the distribution of goshawk nests from satellite-mapped data on spatial resources, with reasonable out-of-area predictive ability and similarity to resource requirements of bears and wolves. These three papers from Utah,

with a fourth, by Sonsthagen, Rodriguez, and White on annual movements of the same satellite-tracked goshawks, will for many readers be the most remarkable in the volume. Goshawks seem not to have previously been tracked by satellite and certainly not in such numbers. In view of low tracking accuracy from the ARGOS system, differences in habitat use between seasons and between resident and migrant hawks are likely to be even more robust than results suggest, because significance levels are probably reduced by noise. However, the low accuracy will have overestimated home ranges. Moreover, 21 of the adult female hawks produced stationary, cold-transmitter readings before the following April and none among 11 survivors tracked the following summer reproduced successfully, which indicates a high impact of tags; such an impact may have biased movements and survival.

Another North American paper with a focus on habitat is by Stephen DeStefano, Michael McGrath, Steven Desimone, and Sonya Daw, on goshawks in inland Washington and Oregon. There they found weak tendencies for greatest persistence of nesting in areas that retained most forest with mid- and late seral stages, and productivity was lowest in one of three areas with least mammals in the diet. Moving further north, into Canada, Frank Doyle reviews evidence that mainland goshawks coexisting with abundant lagomorph populations may be little impacted by timber harvest, compared with hawks on islands with few lagomorphs. Another theme of this paper is that collection of robust data on nest density and productivity is likely to be more useful for monitoring goshawks than observing hawks in migration or in winter.

Similar comments on the need for robust reproductive data that are comparable across studies, and also on winter diet and foraging, are found in the paper by Clint Boal, David Andersen, Pat Kennedy, and Aimee Roberson. As well as reviewing nesting habitats, diet, and productivity in the Great Lakes region, these authors include data on home range, residency, and mortality for 28 breeding adult goshawks. Further eastward, the theme of describing nest habitat, productivity and diet is continued by Trevor Becker, Dwight Smith, and Thomas Bosakowski for 16 nests in Connecticut. Bosakowski and Smith provide similar data for goshawks in the nearby East Coast states of New York and New Jersey, which have been re-colonized following re-afforestation. In addition, the latter paper includes comments on migratory movements of goshawks in the eastern US.

Habitat change is also addressed by one of the two papers from Europe. Risto Tornberg, Erkki Korpimäki, and Patrik Byholm review 12 multi-year studies of breeding and winter ecology in Fennoscandia. From the nationwide counts of prey populations, there are indications that Goshawks may have subtle impacts on populations of their main prey, woodland grouse, especially because extensive radio tagging shows that healthy populations may contain many non-breeders. There is evidence of converse effects too, with variation in goshawk numbers and body-size linked to impacts on prey of recent changes in forest management.

Returning to the southwest of North America, four papers concentrate on seasonal and spatial variation in breeding biology. Andi Rogers, Michael Ingraldi, and Stephen DeStefano use video recording to show that although prey deliveries at 10 nest sites in Arizona declined after a peak at a nestling

age of 15–20 d, an increase in size of prey caused biomass per day to increase throughout the season. Marc Bechard, Graham Fairhurst, and Gregory Kaltenecker analyze 11 yr of data on occupancy and productivity for a study area in Nevada, compared to 10 yr of similar data from Idaho. They also provide records of natal dispersal movements and adult turnover. These are the longest data sets from North America in this volume.

From another multi-year study in the southwest US, Richard Reynolds and the late Suzanne Joy provide data on productivity, turnover, and survival of adult goshawks of both sexes on the Kaibab Plateau. Useful analytic techniques are introduced, including Mayfield estimates to correct late-finding bias, and distance thresholds to increase information from nearest-neighbor-distance analyses of nest spacing. In the fourth site-specific study, John Keane, Michael Morrison, and Michael Fry use 4 yr of data to indicate that large brood size in the California Sierra Nevada correlated with early laying and high pre-laying mean temperature, while abundance and frequency in goshawk diet of Douglas squirrels (*Tamiasciurus douglasii*) correlated with cone crops.

The remaining six papers are essentially reviews. At the end of the *Regional* section of the volume, Christian Rutz, Mick Marquiss, Rob Bijlsma, and I consider factors that may limit goshawk populations across Europe. We discuss why goshawks are more focussed on woodland and eating mammals in North America and note that goshawk colonization of European towns shows how well this species can adapt to habitat change. The creation of a database for the inter-continental comparisons raised issues of data standards. Such meta-analyses would be most robust if biologists always (1) climbed trees to assess productivity, (2) collected individual-unique prey remains in diet studies, (3) adopted in Europe the habitat measures used in North America (e.g. canopy cover in nest stands), (4) recorded nest density and percentage of forest in North American study areas, and (5) estimated mean nearest-neighbor nest distances in case these prove better than density for investigations of population variation in strongly heterogeneous landscapes.

In the last paper in the *Ecology* section of the volume, Richard Reynolds, Susan Salafsky, and David Wiens consider how goshawk populations are affected by predators, competitors, weather, and habitats for nesting, provisioning, and winter foraging. They concur, from the many recent studies of goshawks in North America, with results obtained earlier by studying goshawks in European habitats, namely that goshawks can be quite flexible in breeding habitat but require habitats good for prey populations and hunting them (Kenward and Widén 1989).

This sets the scene for the point at which work on goshawks in North America has gone beyond the situation in Europe, into monitoring and practical habitat planning for goshawk conservation, as described in the following *Management* section. At the start of this section, Christina Hargis and Brian Woodridge consider how goshawk populations could be monitored at the regional scale across North America. They propose standardized use of a broadcast acoustical survey during incubation and nestling periods, in 688 ha blocks at 5-yr intervals, to indicate change in presence of breeders for analysis in relation to covariates such as changing habitat.

In the final two papers, Richard Reynolds, Douglas Boyce, and Russell Graham, give a preliminary assessment of the ecosystem-based conservation strategy developed for goshawks in the southwestern US. Their principle is to conserve the whole food web as well as breeding and foraging habitats, by summing forest habitat elements required for nesting, foraging and the needs of four main prey species, and then planning to ensure an adequate proportion of each vegetation structure stages in the long term (which must be as much as 200 yr for the oldest trees). This principle is embedded in the management guidelines for the southwestern US that were adopted in 1992. These are considered in the second paper, in which Boyce leads a look at the status of goshawks on land managed by the USDA Forest Service. The management guidelines are now widely praised as a pioneering wildlife management initiative, developed by consensus of many interests for use in the wider countryside beyond reserves and management. Their interest in maintaining prey populations benefits other species than goshawks, including humans in that initiation of low-intensity

ground fires is recommended to clear inflammable debris and hence deter crown fires.

I have left a long introductory paper by John Squires and Pat Kennedy until last, because it includes all the topics of the others and yet goes beyond them. As the authors point out, it does not attempt to consider all the literature (especially from Europe) and passes lightly over issues that the authors have reviewed thoroughly elsewhere. However, it is the most comprehensive yet concise account of goshawk biology and politics in North America that is available in English.

The papers in this volume provide an excellent overview of the extensive recent work on goshawks in Europe and North America. On both continents, studies have evolved from the descriptive to the correlative, to multi-site, multi-year studies and now to compilations of data for meta-analyses. In Europe, population and predation studies have become more sophisticated through radio tagging and by using extensive data on prey demography. In North America, goshawk biologists are applying advanced remote sensing technology and linking goshawk conservation with silviculture. Differences between goshawks in Europe and North America continue to raise challenging questions, and Europeans continue to produce at least as many publications on the Northern Goshawk as their North American colleagues.

Ultimately, conservation of goshawks may benefit from many interests and subtle socio-economic approaches. For instance, might goshawks be as amenable as Peregrine Falcons to introduction by falconers for urban living? It may be hoped that innovations in the coming decade also include greater inter-continental liaison, to transfer data standards and understanding of how the Northern Goshawk and other species respond to changing land use.

Studies in Avian Biology No. 31:5–7

TOWARD A BETTER UNDERSTANDING OF THE NORTHERN GOSHAWK

MICHAEL L. MORRISON

WHY THIS ASSESSMENT?

The Northern Goshawk (*Accipiter gentilis*) is the largest member of the genus *Accipiter*, a group of hawks that contains 47 species worldwide. The Northern Goshawk occurs throughout the Holarctic region in wooded environments. Most species in this genus feed primarily on birds and mammals and frequent wooded environments.

Much controversy has arisen during the past several decades regarding the conservation status of the goshawk in North America. In the 1970s, concerns about the effects of forest management on nesting habitat of goshawks were raised in the western US (Reynolds 1971, Bartelt 1977). In the 1980s, further concerns were raised about the large foraging area beyond nest areas (Reynolds 1989, Crocker-Bedford 1990). Petitions to list the Northern Goshawk as threatened have been filed with the USDI Fish and Wildlife Service on several occasions. Although these petitions have been denied, they indicate the level of concern held by many regarding the status and trend of the population.

In response to concerns about the status of goshawk populations in the southwestern US, the Southwestern Region of the USDA Forest Service (USFS) assembled a goshawk scientific committee (GSC) in the fall of 1990. Composed of research and management scientists, the GSC was charged with developing forest management recommendations to protect and enhance goshawk habitat in order to conserve goshawk populations. The GSC produced a habitat conservation strategy entitled *Management recommendations for the Northern Goshawk in the southwestern United States* (Reynolds et al. 1992). This conservation strategy has now been applied on national forests in the Southwest. The management recommendations of Reynolds et al. (1992), however, were designed specifically for southwestern forests. Because important members of the suite of goshawk prey and the ecology of forests differ from one forest type to another, the management recommendations have limited applicability outside of the Southwest. Therefore, additional conservation strategies are needed for other regions and forest types within the range of the goshawk. Although the conceptual approach of Reynolds et al. (1992) is applicable to any system, ecological differences among forest types require that the approach be modified for each situation.

To help expand on the knowledge and recommendations contained in Reynolds et al. (1992), a symposium was held in 1993 to assess the status of the goshawk across North America. The resulting publication (Block et al. 1994) synthesized existing information through a series of contributions and made recommendations on management and additional research.

During the 10 yr since publication of Block et al. (1994) many studies have been conducted on the status, ecology, and conservation of the Northern Goshawk. Nevertheless, controversy continues regarding the status of the species, appropriate management and conservation strategies, and the proper legal status that should be applied. Reflecting the uncertainly surrounding the status of the goshawk, the Raptor Research Foundation, Inc., and The Wildlife Society formed a joint committee to review information regarding the status of the population in the contiguous US west of the 100th meridian. This committee published its findings in 2004, finding that existing data related to the goshawk population trend are inadequate to assess population trend west of the 100th meridian. They concluded that small samples, nests located through ad hoc sampling generally associated with management activities, and an inability to extrapolate results from local studies to the scale of the review area, limited the committee's ability to draw conclusions on population trend, genetic structure, and habitat relationships (Andersen et al. 2004).

As such, individuals with the USDA Forest Service, Rocky Mountain Research Station felt that scientists and managers alike would benefit from a compilation of papers that updated previous works and synthesized the current statue of knowledge on the species. All contributions were solicited by Richard Reynolds, William Block, and me to ensure that much of North America, including Canada, was included. In addition, I solicited several contributions from Europe so contrasts between the status and management of the species could be compared with North America. A few additional, relatively site-and-time specific studies were added after I was contacted by several researchers that learned of this project.

Thus, this document was prepared to expand beyond Reynolds et al. (1992), Block et al. (1994), and Anderson et al. (2004), and to assess the existing body of knowledge, and present a substantial amount of previously unpublished data on the biology and ecology of goshawks. Although this assessment does not provide comprehensive management recommendations for specific forest types, it does provide the background needed for identifying and synthesizing information on the use of habitats and prey by goshawks in different forests so that locally specific conservation strategies can be developed.

APPROACH AND SCOPE OF ASSESSMENT

The goal of this assessment is twofold—to amass existing knowledge on the distribution, abundance, biology, ecology, and habitat needs of the goshawk in North America, and to provide a framework for synthesizing this information in a manner that conservation strategies specific to regional and local forest types can be developed.

We were especially fortunate to have Robert Kenward prepare a detailed foreword that reviewed and synthesized all of the contributions in the volume. Given Kenward's extensive experience with the goshawk, his contribution substantially enhances the value of this volume.

This volume begins with a very detailed assessment of the current state of knowledge regarding goshawk ecology by Squires and Kennedy. They review and synthesize existing data, identify gaps in our knowledge, and provide suggestions on research and management directions. Squires and Kennedy expended considerable effort to bring this contribution together, and it sets an excellent framework for the papers that follow.

I divided the body of the volume into three major parts, entitled *Regional*, *Ecology*, and *Management*. As the name implies, the regional section presents papers dealing with the status and trends of goshawks across North America and Europe. Included in these papers are many large data sets that quantify demography and nesting ecology, dispersal, and other life history traits. The ecology section presents contributions that more narrowly focus on one or a few aspects of goshawk ecology, including prey consumption and foraging ecology and movements. As shown in these papers, the use of satellite telemetry is greatly enhancing our understanding of goshawk movements and habitat use. The management section provides guidance on how we can use the existing data to manage and conserve the species. In particular, Hargis and Woodbridge present a comprehensive design for monitoring goshawk populations at the bioregional scale, and Reynolds et al. develop an ecosystem-based strategy for conserving the species. The final chapter by Boyce et al. summarizes the state of knowledge on science and management of the Northern Goshawk.

Because of the controversy surrounding the status and management of the goshawk, I think it is valuable to briefly outline the review process used in this volume. I served as the review editor and obtained two peer reviews for all contributions; most reviews were obtained from scientists not involved with this volume. I then synthesized the review comments, provided additional comments, and returned the manuscripts to the author(s) for revision. Manuscripts were also sent through a thorough review of study design and statistical methods, conducted by qualified statisticians. The revised manuscripts, along with all review comments, were then forwarded to *Studies in Avian Biology* editor Carl Marti. Marti reviewed all of the materials, provided additional comments as he deemed necessary, and made the final decision on acceptance of all manuscripts. Thus, each paper has undergone a review process that exceeds that applied by most scientific journals.

This volume adds substantially to the existing knowledge of the Northern Goshawk and provides useful guidance for management and conservation of the species. Additionally, weaknesses in our understanding of the species are identified, and recommendations are made for closing the gap between what we know and what we need to know to ensure that the species is perpetuated.

ACKNOWLEDGMENTS

William Block is thanked for organizing the completion and funding of this volume; without his efforts this project would not have been completed. Support from Richard Holthausen was key in seeing this volume come to fruition. Funding was provided by the USDA Forest Service, Rocky Mountain Forest Research Station, Fort Collins, Colorado, and through the USDA Forest Service, Fish, National Wildlife, Fish and Rare Plants Office, Washington, DC. Richard Reynolds is thanked for making initial contacts with some of the contributors and helping to outline the contents. Carl Marti, is thanked for ensuring that all contributions met the high quality expected in *Studies in Avian Biology*. Joyce VanDeWater is thanked for preparing the cover artwork. The following individuals reviewed contributions to this volume: Elizabeth Ammon, David Anderson, Paul Beier, Dixie Birch, William Block, Tom Bosakowski, Jeff Brawn, Jimmy Cain, Cole Crocker-Bedford, Derick Craighead, Dick DeGraaf, Kate Engle, Sean Finn, Joe Ganey, Paul Hardy, Stacia Hoover, Mollie Hurt, Michael Kochert, Kevin Kritz, Amy Kuenzi, Don Lyons, Bill Mannan, Michael McGrath, Jean Morrison, Ian Newton, Vincenzo Penteriana, Dianna Queheillalt, Marty Raphael, Lourdes Rugge, Len Ruggerio, Shane Romsos, Steve Rosenstock, Vidar Selas, Helen Snyder, Karen Steenhof, Pat Ward, Brian Woodbridge, and Marico Yamasaki. Rudy King and Dave Turner provided statistical review of all manuscripts. Cecelia Valencia translated the abstracts into Spanish.

Studies in Avian Biology No. 31:8–62

NORTHERN GOSHAWK ECOLOGY: AN ASSESSMENT OF CURRENT KNOWLEDGE AND INFORMATION NEEDS FOR CONSERVATION AND MANAGEMENT

JOHN R. SQUIRES AND PATRICIA L. KENNEDY

Abstract. The contentious and litigious history associated with managing Northern Goshawks (*Accipiter gentilis*) has focused much research attention toward understanding this species' life history. Results from these studies address many key information needs that are useful to managers and decision makers, but many pressing information needs exist to address key conservation questions. Our goal was to assess the current state of knowledge in light of recent research. We focused on published information, but we also include unpublished studies if necessary to address key information needs. We included key European studies, for areas where there is little information for North American populations. Based on our assessment of current knowledge, we review goshawk conservation and management in terms of threats, ecological relationships; information needs, survey and monitoring, managing in the face of uncertainty, and the increasing demands for science-based management. We conclude by offering our understandings or qualified insights relative to some of the most salient issues confronting goshawk conservation and management.

Key Words: *Accipiter gentilis*, goshawk ecology, goshawk management, Northern Goshawk.

ECOLOGÍA DEL GAVILÁN AZOR: UNA VALORACIÓN DEL CONOCIMIENTO ACTUAL Y DE LAS NECESIDADES DE INFORMACIÓN PARA EL MANEJO Y LA CONSERVACIÓN

Resumen. La contenciosa y discordante historia asociada al manejo del Gavilán Azor *(Accipiter gentilis)* ha enfocado la atención de investigación hacia el entendimiento de la historia de la vida de esta especie. Los resultados de estos estudios dirigen mucha información clave necesaria que es útil para administradores y los tomadores de dediciones, sin embargo, existen muchas necesidades urgentes de información, para dirigir preguntas clave. Nuestro objetivo fue valorar el estado actual del conocimiento sobre investigación reciente. Nos enfocamos en información publicada, pero también incluimos estudios no publicados si era necesario, para dirigir necesidades de información clave. Incluimos estudios Europeos clave, para áreas donde existe poca información para poblaciones de Norte América. Basados en nuestra valoración del conocimiento actual, revisamos la conservación y el manejo del gavilán, en términos de amenazas , relaciones ecológicas, necesidades de información, estudio y monitoreo, incertidumbre en el manejo, y en las crecientes demandas por el manejo basado en la ciencia. Concluimos ofreciendo nuestros conocimientos o ideas relacionadas a algunas de las cuestiones más sobresalientes enfrentadas en la conservación y el manejo del gavilán.

Since the early 1980s, researchers have investigated how forest management impacts Northern Goshawk (*Accipiter gentilis,* hereafter referred to as goshawk) populations (Reynolds et al. 1982, Moore and Henny 1983, Reynolds 1983). Crocker-Bedford's (1990) contention that goshawk populations in the Southwest were dropping precipitously catalyzed state and federal agencies to begin research programs. The goshawk has been proposed for listing several times under the Endangered Species Act (ESA) and its status has been, and still is, the object of considerable litigation (Peck 2000).

Many aspects of goshawk ecology are poorly understood putting decision-makers in the difficult position of having to make important management decisions based on incomplete information. Increasingly, decision-makers are also being asked via the courts and public opinion to define what is defensible information given our limited knowledge and high uncertainty regarding many aspects of goshawk ecology. The primary goal of this paper is two-fold. First, we provide a thorough literature review of goshawk ecology to define our current state of knowledge. Second, based on these understandings, we discuss pressing management issues and information needs. This second goal also includes discussions of data quality standards because they help define defensible information that in turn affects goshawk research and management. We conclude by providing qualified insights which are an attempt to embrace science while

8

recognizing uncertainty (Ruggiero et al. 2000). Qualified insights are specific statements that are backed by the balance of scientific evidence (Ruggiero and McKelvey 2000); these statements help communicate to land managers and decision makers the critical issues in a distilled format.

To describe our current state of knowledge, we drew primarily from the recent reviews of Squires and Reynolds (1997) and Kennedy (2003) and updated these reviews with new information. Not all publications on goshawks were referenced in this assessment, nor were all published material considered equally reliable. Literature that was not included does not mean these studies were inferior scientifically. Rather, the results were not directly relevant to our assessing the current state of knowledge relative to management and conservation. We preferentially referenced peer-reviewed literature because this is the accepted standard in science. Non-refereed publications or reports were regarded with greater skepticism, but were included if these papers addressed important information gaps not reported in published literature. Moreover, we recognize that researchers in Europe have many important insights regarding this species, but we do not know how well these understandings can be generalized to North American populations. Thus, we included European publications that were particularly relevant to important information gaps, but we did not exhaustively review studies outside North America. Further, we downplayed certain topics that are important, but were either too extensive to cover in this paper or were better addressed in a different format. For example, we did not rigorously discuss the ecology of individual prey species nor did we discuss the forest ecology associated with the many habitat types used by goshawk. We minimized our discussions of distribution and systematics because this was reviewed in Squires and Reynolds (1997) and little new published information is available on this topic. We also did not discuss field identification due to the many excellent field guides that provide a better format (Wheeler and Clark 1995, Wheeler 2003). Finally, in reporting the current state of knowledge, we could not conduct a comprehensive meta-analysis of goshawk literature nor did we conduct new analyses aimed at addressing conservation concerns. For example, we did not examine current federal land management plans to discern the direction of forest management relative to goshawks, nor did we analyze geographic information systems (GIS) and other spatial data to assess habitat trends like changes in the abundance and spatial arrangement of mature forests. Thus, we only discuss key conservation issues and information needs based on the current state of knowledge and our collective experience researching goshawks.

DISTRIBUTION AND SYSTEMATICS

SUBSPECIES IN NORTH AMERICA

Approximately 8–12 subspecies of goshawks exist worldwide depending on the taxonomic source (Brown and Amadon 1968, del Hoyo et al. 1994, Squires and Reynolds 1997). Although some authorities recognize three subspecies in North America (Johnsgard 1990), the American Ornithologists' Union (1998) recognizes only two—*A. g. atricapillus* and *A. g. laingi*. *A. g. atricapillus* breeds throughout Alaska, Canada, and the mountains of the western and eastern US. *A. g. laingi*, breeds on Queen Charlotte and Vancouver Islands (Taverner 1940, Johnson 1989), possibly extending north to Baranof Island in southeast Alaska or Prince William Sound in south-central Alaska (Webster 1988, Iverson et al. 1996, Cooper and Stevens 2000). A third subspecies, *A. g. apache*, is not recognized by the AOU as a legitimate subspecies, but its putative distribution is from southern Arizona south to Jalisco in the mountains of Mexico (van Rossem 1938). The USDI Fish and Wildlife Service (USFWS) (USDI Fish and Wildlife Service 1998a) considers the validity of this subspecies to be unresolved; *A. g. apache* is recognized by some scientists (Snyder and Snyder 1991, Whaley and White 1994). The Eurasian subspecies (*A. g. gentilis*) is larger in size and body weight than any of the North American subspecies (del Hoyo et al. 1994).

NORTH AMERICAN BREEDING DISTRIBUTION

In North America, *A. g. atricapillus* breeds from boreal forests of north-central Alaska to Newfoundland and south to western and southwestern montane forests in the US, and locally in the mountains of northwestern and western Mexico (Fig. 1). In central to eastern North America, goshawks breed in the western Great Lakes region and eastward to Pennsylvania, central New York, northwestern Connecticut, and locally south in montane habitats at least to West Virginia and possibly eastern Tennessee and western North Carolina (Brown and Amadon 1968, Squires and Reynolds 1997, USDI Fish and Wildlife Service 1998a). Factors that limit the southern extent of the goshawk range are unknown (Kennedy 1997).

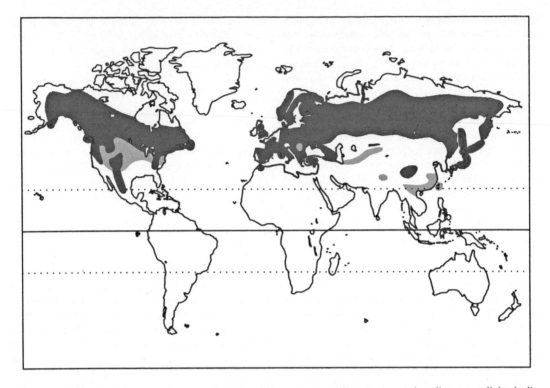

FIGURE 1. Global distribution of the Northern Goshawk. Dark shading delineates current breeding range; light shading indicates areas occupied by goshawks outside the breeding season or in areas where breeding has not yet been documented (from del Hoyo et. al. 1994).

Although few data exist regarding historical changes, Squires and Reynolds (1997) suggested the distribution of the goshawk in the northern and western portions of its range is relatively unchanged since Europeans settled North America. However, the goshawk's range may have been more widespread in the eastern US before the extinction of the Passenger Pigeon (*Ectopistes migratorius*) in the early 1900s, because the pigeon may have been an important prey species. The goshawk's range may also have been more extensive before the substantial deforestation of this region, which reached a peak at the end of the 19th century (Kennedy 1997). Some evidence suggests these populations may be recovering as forests re-establish and mature (Speiser and Bosakowski 1984, Kennedy 1997). For example, during the mid-1950s in Massachusetts, nesting was restricted to the western part of the state, but the species now nests throughout the state (Veit and Petersen 1993). In Minnesota and Wisconsin, the goshawk is currently nesting in more counties then was documented historically (Janssen 1987, Rosenfield et al. 1998, Roberson et al. 2003). Evidence that eastern goshawk populations may be expanding or reoccupying their former range should be interpreted cautiously; such reports could merely reflect increased search efforts (Kennedy 1997).

NORTH AMERICAN WINTER DISTRIBUTION

Goshawks winter throughout their breeding range, extending south to southern California (Small 1994, Squires and Reynolds 1997) and northern and central Mexico (Sonora, Sinaloa, Durango, and Chihuahua). Wintering goshawks are occasionally observed in the lower Colorado River valley of Arizona (Rosenberg et al. 1991), northern and central Texas (Oberholser 1974), and north to Arkansas (James and Neal 1986). During incursion years, a few recorded sightings of goshawks were documented for Missouri (Robbins and Easterla 1992), in the Appalachian Mountains of Tennessee (Robinson 1990), and east to the Atlantic Ocean (Root 1988, American Ornithologists' Union 1998). Christmas Bird Count (CBC) data suggest goshawks generally avoid wintering in southeastern North America (Root 1988), but occasionally winter in northern portions of the Gulf States, including west-central Florida (American Ornithologists' Union 1998).

LEGAL AND ADMINISTRATIVE STATUS IN THE UNITED STATES

History of Goshawk Litigation

Accipiter gentilis atricapillus

Based on findings of Crocker-Bedford (1990) and unpublished research conducted on the Kaibab National Forest in Arizona, environmental organizations sought more extensive protection of goshawk habitat. They thought that current logging practices threatened goshawk viability and thus, violated the National Forest Management Act (NFMA) (Peck 2000). This resulted in a series of legal actions that extend from 1990, when environmental groups first formally requested the Southwestern Region (Region 3) of the USDA Forest Service (USFS) to halt timber harvest in southwestern forests on the Kaibab Plateau, to the present time (Table 1). A goshawk scientific committee (GSC) and a goshawk task force were formed to review goshawk management needs in the Southwest Region of USFS. The GSC produced the *Management Guidelines for the Northern Goshawk in the Southwestern Region* that provides the current basis for goshawk management in this USFS Region (Reynolds et al. 1992).

In September 1991, the USFWS was petitioned to list the goshawk as endangered west of the 100th meridian, and later was listed as a candidate, or category 2 species, under the ESA (Table 1). In June 1992, the petition was denied on taxonomic grounds (no evidence suggests that goshawks west of the 100th meridian are a distinct population), and suits were subsequently filed to reverse the action. From this, the courts claimed the USFWS's findings were arbitrary and capricious and ordered the agency to issue another decision. In 1996, the USFWS issued another decision again denying listing based on taxonomic reasons and the courts again did not support this decision. Thus, in 1997 the USFWS issued a positive 90-d finding that sufficient evidence existed to warrant a status review. They completed their status review in 1998 and concluded there was insufficient evidence to support listing the goshawk under the ESA. This decision has been supported by the courts (Center for Biological Diversity vs USFWS No. 01-35829 [Ninth Circuit Court Decision CV-99-00287-FR issued 21 July 2003]). Also, a recent technical review of this decision by a joint committee of scientists from The Raptor Research Foundation (RRF) and The Wildlife Society (TWS) (Andersen et al. 2005) found that available habitat and demographic information are not sufficient to evaluate goshawk demographic trends.

The USFWS based its decision not to list the goshawk on a review of existing data and the findings of a status review team of nine biologists (including two USFS biologists). The status review team found it was not possible to determine whether goshawk population numbers in the review area were stable, increasing, or decreasing, and concluded the distribution of breeding goshawks in the West did not appear to have changed from the historical range. The USFWS also concluded the goshawk is a forest habitat generalist and is not dependent solely on old-growth forests.

In 1995, the Southwestern Region of the USFS (Region 3) issued an environmental impact statement (EIS) to modify its forest plans to incorporate the Reynolds et al. (1992) goshawk guidelines. The final EIS (FEIS) claims the goshawk is a habitat generalist and this claim was challenged by a consortium of conservation groups, individuals, and state agencies. In November 2003, the U.S. Ninth Circuit Court of Appeals ruled the USFS had inadequately disclosed responsible scientific opposition in preparing the final environmental impact statement for southwestern forests. The court recently reversed and remanded the decision stating the EIS violated the National Environmental Policy Act (NEPA) because it did not review the opposing scientific information that indicated the goshawk was a habitat specialist (Center for Biological Diversity and Sierra Club v. U.S. Forest Service, No.02-16481 [9th Circuit Court opinion No. CV-00-01711-RCB issued 18 November 2003]). The USFS has written a Draft Supplement to the FEIS evaluating the scientific debate over goshawk habitat preferences. The public comment period on the Draft Supplement closed November 2004. Interestingly, the recent RRF-TWS review of the USFWS decision (Andersen et al. 2005) concluded goshawks use late-successional forests in almost all landscapes where they have been studied. However, they also concluded the species demonstrates considerable versatility in habitat use, and thus, assessing its status based solely on the distribution of late successional forest is not warranted based on the current understanding of goshawk-habitat relationships.

Accipiter gentilis laingi

In May, 1994, a petition was filed to list the Queen Charlotte subspecies as endangered under the ESA (Table 2). Twelve months later, the USFWS decided the listing was not warranted. The USFWS acknowledged that continued large-scale removal of old-growth forest in the Tongass National Forest

TABLE 1. THE HISTORY OF LEGAL AND ADMINISTRATIVE ACTIONS RELATIVE TO THE STATUS AND MANAGEMENT OF NORTHERN GOSHAWKS IN THE UNITED STATES (ADAPTED FROM KENNEDY 2003).

Date	Legal or administrative action
February 1990	Formal request to Region 3 regional forester to suspend all harvesting in goshawk territories until long-term survival was assured.
August 1990	Region 3 regional forester organized a goshawk scientific committee (GSC) and goshawk task force (GTF) to review goshawk management needs in USFS Region 3.
September 1991	Petition filed to list the goshawk (*A. g. atricapillus*) as endangered west of 100th meridian.
January 1992	The goshawk (all subspecies) was listed as a candidate species (category 2) for possible future listing under the ESA throughout its range in the US. Category 2 species were those species for which there was inadequate data to justify a listing proposal under ESA at that time.
	The USFWS issued a 90-d finding that the petition did not present substantial information to indicate the goshawk in the western US should be listed. However, the USFWS concluded that the the petition presented substantial information indicating that goshawk population declines and loss or modification of habitat may be occurring. Therefore, the USFWS initiated a status review for the goshawk throughout its range in the U. S. They specifically solicited information to be used to evaluate the potential for distinct population segments within the range of the goshawk.
	GSC produced the Management Guidelines for the Northern Goshawk in the Southwestern Region (Reynolds et al. 1992).
June 1992	USFWS issued a 90-d finding that the petition did not present substantial information to indicate the goshawk in the western US should be listed (57 FR 474). The USFWS found that the petition presented no evidence of reproductive isolation or genetic differentiation between the western and eastern goshawk populations. They also concluded that goshawk habitat was contiguous throughout North America.
1992–1995	Reynolds et al. (1992) generated intense controversy. The focus of the controversy was whether or not the goshawk was a forest generalist. Reynolds et al. (1992) claimed goshawk populations were regulated by prey availability and that data suggest the goshawk is a prey generalist and thus, hunts in heterogeneous landscapes. The opposing state agencies and environmental groups claimed (without any supporting data) the goshawk was an old-growth obligate. Other concerns are detailed in Peck (2000).
1996	Region 3 regional forester issued a record of decision (ROD) to amend all regional forest plans to include the Reynolds et al. (1992) guidelines as well as recommendations from the Mexican Spotted Owl. This ROD is to be in effect for 5–10 yr until the forest plans are revised (scheduled to be completed by 2003) (Cartwright 1996). This is the only region to implement Reynolds et al. (1992) on a regional basis.
February 1996	The U.S. District Court found the June 1992 finding to be arbitrary and capricious, and remanded the finding to the USFWS for a new 90-d determination [926 F. Supp. 920 (D. Ariz. 1996)].
June 1996	USFWS issues a second 90-d finding, again determining the petition does not present substantial information that listing the goshawk in the western US may be warranted (61 FR 28834-35).
September 1996	Suit filed to overturn denial.
June 1997	Court overturns second 90-d finding as arbitrary and capricious, also finding the USFWS national policy on listing populations to be illegal (980 F. Supp. 1080 [D. Ariz. 1997]). The USFWS final policy on distinct population segments (DPS) allowed for only one subspecies per distinct population segment. The USFWS claimed, in the 1997 phase of the litigation, that there were three subspecies of Northern Goshawk west of the 100th meridian, (1) *A.g. atricapillus*, (2) *A.g. laingi*, and (3) *A.g. apache*. The court found this aspect of the DPS policy arbitrary and capricious because the ESA specifically states that in the definition of species, a species may include any subspecies and any distinct population segments of any species. If congress had intended a DPS contain only one subspecies, it would have allowed only the listing of DPSs of subspecies. The court then remanded the case back to the USFWS, which led to the positive 90-d finding in September 1997 (Ellen Paul, Executive Director, Ornithological Council, pers. comm.).
September 1997	USFWS issues a positive 90-d finding on western petition (62 FR 50892). It was then required to conduct a full status review by June 1998.
	Candidate status dropped. Prior to 1997, the USFWS maintained a category 2 list that included species whose status was unknown but of concern due to declines in population trend or habitat. These were also referred to as candidate species. Thus, the goshawk was no longer considered a candidate for listing due to the lack of information supporting a proposed rule (M. Nelson, Chief, Branch of Candidate Conservation, USFWS, pers. comm.).

TABLE 1. CONTINUED.

Date	Legal or administrative action
June 1998	USFWS issues negative 12-mo finding, finding the petition to list the goshawk in the western US as not warranted. (63 FR 35183). See summary of these findings in the text.
February 1999	Suit filed to overturn June 1998 90-d finding.
May 2000	Suit filed against the Sitgreaves National Forest to halt a timber sale which contained 5 of the 42 known goshawk territories on this forest (Center for Biological Diversity v. Bedell U. S. District Court, District of Arizona case No. 3:00-cv-00849-SLV). The suit alleged that the goshawk population on the Sitgreaves is in serious decline and would be extripated in 40 yr if it was a closed population. This case was dropped in 2002 after the parties reached an agreement with the USFS.
September 2000	Suit filed to challenge logging on 3,240,000 ha of forest in the Southwest (Center for Biological Diversity v. Bosworth Civil-01711-PHX-RCB, U. S. District Court, District of Arizona). The plaintiffs have asked for an injunction on logging within goshawk habitat on 11 Arizona and New Mexico national forests until the USFS prepares a new goshawk conservation plan.
June 2001	The USFWS's decision not to list the goshawk as a threatened or endangered species was upheld by a federal judge, who found the USFWS's decision not arbitrary and capricious (U.S. District Court, District of Oregon, Civil No. 99-287-FR).
November 2003	U. S. Ninth Circuit Court of Appeals ruled the USFS had inadequately disclosed responsible scientific opposition in preparing the final environmental impact statement for southwestern forests. The Court recently reversed and remanded the decision stating the EIS violated NEPA because it did not review the opposing scientific information that indicated the goshawk was a habitat specialist (Center for Biological Diversity and Sierra Club v. U.S. Forest Service, No.02-16481 (9th Circuit Court opinion No. CV-00-01711-RCB). Case was sent back to district court.
September 2004	The USFS, Southwestern Region has prepared a draft supplement to the final EIS for amendment of forest plans in Arizona and New Mexico to disclose, review and assess scientific arguments challenging the agency's conclusions over goshawk habitat preferences. The supplement will update the final EIS, which amended the 11 forest plans in the Southwesten Region for goshawks. Public comment period closed November 2004. No further updates are available.

would adversely affect the Queen Charlotte Goshawk in southeast Alaska, but that revised land-use strategies would ensure goshawk habitat conservation. Thus, the USFWS believed the proposed actions to protect goshawks would preclude the need for listing. In September 1996, the U.S. District Court (District of Columbia) remanded the 12-mo finding to the Secretary of Interior, instructing him to reconsider the determination "on the basis of the current forest plan, and status of the goshawk and its habitat, as they stand today." In May 1997, the USFS revised the Tongass Land Management Plan, and the USFWS was granted a 90-d extension to reevaluate the status of the goshawk under the new plan. In April 1998, a suit was filed to overturn the USFWS's refusal to list the Queen Charlotte Goshawk as an endangered species. In August of that year, the U.S. District Court overruled the USFWS's decision not to list the Queen Charlotte Goshawk on the basis that the agency did not use the best available science. However, the U.S. Ninth Circuit Court stated in June 2000 that the district court had exceeded its authority in ordering the government to conduct a population count, stating that the district court is to only consider if the USFWS used the best available science. In May 2004, the U.S. District Court ordered the USFWS to determine if the

Queen Charlotte Goshawk is endangered or threatened on Queen Charlotte Island. In December 2005, USFWS requested public comments on the status of the Queen Charlotte Goshawk throughout its range. This comment period closed February 2006.

In summary, over a decade of litigation over the federal status of *A. g. laingi* and *A. g. atricapillus* has been conducted, respectively. No changes in listing status have resulted from this litigation.

SENSITIVE SPECIES DESIGNATION

The goshawk is listed as a species of concern in all regions of the USFWS and is on the USFS sensitive species list for all regions. The Bureau of Land Management (BLM) lists the goshawk as a sensitive species in six states.

USDA FOREST SERVICE, REGION 3 GUIDELINES FOR SOUTHWESTERN FORESTS AND OTHER MANAGEMENT PLANS

As mentioned in the previous section, the GSC, as assembled by the USFS's Southwestern Region, completed a document in 1992 titled *Management Recommendations for the Northern Goshawk in the*

TABLE 2. THE HISTORY OF LEGAL AND ADMINISTRATIVE ACTIONS RELATIVE TO THE STATUS AND MANAGEMENT OF THE QUEEN CHARLOTTE SUBSPECIES OF NORTHERN GOSHAWKS (*A. G. LAINGI*) IN THE UNITED STATES (ADAPTED FROM KENNEDY 2003).

Date	Legal or administrative action
May 1994	Petition filed to list the Queen Charlotte Goshawk (*A. g. laingi*) as endangered. The petition was based largely upon potential present and impending impacts to the Queen Charlotte Goshawk caused by timber harvest in the Tongass National Forest.
August 1994	USFWS published a positive 90-d finding (59 FR 44124) stating substantial information was presented in the petition indicating the requested action may be warranted.
May 1995	After a 12-mo status review, USFWS decided listing was not warranted (60 FR 33784). In the 12-mo finding, the USFWS acknowledged that continued large-scale removal of old-growth forest in the Tongass National Forest would result in significant adverse effects on the Queen Charlotte goshawk in southeast Alaska; however, at that time the USFS was revising land use strategies to ensure goshawk habitat conservation. The USFWS believed the proposed actions to protect goshawks would preclude the need for listing.
November 1995	Suit filed against the Department of the Interior and the USFWS for their refusal to list the Queen Charlotte goshawk or designate critical habitat [U.S. District Court, District of Columbia (95-cv-02138-SS)].
September 1996	The U.S. District Court remanded the 12-mo finding to the Secretary of Interior, instructing him to reconsider the determination "on the basis of the current forest plan, and status of the goshawk and its habitat, as they stand today." [Southwest Center for Biological Diversity v. Babbitt, 939 F. Supp. 49, 50 (D.D.C. 1996)]
December 1996	USFWS reopens comment period (61 FR 64497) to gather all new information for review. It was extended until 4April 1997 through three subsequent notices (61 FR 69065, 62 FR 6930, and 62 FR 14662). The USFWS has reevaluated the petition and the literature cited in the petition, reviewed the Tongass Land Management Plan and other available literature and information, and consulted with biologists and researchers knowledgeable of northern goshawks in general, and the Queen Charlotte Goshawk in particular. The 1979 Tongass National Forest Land Management Plan, as amended, formed the basis for evaluating the status of the goshawk on the Tongass National Forest.
May 1997	The USFS issued a revised Tongass Land Management Plan. Consequently, the review of the 1979 Tongass Land Management Plan no longer represented the current plan as specified by the court ruling. The USFWS was, therefore, granted a 90-d extension to reevaluate the status of the goshawk under the provisions of the 1997 Tongass Land Management Plan
June 1997	USFWS re-extends comment period.
September 1997	USFWS again finds that a listing of the subspecies is not warranted (62 FR 46710)
April 1998	Suit filed to overturn the USFWS's refusal to list the Queen Charlotte Goshawk as an endangered species [U.S. District Court, District of Columbia (No. 98cv934)].
July 1999	U.S. District Court for the District of Columbia ordered the USFWS to conduct an actual on-site population count. This decision was appealed by the USFWS and a decision was rendered in June 2000 overturning the District Court's decision (Southwest Center for Biological Diversity v. Babbitt 215 F. 3d85). The Court of Appeals sent the case back to District Court.
July 2000	A magistrate of the U.S. District Court for the District of Columbia found that the USFWS failed to make a specific finding as to conservation of the subspecies on Vancouver Island, which constitutes a third of the subspecies' geographic range.
May 2004	U.S. District Court, District of Columbia rejected the magistrate's finding but ordered the USFWS to determine if Vancouver Island is a significant portion of the range and to determine whether or not the Queen Charlotte Goshawk is endangered or threatened on Queen Charlotte Island.
December 2005	USFWS seeks public comment as to the status of the Queen Charlotte Goshawk throughout its range, for the purpose of determining the significance of the Vancouver Island population in relation to the taxon as a whole (70 FR 4284). Comment period closed February 2006.

Southwestern United States (Reynolds et al. 1992). Reynolds et al. (1992) developed these guidelines for southwestern goshawk habitat (ponderosa pine [*Pinus ponderosa*], mixed conifer, and spruce-fir forests). They assessed information available on goshawk ecology, with particular attention on goshawk prey and the ecology of key prey species in

the region, as well as ecology of the forests used by goshawks and local silvicultural practices. The recommendations are designed to provide breeding season habitat for the goshawk and 14 of its key prey species (Fuller 1996).

Reynolds et al. (1992) has the following primary components: (1) no timber harvest in three nest areas (12.1 ha each) per home range, (2) provide three additional nest areas within each home range for future use by goshawks which can receive intermediate treatment or prescribed burning, (3) timber harvest rotation in the post-fledging family area (PFA, 170 ha) and foraging area (2,185 ha) to maintain always a minimum of 60% in late-successional forests (tree classes: 31–46 cm, 46–62 cm, and 62+ cm), (4) restricted management season in nest areas and PFA during the winter season (October through February), (5) openings of 0.4–1.6 ha depending on forest type, and (6) maintenance of reserve trees (1.2–2.4/ha), canopy cover, snag densities (0.8–1.2/ha), downed logs (1.2–2/ha), and woody debris (11.2–13.6 metric tons/ha) in all harvest areas with amount depending upon forest type (Bosakowski 1999).

These recommendations were designed to return current forest conditions (which have been impacted by grazing, fire suppression, and timber management) to relatively open forests dominated by mature trees interspersed with patches of various successional stages. The applicability of this approach to managing goshawk landscapes may not be limited to southwestern forests. As noted by Fuller (1996), the recommendations made by Reynolds et al. (1992) could be used as a model for assessments and strategies in other areas and for other species. However, similar to many wildlife management plans, these recommendations (Reynolds et al. 1992) still remain as an untested hypothesis. Although these guidelines have been adopted by the USFS in Arizona and New Mexico (USDA Forest Service 1995, 1996), their effectiveness at enhancing goshawk population persistence in this landscape has not been evaluated and has been questioned (Greenwald et al. 2005). Braun et al. (1996) and Drennan and Beier (2003) have expressed concerns about the single-species focus of these guidelines and question the practice of managing landscapes for goshawks. According to Bosakowski (1999), some national forests in the Pacific Northwest are providing similar management to that prescribed by Reynolds et al. (1992) for nest sites and PFAs, but no management is being conducted on the foraging areas. Graham et al. (1994) extended the ideas of Reynolds et al. (1992) stressing that forest conditions are temporally and spatially dynamic. Instead of managing individual home ranges, they suggested goshawk management should focus on managing large forest tracts as sustainable ecological units.

For the Olympic Peninsula in Washington, Finn et al. (2002a) developed goshawk habitat-management recommendations based on their analysis of local goshawk nesting habitat at multiple spatial scales. Their results suggest goshawk use of the landscape on the Olympic Peninsula as nesting habitat will be maximized when at least 54% of the home range is late-seral stage forest (defined as >70% coniferous canopy closure with >10% of canopy from trees >53 cm diameter at breast height (dbh) and <75% hardwood/shrub) and no more than 17% is stand initiation (regenerating clearcuts; conifers <7 yr old, <10% coniferous canopy closure). Finn et al. (2002a) also suggest reducing the amount of landscape contrast and edge density (indices of spatial heterogeneity) within home ranges may increase occupancy and maintain potential nest areas.

Goshawk biologists generally agree that goshawk management requires providing suitable nest stands and a large landscape for foraging. However, the need for managing intermediate scales (e.g., PFA) and very small scales (the nest site) is still open to debate.

FOOD HABITS AND ECOLOGICAL RELATIONSHIPS WITH PREY

FOOD HABITS DURING NESTING

Goshawks are opportunistic predators that kill a wide assortment of prey varying by region, season, vulnerability, and availability. Main foods include small mammals, ground and tree squirrels, rabbits and hares, large passerines, woodpeckers, game birds, and corvids (Squires and Reynolds 1997). Goshawks are classified as prey generalists (Squires and Reynolds 1997) and typically forage on a suite of 8–15 species (Reynolds et al. 1992). As with other raptors, the food habits of goshawks have been determined by examination of stomach contents and food removed from crops of nestlings, or more commonly, direct observation of nests, prey remains, and regurgitated pellets (Lewis 2001). Potential biases exist in most of these raptor food habits methods and these biases in *Accipiter* diets are well summarized by Bielefeldt et al. (1992), Younk and Bechard (1994a), Watson et al. (1998), and Rutz (2003a).

Goshawks forage long distances for relatively large-bodied birds and mammals. In Oregon, average prey mass was 307 g (SD = 364, range = 17.6–1,505 g, Reynolds and Meslow 1984); avian prey averaged 195.5g (SD = 207, range = 17.6–1,505.0 g) and mammalian prey averaged 445.2 g (SD = 415, range = 36.8–1,118.6 g). Males can kill prey 2.2 times their mass (approximately 1,600 g), which is proportionally similar to the largest hares (2,700–3,670 g) killed by females (2.4 x female mass, Kenward et al. 1981).

Although potential prey species are extensive (Appendix 1, Squires and Reynolds 1997), a few taxons are prevalent in most diets. Sciurids occur in most goshawk diets due to their high abundance and broad distribution (USDI Fish and Wildlife Service 1998a). Several studies have documented Douglas squirrels (*Tamiasciurus douglasii*) and red squirrels (*Tamiasciurus hudsonicus*) as important prey (Mendall 1944, Meng 1959, Reynolds et al. 1994, Watson et al. 1998, Clough 2000, Squires 2000,) and they may be especially important during the winter when other prey are unavailable (Widén 1987). Rabbits and hares are also used extensively by goshawks (Reynolds and Meslow 1984, Kennedy 1991, USDI Fish and Wildlife Service 1998a, Clough 2000). Cottontail rabbits (*Sylvilagus* spp.) are abundant in a variety of habitats and are distributed throughout the goshawk's range (USDI Fish and Wildlife Service 1998a) and snowshoe hares (*Lepus americanus*) are also important prey, particularly in northern forests (Mendall 1944, McGowan 1975, Doyle and Smith 1994). In the Yukon, Doyle and Smith (1994) found a positive correlation between goshawk breeding success and a snowshoe hare population peak.

Gallinaceous birds (primarily grouse and pheasants) are particularly important prey for North American (Mendall 1944, McGowan 1975, Gullion 1981a, b; Gullion and Alm 1983, Apfelbaum and Haney 1984) and European Goshawks (Kenward 1979, Sollien 1979 *in* USDI Fish and Wildlife Service 1998a, Kenward et al. 1981, Lindén and Wikman 1983, Tornberg 2001) at northern latitudes. Fluctuations in grouse populations have been shown to affect goshawk productivity, including number of nesting pairs, and number of young per active nest (Lindén and Wikman 1983, Sollien 1979 *in* USDI Fish and Wildlife Service 1998a). Tornberg et al. (1999) analyzed skin and skeletal measurements collected from 258 museum specimens of Finnish Goshawks dated between 1961 and 1997. They reported that as grouse decreased in abundance over this 36-yr period, they were replaced by smaller prey in the goshawk breeding season diet. They also observed morphological shifts in both males and females probably as a result of selective pressures due to changes in prey size.

American Robins (*Turdus migratorius*; Grzybowski and Eaton 1976, Reynolds and Meslow 1984, Kennedy 1991, Squires 2000), corvids (*Corvus* spp.; Meng 1959, Eng and Gullion 1962,

Gullion 1981b), jays (Beebe 1974, Bloom et al. 1986, Kennedy 1991, Bosakowski et al. 1992, Boal and Mannan 1994), and woodpeckers (Schnell 1958, Eng and Gullion 1962, Erickson 1987, Allen 1978, Reynolds and Meslow 1984, Reynolds et al. 1994) are also common prey items found in many parts of the goshawk's range. Northern Flickers (*Colaptes auratus*) are particularly important in many goshawk diets (Grzybowski and Eaton 1976, Reynolds and Meslow 1984, Bloom et al. 1986, Kennedy 1991, Boal and Mannan 1994, Squires 2000).

Goshawks occasionally feed on carrion (Sutton 1925, Squires 1995). Sutton (1925) reported that a goshawk was shot while feeding on a dead bear. Squires (1995) described that goshawks fed on gut piles of mule deer (*Odocoileus hemionus*) left by hunters, and on a bison (*Bos bison*) skull in Montana. It is unclear if goshawks feed on carrion whenever available, or only during periods of low prey availability.

HABITAT NEEDS OF PREY SPECIES

The habitat requirements of important prey species include early seral to mature forests and forest openings. Interspersion (the degree of intermixing of vegetation structural stages) and canopy cover have varying effects on different goshawk prey species (Reynolds et al. 1992). For example, red squirrels respond negatively to a high level of interspersion of structural stages and select closed older forests to attain high-density populations (Klenner and Krebs 1991, Larsen and Boutin 1995). Grouse, on the other hand, respond positively to high interspersion of openings and older forests. Other prey species, such as American Robins, are habitat generalists and are abundant in most structural stages (Reynolds et al. 1992). Although goshawks hunt species with diverse habitat requirements (and a detailed analysis of these requirements is beyond the scope of this paper), several habitat features appear to be important to a variety of species (Reynolds et al. 1992, USDI Fish and Wildlife Service 1998a). These features include snags, downed logs (>30 cm in diameter and 2.4 m long), large trees (>46 cm in diameter), openings and associated herbaceous and shrubby vegetation, interspersion, and canopy cover. Reynolds et al. (1992) stressed the need for large trees scattered throughout the foraging area because this component often occurs in clumps with interlocking crowns that provide unique hiding, feeding, den, and nesting areas for many prey species (USDI Fish and Wildlife Service 1998a). Reynolds et al. (1992) emphasized that foraging areas used by goshawks should include a variety of habitat types and structural classes. In southwestern pine forests, they recommended foraging habitat include a mosaic of vegetation structural stages interspersed throughout the area and consist approximately of 20% each of old, mature, middle-aged, and young forests, 10% in the seedling-sapling stage, and 10% in the grass-forb-shrub stage. The 60% of the stands that consist of older age classes should have relatively open understories with a minimum of 40–60% canopy cover (Reynolds et al. 1992).

Reynolds et al. (1992) speculated that small to medium openings (<1.6 ha) and various seral stages scattered throughout goshawk foraging habitat enhances availability of food and habitat resources for prey and limits negative effects of large openings and fragmentation on distribution and abundance of prey species that use interior forests. Forests that provide adequate populations of major prey are predicted to have well-developed herbaceous and shrubby understories associated with small to medium openings that provide cover and food for many small mammals and birds in the form of seeds, berries, and foliage.

Winter Food Habits and Seasonal Dietary Shifts

Little is known regarding the winter diets of goshawks in North America. In northern Arizona, Drennan and Beier (2003) found winter diets were dissimilar to those in summer, in part because of the absence of hibernating species, and this reduction in prey diversity may result in individual goshawks specializing on specific species in the winter. Wintering goshawks from this population appeared to specialize on only two species of large-bodied prey—cottontails and Abert's squirrels (*Sciurus aberti*).

Given that most dietary information is limited to the nesting season, we poorly understand seasonal changes in diet selection. The limited available data indicate diet composition may change considerably from breeding to non-breeding seasons. For example, in Swedish boreal forests, birds dominated the diet during nesting, accounting for 86% of prey number and 91% of biomass (Widén 1987). However, the European red squirrel (*Sciurus vulgaris*) was the dominant prey both in terms of numbers (79%) and biomass (56%) during the winter. The proportion of European red squirrels in goshawk diets was high during winters of both high and low squirrel numbers. Seasonal dietary shifts are at least partially due to different migration, estivation, and hibernation behaviors among suites of locally available prey.

During nesting, goshawks may shift their diets to include more fledgling passerines (Zachel 1985,

Lindén and Wikman 1983, Widén 1987, Tornberg and Sulkava 1990), and overall prey diversity may peak as juvenile passerines and other birds become available (Wikman and Tarsa 1980, Marquiss and Newton 1982). In Nevada, goshawks ate more birds such as American Robins and Northern Flickers as Belding's ground squirrels (*Spermophilus beldingi*) began estivation in mid-summer (Younk and Bechard 1994a). In Arizona, no significant difference was found in proportions of mammals and avian prey taken throughout the nesting season (Boal and Mannan 1994).

COMMUNITY ECOLOGY

Goshawks exist within ecological communities composed of interacting species. Thus, goshawk populations are affected by various predatory, competitive, symbiotic, and mutualistic interactions. The importance that community relationships play in structuring goshawk populations is mostly unknown. For example, many anecdotal observations have been made of predatory interactions between goshawks and other raptors, but we do not know how predatory interactions may structure goshawk demography or habitat-use patterns. The lack of knowledge concerning community relationships in North America is an important information need. Only through improved understandings of basic ecological relationships, can we hope to predict how the human-induced changes to the environment may help or hinder goshawk populations.

Functional and Numeric Responses with Prey

A study quantifying numerical and functional responses of breeding goshawks to their prey was conducted by Tornberg (2001) in northern boreal forests of Finland. His objective was to evaluate the impact of goshawk predation on grouse numbers and multiannual cycling patterns. Four grouse species constituted >40% of the goshawk diet during the breeding season in this area from 1988–1998. The numerical response of goshawks to grouse was relatively weak. Goshawk breeding density and site occupancy fluctuated negligibly, but the production of young tended to lag one year behind Black Grouse (*Tetrao tetrix*) density. A functional response of goshawks to changes in grouse numbers was found only in spring when all four grouse species were combined. No patterns were found for individual species, which probably is due to goshawks switching between grouse species. Tornberg suggested the weak response is due to goshawks treating different grouse species as one. Numerical and functional responses of goshawks to prey warrants further investigation particularly in areas where goshawk predation may be interfering with conservation efforts of its prey species.

DO GOSHAWKS LIMIT PREY?

The role of raptors in limiting or regulating prey populations has recently become a hot topic in research, particularly in Europe where raptors are still persecuted (albeit illegally) for their predation on galliformes, a popular harvested taxa (Korpimäki and Krebs 1996, Krebs 1996, Redpath and Thirgood 1999, Thirgood et al. 2000, Tornberg 2001). As noted in earlier sections, goshawks are a significant predator of forest-dwelling birds and small mammals. In areas where they are abundant, they could potentially regulate populations of their prey, particularly in areas where they specialize on a few prey species, e.g., boreal forests (Tornberg 2001).

Goshawk predation plays a major role in grouse demography in Europe (Angelstam 1984, Wegge et al. 1990, Swenson 1991, Valkeajärvi and Ijäs 1994). Two studies have estimated goshawks remove roughly between 15–25% of grouse populations during the breeding season (Lindén and Wikman 1983, Widén 1987). Tornberg (2001) found the impact of goshawk predation on grouse varied by species. Losses were highest for Willow Grouse (*Lagopus lagopus*) and lowest for Capercaillie (*Tetrao urogallus*). On average goshawks took 6% of grouse chicks. On an annual basis breeding goshawks took 2–31% of the August grouse population. The most reliable estimates of the goshawk's share of grouse total mortality were for Black Grouse and Hazel Grouse (*Bonasa bonasia*) of which 35% and 40% were removed, respectively.

The contribution of goshawk predation to limiting Eurasian Kestrel (*Falco tinnunculus*) and European red squirrel populations in coniferous forests in northern England has been reported by Petty et al. (2003a, b). Goshawks were extirpated from this area toward the end of the 19th century as a result of deforestation and intense persecution. They were reintroduced in the early 1970s and increased in numbers until 1989, after which their numbers stabilized. This area also contains the largest remaining population of European red squirrels in England and a declining population of Eurasian Kestrels.

Petty et al. (2003a, b) used a number of correlative approaches to explore the role of goshawk predation on both species from 1973–1996. They found no evidence that goshawk predation is a major factor limiting densities of European red squirrels and concluded that conservation management for sympatric populations of red squirrels and goshawks are compatible (Petty et al. 2003b). However, Petty et al. (2003a) did find a significant negative relationship between Eurasian Kestrel and goshawk numbers. Goshawks killed many adult Eurasian Kestrels in the early spring, prior to breeding, when predation would have the most impact on breeding population levels, and there was a temporal trend for this predation to be inversely density-dependent. Petty et al. (2003a) also estimated that goshawks removed more Eurasian Kestrels than were recorded each spring in the study area and concluded the decline of the Eurasian Kestrel was mainly due to goshawk predation.

These correlative studies suggest that goshawk predation may limit prey abundance and productivity in some cases, but without experimental tests of this phenomenon it is difficult to infer cause and effect. The role of goshawk prey regulation in southern latitudes where they are more prey generalists is unknown. Also, information on goshawk impacts on North American prey populations is nonexistent.

GOSHAWKS AS PREY

Although goshawks are formidable predators, they are occasionally killed by other predators, and predatory interactions may regulate some populations. The literature describing predation on goshawks mostly consists of anecdotal observations, with little information regarding population responses. For example, we know that Great Horned Owls (*Bubo virginianus*) kill adults and nestlings (Moore and Henny 1983, Rohner and Doyle 1992, Boal and Mannan 1994, Woodbridge and Detrich 1994). Erdman et al. (1998) reported a Great Horned Owl feeding a female goshawk to its young. Several studies have indicated that predation on goshawk nestlings may increase during periods of low goshawk food availability because female goshawks may be required to spend more time away from the nest foraging instead of protecting young (Zachel 1985, Rohner and Doyle 1992, Ward and Kennedy 1996, Dewey and Kennedy 2001). In Europe, Eurasian Eagle Owls (*Bubo bubo*) eat nestlings between 13–38 d, and often eat the entire brood over several consecutive nights (Tella and Mañosa 1993). Squires and Ruggiero (1995) documented that eagles (Golden Eagles [*Aquila chrysaetos*], and Bald Eagles [*Haliaeetus leucocephalus*]) were abundant in the area) killed goshawks in wintering areas. Mammalian predators include pine martens

(*Martes americana*; Paragi and Wholecheese 1994*)* fishers (*Martes pennanti*; Erdman et al. 1998), wolverine (*Gulo gulo*, Doyle 1995), and raccoons (*Procyon lotor*, Duncan and Kirk 1995). One-half of nestling mortalities (N = 12) in New Mexico were attributed to predation (Ward and Kennedy 1996). In Minnesota, Boal et al. (2005a) reported that out of five adult goshawks depredated during the 1998–2000 breeding seasons (four females, one male), two deaths were caused by mammalian predation, two were caused by Great Horned Owls, and one was caused by a diurnal raptor.

We speculate that Great Horned Owls are the dominant predator of goshawks in North America due to their wide distribution, abundance, and capacity to prey on large raptors (Orians and Kuhlman 1956, Luttich et al. 1971, McInvaille and Keith 1974, Houston 1975). Goshawks aggressively defend their nests against predators during the day. However, they are less capable of doing so at night and most reports of predation by Great Horned Owls are losses of nestlings, although adults are occasionally taken (Rohner and Doyle 1992). The effect of Great Horned Owl predation on goshawk populations is unknown (USDI Fish and Wildlife Service 1998a), but predation rates as high as 49% have been reported for Red-tailed Hawks (*Buteo jamaicensis*; Luttich et al. 1971). The ability of Great Horned Owls to kill large raptors indicates they can potentially have an impact on goshawk populations, especially by reducing nestling survival. Great Horned Owls begin nesting earlier than goshawks and occasionally lay eggs in goshawk nests, forcing goshawks to construct or use alternative nest areas (Reynolds et al. 1994, Woodbridge and Detrich 1994). Alternative nest sites are often in close proximity, which may increase the potential for reciprocal predation between the goshawk, the owl, and their progeny (Gilmer et al. 1983, Rohner and Doyle 1992).

Erdman et al. (1998) suggested fisher predation is a major cause of nest failure and incubating female mortality in northeastern Wisconsin, with annual turnover rates of nesting females exceeding 40%. Metal baffles have been used on nest tree trunks in this area since 1988 to reduce predation by mammals (Erdman et al. 1998), but the effectiveness of this technique has not been tested. Duncan and Kirk (1995) reported that Great Horned Owls, raccoons and fishers are the most significant predators of goshawks in Canada.

Predation is a natural mortality factor in raptor populations. It is unknown if predation of goshawks is increasing due to forest management or even if predation rates are significantly reducing

survival. However, studies on passerines suggest that predation rates increase in forested communities with increased fragmentation and/or a reduction of canopy cover (Manolis et al. 2000, Zanette and Jenkins 2000).

COMPETITION

Intra-specific competition

In territorial species, interference competition from conspecifics could give rise to an inverse relationship between density and population growth rate. Krüger and Lindström (2001) analyzed a 25-yr data set (1975–1999) of a German goshawk breeding population to evaluate the site-dependent population regulation and the interference competition hypotheses. The site-dependent population regulation hypothesis was first proposed by Rodenhouse et al. (1997) and it integrates habitat heterogeneity, despotic settlement patterns of territories, and density-dependent reproduction. Under this hypothesis, the productivity of high quality territories is independent of population density because they are always settled first, while the progressive addition of lower quality territories at higher densities will lead to a decline in mean per-capita productivity, leading potentially to density-dependent population regulation. Site-dependent population regulation (Rodenhouse et al. 1997) calls for a territory settlement pattern that follows the ideal pre-emptive distribution (a form of the ideal free distribution that accounts for territorial behavior [Fretwell and Lucas 1970, Pulliam and Danielson 1991]), where high quality territories are inhabited first, and these occupied territories are not available for settlement by other birds. Territory settlement patterns in goshawks likely follow this pattern.

Krüger and Lindström (2001) analyzed territory settlement patterns and breeding performance and modeled per capita growth rate using standard time-series analyses and model-selection procedures. In their study area, territories that were occupied earlier and more often had a higher mean brood size; fecundity did not change with increasing density in these territories. A strong negative relationship occurred between mean number of young per breeding pair and its coefficient of variation, suggesting that site-dependent population regulation was more likely regulating this population than interference competition. Although the evidence is correlative, site-dependent population regulation may be a key process structuring goshawk nesting populations in Europe. Based on population modeling, Krüger and Lindström also concluded the most important factors affecting population growth were habitat quality, weather conditions during the late breeding period, and density. This study is an important step toward understanding population regulation of goshawks. However, we still do not understand what other factors may regulate goshawk populations, or if these results are applicable to North American populations.

In Arizona, Reich et al. (2004) used a Gibbsian pair-wise potential model to describe and predict the spatial dependency of goshawk nests based on territoriality and forest structure. Nest locations were regularly distributed at a minimum distance of 1.6 km between active nests. Spatial analysis based on nest spacing and habitat variables indicated that potential goshawk nests locations were abundant and randomly distributed throughout the landscape. This result supported the notion that the number of high quality nest locations did not limit this goshawk population. Rather, territoriality in the form of non-compressible goshawk territories appeared to limit the local nest density. Thus, goshawks must choose potential high-quality sites within an area delineated by neighboring territories. At a broader scale, the overall territory density may reflect characteristics of prey populations throughout the area.

Inter-specific competition

The extent to which inter-specific competition for habitat as well as prey by potential competitors, such as the Red-tailed Hawk and Great Horned Owl, affect goshawk habitat use is not well understood. In addition, these potential competitors also function as potential predators making the effect of their presence difficult to interpret. Goshawks may be excluded from nest areas by other raptors, although it is common for goshawks and other raptors to nest close to one another (Reynolds and Wight 1978). Great Horned Owls, Spotted Owls (*Strix occidentalis*), and Great Gray Owls (*Strix nebulosa*) often breed in nests previously built by goshawks (Forsman et al. 1984, Bryan and Forsman 1987, Buchanan et al. 1993). In Minnesota, Great Gray Owls have been observed using nests previously used by goshawks with the goshawk pair building a new nest or using an alternative nest nearby (N = 3; A. Roberson, pers. obs.). Although Cooper's Hawks (*Accipiter cooperi*) and goshawks have a similar preference for nest habitat (Reynolds et al. 1982, Moore and Henney 1983, Siders and Kennedy 1996), and nest in the same stands (P. L. Kennedy, unpubl. data), Cooper's Hawks are smaller than goshawks and begin nesting later (Reynolds and Wight 1978); thus, they are unlikely to be effective nest site competitors.

This size effect on potential inter-specific competition has also been demonstrated for the Common Buzzard (*Buteo buteo*) which is a smaller-bodied raptor nesting sympatrically with the European goshawk. Krüger (2002a) recently did a multivariate discriminate analysis of nest site characteristics of the Common Buzzard (hereafter referred to as buzzard) and European Goshawk (392 nests of both species combined). His results showed substantial overlap between the two species and he concluded that this is good evidence for competition for optimal nest sites. The utility of niche overlap data for evaluating competition is debatable, but it suggests the buzzard might be constrained by the larger-bodied European goshawk in its nest site selection. Krüger (2002b) then experimentally examined the behavioral interactions between buzzards and European Goshawks and their effects on buzzard breeding success and brood defense using dummies and playback calls. Buzzards had significantly lower breeding success when presented with a goshawk dummy compared to control broods but there was no effect of buzzard dummies on buzzard reproductive success. European Goshawks were far more aggressive against an intra-specific dummy than buzzards. Krüger concluded that buzzards perceive a goshawk more as a potential predator than a competitor.

In addition to nest site competitors, several species of hawks and owls, and numerous mammalian predators, can potentially compete with goshawks for prey (USDI Fish and Wildlife Service 1998a). The Red-tailed Hawk and Great Horned Owl prey on many of the same species as goshawks (Fitch et al. 1946, Luttich et al. 1970, Janes 1984, Bosakowski and Smith 1992, La Sorte et al. 2004), although neither has the same degree of dietary overlap with goshawks as does the Cooper's Hawk, which also forages in the same habitat (Storer 1966, Reynolds and Meslow 1984, Bosakowski et al. 1992). Because both the Red-tailed Hawk and Great Horned Owl are more abundant in open habitats, such as meadows, edge, forest openings, and woodlands (Spieser and Bosakowski 1988, Johnson 1992), "the extent to which they coexist and compete for food with goshawks probably varies by the openness of forest types and extent of natural and anthropogenic fragmentation of a forest" (USDI Fish and Wildlife Service 1998a).

Determining whether fragmentation has altered inter-specific relationships between generalist avian predators and goshawks has received little research attention. Changes to forested habitats may render habitat more accessible and attractive to competing species such as Red-tailed Hawks and Great Horned

Owls, thereby potentially decreasing habitat available to goshawks (USDI Fish and Wildlife Service 1998a). However, we do not know whether this is a linear relationship or if some threshold level of fragmentation exists where these species may have a negative impact on populations of goshawks via increased predation and/or competition. Johnson (1992) surveyed 469 calling stations for Spotted Owls and Great Horned Owls along 28 roadside routes (total surveyed = 536 km). Landscapes (500-ha plot) surrounding Great Horned Owl detections contained more shrub-forb and shelterwood, less mature-old growth and mature habitat, had a higher ratio of linear edge to mature and old growth area, and were higher in elevation than landscapes surrounding Spotted Owls. The responses of Great Horned Owl declined with increasing amounts of old forests; the greatest number of detections was associated with landscapes containing only 10–20% old growth. Few Great Horned Owls were detected in landscapes containing >70% old growth. Johnson's results are consistent with the prevailing notion that Great Horned Owls are habitat generalists that are most abundant in fragmented landscapes (Houston et al. 1998). It would be very fruitful to both goshawk and Spotted Owl management if current research efforts on the effects of forest fragmentation on Barred Owl (*Strix varia*) expansion into Spotted Owl habitat (Dark et al. 1998, Kelly et al. 2003) were expanded to include Great Horned Owls.

Red-tailed Hawks and goshawks are sympatric on the Kaibab Plateau in northern Arizona. La Sorte et al. (2004) compared habitat differences of Red-tailed Hawk (N = 41) and goshawk (N = 41) nests at two spatial scales—fine scale (0.08 ha) and mid-scale (1,367 ha). At both scales, Red-tailed Hawks were more variable in their habitat-use compared to goshawks. At the fine scale, Red-tailed Hawks selected steep, north-facing slopes with dense understories, while goshawks consistently chose moderate slopes, tall trees, and open understories. The fine-scale differences at nests were attributed to the approaches each species uses to enter nest sites. Red-tailed hawks enter their nest from above the canopy, whereas goshawks enter the nest from below the canopy. Typically, Red-tailed Hawks also nested in areas with commanding views of the surrounding country compared to goshawks that consistently nested in the canopy of mature forests where views are more limited. At the mid-scale, forest fragmentation was greater around Red-tailed Hawk nests, whereas goshawks consistently associated with patches of continuous forests and level terrain. Thus, goshawk habitat would be reduced at both scales with increased fragmentation and Red-tailed Hawk habitat would increase. Results from both Johnson (1992) and La Sorte et al. (2004) indicated that habitat fragmentation can increase the potential for increased abundance of potential competitors and avian predators, like Great Horned Owls and Red-tailed Hawks, but empirical data that demonstrates whether competition is truly affecting the viability of goshawk populations are lacking.

A variety of mammalian carnivores, including foxes (*Vulpes* spp.), coyotes (*Canis latrans*), bobcats (*Lynx rufus*), Canada lynx (*Lynx canadensis*), weasels (*Mustela frenata*), and pine martens, are also sympatric with goshawks in most North American forests and feed on some of the same prey species as goshawks, such as rabbits and hares, tree and ground squirrels, grouse, and other birds (USDI Fish and Wildlife Service 1998a). Erlinge et al. (1984) demonstrated the combined consumption of large numbers of small vertebrates by numerous sympatric species of carnivores, owls, and hawks in Sweden resulted in food limitations to the suite of predators.

SPATIAL USE AND HABITAT PREFERENCES

Goshawks use broad landscapes that incorporate multiple spatial scales to meet their life requisites. This requires that we understand the spatial-use patterns of goshawks as use of habitat types may vary across multiple scales. This is an ambitious goal, given our imperfect understanding of the spatial-use patterns of goshawks. We recognize at least three-levels of habitat scale during the breeding season—the nest area, post-fledging area (PFA), and foraging area (Reynolds et al. 1992, Kennedy et al. 1994; Fig. 2).

Goshawks nest in most forest types found throughout their geographic range (Squires and Reynolds 1997). In eastern deciduous forests, goshawks nest in mixed hardwood-hemlock stands of aspen (*Populus* spp.), birch (*Betula* spp.), beech (*Fagus* spp.), maple (*Acer* spp.), and eastern hemlock (*Tsuga canadensis*; Speiser and Bosakowski 1987, Kimmel and Yahner 1994, Boal et al. 2005b). In western North America, goshawks nest in forests that include Douglas-fir (*Pseudotsuga menzesii*), various species of pines, and aspen (Reynolds et al. 1982, Hayward and Escano 1989, Bull and Hohmann 1994, Younk and Bechard 1994a, Siders and Kennedy 1996, Squires and Ruggiero 1996, Daw and DeStefano 2001, McGrath et al. 2003). In the Black Hills of South Dakota, and throughout the Southwest, goshawks nest primarily in ponderosa pine and mixed conifer forests (Erickson 1987, Crocker-Bedford and

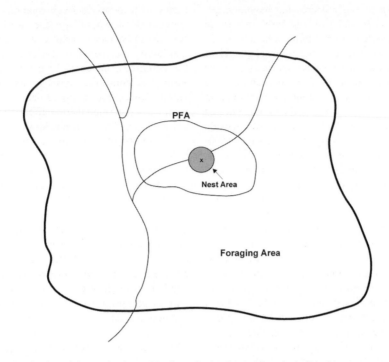

FIGURE 2. Three levels of spatial organization at Northern Goshawk nest sites, including the nest area, post-fledging area (PFA), and foraging area.

Chaney 1988, Kennedy 1988, Reynolds et al. 1994, Siders and Kennedy 1996). Paper birch (*Betula papyrifera*) is a dominant nest stand for goshawks in interior Alaska (McGowan 1975). Goshawks also occasionally nest in tall willow communities along arctic rivers (Swem and Adams 1992).

Nest-site habitat for the goshawk has been described throughout much of its range in North America and Europe (Shuster 1980, Reynolds et al. 1982, Moore and Henny 1983, Hayward and Escano 1989, Bull and Hohmann 1994, Lilieholm et al. 1994, Squires and Ruggiero 1995, Siders and Kennedy 1996, Patla 1997, Squires and Reynolds 1997, Rosenfield et al. 1998, Daw and DeStefano 2001, McGrath et al. 2003). Several studies in the US and Europe have compared habitat characteristics at nest areas to those available habitats within home ranges or landscapes and can be used to draw some conclusions about goshawk nesting habitat preferences (Speiser and Bosakowski 1987, Kennedy 1988, Bosakowski and Speiser 1994, Hargis et al. 1994, Squires and Ruggiero 1996, Penteriani and Faivre 1997, Selås 1997b, Clough 2000, Daw and DeStefano 2001, McGrath et al. 2003). A few breeding foraging habitat preference studies (Widén 1989, Bright-

Smith and Mannan 1994, Beier and Drennan 1997, Lapinski 2000, Boal et al. 2005a) and three post-fledging habitat preference studies have been conducted (Clough 2000, Daw and DeStefano 2001, McGrath et al. 2003). Comparisons among studies are difficult and may not be meaningful due to differences in methodology.

Goshawk winter habitat preferences are unclear due to a paucity of studies on this topic. Winter habitat studies have been conducted primarily in Europe (Kenward et al. 1981, Tornberg and Colpaert 2001) but three studies (Iverson et al. 1996, Stephens 2001, Drennan and Beier 2003) have been conducted in North America. Winter habitat used by the goshawk is likely more variable then breeding habitat and is likely influenced by its local migratory status. In areas where goshawks are residents, breeding pairs can remain on their breeding season home ranges during the non-breeding season (Boal et al. 2003). However, migratory populations may overwinter in very different habitats from their breeding season home ranges such as low-elevation shrub-steppe. Currently, it is unknown how changes in landscape pattern affect seasonal changes in habitat selection; additional research is needed at larger spatial scales (USDI Fish and Wildlife Service 1998a).

HOME RANGE

In North America, home ranges during nesting vary between 570–5,300 ha, depending on sex, habitat characteristics, and choice of home range estimator (Squires and Reynolds 1997, Boal et al. 2003); extremely large home ranges up to 19,500 ha were documented in southeast Alaska (Iverson et al. 1996). The male's home range is usually larger than the female's (Hargis et al. 1994, Kennedy et al. 1994, but see Boal et al. 2003). Home ranges, excluding nest areas, appear not to be defended and may overlap adjacent pairs. Birds usually have one to several core-use areas within a home range that include nest and primary foraging sites. Core areas have been estimated to be approximately 32% of home range area in one population in New Mexico (Kennedy et al. 1994). Shapes of home ranges vary from circular to almost linear and may be disjunct depending on habitat configuration (Hargis et al. 1994). In Minnesota, home range overlap between members of breeding pairs was typically ≤50% suggesting that home range size of individual hawks used in management plans may substantially underestimate the area actually used by a nesting pair (Boal et al. 2003).

The correlation of home range size to habitat use and preference of foraging goshawks is poorly understood for North American populations (Squires and Reynolds 1997). Although comparison of home range sizes may be useful, particularly on a local scale, it is also important to consider prey and foraging habitat abundance and availability, which likely influence home range size (Keane and Morrison 1994, Keane 1999). For example, T. Bloxton and J. Marzluff, (unpubl. data) recently studied the influence of an unusually strong La Niña event (occurred in late 1998 and early 1999 and caused unusually high levels of winter precipitation followed by a cold spring) on prey abundance, space use and demography of goshawks breeding in western Washington from 1996–2000. They noted a decline in abundance indices unadjusted for detectability of nine prey species following the La Niña event. Home range sizes more than doubled during this time period suggesting that weather can also have a major influence on home range size via modification of prey abundance.

Goshawks may shift home ranges after breeding (Keane and Morrison 1994, Hargis et al. 1994). In California, females (N = 7) expanded home ranges after the nestling stage from 520 ha (SD − 390 ha) to 1,020 ha (SD = 820 ha); two males expanded their ranges from 340–1,620 ha and from 950–2,840 ha (Hargis et al. 1994). A female from this population shifted its home range 9 km after young fledged. In northern California, home ranges of males (N = 5, 95% minimum convex polygon) increased from 1,880 ha during nesting (June–15 August; range = 1,140–2,950 ha) to 8,360 ha (range = 1,340–15,400 ha) during the non-breeding season (15 August 1992–March 1993); home ranges of females increased from 1,280 ha (range = 690–3,280, N = 5) to 3,180 ha (range = 1,220–4,010 ha) during the same period (Keane and Morrison 1994).

In the few studies that have estimated winter ranges, they were larger on average than breeding season ranges. In northern Finland, winter range size was 3,283–9,894 ha for males (N = 4) and 2,753–6,282 ha for females (N = 11). The variation in range size was due to different estimators. The average size of core use areas of 12 goshawks wintering in Utah was 2,580 ha ± 2,530 ha (Stephens 2001), but winter range size was highly variable (range = 1,000–7,950 ha). Stephens attributed the large variance to three of the goshawks that wintered in landscapes fragmented by agriculture, where home ranges were very large (2,610–7,950 ha).

A study of goshawks in Sweden reported that goshawk winter range size was an inverse function of prey availability (Kenward et al. 1981). At Fortuna, Sweden where pheasants are regularly released, the average goshawk winter home range was 2,000 ha while at Segersjo, where only wild pheasants were present, the average winter range was 5,400 ha (Kenward et al. 1981).

NEST AREA

The area immediately surrounding the nest tree, referred to as the nest site or nest area (Steenhof 1987, Fig. 2), often contains alternative nests and may be reused in consecutive years (Palmer 1988). The nest area includes the forest stand containing the nest tree(s) although definitions beyond the nest stand have varied by location and study. Reynolds et al. (1992) defined a nest area as approximately 12 ha in size that is the center of movements and behaviors associated with breeding from courtship through fledging. Nest stands of goshawks can be delineated based on unique vegetative characteristics (Reynolds et al. 1982, Hall 1984, Kennedy 1988) or homogeneous forest structure (Squires and Ruggiero 1996).

Nests and nest trees

Goshawks nest in both deciduous and coniferous trees (Palmer 1988, Squires and Reynolds 1997) and appear to choose nest trees based on size and structure more than species of tree (Squires and Reynolds 1997). Goshawks often nest in one of the largest trees in the stand (Reynolds et al. 1982, Saunders 1982, Erickson 1987, Hargis et al. 1994, Squires and Ruggiero 1996), with height and diameter of nest trees varying geographically and with forest type. In Wyoming (Squires and Ruggiero 1996) and California (Saunders 1982), goshawks chose nest trees that had larger diameters than other trees in the nest stand. However, in the eastern forests along the New York-New Jersey border only four of 32 nests were built in the largest tree of the nest area (Speiser and Bosakowski 1989).

Nests are large, often conspicuous structures, that average about 90–120 cm in length, 50–70 cm in width, and 60 cm in depth (McGowan 1975, Allen 1978, Bull and Hohmann 1994). Nests are constructed from thin sticks (<2.5 cm diameter) with a bowl lined with tree bark and greenery. Nests are typically built on large horizontal limbs against the trunk, or occasionally on large limbs away from the bole (Saunders 1982). In eastern forests, nests were usually constructed in primary crotches, with the remainder in secondary crotches or limb axils (Speiser and Bosakowski 1989). Trees with the preferred triple or quadruple crotch branch structures were uncommon in eastern forests suggesting that goshawks actively selected this characteristic when choosing nest trees. In the west, nests are constructed in the primary crotches in aspens or on whorled branching in conifers (Squires and Ruggiero 1996), usually with a southerly exposure relative to the nest-tree bole (Moore and Henny 1983, Squires and Ruggiero 1996). Occasionally, nests are also built on mistletoe clumps (Shuster 1980, Reynolds et al. 1982) or rarely in dead trees (McGrath et al. 2003). Shuster (1980) reported goshawks deserted nest trees (N = 3) that died of beetle infestation, but there are other instances where beetle-killed trees have been used as nest trees for several seasons (T. Dick and D. Plumpton, unpubl. data). Successful nests have been recorded in dead white pines (*Pinus strobus*) in Minnesota (M. Martell and T. Dick, unpubl. data) and Porter and Wilcox (1941) reported a successful nest in a dead aspen tree in Michigan. Snag nesting is a common practice for goshawks nesting in northeastern Utah (S. R. Dewey and P. L. Kennedy, unpubl. data).

The height that goshawks build nests is significantly correlated with nest-tree height (Kennedy 1988, McGrath et al. 2003). Thus, nest heights vary according to tree species and regional tree-height characteristics. Mean nest heights from select populations include 9 m (range = 4.5–16.2 m, N = 41), Alaska (McGowan 1975); 16.8 m (range = 13.4–23.8 m, N = 13), California (Saunders 1982); 16.9 m (SD = 4.5 m, N = 12), New Mexico (Kennedy 1988); 16.2 m (SD = 5.5, range = 4.6–27.4 m, N = 62), Oregon (Reynolds et al. 1982); 13.0 m (SE = 0.48, range = 4.4–30 m, N = 82) Oregon and Washington (McGrath et al. 2003); 11.9 m (SE = 0.4 m, range = 5.1–15.8, N = 39), Wyoming (Squires and Ruggiero 1996); and 7.4 m (SE = 0.7, N = 10) in spruce (*Picea* spp.), 5.8 m (SE = 0.4, N = 6) in aspen, Yukon, Canada (Doyle and Smith 1994). The average height of North American nests was reported by Apfelbaum and Seelbach (1983) as 11.8 m (range = 6.1–25.7 m).

Alternative nests

Typical goshawk breeding areas contain several alternative nests that are used over several years (Reynolds and Wight 1978, Speiser and Bosakawski 1987, Reynolds et al. 1994, Woodbridge and Detrich 1994, Reynolds and Joy 1998). The reason for using alternative nests is unknown, but may reduce exposure to disease and parasites. Although goshawks may use the same nest in consecutive years, nest areas may include from one–eight alternative nests that are usually located within 0.4 km of each other (Reynolds and Wight 1978, Speiser and Bosakawski 1987, Reynolds et al. 1994, Woodbridge and Detrich 1994, Reynolds and Joy 1998, Dewey et al. 2003). Alternative nests can be clumped in one–three nest stands or widely distributed throughout the bird's home range. In northern California, an average of 2.6 nests was used per pair, and only 44% of nest attempts were in the previous year's nest. The mean distance between nests for this California population was 273 m (SE = 68.6 m, range = 30–2,066 m, N = 65 nests, Woodbridge and Detrich 1994). In Oregon, alternative nests were 15–150 m apart, most 60–90 m (Reynolds and Wight 1978). In Arizona, average distance moved from 1991 nests to 1992 alternative nests was 266 m (SD = 157 m, range = 100–635 m, N = 17, Reynolds et al. 1994).

Nest stands

Although the goshawk is considered a habitat generalist at large spatial scales and uses a wide variety of forest types, it nests in a relatively narrow range of structural conditions (Reynolds et al. 1992, Squires and Reynolds 1997). Goshawks prefer mature forests with large trees, relatively closed canopies (50–90%), and open understories (Moore and Henny 1983, Speiser and Bosakowski 1987, Crocker-Bedford and Chaney 1988, Kennedy 1988,

Hayward and Escano 1989, Reynolds et al. 1992, Squires and Ruggiero 1996, Penteriani and Faivre 1997, Selås 1997b, Squires and Reynolds 1997, Daw et al. 1998, Daw and DeStefano 2001, Finn et al. 2002b, La Sorte et al. 2004). McGrath et al. (2003) stated that canopy-cover values of goshawk nest stands may vary due to methodological and site differences. McGrath et al. also compared tree basal area among North American goshawk studies and found that basal area at nest sites ranged from 28.5–50.8 m^2 ha^{-1} compared to 20.7–42.4 m^2 ha^{-1} at random sites; McGrath et al. believed that basal area metrics might better capture site conditions at nest sites compared to canopy cover. Due to frequent bias in goshawk nest detection methods, however, goshawk selection of mature forests over other forest stages has been demonstrated in only a few studies (Squires and Ruggiero 1996, Clough 2000). Squires and Reynolds (1997) state that nests are frequently found near the lower portion of moderate slopes, close to water, and often adjacent to a canopy break. Nesting in stands more dense than surrounding forests may reduce predation and, in combination with north slopes, may provide relatively mild and stable micro-climates (Reynolds et al. 1992). Daw et al. (1998) summarized data from goshawk habitat studies in the West and concluded goshawks tend to select nest stands that are characterized by relatively large trees and relatively high canopy closure (>50–60%), regardless of region or forest type.

Reynolds et al. (1982) reported goshawks in Oregon nesting in dense, mature or old-growth conifers with a mean tree density of 482 trees (>6 cm)/ha and a range of 273–750 trees/ha. Nest areas included forests with few mature trees and dense understory trees to forests with closed mature canopies and sparse understory trees. Most nest areas were in old forests, with only 5% in second growth forests and 4% in mature lodgepole pine (*Pinus contorta*) or mixed stands of mature lodgepole and ponderosa pine. The lodgepole nest areas had relatively open, single-layered canopies (166 trees/ha, 38% canopy closure). In their Oregon study area, Daw et al. (1998) found nests that were located systematically were in areas with an average of 16.4 large trees (>53 cm dbh/ha) and a mean canopy closure of 72.4%. Daw and DeStefano (2001) compared goshawk nest stands to stands with random points in Oregon and found goshawks nested more frequently in stands with dense canopy and late forest structure (i.e., trees >53 cm dbh, canopy cover >50%), but rarely in stands with mid-aged forest structure. They also found nests were positively associated with small dry openings. They reported that average nest-

stand size in older forests was about 100 ha (range = 3–375 ha), but emphasized that stand quality is more important than stand size.

Siders and Kennedy (1996) described the range of stand conditions used by goshawks in northern New Mexico. They reported goshawks used nest trees ranging from 25–31 m in height and 43.3–56.7 cm dbh. Canopy closure at the nest tree was 58–74% and 60–70 % at nest areas. Nest areas had 31–40 m^2/ha basal area, with an overall area density of 800–1,400 trees/ha and overstory trees were spaced 4.8–6.8 m apart. Nest areas were composed of 2.8–8.0% mature, 2.1–11.1% large, 5.2–32.8% pole, and 16.8–85.6% sapling trees. Tree densities by age class were 460–970 sapling trees/ha, 130–370 pole trees/ha, 55–115 large trees/ha, and 53–90 mature trees/ha.

Nest stands of south-central Wyoming goshawks ranged from 0.4–13.0 ha (Squires and Ruggiero 1996). Slopes were more moderate (~11%) than available topography but there was no preference for aspect. Tree densities at nest sites were lower than at random sites but densities of large tress were higher than at random sites. Nest stands were not old-growth in the classic sense of being multi-storied stands with large diameter trees, high canopy closure and abundant woody debris. Rather nest stands were in even-aged, single-storied, mature forests stands of lodgepole pine with high canopy closure (65%), similar to what has been documented in other regions.

In northern California, canopy closure at nests ranged from 53–92% (Saunders 1982), and in northern Arizona, goshawks preferred nest areas that had the greatest canopy closure available, averaging 76%, which was 18% greater than in 360 reference areas (Crocker-Bedford and Chaney 1988). In eastern California, Hargis et al. (1994) reported home range locations used by goshawks were similar to nest areas, and both had greater canopy cover, greater basal area, and more trees/ha than a random sample from the study area.

Despite differences in some habitat characteristics, high canopy closure and tree basal area at nest areas were the most uniform habitat characteristic between study areas in northern Idaho and western Montana (Hayward and Escano 1989). Tree basal area ranged from 29–54 m^2/ha, with most (60%) nest stands between 39 and 46 m^2/ha.

Although goshawks appear to select relatively closed-canopy forests for nesting (Daw et al. 1998), exceptionally they will nest in more open forests (USDI Fish and Wildlife Service 1998a). Goshawks nest in tall willow communities along major drainages in arctic tundra (Swem and Adams

1992), riparian cottonwood (*Populus* spp.) stands (White et al. 1965) and in small stands of aspen in shrub-steppe habitat (Younk and Bechard 1994a). In Oregon, Reynolds et al. (1982) reported seven nest areas had an average canopy closure of 59.8%, although three nests were located in stands of mature lodge-pole pine that were relatively open (38% canopy coverage). Also, Hargis et al. (1994) reported 31% as the average canopy closure of goshawks nest stands in eastern California which was low compared to other studies.

Aspect and slope in nest areas may influence microclimate and goshawk habitat selection but the data are equivocal. Studies conducted in Oregon (Reynolds et al. 1982, McGrath et al. 2003), Idaho, and Montana (Hayward and Escano 1989, Clough 2000) found a significant number (40–60%) of goshawk nest locations on slopes with northwest to northeast-facing aspects. Bosakowski and Speiser (1994) compared goshawk nest sites to random points throughout their study area in New York and New Jersey and found goshawks avoided nesting on slopes with southerly aspects. Average slopes in nest areas were 9% (range = 0–75%) in Oregon (Reynolds et al. 1982) 14% in northeastern Oregon (Moore and Henny 1983), and between 15–35% slope in Idaho and Montana (Hayward and Escano 1989). Although goshawks nesting in New Mexico (Siders and Kennedy 1996) and Wyoming (Squires and Ruggiero 1996) did not exhibit a preference for aspect, most nests were found on moderate slopes. Alternatively, goshawks nesting in the Kaibab Plateau of northern Arizona selected nest sites on gentle slopes (9.6°) with no aspect directionality. Goshawks nesting in northwestern California used slopes averaging 42%, which are some of the steepest slopes recorded (Hall 1984). In contrast, 64% of goshawk nest sites in interior Alaska were on southern aspects with 16% of nests on the upper portion of the slope, 46% on the middle slope, and 38% on the lower slope (McGowan 1975). Clear topographic patterns at goshawk nest sites do not appear to exist.

Penteriani et al. (2001) described goshawk nest site preferences in France by using a multi-scale analysis: nest tree, nest stand (1 ha) and landscape to compare 50 goshawk nest sites with random plots. The landscape was defined as a circular plot with a 2-km diameter centered on each of the 50 active nest trees and random points. Plot diameter was equal to the minimum nearest-neighbor distance. Avian abundance was estimated in each landscape plot as an index of prey availability. Their stepwise logistic regression showed that four nest stand structural variables (larger average dbh, larger crown volume,

higher flight space and shorter distance to trails) and two landscape variables (low avian prey richness for both 100–500 g and 501–2,000 g prey size classes) were significant predictors of goshawk nest sites as compared to random sites. Their results support the results of Beier and Drennan (1997) who argue that goshawks apparently select habitat based on forest structural characteristics and not prey abundance.

Several authors have noted that goshawks often nest near water (Bond 1942, Squires and Reynolds 1997, Shuster 1980, Reynolds et al. 1982, Hargis et al. 1994). Shuster (1980) found all nests in aspen stands were near running water and those nests in pine stands were 10–450 m from water sources. Most South Dakota nests were found within 0.84 km of water although several nests were not within 1 km of a water source (Bartelt 1977). Conversely, some studies have shown that nests are not associated with water (Speiser and Bosakowski 1987, Crocker-Bedford and Chaney 1988) and the potential functional significance of water to goshawk nest sites has not been investigated.

Goshawks commonly nest close to forest openings such as meadows, forest clearings, logging trails, dirt roads, and fallen trees (Gromme 1935, Reynolds et al. 1982, Hall 1984, Erickson 1987, Hayward and Escano 1989). Although the function of forest openings near nests is unclear, openings may help goshawks access or locate their nests (USDI Fish and Wildlife Service 1998a, Boal et al. 2005b).

POST-FLEDGING AREA

Post-fledging areas (PFA) may represent defended portions of the territory (Reynolds et al. 1992; Fig. 2). The PFA surrounds the nest area and is defined as the area used by the family group from the time the young fledge until they are no longer dependent on the adults for food (Reynolds et al. 1992, Kennedy et al. 1994). Reynolds et al. (1992) also assumed that all alternative nests were within the PFA. During the fledgling-dependency period the activities of young are centered near their nests, but they move farther from the nest over time (Zachel 1985, Kenward et al. 1993a, Kennedy et al. 1994, Kennedy and Ward 2003). Post-fledging areas may be important to fledglings by providing prey items on which to develop hunting skills, as well as cover from predators and prey. The PFA (originally described as the post-fledging family area) was conceptualized by Reynolds et al. (1992) and empirically supported by studies of family movement patterns (Kenward et al. 1993a, Kennedy et al. 1994, and Kennedy and Ward

2003). Kennedy et al. (1994) estimated PFA size to be approximately 170 ha in New Mexico. However, PFA size and the functional significance of this spatial scale to goshawk management needs further evaluation because it may vary based on local conditions (McClaren et al. 2005).

The first evaluation of PFA habitat was conducted by Daw and DeStefano (2001). They compared forest structure around 22 nests with forest structure around random points. Comparisons were made at six spatial scales from the nest stand up to a 170-ha PFA. They found that within circles of 12-ha and 24-ha plots around nests, late forest structure was more abundant than around random points. They also reported forest structure at the PFA-scale was dominated by dense-canopied forest and always contained wet meadows.

Reynolds et al. (1992) hypothesized the PFA would be intermediate in heterogeneity between the nest area and home range. This concept was recently supported by a study conducted by Finn et al. (2002a). Finn et al. (2002a) compared occupancy patterns of goshawks (during 1996–1998, N = 30) nesting on the Olympic Peninsula, Washington to habitat structure, composition, and configuration measured at three spatial scales (39 ha nest area, 177 ha PFA; and 1,886 ha home range). Occupied historical sites tended to have a high proportion of late-seral forest (>70% canopy closure of conifer species with >10% of the canopy trees >53 cm dbh), reduced stand initiation cover, and reduced landscape heterogeneity at all three scales, but only the two larger scale models predicted occupancy successfully. Habitat conditions at the nest-area scale were more similar between occupied and unoccupied sites than were habitat conditions in PFAs or home ranges. Also, goshawks occupied areas with more heterogeneity and more early stand initiation forest within their home range than within the PFA.

McGrath et al. (2003) further evaluated this question of goshawk habitat at various spatial scales in an intensive field and modeling study. They compared nesting habitat on four study areas in eastern Oregon and Washington during 1992–1995. Eight habitat scales ranging from 1–170 ha (PFA scale) surrounding 82 nests and 95 random sites were analyzed to describe goshawk nesting habitat at biologically relevant scales and to develop models that could be used to assess the effects of forest management on habitat suitability. At the 1-ha scale, the stage of stand development, low topographic position, and high stand basal area reliably discriminated between nests and random sites. At this small scale, the stem exclusion phase of stand development was preferred, whereas understory re-initiation and old-growth phases were used in proportion to their availability. At larger scales, the middle stages of stand development consisting of stem exclusion and understory re-initiation (both with canopy closure >50% and greater habitat heterogeneity), were more common around nests than random sites. These effects were prevalent up to 83 ha. They provide convincing evidence that in their study area, a core area around goshawk nests where the forest is characterized by large trees with high canopy closure and this core is surrounded by a heterogeneous landscape with forest cover types that are equally abundant. Although the functional significance of this 83-ha area has not been demonstrated, they speculate the habitat conditions within 500 m (approximately 80 ha) may provide the PFA-like conditions described by Reynolds et al. (1992) and Kennedy et al. (1994) in this area. Recently, La Sorte et al. (2004) found that goshawk nests in northern Arizona were consistently associated with regions of continuous forest and gentle terrain out to 645 m from the nest site. They concluded that this non-fragmented, forested area represents the PFA which Kennedy et al. (1994) estimated as a circle centered at the nest with a radius of 732 m. This literature suggests that PFAs likely exist and occur at the scale of 80–200 ha, but vary in size depending on local environmental conditions (i.e., availability of vulnerable prey and predation risk).

FORAGING AREAS

Goshawk nesting habitat is well described at the nest-tree and nest-stand levels, but how goshawks use habitats away from their nests during the nesting season is poorly understood. A few studies have been conducted in North America that describe breeding season foraging habitat (Austin 1993, Bright-Smith and Mannan 1994, Beier and Drennan 1997, Good 1998, Lapinski 2000, Finn et al. 2002a, Boal et al. 2005b). These studies have defined foraging habitat in a variety of ways, which limits our ability to make cross-study comparisons. These definitions include: (1) all habitat within a home range not included in the nest area, (2) habitat at locations of goshawks obtained by radio tracking tagged birds, and (3) habitat at known kill sites located by detailed tracking of radio-tagged birds. Home range analyses estimate home range size based on locations of radio-tagged birds or assume the home range can be represented by a circular area centered on the nest.

Results from some studies suggest goshawks forage in all forest types, but appear to select forests with a high density of large trees, greater canopy cover and high canopy closure, high basal area and relatively open understories in which to hunt (Beier and Drennan 1997, Finn et al. 2002a, Greenwald et al. 2005). However, other studies report a tolerance for a broad range of forest structures (Kenward 1982, Widén 1989, Austin 1993, Bright-Smith and Mannan 1994, Hargis et al. 1994, Beier and Drennan 1997). Beier and Drennan (1997) suggested goshawks in their northern Arizona study area forage in all types of forest stands. It is also important to note that while some habitats may be avoided by foraging goshawks, they may actually be important in terms of prey production (Boal et al. 2005b).

In southwestern Yukon, Canada, 33% of goshawk kills were in dense forest cover although only 18% of the area contained this cover type (Doyle and Smith 1994). Hargis et al. (1994) found goshawks foraging in forest stands with higher basal area, more canopy cover, and more trees in large diameter classes than were randomly available.

Goshawks can also hunt openings and along edges. Shuster (1980) observed goshawks hunting in openings and clear-cuts in Colorado. In Nevada, three males foraged in open sagebrush away from trees (based on 13 visual locations) and along the edge of aspen groves to hunt Belding's ground squirrels in sagebrush (Younk and Bechard 1994a). In Europe, Kenward (1982) collected detailed movement data on four radio-tagged goshawks. These birds spent a substantial amount of time hunting along edges and crossing openings between woodlands. These studies indicate that goshawks hunt in open and edge habitats; however, the degree to which they rely on these edges for prey is unclear.

Reynolds and Meslow (1984) assigned bird and mammal prey species in forested habitat to four height zones (ground-shrub, shrub-canopy, canopy, and aerial) based on where each species spends most of its time. They found 40% of prey species in goshawk diets were zone generalists, 35% were most often in the ground-shrub layer, and the remaining prey was evenly distributed between shrub-canopy and canopy layers. Reynolds et al. (1992) indicated large-bodied prey might be more important to breeding goshawks than smaller prey. In the Reynolds and Meslow (1984) study, large-bodied mammals and avian prey were primarily associated with lower forest strata or were zone generalists. In Arizona, 62% of prey were captured from the ground-shrub zone, 25% were zone generalists, and 13% were from the shrub-canopy and canopy zones with highly aerial prey, such as swallows, rarely present in the diet (Boal and Mannan 1994).

DeStefano and McCloskey (1997) reported that in the coast ranges of Oregon, goshawks are rare even though goshawk prey species are varied and abundant. Forests in this area contain high understory stem densities and dense undergrowth, which may make prey species difficult to capture. DeStefano and McCloskey (1997) suggested that if a relationship between vegetation structure and prey availability does exist, these forest conditions might limit prey availability to goshawks.

In southcentral Wyoming, Good (1998) described foraging habitat of five male goshawks at nest sites. He examined four factors at each kill site: prey abundance, habitat characteristics, landscape patterns, and habitat needs of prey species. Similar to Beier and Drennan's (1997) study, Good (1998) found the relative use of kill areas correlated with habitat characteristics rather than prey abundance. The majority of goshawks (N = 3) in his sample returned most often to sites with more mature forests, gentler slopes (6–60%), lower ground coverage of woody plants (1–30%) and greater densities of large conifers (23–37.5 cm dbh, range = 0–11 stems/0.04 ha). Goshawk kill areas were often associated with small natural openings, as were many prey species. Good also suggested that goshawks may return to areas more often where large numbers of prey are present because two individuals in his sample regularly returned to kill sites with high prey abundance.

In western Washington, Bloxton (2002) identified 52 kill sites of 13 goshawks (seven adult males, one juvenile male and five adult females). Goshawks killed prey in stands that ranged from 13-yr-old regeneration stands to 200-yr-old stands; all forest types were hunted except recent clearcuts and shrub-sapling states. Although much variation was associated with kill sites, goshawks made kills in mature forests more than expected based on availability. Goshawks tended to hunt in stands with larger diameter trees and avoid areas composed primarily of small trees (saplings-pole). Kill sites also had greater overall basal area, greater total snag density, and greater small snag density, but the number of large snags did not differ between use and random sites. The forest understory characteristics seemed to have little effect where goshawks killed prey, except that kill sites had 35% less tall understory cover compared to random sites.

WINTERING AREAS

The European studies suggest that prey abundance and not habitat per se may be an important factor affecting habitat use by goshawks during the winter, particularly at northern latitudes (Sunde 2002). However, a recent study of forest structure and prey abundance at goshawk winter kill sites by Drennan and Beier (2003) suggested that goshawks select winter foraging sites in northern Arizona based on forest structure rather than prey abundance. In their northern Arizona study area, kill sites of 13 radio-tagged adult goshawks (six males and seven females) had more medium-sized trees and denser canopies than nearby paired sites that lacked evidence of goshawk use. Prey abundance indices were nearly equal at used and reference plots. This pattern is consistent with their results for breeding season foraging habitat in the same study area (Beier and Drennan 1997). However, the results of both Arizona studies need to be interpreted cautiously because they used prey abundance indices that do not account for detection probabilities which has been demonstrated to be difficult to interpret by numerous authors (Buckland et al. 2001).

In the winter, goshawks have been reported to use a variety of vegetation types, such as forests, woodlands, shrub lands, and forested riparian strips in search of prey (Squires and Ruggiero 1995, Drennan and Beier 2003). In northern Arizona, adult goshawks continued to use their breeding season home ranges in ponderosa pine and most males moved into lower elevation, pinyon-juniper woodlands during the winter (Drennan and Beier 2003). Squires and Ruggiero (1995) documented that four goshawks, which nested in south-central Wyoming, were short-distance migrants (range = 65–185 km from nesting area). These four goshawks wintered in aspen with mixed conifer stands, large stands of spruce-fir, lodgepole pine, and cottonwood groves surrounded by sagebrush.

Stephens (2001) analyzed landscapes of winter home ranges of 12 goshawks breeding in the Uinta Mountains in Utah. This is the largest sample size of winter birds observed in North America. The four core range habitat types were: (1) mixed-conifer forests at higher elevations composed primarily of lodgepole pine, subalpine fir (*Abies lasiocarpa*), and/ or Douglas fir, (2) woodlands composed primarily of pinyon-juniper and agricultural areas adjacent to the woodland, (3) a combination of the first two habitat types, and (4) lowland riparian areas adjacent to salt-desert scrub. The birds demonstrated a preference for habitats 1, 3 and 4. These data indicate this sample of goshawks had winter home ranges with a higher diversity of vegetation types and more patches than the rest of the study area. Stephens (2001) speculated these areas may have supported a more diverse prey base. His data also support the observations of

Drennan and Beier (2003) that birds will winter in habitats not used for nesting, i.e., pinyon-juniper woodland.

Widén (1989) tracked radio-tagged goshawks (N = 23 males; 20 females) in Sweden that wintered in highly fragmented forests interspersed with clear cuts, wetlands and agricultural lands. In this study, goshawks killed more than half of their prey in large (>40 ha) patches of mature forests (70 yr old) and used these areas significantly more than what was proportionately available. Young and middle-aged forests were used by goshawks in proportion to abundance. Mature forests allowed goshawks to hunt while remaining undetected by prey, but were also open enough for birds to maneuver when attacking prey (Widén 1989).

In England, Kenward (1982) tracked four goshawks that spent 50% of their time in and took 70% of their prey from the 12% of woodland contained within their home ranges. Another study conducted in agricultural areas of England (Kenward and Widén 1989) reported wintering goshawks used edge habitats for foraging. Differences in habitat use may be attributed to different prey distributions (Kenward and Widén 1989). Kenward and Widén (1989) reported that in boreal forests, goshawks prey primarily on squirrels found distributed throughout the forest, whereas in agricultural areas goshawks hunt near forest edges where prey are more abundant. Goshawk home ranges in agricultural areas were smallest where prey densities were greatest, and were largest in areas that contained the least woodland edge, suggesting that prey distribution and availability was the factor that determined the distribution of goshawks during winter (Kenward and Widén 1989).

A recent study by Tornberg and Colpaert (2001) monitored winter habitat use of 26 radio-marked goshawks in northern Finland. These were birds that were trapped in the winter so their residency status was unknown. However, the species is a resident in the northern boreal forest of Finland. Harmonic mean centers of their winter ranges were concentrated near human settlements where they preyed upon human commensals, e.g., brown rats (*Rattus norvegicus*). Goshawks preferred deciduous and mature coniferous forests and avoided open areas such as large fields and bogs. They also avoided very heterogeneous sites, which the authors attribute to avoidance of areas of dense vegetation and not edges as was noted in Sweden by Widén (1989). In Finland, they preferred small to medium-sized patches (<30 ha) of forests and avoided large patches (>30 ha). The results of this study differ from that of Widén (1989) in Sweden where goshawks showed a strong preference for large patches of mature forest. Tornberg and Colpaert (2001) suggested these differences were due to differences in prey preferences. Goshawks in Sweden mostly took squirrels, which reached their peak densities in old spruce forests. In Finland, wintering goshawks preyed mostly on species associated with deciduous forests (Black Grouse) and early seral stages (mountain hares [*Lepus timidus*]), or urban areas (brown rats).

SEASONAL MOVEMENTS AND DISPERSAL

Movements of goshawks beyond home range boundaries include migration, natal dispersal, and breeding dispersal. Migration is seasonal movement between breeding and non-breeding home ranges. Natal dispersal is defined as movement between a bird's natal area and its first breeding area, whereas breeding dispersal is defined as movements by adults between years among breeding areas (Greenwood 1980, Greenwood and Harvey 1982). Migration and dispersal are important components of population dynamics, yet are poorly understood for most bird populations (Lebreton and Clobert 1991, Newton 1998) including goshawks in North America.

FALL MIGRATION

Goshawks are partial migrants (Squires and Reynolds 1997) meaning that some individuals maintain year-round occupancy of nest territories while other individuals in the population undergo seasonal movements to wintering areas (Berthold 1993). Sonsthagen (2002) used satellite telemetry to monitor migratory movements of 34 female goshawks breeding throughout the state of Utah. She found the goshawks moved throughout Utah and inconsistently used existing forest corridors when they left their nesting territories. The 34 female goshawks exhibited a variety of movement patterns. However, her data support previously reported patterns based on band returns (Reynolds et al. 1994, Hoffman et al. 2002) and radio telemetry (Squires and Ruggerio 1995, Stephens 2001) that goshawk migrations involve short-distance movements (<500 km). Of the 34 birds fitted with platform transmitter terminals (PTT), 19 wintered near their breeding area and 15 were migrants. The migrants moved 49–613 km to wintering areas and only two birds moved >500 km. Band return data from the European subspecies suggest short-distance movements or wandering during the non-breeding season occurs for birds that reside in southern latitudes (Bühler et

al. 1987) and longer-distance migrations are more common for populations from northern latitudes (Hoglund 1964a).

The degree to which populations are partially migratory may relate to food availability on breeding areas during winter. At Kluane, Yukon, goshawks were year-round residents during periods of high snowshoe hare abundance, but winter sightings sharply declined when hare densities were low (Doyle and Smith 1994). In southeast Alaska, males maintained loose association with their nesting home range throughout the non-breeding season (Alaska Department of Fish and Game 1993), but some females moved up to 56 km from nesting home ranges. In Minnesota, 27 of 28 radio-tagged goshawks were recorded within 12.4 km of their nest during three consecutive winters (Boal et al. 2003).

Approximately every 10 yr, large numbers of goshawks are observed migrating to southern wintering areas apparently in response to low prey abundance at northern latitudes (Mueller and Berger 1968, Mueller et al. 1977, Doyle and Smith 1994); incursions usually last at least 2 yr (Squires and Reynolds 1997). The periodic invasions of goshawks along the western shore of Lake Michigan from 1950–1974 were correlated with 10-yr population declines in Ruffed Grouse (*Bonasa umbellus*) and snowshoe hares (Mueller et al. 1977). Irruptive movements of goshawks are composed primarily of adults (Sutton 1931, Mueller et al. 1977); juvenile proportions are variable, probably dependent on reproductive success during the previous nesting season. Incursion years in North America summarized by Palmer (1988) and Squires and Reynolds (1997) include: winters 1859–1860, 1870–1871, 1905–1907, 1917–1918, 1926–1928, 1935–1936, 1952–1954, 1962–1963, 1972–1973, 1982–1983, and 1992–1993. In 1972–1973 near Duluth, Minnesota, observers counted 5,352 goshawks which dwarfed previous counts (Hofslund 1973). In other areas, migration counts indicate some populations irrupt on a 4-yr cycle (Nagy 1977). As noted by Boal et al. (2003), we do not understand the factors that influence goshawk residency patterns.

Fall migrations generally commence after young disperse from natal areas (Palmer 1988) and occur between mid-September and mid-December. Heintzelman (1976 in Bosakowski 1999) shows the fall migration season for goshawks extends from mid-September through November at Hawk Mountain, Pennsylvania. In New Jersey, the peak fall migration occurs mid to late October (Bosakowski 1999). From 1970–1994 counts of migrant goshawks ranged from 27–347 for Hawk Mountain; 106–5,819 for Hawk Ridge, Minnesota; 9–75 for Cape May, New Jersey; and 63–252 for Goshute Mountain, Nevada. These numbers are difficult to interpret because they are a function of number of observers and observer detection probabilities.

Spring migration is far less pronounced and poorly understood (Squires and Reynolds 1997). In Wyoming, four radio-tagged goshawks exhibited short distance migration (range = 65–185 km) beginning in mid-September and returned to nest sites between 23 March and 12 April 1993 (Squires and Ruggiero 1995). Breeding birds in northeast Utah also returned to their nest sites in March but their winter locations were unknown (Dewey et al. 2003). Habitat used by goshawks during migration has never been documented.

WINTER MOVEMENTS

Winter movements are better understood for European populations. In Fennoscandia, wintering goshawks move in a northeast or southwest direction; the orientation of these movements may be due to geographical constraints or enhanced chances of recovery in certain directions (Marcström and Kenward 1981a). Juveniles tended to move farther than adults, approximately 70% of movements were between 1–50 km, but 4% were >500 km. Juvenile males tended to move further than juvenile females, and adult males were more sedentary (approximately 80% of movements were <20 km) than adult females. However, the movements of females were highly variable with 46% of females moving <10 km and 9% >500 km. In the boreal forests of Sweden, banded goshawks moved from boreal forests to agricultural regions where prey was more abundant; juveniles moved greater distances than adults (Widén 1985b). In Sweden, the migratory movements of goshawks banded as nestlings varied from 50–200 km depending on region (Hoglund 1964a).

DISPERSAL

Information on dispersal is important for investigating issues of population isolation and demography (Johnson and Gaines 1990, Stenseth and Lidicker 1992). Dispersal and mortality may be more important than reproduction in governing population dynamics, but given these processes occur mainly outside of the nesting period, they are difficult to measure (Braun et al. 1996).

Natal dispersal

Given that natal dispersal involves a complex series of movements (Walls and Kenward 1995, 1998), the final natal-dispersal distance is a function of the cumulative history of movements during the dispersal process (Dufty and Belthoff 2001, Wiens 2001). Successful dispersal is critical to the genetic and demographic viability of populations (Greenwood 1980, Arcese 1989, Wiens 1996). Little is known about the habitats used by goshawks during dispersal, or their dispersal directions and distances. The limited information that is available comes from recapture of marked birds, band returns, radio telemetry, and satellite telemetry.

On the Kaibab Plateau, Reynolds et al. (unpubl. data) reported that 24 of 452 fledglings banded were recruited into the local breeding population. Mean natal dispersal distance was 14.7 km (SD = 8.2, range = 3.4–36.3 km) and did not differ among sexes for the recruits. Five banded juveniles found dead outside of the study area demonstrated a potential for long-distance natal dispersal (181 ± 137 km, range = 52–442 km). In addition, two band recoveries in the southwestern US of birds banded that year were 130 km (Kennedy and Ward 2003) and 176 km (Reynolds et al. 1994) from their natal nest. Distances from natal nest areas, for recoveries of juveniles radio-tagged in New Mexico, ranged from 5.5–130 km (N = 16; P. L. Kennedy and J. M. Ward, unpubl. data).

Kennedy and Ward (2003) experimental results suggest that natal dispersal in New Mexico was regulated by food availability for at least the first 4 mo post-fledging. After independence, radio-tagged control birds were never located in their natal areas and by the end of September in 1992 and 1993 they had all left the study area. However, treatment (provided with supplemental food at the natal area) birds remained on the study area for the duration of the experiment (late October in 1992 and late November in 1993). These results support the idea that juveniles monitor their environment at a local scale to make dispersal decisions. These results are corroborated by correlative studies conducted by Byholm et al. (2003) on factors influencing natal dispersal in the European subspecies. Byholm et al. (2003) analyzed 12 yr of band-return data for birds hatched over a wide area in Finland and found local prey availability (as indexed by grouse census data) influenced dispersal distances; juvenile European goshawks remained nearer to the natal area when local grouse density was high than when grouse were scarce.

Breeding dispersal

Goshawk breeding dispersal includes movements between alternative nests within a breeding area, and movements of individuals from one breeding area to another. Although movements of a pair between alternative nests are not important demographically, they may confound detection and interpretation of movement by pairs or individuals to a different breeding area and these two types of movement can only be distinguished when individuals are marked (USDI Fish and Wildlife Service 1998a). Breeding dispersal could result from death of a mate, or may represent an attempt to acquire a better mate or breeding area (USDI Fish and Wildlife Service 1998a), and may be induced by low productivity (Reynolds et al. 1994). The factors influencing breeding dispersal may differ from those influencing natal dispersal, but the probability of remaining close to the natal area is positively related to survival and/or reproductive success (Byholm et al. 2003).

Reynolds et al. (1994) reported that in northern Arizona, three birds that moved from one breeding area to another in consecutive years all produced more young after the move. Reynolds et al. (unpubl. data) reported results of a study of 259 banded adult goshawks breeding in the same study area. Mean breeding dispersal distance for males was 2.4 ± 0.6 km (range = 1.9–3.5 km, N = 6) and for females was 5.0 ± 2.3 km (range = 2.4–9.0 km, N = 11). Both male and female mean breeding dispersal distances were close to the nearest-neighbor distance ($\bar{x}$ = 3.8 km, SD = 3.2, N = 97), indicating that dispersers moved to neighboring territories. In northern California, Detrich and Woodbridge (1994) reported higher rates of breeding dispersal. Over 9 yr, 18.2% of females (N = 22) and 23.1% of males (N = 13) were found breeding in more than one breeding area. Breeding dispersal distances for females averaged 9.8 km (range = 5.5–12.9 km) and for males averaged 6.5 km (range = 4.2–10.3 km). Similar to natal dispersal, detection of maximum breeding dispersal distances is likely constrained by size of study areas and resighting technique (Koenig et al. 1996).

DEMOGRAPHY AND POPULATION ECOLOGY

Goshawk populations fluctuate in response to changes in survival, reproduction, immigration, and emigration. Population ecology is concerned with determining how factors such as genetics, population density, distribution, age structure, resource abundance and availability, habitat distribution, competition, and climate influence these population parameters. Understanding a species' population biology is also mandated by the NFMA that requires the USFS to maintain viable populations of native vertebrates. The ESA reinforces the NFMA by identifying distinct population segments as an appropriate level of protection. These laws, coupled with life-history attributes of goshawks, underscore the pressing need to determine how population vital rates may vary relative to forest management and other human-induced changes to landscapes.

Population Vital Rates

Longevity

Goshawk longevity is poorly documented because few studies are long term and inherent difficulties exist for following individual birds over time. Age records for wild birds include a 6-yr-old bird in Alaska (McGowan 1975), 6- and 7-yr-old birds in northern California (Detrich and Woodbridge 1994), a 9-yr-old bird in New Mexico (P. L. Kennedy, unpubl. data), an 11-yr-old male in Minnesota (Boal et al. 2002), and a 12-yr-old female in Wisconsin (Evans 1981). Bailey and Niedrach (1965) reported a captive bird living 19 yr.

Survivorship

Survival estimates are poorly documented. We do not understand how seasonal, temporal, spatial, or environmental factors affect goshawk survival, nor do we understand how survival patterns vary by sex and age class. Annual juvenile survival can vary from 0.16–1.00 with most estimates occurring between 0.37–0.57 (Table 3). Average annual adult survival varies from 0.70–0.87 independent of estimation technique and geography (Table 4). However the standard errors of these estimates vary from 0.05–0.1; this low precision limits their utility for estimating annual trends in survival.

Estimated age-specific mortality rates of Finnish and Swedish birds based on banding recoveries (N = 552, years 1950–1966) assuming a 60% reporting rate were: 66% year 1, 33% year 2, 19% year 3, 19% year 4, and 11% for years 5+ (Haukioja and Haukioja 1970). Survivorship between banding and recovery was 287 d for birds banded in Sweden and 221 d for those in Finland (Hoglund 1964a). Winter survival favors birds of higher body mass; males appear to be more vulnerable to food shortage than females (Marcström and Kenward 1981b).

TABLE 3. ESTIMATED POST-FLEDGING SURVIVORSHIP CALCULATED FOR JUVENILE (0–1 YR OF AGE) NORTHERN GOSHAWKS.

Location	Year(s)	Time monitored survivorship (SE)	Annualized survivorship	N	Months post-fledging[a]	Source
North America						
Alaska	1992–1993	0.50 (NA)	0.16	14	4.5	Titus et al., unpubl. data
Northern New Mexico	1992	0.91 (0.09)[b]	0.81	12	5.5	Ward and Kennedy 1996
	1992	0.93 (0.06)[c]	0.85	15	5.5	
	1993	1.00 (0.0)[b]	1.00	9	7	
	1993	0.67 (0.27)[c]	0.50	3	7	
Northeastern Utah	1996	0.87 (0.1)[b]	0.56	15	3	Dewey and Kennedy 2001
	1996	0.89 (0.07)[c]	0.57	18	3	
	1997	1.00 (0)[b]	1.00	19	3	
	1997	0.56 (0.12)[c]	0.43	18	3	
Europe						
Sweden	1980–1987	0.86 (NA)	0.55	22	3	Kenward et al. 1999
	1980–1987	0.69 (NA)	0.48	22	6	
	1980–1987	0.52 (NA)	0.52	22	12	
Fennoscandia	1950–1966	0.37 (NA)[d]	0.37	55	12	Haukioja and Haukioja 1970
Northern Finland	1991–1995	0.50 (NA)	0.37	7	5	Tornberg and Colpaert 2001

[a] The number of months monitored after fledging.
[b] Treatment in supplemental feeding experiment.
[c] Control in supplemental feeding experiment.
[d] Estimated from banding.

TABLE 4. ESTIMATED MEAN SURVIVORSHIP RATES FOR ADULT FEMALE[a] NORTHERN GOSHAWKS.

Location	Year(s)	Survivorship (SE)	N	Source	Method
North America					
Alaska	1992–1996	0.72 (NA)[b]	39	Iverson et al. 1996	Radio tracking
Northern Arizona	1991–1996	0.87 (0.05)	99	Reynolds and Joy 1998	Mark-resight
Northern California	1983–1992	0.70 (0.10)	40	DeStefano et al. 1994b	Mark-resight
Northern New Mexico	1984–1995	0.86 (0.09)[b]	45	Kennedy 1997	Mark-resight
Europe					
Sweden	1980–1985	0.79 (NA)	132	Kenward et al. 1999	Radio tracking
Fennoscandia	1950–1966	0.86 (NA)[b]	552	Haukioja and Haukioja 1970	Mark-resight
Northern Finland	1991–1995	0.75 (NA)[b]	19	Tornberg and Colpaert 2001	Radio tracking

[a] Insufficient data available to estimate male survival rates in all studies.
[b] Annual survivorship reported for adults (male and female combined).

Age at first breeding

During the breeding season, goshawks can be categorized as: subadults (1–2 yr) with primarily juvenile feathers, young adults (2–3 yr) with primarily adult plumage and some juvenile feathers, and adults (>3 yr) with full adult plumage (Bond and Stabler 1941, Mueller and Berger 1968, Henny et al. 1985, Reynolds et al. 1994). Although females occasionally nest as subadults, this has not been documented

for males (USDI Fish and Wildlife Service 1998a). Hoglund (1964a) examined testicular development of 10 subadult males and found the size was variable and only one contained viable sperm suggesting juvenile males may not be physiologically capable of breeding.

Proportion of subadults and juveniles varies geographically from <5% in Oregon (Reynolds and Wight 1978, Henny et al. 1985) and New Mexico (P. L. Kennedy, unpubl. data) to 50% in Nevada (Younk and Bechard 1994a). In New York and New Jersey, only two females (N = 35 nesting attempts) were in immature plumage and all males (N = 18) were in adult plumage (Speiser and Bosakowski 1991). In Alaska, subadult females occupied 33% (N = 16) of active nests during the only year that subadults nested (McGowan 1975). Reynolds et al., (unpubl. data) reported the mean age of first breeding for 24 young goshawks recruited into their natal breeding population in Arizona as 3.2 yr ± 1.1 (range = 2–5 yr) for males and 4.3 ± 1.9 (range = 2–8 yr) for females. They suggested that low recruitment rates and delayed age of first breeding could indicate a stationary, saturated population of breeders on the study area.

Clutch size

Goshawks usually lay one clutch per year. Renesting appears to be rare but does occur following egg loss, especially if loss is during early incubation (Zirrer 1947, Squires and Reynolds 1997). Clutch sizes are usually two–four eggs, rarely one and five. In North America, the mean clutch size was 2.7 eggs (SD = 0.88, N = 44; Apfelbaum and Seelbach 1983). The average clutch size was 3.2 eggs (SD = 0.45, N = 5; Reynolds and Wight 1978) in Oregon, and 3.2 (range = 1–4, N = 33) in Alaska (McGowan 1975). In Nova Scotia (N = 47), 34 % of nests contained two eggs; 49 %, three eggs; and 17%, four eggs (Tufts 1961). In Great Britain, average clutch size was 4.0 (SE = 0.11, range = 2–5, N = 47); of these clutches, 2% contained two eggs; 21%, three eggs; 55%, four eggs, and 21%, five eggs (Anonymous 1990).

REPRODUCTIVE SUCCESS

Goshawk fecundity is difficult to estimate, but clearly there is considerable spatial and temporal variation across the species' range (Squires and Reynolds 1997). Given the inherent difficulties of directly measuring fecundity, indices of reproductive success are used that require specific terminology (Steenhof 1987). An occupied breeding area is an area with evidence of fidelity or regular use by goshawks that may be exhibiting courtship behavior and may attempt to breed. An active breeding area or nest is an area or nest in which eggs are laid. A successful breeding area or nest is one in which at least one young is fledged. Nesting success is the proportion of active nests that fledge at least one young, or occasionally the proportion of occupied breeding areas that fledge at least one young. Productivity is the mean number of young

fledged per successful nest, the mean number of young produced per active nest, or the mean number of young per occupied breeding area. Estimates of these parameters are often overestimated due to the greater probability of detecting breeding versus non-breeding pairs and successful versus unsuccessful nests (Mayfield 1961, Miller and Johnson 1978, Johnson 1979, Hensler and Nichols 1981, Steenhof and Kochert 1982, Reynolds and Joy 1998, Manolis et al. 2000).

Nesting success and productivity

Estimates of annual nesting success range from 8–94% (Squires and Reynolds 1997, Lapinski 2000, Boal et al. 2005a). Mean nest success ranges from 76–95% in western North America (Table 5). Productivity, defined as the number of young fledged per nest where eggs were laid, is the most commonly used statistic quantifying raptor reproduction (Newton 1979a). It is also common to consider young observed at 80–90% of fledging age as surviving to fledge (Steenhof 1987). Productivity ranges from 1.2–2.0 young per active nest and 1.4–2.7 young per successful nest in western North America (Table 5). Most populations produce between 2.0–2.8 fledglings per successful nest (Squires and Reynolds 1997). In Arizona (N = 98 nests), 85% of nests successfully fledged young, 3% either did not lay eggs or clutches were lost during early incubation, 6% of clutches were lost during incubation, and 6% failed during the nestling period (Reynolds et al. 1994). The highest estimates of productivity in North America are from the northern portion of the goshawk's range in Yukon, Canada, and interior Alaska (McGowan 1975, Doyle and Smith 1994). Although productivity is high for northern populations, it can be highly variable. In the Yukon, the number of fledglings/successful nest varied from zero in 1992 to 3.9 in 1990 (Doyle and Smith 1994).

In long-lived raptors, research suggests some nest areas consistently fledge more young than others, with the majority of young in the population being produced by a few females that are breeding in high quality nest areas. McClaren et al. (2002) evaluated whether or not number of young fledged varied spatially and temporally among goshawk nest areas within three study areas where long-term reproductive data from goshawks were available: Vancouver Island, British Columbia, Jemez Mountains, New Mexico, and Uinta Mountains, Utah. Their analysis indicated minimal spatial variation in nest productivity within the three study locations. Rather, nest areas exhibited high temporal variability in nest

TABLE 5. REPRODUCTION STATISTICS IN WESTERN NORTHERN GOSHAWK POPULATIONS IN NORTH AMERICA.

Location	Year(s)	N active nests[a]	N successful nests[b]	Mean N young / active nest	Mean N young / successful nest	Mean nest success (%)[c]	Source
Alaska	1971–1973	33	NA	2.00	2.70	NA	McGowan 1975
Arizona	1990–1992	22	20	1.90	2.20	91	Boal and Mannan 1994
Central Arizona	1990–1991	NA	23	NA	1.72	NA	Dargan 1991
Northern Arizona	1988–1990	NA	NA	1.68	2.00	82	Zinn and Tibbitts 1990
Northern Arizona	1991–1996	273[d]	224[d]	1.55[d]	1.88[d]	82[d]	Reynolds and Joy 1998
Southeastern Arizona	1993–1994	14	11	1.50	1.90	79	Snyder 1995
California	1981–1983	181	164[d]	1.71	1.89[d]	91[d]	Bloom et al. 1986
California	1987–1990	23	18	1.39	1.77	78	Austin 1993
California	1984–1992	84	73[d]	1.93	2.22[d]	87[d]	Woodbridge and Detrich 1994
Idaho-Wyoming	1989–1994	68	62	1.96	2.11	91	Patla 1997[e]
Northcentral New Mexico	1984–1955	80	NA	1.30	NA	NA	McClaren et al. 2002
Oregon-Washington	1994	81	73[d]	1.64	1.82	90	McGrath et al. 2003
Oregon	1992	12	10	1.20	1.40	83	Bull and Hohmann 1994
Oregon	1992–1993	50	NA	1.28[d]	NA	NA	DeStefano et al. 1994a
Oregon	1969–1974	48	NA	1.70	NA	90	Reynolds and Wight 1978
Northeastern Utah	1991–1999	118	NA	1.30	NA	NA	McClaren et al. 2002
South Dakota	1972–1976	17	13	1.35[d]	1.77[d]	76[d]	Bartelt 1977
Vancouver Island, British Columbia	1991–2000	51	NA	1.59	NA	NA	McClaren et al. 2002
Mean[f]	---	---	---	1.59	1.95	86	---

[a] An active nest is one in which at least an egg is laid or is inferred to be laid by a female (e.g., a bird seen in incubation posture).
[b] A successful nest is one that fledges at least one young.
[c] Nesting success is the proportion of active territories that successfully produce young.
[d] Estimated from data presented.
[e] Study done in the Targhee National Forest and encompasses more than one state.
[f] Mean calculated for numeric entries only and not across all studies (i.e., NA entries were ignored).

productivity within each study area. These results suggest temporal patterns, such as local weather and fluctuating prey populations, influenced goshawk reproduction more than spatial patterns such as habitat characteristics. They concluded nest productivity may inadequately reflect spatial patterns in goshawk reproduction; spatial variability among nest areas in adult and juvenile survival rates may instead reflect variation in habitat quality.

The age of pair members also impacts productivity. In Arizona, young-adult to adult pairings produced fewer fledglings per active site (1.1 fledglings, $SD = 0.9$, $N = 9$) than adult-adult pairings (2.3 fledglings, $SD = 0.8$, $N = 21$, Reynolds et al. 1994); young-adult females and young-adult males were similarly productive. However, in Nevada, young females were as productive as older birds (2.54 vs. 3.0 young per nest, $N = 11$), but fledged young at a later date (Younk and Bechard 1994a).

Unsuccessful nests usually failed early in the breeding season, before or soon after laying (Widén 1985b). Dead nestlings, usually <10 d, are frequently found below nests with the cause of death unknown (Reynolds and Wight 1978). Pairs rarely fail after nestlings are 3-wk old. In New Mexico, nestling survival varied from 100% (six nests) at control nests (pairs not receiving supplemental-feeding) in 1992, to 37% at eight control nests in 1993 (Ward and Kennedy 1996). In Utah, nestling survival varied from 67% (6 nests) at control nests in 1996, to 57% at seven control nests in 1997 (Dewey and Kennedy 2001). In Alaska, nestling survival estimated at 98% (1971–1973, $N = 33$, McGowan 1975). On the Baltic island of Gotland, 3% ($N = 73$) of radio-tagged males and 8% of females that fledged died before dispersal (Kenward et al. 1993c).

Causes of nest failure include human disturbance, i.e., shooting of adults, recreational use of an area, and logging activities (Hoglund 1964a, Hennessy 1978, Bühler et al. 1987), disease (McGowan 1975, Ward and Kennedy 1996), inclement weather (Hennessy 1978, Boal et al. 2005a), avian predation (Hennessy 1978, Ward and Kennedy 1996, Boal et al. 2005a) and mammalian predation (McGowan 1975, Hennessy 1978, Doyle and Smith 1994, Erdman et al. 1998, Boal et al. 2005a). From 1998–2000 in northern Minnesota, 21% of all nesting attempts failed ($N = 43$) and 52% of these failures were a result of documented or possible depredation from a suite of predators and 35% of the failures were due to inclement weather. Food limitation can result in higher predation rates on nestlings because female goshawks must spend more time foraging and less time defending their young (Ward and Kennedy 1996, Dewey and Kennedy 2001).

Siblicide and cannibalism occurs, especially during periods of food deprivation (Kenward et al. 1993b, Boal and Bacorn 1994, Estes et al. 1999). Estes et al. (1999) presented evidence supporting the hypothesis that siblicide is a mechanism for brood reduction during periods of low food availability. Kenward et al. (1993b) documented that at hatching, nestling sex ratio was 1:1 but females predominated in broods that lost most offspring suggesting siblicidal interactions favor the larger females.

Proportion of pairs breeding

The proportion of goshawks that nest in a given population is difficult to determine, and poorly understood. Widén (1985b) reported 67% of adults radio-tagged ($N = 12$) during winter in Sweden were later found breeding. In northern Arizona, Reynolds and Joy (1998) found the proportion of pairs ($N = 478$ breeding area-years) annually laying eggs declined from 77–87% in 1991–1993 to 22–49% in 1994–1996 with low rates likely occurring during periods of low prey abundance.

ENVIRONMENTAL FACTORS AFFECTING PRODUCTIVITY AND POPULATION DYNAMICS

Weather

Cold spring temperatures and exposure to cold and rain can cause egg (Hoglund 1964a) and nestling mortality (Zachel 1985). Yearly variation in climatic conditions can impact productivity and other demographic parameters (Elkins 1983). Bloxton (2002) demonstrated a profound pattern of reduced survival rates of adult goshawks (with most mortalities occurring during winter) and an almost complete cessation of reproduction after an unusually strong La Niña event. This period (late 1998–early 1999) had unusually high levels of winter precipitation followed by a cold spring. Abundance indices of nine prey species (unadjusted for detection probabilities thus limiting their interpretation) declined following the La Niña winter, and goshawks generally abandoned reproductive attempts during the pre-laying period or failed during incubation. Abandoning reproductive efforts presumably helped goshawks improve their body condition throughout the summer. Bloxton's (2002) results suggest the indirect effects of weather (reducing prey abundance) are more important than direct effects (hypothermia, freezing eggs, and reduced foraging caused by precipitation interference) in influencing goshawk populations.

In Germany (Kostrzewa and Kostrzewa 1990, 1991), Italy (Penteriani 1997), and the US (Idaho; Patla 1997) high levels of spring precipitation negatively impacted goshawk reproduction whereas warm spring temperatures favored goshawk reproduction. Nestlings had retarded development during cold, wet springs (Kostrzewa and Kostrzewa 1990). Conversely, in British Columbia, high rainfall in May was associated with increased goshawk reproduction (Doyle 2000). In Germany and British Columbia, winter weather and breeding success the following season were not related.

Food availability

Prey abundance and availability are important habitat attributes that elicit demographic and population responses of goshawks (Lindén and Wikman 1983, Doyle and Smith 1994, Ward and Kennedy 1996, Squires and Reynolds 1997, Dewey and Kennedy 2001). In their literature review, Squires and Reynolds (1997) reported prey abundance strongly affects breeding area occupancy and productivity. However, Ward and Kennedy (1996) in New Mexico and Dewey and Kennedy (2001) in Utah experimentally determined that goshawks have a demographic response to a super-abundance of available food during some years, but not other years suggesting that food is not always limiting during the breeding season. These results imply that regional-goshawk populations may only be food-limited during periods when cyclic prey species populations are at low densities (Kennedy and Andersen 1999).

Correlative evidence from North America and Europe suggests goshawk reproduction at northern latitudes may be related to cyclic snowshoe hare and grouse (various species) populations (southern coast of Finland, Lindén and Wikman 1983; southwestern Yukon, Doyle and Smith 1994, Doyle 2000; northeastern Wisconsin, Erdman et al. 1998). The most dramatic example of this relationship occurred in the Yukon where goshawks breeding in peak snowshoe hare years fledged 2.8 young/active nest and 3.9 young/successful nest, compared to years when hare populations were at their lows, and no active goshawk nests were located (Doyle and Smith 1994). In Finland, the proportion of nonbreeding pairs increased from 35–52% in an apparent response to declining grouse populations (Lindén and Wikman 1983). In northeastern Wisconsin, Erdman et al. (1998) monitored the productivity of goshawks from 1968–1992; this is the longest dataset published on reproduction for any goshawk population. Fledglings per nesting attempt ranged from a high of 3.2 in 1978

to lows of 0.8 in 1983 and 1989. They found annual productivity was directly related to an index of prey they developed based on prey remains and pellets containing snowshoe hare and Ruffed Grouse, but the mathematical calculations were not reported. Overall, it appears that certain prey items are particularly important for goshawk reproduction and the abundance of these prey may strongly influence reproductive success (Tornberg and Sulkava 1991).

In addition to prey abundance, it is also important to consider whether prey items are *available* to goshawks. For example, even a high abundance of hares may have low availability to goshawks in a dense aspen regeneration or other habitats where goshawks are unable to effectively hunt (T. Dick and D. Plumpton, unpubl. data, Drennan and Beier 2003). Thus, preferences in goshawk foraging habitat are likely determined, in part, by habitat characteristics that influence their ability to access prey as well as prey abundance (Reynolds et al. 1992, Drennan and Beier 2003).

Based on the assumption that goshawk populations are regulated by food availability, Reynolds et al. (1992), emphasizes that forest management practices may strongly influence the availability of prey items for the goshawk, thus being a determining factor in the long-term persistence of the species (Kennedy and Andersen 1999). Beier and Drennan (1997) and Drennan and Beier (2003) concluded that goshawks did not select foraging areas based on prey abundance, but rather selected areas with higher canopy closure, greater tree density, and greater density of trees >41 cm dbh than on contrast plots. They suggest that goshawk morphology and behavior are adapted for hunting in moderately dense, mature forests, and that prey availability is more important than prey density in habitat selection. Drennan and Beier (2003) also hypothesize that goshawk habitat selection may be a two-tiered process. First, goshawks select broad landscapes that support abundant populations of large-bodied prey, before selecting moderately dense stands of mature forests where they can use their maneuverability to capture prey.

Reynolds et al. (1992) emphasized that goshawk prey species depend on a variety of habitats distributed in a mosaic across the landscape, because many important prey such as sciurids (Carey et al. 1992, Carey 1995) and birds (Schwab and Sinclair 1994) are more abundant in old-growth and mature forests compared to young or regenerating forests. Arthropods, the prey base for many forest-dwelling insectivores, which may in turn be prey for goshawks, are significantly less abundant along edges and in small woodlots (Burke and Nol 1998, Zanette et al. 2000) suggesting food supplies may be reduced by forest fragmentation. Carey et al. (1992) and Carey (1995) demonstrated that sciurid populations were more abundant and remained at relatively constant levels in old-growth forests in comparison to managed second-growth stands. Similarly, Schwab and Sinclair (1994) reported avian populations were more abundant and diverse in mature forests than in younger forests. However, Sallabanks et al. (2001) found little evidence of structural-class specializations by breeding birds in grand fir (*Abies grandis*) forests in northeastern Oregon.

Clearly, a pressing need exists to understand how prey species are influenced by changes in forest structure and pattern resulting from forest management. This information is needed before we can develop sound conservation plans for goshawks (Kennedy and Andersen 1999).

POPULATION DENSITY

Breeding density

Given their large home ranges, nesting goshawks are distributed across broad landscapes at low breeding densities. Determining breeding density of goshawks requires extensive nest searches over large areas (Kennedy and Stahlecker 1993, Joy et al. 1994). This technique relies on several assumptions, including that surveys are complete (i.e., a census) and accurate. This assumption is problematic because non-breeding birds often go undetected (USDI Fish and Wildlife Service 1998a). Nest surveys that attempt to census breeding density require intensive, systematic searches of large areas, and need to be repeated over several years to detect pairs that do not breed every year (Reynolds and Joy 1998). Nest searches are often conducted only in suitable habitat; thus, many studies actually report ecological density (birds per unit of suitable habitat) rather than crude density (birds per unit area; USDI Fish and Wildlife Service 1998a); this may bias our understanding regarding the habitat-use patterns and density of nesting goshawks (Squires and Reynolds 1997).

Densities of nesting goshawks are low, but highly variable seasonally and spatially among and within populations (Kennedy 1997, Squires and Reynolds 1997). The density of mid-latitude populations in the western half of North America, ranges from 3.6–10.7 pairs/100 km² (Squires and Reynolds 1997). In Pennsylvania, the density was 1.2 pairs/100 km², but the density of this and other eastern populations may increase as populations recover (Kimmel and Yahner 1994). Densities in the range of 10–11

occupied nests per 100 km² were reported for three study areas: Arizona (Crocker-Bedford and Chaney 1988), California (Woodbridge and Detrich 1994), and the Yukon (Doyle and Smith 1994). In Montana, the estimated density was 4.6 nests/100 km² during 1998 (Clough 2000). Kenward et al. (1991) reported broad-scale density estimates based on various European studies as 3,000 or more breeding pairs in France, Germany and Spain, and at least 14,000 pairs in Scandinavia.

Density varied from 33–270% during 2 yr in Oregon (DeStefano et al. 1994a). The Bly study area censused by DeStefano et al. (1994a) in 1993 was the same study area censused by Reynolds and Wight (1978) in 1974. The number of occupied nest sites located on this study area (N = 4) did not change over the 21-yr period and thus, densities were equivalent (3.6 birds/100 km² in 1974 and 3.8 birds/100 km² in 1993; variation due to slightly more area censused in 1974).

Density of non-breeders

Currently, no effective survey methods are available for detecting non-breeders. Non-breeding individuals may play significant roles in goshawk demography as they do in other species (Newton 1991, Hunt 1998). Nonbreeding individuals may buffer populations during stress, stabilize breeding population abundance by quickly filling in when breeders die, or serve to quickly increase the breeding density during periods of prey abundance (Iverson et al. 1996, Hunt 1998). Although it is difficult to estimate the proportion of the adult population made up of nonbreeders, several studies in Europe have indicated a substantial portion of the population does not breed (Kenward et al. 1990). Widén (1985b) estimated one third of the adult, sedentary population in his Swedish study area was non-breeding. In Finland, Lindén and Wikman (1983) estimated 35–52% of the goshawks were non-breeders, with higher proportions occurring during periods of low grouse populations.

Winter density

Winter densities are also difficult to estimate and are currently unavailable. The only index of winter abundance for North American goshawks was estimated by Doerr and Enderson (1965) for the foothills of the Front Range near Colorado Springs, Colorado. They operated six–eight traps in this area from 14 November 1963 to 14 April 1964. All traps traversed a 1,000-m section within the upper sonoran and montane life zones. They caught 13 goshawks between

November and January. No birds were caught after 4 February. The un-calibrated index of abundance ranged from 0.24–0.78 goshawks per trap day during this period. The authors concluded goshawks were relatively common in this area until February, after which no birds were present. However, they could have been present but not trappable.

METAPOPULATION STRUCTURE

Metapopulation structure is the degree that individual populations interact with one another throughout broad landscapes (Levins 1969, 1970; Hanski 1982). Knowing the connectivity among populations has conservation ramifications because it affects population persistence from genetic, demographic, and environmental perturbations (Shaffer 1981, Gilpin 1991). We are unaware of literature discussing goshawk population dynamics within a metapopulation framework. We speculate that metapopulation structure is poorly defined given that goshawk are continuously distributed across the western US and are highly mobile. However, clinal differences exhibited across western populations, plus distinct subspeciation suggests some degree of population structuring. Additional genetic sampling and movement studies are needed to address this important information need.

MORTALITY FACTORS

Goshawks die from a wide variety of causes including accidents, starvation, predation, and disease. The degree to which these factors contribute to total mortality found in North American populations has only been evaluated quantitatively for juveniles in New Mexico (Ward and Kennedy 1996) and Utah (Dewey and Kennedy 2001). The cause of death for 12 juveniles in New Mexico was predation (50%), accident (8.3%), spinal injury (8.3%), disease (8.3%), and unknown causes (25%; Ward and Kennedy 1996). In Utah, 12 necropsied juveniles died of starvation (25%), siblicide (16.7%), accident (8.3%), predation (8.3%), blood loss (8.3%), and unknown causes (33.3%; Dewey and Kennedy 2001). Bloxton et al. (2002) reported that two adult females on separate occasions died from apparent choking on mammalian prey. Boal et al. (2005a) monitored the survival of 33 adult goshawk territory holders over a 3-yr period in northern Minnesota (32 were radio tagged). Nine goshawks, eight of which were radio tagged, died during this study. Five (56%; four females and one male) of these nine mortalities occurred during the breeding seasons and were from

predation. The remaining mortalities (one female and three males) occurred during the winter months. The female that died during the winter had been shot and the mortality of one male appeared to also be due to human actions. Causes of death could not be verified for the other two male goshawks.

On the Baltic island of Gotland, natural mortality agents included starvation (37%), disease (7%), a combination of starvation and disease (22%), and trauma (33%, including two birds killed by other goshawks). Trauma induced mortalities include shooting, trapping, injuries (Jälefors 1981), and roadkills (Keran 1981); shooting, trapping and poisoning are especially common mortality factors for European populations but human persecution also occurs in North America (Boal et al. 2005a). Of 11 adult recoveries in Britain, two were killed on roads, eight were shot, trapped, or poisoned, and the cause of remaining death was unknown (Marquiss and Newton 1982).

DISEASE AND PARASITES

Although disease has been documented in wild goshawks (Redig et al. 1980, Ward and Kennedy 1996, Lierz et al. 2002a, b), disease has not been shown to significantly affect the long-term persistence of goshawk populations (USDI Fish and Wildlife Service 1998a). However, disease ecology is poorly understood and mortality by disease is difficult to identify without a detailed necropsy on fresh mortality samples. Traditional ecological analyses have largely ignored the importance of disease in mediating ecosystem function and biodiversity (Real 1996) and numerous emerging infectious diseases are developing that pose a substantial threat to wild animal populations (Daszak et al. 2000). For example, the potential impact of West Nile virus on goshawks is unknown. Given our poor state of knowledge, we must assume that disease could play a role in regulating some goshawk populations.

Bacterial diseases include tuberculosis (*Mycobacterium avium* infection; Lumeij et al. 1981) and erysipelas (*Ersipelas insidiosa* infection; Schröder 1981). Symptoms for tuberculosis included loss of balance, leg weakness, trembling and convulsions, necrotic lesions under tongue, necrotic mass in lung, air sacs, and base of heart, and millet-size to walnut-size yellow-white foci in major organs, especially liver and spleen (Lumeij et al. 1981, Schröder 1981). Ward and Kennedy (1996) reported the cause of death of a nestling in New Mexico as heart failure due to severe fibrinous pericarditis on the heart caused by *Chlamydia tsittaci* and *Escherichia* coli.

Mortality from diseases may be exacerbated by changes in other limiting factors such as food shortage (Newton 1979a). The fungal disease from the genus *Aspergillus* can produce granulomas throughout lungs and air sacs when chronic. Of migrants captured at Hawk Ridge in Minnesota, 53% (N = 49) had *Aspergillus* in 1972 (an invasion year) compared to only 7% (N = 45) in 1973 (a non-invasion year; Redig et al. 1980). Redig et al. (1980) suggested trapped goshawks were birds emigrating from northern forests due to low prey abundance, and the epizootic was the result of increased stress from reduced prey availability or migration (Redig et al. 1980).

Internal parasites are common and heavy infestations of ectoparasites, like lice (*Degeeriella nisus vagrans*), may occur in weakened birds (Keymer 1972, Lierz et al. 2002b). Greiner et al. (1975 *in* USDI Fish and Wildlife Service 1998b) estimated 56% of North American birds had blood parasites, including *Leucocytozoon*, *Haemoproteus*, *Trypanosoma*, and microfilariae. *Trichomoniasis* can be transmitted to accipiters that ingest infected prey, usually columbids, which are hosts to *Trichonomonas gallinae*, a parasitic protozoan (Boal et al. 1998). This parasite may cause severe lesions, usually a stomatitis that obstructs the buccal cavity and pharynx and causes the disease known as frounce, a disease of the crop that may be contracted by feeding on fresh pigeons. Beebe (1974) speculated that some goshawk populations may be threatened by ingesting *Trichonomonas* spp. from pigeons, however, data are lacking. In Alaska, 71% of goshawks (N = 31) had parasites (45% had cestods, 32% trematodes, and 7% had both; McGowan 1975). Sarcocystis parasites can cause encephalitis (Aguilar et al. 1991).

POPULATION TRENDS

No long-term indices of population trends are available for goshawks derived from standardized, widespread surveys in North America (Braun et al. 1996, Kennedy 1997). In addition, insufficient data are available to make a status determination throughout the entire breeding range (Andersen et al. 2005). Breeding Bird Survey (BBS) and CBC data are potential sources of information for estimating rangewide goshawk population trends, but they are inadequate because of low number of routes (25 during 1997–2001 with goshawk detections) and low detection rates on routes (from 1997–2001 no goshawks were observed in Kansas and Nebraska, and an average of 2.6, 2.8, and 1.4 sightings/year were observed across all routes in Colorado, Wyoming, and South Dakota, respectively). CBC data are also inadequate

to estimate goshawk population trends because of low encounter rates.

Some authors have speculated that goshawk populations and reproduction may be declining in the western US (Bloom et al. 1986, Crocker-Bedford 1990, Zinn and Tibbitts 1990). However, Kennedy (1997, 1998) concluded that current sampling techniques may be insufficient to detect population trends and that data are lacking to indicate whether goshawk populations are declining, increasing, or stationary. Andersen et al. (2005) concurred with these conclusions. The difficulty in accurately measuring goshawk population trends is due to multiple factors: (1) goshawks are secretive in nature and difficult to survey, (2) many studies have small sample sizes and are temporally and spatially limited in scope, (3) potential biases exist in nest detection methods used in some studies, and (4) research methods, data analyses and interpretation are not consistent among studies, making comparisons across studies difficult (Andersen et al. 2005, Boyce et al. 2005). The development of a reliable population model is further complicated by the spatial and temporal variation in goshawk populations (Kennedy 1997, McClaren et al. 2002).

In response to Kennedy (1997), Crocker-Bedford (1998) stated the rate of population change for goshawk populations in the US may be impossible to calculate because the species is sparsely distributed, measurements of population parameters vary with prey cycles and weather, and immigration, emigration, and survival are difficult to estimate. Crocker-Bedford (1998) suggested that instead of trying to demonstrate a decline in goshawk populations, habitat relationships of goshawks should be examined to evaluate the amount of habitat destruction or modification that has or is occurring. Kennedy (1998) responded that habitat monitoring should augment demographic studies, not replace them, and suggested that once goshawk habitat is well-defined and demographic data are available from several study areas, a model (or models) that predicts the relationship between nesting and winter habitat and population trends and/or performance could be developed. Andersen et al. (2005) concluded in their recent review of the goshawk literature that assessing the status of goshawks based solely on the distribution of late-successional forests is not appropriate based on the current understanding of goshawk-habitat relationships.

Extensive cutting of eastern forests earlier this century may have reduced populations, but goshawk numbers may be recovering as reforested areas mature (Speiser and Bosakowski 1984). Expanding distributions of goshawks in Connecticut (Bevier 1994), New York (Andrle and Carroll 1988), Pennsylvania (Brauning 1992), and Michigan (Brewer et al. 1991) suggest regional increases. During the mid-1950s, goshawks only nested in western Massachusetts, but now have expanded throughout the state (Veit and Petersen 1993). Similarly, in Minnesota, goshawks formerly nested only in the southeastern region of the state, but their breeding distribution has expanded northward and westward into east-central, central, north-east and north-central regions of the state (Janssen 1987). The breeding distribution of known goshawk nests in Wisconsin (northern two-thirds of the state) is more extensive currently then what was documented in the 1960s (Rosenfield et al. 1998). However, we do not know to what extent the apparent increase in these Great Lakes populations is due to increased search effort.

At Hawk Ridge in Duluth, Minnesota, more goshawks are banded than anywhere else in North America (Palmer 1988). Data from Hawk Ridge indicate that 1972 and 1982 were years of heavy goshawk migration (Evans 1983). Annual totals for the peak migration in the early 1990s (>2,200) were less than those of 1982 (5,819) or 1972 (>5,100; Evans 1981). Do these migration count data suggest anything about goshawk population trends? Smallwood (1998) and others have suggested that goshawk abundance should be evaluated based on changes in migratory counts. The utility of migration counts for monitoring population trends has been much debated (Bildstein 1998). To track population change, a constant proportion of the index (e.g., numbers of goshawk seen per day) to the true population size must be maintained. If this does not occur, then the proportion must be estimated. These validation studies have not been conducted on the goshawk for a local area or range wide, so the trends in the current migration count data are difficult to interpret (Kennedy 1998, Andersen et al. 2005), especially given the periodic incursions from northern populations.

Trends in migration counts could reflect distributional changes or changes in residency patterns rather than changes in population size. For example, CBC data suggest that numbers of the closely related Sharp-shinned Hawk (*Accipiter striatus*) are increasing. However, more Sharp-shinned Hawks, may over winter in North America because of warmer winter climates and/or the abundance of bird feeders that provide a stable over-winter food source (see review in Bildstein 1998). This could account for the recent lower counts of Sharp-shinned Hawks at northern migration stations. Since goshawk migrations are characterized by irruptive invasions, migration counts of this species are more likely to reflect changes in residency patterns than changes in abundance (Bednarz et al. 1990, Titus and Fuller 1990).

Recently, Hoffman et al. (2002) analyzed goshawk band encounter locations accumulated between 1980 and 2001, from birds banded or recaptured at four western migration stations. Their results (although limited by sample size) suggest that migration counts of goshawks generally reflect relatively localized movements (i.e., 400–500 km or less). They hypothesize counts of hatching-year birds, except in invasion years, may therefore serve as an indicator of regional productivity. This hypothesis requires further testing to determine if counting hatching-year birds at regional migration stations could be used to monitor regional productivity.

Three European studies have monitored population trends and one review of regional data in Fennoscandia has been published. Thissen et al. (1982) did a coarse-grain analysis of trends in the number of breeding pairs in the Netherlands for 1950–1981. Based on a review of the literature for the Netherlands and their own data, they concluded that Dutch goshawk populations have increased considerably during the 20th century (180–200 pairs in 1955 to >400 pairs in 1981). They also hypothesized that the steady upward trend from 1900 was interrupted by a population crash during the 1960s, presumably caused by pesticide contamination. After pesticides were banned population growth continued. They further speculated that the major factors contributing to this increase are: the extension of suitable habitat by reforestation, the increase of food abundance (Wood Pigeon [*Columba palumbus*] and Rock Dove [*Columba livia*]), and declines in persecution by humans.

Kenward et al. (1999) estimated the finite rate of population change (lambda, λ) for a population of goshawks in Sweden. They estimated age-specific survival and productivity based on both radio-tagged birds and banded birds and used these estimates in a deterministic, staggered-entry population model. Their demographic estimates are based on the largest sample size reported for goshawks and one of the largest ever reported for any diurnal raptor (318 radio-tagged goshawks, 446 banded birds, and 39 nest territories; data collected for 8 yr from 1980–1987). Lambda was estimated to be 1.0 for males and 0.98 for females, which would be a 2%/year decline for females. However, if the demographic estimates were modified to reflect the estimated range of variation in these values, (e.g., 8% standard error of female survival rate estimates and productivity),

$\lambda = 0.98$ for females would not likely differ from $\lambda = 1$. Because Kenward et al. (1999) did not run a stochastic population model, the effects of demographic variance on the precision of λ are not known.

Krüger and Lindström (2001) monitored occupancy and productivity of all known nests in two 125-km^2 study areas in Germany. They assumed an annual census of all pairs in each study area. The number of breeding pairs fluctuated between six and 18 during the 25 yr of study (1975–1999). Highest densities in the study area were found at the end of the 1970s, after which the sample of nests decreased sharply during the 1980's. During the last decade, the number of nests returned, albeit with fluctuations, to the level at the study onset.

GENETICS

Goshawks exhibit clinal variation in size and coloration (Squires and Ruggiero 1996). The largest goshawks are in the southwestern US and they decrease in size north to the Pacific Northwest; however, the smallest individuals are on the Queen Charlotte Islands, British Columbia. Size then increases from the Pacific Northwest northward through Canada to Alaska (Whaley and White 1994). In British Columbia, wing and culmen length of individuals measured from coastal islands are 2–3% smaller than those of birds from the adjacent mainland (Johnson 1989). Both *A. g. apache* and *A. g. laingi* have darker coloration compared to other populations (van Rossem 1938, Taverner 1940, Johnson 1989) suggesting genetic differences among populations.

Sonsthagen et al. (2004) and Bayard de Volo (2005) characterized genetic structure and gene flow of breeding populations in Utah and northern Arizona, respectively. The Utah population had moderate heterozygosity (50%) similar to levels found in other medium-sized, highly mobile birds. Sonsthagen et al.'s analyses suggested the functional breeding population in Utah extends beyond their sampled area; gene flow is likely maintained by natal dispersal. De Volo et al. (2005) reported high levels of heterozygosity (81%) in the northern Arizona population and also concluded that this high genetic variability occurred because this population was connected to other populations via migration and gene flow from natal dispersal. Sonsthagen et al. observed differences in the haplotype distribution between northern and southern forests in Utah. They speculated that these differences may be caused by clinal variation in haplotype frequencies across western North America. Alternatively, this subdivision

may reflect a contact zone occurring at the southern forests between *A. g. atricapillus* and goshawks of southern Arizona and the Mexican Plateau.

BREEDING BIOLOGY AND DEVELOPMENT OF YOUNG

PARENTAL ROLES

Typical of most raptors, male goshawks primarily provision the nest while the larger female defends the site from intruders. However, the degree to which females depend on males for food may depend on prey abundance and thus, delivery rates. Males mostly provision females during pre-laying and early nestling stages, but there is considerable variability. Some females begin hunting during the mid-nestling period while others depend on the male for food until fledging (Younk and Bechard 1994a, Dewey and Kennedy 2001). In Wyoming, males delivered 71% of prey items and females 29% (Good et al. 2001). This relatively high level of female foraging may be attributed to the fact that intensive telemetry was combined with nest observations to accurately assign deliveries to a particular bird. In Alaska, two females provided 12.1% and 8.8% of food delivered to nest during the nestling period (11–28 d; Zachel 1985). These females delivered prey even though the males had already delivered prey. In California, the male provided 85% of food items and the female 15% (Schnell 1958).

FIDELITY TO MATES AND NEST SITES

Pair fidelity has been estimated in birds using genetic analysis to measure the prevalence of extra-pair fertilizations (EPF) or by observing banded birds. Goshawks are monogamous, territorial birds that build nests within large home ranges. Thus, we expect that EPF would be low, but few data are available. Based on genetic analyses of 103 adults and 122 nestlings from 64 nests in northern Arizona, Gavin et al. (1998) found that EPFs were infrequent for this population (9.4% in 1991, 0% in 1992 and 1993). This result is consistent with the species' life history and densities, which probably limits EPFs.

Determining pair fidelity to mates is difficult because the fate of pair members is usually unknown, and mate fidelity can be confounded with mortality. It is also difficult to determine site fidelity given the difficulty of locating alternative nest areas and the goshawk's ability to nest many kilometers from the site used the previous year (J. Squires, unpubl. data). Nonrandom, non-systematic, or incomplete searches would bias results, especially when based on birds without telemetry.

In California, mates were retained in 18 of 25 pairs where mates were identified in consecutive years (Detrich and Woodbridge 1994); an unknown number of the 28% of remaining birds that found new mates may be due to mortality of the previous mate. Detrich and Woodbridge (1994) observed three pairs for 5 yr and documented that two males and two females bred in three different combinations. Another male bred with three different females in the same territory over a 6-yr period. In northern California, males occupied the same nest area in consecutive years 76.5% (N = 17) of the time, compared to 71.4% for females (N = 49; Detrich and Woodbridge 1994).

In northern Arizona out of 259 adult goshawks banded between 1991 and 2003, six instances of breeding dispersal by males occurred for a rate of 4.9/100 opportunities, and 11 instances by females (6.3/100 opportunities). Only 16% (N = 17) of breeding dispersals had a failed nesting attempt the previous year, whereas mates that failed to return preceded 88% of dispersals. However, most goshawks remained on their territories in subsequent years despite a mate that failed to return (R. Reynolds et al., unpubl. data).

PRE-LAYING PERIOD

Copulation

Goshawk copulations are short (9.3 ± 0.7 sec [s.e.], N = 10) and among the most frequent among birds (518 copulations/clutch, Møller 1987, Palmer 1988). High copulation frequency may help ensure paternity, since the male is often away foraging during egg-laying. In Denmark, Møller (1987) reported two major peaks in copulation frequency. The first was 31–40 d before laying, and the other immediately before and during egg laying. Copulations are most frequent in the morning when egg laying occurs with a minor activity peak in afternoon.

Nest construction

Observations of nest building are few In Alaska, nest construction begins soon after birds return to territories, even with snow still present on nest bowls (McGowan 1975). Females begin repairing old nests or build new structures during courtship by gathering sticks from the forest floor or breaking them from trees (Zirrer 1947). Additional nesting material is added throughout incubation. Males

occasionally assist with nest construction (Schnell 1958, Lee 1981a).

It is unclear why goshawks often add greenery, usually conifer sprigs, to the nest structure. Possibly there is a hygienic function or it communicates occupancy to neighboring birds. Females place greenery in nests throughout the nestling stage by pulling at the base of live sprigs until they break off (Schnell 1958). Sprigs are then dropped on the nest, but usually not incorporated into the structure.

INCUBATION

Egg laying

Timing of clutch completion ranges from early April–early June, varying among pairs, geographic areas, and years, but completed on average between late April and mid-May (Reynolds and Wight 1978, Henny et al. 1985, Speiser and Boskowski 1991, Bull and Hohmann 1994, Reynolds et al. 1994, Younk and Bechard 1994a, Dewey et al. 2003). Cold, wet springs may delay incubation (Younk and Bechard 1994), as does high elevation (Henny et al. 1985; but see McGown 1975, Reynolds and Wight 1978).

Female goshawks become sedentary as egg laying approaches, presumably to sequester the energy reserves necessary for egg formation (Reynolds 1972, Newton 1979a, Lee 1981a, Speiser and Bosakowski 1991); the male delivers prey directly to the female during this time, but may occasionally help with incubation (Boal et al. 1994). Eggs are laid at 2–3 d intervals (Beebe 1974, Cramp and Simmons 1980); a clutch of four eggs may take 8–9 d to complete (Anonymous 1990). In Denmark, eggs were laid early in the morning (05:28, SD = 9 min, N = 4; Møller 1987).

Females occasionally lay replacement clutches 15–30 d after initial egg loss (Cramp and Simmons 1980), but this appears to be rare (Marquiss and Newton 1982). In Oregon, a bird that failed 24 April completed a second clutch on 15 May (Henny et al. 1985). Although renesting attempts are uncommon, Zirrer (1947) observed a pair that repeatedly attempted to renest.

Incubation length

Females are primarily responsible for incubating eggs (Zirrer 1947), but males may assist for short periods after a food delivery (Lee 1981a, P. L. Kennedy, unpubl. data). Females remain on eggs up to 244 min continuously with short breaks not over

10 min in length (Allen 1978). The incubation period has been estimated at 30–44 d (Brown and Amadon 1968, Snyder and Wiley 1976, Reynolds and Wight 1978, Cramp and Simmons 1980). Differences among estimates may be attributed to individual, geographic, or annual variation, to measurement error (USDI Fish and Wildlife Service 1998a), or prolonged pipping (Palmer 1988). Incubation usually begins with the first or second egg laid, resulting in partial asynchronous hatching. Pipping of eggs may take up to 50 h (Palmer 1988).

NESTLING PHASE

Goshawks hatch from late May through June (Reynolds and Wight 1978, Dewey et al. 2003) but dates vary considerably. The nestling period varies from 37–45 d (Dixon and Dixon 1938, Reynolds and Wight 1978, Newton 1979a, Kenward et al. 1993a, Boal 1994, Kennedy and Ward 2003) and young generally fledge between late June and late July (Reynolds and Wight 1978, Reynolds et al. 1994, Kennedy and Ward 2003). Males develop faster and fledge sooner than females (Reynolds and Wight 1978, Kenward et al. 1993b, Boal 1994).

The size of goshawk broods typically varies from one–three nestlings. In Arizona 28% of 224 successful broods had one young, 50% had two young and 22% had three young (Reynolds and Joy 1998). However, there may be considerable seasonal and geographic variation in brood size. Nestlings are born semi-altricial and nidiculous, requiring much parental care. Females brood nestlings almost continually for 9–14 d following hatch (Schnell 1958, Boal 1994, Dewey and Kennedy 2001). Brooding at night ceases by 24 d of age except during wet, cold weather (Boal 1994). Females do most of the brooding, but males may occasionally brood young while the female feeds (Schnell 1958, Lee 1981a). Females continue to feed and protect young throughout the nestling stage, whereas the males primarily hunt for the brood (Squires and Reynolds 1997, Dewey and Kennedy 2001).

Nestlings grow rapidly while in the nest; see Schnell (1958), Boal (1994), and Squires and Reynolds (1997) for descriptions of growth and development. Females generally feed nestlings until they are approximately 25 d of age (Schnell 1958, Lee 1981a); males also occasionally feed nestlings, especially when the female is not present (Allen 1978, Zachel 1985). By 32–34 d of age, nestlings are 90% feathered and their tail is approximately two-thirds of adult length (Boal 1994). Nestlings of this age can feed themselves and beat their wings

vigorously as they run and hop or momentarily lift from the nest. Nestlings start leaving the nest to perch nearby at 34–35 d (Boal 1994).

Ward and Kennedy (1996) hypothesized that food supplementation during the nestling and fledgling depedency periods affected young goshawk survival not by limiting starvation, but by causing the adult female goshawk to modify her behavior and spend increasing time in the nest stand, allowing more constant protection from predators. Dewey and Kennedy (2001) experimentally tested their hypothesis and found female nest attentiveness is a function of food availability in the nest stand.

Goshawks will aggressively defend their nest stand from human intruders. However, considerable individual, geographic, and seasonal variation occurs in nest-defense behavior. Adult females are particularly defensive toward human intruders later in the nestling period (Boal and Mannan 1994). In New York and New Jersey, females brooded the young for a few days following hatching, and only rarely attacked intruders entering the nest stand during this period (Speiser and Bosakowski 1991).

FLEDGLING DEPENDENCY PHASE

The fledgling dependency period is an important period of transition during which the young learn to hunt and protect themselves (Reynolds et al. 1992). Feather growth is not yet complete at fledging (Bond 1942, Kenward et al. 1993a), so young are initially incapable of sustained flight and may have special habitat requirements. Fledglings may delay departing from nest areas when they are fed additional food by researchers suggesting that early dispersal may be in response to food shortages (Kenward et al. 1993a; Kennedy and Ward 2003). Sibling groups of both sexes continue to associate in cohesive units until flight feathers harden (Kenward et al. 1993a). Recent fledglings depend on their parents for food while their feathers harden and they learn to hunt. The distance that fledglings move from the nest gradually increases as they gain independence (Kennedy et al. 1994; Kennedy and Ward 2003). For the first 3 wk after fledging, juveniles in New Mexico remained within 300 m of the nest, and ranged to a mean distance from the nest of 1,955 m by 8 wk after fledging (Kennedy et al. 1994). In Arizona, dispersal from nest areas began in mid August and was completed by late August (Reynolds et al. 1994). On the Baltic island of Gotland, dispersal was often abrupt with approximately 90% of fledglings dispersing from their nest areas between 65–90 d of age (Kenward et al.

1993a). By day 95, 98% of the fledglings dispersed with females moving significantly later than males.

COURTSHIP AND FORAGING BEHAVIOR

COURTSHIP AND PRELAYING BEHAVIOR

Little is known regarding the timing of courtship behavior, but it appears to vary. Most pairs return to nesting territories by March (Zirrer 1947, Beebe 1974, Reynolds and Wight 1978, Roberson 2001, Dewey et al. 2003) through early April (McGowan 1975, Dewey et al. 2003). However, pairs in some regions may return as early as February (Lee 1981a, Speiser and Bosakowski 1991) or remain near their nest year-round (Boal et al. 2003). In Wyoming, migratory adults equipped with transmitters returned to nest areas from 23 March–12 April (Squires and Ruggiero 1995). The phenology of courtship may vary by residency patterns; resident birds may initiate courtship earlier in the season compared to migrants (Dewey et al. 2003).

Courtship behavior may include sky-dance displays when from brief soaring flights, the male dives at the female with closed wings well above the forest canopy, or initiates a direct aerial chase below tree canopy (Beebe 1974, Palmer 1988). Both birds then fly slowly about 1 m apart, with deep, slow wing beats, holding their wings above the body dihedral. The bird's flight undulations may be shallow or they can consist of spectacular dives. Zirrer (1947) describes this flight as wavy gliding approximately 3–6 m above the canopy; at times pair members are close together and then far apart. Pair members may be silent during the display or may be highly vocal, uttering wails and chatters. White under-tail coverts may also be flared 10 cm on either side of the tail (Beebe 1974). Prey plucking (Schnell 1958), frequent copulations (Møller 1987), pre-laying vocal activity (Penteriani 2001, Penteriani et al. 2002a), and conspicuous perching (Lee 1981a) may also serve courtship functions.

FORAGING BEHAVIOR

Hunting methods

Goshawks exhibit behavioral and morphological adaptations for hunting in forests (Squires and Reynolds 1997). Goshawks have been described as sit-and-wait predators that perch briefly while searching for prey before changing perches (Pianka 1983, and Schoener 1971, 1984). Radio-telemetry studies in Sweden (Kenward 1982, Widén 1984) and

in Utah (Fischer 1986) demonstrate that goshawks forage by perching for a few minutes to search for prey, before flying to a new hunting site. Kennedy (1991) confirmed similar results, but she defined the search strategy used by goshawks as saltatory searching. Evans and O'Brien (1988) originally defined saltatory searching as hunting using a stop-and-go pattern where the animal frequently shifts locations when searching for food. The main difference between ambush, i.e., sit-and-wait search, and salutatory searching is the frequency of repositioning moves (O'Brien et al. 1989, 1990). In Sweden, flights between perches averaged 84 s for males and 96 s for females (median flight time is 24 s for males and females, Widén 1984). Males when foraging then remained perched for an average of 8 min, 36 s compared to 10 min, 24 s for females (median perch time 3 min for both). The search method used by foraging goshawks is very different from cruise foragers that hunt prey while moving. Only 3% of prey was attacked from goshawks in flight (Kenward 1982). Attacks on winged quarry rarely last >1 km before the hawk overtakes its prey. In Washington, Bloxton (2002) noted that goshawks may vary their foraging methods by habitat type. Goshawks used salutatory searching 72% of the time overall; this foraging method was used 96% of the time in forest stands >30 yr old. However, goshawks were observed using low soaring foraging on 13% of foraging bouts, generally when hunting young, dense stages of sapling-pole forests.

Goshawks also hunt by flying rapidly along forest edges, across openings, and through dense vegetation to surprise prey (Johnsgard 1990). Goshawks have short, powerful wings and long tails that are highly adapted for rapid acceleration and maneuverability in trees. Most goshawk prey occupies the ground-shrub zone so attacks are usually directed at that zone (Reynolds and Meslow 1984). If the hawk is undetected by prey, the attack may consist of a smooth, silent, accelerating glide that ends in a capture strike without a wing beat (Beebe 1974). However, if detected, the hawk rapidly pumps its wings to capture its intended quarry. Goshawks kill prey by driving their talons into the quarry using a kneading action immediately after impact; their strong feet and bill are capable of killing a wide variety of large-bodied prey.

Foraging success and prey delivery rates

Goshawks deliver prey to the nest one item at a time throughout the day, but peak delivery periods include early morning (0600–0700 H) mid-morning

(0900-1100 H), and late afternoon and evening, (1600–2000 H; Schnell 1958, Allen 1978, P. L. Kennedy, unpubl. data). Foraging success and prey delivery rates vary according to brood size, stage of nestling development, habitat type and prey species, but these relationships have not been thoroughly studied. In Wyoming, the average prey delivery rate from eight females was 0.23 items/hr (Good et al. 2001). This was similar to the average delivery rate for goshawks in Arizona (0.25 items/hr, N = 381 deliveries; Boal and Mannan 1994) and Nevada (0.31 items/hr, N = 51 deliveries; Younk and Bechard 1994a). In California, Schnell (1958) reported 3.9 prey deliveries/day for a single nest. A pair supporting three nestlings brought 34.8 kg of prey during the first 53 d after hatch, or approximately 11.5 kg per nestling (Zachel 1985). In Washington, male goshawks returned to their nests with prey every 4.8 ± 0.6 hr (N = 126 visits by nine birds; Bloxton 2002). He found small prey were generally returned to the nest immediately following capture, whereas larger prey, such as pigeons (360 g), were decapitated and plucked before delivery. Grouse (500–1,000 g) were decapitated, plucked and parceled into two pieces for separate deliveries.

Foraging distance from nest

Male goshawks generally forage away from the immediate nest site (Kennedy 1991, Good 1998). In New Mexico, males hunted between 0.8 and 8 km from the nest (Kennedy 1991). In south-central Wyoming, the average kill distance from the nest was 1,885 m (SD = 1,181m), but was highly variable and could be up to 5,456 m from the nest (Good 1998). Of 37 Ruffed Grouse banded in Minnesota, nine were killed by goshawks within 1,097–2,515 m of the nest, and 26 were killed within a 1.6 km radius of the nest (Eng and Gullion 1962). Large goshawk home ranges coupled with long foraging distances indicate these hunters forage over large areas surrounding their nests. However, female goshawks will attack prey from their nest or within the nest stand. Schnell (1958) observed a female hunting ducklings from her nest.

From central-place-forging theory, we expected a relationship between prey size and distance that goshawks are willing to forage from their nests (Orians and Pearson 1979), and that this relationship would be influenced by habitat use (Rosenberg and McKelvey 1999). In Washington, Bloxton (2002) used radio telemetry (N = nine males, five females) to determine that goshawks traveled an average of 2.2 km from their nests; the average maximum distances was 5.0 km, and 10.2 km was the farthest

a breeding goshawk traveled from the nest during the breeding season. Consistent with central-place-foraging theory, the further they foraged the larger the prey item returned to the nest (N = 28 deliveries pooled across eight hawks, r = 0.42, P = 0.02). Generally, if the birds traveled over 4 km from the nests, they did not return with small prey.

Caching

Caching surplus prey when nestlings are present or for future use has been observed for many species of raptors (Newton 1979a). Goshawks cache prey on branches near the tree trunks, or wedge the item in a crotch between branches (Zachel 1985). Caching rates have not been quantified for this species. Schnell (1958) observed a single nest in California and noted that a female cached food primarily when nestlings were <1 mo old and needed frequent feedings. Most cached items were fed to nestlings the same day, but some were fed at least 32 h after a kill (Schnell 1958).

Plucking perches

Goshawks may repeatedly use particular perches near their nests for plucking prey. Plucking perches may be downed logs, stumps, or old nests, but preferred perches are usually low (<1 m), bent-over trees or saplings (Schnell 1958, Reynolds and Meslow 1984, Bull and Hohmann 1994). Plucking perches are often located in denser portions of the secondary canopy and are often up-slope and fairly close to the nest (Hall 1984). Distances of plucking perches from nests averaged: Oregon, 45 m (range = 27–74 m; Reynolds et al. 1982); north-eastern Oregon, 42 m (range = 7–200 m; Bull and Hohmann 1994); California, 69 m (range = 30–130 m; Schnell 1958). However, these distances may be underestimates because distant perches are difficult to locate.

SOCIAL BEHAVIOR

Goshawks are solitary outside the breeding season. During migration, they may be observed with other raptors but these interactions are not considered social. Pair members have few interactions during winter as they often use separate wintering areas (J. Squires, unpubl. data). After fledging, siblings of both sexes often remain together in cohesive groups near the nest until dispersal (Reynolds and Wight 1978, Kenward et al. 1993b). Fledglings will also visit adjacent nests where they can be fed by the resident adults (Kenward et al. 1993b).

GOSHAWK CONSERVATION AND MANAGEMENT

THREATS

A number of factors are cited by researchers and managers as potentially detrimental to current and future goshawk viability. These include, but may not be limited to, habitat alteration, direct human disturbance, pesticides and other contaminants, and harvest for falconry. However, the primary concern throughout the range of the goshawk is habitat alteration due to timber and fire management practices. The issues cited by researchers, agency personnel, and others as potential threats to habitat caused by various silvicultural treatments include forest fragmentation, creation of even-aged and monotypic stands, potential increases in area of younger age classes, and loss of tree species diversity.

Habitat alteration due to timber and fire management practices

A number of studies describe structural characteristics of goshawk nest stands and goshawk landscapes but few data are available on the effects of logging within the nest stand on demographic performance, particularly in an experimental or quasi-experimental framework. Although only a few studies have been conducted on the responses of goshawks to forest management practices, clearly some level of habitat change will render a landscape unsuitable for goshawks (USDI Fish and Wildlife Service 1998b). This level or threshold may vary spatially or temporally across the range of the goshawk. Effects analysis of forest management on goshawk populations should consider the spatial relationships among different functional levels of habitat use by goshawks, including nesting habitat, foraging habitat, winter habitat, and important prey species and their habitat requirements.

Forest management can impact structure, function, and quality of both nesting and foraging habitat by removing nests and nest trees, modifying or removing entire nest stands, and removing canopy and mature trees, snags, and downed wood (Reynolds 1989, Crocker-Bedford 1990, Bright-Smith and Mannan 1994, Woodbridge and Detrich 1994, Beier and Drennan 1997, Desimone 1997, USDI Fish and Wildlife Service 1998a). Reduction and fragmentation of habitat may also favor early successional competitors and predators such as Red-tailed Hawks and Great Horned Owls (Woodbridge and Detrich 1994).

Forest-management practices, such as the use of controlled fire and thinning, may improve habitat for goshawks by opening up dense understory vegetation, creating snags, downed logs, woody debris, and other conditions that may benefit goshawks and their prey (Reynolds et al. 1992, Graham et al. 1999b). To determine the effect of silvicultural prescriptions on potential nest habitat, expected post-harvest stand density and canopy closure should be compared to local definitions of mean structural attributes of nest area habitat (USDI Fish and Wildlife Service 1998a). For example, in the temperate rainforests of southeastern Alaska, forest management would need to account for long fire-return intervals that produce old growth forests. These prescriptions could differ markedly from those for managing goshawks in the Southwest hwere frequent fires are assumed to affect the structure of ponderosa pine communities (but see Baker and Ehle 2001, Schoennagel et al. 2004). McGrath et al. (2003) provides a good example of modeling the putative effects of forest management. For central Washington, they simulated the effects of three silvicultural prescriptions (no harvest, commercial thin, and implementation of Spotted Owl guidelines) on goshawk nesting habitat over a 100-yr interval. All three management scenarios failed to maintain a modeled nesting population over a 100-yr period, until habitat heterogeneity was increased by simulated thinning. Although this study provides a good example of predicting how forest management may be used to enhance nesting populations, it also illustrates how important it is to understand basic ecological relationships. For example, it has not been well established that habitat homogeneity, per se, reduces population persistence. Thus, the underlying assumptions of models need to be clearly articulated and validated, including the extent that model predictions can be generalized to the diverse habitats used by nesting goshawks.

Negative effects of timber harvest on goshawk nest habitat can be described as the area of potentially suitable forest that meets local definitions of suitable habitat from nest habitat studies, and that is modified to a condition no longer meeting the definition (USDI Fish and Wildlife Service 1998a). Desimone (1997) prescribed little or no habitat alteration within aggregate nest stands and Bright-Smith and Mannan (1994) stated that tree harvest methods that create large areas with reduced canopy cover of less than 35–40% may be particularly detrimental to potential goshawk foraging habitat. Reynolds (1989) stated that practices such as selective overstory removal or patch and clearcut harvesting, resulting in either a complete removal of trees or a reduction of the stem density and canopy cover throughout management units, lower the quality of goshawk nesting habitat. Reduction of canopy closure may result in increased solar radiation and heat stress, reduced buffering from adverse weather, and increased visibility to predators, all of which may singly, or in combination, affect goshawk nesting success (USDI Fish and Wildlife Service 1998b).

Using a quasi-experiment, Penteriani and Faivre (2001) tested some of these assumptions within nest-stand harvest. They examined the effects of shelterwood harvest within nesting stands on European goshawk occupancy and productivity. During this long-term study (1984–1995 in Italy and 1993–1999 in France) they compared trends in occupancy and productivity in logged and unlogged stands and also assessed the logging effects on the same nesting stand (N = nine stands) before and after timber harvest. They found no difference in productivity of goshawk pairs reproducing in unlogged vs. logged stands. When considering the same nesting stand, before and after timber harvest, they noted no short-term differences in productivity. However, they observed that 87.5% of goshawk pairs nesting in logged stands moved away only when the original stand structure was altered by >30% and then the birds moved only to the nearest neighboring mature stand. Although sample sizes were small, the results of this study suggest goshawks can tolerate some levels of timber harvesting within the nesting stand (if harvest is avoided from February through August), as long as cover reduction does not exceed approximately 30%. The applicability of this study to other timber management practices and other portions of the goshawk range is unknown.

The duration to which forest-management impacts goshawks has not been formally studied across the species' range. In areas that support populations that depend on old and/or complex forest structures, the duration of management impacts could be much longer compared to populations that occupy forests that are primarily structured by frequent natural disturbances. However, efforts to determine the duration of impacts need to account for specific habitat needs, the spatial context of the surrounding landscape, and the structure of important micro-sites. We do not always assume that pristine or non-managed forests provide optimal habitat. For example, nest stands in ponderosa pine may be improved by thinning from below to prevent infilling with other tree species (Reynolds et al. 1992) or to promote habitat heterogeneity (McGrath et al. 2003).

Relatively few studies have addressed the size of forest patches selected by goshawks for nesting

(USDI Fish and Wildlife Service 1998a). Based on observations of feathers, whitewash, and prey remains, Reynolds (1983) defined the nest area as approximately 12 ha of intensified use surrounding the nest. Woodbridge and Detrich (1994) suggested that although small (12–24 ha) stands were used successfully for nesting, goshawks preferred larger (34–80 ha) stands for nesting because occupancy rates of forest stands used for nesting decreased with decreasing stand size. The larger (60 ha) core area reported by McGrath et al. (2003) further supports the hypothesis that larger patches of mature forest surrounding goshawk nests may be important (USDI Fish and Wildlife Service 1998a).

Although assessment of habitat condition for goshawk nest areas is often made at broad scales, evidence suggests that landscape features such as slope, aspect, riparian vegetation, meadows, drainages, water, and other features affect location of goshawk nest areas (Allison 1996). Timber harvests associated with these physiographic features may have a disproportionate effect on habitat suitability if selection of nest areas by goshawks is at least partially dependant on them (USDI Fish and Wildlife Service 1998a) and nesting habitat is limiting.

One of the limitations of studies investigating the effects of timber harvest on goshawk nesting habitat is that few studies have investigated goshawk habitat in forests not managed for timber harvest. Studies of goshawk habitat relations conducted on timberland may reflect the history of timber harvest in those areas. Studies of goshawk habitat in protected areas, would provide baseline data that could be used to compare with habitat data from forest lands to determine the degree to which timber management influences goshawk habitat preferences. Finn et al. (2002a, b) included nest sites within Olympic National Park as well as on managed forest lands. They used the park to document that loss of mature forest in managed landscapes was detrimental to goshawk site occupancy and productivity on the Olympic Peninsula.

Habitats used for foraging by goshawks in North America have been documented in a small number of telemetry studies (Austin 1993, Bright-Smith and Mannan 1994, Hargis et al. 1994, Beier and Drennan 1997, Boal et al. 2005b). These studies suggest goshawks select foraging areas with specific structural attributes, including old or mature forest stands with open understories, relatively high canopy closure, large trees, and high stem densities. It is possible; however, that actual foraging habitat selection occurs at spatial and temporal scales difficult to investigate using radio telemetry (USDI Fish and

Wildlife Service 1998a). Small openings, tree fall gaps, edges, riparian zones, and rock outcrops are examples of small-scale landscape elements that may be important to foraging goshawks (Squires and Reynolds 1997). It cannot be assumed, however, that adequate prey will necessarily be available in openings created by timber harvests, which often result in dense re-growth where goshawks would be unlikely to detect or capture prey (USDI Fish and Wildlife Service 1998a). Also, populations of many prey species are linked to structural attributes such as snags, large logs, large trees, soil organic horizon depth for fungi, and hardwoods for mast, and these may not be maintained under silvicultural prescriptions, unless specifically designed to maintain them (Reynolds et al. 1992, USDI Fish and Wildlife Service 1998a).

Goshawk foraging habitat can be maintained or restored through means such as protection of specific areas, control of tree spacing and canopy layering, and management strategies that sustain the structure, function, and ecological processes of forests that are important to goshawks (Reynolds et al. 1992, USDI Fish and Wildlife Service 1998a). Widén (1997) claims goshawk declines in Fennoscandia from the 1950s to the 1980s are a result of changes in forest management practices that have altered goshawk foraging areas in this region. In the 1950s, forest management practices changed from selective cutting to clear cutting, replanting, and thinning. As a result of this intensive management, the boreal forest landscape of Fennoscandia is a highly fragmented patchwork of clearcuts and forest stands in different successional stages and the proportion of old-growth forest has declined dramatically (<5% of Swedish forests are old growth). Widén develops a cogent argument that suggests this landscape change has caused goshawk declines by reducing the availability of foraging habitat not nesting habitat. Goshawks can successfully nest in patches of mature or old-growth forest as small as 0.4 ha, but their foraging ranges cover 2,000–6,000 ha, and in boreal forests in Europe they prefer large patches of mature forest for hunting. He suggests changes in the boreal landscape have resulted in a deterioration of goshawk hunting ranges, making it more difficult for them to secure adequate food for breeding. This factor is probably more important than a shortage of nest sites. He also notes declining prey densities may be associated with forestry which would affect goshawk numbers.

Although we know goshawk demography is strongly influenced by prey availability, the degree to which forest management positively or negatively influences prey availability is not well documented. This is because most investigations of the effects of forest management on goshawk prey typically correlate avian or mammalian abundance—usually not both—with timber management using one–three replicates studied over 1–2 yr. They are also generally conducted on too small of a spatial scale to be relevant to the goshawk (Marzluff et al. 2000). Marzluff et al. (2000) and Sallabanks et al. (2000) suggest some on-going avian studies are correcting these limitations by expanding their scale of investigation, using sound experimental design and relating forest management to avian demography. Such studies will increase our understanding of how forestry affects goshawk prey, particularly if they successfully identify the mechanisms that relate silviculture to prey population processes.

Fire suppression

Goshawks from most populations occupy forests that are structured by fire. Understanding the extent and duration of how fire effects goshawk habitat may become even more pressing in light of changing climates relative to global warming (Dale et al. 2001). The effects of fire suppression on goshawk populations have not been formally researched. Thus, our assessment of how fire suppression may structure goshawk habitat is conjectural at this point based on our understanding of goshawks and fire ecology.

We think the effects of fire suppression on goshawk habitat will vary due to the complex fire regimes found across the species' distribution. To assess the effects of fire suppression, it is important to distinguish between natural understory and stand-replacing fire regimes (Brown 2000). Historically, natural understory fire regimes dominated ponderosa pine communities, with fire-return intervals of 2–15 yr in many stands (Covington and Moore 1994a, but see Baker and Ehle 2002, Schoennagel et al. 2004). These low-intensity fires were readily suppressed resulting in increased fuel loads that increased the risk of stand-replacing fires in ponderosa pine communities (Covington and Moore 1994a, Allen et al. 2002). The impacts are clear—the density of ponderosa pine forests has increased, the herbaceous layer has almost disappeared and stream flow has been reduced significantly. The shift in community structure of ponderosa pine has also been exacerbated by grazing, logging, and invasive exotics (Allen et al. 2002). Fires now burn over larger areas and are more intense compared to earlier times, and crown fires are becoming common because dense stands of saplings provide ladders that carry fire from the forest floor to the tree canopy (Covington and Moore 1994a). Thus, we speculate that fire suppression may have significantly altered goshawk habitat in ponderosa pine communities.

However, goshawks nesting in northern boreal forests occupy stands that support high-severity, stand-replacing fires that kill most of the canopy either through intense ground fires or flames in the tree crowns (Agee 2000, Turner et al. 2003). The behavior of fires in these habitats can be extreme with daily spread rates of 100 m /min and 13–18 m flame lengths (Kiil and Grigel 1969). The fire-return intervals in subalpine forests tend to be long, ranging from 60 yr in jack pine (*Pinus banksiana*) to 300–350 yr in western boreal stands of spruce (Turner et al. 2003, Agee 2000). Although fires in subalpine forests are often infrequent, they can burn large areas when severe droughts govern regional weather (Turner and Romme 1994, Turner et al. 2003). Thus, infrequent but large-scale fires account for most of the total burned area (Agee 2000, Turner et al. 2003). For example, of over 200 fires between 1972 and 1988 in primarily lodgepole pine forests of Yellowstone National Park, 83% went out by themselves after burning only 0.5 ha (Renkin and Despain 1992). However, the extreme drought and high winds in 1988 produced conditions that burned over 250,000 ha in the Park (Renkin and Despain 1992). Under such extreme fire-weather conditions, variations in fuel structures are of little importance (Bessie and Johnson 1995), and fire suppression has little influence on recent fire behavior during big-fire years (Schullery 1989, Turner et al. 2003, Romme et al. 2004). Effective fire suppression may have been especially difficult in the past because subalpine forests are often in high, remote areas and fire-fighting aircraft have only been available since World War II (Schullery 1989). Thus, we believe that past fire suppression in northern and subalpine conifer forests may have had little effect on goshawk habitat.

On 21 November 2003, Congress passed HR 1904, the Healthy Forests Restoration Act of 2003 with the intent of reducing the threat of catastrophic wildfire to human communities and forest and range lands. New procedures provided under NEPA allow priority fuels reduction and forest restoration projects identified through collaboration with state, local and tribal governments to move forward more quickly. In 2002, federal land management agencies thinned a record 910,000 ha, an increase of 405,000 ha over FY 2000 levels (http://www.USDA.gov [2 Feb 2006]). In 2003, the agencies broke the previous record and treated an additional 1,050,000 ha. Nearly 65% of forest restoration dollars have been invested in the wildland-urban interface, including private lands that surround human communities most at risk from wildfire. From 2001–2003, agencies treated 2,800,000 ha,

and expect to treat 3,800,000 ha by the end of FY 2004 (http://www.USDA.gov [2 Feb 2006]). Thus, forest structures across broad landscapes are being altered as healthy forest initiatives are implemented across the western US. We are unaware of any broad-scale efforts to evaluate the potential effects of the healthy forest initiatives on goshawk populations. In ponderosa pine communities, forest management such as thinning from below may be a necessary first step in restoring goshawk habitat, before prescribed fire can be introduced (Reynolds et al. 1992). However, in other forest types where thinned trees are not consistent with natural forest pattern, there could be a significant negative effect based on reduction in canopy closure. Thus, the degree to which healthy forest initiatives affect goshawk populations will depend on the forest type, extent, spatial arrangement, prescription, and considerations to micro-site requirements (e.g., spatially distributed nest stands) relative to management actions.

Human disturbance

The USFWS (USDI Fish and Wildlife Service 1998a) reported that disturbance generally does not appear to be a significant factor effecting the long-term survival of any North American goshawk population. However, human disturbance such as timber harvesting near nests can cause failure, especially during incubation (Anonymous 1989, Boal and Mannan 1994). Logging activities such as tree cutting, loading, and skidding within 50–100 m of a nest can cause abandonment even with 20-d-old nestlings present (J. Squires, unpubl. data). Camping near nests has also caused failures (N = 2; Speiser 1992). Goshawks in Britain, central Europe, and Japan nest in close proximity to humans in rural landscapes suggesting that some populations are not especially prone to disturbance (Krüger and Lindström 2001, Krüger 2002a, P. L. Kennedy unpubl. data). Lee (1981b) documented that two pairs of goshawks nesting in a ski resort were able to fledge young successfully where they were subjected to daily disturbance in winter and summer due to skiers, snowmobilers, construction, hikers, and horseback riders.

Disturbances associated with research are usually short in duration and believed to have little impact on nesting birds (Squires and Reynolds 1997). Climbing nests for short periods after young have hatched does not cause desertion, nor does banding or attaching transmitters to the adults. The percentage of nesting pairs that successfully raised young with radios (83%, N = 8, 1988–1989) was similar to those without radios (82%, N = 10, 1987–1990; Austin 1993;

but see Reynolds et al. 2003 for effects of transmitter mounts on adult male survival).

Invasive species

The goshawk is not known to interact strongly with any exotic species. Rock Doves and European Starlings (*Sturnus vulgaris*) are consumed by goshawks, but are not documented as frequent prey in diet analyses. No information is available regarding the influence of exotic plant invasions on goshawk habitat and prey. However, the most important exotic plant invasions are occurring on unforested lands at lower elevations where changes in plant communities could influence winter goshawk habitat and prey populations (Stohlgren et al. 2003).

Shooting and trapping

In North America, shooting, trapping, and poisoning are generally illegal and not considered an important mortality factor. However, in the early to mid-1900s, some states like Pennsylvania paid bounties on goshawks, but the effects this had on populations is unknown. European populations were more actively persecuted in efforts to protect private game-bird farms. On the Baltic island of Gotland, 36% of mortalities of radio-tagged birds (N = 67) were killed by humans (Kenward et al. 1991); juveniles were more likely to be shot than adults.

Pesticides and other contaminants

In the early 1970s, pesticide levels were high in Peregrine Falcons (*Falco peregrinus*), Ospreys (*Pandion haliaetus*), Sharp-shinned Hawks, and other raptors in the US, but were low in goshawks (Snyder et al. 1973, Reynolds and Wight 1978). Goshawks, during the 1972–1973 invasion years, contained less organochlorine and polychlorinated biphenols (PCB) residues than other raptors (Havera and Duzan 1986), probably because these birds were from non-agricultural, northern forests. The primary prey species of goshawks tend to accumulate less pesticide in their tissues compared to other accipiters (Rosenfield et al. 1991). The USFWS concluded pesticides and other contaminants appear to have not significantly affected goshawks in the US (USDI Fish and Wildlife Service 1998a).

Kenntner et al. (2003) recently analyzed levels of organochlorine pesticides, PCBs and heavy metals in organ samples of 62 free-ranging goshawks found dead or injured in three regions of Germany from 1995–2001. The contaminant burdens varied significantly among the three regions presumably due to differences in the legislative restrictions on the use of these chemicals in agriculture and forestry prior to German reunification. Extraordinarily high residues of PCBs and DDE, the main metabolite of DDT, were found in livers of goshawks inhabiting Berlin. However, these levels were not high enough to be indicative of acute poisoning and were far below suspected lethal levels in raptors. Levels of contamination were negatively correlated with goshawk age and body condition. Lead concentrations indicative of acute poisoning was detected in one bird and suggested in two other birds. All other heavy metal concentrations were low.

Falconry

Goshawks have been trained for falconry for at least 2,000 yr and were favored among Asian, Middle Eastern, and north European falconers (Cooper 1981). During the 18th century, falconry declined as guns became generally available and goshawks were then viewed as competitors for game. Since World War II, interest in falconry increased and spread to North America. Modern-day falconers value goshawks for their willingness to hunt a variety of prey and their aggressive dispositions (Beebe 1976). In an environmental assessment on falconry and raptor propagation regulations, the USFWS (USDI Fish and Wildlife Service 1988) concluded falconry is a small-scale activity that has no significant biological impact on raptor populations. Mosher (1997) examined data reported by Brohn (1986) and falconers' annual reports and concurred with the conclusions reached by the USFWS. Although falconry has been listed as a potential threat in the western Great Lakes Region (Noll West 1998), no evidence indicated that falconry has an impact on North American populations.

In Britain, Kenward et al. (1981d) determined that captive goshawks had relatively constant annual mortality of about 22% (N = 216 birds) from accidents, infectious diseases, and other clinical conditions. Approximately one-third of the goshawks were eventually lost or released resulting in 13% successfully re-entering the wild in Britain. Once released to the wild, captive goshawks did not require supplemental feeding after they had killed at least twice for themselves.

ECOLOGICAL RELATIONSHIPS WITHIN A MANAGEMENT CONTEXT

To illustrate the ecological linkages described above and how threats may affect these relationships, we constructed an envirogram for the goshawk nesting in the northern Rocky Mountains (Fig. 3). Envirograms hypothesize the ecological linkages among direct and indirect factors and abundance of a species at a particular time and place (Andrewartha and Birch 1984). Envirograms help researchers and managers organize prior knowledge that spans multiple ecological levels while maintaining a focus on ecological factors and processes that directly or indirectly affect the size of a focal population (James et al. 1997). These ecological flow charts are developed using a standardized conceptual framework following the logic and terminology of Andrewartha and Birch (1984). We have used a modification of their approach developed by James et al. (1997) for the Red-cockaded Woodpecker (*Picoides borealis*).

Envirograms depict each organism within the context of a centrum and web. The centrum is comprised of factors that directly affect the organism's abundance such as resources, hazards, or mates. Resources are environmental components that enhance the organism's chance of survival and reproduction and are either negatively or not influenced by the abundance of the organism, e.g., the goshawk's prey. Hazards reduce survival and reproduction in the focal population, and in turn, benefit from increases in the organism's abundance. Mates convey a positive-positive relationship. Indirect factors comprise the web and include anything that can affect a species by modifying its centrum, including the effects of individuals of the focal species on their own populations. Flow in an envirogram tends from distal indirect influences in the web toward the most proximate direct effects on the organism's population as shown in the centrum (Ward 2001). Similar to James et al. (1997) this envirogram contains sub-models for limiting resources and hazards.

The number of factors and interactions depicted in an envirogram are limited only by the knowledge of the organism's ecology. We constructed the goshawk envirogram based on the information presented in this document and in Kennedy (2003). This envirogram is basically a hypothesis that could be used to develop models with goshawk abundance as the response variable and the factors influencing abundance as dependent variables. Figure 3 is not comprehensive, simply a schematic of possible interactions with an emphasis on the potential effects of forest management on the direct and indirect factors that could influence goshawk populations in the interior mountains of western North America. A wide variety of alternative envirograms could be developed with existing information and these models could be evaluated against empirical data

using a wide variety of techniques. Site-specific envirograms could be used in conjunction with the silvicultural concepts presented in Reynolds et al. (1992) to develop regional or local management plans to prevent goshawk population declines.

In Fig. 3, current management practices that might influence goshawk numbers are indicated by ovals. As indicated in earlier sections, timber-management practices can have a profound influence on all direct and indirect processes that influence goshawk numbers. Progressively more indirect effects appear in the columns of the web. For example, in the sub-model for nest-site availability, if the number of large trees available for nest sites is limiting, the rate of maturation of younger trees must be balanced by the number of older trees lost to harvest and death for population stability. However, nest sites in good condition can be usurped by competitors and the abundance of competitors may be influenced by habitat fragmentation from timber harvest and fire. The other sub-models reflect other management activities that we think influence goshawk abundance and have been discussed in more detail in earlier sections. The pathways could be made more specific if information was available on the types of management actions a management unit is conducting that might negatively impact or enhance goshawk populations.

INFORMATION NEEDS

Effective sensitive-species programs are firmly grounded in ecological knowledge that supports management recommendations (Squires et al. 1998). Understanding the ecological characteristics associated with a given ecosystem such as food webs, predatory relationships, disturbance patterns, and vegetative structure and landscape characteristics are essential for providing the specific habitat needs of sensitive species within the constraints of ecosystem function. To empirically evaluate the envirogram in Fig. 3 and ultimately determine the effects of forest management on goshawk abundance, we need additional information on many aspects of goshawk ecology. The winter ecology of goshawks is almost completely unknown. In addition, positive and negative effects of timber management on goshawk resources need to be rigorously evaluated, ideally with forest-management experiments. We do not know the thresholds above which forest fragmentation may alter competitive interactions, such as increasing Red-tailed Hawks and Great Horned Owls, which ultimately could affect population persistence. Finally, a pressing need exists to assess habitat needs at broader spatial scales, and to have

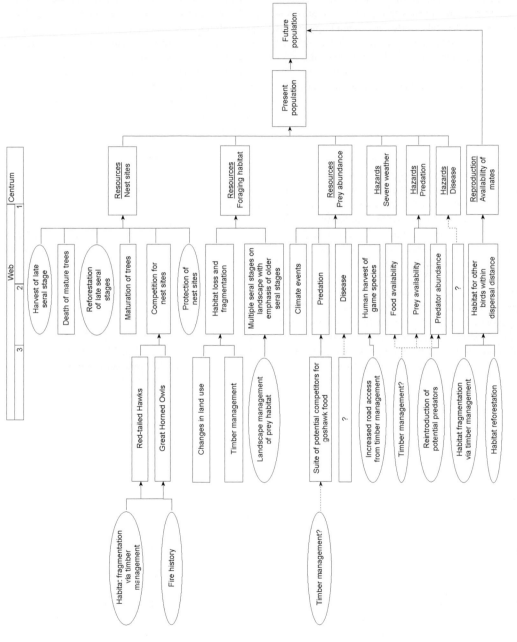

FIGURE 3. Envirogram for the Northern Goshawk in the interior mountain western North America (modified from Kennedy 2003).

the necessary spatial data to monitor changes in forest structure and composition from management across broad landscapes.

Information needs are easy to list, but are often ignored. In many cases, it is exceedingly difficult for agencies to fund the acquisition of new information, and in other cases, decision makers resist new understandings. Successful sensitive species programs depend on a strong commitment by line officers at all levels (Squires et al. 1998). To foster that commitment, researchers must communicate with line officers throughout the planning process; participation builds ownership.

Winter ecology

Given the goshawk's life-history strategy and our understanding of population regulation in similar long-lived avian species (Newton 1998), it is highly likely that over-winter survival of juveniles and adults and the condition of the female entering the breeding season has a stronger influence on goshawk population regulation then conditions that occur after breeding is initiated. However, as indicated earlier, our understanding of goshawk winter ecology is poor. In areas such as Minnesota where goshawks appear to be year-round residents (Boal et al. 2003) they may use similar habitats year-round (Boal et al. 2002). However, the limited evidence on goshawk populations in the inter-mountain west suggest these populations are migratory or partially migratory (Squires and Ruggerio 1995, Dewey et al. 2003) and during the winter are regularly found in open habitats or forest-shrubland ecotones (J. Kirkley, unpubl. data.). Therefore, unlike the Spotted Owl, goshawk habitat requirements may be dramatically different for different stages of its annual cycle. Do we mange the goshawk as a forested species during the breeding season and as a rangeland species during the winter? More information is needed on goshawk winter habitat selection patterns and winter diet before these types of basic management questions can be addressed.

Forest management experiments

As recommended by DeStefano (1998) and Kennedy (1998), on-site experiments are necessary to clearly understand how goshawks and their prey and competitors are affected by forest management. To date, Penteriani and Faivre (2001) have conducted the only experimental analysis of goshawk responses to silvicultural treatments. The absence of such studies in the literature is perplexing considering

these quasi-experiments are being implemented continuously in the form of timber harvests near goshawk nests. Most federal timber sales are identified years before the sale allowing for collection of adequate pre-treatment data. Monitoring pre- and post-treatment movements of even a limited sample could provide fascinating qualitative insights into goshawk responses to harvest and could be the basis for designing future experiments. Also, measurements of prey responses to experimental harvests could be conducted at the same time. We surmise that we would learn more and spend fewer resources about goshawk responses to forest management using this approach then we have learned from the many correlative studies conducted on this topic.

Management databases

Without a database that clearly summarizes past and future management activities conducted by each land management agency, it is impossible to evaluate threats to goshawk nesting habitat and develop potential conservation scenarios. GIS databases that summarize the location, date, and sizes of management activities are needed to assess how goshawk habitat is being enhanced or reduced as indicated in Fig. 3. Spatial databases that relate predicted immediate and long-term changes to forest composition and stand structure are most needed. Spatial databases could also be used to identify the stands that should be monitored to evaluate predicted changes. These spatial databases could be used as a part of the forest-plan development process. Spatial information would also streamline the environmental-assessment process where cumulative effects of forest management are evaluated at the forest and regional scale.

SURVEY AND MONITORING

Population monitoring

Information on goshawk populations is generally obtained by monitoring nesting activity at local scales (Roberson et al., unpubl. data; Kennedy 2003; Hargis and Woodbridge, *this volume*). Although goshawk demographic studies have significantly increased understanding of goshawk population dynamics, no studies to date have generated adequate empirical stage-specific estimates of survival and fecundity for estimating population growth rates (λ) using matrix projection models at the local scale, and demographic data are unavailable to estimate λ over broader spatial extents. In addition, nesting densities are difficult to estimate due to the bird's low detectability and uncommon status, so trends in this parameter are not available (Kennedy 1997).

A viable alternative to monitoring goshawk demographics is estimating trends in site occupancy. Territory occupancy is a reliable index of habitat quality and productivity in breeding raptors (Sergio and Newton 2003). Although, goshawk site occupancy has been monitored in several populations across the species range (Kennedy 1997, 2003), these data have limited utility for monitoring goshawk population trends because standard protocols are not regularly used to determine site occupancy, and analytical techniques for estimating detection probabilities of site occupancy have not been available. Failing to account for imperfect detectability will result in underestimates of site occupancy (MacKenzie et al. 2003). MacKenzie et al. (2002, 2003) addressed this problem by developing analytical approaches to estimate site occupancy rates when detection probabilities are imperfect (<1.0). This is a likelihood-based method that allows for the incorporation of covariates, e.g., habitat type or patch size, into detection probability estimates. These new analytical approaches have considerable promise for monitoring goshawk population performance at large spatial scales. Hargis and Woodbridge (*this volume*) describe a bioregional monitoring program for northern goshawks that is based on this approach.

Habitat-based monitoring

Kennedy and Andersen (1999) suggested that if goshawk habitat can be well-defined and demographic data are available from several study areas for an analysis of population trends, a model or models that predict(s) relationships between preferred breeding season and winter habitat and population trends and/or performance could be developed. The rationale for switching to habitat-based monitoring has been clearly articulated by Roloff and Haufler (1997) and Lint et al. (1999) and includes cost-effectiveness in emphasizing the ecosystem rather than single species and the ability to develop a more proactive management program.

Preliminary habitat models based on available habitat information could be developed to predict goshawk habitat (Kennedy and Andersen 1999, McGrath et al. 2003). These models could be independently validated and modified based on validation results in an iterative process. Kennedy (1997, 1998) suggested the most efficient way to identify consistent patterns in data collected in multiple studies is to conduct meta-analyses of the existing habitat literature. However, meta-analysis is only an approach for model parameterization; it is not a replacement for model testing and validation. The habitat models would require testing with demographic data before such an approach could be implemented. If models can be developed to predict goshawk population performance, then monitoring programs could switch emphasis from population-based to habitat-based monitoring.

Although goshawks may select habitat on the basis of structural characteristics and prey availability, they are also at the mercy of unpredictable factors such as drought, severe storms, or predation (Penteriani et al. 2002b). Habitat models would need to incorporate these stochastic processes to accurately predict population performance. If habitat models do not adequately predict population performance and it is determined that habitat features have little affect on goshawk population dynamics, a strictly habitat-based monitoring program may have limited ability to predict changes in goshawk demographic performance and population-based monitoring would need to be continued (Kennedy and Andersen 1999).

PROCEEDING IN THE FACE OF UNCERTAINTY

Based on our review of goshawk ecology, it is clear that many life-history attributes of this species are unknown. It is a daunting task to gain the complex ecological knowledge needed to manage top-level carnivores, like goshawks. Land managers are being forced to make land-use decisions based on limited information that varies in reliability. Thus, land mangers are in the difficult position of having to use best available information while making a conscious decision regarding how to proceed in the face of uncertainty.

Science represents a rigorous, systematic approach by which humans gain understanding of nature. Competing ideas regarding how the world works are measured against observations. Research and reliability of knowledge gained from research depend on appropriate application of the scientific method. Unfortunately, not all research in wildlife ecology and management results in reliable knowledge. Unreliable knowledge can result from inappropriate application of the scientific method in the design and implementation of these studies (Romesburg 1981, Nudds and Morrison 1991) and/ or confusing subjective, political values with objective, technical knowledge (Nudds and Morrison 1991, Kennedy 1997, 1998, White and Kiff 1998). Obtaining reliable knowledge on wide-ranging predators, like goshawks, is expensive. Thus, the problem of how to make defensible decisions in the face of uncertainty is a problem that will persist for the foreseeable future.

Society could do much to reduce the uncertainties associated with managing species, but often does not provide the financial or political will. If limited data are available, formal modeling structures can account for uncertainty (Todd and Burgman 1998). Usually, however, few data are available and uncertainty is addressed using ad hoc methods that lack rigorous quantification.

The Delphi approach

The Delphi method is a way to address uncertainty by seeking a consensus of scientific opinion rather than to generate new knowledge (Ziglio 1996). It is common for agencies to assemble panels of experts and ask them their opinion regarding the potential impact of management decisions. For example, the forest ecosystem management assessment team (Forest Ecosystem Management Assessment Team 1993) involved over 70 experts that had special knowledge of species or species groups (Meslow et al. 1994, Ruggiero and McKelvey 2000). Delphi methods, in their various forms, are appealing because they are quick, require no new knowledge, and have been accepted by the courts (Ruggiero and McKelvey 2000). Delphi is also appealing in that it logically follows that species experts should better understand potential impacts compared to local biologists and managers. However, despite these strengths, the primary appeal of Delphi in conservation planning is its expedience (Ruggiero and McKelvey 2000).

Although Delphi methods are quick and require no new information, scientifically they are inappropriate for conservation decisions (Ruggiero and McKelvey 2000). The collective opinions of experts cannot be reproduced; they have an unknown error factor, and an unknown relationship to the species' ecology. In addition, expert opinions do not represent independent votes regarding potential effects. Species-experts often read the same scientific journals, attend the same conferences, and receive similar technical training. Science has many examples of commonly held beliefs that were later proved wrong. Although in the past, Delphi has been admissible the courts, this acceptance may change with new data-quality standards. Thus, in the future, Delphi methods may not provide a defensible method for addressing the uncertainties associated with goshawk conservation and management.

Inductive science

We believe that scientific investigation is the only defensible way for addressing the uncertainties associated with species management. Romesburg (1981) argued that much wildlife science was compromised with respect to providing the reliable knowledge required to make management decisions. He stated that good science based on the hypothetic-deductive (H-D) method is best able to provide reliable knowledge. This method employs three steps: (1) observation and induction (the use of repeated observations to discover laws of association), (2) hypothesis formulation, and (3) tests of these hypotheses, preferably with experimentation. It also includes a methodology for dealing with uncertainty. Romesburg (1981) pointed out that some accepted knowledge about wildlife is untested hypotheses about observations because many studies go through the first two steps but not the third. Induction can provide us with reliable knowledge about associations such as the association of goshawks with forests having certain structural characteristics. However, this method does not provide the mechanism for understanding the processes that underlie this association nor does it provide reliable knowledge about cause and effect. Thus, we can describe the structure of forests used by goshawks, but we cannot ascertain which characteristics are important or why, without application of the H-D method. We can describe patterns through induction but need the H-D method to understand why these patterns occur and which components of those patterns are important. In terms of management, understanding why a pattern has occurred and what caused it are important for predicting effects when observed patterns are changed via management or other processes (USDI Fish and Wildlife Service 1995b).

As Nudds and Morrison (1991) point out, resistance to using the H-D method in wildlife biology is common. The resistance includes claims that: (1) nothing is yet known about a system so hypotheses are not apparent, (2) funding agencies do not support tests of hypotheses, and (3) the H-D method is impossible if experiments are impractical. Nudds and Morrison address the first challenge by admitting there will always be a need for new data from which to generate testable hypotheses. This challenge just reflects the need for more research. The second addresses the difficulty to fund hypothesis tests. This is certainly true given the tight budget constraints facing most agencies, but administrators are recognizing the need. For example, the USFS has embraced the concept of adaptive management that is management based on the evaluation of results from experimentation, evaluation, and new management experiments (Walters and Holling 1990). Administrators are realizing they should be able to justify why they spend money on tests of hypotheses that explicitly evaluates the cost-effectiveness of their management actions.

The third challenge that the H-D method is impractical to implement assumes the method only allows for manipulative, controlled, and replicated experiments. However, this argument rests on a very narrow definition of experimentation. As Nudds and Morrison (1991) and Murphy and Noon (1991) point out, this challenge does not recognize what is most important about the H-D approach is the attempt to falsify hypotheses and erect better ones. H-D research is not characterized by whether or not it is experimental, because hypotheses can be evaluated with non-experimental data (Ratti and Garton 1994). Data collected in non-experimental or descriptive studies are more limited in terms of their reliability (e.g., one can not infer cause and effect from non-experimental data), but they can be used to test hypotheses and are certainly better then ignoring hypothesis testing completely. Well-designed descriptive studies that include unbiased sampling techniques, adequate sample sizes, and appropriate statistical tests can be used to evaluate management hypotheses.

DEMANDS FOR SCIENCE-BASED MANAGEMENT

The ESA requires that we use best scientific data when conserving species that are listed as threatened or endangered on the federal level and the ecosystems upon which they depend (Smallwood et al. 1999). This approach should apply to management of sensitive species such as the goshawk. Squires et al. (1998) surveyed USFS wildlife biologists across the country asking them to list two general information needs that would be most useful for managing sensitive species. The biologists responded that information regarding natural range of variation in population characteristics, as well as autecological habitat relationships were their top information needs. Clearly, management of sensitive or listed species should be science based as described above and not based on subjective judgments as is commonly the case (Nudds and Morrison 1991, Kennedy 1997, Smallwood et al. 1999).

Agencies are subjected to increasing congressional and judicial pressures to base their policies and management actions on good science (Data Quality Act enacted in 2002; U. S. Supreme Court, Daubert v. Merrell Dow Pharmaceuticals [113 S.Ct. 2786, 1993 decision; Tellus Institute 2003]). Thus,

land managers and decision makers not only have to determine if their management actions have a scientific basis, but they also must evaluate the quality of the underlying science in terms of peer review, clear objectives, adequate sample sizes, correct statistical analyses, and appropriate methods. In 2003, the Coalition of Arizona-New Mexico counties, the Washington Contract Loggers Association, the Northern Arizona Loggers Association, and a forestry company, Olsen & Associates, jointly submitted industry sponsored data-quality petitions challenging the USFS's decision to restrict logging in order to protect goshawk habitat according to USFS, Region 3 (Reynolds et al. 1992). In a detailed 281-page petition, the petitioners challenged the report as inaccurate, biased and arbitrary. Issues such as nest stand and foraging habitat conditions and canopy cover were contested. The other petitions filed by the industry groups challenged amendments to forest plans and goshawk management in the Black Hills National Forest that followed similar habitat recommendations as in the Southwest. The Center for Biological Diversity, with nine environmental groups co-signing, submitted comments requesting the USFS to reject the petitions because they failed to meet legal requirements and were intended to circumvent the forest planning process (http://www.ombwatch.com [2 February 2006]).

In July 2003, the USFS Rocky Mountain Research Station issued a response letter to the industry petitioners stating, that while eight minor errors were in the document, the inaccuracies did not affect desired forest conditions or specific management recommendations. In addition, Reynolds et al. (1992) had received peer review that was well beyond the norm—19 scientists and managers at universities, state wildlife agencies, and governmental agencies—prior to publication. The letter concluded that the claims of the petitioners had no substantive merit, and that the Reynolds et al. (1992) would not be retracted (http://www.fs.fed.us/qoi/documents/2003/07/rfc3001response.pdf [2 February 2006]).

This example illustrates the high level of scrutiny that management recommendations for sensitive species, like goshawks, can receive. It also illustrates the importance and central role that good science plays in resource decision making, and how data-quality standards can substantially impact the scientific underpinnings of management decisions. Forest planning in the Southwest would have been disrupted greatly had Reynolds et al. (1992) been rescinded due to lack of peer review or was found lacking in other data-quality issues.

CONCLUSIONS

In conservation planning, a fundamental mismatch often occurs between the state of knowledge and the feasibility of obtaining specific knowledge, and the actions that society would have land managers take towards species conservation (Ruggiero and McKelvey 2000). In this paper, we assessed the current knowledge concerning goshawk ecology, and we discussed the pressing information needs for conservation and management. The uncertainty associated with goshawk management is similar to issues confronted by the lynx science team when asked to define appropriate management for Canada lynx (*Lynx canadensis*), a species with a life history that also is poorly understood (Ruggiero et al. 2000). Ruggiero and his colleagues define what they called qualified insights that were an attempt to embrace science while recognizing uncertainty (Ruggiero and McKelvey 2000). Qualified insights are specific statements that are backed by the balance of scientific evidence, but they are fundamentally subjective because they are based on scientific judgment. The specific linkage between data and inference is what separates this method from opinion-based methods, i.e., Delphi. The statements are qualified because the relationships are scientifically known for given areas, and we then infer the degree that these understandings can be transferred to outside areas with local knowledge.

The qualified insights that we offer are based on: (1) our review of the current state of knowledge, (2) the degree this information is applicable to different subspecies and populations, and (3) our combined experience researching goshawks. These insights are on topics of key management concern and for which sufficient information is available to form some preliminary conclusions. The conclusions we present as qualified insights are our attempt to distill our current understandings to the most salient issues affecting goshawk management and conservation. However, we offer these insights fully recognizing our imperfect knowledge of this species' life history. Our conclusions are best viewed as testable hypotheses that merit further research and testing.

ARE GOSHAWK POPULATIONS DECLINING?

The goshawk has been proposed for listing several times under the ESA and its status has been and still is the object of considerable litigation. It is currently not listed as a threatened species but is considered a sensitive species or a species of concern by most governmental agencies and non-governmental organizations within the Rocky Mountain Region (Region 2) of USFS. Kennedy (1997) evaluated the demographic data available on goshawks through 1996 and concluded that no evidence showed goshawk populations were declining. The USFWS published a status review in 1998 (USDI Fish and Wildlife Service 1998a) and their review supported Kennedy's (1997) conclusions as did a recent technical review of the USFWS status review (Andersen et al. 2005).

No new demographic evidence suggests a decline in goshawk populations. Existing data, including those from migration counts, trends in BBS data, estimates of production, breeding distribution, detection surveys, local studies of population dynamics, and estimates of breeding density are inadequate to assess population trends in goshawks west of the 100th meridian. Although these studies have significantly increased understanding of goshawk distribution and population dynamics, no studies to date have generated adequate empirical stage-specific estimates of survival and fecundity for estimating lambda (λ). Demographic data are unavailable to estimate λ at the scale of western North America. In addition, densities are difficult to estimate due to the bird's low detectability and uncommon status, so trends in this parameter are also not available.

Four European studies have reported on population trends in various locales (Thissen et al. 1982, Widén 1997, Kenward et al. 1999, Krüger and Lindström 2001). Three of the four studies concluded that goshawk populations were stable or increasing (Thissen et al. 1982, Kenward et al. 1999, Krüger and Lindström 2001). One study (Widén 1997) concluded that goshawk populations in Fennoscandia declined by 50–60% from the 1950s to the 1980s. The trend since the 1980s is unknown.

We conclude that no evidence shows that North American goshawk populations are declining. However, we cannot separate the following hypotheses given the nature of the available evidence: the goshawk is not declining, or it is declining but there is not sufficient information to detect the declines. The majority of the data from Europe suggest that the species is not in jeopardy of extinction globally, although populations might be declining in regional pockets, e.g., Fennoscandia.

WHAT FACTORS LIMIT GOSHAWK POPULATIONS?

Experimental evidence shows that food during the breeding season limits goshawk reproduction (Ward and Kennedy 1996, Dewey and Kennedy 2001) and recruitment via natal dispersal (Kennedy and Ward

2003). Predation also limits goshawk reproduction and is influenced by food availability (Dewey and Kennedy 2001). Whether or not food and predation are additive or synergistic (as demonstrated in Song Sparrows [*Melospiza melodia*]; Zanette et al. 2003) has not been determined. The role of food and predation in limiting over-winter survival is unknown. Weather during the breeding season influences goshawk productivity, but the effect of weather on regulating populations is also unknown.

Strong correlative evidence demonstrates that goshawk population growth rate is also regulated by density-dependent territoriality (Krüger and Lindström 2001). In a German population, territories that were occupied more often and earlier had a higher mean brood size, and fecundity did not increase with increasing density in the best territories. Increased usage of poor territories at high densities results in a decrease in per capita reproductive success (Krüger and Lindström 2001). The site factors that influenced territory quality were not identified in this study.

We conclude that goshawk breeding populations are limited by food, predation, and density-dependent territoriality. High-quality territories which are regularly occupied and very productive likely contain high abundance of prey, low abundance of predators, and forest structural characteristics that enhance prey acquisition and predator avoidance. The factors regulating winter populations and the effect of winter conditions on breeding populations are unknown.

WHAT ARE THE PRINCIPAL HABITAT ATTRIBUTES AND RELEVANT SPATIAL SCALES OF NEST HABITAT?

Goshawks nests in many forest types throughout their range (Squires and Reynolds 1997). These forests include mixed hardwood-hemlock stands in the eastern deciduous forests (Speiser and Bosakowski 1987), various pine and aspen forests in western North America (Reynolds et al. 1982, Hall 1984, Younk and Bechard 1994a, Siders and Kennedy 1996, Squires and Ruggiero 1996, Clough 2000, McGrath et al. 2003), and ponderosa pine-mixed conifer forest (Erickson 1987, Crocker-Bedford and Chaney 1988, Kennedy 1988, Reynolds et al. 1994, Siders and Kennedy 1996). Within these types, there are at least three levels of habitat scale that appear to be biologically important during the breeding season—the nest area, the PFA, and the foraging area (Reynolds et al. 1992, Kennedy et al. 1994). How the size of these areas may differ among populations is not well understood.

Nest areas include forests with a narrow range of structural conditions (Reynolds et al. 1992, Squires and Reynolds 1997). Nest areas are usually mature forests with large trees, relatively closed canopies (60–90%), and open understories (Reynolds et al. 1982, Moore and Henny 1983, Speiser and Bosakowski 1987, Crocker-Bedford and Chaney 1988, Kennedy 1988, Hayward and Escano 1989, Reynolds et al. 1992, Squires and Ruggiero 1996, Penteriani and Faivre 1997, Selås 1997b, Squires and Reynolds 1997, Daw et al. 1998, Daw and DeStefano 2001, Finn et al. 2002b, McGrath et al. 2003). Within nest areas, goshawks usually nest in one of the largest trees (Reynolds et al. 1982, Saunders 1982, Erickson 1987, Hargis et al. 1994, Squires and Ruggiero 1996) with some exceptions (Speiser and Bosakowski 1989). Limited data also suggest that forest structure may be more important than prey abundance when selecting nest sites (Beier and Drennan 1997, Penteriani et al. 2001). Although understanding the structural characteristics of nest areas and nest trees is one of the best known aspects of goshawk ecology, it is still difficult to compare preference relationships among studies due to different field methods and biased nest-search methods.

The PFA was conceptualized by Reynolds et al. (1992) and empirically supported by studies of family movement patterns (Kennedy et al. 1994, Kenward et al. 1993a, and Kennedy and Ward 2003). The function of the PFA is unclear, but it may be important to fledglings by providing prey items on which to develop hunting skills or may provide cover from predation (Reynolds et al. 1992). PFAs are usually in mature forests with dense canopies and small openings (Daw and DeStefano 2001, Finn et al. 2002a, McGrath et al. 2003); these structural components appear to be important to site occupancy (Finn et al. 2002a). The size of the PFA was originally estimated at 170 ha (Kennedy et al. 1994), but a study by McGrath et al. (2003) found late-seral forests, high understory growth, and high canopy cover (50%) were more common around nests compared to random sites up to 83 ha. McClaren et al. (2005) measured PFA size for *A. g. laingi* on Vancouver Island, British Columbia, and mean PFA size for 12 juveniles at 12 nests was approximately 60 ha. PFAs likely vary in size depending on local environmental conditions and perhaps there are sub-specific differences in use of habitat by fledglings.

Goshawks use an array of habitat types in foraging areas, but often select forests with a high density of large trees, greater canopy cover, high tree basal area, and open understories (Doyle and Smith 1994,

Hargis et al. 1994, Beier and Drennan 1997), but with much variation (Kenward 1982, Widén 1989, Austin 1993, Bright-Smith and Mannan 1994, Hargis et al. 1994, Younk and Bechard 1994a, Beier and Drennan 1997). Habitat structure may be more important than prey abundance where goshawks kill prey (Beier and Drennan 1997, Good 1998, Bloxton 2002), again with exceptions (Kenward and Widén 1989).

We conclude that at least three spatial scales are biologically important to nesting goshawks—the nest area, the PFA, and the foraging area. Habitat structure may be as important as prey abundance when selecting nest areas and PFAs. The principal structural components include a high density of large trees, high canopy closure, and high tree basal area than generally available in the landscape; these components are provided in mature forests. Foraging areas are more heterogeneous, but often include mature-forest components.

Are Goshawks Habitat Specialists or Generalists?

Goshawks in western North American breed in forested habitats, and in most places appear to select old-growth and mature forests for nesting. Goshawks often place their nests in the larger or largest trees in a stand, and stands in which nests are placed tend to be older than adjacent stands. However, not all goshawk territories are equally suitable. Thus, nesting habitat diversity may increase with nesting density because lower-quality territories are more regularly occupied at higher densities. These lower-quality territories may have different structural characteristics than high quality territories.

A core area seems to exist around goshawk nests (<100 ha) where the forest can be characterized by large trees with high canopy closure, and this core is surrounded by a heterogeneous landscape with a variety of forest cover types and seral stages. Within this heterogeneous landscape, goshawks may forage selectively in forests with a high density of large trees, greater canopy cover, high tree basal area, and open understories.

The limited data on winter-habitat-use patterns suggest that winter-habitat diversity is greater then breeding-season habitat diversity. During the winter, goshawks use forests as well as non-forested habitats and their habitat-use patterns are partially dictated by residency patterns. Year-round they hunt a wide variety of prey species that occur in a variety of habitat types.

We conclude that goshawks have a strong preference for mature and old-growth forests, but this preference is dependent on nest density, scale, and season; this preference seems strongest within approximately 100 ha of the nest stand. As nest density increases, low quality habitats are more likely to be occupied and thus, nesting habitat diversity used by the population may increase. As spatial scale increases from the nest site to the landscape in which home ranges are embedded, habitat heterogeneity increases. Goshawks are more of a habitat generalist at these larger spatial scales then at the scale of the nest site. Finally, the limited data on non-breeding habitat use patterns suggest that goshawks are more of a habitat generalist during the non-breeding season then during the breeding season.

What Human Activities Most Affect the Persistence of Goshawk Populations?

Forest management can have an impact on the structure and function of goshawk habitat (Reynolds 1989, Crocker-Bedford 1990, Bright-Smith and Mannan 1994, Woodbridge and Detrich 1994, Beier and Drennan 1997, Desimone 1997, USDI Fish and Wildlife Service 1998a, Greenwald et al. 2005). Habitat fragmentation may also favor early successional competitors and predators (Woodbridge and Detrich 1994). Forest management, such as controlled fire and thinning, may improve or degrade habitat depending on implementation, especially as they affect the density of large trees and canopy closure. Forest management that reduces the size of nest stands may decrease occupancy rates (Woodbridge and Detrich 1994). Few studies have directly assessed the impacts of timber management on goshawk populations, but limited data suggest goshawks can tolerate timber harvesting near their nesting area below some threshold (Penteriani and Faivre 2001, McGrath et al. 2003). The effects of forest management on prey populations vary by species, and specific effects are poorly documented.

Although human persecution may have had an impact on goshawk populations in the past, it is not believed to be a factor affecting the persistence of North American populations. Likewise, pesticides and other contaminants do not appear to have an impact on North American populations (Snyder et al. 1973, Reynolds and Wight 1978, Rosenfield et al. 1991, USDI Fish and Wildlife Service 1998a), but this topic has received little study in North America. Recent European data suggest some populations of goshawks still show high levels of organochlorines and PCBs (Kenntner et al. 2003), but the effect of these levels on population persistence is unknown. The populations with high levels of contaminants occur in areas where regulatory control of the use of these chemicals is less stringent then in the US. Although falconry may impact local populations (Noll West 1998), it is not at a sufficient scale to affect North American populations (Brohn 1986, USDI Fish and Wildlife Service 1988, Mosher 1997).

We conclude that forest management—cutting, thinning, and controlled burning—is the primary human-caused activity that has an impact on goshawk populations. These impacts can either enhance or degrade goshawk habitat depending on type and extent of habitat alterations. Effects of timber management on goshawks are poorly documented, especially relative to prey populations and community interactions. The impacts associated with human persecution, pesticides, and falconry are negligible.

Is Goshawk Monitoring Feasible Given Current Tools?

Information on goshawk populations in North America is generally obtained by monitoring nesting activity at local scales (Roberson et al., unpubl. data; Hargis and Woodbridge, *this volume*). These local monitoring programs typically focus on trends in reproduction which indicate extensive temporal and spatial variation and are difficult to interpret in the absence of survival data (McClaren et al. 2002). When survival has been estimated, it is usually based on mark-resighting techniques and the studies have insufficient sample sizes (<100 birds) to estimate survival with acceptable levels of precision (DeStefano et al. 1994b, Kennedy 1997). Although demography data are vital to determining trends in goshawks populations, funding for the goshawk waxes and wanes as the threat of listing the goshawk comes and goes (DeStefano 1998). This is counterproductive to implementing the long-term, large-scale studies needed to evaluate goshawk demographics. Estimating the rate of population change for a non-listed species such as the goshawk may simply be too difficult and take too long to provide meaningful information for listing decisions and other management concerns.

Documenting the distribution of all forest structural stages, including mature and old-growth forests, would be an important step in goshawk management. Such documentation will be important for a number of wildlife species, including the goshawk and has been suggested by Crocker-Bedford (1998), DeStefano (1998), and Smallwood (1998). Although methods to gather and compile data on current forest conditions need to be improved, assessing goshawk status based solely on the distribution of old-growth or mature forests is not appropriate at present because our current understanding of goshawk-habitat relations is poor.

A viable alternative for monitoring goshawk population performance in a rigorous and cost-effective manner is estimating trends in site occupancy (presence or absence of breeding goshawks at a site). Currently the most accurate field method for determining site occupancy is dawn vocalization surveys (Dewey et al. 2003). If these surveys are conducted in a sampling framework that allows for estimation of detection probabilities (MacKenzie et al. 2002, 2003), trends in site occupancy could be used as an index of goshawk population performance. Hargis and Woodbridge (*this volume*) describe a bioregional monitoring program for northern goshawks that is based on this approach.

We conclude that the best current method available for monitoring goshawk population performance is monitoring trends in site occupancy. We recommend using dawn vocalization surveys as described by Dewey et al. (2003) and estimating detection probabilities of these surveys with recent analytical procedures described by MacKenzie et al. (2002, 2003).

Is Goshawk Management a Serious Issue in Terms of Feasibility and Need?

Goshawks have life-history attributes that are specialized in terms of their morphology and their use of nest habitat. The mature forests that provide nesting and foraging habitat for goshawks are often the same areas that are important for producing forest products. As such, forest management does potentially impact goshawk populations. The density of nesting goshawks tends to be low, and is limited through a combination of food availability, predation, and density-dependent territoriality. Low density and general rarity makes it difficult to assess long-term population trends of regional and local populations. Although monitoring the effects of forest management on goshawks is difficult, it is possible given adequate funding and political will.

We conclude that goshawks have life-history attributes that make them sensitive to changes in forest structure and composition. These attributes also make it difficult to monitor population responses to habitat alterations. Thus, goshawk management is a serious issue because management agencies need concerted efforts to monitor goshawk responses to their management actions within an experimental context. This is necessary before the effects of forestry on goshawk populations are elucidated across the broad landscapes that are congruent with goshawk spatial-use patterns.

ACKNOWLEDGMENTS

We acknowledge G. D. Hayward (USDA Forest Service, Region 2) for providing the original conceptual and logistical support for Kennedy (2003) that was the partial basis for this document. We acknowledge W. M. Block (Project Leader, Rocky Mountain Research Station) for providing financial support. Finally, we thank M. L. Morrison and C. D. Marti for their encouragement and patience during this project. The material on the legal and administrative history was greatly enhanced by discussions with E. Paul. C. Coiner and J. Dick assisted with graphics and copy editing, and R. N. Lehman assisted with the literature review.

DEMOGRAPHY OF NORTHERN GOSHAWKS IN NORTHERN ARIZONA, 1991–1996

RICHARD T. REYNOLDS AND SUZANNE M. JOY

Abstract. We studied 282 nesting attempts on 107 territories of Northern Goshawks (*Accipiter gentilis*) on the Kaibab Plateau in northern Arizona from 1991–1996. Mark-recapture methods were used to estimate recruitment, turnover of adults on territories, fidelity to territories by adults, and apparent annual survival of breeding adults. Territories were regularly spaced at a mean nearest-neighbor distance of 3.9 km. Annual proportion of pairs breeding and recapture rates were high in 1991–1993, sharply declined in 1994, and partially recovered in 1995–1996. Average annual turnover of breeding goshawks was 42% for males and 25% for females. Breeding males stayed on their territories from one breeding year to the next in 97% of cases and females in 95% of cases. Of 64 capture-recapture models evaluated in program SURGE, the model with the lowest AIC $\{Phi_s, P_t\}$ showed that, while survival differed between genders, it was constant for both genders over years. Probability of recapturing a goshawk varied with time (0.15 in 1994; 0.66 in 1992) but not with gender; recaptures were lowest in years when few of the territorial goshawks nested and highest when the majority of pairs nested.

Key Words: *Accipiter gentilis*, Arizona, capture-recapture, demography, Kaibab Plateau, nesting success, Northern Goshawk, reproduction, survival, territory fidelity, turnover.

DEMOGRAFÍA DE GAVILANES AZOR EN EL NORTE DE ARIZONA, 1991–1996

Resumen. Estudiamos 282 intentos de anidación en 107 territorios de Gavilanes Azor (*Accipiter gentilis*), en la meseta de Kaibab en el norte de Arizona, de 1991–1996. Métodos de Marqueo-recaptura fueron utilizados para estimar aislamiento y reemplazo de adultos en los territorios, fidelidad de los adultos al territorio, y sobrevivencia anual aparente de adultos reproductores. Los territorios fueron espaciados regularmente a una distancia vecino-cercano media de 3.9 km. La proporción anual de parejas reproductoras y las tasas de recaptura fueron altas en 1991-1993, declinaron agudamente en 1994, y se recuperaron parcialmente en 1995–1996. El promedio anual de reemplazo de gavilanes reproductores fue de 42% para machos y de 25% para hembras. Los machos reproductores permanecieron en sus territorios por un año reproductivo al otro en un 97% de los casos, y las hembras en el 95% de los casos. De 64 modelos captura-recaptura estudiados en el programa SURGE, el modelo con el más bajo AIC $\{Phi_s, P_t\}$ mostró que, mientras la sobrevivencia difirió entre géneros, la sobrevivencia fue constante para ambos géneros a través de los años. La probabilidad de recapturar al gavilán varió con el tiempo (0.15 in 1994; 0.66 in 1992), pero no con el género; las recapturas fueron más bajas en los años en los cuales menos gavilanes territoriales anidaron, y más altas cuando la mayoría de las parejas anidó.

The effects of forest management on Northern Goshawk (*Accipiter gentilis atricapillus*) populations has been the focus of much research since the early 1970s (Boyce et al., *this volume*; Block et al. 1994). It has been hypothesized that harvesting older forests causes declines in goshawk populations by changing the structure of its habitat, the abundance and availability of its prey, and numbers of its predators and competitors. Collection of demographic data such as birth, death, emigration, and immigration rates is important for understanding how each of these is affected by forest management and for assessing goshawk population trends. Such understanding is also useful in developing conservations plans that guide resource management and conservation of species. We have conducted a long-term study of the ecology, diets, genetics, limiting factors (habitat, food, and predators), and vital rates of a goshawk population on

the Kaibab Plateau in northern Arizona (Reynolds et al. 1994, Reynolds and Joy 1998, La Sorte et al. 2004, Reich et al. 2004, Reynolds et al. 2004). We report on the distribution and density of breeding pairs, interannual variations in proportion of pairs breeding and reproduction, fledgling sex ratio, territorial fidelity, and survival of adult goshawks on the Kaibab Plateau from 1991–1996. This paper is an update of an unpublished report to the Arizona Heritage Program (Reynolds and Joy 1998). It is our intent to present data, collected over the short-term, that will help assess the value of data from what has now become a long-term study of goshawk ecology and demographics.

STUDY AREA

The study area was all of the Kaibab Plateau above 2,182 m elevation (encompasses 1,732 km²), including both the Kaibab National Forest and the Grand Canyon National Park-North Rim (GCNP). The Kaibab Plateau is an oval-shaped (95 × 55 km), limestone plateau that rises from a shrub-steppe plain at 1,750 m elevation to its highest point at 2,800 m, and is dissected by moderately sloping drainages (Rasmussen 1941). The plateau is bounded by escarpments of the Grand Canyon of the Colorado River on its south side, and by steep slopes on the east, and gentle slopes on the north and west sides, that descend to the plain. Pinyon-juniper (*Pinus edulis-Juniperus* spp.) woodlands occur below the study area, and ponderosa pine (*Pinus ponderosa*), mixed conifer, and spruce-fir (*Picea* spp.-*Abies* spp.) forests predominant on the study area (Reynolds et al. 1994). Structure and composition of forests on the Kaibab Plateau are described in Rasmussen (1941) and White and Vankat (1993), and forest management history is described in Burnett (1991) and Reynolds et al. (1994). Several narrow meadows occur on top of the Kaibab Plateau containing grasses and herbaceous vegetation. Annual precipitation on the Kaibab Plateau averages 67.5 cm, with winter snow packs of 2.5–3.0 m (White and Vankat 1993). Winters are cold and summers are cool. A drought period typically occurs in May and June, followed by a mid- to late-summer monsoon season with frequent (2–4/wk) thunderstorms and heavy showers.

METHODS

FIELD METHODS

We defined territory as an area used by a single pair of goshawks during a nesting season. Territories typically contained multiple alternate nests used by the resident goshawks over years (Reynolds et al. 1994). The size of a goshawk territory (defended area) is unknown, but may be an area whose radius is half the distance between adjacent territories. An occupied territory was defined as a territory in which goshawks were observed on two or more occasions, or a single observation of an adult goshawk combined with the presence of molted feathers, feces, and new nest construction in a season. An active nest (and territory) was a nest in which eggs were laid, and failed nests were nests in which eggs or nestlings were lost (none fledged). A cohort of territories was a year's set of territories that contained active goshawk nests (in a few cases occupied by non-breeding goshawks). New territories found in a particular year were not included in that year's cohort of territories but were added to the next year's cohort (see below).

A nest area was a 15–20 ha area surrounding a nest that included prey plucking sites, tree-roosts of the adult goshawks, and one or more alternate nests.

We began searches for goshawk nests (and territories) in the northwest of the Kaibab Plateau in 1991. We also visited historical (pre-1991) nest structures that were on record at the USDA Forest Service Kaibab National Forest that had been identified by forest managers prior to 1991 (see Crocker-Bedford 1990). In subsequent years (1992–1996), searches for nests and territories were expanded to the north, east, and south. At the end of the 1996 breeding season about 80% of the Plateau had been searched; only the extreme south-central portion of the Plateau had not been searched. Nest searches were conducted by systematically walking large areas (1,600–2,400 ha) while inspecting all trees for goshawk nests, and by broadcasting goshawk vocalizations from stations on transects in 2,400–4,800 ha areas using procedures and a broadcast-station distribution described by Kennedy and Stahlecker (1993) and Joy et al. (1994). Nest searches began each April and ended at the close of the post-fledging dependency period (mid-August).

We used a protocol consisting of three sequential components for annually determining the status of nests within territories. In initial visits, all goshawk nests discovered in this study, as well as all historical nests discovered prior to 1991, were visited within the first week post-egg laying (initial visits required one-person-day of effort per territory; historical nests not in known territories were visited independent of territory visits). If goshawks were not using a previously known nest within a territory, a foot search (effort of three–four person-days/territory) was conducted within an 800-m radius from the most recently used nest within a territory. If an active nest was not located in a foot search, a 1,500-m radius area, also centered on the last known active nest, was broadcast (effort of six–seven person-days/territory) with broadcast station distribution and at-station procedures as described in Joy et al. (1994). Once located, all active nests were visited weekly to determine the status of nesting attempts and to trap, band, or re-sight breeding adults. Nest trees were climbed once during the late nestling period to count and band nestlings. Nesting success in studies involving annual nest searches can be overestimated because nests failing early in a season are less likely to be detected than successful nests (Steenhof and Kochert 1982). To control for this, we determined the proportion of territories with breeding goshawks, the production of young, and nesting success only for nests in the previous year's cohort of territories;

that is, only for territories in which monitoring of goshawks and nests began early in a breeding season. However, some active nests were not found until later in the breeding season. We compared annual estimates of nest success in each cohort of territories to annual nest survival in each cohort estimated with the Mayfield (1961) method. This method estimates nest survival based on days of exposure regardless of when in a breeding season nests are found. We made weekly Mayfield visits to nests in 1992–1996. Beginning and ending dates of the incubation and nestling periods were estimated by back-dating from the estimated age of nestlings (see Boal 1994) or known egg laying, hatching, and fledging dates. From these, annual mean dates of egg laying, hatching, and fledging were determined. Days of exposure were calculated using a 32-d incubation period and a 35-d nestling period (Reynolds and Wight 1978). Standard errors of the Mayfield estimates of nest survival were calculated after Johnson (1979).

Nesting adults were trapped in nest areas with dho-gaza traps baited with a live Great Horned Owl (*Bubo virginianus*) during the nestling and early fledgling stages (Bloom 1987), or with falling-end Swedish goshawk traps (Kenward et al. 1983) baited with domestic pigeons (*Columba livia*) (Reynolds et al. 1994). The age (juvenile = 0 yr; adult 1 = 1 yr; adult 2 = 2 yr; adult 3 ≥3 yr) of goshawks was determined by plumage, and gender by behavior prior to capture and by morphometrics subsequent to capture (Reynolds et al. 1994). Fledglings were captured during the last 2 wk of the nestling period by climbing to nests. Adults and fledglings were weighed, measured, and fitted with USGS aluminum leg bands and colored leg bands with unique two-character alpha-numeric codes readable from up to 80 m with 20–40 power spotting scopes (Reynolds et al. 1994).

Locations of nest trees were recorded with global positioning system (GPS) (Trimble Navigation Ltd. 1992, Trimble Navigation Ltd. 1994) and mapped in ArcView (ESRI 1998) geographical information system (GIS). GPS coordinates for each nest tree were generated in the Universal Transverse Mercator (UTM) projection and verified using field plots, topographical knowledge, and site visits. Digital elevation models (DEMs) of 32 7.5-min USGS quadrangles were latticed together to produce a single DEM of the Kaibab Plateau.

DATA ANALYSIS

We used UTM coordinates of all nests and ArcView (ESRI 1998) to calculate distances between alternate nests within territories, nearest-neighbor distances among territories, and breeding-dispersal distances. Mean distance between alternate nests within territories was calculated as the mean of distances among all possible combinations of alternate nests within a territory (e.g., nest A-B, B-C, C-A). The nearest-neighbor distances among territories of adjacent pairs of goshawks were calculated as distances between centroids of territories, where territory centroids were the weighted geographic mean of coordinates between alternate nests in a territory (generated in ArcView; ESRI 1998). Means were weighted by the number of times a nest was used during the study period (a nest used in 2 yr was closer to the centroid than a nest used once). In territories in which only one nest was used, the single nest was the centroid for that territory. Nearest-neighbor distances between territory centroids were calculated without using reciprocal measures between nearest-neighbors (Diggle 1983).

Ripley's k-function (Ripley 1981, S-PLUS 1995) was used to model the distribution of 103 territory centroids (four territories in the southeastern portion of the GCNP where excluded due to incomplete nest searches there). This procedure counts centroids that fall within a designated distance of each centroid to provide a measure of dispersion, corrected for edge effects (Cressie 1991). Observed counts [L(t)] were plotted against the distances at which the counts were made and compared with 95% dispersion (confidence) envelopes estimated from 100 populations of 100 points simulated under complete spatial randomness (CSR process). Points below the envelopes reflect regular (simple sequential inhibition [SSI]) spacing; points within the envelopes reflect random spacing, and points above envelopes reflect aggregated spacing (Neyman-Scott). We modeled the k-function of centroids to 15 km to capture all possible inter-territory distances. The Cramer-von-Mises goodness-of-fit statistic (Cressie 1991) was used to test the null hypothesis that the data were from a CSR process at the $\alpha = 0.05$ level. Rejection of the null hypothesis required fitting the data to the alternative k-function of a regular (Pielou 1960, Strauss 1975) or aggregated (Neyman and Scott 1957) process and comparing the centroids' distribution against the appropriate simulation envelope. Alternate distributions were followed by a Cramer-von-Mises goodness-of-fit (Cressie 1991) test of suitability of the alternate process. All spatial analyses were performed using S-PLUS (1995) and the spatial library developed for S-PLUS by Reich and Davis (2002).

Territory fidelity was calculated from bird years, the number of successive years in which goshawks

TABLE 1. NUMBER OF NORTHERN GOSHAWK TERRITORIES UNDER STUDY AND THEIR ANNUAL STATUS (ACTIVE, OCCUPIED, UNKNOWN) ON THE KAIBAB PLATEAU, ARIZONA, 1991–1996.

Territories	Year					
	1991	1992	1993	1994	1995	1996
Total	37	64	82	88	100	107
Active	36	59	67	21	53	46
Occupied	1	2	6	13	20	23
Status unknown	0	3	9	54	27	38

were recaptured/re-sighted and, thus, were known to have stayed on the same territory or moved to a new territory (Newton and Wyllie 1996). Turnover is the replacement of a banded goshawk on a territory in a previous season by a new goshawk in a current season. A goshawk may be replaced on a territory due to its death or breeding dispersal. Turnover opportunities were cases where the identity of a male or female on a territory was known in successive years. The demographic portion of this study consisted of capturing, banding, and releasing nesting goshawks, followed by recapturing or re-sighting them in subsequent breeding seasons. Age, sex, and reproductive status of individuals were determined as described above. All nest trees were climbed within 14 d of fledging to band and count nestlings.

The number of young in nests at banding was our estimate of productivity. For nests found late in a breeding season (mostly in new territories), productivity was estimated by counting fledged young during the post-fledgling dependency period. Sex ratio was estimated by counts of male and female nestlings at banding. Nestlings were sexed on the basis of body mass and tarsus-metatarsus length. Only broods where the sex of all brood members was determined were used to estimate sex ratio. Capture-recapture histories of individual goshawks provided for parameter estimation and hypothesis testing in capture-recapture analysis of survival. Capture is defined as the capturing or re-sighting (i.e., reading a goshawk's alpha-numeric color band with telescopes) of individual goshawks. Estimates of annual survival rates were calculated using Cormack-Seber-Jolly open population models in program SURGE (Pollock et al. 1990, Franklin et al. 1996). Akaike's Information Criterion (AIC) was used to identify models that best fit the data (Akaike 1973, Anderson et al. 1985, Burnham et al. 1992, Franklin et al. 1996). Goodness-of-fit tests in program RELEASE were used to evaluate how well the data met the assumptions in the capture-recapture models (Pollock et al. 1985, Burnham et al. 1987).

RESULTS

NUMBER AND OCCUPANCY OF TERRITORIES

Numbers of territories in the study increased annually as searches for new territories were expanded (Table 1). By the end of the 1996 breeding season, about 95% of the national forest lands, and about 30% of the GCNP, had been searched for goshawk nests. A final total of 107 territories were located (Fig. 1), resulting in 478 territory-years of study. All but two of the 107 territories contained active nests in one or more breeding seasons. The two exceptions were territories occupied two or more years by goshawks that built new nests or

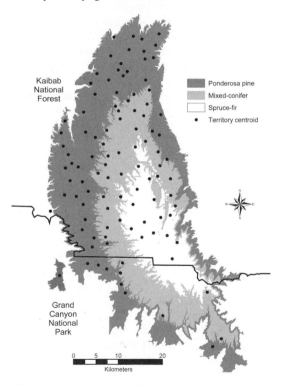

FIGURE 1. Locations of 107 Northern Goshawk territories on the Kaibab Plateau, Arizona, 1991–1996.

reconstructed old nests, but were not known to have laid eggs during the study.

From 1991 through 1993, the increase of territories with active nests was proportional to increases in territories under study (Table 1). However, in 1994 numbers of territories with active nests declined to 21, increased to 53 in 1995, and declined again to 46 in 1996. Annually, variable numbers of territories with unknown status reflected the difficulty of unambiguously determining the occupancy status (presence or absence) of goshawks on territories in years when they did not lay eggs. This ambiguity results from the difficulty of proving that goshawks are not present despite 8–12 person-days of searching for pairs in known territories.

Nesting Success and Productivity

The proportion of pairs breeding in the prior year's cohort of territories was highest in 1992 and 1993, declined in 1994, and partially recovered in 1995 and 1996 (Table 2). Annual percent of nests failing did not significantly differ among years (14–28%). Annual nesting success was similar for the cohort of territories and Mayfield estimates; the two estimates differed by no more than 4% in any year, and neither was consistently higher or lower than the other (Table 2).

In 1996, the first three cohorts of territories (1991–1993) had 6, 5, and 4 yr of data on territory status, respectively. The overall decline in the proportion of territories active from 1992–1994 is reflected in the declining numbers of years newly discovered territories in each of the first three territory cohorts were active in subsequent years. For the 36 new territories discovered in 1991, the largest proportion (31%) was active for five of the six (83% of years) subsequent study years, for the 27 new territories in the 1992 cohort, the largest proportion (41%) was active in three of the five (60% of years) years, and for the 18 new territories in the 1993 cohort, the largest proportion (50%) was active in two of the four (50% of years) years (Table 3).

Brood size on the Kaibab Plateau ranged from one to three nestlings (median = 2); 63 (28%) of a total 224 successful broods had one young, 112 (50%) had two young, and ten (22%) had three young. Mean number of fledglings produced per active and successful nests generally declined from the better breeding years in 1991–1993 to lows in 1994–1996 (Table 4), but nesting success remained relatively constant over years (Table 2).

Of 282 nesting attempts in which eggs were laid on the Kaibab Plateau, 46 (16%) were known to have failed. Of the 46 failures, 16 (35%) failed during incubation and 30 (65%) failed during the nestling stage. Of clutches that failed during incubation, four contained both fertile and infertile eggs, three contained only fertile eggs, and 12 contained only infertile eggs. Mean clutch size of failed nests was 1.6 eggs (sd = 0.63; range = 1–3 eggs). Nest failures in the nestling period typically occurred in the first two wks after hatching. Except in the 12 clutches with infertile eggs, we were unable to determine causes of nest failures. Eggs buried under fresh greenery in nests were recovered from 15 nests that fledged young; three of these nests contained buried fertile eggs (dead embryo), and 12 contained infertile eggs.

Nestling Sex Ratio and Recruitment

We determined the sex of each nestling in 125 broods. Combining years, there were 126 females

TABLE 2. Number of territories in cohort (know territories from previous years), number and percent of territories with active nests, number and percent with failed nests, and two estimates of nesting success (the Mayfield [1975] estimate of nest survival and our cohort method) of Northern Goshawks on the Kaibab Plateau, Arizona, 1991–1996.

	Year				
Territories	1992	1993	1994	1995	1996
Territories in cohort	37	64	82	88	100
Territories with active nests	32	49	18	44	40
% with active nests	87[a]	77[a]	22[b]	50[c]	40[bc]
Number with failed nests	6	7	5	11	9
% failed nests	19[a]	14[a]	28[a]	25[a]	23[a]
% successful	81	86	72	75	77
Mayfield estimate	0.79	0.83	0.75	0.76	0.73
se, Mayfield estimate	0.002	0.001	0.003	0.001	0.002

[a, b, c] Within rows, numbers followed by the same letter are not significantly different according to pairwise comparisons of multiple proportions ($\alpha = 0.05$) (Goodman 1964).

TABLE 3. NUMBER AND PROPORTION OF NEW NORTHERN GOSHAWK TERRITORIES DISCOVERED EACH SUCCESSIVE YEAR (1991–1996) THAT CONTAINED ACTIVE NESTS (EGGS LAID) IN N NUMBERS OF YEARS (NOT NECESSARILY CONSECUTIVE) ON THE KAIBAB PLATEAU, ARIZONA, 1991–1996.

Year	New territories found	Number of years with active nests					
		1	2	3	4	5	6
1991	36	0.06 (2)[a]	0.14 (5)	0.28 (10)	0.14 (5)	0.31 (11)	0.08 (3)
1992	27	0.04 (1)	0.33 (9)	0.41 (11)	0.15 (4)	0.07 (2)	
1993	18	0.28 (5)	0.50 (9)	0.11(2)	0.11 (2)		
1994	6	0.33 (2)	0.67 (4)				
1995	11	0.73 (8)	0.27 (3)				
1996	7	1.00 (7)					

Notes: Two territories were occupied by goshawks but never had active nests in the study (one occupied in 1991, one in 1995). Total number of territories under study in 1996 was 107.

[a] Number of territories with active nests in parentheses.

TABLE 4. NUMBER OF ACTIVE (EGGS LAID) AND SUCCESSFUL (FLEDGED AT LEAST ONE YOUNG) NESTS, AND MEAN NUMBER AND STANDARD DEVIATION (SD) OF FLEDGLINGS PER ACTIVE AND PER SUCCESSFUL NORTHERN GOSHAWK NEST ON THE KAIBAB PLATEAU, ARIZONA, 1991–1996.

	Year					
	1991	1992	1993	1994	1995	1996
Active nests[a]	36	59	64	21	49	44
Fledglings/active nest	2.0[c]	1.8[cd]	1.7[cd]	1.2[d]	1.3[d]	1.3[d]
SD	0.79	1.05	1.00	0.93	0.92	0.90
Successful nests[b]	34	49	54	15	39	33
Fledglings/successful nest	2.1[cd]	2.2[c]	2.0[ce]	1.7[ce]	1.6[e]	1.7[de]
SD	0.64	0.72	0.74	0.62	0.71	0.59

[a] Number of nests where exact number of fledglings was determined.

[b] Successful nests fledged ≥1 young.

[c, d, e] Within rows, means followed by the same letter are not significantly different according to the Tukey-Kramer multiple comparison procedure (α = 0.05).

(54.3%) to 106 males (45.7%), not significantly different from a 1:1 sex ratio ($\chi^2 = 1.72$; df = 1; P = 0.212). Of the 256 nestlings banded as nestlings on the study area, only six (three males; three females) (2%) were subsequently recaptured as breeding adults on the study area. Males were 3–5 yr-old ($\bar{x} = 4.0$ yrs-old) and females were 2–4 yr-old ($\bar{x} = 2.7$ yr-old) at recruitment.

TERRITORY DISPERSION

Ripley's k-function (Fig. 2) showed that territory centroids were spaced regularly at distances of 1.4–2.5 km, distributed randomly at distances of 2.5–5.0 km, and appeared aggregated at distances >8.5 km. We rejected (Cramer-von-Misses; P <0.001) the null hypothesis of a CSR process in overall distribution. Because clustering evident at large (>8.0 km) inter-centroid distances was assumed to reflect the shape of the study area and not true territory aggregation, we tested only the alternative spatial distribution of centroids between distances of 0–2.5 km. This range of distances was correctly modeled using the SSI process (Cramer-von-Misses; P = 0.98; Fig. 3) indicating a regular distribution of centroids at these distances. The minimum distance between territory centers was 1.4 km. The mean nearest-neighbor spacing of the 103 territory centroids (excluding four territories in areas not fully searched) was 3.9 km (SD = 0.322 km). This is 0.9 km less than the mean distance between centroids for nests in 59 territories on the Kaibab Plateau in 1992 (Reynolds et al. 1994), and reflects the addition of 44 territories in an area only slightly larger than the area containing the 1992 sample of 59 territories (Reynolds et al. 1994).

We estimated the potential total number of nesting pairs of goshawks on the study area by calculating an exclusive circular area of the average pair of goshawks by using one-half (1.95 km) of the mean nearest-neighbor distances (3.9 km) as a radius and dividing the study area (173,200 ha) by that exclusive area (1,195 ha). We used the mean because the centroids were from a regularly distributed

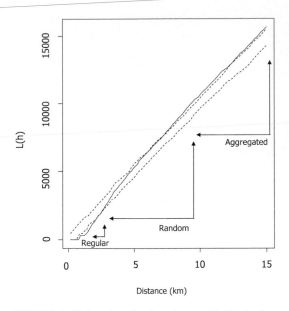

FIGURE 2. K-function showing the spatial distribution (solid line) of Northern Goshawk territory centroids on the Kaibab Plateau (1991–1996) within 0–15 km compared with the distribution of a hypothetical goshawk population modeled under complete spatial randomness (CSR). Regular spacing of centroids is indicated at inter-territory distances where the actual distribution falls below the confidence envelopes for CSR (dashed lines).

population (see above) suggesting that the mean distance was a good estimator of the dispersion of pairs. The extrapolation to the entire study area was reasonable because forests were nearly continuous throughout the study area (Fig. 1). Our estimate of the total breeding population on the study area was 145 pairs. Thus, the 107 territories identified in 1991–1996 comprised about 73% of the potential nesting population on the study area.

SPACING AND USE OF ALTERNATE NESTS

Territorial pairs of goshawks often nest in one or more alternate nests within their territories (Reynolds and Wight 1978, Detrich and Woodbridge 1994, Reynolds et al. 1994). On the Kaibab Plateau, Reynolds et al. (1994) showed that uniquely colored-marked goshawks moved up to 635 m to alternate nests. Of the 105 Kaibab territories in which eggs were laid in 1991–1996, 59 contained two or more alternate nests used during the study: 43 (41%) contained two alternate nests, 12 (12%) contained three alternate nests, and four (4%) contained four alternate nests. Of course, the longer a study, the greater the likelihood that more alternate nests will be used. The mean distance among alternate nests within territories was 489 m (SD = 541; min = 21 m; max = 3,410 m; median = 285 m; N = 103 alternate nests). The distribution of inter-alternate nest distances was strongly right skewed; 89% of alternate nests were within 900 m, and 95% within 1400 m, of one another (Fig. 4). On the Kaibab Plateau, the proportion of pairs that moved annually to alternate nests ranged between 55–76% ($\bar{x}$ = 63%; SD = 8.3%; Table 5). A mean of 27% (SD = 8.5%) of these annual movements were returns to alternate nests used earlier in the study.

TURNOVER ON TERRITORIES

Annual turnover of adults on territories varied from 0–40% for males and from 0–50% for females (Table 6). For the sexes combined, the year with fewest turnovers was 1994—the year with the fewest breeding pairs and the fewest opportunities to detect turnovers had they occurred. The year of highest turnover for males was 1992, and for females, 1995. Male turnovers were relatively constant among years compared to female turnovers. Total turnover for males and females during the 6-yr study was 25% and 19%, respectively (Table 6).

TERRITORY FIDELITY

Tenure on territories by males and females ranged from 1–6 yr. Mean number of years breeding goshawks in the 1991 cohort (N = 36 active territories;

TABLE 5. PERCENT OF PAIRS OF NORTHERN GOSHAWKS THAT MOVED TO AN ALTERNATE NEST WITHIN THEIR TERRITORY EACH YEAR ON THE KAIBAB PLATEAU, ARIZONA, 1991–1996.

| | Year | | | | | |
Movement	1992	1993	1994	1995	1996	Total
Stayed	45 (14)[a]	35 (17)	39 (7)	43 (18)	24 (9)	37 (65)
To new alternate	55 (17)	53 (26)	39 (7)	40 (17)	43 (16)	47 (83)
To prior alternate		12 (6)	22 (4)	17 (7)	32 (12)	16 (29)
Percent of total moving	55 (17)	65 (32)	61 (11)	57 (24)	76 (28)	63 (112)

[a] Number of movements is in parentheses.

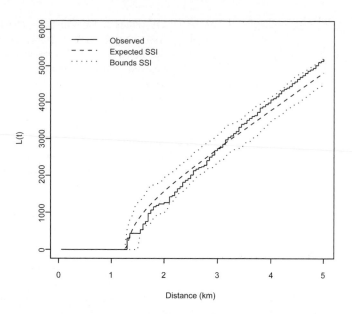

FIGURE 3. K-function showing the spatial distribution (solid line) of Northern Goshawk territory centroids on the Kaibab Plateau (1991–1996) at inter-centroid distances of 0–5 km compared with the distribution of a hypothetical Northern Goshawk population modeled with a simple sequential inhibition (SSI) process (dashed line). The model correctly captures the regular spacing of centroids between 2.5 km and 1.4 km. No territory centroids occurred within 0–1.4 km of other centroids in the actual population. Variegated lines represent 95% confidence limits around the SSI population.

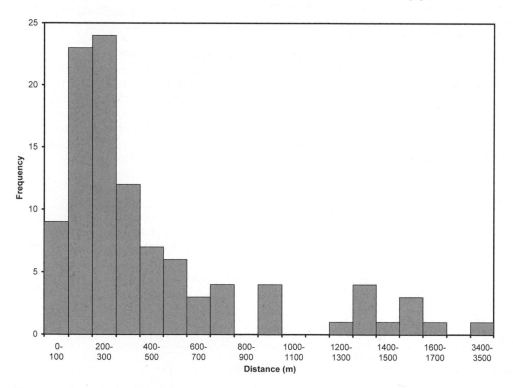

FIGURE 4. Frequency distribution of inter-alternate nest distances within Northern Goshawk territories on the Kaibab Plateau, Arizona, 1991–1996.

TABLE 6. ANNUAL TURNOVER OF MALE AND FEMALE NORTHERN GOSHAWKS IN TERRITORIES ON THE KAIBAB PLATEAU, ARIZONA, 1991–1996.

	1992		1993		1994		1995		1996		Total	
	M	F	M	F	M	F	M	F	M	F	M	F
Turnovers	4	3	3	2	0	0	1	3	1	2	9	19
Opportunities[a]	10	19	12	22	4	5	5	6	5	11	36	99
% turnover	40	16	25	9	0	0	20	50	20	18	25	19

[a] Opportunities = number of breeding seasons (subsequent to year when a breeding goshawk was first banded on a territory) in which either the original or new (= turnover) breeding goshawk was captured/re-sighted on the original territory.

6 yr of study) remained on their territories was 1.4 yr for males and 1.9 yr for females. For the newly discovered territories in the 1992 cohort (N = 27 territories; 5 yrs of study), males remained on territories a mean of 1.6 yr and females 1.8 yr. Too few years were available for meaningful fidelity estimates in later cohorts. Both male and female breeders showed high fidelity to their territories and there was no significant difference in gender fidelity rates (χ^2 = 0.22; df = 1; P = 0.71; Binomial Proportion test). Breeding males remained faithful to their territories in 97% of cases (55 of 57 bird yrs) and females in 94% of cases (92 of 97 bird yrs). In 154 opportunities (bird years) to detect breeding dispersal (change of territory), two males and five females did so; and none of these retained the same mate in the move.

SURVIVAL ESTIMATION

Sample size and goodness-of-fit

During the 6-yr study, we banded 449 goshawks, including 86 males and 87 females that were ≥3 yr old, eight males and 12 females that were 1or 2 yr old, and 256 nestlings. Because only six nestlings banded were recaptured on the study area in subsequent years, we were unable to estimate survival for the juvenile age class (<1 yr old). In addition, only eight male and 12 female 1- or 2 yr-old goshawks were captured, too few to estimate survival rates for these age classes. We therefore combined the 1- and 2-yr-old goshawks with the ≥3 yr old into a non-juvenile age class of goshawks ≥1 yr old. Total number of ≥1-yr-old goshawks included in the capture-recapture analysis was 193 (94 males; 99 females). The number of times these goshawks were captured (or re-sighted) and released (R_j) is displayed in an M-array (Table 7). Annual recapture/re-sighting rates ranged from a low of 15% (1994) to a high of 66% (1992) (model 1; see below). Goodness-of-fit tests in program RELEASE (Burnham et al. 1987) showed no differences in survival or recapture probabilities for males and females. Thus, there was no

lack-of-fit to assumptions of Cormack-Seber-Jolly open population models.

Model selection

Of 64 models examined, the five top models (those with the lowest AIC values) all had time effects, and two of the top five models had time and sex effects, associated with the recapture probabilities (Table 8). In these models, capture probabilities ranged from a high of 0.7 in 1992 to a low of 0.2 in 1994, and in models with sex effects (models 3 and 4) males had lower capture probabilities than females. Lower capture probabilities for males may have resulted from greater difficulties of capturing or resighting males than females, higher male mortality rates, or higher emigration rates. Time effects on recapture probabilities corresponded to the variable annual proportions of goshawk pairs laying eggs. This at least partially reflects the fact that only breeding goshawks could be captured or resighted. Survival varied with sex in all except one (model 4) of the five top models, and three models (models 2, 3, 5) had survival varying with time. The top model ($\{Phi_s, P_t\}$) had males and females surviving at different, but annually constant, rates—0.69 (SE = 0.062) for males and 0.87 (SE = 0.051) for females. The second best model ($\{Phi_{s+T}, P_t\}$) had a sex effect and a linear time trend increasing over years—from 0.54 (SE = 0.13) in 1992 to 0.94 (SE = 0.12) in 1996 for males, and from 0.83 (SE = 0.08) in 1992 to 0.99 (SE = 0.04) in 1996 for females (Figs. 5 a, b). The fourth model (Phi, P_{s+t}) had a no-sex effect survival estimate of 0.82 (SE = 0.048; both males and females). Likelihood ratio tests (LRT) for the top four nested models showed no significant difference in model fit (differences in deviance) among the four models, only two of which contained temporal survival effects. No strong evidence of a time effect on annual survival was found.

DISCUSSION

Mean annual numbers of fledglings produced per active nest on the Kaibab Plateau (range,

TABLE 7. CAPTURE-RECAPTURE DATA IN M-ARRAY FORMAT FOR FEMALE AND MALE NORTHERN GOSHAWKS INITIALLY CAPTURED AS ≥1-YR-OLD ADULTS ON THE KAIBAB PLATEAU, ARIZONA, 1991–1996.

Age class	i	R_i	M_{ij} for $j =$					r_i
			2	3	4	5	6	
Non-juvenile (>1yr) male	1	19	7	2	0	1	0	10
	2	19		8	1	1	1	11
	3	28			5	2	3	10
	4	14				4	0	4
	5	27					4	4
Non-juvenile (>1yr) female	1	28	18	11	3	0	0	21
	2	39		20	0	3	4	27
	3	37			5	4	5	14
	4	11				3	1	4
	5	30					9	9

Notes: R_i is the number of goshawks marked and released on the *i*th occasion in the study, M_{ij} the number of goshawks marked and released on occasion *i* which were recaptured (or re-sighted) on occasion *j*, and r_i the total number of goshawks marked and released on occasion *i* which were later recaptured (= Σm_{ij}).

TABLE 8. TOP FIVE OF 64 AIC RANKED CAPTURE-RECAPTURE MODELS FOR ESTIMATING SURVIVAL OF NORTHERN GOSHAWKS ON THE KAIBAB PLATEAU, ARIZONA, 1991–1996.

Model[a]	Deviance	K	AIC	LRT		
				χ^2	df	P
1. {Phi$_s$, P$_t$}	490.126	7	504.13			
2. {Phi$_{s+T}$, P$_t$}	488.192	8	504.19	1.93[b]	1	0.165
3. {Phi$_{s+T}$, P$_{s+t}$}	487.558	9	505.56	0.64[c]	1	0.424
4. {Phi, P$_{s+t}$}	491.695	7	505.69	4.14[d]	2	0.126
5. {Phi$_{s+t}$, P$_t$}	485.745	10	505.75	4.38[e]	3	0.126
16. {Phi, P$_t$}	497.349	6	509.32	7.22[f]	1	0.007

Note: Model 16 included for comparison to model 1, sex effects vs. no sex effects on survival.
[a] Models that best fit the data are indicated by lowest AIC values. K is the number of estimable parameters for each model. Subscripts associated with Phi (survival) and P (recapture probability) indicate these parameters have a linear time trend (T), a variable time effect (t), a sex effect (s), or some additive effect. Models of Phi and P without subscripts indicate no time or sex effects on survival or recapture rates.
[b] Comparison of model 2 vs. model 1.
[c] Comparison of model 3 vs. model 2.
[d] Comparison of model 4 vs. model 3.
[e] Comparison of model 5 vs. model 1.
[f] Comparison of model 16 vs. model 1.

1.2–2.0 young) were at the lower range of values reported in other North American goshawks (1.7 young/nests in Oregon [Reynolds and Wight 1978], 3.8 young in Utah [Lee 1981a], 2.5 young in Alaska [McGowan 1975], 2.0–2.8 young in Nevada [Younk and Bechard 1994a], 2.6 young in Montana [Clough 2000]), but were similar to production of young per active nest in Oregon (0.3–2.2 young [DeStefano et al. 1994a]). Mean number of young produced per successful nest on the Kaibab Plateau (1.6–2.2 young) was also at the lower end of the range reported elsewhere (3.9 young per successful nest in Canada [Doylele and Smith 1994]), 3.6 young in Utah [Lee 1981a], and 2.0–3.0 young in Alaska [McGowan 1975]). Mean annual nesting success on the Kaibab Plateau (77%; Mayfield method) was lower than some values reported for other goshawk populations (90% in Oregon [Reynolds and Wight 1978]), and 84–100% in Nevada [Younk and Bechard 1994a]), but higher than others (67% in Montana [Clough 2000]). To our knowledge there are no reports of unequal sex ratios of nestling goshawks in North America. However, in a sample of Cooper's Hawk (*Accipiter cooperii*) nestlings (N = 1,337) considerably larger than our sample of goshawks, (Rosenfield et al. 1996) reported a sex ratio significantly skewed in favor of males (54%) over females (46%). A significantly skewed sex ratio in favor of males has also been reported in Harris's Hawk (*Parabuteo unicinctus*) (Bednarz and Hayden 1991).

Goshawk survival varied by gender in four of the top five models, and male survival was lower than female survival in each of the four models. A similar gender effect in survival was also reported for goshawks in California (DeStefano et al. 1994b).

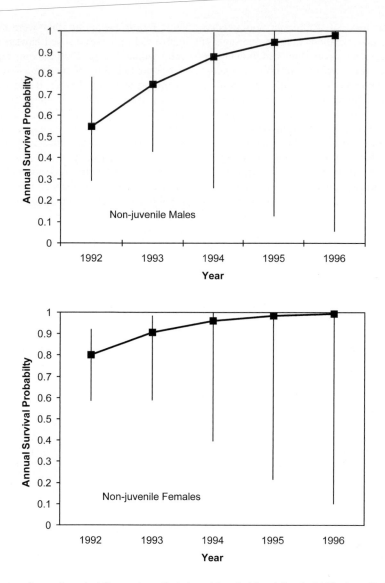

FIGURE 5. Estimates of annual survival for non-juvenile (≥1 yr old) male (a) and female (b) Northern Goshawks under the second-best model (Phis+T, Pt) on the Kaibab Plateau, Arizona, 1991–1996.

While the number of goshawks born, banded, and subsequently recruited as breeders on the Kaibab Plateau was small, ages of Kaibab goshawks at first breeding were greater for males than females. Delayed breeding in males relative to females on the Kaibab Plateau parallels the rarer reports of juvenile males nesting compared to more common reports of juvenile females nesting (McGowan 1975, Reynolds and Wight 1978, Younk and Bechard 1994a). A more advanced age of males at first breeding might result from greater difficulties for males to gain breeding territories. However, the lower apparent survival of males on the Kaibab Plateau argues that there ought

to have been more male vacancies on territories, allowing males to be recruited at younger ages. More years of capture-recapture study of survival, and additional known-aged recruits, are needed to confirm gender effects on survival and recruitment.

The precision of capture-recapture estimates of survival are sensitive to recapture probabilities (Pollock et al. 1990). While our survival estimates of breeding goshawks were based on capture-recapture histories of 193 individuals and 6 yr of study, capture probabilities of these goshawks were quite low in some years (1994 and 1996). A large part of the annual variation in capture probabilities stemmed directly from the difficulties of capturing non-breeders and the large annual variations in the proportions of goshawks breeding. However, some variation in capture probabilities was surely the result of mortality, emigration, or both. While the relative contribution of mortality and emigration to the variable recapture rates was unknown, we argue that emigration of adults from the Kaibab Plateau was likely to have been rare because of a near lifetime fidelity of both genders to their breeding territories (Reynolds, unpubl. data), the lack of detected medium- or long-distance breeding dispersals within our study area (maximum distance of seven known breeding dispersals was 8.6 km, or less than the width of three territories), and that the isolation of our study area would have required emigrants to travel long distances in shrub-steppe habitat to find other suitable forests (Reynolds et al. 2004). Thus, emigration was probably rare, making it likely that mortality was a more important contributor to variation in recapture rates.

Since 1998, the lower survival estimate of male relative to female Kaibab Plateau goshawks has been of concern. However, an analysis of seven additional years (1997–2003) of capture-recapture of breeders on the Kaibab Plateau, showed that survival was the same for both males and females (no sex effects on survival) (Reynolds et al. 2004). Also, in the 2004 analysis, the survival estimates of 14 adult males that had received tail-mounted radio transmitters in 1991 and 1992 was nearly two-thirds lower than survival of males without tail-mounts (0.29 vs. 0.75) (Reynolds et al. 2004). Thus, the lower survival of males vs. females in 1991–1996 likely reflected the reduced survival of these 14 males with tail-mounts. The 14 males also comprised a relatively large proportion of the males included in that 1998 survival analysis.

Goshawk territories on the Kaibab Plateau appeared to be spatially and temporally fixed. Territories were occupied by known (banded) goshawks, most of which remained on the same territories their entire reproductive lives, and, when these goshawks did not return in the spring, they were replaced by new (unbanded or locally-banded hawks) goshawks typically within 1–3 yr. Furthermore, replacement goshawks continued to use the same nests and nest areas as the preceding goshawks. Regular spacing of territories at short nearest-neighbor distances (compare to Reynolds and Wight 1978, but see Woodbridge and Detrich 1994), the nearly complete filling of searched forests with territories, the low recruitment rates of locally produced goshawks and their relatively advanced age when first recruited as breeders, suggest the habitat on the Kaibab Plateau is saturated with territories and that the population of breeders is somewhat stable over years. Low recruitment and advanced age of goshawks at first breeding suggest that territories were occupied and young goshawks had to wait 2–5 yr before territories became available.

ACKNOWLEDGMENTS

This research was supported by the USDA Forest Service's Southwestern Regional Office, Kaibab National Forest, North Kaibab Ranger District, Rocky Mountain Research Station, and a Heritage Program grant from the Arizona Game and Fish Department. For help with nest searching, capturing, and banding goshawks, we thank S. Bedard, C. Boam, C. Erickson, M. Gavin, D. Laing, D. Leslie, J. Seyfried, J. Wiens, R. Brogel, J. Burns, B. Hunt; P. Clark, G. Dilworth, T. Gamberg, L. Hunt, D. Rubinoff, S. Salafsky A. Alfonso, R. Albers, G. Bayluss, K. Boden, R. Brunotte, J. Dudley, S. Dudley, I. Gilmore, K. Kalin, T. Kelley, J. Koloszar, T. Rice, L. Schultz, M. Sherman, J. Sneva, S. Spidle, D. Strait, J. Whittier, and D. Worthington. D. Wiens, S. Bedard, R. Brogel, M. Gavin. E. Forsman and J. Reid provided input on running programs RELEASE and SURGE. V. Thomas developed custom ArcView applications, R. Reich provided guidance with S-PLUS programming, and D. Dean helped with geographic information systems theory. P. Beier, C. Crocker-Bedford, and R. King provided valuable reviews of the manuscript.

ECOLOGY AND HABITAT OF BREEDING NORTHERN GOSHAWKS IN THE INLAND PACIFIC NORTHWEST: A SUMMARY OF RESEARCH IN THE 1990S

STEPHEN DESTEFANO, MICHAEL T. MCGRATH, SONYA K. DAW, AND STEVEN M. DESIMONE

Abstract. During the 1990s, we conducted research on the distribution, productivity, and habitat relationships of Northern Goshawks (*Accipiter gentilis*) in eastern Oregon and Washington. Our research was initiated primarily in response to concerns raised about the status of Northern Goshawks in the western US, and coincided with early attempts to list the species as threatened or endangered under the Endangered Species Act and the publication of management guidelines for goshawks in the southwestern US. To develop baseline information on the status, distribution, and habitat relationships of goshawks in eastside forests (i.e., east of the Cascade Mountain Range) in the Pacific Northwest, we established study areas on three national forests in eastern Oregon in 1992, adding a fourth study area in central Washington in 1994. We focused on the breeding season and nesting habitat because of its primary importance to goshawk ecology and the logistical feasibility of finding nests. Density of breeding pairs ranged from 0.03–0.09/100 ha, and annual productivity ranged from 0.3–2.2 young fledged/nest. Goshawks selected forest stands with trees of larger diameter and greater canopy closure for nesting than available in the landscape. Occasionally nests could be found in large trees in open-canopied stands. As distance increased from the nest site, forest type and structure became more heterogeneous and the prevalence of older-seral-stage forest declined. Dry or wet openings were present in most territories, often within close proximity to nest stands. Goshawks ate a variety of mammalian and avian prey. Mammal species made up a larger portion of prey biomass on two of the national forests, but avian species appeared to be more prevalent in the diet of goshawks in the most northern study area. We recommend that the existing management guidelines for goshawks in the Southwest form a basis for management in the inland Pacific Northwest, particularly with regard to nested spatial concepts, emphasis on management of prey, and the use of silviculture to promote the development and replacement of old growth or late-seral-stage forest. Our research and management recommendations can be used in concert with the Southwestern management guidelines to establish a mix of vegetation structural stages to support goshawk populations, their prey, and other forest wildlife species specifically for the inland Pacific Northwest.

Key Words: *Accipiter gentilis*, density, diet, nests, habitat, inland Pacific Northwest, management recommendations, Northern Goshawk, Oregon, Washington.

ECOLOGÍA Y HÁBITAT DE REPRODUCCIÓN DEL GAVILÁN AZOR EN EL INTERIOR DEL NOROESTE PACÍFICO: UN RESUMEN DE INVESTIGACIÓN SOBRE LA DÉCADA DE LOS NOVENTA

Resumen. Durante la década de los noventa, conducimos investigación sobre la distribución, productividad, y relaciones del hábitat del Gavilán Azor (*Accipiter gentilis*), en el este de Oregon y de Washington. Nuestra investigación fue iniciada principalmente en respuesta a las preocupaciones acerca del estatus de los Gavilanes Azor en el oeste de Estados Unidos, lo cual coincide con los intentos recientes de enlistar a la especie como amenazada o en peligro, bajo el Acto de Especies en Peligro, así como con la publicación de las pautas para el manejo de gavilanes en el suroeste de los Estados Unidos. Para desarrollar información de arranque dele stado, distribución, y relaciones del hábitat de los gavilanes de bosques del lado este (ej. este de la Cordillera Montañosa de la Cascada) en el Noroeste Pacífico, establecimos áreas de estudio en tres bosques nacionales en el este de Oregon en 1992, agregando una cuarta área de estudio en el centro de Washington en 1994. Nos enfocamos en la temporada de reproducción y en el hábitat de anidación, debido a la primordial importancia en la ecología del gavilán y a la viabilidad logística de encontrar nidos. La densidad de parejas reproductoras osciló de 0.03–0.09/100 ha, y la productividad anual osciló de 0.3–2.2 volantones por nido. La densidad de parejas reproductoras tuvo un rango de 0.03–0.09/100 ha, y la producción anual tuvo un rango de 0.3–2.2 volantones/nido. Los gavilanes para anidar, seleccionaron áreas boscosas con árboles de mayor diámetro y mayor cierre de copa, de lo que había disponible en el paisaje. Ocasionalmente, nidos pudieron ser encontrados en árboles grandes con copas abiertas. Conforme la distancia del sitio del nido incrementaba, el tipo de bosque y la estructura se volvía más heterogénea y la preponderancia de bosque en estado seral decayó. Zonas abiertas secas o húmedas estuvieron presentes en casi todos los territorios, a menudo con una estrecha proximidad a los nidos. Los gavilanes comieron una variedad de presas mamíferas y aves. Las especies mamíferas conformaron una porción mayor de la biomasa de presas, en dos de los bosques nacionales, pero las especies de aves parece que prevalecieron más en la dieta de los gavilanes en la parte más al norte del área de estudio. Recomendamos que las guías existentes para el manejo de los gavilanes en el Suroeste, formen una base para el manejo en el interior del Noroeste Pacífico, particularmente respecto a los conceptos espaciales de anidación, énfasis en manejo de presa, y la utilización de silvicultura para promover el desarrollo y el reemplazo de bosque de viejo crecimiento o de estado seral tardío. Nuestra investigación y nuestras recomendaciones de manejo pueden ser utilizadas, en concertación con las guías de manejo del Suroeste, para establecer una mezcla de fases en la estructura de la vegetación, para sostener las poblaciones de gavilán, sus presas, y otras especies silvestres de bosque, específicamente para el interior del Noroeste Pacífico.

In 1992, we began studies on the breeding ecology and habitat relationships of Northern Goshawks (*Accipiter gentilis*) in eastern Oregon. In 1994, we expanded our research to include parts of eastern Washington. This research was initiated because the distribution of nesting pairs and the status of the population in the Pacific Northwest were largely unknown but of concern because of the potential effects of timber harvest on the structure of forest stands (Marshall 1992). This paper represents a synthesis and summary of these findings: some information has been published previously and is cited appropriately, while additional information has not been published and is presented herein.

During the two–three decades before our studies, most of the research and management attention for forest wildlife in the Pacific Northwest was focused west of the Cascade Mountain range in the temperate rainforests of western Oregon and Washington and northwestern California (e.g., Thomas et al. 1990, Forest Ecosystem Management Assessment Team 1993, USDA Forest Service 1993b). The Northern Spotted Owl (*Strix occidentalis caurina*) was a major species of concern because of its close association with late-seral-stage forest (old growth) and the potential impact of extensive and intensive timber harvesting on owl populations on both public and private lands (DeStefano 1998). In 1990, however, attention focused on timber harvesting and another species of forest raptor in a different region of the country—the Northern Goshawk in the southwestern US (Crocker-Bedford 1990). This prompted heightened interest in the goshawk throughout its range in the western US, including forests east of the Cascade range in the inland Pacific Northwest. The USDA Forest Service (USFS) developed management recommendations for Northern Goshawks in the forests of the Southwest (Reynolds et al. 1992). Other regions of the country were obviously interested in the recommendations put forth by Reynolds et al. (1992), but it was unclear if these guidelines would be entirely appropriate for forest management outside of the Southwest.

Reynolds et al. (1992) review of the status of goshawks, especially the potential impact of timber harvest on nesting and reproduction, directed the design of our research. Specifically, we focused on locating nests and making nests the center of habitat studies. We built on the spatial concepts put forth by Reynolds et al. (1992), who specified three nested spatial components used by breeding goshawks: (1) a 10–12 ha nest area, composed of one or more forest stands or alternate nests; (2) a 120–240 ha post-fledging area (PFA), which is an area around the nest used by adults and young from the time of fledging, when the young are still dependent on the adults for food, to independence (Kennedy et al. 1994); (3) and a foraging area that comprises the balance of the goshawks' home range, which Reynolds et al. (1992) estimated as 1,500–2,100 ha based on averages from previous studies.

Our objectives were to: (1) determine the distribution, density, and productivity of nesting goshawks in the coniferous forests of eastern Oregon, (2) examine forest structure and vegetative characteristics around goshawk nests at several scales, including the nest stand (10–12 ha) and an area approximating the PFA (170 ha), (3) determine the historic distribution of nests and potential effects of timber harvest and landscape change, (4) model effects of changes in forest structure as a result of timber harvest to the distribution of goshawk nests, (5) describe goshawk-prey relationships and diet, and (6) evaluate the appropriateness of the southwest management guidelines for the inland Pacific Northwest. Aspects of objectives 1–4 were presented in theses by Daw (1997), Desimone (1997), and McGrath (1997) and several publications; this information is summarized. Information on goshawk-prey relationships and diet and the efficacy of the southwest management guidelines for the Pacific Northwest are newly presented in this paper.

METHODS

STUDY AREAS

We examined Northern Goshawk populations on federal and private lands in four areas of eastern Oregon and Washington: southern, east-central, and northeastern Oregon and central Washington. In southern Oregon, research occurred on all districts of the Fremont National Forest and surrounding lands of the Klamath Province of the Weyerhaeuser Corporation, encompassing >5,000 km². In general, large expanses of lodgepole pine (*Pinus contorta*) interspersed with small stands of ponderosa pine (*Pinus ponderosa*) on higher ground and wet meadows on lower ground dominated the northern half of the study area, while dry, mixed conifer stands interspersed with xeric rocky flats with sagebrush (*Artemisia* spp.) and bitterbrush (*Purshia tridentata*) dominated the southern half. Large blocks of pine plantation were common on Weyerhaeuser lands.

In east-central Oregon, research was conducted on the Bear Valley Ranger District of the Malheur National Forest, encompassing about 1,500 km². This area was characterized by a mix of forest types including ponderosa pine on dry slopes, ponderosa pine and Douglas-fir (*Pseudotsuga menzeseii*) stands on more moist sites, and mixed conifer stands including some Douglas-fir, grand fir (*Abies grandis*), western larch (*Larix occidentalis*), and lodgepole pine on north slopes. Small openings including wet and dry meadows and dry rocky flats were common, and the district surrounded a large, open, flat valley (about 240 km²) dominated by sagebrush and grasses.

In northeastern Oregon, research was conducted on all districts of the Wallowa-Whitman National Forest, as well as lands administered by Boise Cascade Corporation and R-Y Timber Company, encompassing >5,500 km². A mosaic of forest stands occurred throughout this area, including ponderosa pine, lodgepole pine, grand fir, and subalpine fir (*Abies lasiocarpa*) as well as mixed conifer stands of ponderosa pine, Douglas-fir, grand fir, and western larch.

In central Washington, research was conducted on lands surrounding the community of Cle Elum, including the Cle Elum Ranger District of the Wenatchee National Forest and lands managed by the Washington Department of Fish and Wildlife, Plum Creek Timber Company, and Boise Cascade Corporation, encompassing about 3,000 km². Conifer associations included Pacific silver fir (*Abies amabilis*), subalpine fir, grand fir, western larch, Engelmann spruce (*Picea engelmannii*), white pine (*Pinus monticola*), lodgepole pine, ponderosa pine, Douglas-fir, western red cedar (*Thuja plicata*), and western hemlock (*Tsuga heterophylla*) (Franklin and Dyrness 1973).

All study areas were mosaics of various-aged forest stands, dry and wet openings, and burns. The climate in eastern Oregon and Washington was dry, with cold winters providing the majority of precipitation as snowfall. Topography was typically moderately sloped hills and ridges with some deeply-cut drainages in the south to highly variable topographic relief including moderate to steep slopes and high mountain peaks in the north. Elevations generally ranged between 900–3,000 m. Silvicultural practices included a variety of even-aged (e.g., clear-cut and shelter-wood harvests) and uneven-aged (e.g., thinning from below, overstory removal, and group selection) management techniques.

NEST LOCATIONS AND PRODUCTIVITY

We established five survey areas for goshawk nests on the Fremont, Malheur, and Wallowa-Whitman National Forest, which we called density study areas (DSA; DeStefano et al. 1994a). These DSAs ranged from about 9,000–13,000 ha and were composed of forest types representative of the dominant forest tree species on each national forest. Within each DSA, we broadcast taped goshawk calls to elicit a response from goshawks and used the protocol recommended by Kennedy and Stahlecker (1993) and Joy et al. (1994) to search for all goshawk nests in 1992–1994 (DeStefano et al. 1994b, Daw et al. 1998). We made repeated searches of each DSA to locate every territory. In addition, we also located nests opportunistically outside of the DSAs during other field activities, or had nest locations reported to us by wildlife and timber survey crews (Daw et al. 1998).

We visited nests in late July and counted nestlings either just before or just after fledging. A successful nest was any nest that produced more than one fledgling. Nesting phenology dates were based on back-dating from estimated weekly development of juveniles based on plumage characteristics and fledging dates (Boal 1994).

HISTORIC NEST SITES

In 1994, we compiled a list of 102 previously known or historic goshawk territories from the Fremont National Forest and surrounding lands from original data collected by Reynolds (1975, 1978), Reynolds and Wight (1978), Reynolds et al. (1982), the USFS, and Weyerhaeuser Corporation, dating from 1973–1991 (Desimone 1997). We evaluated the credibility of these reported nest locations based on accompanying documentation (e.g., written reports, legal descriptions, and mapped locations), reliability of observers, and number of years the site was known to be active. Records of historic nest sites were only included if there was a confirmed report of young or an incubating goshawk noted in the report. After evaluation of associated documentation, we compiled a list of credible territory locations. These nest locations were then stratified into one of three principal forest cover types, including dry-mixed conifer, ponderosa pine, and lodgepole pine, and a stratified random sample was selected for field survey. We surveyed these sites according to protocol. Searches were conducted ≥2 times during May–August 1994, were centered on the last known nest location, and extended out in a 1,000-m-diameter circle from the last recorded nest location. We classified each nest site as goshawk present, if a goshawk was detected and we had confirmed evidence of nesting, or no response, if no goshawk was detected.

Habitat Characteristics

We measured forest structure and other habitat elements in goshawk breeding territories in Oregon and Washington at several scales, represented by circles of increasing size, all of which were centered on nest trees or random trees (Lehmkuhl and Raphael 1998). Scales ranged from 12–170 ha and had biological or management significance (Daw 1997, Desimone 1997, McGrath 1997). For example, 12 and 170 ha represented the nest and PFA sizes, respectively, recommended by Reynolds et al. (1992) for goshawks in the Southwest, while 24 ha was designated as a management unit for goshawk nests on some forests in eastern Oregon at the time of our study. Woodbridge and Detrich (1994) recommended 52 ha to encompass clusters of nests sites used in different years by a single pair, and 120 ha was an area used for Pileated Woodpecker (*Dryocopus pileatus*) management in some forests in eastern Oregon.

For our earlier studies (Daw 1997, Desimone 1997), we classified forest structure based on current guidelines provided by individual forests (USDA Forest Service 1994a). Forest structure was based on mean diameter at breast height (dbh), density of trees, and amount of canopy cover (Table 1). We also include dry openings (e.g., grass or sagebrush meadows), wet openings (e.g., riparian corridors flanked by wet meadows), and roads (arterial which were paved, collector which were well-used gravel, and local which were sporadically used unpaved). For the latter study (McGrath 1997, McGrath et al. 2003), we used the four stand stages recommended by Oliver and Larson (1996:148), who defined stand initiation as the stage characterized by young trees of various species colonizing the site following disturbance; stem exclusion as the absence of seedlings and saplings with the onset of self thinning and the beginning of crown class differentiation into dominant and subordinate species; under story reinitiation as colonization of the forest floor by advanced regeneration and continued over story competition; and old growth as the irregular senescence of over story trees and recruitment of under story trees into the overstory.

Forest structure was delineated on aerial photographs, and a portion was ground-verified (Daw 1997, Desimone 1997, McGrath 1997). We then compared the habitat variables around nest sites to random points in a use-versus-availability framework among the different scales (Marcum and Loftsgaarden 1980, Manly et al. 1993). We performed use-versus-availability tests in three different ways during the course of our research: (1) at historic nest sites on the Fremont National Forest and surrounding private lands (Desimone 1997), (2) at current (1992–1994) nest stands and surrounding PFA-sized areas around nests on the Malheur National Forest (Daw 1997), and (3) at multiple scales around current nests on national forests and private lands in eastern Oregon and central Washington (McGrath 1997). Details of methods are described in these theses and resulting publications (Daw et al. 1998, Daw and DeStefano 2001, McGrath et al. 2003).

TABLE 1. FOREST STAND CLASSIFICATION CHARACTERISTICS USED DURING STUDIES OF NORTHERN GOSHAWK HISTORIC NEST SITES, CURRENTLY OCCUPIED NEST STANDS, AND POST-FLEDGING AREAS IN EASTERN OREGON, BASED ON USDA FOREST SERVICE (1994A) DESIGNATIONS FOR TREE SIZE (DIAMETER AT BREAST HEIGHT [DBH]) AND CANOPY CLOSURE (DAW 1997, DESIMONE 1997).

Forest vegetation structure	dbh (cm)	Crown closure (%)	Trees per ha ≥53 cm dbh
Late closed	>53	>50	≥15
Late open	>53	<50	≥15
Mid-aged closed	23–53	>50	<15
Mid-aged open	23–53	<50	<15
Early closed	12–23	>50	Not applicable
Early open	12–23	<50	Not applicable
Very early	≤12	<50	Not applicable

Diet and Prey Relationships

We collected goshawk pellets and plucking remains opportunistically during 1992–1994 on the Fremont National Forest, 1992–1996 on the Malheur National Forest, and 1992–1993 on the Wallowa-Whitman National Forest. Each sample was collected between June and September beneath a goshawk nest or plucking post. A sample consisted of all remains collected at the same site on the same day. Fur, feathers, and skeletal remains were separated by picking apart dry pellets and other remains. Mammal and bird remains were compared to study skins and skeletons in collections at Oregon State University, Corvallis, and The University of Arizona, Tucson. We also used a dichotomous key (Verts and Carraway1984) to identify small mammal skeletal remains. A prey item was counted only if it was absolutely not part of other identified prey in the same sample; no attempt was made to estimate prey numbers by counting individual hairs, feathers, or bone fragments within a sample, because they are of little value for counting prey (Marti 1987). Prey were classified into 14 categories and summarized as percent composition and biomass for each study area. Biomass was calculated by multiplying the number of each prey item by the mean weight of that item (DeStefano and Cutler 1998).

Terminology and Statistical Analyses

We classified goshawk nest locations based on occupancy (modified after Postupalsky 1974). An occupied territory was any territory where goshawks attempted to breed, independent of success, where evidence such as an incubating or brooding female, nestlings or fledglings, or eggshell fragments was confirmed. A current territory was any territory first found during the course of our field studies (1992–1994), while an historic territory was any confirmed territory that was initially found during 1973–1991

(the years before our field studies). A successful nest was any nest from which more than one young fledged (Steenhoff and Kochert 1982).

We used chi-square, two-sample t-tests of homogeneity, or Wilcoxon signed-rank tests to compare proportional use of forest structural categories between nest stands and random stands (Zar 1996). For multiple scales (circles) around nests, we used logistic regression with forward stepwise variable selection to test for habitat associations (Hosmer and Lemeshow 1989, Daw 1997, McGrath et al. 2003). Variables were either square-root or natural log transformed when necessary, and included in the model at $P \leq 0.10$ (Daw 1997, Desimone 1997, McGrath 1997). Our binary response variable was coded as either nest (1) or random (0, i.e., not nest), and the effect of explanatory variables was to increase or decrease the odds of a nest occurring. We report $\bar{x} \pm$ SE and considered variables to be significant at $P \leq 0.10$.

RESULTS

Density, Phenology, and Productivity

During 1992 and 1993, we found 20 and 30 occupied goshawk territories in our DSAs, respectively (Table 2; DeStefano et al. 1994a). Nest densities ranged from 0.026–0.088 territories/100 ha, and varied among DSAs and between years. Nesting phenology was similar on all three national forests in Oregon—goshawks laid eggs in late April to early May, eggs hatched during late May and early June, and young fledged from late June–late July. Productivity ranged between 0.3–2.2 fledglings per nest and varied within each forest and between years (Table 3; DeStefano et al. 1994a). However, there was an apparent but weak latitudinal trend in productivity in both years, with productivity declining from south (Fremont National Forest) to north (Wallowa-Whitman National Forest) (Table 3).

TABLE 2. DENSITY OF BREEDING NORTHERN GOSHAWKS IN EASTERN OREGON,1992–1993 (FROM DESTEFANO ET AL. 1994A).

National forest	Primary forest cover	1992			1993		
		Area searched (ha)	Nests	Nest density (per 100 ha)	Area searched (ha)	Nests	Nest density (per 100 ha)
Fremont	Lodgepole	8,780	4	0.046	12,960	8	0.062
	Mixed conifer				10,627	4	0.038
Malheur	Ponderosa pine	9,046	8	0.088	9,046	6	0.066
	Mixed conifer				10,519	9	0.086
Wallowa-Whitman	Mixed conifer	11,396	8	0.070	11,396	3	0.026

TABLE 3. PRODUCTIVITY OF BREEDING NORTHERN GOSHAWKS IN EASTERN OREGON, 1992–1993 (FROM DeSTEFANO ET AL. 1994A).

National forest	Primary forest cover	1992			1993		
		$\bar{x}$	SE	N	$\bar{x}$	SE	N
Fremont	Lodgepole	2.2	0.75	6	2.2	1.08	6
	Mixed conifer				0.3	0.76	3
Malheur	Ponderosa pine	1.9	0.57	10	0.3	0.72	6
	Mixed conifer				1.6	0.89	7
Wallowa-Whitman	Mixed conifer	1.0	0.71	9	0.7	0.76	3

HABITAT RELATIONSHIPS FOR HISTORIC NEST SITES

We compiled a list of 102 historic goshawk territories on the Fremont National Forest and surrounding private lands. Of these, 72 reports were deemed credible. We surveyed for the presence of goshawks at 51 of these sites and categorized vegetation structure around 46 (five sites did not have adequate photographic records) (Desimone 1997).

In 1994, 15 of 51 (29%) historic sites were occupied by adult goshawks. These occupied sites (N = 15) had more mid-aged closed forest (Table 1) and late closed forest (Table 1) than no-response sites (N = 31) in the 12 ha around each nests (Desimone 1997).

Combined mid-aged and late-closed forest comprised 49% (se 7%) of the forest cover in 12 ha around historic occupied nests, versus 19% (SE = 3%) for historic no-response nests (Kruskal-Wallis, P ≤0.045; Desimone 1997). Among current nest sites (i.e., those nests first found during our study in 1992–1993 on the Fremont National Forest; N = 38), 86% were in mid-aged or late structural stage forest with >50% canopy closure in the 12 ha around the nest.

HABITAT RELATIONSHIPS FOR NEST STANDS AND PFAs

On the Malheur National Forest, we compared forest stands that contained goshawk nests to random forest stands without nests at two scales, stand-level (12–50 ha) and PFA-sized (170 ha) circles (Daw 1997, Daw and DeStefano 2001). Both nest stands and random stands were similar in size (103 ± 20 ha and 137 ± 19 ha, respectively; t = 1.23, 54.6 df, P = 0.22). Nests were not distributed among forest stands in the same proportion as stands were available. Late seral-stage forest with large trees and dense canopy cover was used by goshawks for nesting more than it was available, while mid-aged forest was used less (P = 0.03). Stands with open canopies (<50% cover) were used in proportion to availability, but overall use was rare; only two of 22 nests were in open-canopied stands.

At a broader perspective, nest stand attributes within 1 ha of 82 goshawk nests on four national forests (including the Malheur National Forest) and private lands in eastern Oregon and Washington were compared with available habitat at 95 random sites (McGrath 1997, McGrath et al. 2003). Canopy closure, estimated at 43 points within 1 ha of each site, averaged 53% (SE = 1.7, range = 14–89%) around goshawk nests, and 33% (SE = 1.7, range = 3–74%) at random sites. Additionally, canopy closure around the 82 goshawk nest sites was normally distributed about the mean of 53% (P >0.05; Shapiro-Wilk statistic for a test of normality, PROC UNIVARIATE [SAS 1988]). Goshawk nests were not distributed proportionately among the four stages of stand development (i.e., stand initiation, stem exclusion, under story re-initiation, old growth; χ^2 = 19.8, 3 df, P <0.0001). Stem exclusion was used significantly more than expected based on its availability, and stand initiation was used significantly less than expected. Under story re-initiation and old growth stands were used in proportion to their availability in the landscape (McGrath 1997, McGrath et al. 2003).

The forest in PFA-sized circles around goshawk nests was a mix of structural stages. Dense canopy, mid-aged forest was most prominent (37%), followed by dense canopy, late forest (29%), and early forest or regenerating clearcuts (3%) (Daw 1997). All PFA-sized circles contained wet openings ($\bar{x}$ = 7.0 ± 1.2 ha), and 12 of 22 PFA-sized circles contained dry openings ($\bar{x}$ = 3.0 ± 0.7 ha). Dry openings were more prevalent around nests than random points (χ^2 = 3.2, 1 df, P = 0.08), and the presence of dry openings increased the odds of a nest occurring 2.5 times (P = 0.08) (Daw 1997).

HABITAT RELATIONSHIPS FOR MULTIPLE SCALES

McGrath (1997) and McGrath et al. (2003) built on the sample of nests collected on the three national forests in eastern Oregon and added a fourth study area in central Washington. For this analysis, we used 82 goshawk nests and 95 random points, and analyzed forest structure within 1 ha of nest sites and at landscape scales of 10, 30, 60, 83, 120, 150, and 170 ha. The analyses and results were extensive and are reported by McGrath et al. (2003) and can be summarized as follows: (1) by examining goshawk habitat relationships at multiple spatial scales across several study areas, we detected unifying spatial patterns and structural conditions surrounding goshawk nesting habitat, (2) the ability to discriminate goshawk nest sites from available habitat decreased as landscape scale increased, and different factors influenced goshawks at different scales, (3) the presence and arrangement of forest structural types interacted to influence site suitability for nesting, (4) at the 1-ha scale, the stage of stand development (i.e., stand initiation, stem exclusion, understory reinitiation, old growth; Oliver and Larson 1996), low topographic position, and tree basal area reliably discriminated between nests and random sites, (5) low topographic position and basal area were more influential than stand structure, (6) at the landscape scale, modeling indicated that conditions at different scales interact to influence selection of habitat for nesting, (7) a core area exists surrounding goshawk nests in which stem exclusion and understory reinitiation stands with canopy closure ≥50% served as apparent protection against potentially detrimental effects associated with more open forest, and (8) among several models tested, the model that best discriminated between

nests and random sites encompassed 83 ha surrounding the nest and incorporated habitat characteristics from multiple scales nested within that range. This model had a cross-validated classification accuracy of 75%. Positive correlations were found between fledging rate and tree basal area within 1 ha of the nest ($F_{1, 77}$ = 2.89, P = 0.041), and between fledging rate and the percentage of landscape occupied by stem exclusion stands of low canopy closure (i.e., <50%) at landscape scales ≥60 ha ($F_{1, 77}$; 0.041 ≤ P ≤ 0.089).

DIET AND PREY RELATIONSHIPS

We found 153, 197, and 30 unique prey items below nests or at plucking sites on the Fremont, Malheur, and Wallowa-Whitman national forests, respectively (Table 4). By frequency, both birds and mammals comprised about 50% each of goshawk remains from the Fremont and Malheur national forests; birds comprised 60% and mammals 40% on the Wallowa-Whitman National Forest. Prey from the Fremont National Forest was dominated by Northern Flickers (*Colaptes auratus*) (17%) and tree squirrels (*Tamiasciurus* spp., *Tamias townsendii*, and *Glaucomys sabrinus*) (15%). Prey from the Malheur National Forest was dominated by Northern Flickers (20%), American Robins (*Turdus migratorius*)

TABLE 4. PERCENT COMPOSITION AND ESTIMATED BIOMASS OF PREY ITEMS OF NORTHERN GOSHAWKS FROM THREE NATIONAL FORESTS IN EASTERN OREGON (FROM DESTEFANO AND CUTLER 1998).

Species	Fremont (1992–1994) N = 153 % composition	% biomass	Malheur (1992–1996) N = 197 % composition	% biomass	Wallowa-Whitman (1992–1993) N = 30 % composition	% biomass
Rabbit/hare	6.6	27.6	6.6	20.8	0.0	0.0
Ground squirrel	7.2	6.3	11.7	13.9	3.3	5.1
Tree squirrel	15.0	13.3	9.1	10.1	3.3	3.1
Unidentified squirrel	2.6	2.0	8.6	7.9	0.0	0.0
Pocket gopher[a]	3.3	3.2	0.0	0.0	3.3	3.7
Other mammals	1.3	0.9	4.1	0.6	13.3	1.3
Unidentified small mammal	11.8	12.7	7.1	9.2	20.0	24.4
Total mammals	47.8	66.0	47.2	62.5	39.9	37.5
American Robin[b]	5.2	2.1	11.7	5.5	6.7	3.0
Owl	2.0	1.4	1.5	1.3	0.0	0.0
Woodpecker	6.5	2.2	1.5	1.3	3.3	1.2
Northern Flicker[c]	17.0	12.3	20.3	17.6	10.0	8.2
Steller's Jay[d]	8.5	4.4	5.6	3.5	3.3	2.0
Other birds	5.9	7.1	4.1	2.2	23.3	38.6
Unidentified birds	7.2	4.5	8.1	6.1	13.3	9.5
Total birds	52.2	34.0	52.8	37.5	59.9	62.5

[a] *Thomomys* spp.
[b] *Turdus migratorius.*
[c] *Colaptes auratus.*
[d] *Cyanocitta stelleri.*

(12%), and ground squirrels (*Spermophilus* spp.) (12%). Prey from the Wallowa-Whitman National Forest was dominated by Northern Flickers (10%) and American Robins (7%).

By biomass, birds comprised about 35% and mammals 65% of prey items from the Fremont and Malheur national forests; that trend was reversed for the Wallowa-Whitman National Forest (65% birds and 35% mammals) (Table 4). Rabbits (*Sylvilagus* spp.) and hares (*Lepus* spp.) contributed most to biomass of prey from the Fremont and Malheur national forests, although these larger prey were apparently consumed relatively infrequently. Tree squirrels and Northern Flickers made up 13% and 12% of total biomass, respectively, on the Fremont National Forest, while ground squirrels and Northern Flickers made up 15% and 14%, respectively, on the Malheur National Forest. Unidentified birds and small mammals made up 39% and 24%, respectively, on the Wallowa-Whitman National Forest.

DISCUSSION

Our information on the density and productivity of Northern Goshawks only spanned a few years, and thus is inadequate to fully address questions related to the status and population ecology of this species. Longer studies will more adequately provide information on life history parameters (DeStefano et al. 1994b, 1995), but our studies provide at least estimates of breeding densities and productivity over a fairly broad geographic area for a point in time. This information is also useful for comparative purposes, especially when assessing management plans that have been developed for other regions of the goshawk's range, and also stimulates some hypotheses and speculation. For example, densities of nesting goshawks may vary among forest types, with more nests per unit area in ponderosa pine than lodgepole pine.

For the historic nest-site phase of our research, our goal was to examine potential effects of long-term habitat alteration on the distribution of breeding Northern Goshawks based on changes in forest structure over three decades. We determined whether historic territories (i.e., those occupied ≥1 season during 1973–1991) were still occupied, documented changes in forest cover in historic territories between 1973–1994, and compared present conditions of forest vegetation between historic nest sites that were currently occupied and those where goshawks were not detected (no-response sites). Goshawks were more likely to be found in historic territories having a high percentage (about 50%) of mid-aged and late succession forest in closed-canopied conditions. Again, long-term studies will be necessary to fully assess the impact of extensive and intensive timber harvest on goshawk populations, but it appeared on the Fremont National Forest, and likely other parts of the inland Northwest, that a reduction in large trees and canopy cover, either through short-term, high-volume logging or repeated entry into stands over time, reduced the suitability of those stands for occupancy by breeding goshawks.

Our examination of the forest structure around goshawk nests showed selection for forest stands with larger trees and denser canopy than available in the surrounding landscape, which is a consistent finding for breeding goshawks throughout the western US (Squires and Reynolds 1997). Nest sites were often associated with wet or dry openings in the forest. Occasionally, goshawk nests were found in large trees in more open-canopied stands. As distance from the nest increased, so did the mixture of forest types and structure. Dense canopy and late seral stage structure was clearly important at landscape scales close to the nest, but decreased in relative abundance with distance from the nest (Daw and DeStefano 2001, McGrath et al. 2003). In general, Northern Goshawk nesting habitat became less distinguishable from the landscape with increasing area. These results are not surprising considering the heterogeneous landscape and scarcity of remaining large patches of older forest in eastern Oregon and Washington, conditions that are common throughout much of the forested lands in the western US (USDI Fish and Wildlife Service 1998c). Our spatial modeling also showed that timber harvest can be managed to maintain or enhance goshawk nest site suitability over time in the inland Northwest, and that a non-harvest strategy can in some cases be just as detrimental to nesting habitat as can be aggressive, maximum-yield forestry (McGrath et al. 2003). Active management may be required to counteract recent historical changes in the dynamic nature of forests such as fire suppression, overstocking of pole-sized trees, and insect outbreaks (Graham et al. 1994b, McGrath et al. 2003). Further, habitat management based on exclusionary buffers should be re-evaluated in light of the way different habitat factors interact across spatial scales (McGrath et al. 2003). Designation of buffers of a specific size around goshawk nests forces a predetermined restriction on all forest types, which may not be appropriate among different forest types (e.g., ponderosa pine vs. lodgepole pine stands), gives the impression that management is not required beyond the buffer, and ignores the spatial interactions that may be occurring among scales (e.g., nest stand, PFA, and foraging area).

Given the results from Desimone (1997), and the association between occupancy at historic sites and landscape composition, we see an avenue for the implementation of habitat models from McGrath et al. (2003) to maintain or enhance goshawk nesting habitat in an adaptive management context, while monitoring occupancy and productivity over time. Implementation of the models in a management context should be done in a deliberate manner, and be viewed as an experiment. We also offer the caveat that these models were developed in the interior Pacific Northwest, and may not be applicable to other regions or climatic conditions. McGrath et al. (2003) provide several examples of model applications at several landscape scales.

Goshawks in eastern Oregon preyed upon a wide variety of birds and mammals. Lagomorphs, tree and ground squirrels, Northern Flickers, and American Robins were important prey, based on both frequency in prey remains and estimated biomass. The relative importance of these species in the diet of goshawks could change with differences in relative abundance of prey over time (Watson et al. 1998) or as the structure of the forest is altered by succession, fire, or timber harvest (Reynolds et al. 1992). However, many of these or similar common species are likely important sources of energy for goshawks throughout much of their range in North America, and are listed in Reynolds et al. (1992).

The relatively small amount of prey collected from the Wallowa-Whitman National Forest is inadequate for fully assessing diets of goshawks on that forest. However, the results from this forest compared to the Fremont and Malheur national forests stimulate some speculation as to the relationship of prey availability, diet, and productivity of Northern Goshawks in western forests (DeStefano and McCloskey 1997, Watson et al. 1998). Birds appeared to make up a larger portion of the diet in the northernmost forest, the Wallowa-Whitman— about 60% birds and 40% mammals by frequency and biomass. Prey remains on both the Fremont and Malheur were about 50:50 for birds and mammals by frequency and about 35:65 by biomass. Productivity (number of fledglings per nest) may be lower on the Wallowa-Whitman National Forest (0.85 ± 0.74) compared to the Malheur National Forest (1.3 ± 0.73) and Fremont National Forest (1.6 ± 0.86). Birds in general contributed lower biomass than mammals, and high numbers of small birds such as flickers and robins, compared to larger prey such as grouse and hares, in the diet may correlate to lower

productivity in goshawks in any part of their range. The relationship of nutrition to reproductive output and survival of young in raptors is well documented (Ward and Kennedy 1994, 1996). Our data only show this relationship weakly, if at all, but this does underscore the importance of quality as well as quantity of prey in the diet. Larger biomass prey, such as lagomorphs and even squirrels and grouse, likely contributes to higher productivity of goshawks. In regions of the goshawk's range where breeding pairs rely heavily on small birds for prey, such as southeast Alaska and the Olympic Peninsula of Washington, productivity is often low (Finn et al. 2002b). Given the importance of prey abundance and availability in the current version of the goshawk management guidelines (Reynolds et al. 1992), further study on prey biomass, energetics involved in capture, and productivity of nesting goshawks would be interesting and warranted.

Goshawks can also be quite adaptable in the types of cover in which they hunt. Studies have shown that goshawk spend large amounts of time hunting in late-seral-stage forest (Bright-Smith and Mannan 1994, Beier and Drennan 1997). This was likely the case in eastern Oregon as well, but we did commonly observe goshawks hunting in the broad open sagebrush valley adjacent to the Malheur National Forest, and occasionally flying back into the forest with ground squirrels, which made up a measurable portion of prey remains from this forest (12% by frequency and 14% by biomass).

We believe that the management recommendations for goshawks developed by Reynolds et al. (1992) for the southwestern US have major application for the inland Pacific Northwest. The nested spatial concept, consisting of alternate nest sites of 10– 12 ha, within a post-fledging area (PFA) of 170 ha, within a home range of a few to several thousand hectares, is based on the ecology of breeding goshawks and provides a framework for addressing habitat needs at multiple scales. The mixture of cover types among these three spatial scales, as well as across landscapes the size of national forests as outlined by Reynolds et al. (1992) for the Southwest, should be applicable to other regions of the goshawks' geographic range. Reynolds et al. (1992) present desired amounts and spatial patterns of various vegetation structural stages (VSS) to provide a mix of cover types for goshawks and their prey, and to promote old-growth development and replacement. These recommended VSS should be reviewed for the inland Pacific Northwest in light of McGrath et al. (2003). One important caveat is that conservation of existing late-seral-stage forest and silvicultural treatments aimed at promoting the development of forest with old-growth characteristics (e.g., large trees, multi-layered stories, high-canopy volume, abundant and well distributed logs and snags) (Sesnie and Bailey 2003), should be of highest priority, as this is the forest seral stage most under-represented in the inland Pacific Northwest (Everett et al. 1993, Henjum 1996). There may be potential for management of the understory reinitiation stage to promote old growth characteristics in this region. Early successional stage forest and openings are well represented, but managers in eastern Oregon and Washington could focus on the size, distribution, and spatial arrangement of these forest patches and openings, with the southwest management guidelines and McGrath et al. (2003) as templates.

The focus on providing habitat for a variety of goshawk prey, as put forth by Reynolds et al. (1992), is also very appropriate and applicable to the Pacific Northwest. Managing for a diversity of prey species will not only help ensure a variety of prey for goshawks, especially when the periodic abundance of some species is low, but will also move us closer to management for biodiversity. What is most needed now is the systematic implementation and careful documentation of management procedures on the ground and long-term monitoring of the results, with changes made as necessary in an adaptive management framework (Long and Smith 2000).

ACKNOWLEDGMENTS

We thank the large number of employees of the state and federal agencies and timber industry companies, land managers, foresters, and biologists who contributed to this study. Funding was provided by the Oregon Department of Fish and Wildlife, USDA Forest Service, USDI Fish and Wildlife Service, Boise Cascade Corporation, National Council for Air and Stream Improvement, Northwest Forest Resource Council, Oregon Cooperative Wildlife Research Unit, and the Center for Analysis of Environmental Change. Special thanks to E. C. Meslow, R. G. Anthony, G. Keister, R. A. Riggs, L. L. Irwin, G. J. Roloff, R. T. Reynolds, and B. Woodbridge for their involvement in various aspects of these studies. S. P. Finn, M. L. Morrison, and an anonymous reviewer provided valuable comments on the manuscript.

Studies in Avian Biology No. 31:85–99

PREY AND WEATHER FACTORS ASSOCIATED WITH TEMPORAL VARIATION IN NORTHERN GOSHAWK REPRODUCTION IN THE SIERRA NEVADA, CALIFORNIA

John J. Keane, Michael L. Morrison, and D. Michael Fry

Abstract. We studied the association between Northern Goshawk (*Accipiter gentilis*) reproduction and annual variation in prey and weather factors in the Lake Tahoe region of the Sierra Nevada, California, during 1992–1995. The proportion of Northern Goshawk breeding territories occupied varied between years although differences were not statistically significant. However, annual variation was observed in the proportion of Northern Goshawk territories with active nests, successful nests, and in the number of young produced per successful nest. Annual variation in reproduction was associated with variation in late-winter and early-spring temperatures and Douglas squirrel (*Tamiasciurus douglasii*) abundance (February–April). Douglas squirrel abundance, and their frequency and biomass in diets of Northern Goshawks during the breeding period, varied annually in concordance with cone crop production. Northern Goshawk reproduction was greatest in 1992 following both abundant late-winter and early-spring Douglas squirrel populations, which resulted from high cone crop production the previous autumn, and mild late-winter and early-spring temperatures. These results are consistent with the prediction that carnivorous birds require increased energy before breeding in order to reproduce successfully. In the high elevations of the Sierra Nevada, prey availability is reduced during the late winter and early spring because of the migration and hibernation patterns of important prey species and temperatures are near or below the lower critical temperature for Northern Goshawks during this period. In contrast to other prey species, Douglas squirrels are active throughout the year and are available during this period. Thus, our results suggest that forest management and restoration strategies adopted to enhance Northern Goshawk foraging areas should consider management of conifer tree size distributions and species compositions to enhance seed production in terms of frequency over time, number of seeds per crop, and energetic value of seeds by tree species, as these are important habitat elements and ecological processes influencing Douglas squirrel populations. Autecological studies of focal species of concern such as the Northern Goshawk are necessary to provide the basic ecological knowledge required to integrate species level concerns with landscape and ecosystem management perspectives to advance conservation science and improve land management.

Key Words: *Accipiter gentilis,* California, cone-crop production, diet, Douglas squirrel, Northern Goshawk, reproductive success, Sierra Nevada, *Tamiasciurus douglasii,* weather.

PRESA Y FACTORES DEL CLIMA ASOCIADOS CON LA VARIACIÓN TEMPORAL EN LA REPRODUCCIÓN DEL GAVILÁN AZOR EN LA SIERRA NEVADA, CALIFORNIA

Resumen. Estudiamos la asociación entre la reproducción y la variación anual en la presa, así como los factores del clima del Gavilán Azor (*Accipiter gentilis*), en la región de Lake Tahoe de la Sierra Nevada, en California, durante 1992–1995. La proporción ocupada de territorios de reproducción del Gavilán Azor varió entre los años, a pesar de que las diferencias no fueron estadísticamente significativas. Sin embargo, la variación anual fue observada en la proporción de territorios del Gavilán Azor con nidos activos, nidos exitosos, y en el número de juveniles producidos por nido exitosos. La variación anual en la reproducción estuvo asociada con la variación en temperaturas al final del invierno y al principio de la primavera, y con la abundancia de la ardilla de Douglas (*Tamiasciurus douglasii*), febrero–abril. La abundancia de la ardilla de Douglas, y la frecuencia y biomasa en las dietas de los Gavilanes Azor durante el período reproductivo, varió anualmente de acuerdo a la producción de la cosecha de conos. La reproducción del Gavilán Azor en 1992 fue mayor, seguida de poblaciones abundantes de ardillas de Douglas durante el final del invierno y el principio de la primavera, lo cual resultó de una alta producción en la cosecha de conos durante el otoño anterior y las temperaturas blandas durante el final del invierno y el principio de la primavera. Dichos resultados son consistentes con la predicción de que las aves carnívoras requieren un incremento en la energía antes de reproducirse, con el fin de reproducirse exitosamente. En las altas elevaciones de la Sierra Nevada, la disponibilidad de la presa es reducida durante el final del invierno y el principio de la primavera, debido a los patrones de migración e hibernación de especies importantes de presas, y ya que las temperaturas durante este período se acercan o están por debajo de la temperatura crítica de los Gavilanes Azor. En contraste a otras especies de presas, las ardillas de Douglas son activas durante todo el año, y están disponibles durante este período. Es por esto que nuestros resultados sugieren que el manejo forestal y las estrategias de restauración adoptadas para mejorar las áreas de forrajeo del Gavilán Azor, deberían considerar el manejo de las distribuciones en el tamaño de árboles de coníferas, así como la composición de las especies, para mejorar la producción de la semilla en términos de frecuencia a través del tiempo, número de semillas por cosecha y valor energético de las semillas por especie de árbol; ya que estos son elementos importantes del hábitat, así como procesos ecológicos, los cuales influyen las poblaciones de la ardilla de Douglas. Estudios Auto ecológicos de especies focales de interés, tales como los del Gavilán Azor, son necesarios para proveer el conocimiento ecológico básico requerido para integrar las preocupaciones del nivel de especies, con el paisaje y el manejo del ecosistema, con el fin de avanzar en la ciencia de la conservación y de mejorar el manejo de la tierra.

The Northern Goshawk (*Accipiter gentilis*) has been of conservation concern recently in North America due to uncertainty regarding population trends and potential impacts of forest management practices on habitat (Block et al. 1994, Kennedy 1997, DeStefano 1998, Andersen et al. 2004). Northern Goshawks are distributed throughout forests and woodlands of the Holarctic (Brown and Amadon 1968). In North America, Northern Goshawks are found in forested vegetation types ranging across the boreal forest and extending south through the western mountains into Mexico and, in the East, south through the mixed conifer-hardwood forest to approximately New York and New Jersey (Palmer 1988, Squires and Reynolds 1997; Bosakowski and Smith, *this volume*). Conservation strategies for Northern Goshawks will need to be developed at appropriate ecological scales to account for variability in vegetation, climate, diet, and prey dynamics across the broad geographic range of the species (Reynolds et al. 1992, Keane and Morrison 1994, Andersen et al. 2004).

The influence of biotic and abiotic factors on population dynamics has been of fundamental interest to ecologists (Andrewartha and Birch 1954, Lack 1966, Newton 1998). Food and weather are primary limiting factors for raptor populations (Newton 1979a). Studies of Northern Goshawk populations in boreal forests of both the Nearctic and Paleoarctic have demonstrated that annual variation in their reproduction, as well as migration patterns, are associated with cyclic population dynamics of galliformes or lagomorphs, their primary prey in those regions (McGowan 1975, Doyle and Smith 1994, Sulkava et al. 1994, Erdman et al. 1998). Weather factors, specifically temperature and precipitation, are also associated with annual variation in Northern Goshawk reproduction (Kostrzewa and Kostrzewa 1990, Sulkava et al. 1994). Like populations in boreal forests, populations of Northern Goshawks in temperate North American forests also exhibit high variation in reproduction between years (Bloom et al. 1986, Reynolds et al. 1994, Kennedy 1997).

Although breeding season diets have been described for a number of Northern Goshawk populations in these temperate forest systems (Andersen et al. 2004), the data are generally reported as overall summaries of frequency and biomass pooled over multiple years of the study. We are unaware of any studies that have attempted to quantify annual variation in diets, prey abundance, and weather factors associated with annual variation in reproduction.

Consideration of avian ecological energetics provides a foundation for framing questions related to the role of biotic and abiotic environmental factors on annual variation in Northern Goshawk reproduction. Weathers and Sullivan (1993) reviewed the avian ecological energetics literature and suggested that diet is a factor that determines which of two competing hypotheses regarding seasonal energetic patterns applies to species in seasonal environments. Omnivorous or granivorous species follow a reallocation-pattern hypothesis whereby overall energetic requirements are similar between seasons and individuals reallocate energy from thermoregulation in winter to reproductive needs in spring and summer. Carnivorous or insectivorous species follow an increased demand hypothesis, whereby individuals have increased energy demands in the breeding season (Weathers and Sullivan 1993). For example, field metabolic rates of Long-eared Owls (*Asio otus*) increased by 42% (Wijandts 1984), and male Eurasian Kestrels (*Falco tinnunculus*) by 48% during the breeding season as compared to the winter (Masman et al. 1988).

Female raptors require a significant increase in energy intake to acquire the substantial body reserves necessary before egg laying (Hirons 1985). The amount of food required to attain these body reserves is potentially much greater than the food required solely for egg production in large raptors (Newton 1993). Females that do not accumulate these reserves do not lay eggs. Typically, females do not actively hunt during the pre-laying period and the majority of food is provided by the male. Therefore, whether a pair will breed successfully depends on the ability of the male to provide extra food in the early spring which is affected by a number of potential factors that include the individual hunting prowess of the male, prey abundance and availability, and thermal stress induced by weather conditions (Newton 1993).

Our goal was to study the ecology of Northern Goshawks in the Sierra Nevada of California to investigate annual variation in reproduction and its relationship to prey and weather factors. Our specific objectives were to investigate annual variation in: (1) the proportion of Northern Goshawk territories occupied, active, and successfully producing young, (2) the frequency and biomass of each prey species in Northern Goshawk diets during the breeding period, (3) the relative abundance of key prey species, (4) factors affecting the abundance of key prey species, and (5) relationships between weather and reproduction. An understanding of these relationships is necessary to develop an effective conservation strategy for Northern Goshawks and to provide a basis for integrating a single-species perspective with broader ecosystem perspectives to advance conservation and land management in the Sierra Nevada.

STUDY AREA

Our study was conducted within an approximately 950 km^2 area in the Lake Tahoe region (39°00', 120°00') of the Sierra Nevada range of California. Geologically, the region is dominated by the Lake Tahoe Basin, a fault block that has sunk between the uplifted Sierra Nevada and Carson Range fault blocks with Lake Tahoe having formed as a result of volcanic and glacial processes (Whitney 1979). Elevation in the study area ranged from 1,800–2,450 m. The Sierra Nevada is characterized by a Mediterranean climate with hot, dry summers and cool, wet winters (Schoenherr 1992). Average summer and winter temperatures were 14.8 C and -0.8 C, respectively, and total annual precipitation (1 July–30 June) ranged from 41.1–155.5 cm during the study between 1991–1995 (Western Regional Climate Center, Reno, NV, unpubl. data). Primary forest types in the study area consisted of mixed-conifer (ponderosa pine [*Pinus ponderosa*], Jeffrey pine [*Pinus jeffreyi*], white fir [*Abies concolor*], red fir [*Abie magnifica*], and incense cedar [*Libocedrus decurrens*]), red fir, eastside pine (Jeffrey-ponderosa), and lodgepole pine (*Pinus contorta*). Other prominent vegetation types present were montane chaparral (*Arctostaphylus-Quercus-Ceanothus*), riparian, and montane meadow.

METHODS

NORTHERN GOSHAWK REPRODUCTION

We surveyed for Northern Goshawk territories using two survey techniques to meet two objectives during March–September 1991–1995. We used broadcast surveys to inventory and document the location of Northern Goshawk breeding territories across the study area. We used status surveys to monitor occupancy and reproductive status at known Northern Goshawk territories.

Broadcast surveys were conducted by systematically traversing each survey area and broadcasting conspecific calls from sample points at approximately every 200 m (Kennedy and Stahlecker 1993, Joy et al. 1994). Each point was surveyed for approximately 10 min by alternating broadcast calling with silent observation. Territorial alarm calls were used during the incubation and nestling periods and a combination of wailing and territorial alarm calls were used during the fledgling dependency period (Kennedy and Stahlecker 1993). All watersheds in the northern, western, and southern regions of the Lake Tahoe Basin were surveyed. We also surveyed select areas to the north and west of the basin proper that had historic records of nesting activity with no current information on occupancy status or where observations of birds suggested the potential location of Northern Goshawk breeding territories. All areas were surveyed with broadcast surveys a minimum of two times each year. Broadcast surveys were conducted during the nestling and fledgling dependency periods of the breeding season when these methods are most effective (Kennedy and Stahlecker 1993). We also conducted at least one status survey per year in each of the historic sites using a combination of intensive stand searches and broadcast surveys described below.

We considered an area a Northern Goshawk territory if an active nest (i.e., adult incubating, nestlings, or fledglings) was found in any one year of nest monitoring. Thus, we excluded areas where we found old nests but did not detect adult birds or nest attempts during the study as we had no information on when the territory may have been last occupied. Each year we monitored all known nesting areas to document occupancy and reproductive status. Intensive stand searches were used in April–June to determine territory occupancy, estimate laying dates, and nest locations within 0.8 km of known nest trees; each known site was visited two–three times. Intensive stand searches at this time of the breeding period consisted of one or two observers silently traversing the survey area searching for nests or sign (feathers, prey remains, and/or whitewash). If we did not locate an active nest with the early season intensive stand searches, we conducted broadcast surveys and repeated intensive stand searches during the nestling and fledgling dependency periods of the nest cycle to determine territory status. The area within 1.6 km of known nest trees was surveyed a minimum of five times using a combination of broadcast surveys and intensive stand searches. One or two observers systematically traversed the area along transects spaced at approximately 50 m apart visually searching for nests and sign, and broadcast conspecific calls approximately every 150 m to illicit territorial responses. Territorial alarm calls were used during the incubation and nestling periods and a combination of wailing and territorial alarm calls were used during the fledgling dependency period (Kennedy and Stahlecker 1993).

A nest area was classified as occupied if adult birds were detected one or more times within the 1.6 km survey area around known nest locations (February–September). A nest site was considered active in any one year if a nest with an incubating adult or nestlings, or fledglings in the immediate nest area were detected. A nest site was also considered active in that year if a failed nest with either fresh greenery, whitewash at the base of the tree, fresh prey remains, or fresh down on the nest rim was observed indicating that pairs had initiated nest building and egg-laying before abandoning the nest attempt. A nest site was classified as successful if fledglings successfully dispersed from the area. Nest sites were considered inactive if neither adult birds nor an active nest were located. Given that we conducted surveys throughout the entire breeding period and that fledglings are highly vocal and thus detectable during the fledgling dependency period, and remain in the nest area for 4–6 wk after fledgling (J. Keane, unpubl. data), it is likely we would have detected most successful nest attempts. However, we may not have detected pairs that had moved farther than 1.6 km among alternate nest locations between years. Woodbridge and Detrich (1994) reported that known alternate nest sites were within 0.7 km for 85% of 28 pairs in northern California. Reynolds and Joy (1998) reported that >95% of alternate nests were located within 1.6 km of each other. We used chi-square analysis (Sokal and Rohlf 1981) to separately test for differences in the proportion of territories occupied, active, and successful between years, and the proportion of active nests that were successful between years. Only data from known territories were used in these analyses. Data from the initial year in which a territory was located were not used in the analysis. This was done to eliminate potential bias resulting from including only new territories with active nests because search efforts are likely biased towards locating new territories when they have active nests versus when they are unoccupied or occupied but non-nesting. We used one-way analysis of variance (ANOVA; Sokal and Rolhf 1981) to compare the number of young produced per territory and per successful nest among years. Data from all successful nests, including new nests located within each year, were used in the comparison of young produced per successful nest in this analysis.

NORTHERN GOSHAWK DIET

Northern Goshawk diets were determined by collecting prey remains (i.e., feathers, fur, skin, and skeletal parts) and pellets found in the nest area during the nesting period by systematically searching the entire area within approximately 150-m radius circle centered on each active nest. All methods used to quantify raptor diets have associated biases (Marti 1987). Boal and Mannan (1994) reported that estimates based on collections of prey remains are biased towards conspicuous prey species, e.g., mammals, as compared to direct observations of prey delivered to nests. Their observations suggest that mammals may constitute a larger portion of the diet then our data might indicate. However, we think that our estimates of relative annual variation in diet provide a comparative measure of prey species in the diet among years because Collopy (1983) reported that remains analysis, pellet analysis, and direct observation yielded similar rankings of prey taxons for Golden Eagles (*Aquila chrysaetos*) and Northern Goshawks. Prey items were categorized to species based on comparisons with specimens in the bird and mammal collection in the Department of Wildlife, Fisheries and Conservation Biology at the University of California, Davis. Some items were identified only to genus due to difficulty in identifying species (e.g., *Spermophilus* and *Tamias*). Biomass was estimated by calculating mean weights for adult mammal species based on values obtained from museum specimens and mean values reported in Jameson and Peeters (1988). We used adult weights for calculating mammal biomass and used an average weight for all species in a genus for those species identified to genus. Mean values reported in Dunning (1984) were used to calculate biomass for avian species. Following Reynolds and Meslow (1984), we used one half of the adult weight as an estimate of fledgling and sub-adult weights for birds.

We calculated the frequency and biomass contribution of each prey species by year and created eight subgroups of species or taxonomic groups for analysis based on sample size (individual species comprised >5% of total prey by frequency or biomass in most years, or they were grouped into general class of birds or mammals) and identification criteria (pooled *Spermophilus* and *Tamias*).

Douglas squirrel (*Tamiasciurus douglasii*), American Robin (*Turdus migratorius*), Steller's Jay (*Cyanocitta stelleri*), and Northern Flicker (*Colaptes auratus*) were the most frequently recorded prey species and were analyzed as individual species. Additional, infrequently recorded bird species were lumped into the taxonomic group labeled other birds for analysis. Golden-mantled ground squirrel (*Spermophilus lateralis*), Belding ground squirrel (*Spermophilus beldingi*), and California ground squirrel (*Spermophilus beecheyi*) were lumped into the taxonomic group *Spermophilus* for analysis based on the difficulty of identifying prey remains to species. Shadow chipmunk (*Tamias senex*), long-eared chipmunk (*Tamias quadrimaculatus*), lodgepole chipmunk (*Tamias speciosus*) , and yellow-pine chipmunk (*Tamias amoenus*) occurred in the study area and were lumped into the taxonomic group *Tamias* for analysis due to difficulty in identifying prey remains to species. Additional, infrequently recorded mammal species were lumped in the species group labeled other mammals for analysis. We used chi-square analysis (Sokal and Rohlf 1981) to compare the frequency and biomass of each species or taxonomic group in the diet between years.

PREY ABUNDANCE

Point counts (Verner 1985) were used to estimate an index of abundance for bird prey species and Douglas squirrels from autumn 1991 through spring 1994. A total of 312 sample points were established and distributed in grids across Donner Memorial, Burton Creek, Sugar Pine Point, D.L. Bliss, Emerald Bay, and Washoe Meadows California state parks, and across the Angora Creek watershed in the southwestern corner of the Lake Tahoe Basin on land administered by the USDA Forest Service. From a random starting location, each grid was laid out with count points at 300 m intervals along cardinal compass directions. The nearest tree, defined as >2 m in height and >5 cm diameter at breast height (dbh) served as the center of the sample point. Grids were located to provide complete coverage of the watershed or park and Northern Goshawk nesting territories were located within each of the watersheds where prey sampling was conducted. The grids were distributed north to south across the entire study area, with approximately 33 km^2 covered by the prey sampling grids, to provide estimates of prey abundance across the study area.

A random sample of 205 count points was selected from the 312 total points across the study sites for monthly point count sampling to assess the relative abundance of prey species. We attempted to conduct monthly counts at the same 205 points from November 1991 through April 1994. A 7-min point count was conducted at each point count within which the observer recorded all birds and Douglas squirrels heard or seen within distance bands of 0–30 m, 31–60 m, 61–100 m, and >100 m. All counts were conducted within 4 hr after dawn. Approximately 10–15 points were counted per sample day. A total of six observers collected data during the study, with three observers the same throughout the study. All observers were experienced with bird identification and had extensive training on identification and count methods to minimize potential observer bias. Not all points could be counted in each month, largely due to inclement winter weather. Although point-count sampling ended in spring 1994 due to funding constraints, an estimate of Douglas squirrel abundance for spring 1995 was obtained from similar point count sampling conducted at 160 points in six watersheds within the study area, four of which were the same watersheds where we conducted point counts (P. Manley, USDA Forest Service, unpubl. data).

Monthly counts were grouped into four seasonal groups for statistical analysis (autumn = September–November; winter = December–February; spring = March–May; summer = June–August). We calculated an index of abundance defined as the total number of detections per 100 points. We used ANOVA (Sokal and Rohlf 1981) to compare the abundance of each species within each season between years. Lack of data for all four seasons across all 4 yr, and likely differences in detectability among seasons, precluded use of a factorial ANOVA to assess interactions between seasons and years. Scheffe's test was used for multiple comparisons to assess between group differences when ANOVAs indicated significant differences. Only results for species which comprised at least 5% of Northern Goshawk prey items across years are included.

RELATIONSHIPS WITH CONE CROP PRODUCTION

Cone crop production was qualitatively assessed during autumn of each year based on a visual assessment of each of the conifer tree species across the study area (Petty et al. 1995). Cone crop production in the study area was classified subjectively based on an index score relative to the maximum cone production observed in autumn 1991. An extra large crop of cones was produced in autumn 1991 on both ponderosa and Jeffrey pines and white and red fir. Cone production was qualitatively scored in each year relative to this baseline with a score ranging from 0–3 (0 = no cone production observed on any conifer species; 1 = low cone production [cone production observed on one conifer species—individual trees producing small number of cones]; 2 = medium cone production [large numbers of cones within one conifer species or small numbers of cones produced across two or more conifer species]; 3 = high cone production [large numbers of cones across two or more conifer species]).

Based on the observed patterns between Northern Goshawk reproduction, frequency and biomass of Douglas squirrel in the diet, and the relative abundance of Douglas squirrels across the 4 yr of the study, we assessed the relationship of these variables to cone crop production measures. We used simple linear regression analysis (Sokal and Rohlf 1981) to assess the relationship between cone crop production and spring Douglas squirrel abundance, and the proportion of Douglas squirrels in the Northern Goshawk diet for both frequency and biomass across years. We used simple linear regression analysis to assess the relationship between the proportion of Northern Goshawk territories successful and spring Douglas squirrel abundance, and the frequency and biomass of Douglas squirrel in the diet across years.

RELATIONSHIPS WITH WEATHER

We obtained weather data collected from a monitoring station in the study area near Tahoe City, California, operated by the Western Regional Climate Center. Simple linear regression analysis (Sokal and Rohlf 1981) was used to assess the relationships of the proportion of active and successful goshawk territories, and the number of young produced per successful nest, with three measures of weather across years—total precipitation, number of days with recorded precipitation, and mean temperature. The relationships between reproductive and weather variables were examined across the late-winter and early-spring period (February–April). This timeframe corresponded to the pre-laying period of the reproductive cycle when radio telemetry indicated that females began to reduce their ranging behavior and center their activity within or near their nest stands (Keane 1999).

RESULTS

NORTHERN GOSHAWK REPRODUCTION

Northern Goshawk reproduction was monitored on 17–24 nest sites each year of the study (Table 1). The proportion of territories occupied varied across years, ranging from 82–100%, although differences were not statistically significant ($\chi^2 = 3.16$, df = 3, P = 0.37). Both the proportion of territories with active nests ($\chi^2 = 12.70$, df = 3, P = 0.01) and successful nests ($\chi^2 = 8.22$, df = 3, P = 0.04) differed significantly between years. The proportion of territories with successful nests was greatest in 1992 (82%), declined to 47% in 1993 and 37% in 1994, and increased to 58% in 1995 (Table 1).

The proportion of active nests that were successful did not differ significantly between years ($\chi^2 = 2.29$, df = 3, P = 0.51), but nonetheless ranged from a low of 62% in 1993 to a high of 82% in 1992. Of the total 13 nest failures recorded over the 4-yr study period, nine attempts failed during the incubation period from undocumented causes. In each of these cases a previously active nest was abandoned during one of the approximately weekly monitoring visits (two failed nests in 1992, 1993, and 1994; three failed nests in 1995). One nest failed during the nestling period, apparently due to Great Horned Owl (*Bubo virginianus*) depredation. One nesting attempt

TABLE 1. RESULTS OF CHI-SQUARE ANALYSIS OF ANNUAL VARIATION IN THE PROPORTION OF NORTHERN GOSHAWK NEST SITES OCCUPIED, AND WITH ACTIVE AND SUCCESSFUL NESTS, IN THE LAKE TAHOE REGION, CALIFORNIA, 1992–1995.

Variable	1992	1993	1994	1995	Total	P
N territories	17	17	19	24	77	
N occupied	17	14	16	21	68	0.368
Percent occupied	100	82.4	84.2	87.5	88.3	
N active nests	17	13	9	17	56	0.005
Percent occupied	100	76.5	47.4	70.8	72.7	
N successful nests	14	8	7	14	43	0.042
Percent occupied	82.4	47.1	36.8	58.3	55.8	

TABLE 2. RESULTS OF ANOVA FOR ANNUAL VARIATION IN THE NUMBER OF YOUNG PRODUCED PER TERRITORY AND PER SUCCESSFUL NEST (MEAN ± SD) FOR NORTHERN GOSHAWKS IN THE LAKE TAHOE REGION, CALIFORNIA, 1992–1995.

Variable	1992	1993	1994	1995	P
N young/ Territory [a]	2.0 ± 1.22 A	0.8 ± 0.90 B	0.7 ± 1.00 B	1.0 ± 0.93 B	<0.001
N young/ Successful nest [a]	2.4 ± 0.85 A	1.7 ± 0.50 AB	1.9 ± 0.76 AB	1.6 ± 0.51 B	0.005

[a] Numbers with different letters are significantly different (P <0.05) based on multiple comparisons using Scheffe's test.

failed during the early fledging period in 1994 when the single fledgling disappeared from the nest area 5–10 d after fledging. We observed two females during 1993 incubating eggs for approximately 62–65 d. Each of their clutches contained two eggs, from which we collected a total of three eggs. All three eggs were infertile, suggesting that the females may not have attained a sufficient energetic condition to produce viable eggs (Keane 1999).

The number of young produced per territory (F = 6.28, df = 3, P <0.001) and per successful nest (F = 4.53, df = 3, P = 0.01) differed significantly among years (Table 2). More young were fledged per territory in 1992 than the other 3 yr. The number of young per successful nest differed between 1992 and 1995. We documented one incidence of nestling mortality during the nestling period in addition to the nest predation event described above. The remains of two young from a nest containing three young approximately 4 wk old were found at the base of the nest tree during June of 1992 following an overnight snowstorm with 6 cm of snow. The proximate cause of death could not be determined.

Incubation was initiated in mid-April in 1992, the first week of May in 1993, the fourth week of April in 1994, and the first week of May in 1995. The number of young fledged per successful nest was associated with both the earliest laying date (adj. r^2 = 0.92, df = 3, P = 0.03) and the proportion of successful nests fledging three young (adj. r^2 = 0.96, df = 3, P = 0.01). Nine of fourteen successful nests (64%) fledged three young in 1992 whereas one of seven (14%) did in 1994. None of the successful nests fledged three young in 1993 or 1995 (Fig. 1). Thus, the number of young per successful nest was greatest in years when breeding was initiated earlier in the spring.

NORTHERN GOSHAWK DIET

A total of 1,058 individual prey items comprised of 12 mammal and 22 bird species were identified (Keane 1999). Mammals comprised 49% by frequency and 58% by biomass of the prey items identified, whereas birds comprised 51% by frequency and 42% by biomass (Tables 3 and 4). The frequency (χ^2 = 39.602, df = 3, P <0.001) and biomass (χ^2 = 7.87,

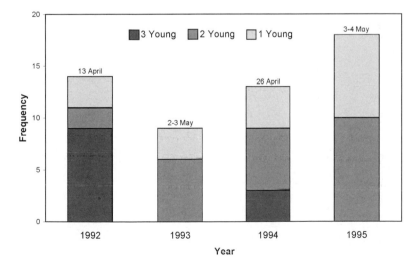

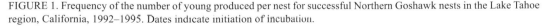

FIGURE 1. Frequency of the number of young produced per nest for successful Northern Goshawk nests in the Lake Tahoe region, California, 1992–1995. Dates indicate initiation of incubation.

TABLE 3. FREQUENCY AND PERCENT OCCURRENCE OF SELECTED SPECIES AND SPECIES GROUPS IDENTIFIED IN PREY REMAINS COLLECTED AT NORTHERN GOSHAWK NESTS IN THE LAKE TAHOE REGION, CALIFORNIA, 1992–1995.

Species	1992 N	1992 %	1993 N	1993 %	1994 N	1994 %	1995 N	1995 %	Total N	Total %
Douglas squirrel	70	32.6	24	14.3	59	14.1	90	34.9	243	23.0
Spermophilus spp.	40	18.6	40	23.8	44	10.6	27	10.5	151	14.3
Tamias spp.	8	3.7	13	7.7	38	9.1	35	13.6	94	8.9
Other mammals	1	0.5	8	4.8	14	3.4	3	1.2	26	2.4
American Robin	11	5.1	12	7.1	70	16.8	3	1.2	96	9.1
Northern Flicker	26	12.1	25	14.9	77	18.5	30	11.6	158	14.9
Steller's Jay	45	20.9	32	19.0	74	17.7	49	19.0	200	18.9
Other birds	14	6.5	14	8.3	41	9.8	21	8.1	90	8.5
Total mammals	119	55.3	85	50.6	155	37.2	155	60.1	514	48.6
Total birds	96	44.7	83	49.4	262	62.8	103	39.3	544	51.4
Total prey items	215	20.3	168	15.9	417	39.4	258	24.4	1,058	100.0

TABLE 4. BIOMASS OF SELECTED SPECIES AND SPECIES GROUPS IDENTIFIED IN PREY REMAINS COLLECTED AT NORTHERN GOSHAWK NESTS IN THE LAKE TAHOE REGION, CALIFORNIA, 1992–1995.

Species	1992 Kg.	1992 %	1993 Kg.	1993 %	1994 Kg.	1994 %	1995 Kg.	1995 %	Total Kg.	Total %
Douglas squirrel	16.34	44.6	5.60	19.2	13.77	21.3	21.01	49.9	56.72	32.9
Spermophilus spp.	8.19	22.3	7.70	26.3	9.82	15.2	5.24	12.5	30.95	17.9
Tamias spp.	0.48	1.3	0.79	2.7	2.30	3.6	2.11	5.0	5.68	3.3
Other mammals	0.17	0.4	2.82	9.6	3.42	5.3	0.50	1.2	6.91	4.0
Northern Flicker	3.69	10.1	3.48	11.9	10.93	17.0	4.26	10.1	22.37	13.0
Steller's Jay	3.87	10.6	3.07	10.5	7.47	11.6	5.04	12.0	19.45	11.3
American Robin	0.77	2.1	0.89	3.0	5.26	8.2	0.23	0.6	7.15	4.1
Other birds	3.14	8.6	4.89	16.7	11.54	17.9	3.69	8.7	23.26	13.5
Total mammals	25.18	68.7	16.91	57.8	29.31	45.4	28.86	68.6	100.26	58.1
Total birds	11.48	31.3	12.33	42.2	35.20	54.6	13.22	31.4	72.23	41.9
Total biomass	36.66	21.2	29.24	17.0	64.51	37.4	42.08	24.4	172.49	100.0

df = 3, 0.02 < P < 0.050) of birds and mammals in Northern Goshawk diets varied among years. The frequency of mammals ranged from 60% in 1995 to 37% in 1994 (Table 3). The biomass of mammals in the prey items ranged from highs of 69% in 1992 and 1995 to a low of 45% in 1994 (Table 4).

Overall the Douglas squirrel was the most frequently recorded species, followed by Steller's Jay, Northern Flicker, and *Spermophilus* spp. (Table 3). Douglas squirrel also contributed the most to total biomass, followed by *Spermophilus* spp., other birds, Northern Flicker, and Steller's Jay (Table 4).

The frequency (χ^2 = 58.035, df = 3, P <0.001) and biomass (χ^2 = 14.20, df = 3, P < 0.01) of Douglas squirrel in the diet varied among years, with both being greater in 1992 and 1995 than in 1993 and 1994 (Tables 3 and 4). The frequency of *Spermophilus* spp. (χ^2 = 23.31, df = 3, P < 0.001), *Tamias spp.* (χ^2 = 14.36, df = 3, P = 0.002), other mammals (χ^2 = 10.49, df = 3, P = 0.015), and American Robins (χ^2 = 54.48, df = 3, P <0.001) in Northern Goshawk prey remains varied in a statistically significant manner among years (Table 3). Other than Douglas squirrel, no significant annual differences were found in the proportion of biomass contributions by the other species or species groups.

PREY ABUNDANCE

Overall, populations of primary prey species exhibited significant differences in relative abundance and high degrees of variation within and among years (Table 5). Douglas squirrel abundance differed significantly among years during all four seasons based on point counts. Squirrel numbers during autumn were greater in 1992 than in 1993, which in turn were greater than in 1991. During winter, squirrel numbers were greater in winter 1991–1992 than in 1992–1993 or 1993–1994. Similarly, spring squirrel numbers were greater in 1992 than in 1993 or 1994. Squirrel numbers were greater in summer 1992 versus 1993. Squirrel numbers were high in spring 1995 with a relative abundance estimate of 114.4 individuals/100 count points and where detected at 64% of the count points (frequency of detection of 0.64; P. Manley, unpubl. data). Over the 4-yr study, spring Douglas squirrel numbers were high in 1992 and 1995 and low in 1993 and 1994.

Steller's Jay abundance differed significantly among years during each of the four seasons (Table 5). During autumn, Steller's Jay numbers were greater in 1993 than in 1994. Steller's Jay numbers were greater in winter 1991–1992 than during 1992–1993 and 1993–1994. Steller's Jay numbers

were greater in spring 1993 than in 1992 or 1994 and greater in summer 1992 than summer 1993. Northern Flicker abundance differed significantly among years during autumn, winter, and summer (Table 5). Northern Flicker numbers were greater in autumn 1991 and 1992 versus 1993, greater in winter 1991–1992 versus 1992–93 and 1993–1994, and greater in summer 1992 versus 1993 (Table 5). American Robin abundance differed significantly among years only during the spring (Table 5). American Robin numbers in spring 1994 were lower than in 1992.

RELATIONSHIPS WITH CONE CROP PRODUCTION

High cone crop production (score = 3) was recorded in autumn 1991 and autumn 1994 when ponderosa, Jeffrey, and sugar pines, and white and red firs produced large numbers of cones. No cone crop production (score = 0) was noted in autumn 1992. Cone crop production was low (score = 1) in autumn 1993 when only a low proportion of white fir produced low numbers of cones.

The proportion of territories with successful nests, the number of young per territory, the frequency and biomass of Douglas squirrel in the diet, the winter and spring abundance of Douglas squirrel, and cone production varied in a similar pattern with one another over the four years of the study (Fig. 2). The overall pattern was that each of the aforementioned variables was relatively high in 1992, declined in 1993 and 1994, and then increased again in 1995. The frequency (adj. r^2 = 0.89, df = 3, P =0.04) and biomass (adj. r^2 = 0.85, df = 3, P = 0.05) of Douglas squirrel in the diet varied with spring Douglas squirrel abundance. Spring Douglas squirrel abundance (adj. r^2 = 0.89, df = 3, P = 0.04), and the frequency (adj. r^2 = 0.87, df = 3, P = 0.04) and biomass (adj. r^2 = 0.90, df = 3, P = 0.03) of Douglas squirrels in the Northern Goshawk diet, varied in concordance with cone crop production. Spring Douglas squirrel abundance accounted for a high proportion of the variation observed in the proportion of territories with successful nests between years, although the relationship was not statistically significant (adj. r^2 = 0.71, df = 3, P = 0.10).

RELATIONSHIP WITH WEATHER

Total precipitation recorded during late-winter and early-spring differed by a factor of about four among years (Table 6). Total precipitation was lower during 1992 and 1994, about 50% greater in 1993, and about 300% greater in 1995. In addition

TABLE 5. RELATIVE ABUNDANCE (N/100 COUNT POINTS) AND FREQUENCY OF OCCURRENCE OF SELECTED NORTHERN GOSHAWK PREY SPECIES ESTIMATED FROM POINT COUNTS IN THE LAKE TAHOE REGION, CALIFORNIA, FALL 1991 THROUGH SPRING 1994. ANOVA WAS USED TO TEST FOR ANNUAL VARIATION IN SPECIES RELATIVE ABUNDANCE WITHIN SEASONS AMONG YEARS

Species Season	1991–92			1992–93			1993–94			P
	Mean[a]	SE	Frequency	Mean	SE	Frequency	Mean	SE	Frequency	
Douglas Squirrel										
Fall	147.4 A	10.88	0.78	386.1 B	8.03	0.95	272.6 C	7.37	0.91	<0.0001
Winter	125.8 A	5.13	0.69	61.2 B	5.51	0.44	84.1 B	6.68	0.47	<0.0001
Spring	132.9 A	4.63	0.74	48.9 B	3.13	0.36	55.1 B	4.72	0.43	<0.0001
Summer	292.7	6.78	0.94	156.8	5.57	0.73		–[b]		<0.0001
Steller's Jay										
Fall	137.7 AB	9.84	0.76	165.9 A	7.16	0.71	112.6 B	6.48	0.53	<0.0001
Winter	74.4 A	5.03	0.43	30.5 B	6.73	0.20	10.5 B	2.91	0.07	<0.0001
Spring	162.4 A	5.89	0.75	200.0 B	8.01	0.73	132.4 A	9.73	0.56	<0.0001
Summer	165.0	5.72	0.79	126.7	4.82	0.68		––		<0.0001
Northern Flicker										
Fall	42.1 A	5.70	0.37	30.5 A	2.41	0.24	20.6 B	1.96	0.18	<0.0001
Winter	11.5 A	1.58	0.10	0.9 B	0.62	0.01	1.4 B	0.83	0.01	<0.0001
Spring	44.0	2.48	0.39	38.4	2.66	0.31	36.7	4.38	0.27	0.1933
Summer	46.7	3.36	0.36	28.9	2.36	0.23		––		<0.0001
American Robin										
Fall	33.3	8.69	0.20	20.7	6.49	0.09	23.6	2.85	0.16	0.5933
Winter	2.9	1.10	0.02	0.9	0.62	0.01	0.7	0.48	0.01	0.1878
Spring	79.2 A	5.25	0.49	64.3 AB	6.29	0.38	53.5 B	5.45	0.34	0.0227
Summer	47.8	3.06	0.36	52.5	3.40	0.37		––		0.3024

[a] Numbers with different letters are significantly different (P <0.05) based on multiple comparisons using Scheffe's test.
[b] Data not available for this sample period.

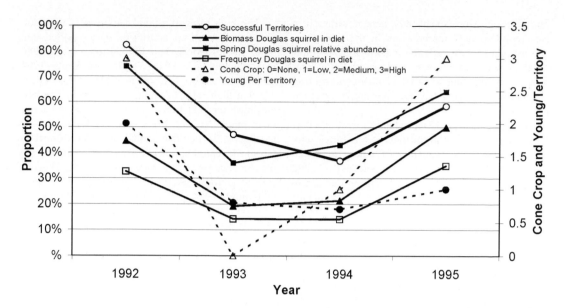

FIGURE 2. Relationship among percent nest success, number of young fledged per territory, percent Douglas squirrel recorded in Northern Goshawk diets by frequency and biomass, spring Douglas squirrel abundance based on percent of counts where squirrels were recorded, and an index of cone crop production for northern goshawks in the Lake Tahoe region, California, 1992–1995.

TABLE 6. TEMPERATURE AND PRECIPITATION RECORDED DURING THE PRE-INCUBATION PERIOD (FEBRUARY–APRIL) FOR NORTHERN GOSHAWKS IN THE LAKE TAHOE REGION, CALIFORNIA, 1992–1995.

	Year			
Variable	1992	1993	1994	1995
Mean temperature (°C)	4.4	1.7	2.6	1.3
Total precipitation (cm)	18.7	33.0	20.7	66.2
Days with precipitation (≥0.025 cm)	22	28	24	33

to high total amounts, snow and rain storms continued through May and mid-June in 1995 (J. Keane, pers. obs.). Late-winter and early-spring mean temperatures were higher in 1992 than in the other three years (Table 6). The number of young produced per successful nest was positively associated with warmer late-winter and early-spring mean temperature (adj. $r^2 = 0.999$, df = 3, P = <0.001; Table 7).

DISCUSSION

Northern Goshawks in our study area exhibited significant annual variation in reproduction. We propose that this annual variation was the result of both prey and weather factors that determined whether Northern Goshawks were able to attain the necessary energetic condition required for successful

TABLE 7. RESULTS OF REGRESSION ANALYSES OF THE PROPORTION OF NORTHERN GOSHAWK TERRITORIES WITH ACTIVE AND SUCCESSFUL NESTS, AND THE NUMBER OF YOUNG PER SUCCESSFUL NEST, AGAINST TEMPERATURE AND PRECIPITATION VARIABLES RECORDED DURING THE PRE-INCUBATION PERIOD (FEBRUARY–APRIL) IN THE LAKE TAHOE REGION, CALIFORNIA, 1992–1995.

	Proportion of territories active		Proportion of territories successful		Young/successful nest	
Weather variables	adj. r^2	P	adj. r^2	P	adj. r^2	P
Mean temperature	-0.060	0.459	0.131	0.351	0.999	<0.001
Total precipitation	-0.484	0.895	-0.496	0.949	0.320	0.261
Days with precipitation	-0.432	0.786	-0.411	0.757	0.662	0.120

reproduction. More specifically, annual variation in Northern Goshawk reproduction in the study area was associated with variation in both Douglas squirrel abundance and late-winter and early-spring temperature. In turn, annual variation in Douglas squirrel abundance was associated with cone crop production patterns.

Northern Goshawk reproduction was greatest in terms of both the proportion of territories with successful nests and number of young produced per successful nest in 1992. The success of 1992 was associated with high cone crop production in autumn 1991 and increased relative abundance of Douglas squirrels during winter and spring. The abundance of Douglas squirrels was manifest through greater frequency and biomass of squirrels in Northern Goshawk diets. Warmer temperatures in late winter and early spring were also positively associated with nesting success. Northern Goshawk reproduction was lower in both 1993 and 1994, with each of these breeding seasons preceded by low cone crop production and lower winter and spring Douglas squirrel abundance relative to 1992. Late-winter and early-spring mean temperatures preceding each of these breeding seasons were also lower relative to 1992.

The proportion of territories with successfully reproducing pairs increased in 1995 following high cone crop production in autumn 1994, increased relative abundance of Douglas squirrels in spring 1995 and increased frequency and biomass of squirrels in the diet. However, relative to 1992, the proportion of successful pairs was lower, fewer young were produced, and birds initiated laying 3 wk later in 1995. We think that these differences were a result of low late-winter and early-spring temperatures in 1995. Mean temperatures in late winter and early spring 1995 were the lowest that occurred during the study. Additionally, total precipitation during the preceding winter and spring was 300% greater, and high amounts of precipitation occurred in March and April during 1995 relative to 1992. Thus, we hypothesize that weather factors may have interacted to moderate the effect of cone crop production on Northern Goshawk reproduction in 1995 relative to 1992. We conclude that annual variation in Northern Goshawk reproduction during our study in this region of the Sierra Nevada was a result of an interaction between food and weather. Reproduction was greatest in years following high cone crop production, which positively affected Douglas squirrel abundance, and mild late winter and early springs with higher temperatures and low total precipitation.

The high rates of annual variation in reproduction we observed are similar to those reported from other studies (McGowan 1975, Bloom et al. 1986, DeStefano et al. 1994a, Doyle and Smith 1994, Sulkava et al. 1994, Erdman et al. 1998), indicating that high rates of annual variation in Northern Goshawk reproduction is a consistent pattern across their range. Studies from northern forest systems have demonstrated that annual variation in Northern Goshawk reproduction is linked with cycles in key prey species (snowshoe hare and galliformes) occurring at periodic intervals (McGowan 1975, Doyle and Smith 1994, Sulkava et al. 1994, Erdman et al. 1998). Weather factors have also been shown to affect Northern Goshawk reproduction. Kostrzewa and Kostrzewa (1990) reported a negative correlation between the proportion of pairs laying eggs and March–April precipitation, while the number of fledglings per successful nest was positively correlated with April–May temperature and negatively correlated with the number of days with precipitation in May for a Northern Goshawk population in Germany. Sulkava et al. (1994) reported a negative correlation between the initiation of nest building and February–March temperature for Northern Goshawks in western Finland. Northern Goshawk populations in temperate western North American forests also exhibit high rates of annual variation in reproduction. Bloom et al. (1986) reported that the proportion of territories active in a year ranged from 27–86% during 1981–1983 based on a sample of monitored territories throughout the Sierra Nevada and White Mountains in California. Similarly, the proportion of territorial pairs laying eggs varied from 22–86% on the Kaibab Plateau in Arizona during the 1990s (Reynolds and Joy 1998). However, to date no studies have directly addressed both the biotic and abiotic environmental factors associated with documented patterns of annual variation in Northern Goshawk reproduction in these systems. Our results indicate that both biotic and abiotic factors are associated with annual variation in Northern Goshawk reproduction and that interactions among multiple factors likely determine whether individuals can successfully reproduce.

Northern Goshawks are resident in the Lake Tahoe region, exhibiting increases in home range sizes by a factor of three-four during winter relative to the breeding season, and appear to initiate breeding in February when females concentrate their activity in the nest stand (Keane 1999). Initiation of egg-laying varied over approximately a 3-wk period ranging from mid-April in 1992 to early-May in 1993 and 1995. It is during this late-winter and early-spring period before egg-laying that females must accumulate sufficient body reserves to reproduce successfully. The accumulation of body reserves is affected by both the energetic condition of the birds at the end of winter as they initiate breeding and their ability to acquire needed reserves prior to laying (Newton 1993). Mean low temperatures during this period ranged from -2.2–4.0 C. Results from laboratory studies of Northern Goshawk basal metabolic rates indicate that they have a lower critical temperature of approximately 1.7 C (J. Keane, unpubl. data). Thus, at this time of year goshawks may be experiencing increased energetic demands for thermal requirements in addition to the needed reserves to produce eggs successfully. We suggest that consideration of the timing of these increased energy requirements in conjunction with the natural history of key prey species explains the patterns we detected between Northern Goshawk reproduction, diet, prey abundance, cone crop production and temperature.

Of the prey species comprising at least 5% of prey items or biomass in most years of the study, American Robins and Northern Flickers are facultative migrants at high elevations in the Sierra Nevada and in the study area (Grinnell and Miller 1944, Beedy and Granholm 1985, Gaines 1988, Keane 1999). Both species forage to a large extent on the ground and hence most individuals emigrate from the higher elevations and apparently move up or down in altitude and north or south in response to snow cover, with large numbers of individuals of both species present in the lower elevation oak woodlands during winter (Block 1989, J. Keane, pers. obs.). Steller's Jays apparently are partial migrants at higher elevations in the Sierra Nevada, with some segment of the population emigrating in the winter and others being resident (Grinnell and Miller 1944). Golden-mantled and Belding ground squirrels hibernate during winter, with their active period being later in the year with increasing elevation in the Sierra Nevada (Bronson 1979). Golden-mantled ground squirrels became active in mid-March following the mild winter and early meltout in 1992. Conversely, they did not appear to become active till mid- to late-April in years following heavy snow and lingering snowpacks (J. Keane, pers. obs.).

In contrast to breeding season studies of Northern Goshawk diets in other North American forest systems (Boal and Mannan 1994, Doyle and Smith 1994, Reynolds et al. 1994, Erdman et al. 1998, Andersen et al. 2004), galliformes or lagomorphs did not constitute a significant proportion of the breeding period diet in our study area. Since male

goshawks are the primary prey providers during the breeding period, perhaps during winter, when the larger females are foraging, galliformes and lagomorphs comprise a larger proportion of the diet. On one occasion we flushed an adult female off of a snowshoe hare kill during January (J. Keane, pers.obs.). The Lake Tahoe race of the snowshoe hare (*Lepus americanus tahoensis*) was the only lagomorph in the study area and is listed as a mammalian subspecies of special concern in California (Williams 1986). Little information exists regarding their distribution and abundance, although they appear to be relatively uncommon (Williams 1986). Additionally, Blue Grouse (*Dendragapus obscurus*) abundance appeared to be low based on our point count sampling (Keane 1999). Thus, the apparent low abundance of galliformes and lagomorphs in our study area may be the reason why these two prey species groups were not associated with annual variation in reproduction or frequently recorded in the diet in our study area.

Douglas squirrels are resident and active year round (Ingles 1965, Smith 1968), and are available during the late-winter and early-spring period when Northern Goshawks experience increased energy demands necessary for successful reproduction. Douglas squirrels feed primarily on seeds and fungi, and their populations vary annually in response to cone crop production, as manifested through increased over-winter survival and both earlier and greater reproduction in springs following years of high cone crop production (Smith 1968, Sullivan and Sullivan 1982). Our data indicate that Northern Goshawks respond functionally, as evidenced through increased frequency and biomass of squirrels in the diet, and numerically, as evidenced by higher reproduction, to increased Douglas squirrel populations following high cone crop production. This relationship in turn appears to be affected by an interaction with temperature. Colder temperatures, as well as greater precipitation, during late winter and early spring likely affect Northern Goshawk energetic dynamics through increased energetic stress, and may influence prey availability by reducing hunting success or by directly affecting the migration, hibernation, and abundance of prey. Thus, considering the energetic strategy of raptors, our observations on diet, prey abundance, and weather, the data suggested that Northern Goshawk reproduction during our study was associated with both specific prey (Douglas squirrel) and temperature factors. If true, Northern Goshawk reproduction in this region of the Sierra Nevada should be greatest, in terms of the proportion of territories with successful nests and young produced per successful nest, in years following high cone crop production and mild late-winter and early-spring weather, such as we observed in 1992. Our observational study was conducted over a 4-yr period that included annual variation in prey, weather, and cone crop production, along with various combinations of each of the factors. We recommend that observations be continued over longer time periods and in other study areas to assess if the patterns regarding the importance of specific prey species and weather factors during the pre-laying period are generally supported. Additionally, carefully crafted experimental studies might be used to assess the degree to which Northern Goshawks are energy limited during the pre-laying period.

CONSERVATION IMPLICATIONS FOR NORTHERN GOSHAWK MANAGEMENT IN THE SIERRA NEVADA

Prey abundance is a primary environmental limiting factor influencing raptor populations such that densities can vary in concordance with variation in prey abundance across landscapes (Newton 1986). Managing forests to provide prey is recognized as a primary need for managing habitat for Northern Goshawks (Kenward and Widén 1989, Reynolds et al. 1992, Widén 1997). Reynolds et al. (1992) recommended managing forests in the southwestern US as interspersed mosaics of structural stages with the goal to provide for a diversity of habitat for Northern Goshawk prey. Although we recorded a total of 22 bird and 12 mammal species in the diets of Northern Goshawks in our study area, our results suggest that the Douglas squirrel may be a particularly important prey species associated with annual variation in Northern Goshawk reproduction. This evidence suggests that management of Northern Goshawk foraging habitat in this study area, while needing to consider the habitat requirements of the full suite of other prey species, might be weighted towards managing habitat for Douglas squirrels. This would seem to be an appropriate additional focus for management because it targets factors that directly affect Northern Goshawk fitness. Further information on Northern Goshawk habitat and prey use patterns, and their demographic response, both in reproduction and survival, to variation in forest structure and composition is needed to assess conservation strategies.

Observational and experimental studies have demonstrated that Douglas squirrel, as well as the closely related red squirrel (*Tamiasciurus hudsonicus*), populations vary in concordance with cone crop production (Smith 1968, 1970, Kemp and Keith 1970, Sullivan and Sullivan 1982, Buchanan et al.

1990, Sullivan 1990). A greater proportion of females breed, litter sizes are larger, and over-winter survival is greater in response to cone crop production (Smith 1968, Sullivan and Sullivan 1982). Douglas squirrels are territorial with territory size inversely related to food availability (Smith 1968). Territories are a critical resource in that they provide the mechanism for squirrels to survive over the winter by caching food (cones and fungi) and squirrels without a territory experience high mortality (Smith 1968). Kemp and Keith (1970) proposed that red squirrel territories differ in quality across a continuum, with high-quality territories occupied year-round and able to provide sufficient food sources for individuals to survive through intervals between cone crops. They noted that high-quality territories encompassed mature conifer trees capable of cone production. These observations suggest that one goal of Douglas squirrel habitat management in the Sierra Nevada should be to target vegetative structure and composition that can provide high quality squirrel habitat as measured by survival and fecundity. Currently no data are available relating habitat structure and composition to habitat quality for Douglas squirrels in the Sierra Nevada.

Factors related to cone crop production dynamics should be a management focus when considering management of habitat for Douglas squirrels. Cone crop production differs in both magnitude and frequency across tree-size classes and between conifer species (Fowells and Schubert 1956, Burns and Honkala 1990). Cone production is greater by mature conifers in terms of both magnitude (number of cones per tree) and frequency (periodicity of cone production) relative to younger, smaller conifers. Further, seeds from different tree species differ in their caloric value (Smith 1968). Therefore, changes in tree size distributions and species composition may affect cone crop production dynamics and related trophic dynamics. We hypothesize that cone crop production by ponderosa and Jeffrey pines, because of the large size of their seeds, may be particularly important in influencing the absolute amounts of primary productivity generated through cone crop production in the forests in our study area.

Northern Goshawks are distributed across a wide elevational gradient and across several forest vegetation types in the Sierra Nevada (Zeiner et al. 1990). Further work is needed to determine the degree to which the results of our study are applicable across the full range of the species in the Sierra Nevada. Specifically, comparable studies are needed to assess ecological relationships in west side mixed conifer forests between 750–1,500 m elevation and in eastside pine forests. Both of these forest types have been highly affected by human management activities (Franklin and Fites-Kaufmann 1996). Douglas squirrels reach the edge of their distribution in the eastern Sierra Nevada and work is needed to assess their importance to Northern Goshawks in the relatively drier forests of the eastside in order to improve our ability to manage for prey habitat requirements. In west side mixed-conifer forests, presumably, winters would be relatively less severe but perhaps more variable at lower elevations and snow melt should occur earlier in the spring. This would make prey species affected by snow cover (American Robins, Northern Flickers, and golden-mantled and Belding ground squirrels) more available. Further, additional species (e.g., western gray squirrel [*Sciurus griseus*] and brush rabbit [*Sylvilagus bachmani*]) may be available to Northern Goshawks at these elevations, although the ability of male Northern Goshawks to regularly capture adult gray squirrels because of their large size has been questioned (Kenward 1996).

Increasing emphasis has been focused on the need to link species-based perspectives with ecosystem and landscape level perspectives that consider ecological processes in order to advance conservation science and improve ecological understanding (Karr et al. 1992, Noss et al. 1997, Thomas 1999). Seed production has been demonstrated to affect numerous species and ecological interactions in forest systems (Smith 1970, Smith and Balda 1979, Mattson et al. 1992, Benkman 1993, Pucek et al. 1993, Ostfeld et al. 1996, Wolff 1996, this study). Thus, cone crop production might be viewed as an important bottom-up trophic effect in forested systems that generates pulses of primary productivity at irregular intervals into these systems. In turn these pulses of primary productivity may affect species populations throughout forest communities through both direct and indirect interactions. Understanding factors that generate population dynamics for species in fluctuating or periodic environments have implications for population viability assessments (Beissinger 1995).

The structure and composition of forests in the Sierra Nevada have been significantly modified as a result of human management activities in the past 150 yr. Timber harvest and fire suppression practices have resulted in a reduction in the proportion of late-seral and old-growth forests, reduced the number of large trees, and reduced the pine component and increased the fir component throughout the range (McKelvey and Johnston 1992, Franklin and Fites-

Kaufmann 1996). Given that the magnitude and frequency of cone production increases with increasing conifer size and that the energy value of seeds differs between tree species, changes in the distribution, abundance, and species composition of large trees and mature and old-growth vegetation classes would be predicted to affect cone crop production dynamics. These changes may have implications for a number of additional species and interspecific interactions in these systems (Bock and Lepthien 1976, Zielinski et al. 1983, Spencer 1987, Benkman 1993, Reitsma et al. 1990, Darveau et al. 1997, Ruggerio et al. 1998). Ecologists have recognized the increasing need to meld single-species conservation approaches with ecosystem- and landscape-scale perspectives in order to more effectively address conservation issues (Franklin 1993, Harris et al. 1996, Noss et al. 1997). Detailed autecological studies of focal species of concern, such as the Northern Goshawk, are essential and can begin to provide an understanding of environmental factors relevant to the conservation of both the species and the structure and function of the system (Woolfenden and Fitzpatrick 1991, James et al. 1997, Derrickson et al. 1998).

ACKNOWLEDGMENTS

G. Walter (California Park Service), R. Robinson (California Tahoe Conservancy), P. Manley (USDA Forest Service), the USDA Forest Service Region 5 Wildlife Ecology Program, the Department of Environmental Science, Policy and Management at University of California, Berkeley, and the Department of Animal Sciences, Graduate Group in Ecology, and Center for Ecological Health at University of California, Davis provided financial and logistical support. M. Sureda, D. Ward, T. Tennant, A. Duerr, N. Sureda, B. McBride, L. Oeschlii, K. Blewjas, B. Sacks, J. Neal, A. Scales, J. Hammond, and D. Hines provided field assistance. K. Erwin, Q. Youngblood, G. Wilson, T. Mark, M. Tierney, and D. Lipton of the USDA Forest Service, and D. Preatzel, J. Dowling, and T. Beedy provided information on Northern Goshawk locations in the study area. R. Cole provided access to specimen collections at University of California, Davis. M. L. Johnson, D. W. Anderson, B. M. Marcot, S. B. DeStefano, and two anonymous referees reviewed earlier drafts of this manuscript. Our gratitude is extended to all.

Studies in Avian Biology No. 31:100–108

OCCUPANCY, PRODUCTIVITY, TURNOVER, AND DISPERSAL OF NORTHERN GOSHAWKS IN PORTIONS OF THE NORTHEASTERN GREAT BASIN

MARC J. BECHARD, GRAHAM D. FAIRHURST, AND GREGORY S. KALTENECKER

Abstract. We determined the occupancy, productivity, turnover, and dispersal distances of Northern Goshawks (*Accipiter gentilis*) in two areas of the northern Great Basin in northeastern Nevada and southern Idaho from 1992–2003. Occupancy of nesting territories declined in both study areas over the 10–11 yr study period but the decline was statistically significant (P <0.05) only in northeastern Nevada where it decreased from a high of 83% in 1997 to a low of only 23% in 2002. The average productivity of goshawk breeding pairs did not change significantly in either study area, but it was lowest in southern Idaho at only 1.5 ± 0.6 young/breeding pair and highest in northeastern Nevada at 2.3 ± 0.8 young/breeding pair. Males bred mostly at 3yr of age and females bred at 2 yr of age with both sexes residing in nesting territories an average of 2 yr. We found no difference in the number of nesting territories used by either sex with 88% of adults using only one nesting territory, 10% using two nesting territories, and 2% using three nesting territories. Turnover of males and females ranged from 12.5–22.9% and 16.2–30.0%, respectively, and did not differ significantly. Breeding dispersal of males and females ranged from only 2.1–5.8 km but natal dispersal was 19.1 km for males and 96.4 km for females indicating that the female segment of the population was the dispersing sex. Several goshawks captured on migration at the Goshutes Mountains in northeastern Nevada were reencountered as breeding adults in both southern Idaho and northern Nevada suggesting that Northern Goshawks in the northeastern section of the Great Basin constitute a large metapopulation consisting of several subpopulations occupying the isolated mountain ranges of Nevada, Utah, and southern Idaho. With dispersal distances of nearly 100 km, female goshawks are capable of being recruited into breeding populations throughout the northeastern segment of the Great Basin.

Key Words: *Accipiter gentiles*, adult turnover rates, dispersal distance, nesting territory occupancy, Northern Goshawk, northern Great Basin, population dynamics.

OCUPACIÓN, PRODUCTIVIDAD, REEMPLAZO Y DISPERSIÓN DEL GAVILÁN AZOR EN PORCIONES DE LA GRAN CUENCA DEL NORESTE

*Resumen*Determinamos la ocupación, productividad, reemplazo y distancia de dispersión del Gavilán Azor (*Accipiter gentilis*), en dos áreas del norte de la Gran Cuenca, en el noreste de Nevada y el sur de Idaho, de 1992–2003. La ocupación de territorios de anidación declinó en ambas áreas de estudio, sobre el período de 10–11 años, pero el descenso fue estadísticamente significativo (P <0.05) solamente en el noreste de Nevada, donde declinó de un elevado 83% en 1997 a tan sólo 23% en el 2002. El promedio de productividad de las parejas reproductivas de gavilanes no cambió significativamente en ninguna de las áreas de estudio, pero fue más baja en el sur de Idaho, con solo 1.5 ± 0.6 crías sobre parejas reproductivas, y más alta en el noreste de Nevada con 2.3 ± 0.8 crías sobre parejas reproductivas. Los machos se reprodujeron hasta casi los 3 años de edad y las hembras a los 2 años, ambos sexos residiendo en los territorios de anidación por un promedio de 2 años. No encontramos diferencia en el número de territorios de anidación utilizados, ya sea por sexo, con 88% de adultos utilizando solo un territorio para anidar, 10% utilizando dos territorios de anidación, y 2% utilizando tres territorios de anidación. El reemplazo de machos y hembras tuvo un rango de 12.5–22.9% y 16.2–30.0% respectivamente, y no diferenció significativamente. La dispersión de machos y hembras reproductivas tuvo un rango de tan solo 2.1–5.8 km, pero la dispersión de las crías fue de 19.1 km para los machos y de 96.4 para las hembras, indicando que la población del segmento de hembras era el sexo dispersor. Algunos gavilanes capturados durante la migración en las Montañas Goshutes en el noreste de Nevada, fueron reencontrados como adultos reproductores, tanto en el sur de Idaho, como en el noreste de Nevada, sugiriendo que los Gavilanes Azor en la sección noreste de la Gran Cuenca, constituyen una gran metapoblación, que consiste en varias subpoblaciones, las cuales ocupan las aisladas cordilleras montañosas de Nevada, Utah y el sur de Idaho. Con distancias de dispersión de cerca de 100 km, las hembras gavilán son capaces de ser reclutadas dentro de las poblaciones reproductivas, a lo largo del segmento noreste de la Gran Cuenca.

The Northern Goshawk (*Accipiter gentilis*) is the largest member of the genus *Accipiter* in North America and it occurs in boreal and temperate forests throughout the continent (Squires and Reynolds 1997). The goshawk is considered a forest habitat generalist with specific habitat requirements associated with nest sites (Dixon and Dixon 1938, Schnell 1958, Kenward 1982, Moore and Henny 1983, Crocker-Bedford and Chaney 1988, Lilieholm et al. 1993, Hargis et al. 1994, Beier and Drennan 1997, Rosenfield et al. 1998). In North America, nests occur in either mature coniferous, deciduous, or mixed conifer-hardwood forests with large trees, high canopy closure, and sparse ground cover (Reynolds et al. 1982, Speiser and Bosakowski 1987, Hayward and Escaño 1989, Siders and Kennedy 1994, Squires and Ruggiero 1996). Goshawks feed opportunistically on a wide diversity of prey species but main foods include ground (*Spermophilus* spp.) and tree squirrels (*Sciurus* spp.), lagomorphs (*Sylvilagus* and *Lepus* spp.), large passerines, woodpeckers, and game birds (Squires and Reynolds 1997). Partially migratory, goshawks winter throughout their breeding range but some individuals do make short movements to lower elevations during winter. Irruptive movements in northern populations to more southern latitudes in winter occur at approximately 10-yr intervals and these apparently coincide with population lows of the snowshoe hare (*Lepus americanus*) and grouse (Squires and Reynolds 1997).

Due to concerns raised over possible declining populations since the late 1980s, the USDI Fish and Wildlife Service listed the goshawk as a category 2 species of concern in 1991 (USDI Fish and Wildlife Service 1992a, 1992b) and it kept that status until the category was eliminated in 1996. It continues to be listed as a sensitive species in Regions 3, 4, and 5 of the USDA ForestService (Kennedy 1997). Information on the breeding biology and status of populations across the goshawks' western range is limited making evaluations of these various listings troublesome. Because of this situation, we undertook a study in the northeastern portion of the Great Basin in an attempt to better document the dynamics of the breeding population of goshawks in this portion of the species' North American range.

STUDY AREA

Our study included portions of two national forests, the Independence and Bull Run Mountains of the Humboldt-Toiyabe National Forest in northeastern Nevada and the Cassia and Sublett Divisions of the Sawtooth National Forest in southern Idaho

(Fig. 1). These areas are situated in the northeastern segment of the Great Basin Region of North America. Our study area in northeastern Nevada included most of the Independence and Bull Run Mountains. These mountain ranges are approximately 150 km long and 10–30 km wide and range from 1,700 m on the valley floor to >3,000 m in elevation on the highest peaks. Vegetation in the area is mostly open sagebrush (*Artemisia tridentata*) steppe habitat that contains highly-fragmented stands of mixed conifer (*Pinus albicaulis, Pinus flexilis,* and *Abies lasiocarpa*) and aspen (*Populus tremuloides*) stands at >2,500 m elevation, and aspen stands in riparian areas and natural drainages at lower elevations (Loope 1969). The Sawtooth National Forest is characterized by a very diverse assemblage of physical features that range from broad stretches of flat to rolling semi-arid plains interspersed with shallow to deep canyons, high elevation desert plateaus (>2,500 m), and infrequent mountain ranges in the southern portion of the forest to strongly glaciated valleys, steep terrain, rugged ridges, and mountain peaks with cliffs and talus slopes in the forests' northern areas (USDA Forest Service 1987). Our study areas in the Cassia and Sublett Divisions of the Sawtooth National Forest are mainly classified as shrubsteppe habitat with fragmented stands of conifer trees (either lodgepole pine [*Pinus contorta*] or subalpine fir, 7,181 ha), mixed conifer (subalpine fir and lodgepole pine) and aspens (1,438 ha), and aspen stands (7,572 ha; USDA Forest Service 1980, 1991a). Over 80% of these stands are classified as mature (70–150-yr old), and stand size averages from only 4 ha for conifer stands to16 ha for aspen stands (USDA Forest Service 1980).

METHODS

We annually searched forest patches in each study area that had histories of occupancy by breeding goshawks, which we defined as historic nesting territories. We also searched all nearby forest patches that appeared to support suitable aspen stands for breeding goshawks where alternative nest sites and any possible new nesting territories may have been located. Searches were conducted on foot during May and we thoroughly searched each forest patch for evidence of breeding goshawks. We confirmed that breeding attempts had taken place by observing goshawks showing breeding behaviors such as copulation, incubation, or nest building activity (Postupalsky 1974, Steenhof 1987, Steenhof et al. 1999). Locations of occupied nest trees within nesting territories were recorded using

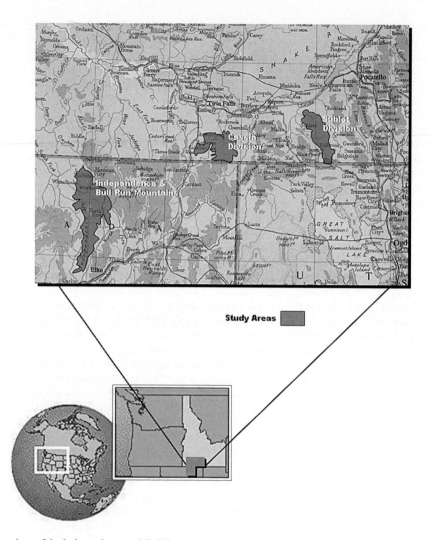

FIGURE 1. Locations of the Independence and Bull Run Mountains study area of the Humboldt-Toiyabe National Forest in northeastern Nevada and the Cassia Division and Sublet Division study areas of the Sawtooth National Forest in southern Idaho from 1992–2003.

global positioning system (GPS) coordinates and marked on topographic maps. In April of 1992 and 1994–1996, the study area in northeastern Nevada was also searched via helicopter prior to emergence of aspen catkins to document early occupancy of nesting territories. Because many adults were individually marked with color bands, we also attempted to identify each adult we observed during occupancy checks using 10× binoculars and 20–60× spotting scopes. During June, we rechecked all nesting territories on foot to verify breeding, record and age nestlings in nests, and identify any breeding adults that were not previously identified. We estimated the productivity of breeding pairs by climbing nest trees and counting young when they were 30–31 d old,

or 80% of fledging age (Steenhof 1987). Because of logistical restraints, we did not revisit nesting territories to confirm fledging. Nestlings were banded with USGS aluminum bands and colored, aluminum bands bearing alpha-numeric codes for future identification. Sex of nestlings was determined by tarsus width and age estimates were based on plumage characteristics (Boal 1994). If breeding adults were not marked, we trapped them using a Great Horned Owl (*Bubo virginianus*) lure and dho-gaza net (Bloom 1987) and they were also banded with USGS Bird Banding Laboratory aluminum leg bands and colored, aluminum leg bands with alpha-numeric codes. We did not begin trapping and color-marking goshawks in southern Idaho until 2000.

To determine residency, we used the average number of years individual goshawks were observed in either of the two study areas, and, to estimate nesting territory turnover, we used the percent of territories where individuals were replaced by new goshawks in subsequent years. Natal dispersal distances, or the distance between the natal site and first breeding site (Greenwood 1980), and breeding dispersal distances, or the distances between subsequent breeding sites (Greenwood 1980), were calculated with the point feature distance matrix extension in ArcView GIS v. 3.2a (Environmental Systems Research Institute, Redlands, CA).

For statistical analysis, we considered reproductive measures as continuous variables, which allowed us to compare our results with other studies. However, for analyses through time, we considered reproductive measures as categorical response variables. Occupancy, failure, and turnover were considered binomial (i.e., occupied or not occupied, failed or not failed, same adult or different adult), and productivity was considered a multinomial count, thereby allowing us to model reproductive statistics through time using logistic regression analyses. For modeling, we used the generalized estimating equations (GEE) method in PROC GENMOD (SAS Institute Inc. 2001) with a logit link function and binomial distribution for binomial data, and a log link function and Poisson distribution for count data. Rather than taking an annual average occupancy across all nesting territories and regressing with year, our analysis modeled responses on a nesting territory level. This approach had several advantages in that it allowed us to use all data collected from all nesting territories, regardless of how many years a territory was surveyed, and it solved problems associated with sample independence and the binomial distribution of our data (Allison 1999).

RESULTS

NESTING TERRITORY OCCUPANCY AND PRODUCTIVITY

During the 11-yr period we monitored goshawks in the study area in northeastern Nevada, a total of 41 nesting territories were located. Because of years with heavy snowpack, not all nesting territories were surveyed every year but we surveyed an average of 32 ± 4.74 nesting territories annually (range = 24–41; Table 1). Mean annual nesting territory occupancy was 62.3 ± 18.8% and varied from a high of 83.3% in 1997 to a low of 22.6% in 2002. Occupancy of individual nesting territories ranged from 11–100%. There was a significant annual decline (21.5%) in the odds that sites would be occupied over the 11-yr study period (odds = 0.7851, P <0.0001). A total of 22 nesting territories were identified over the 10-yr study period in southern Idaho (Table 1). All 22 of the nesting territories were surveyed each year. Nesting territory occupancy averaged 39.5% and ranged from a high of 59.1% in 1995 and 2000 to a low of 13.6% in 1999. Occupancy of individual nesting territories ranged from 0–100%. We also observed a decline in territory occupancy by Northern Goshawks in southern Idaho, but logistic regression analysis indicated that the decline over the 10-yr period was not statistically significant (odds = 0.9502, P <0.2922).

TABLE 1. OCCUPANCY OF NORTHERN GOSHAWK NESTING TERRITORIES IN THE INDEPENDENCE AND BULL RUN MOUNTAINS OF THE HUMBOLDT-TOIYABE NATIONAL FOREST IN NORTHEASTERN NEVADA AND THE CASSIA AND SUBLET DIVISIONS OF THE SAWTOOTH NATIONAL FOREST IN SOUTHERN IDAHO, 1992–2002.

| | Nevada | | Idaho | |
Year	N territories surveyed	% occupancy	N territories surveyed	% occupancy
1992	27	81.5	–	–
1993	32	78.1	–	–
1994	37	70.3	15	54.5
1995	37	73.0	22	59.1
1996	41	73.2	22	41.0
1997	24	83.3	22	13.6
1998	33	54.6	22	27.2
1999	33	51.5	22	36.3
2000	33	54.6	22	59.1
2001	30	43.3	22	31.8
2002	31	22.6	22	41.0
2003	–	–	22	31.8

Breeding pairs of goshawks in northeastern Nevada produced a total of 478 young during the 11-yr study period for a mean productivity of 2.27 ± 0.76 (N = 211) young/breeding pair (Table 2). Annual productivity was lowest in 2002 ($\bar{x} = 1.43 \pm 1.40$ young/breeding pair, N = 7) and highest in 2000 ($\bar{x} = 3.39 \pm 0.78$ young/breeding pair, N = 18). We found no significant interaction between location and year on productivity per breeding pair, and no significant trend in overall productivity (odds = 0.9853, P = 0.2020) or the productivity of individual nesting territories (odds = 0.8674, P = 0.1090) over the duration of the study. Breeding pairs of goshawks in southern Idaho produced a total of 72 young during the 10-yr study period for an average productivity of 1.49 ± 0.60 (N = 48) young/breeding pair (Table 2). Despite a decline from an average high of slightly over 2 young/breeding pair in 1999 to a low of 0.83 young /breeding pair in 2002, regression analysis of productivity over the 10-yr period did not show a significant decline (odds = 1.017, P = 0.5598).

The number of young produced by successful breeding pairs of goshawks in northern Nevada and southern Idaho averaged 2.64 ± 0.57 (N = 181) and 2.04 ± 0.65 (N = 65), respectively (Table 2). Here also, we did not detect a significant decline in the productivity of successfully breeding pairs of goshawks in either northern Nevada (odds = 1.003, P = 0.9047) or southern Idaho (odds = 0.9152, P = 0.1913) during the study period.

DEMOGRAPHICS, INDIVIDUAL IDENTITY, AND TERRITORY AND MATE TURNOVER

We banded 102 adult goshawks (60 females, 42 males) in northeastern Nevada over the 11-yr study period. Fifty-five of the females and 34 of the males were aged at banding. Mean age of breeding females was 2.0 ± 1.06 yr (mode = 3, N = 55) and mean age of breeding males was 3.0 ± 0.24 yr (mode = 3, N = 34). Males were significantly older than females ($\chi^2 = 14.83$, P = 0.0001) and females were more likely to be breeding as 2-yr olds and males as 3-yr olds (G = 21.37, P <0.0001). Based on re-sightings, residence time in the study area averaged 2.0 ± 2.0 yr for females (range = 1–10, mode = 1, N = 59) and 2.0 ± 1.38 yr for males (range 1–7, mode = 1, N = 42), but no significant difference was found between the sexes in the number of years they remained in the study area (G = 5.47, P = 0.2422). Both sexes used from 1–3 different territories for breeding (mode = 1 for both sexes) and, again, we found no significant difference in the number of territories used by either sex (G = 2.27, P = 0.3230). Combining all adults, 88% used one nesting territory, 10% used two different territories, and only 2% used three different territories.

Of the 359 territory years surveyed in northeastern Nevada, we determined individual identities of female breeding goshawks at 151 territories and male breeding goshawks at 93 territories for a total of 244 individually identified breeding goshawks over the 11-yr study period. Of the 109 cases where the identity of either member of breeding pairs was known in two consecutive years, 74 were females and 35 were males. Female turnover occurred 12 times (16.2%/yr) and male turnover occurred 8 times (22.9%/yr), but the difference in turnover rates between the sexes was not significant (Table 3). Combining turnover for both sexes, there was a significant annual increase in the likelihood that a known-identity adult would remain on the same territory the following year (odds = 0.7950, P = 0.0245), but this increase

TABLE 2. PRODUCTIVITY OF NORTHERN GOSHAWK BREEDING PAIRS IN THE INDEPENDENCE AND BULL RUN MOUNTAINS OF THE HUMBOLDT-TOIYABE NATIONAL FOREST IN NORTHEASTERN NEVADA AND THE CASSIA AND SUBLET DIVISIONS OF THE SAWTOOTH NATIONAL FOREST IN SOUTHERN IDAHO, 1992–2002. NUMBERS IN PARENTHESES INDICATE SAMPLE SIZE.

	Nevada		Idaho	
Year	Young/breeding pair	Young/successful pair	Young/breeding pair	Young/successful pair
1992	2.77 ± 0.92 (22)	2.90 ± 0.70 (21)	–	–
1993	2.08 ± 1.14 (24)	2.38 ± 0.86 (21)	–	–
1994	2.47 ± 1.22 (19)	2.76 ± 0.90 (17)	1.58 ± 1.16 (12)	2.11 ± 0.78 (9)
1995	1.84 ± 1.40 (25	2.56 ± 0.92 (18)	1.38 ± 0.96 (13)	1.80 ± 0.63 (10)
1996	2.43 ± 0.94 (30)	2.61 ± 0.68 (28)	1.67 ± 1.00 (9)	1.87 ± 0.83 (8)
1997	2.05 ± 0.85 (19)	2.17 ± 0.71 (18)	1.00 ± 1.00 (3)	1.50 ± 0.71 (2)
1998	2.22 ± 1.17 (18)	2.67 ± 0.62 (15)	1.00 ± 0.00 (2)	1.00 ± 0.00 (2)
1999	1.53 ± 1.33 (17)	2.17 ± 1/03 (12)	2.12 ± 1.13 (8)	2.43 ± 0.79 (7)
2000	3.39 ± 0.78 (18)	3.39 ± 0.78 (18)	1.87 ± 1.55 (15)	2.08 ± 0.92 (10)
2001	1.92 ± 1.55 (13)	2.50 ± 1.27 (10)	1.15 ± 1.21 (13)	2.14 ± 0.69 (7)
2002	1.43 ± 1.40 (7)	2.50 ± 0.58 (4)	0.83 ± 1.11 (12)	2.00 ± 0.71 (5)
2003	–	–	3.00 ± 1.41 (7)	3.50 ± 0.555 (5)

TABLE 3. ANNUAL TURNOVER OF BREEDING GOSHAWKS AT NESTING TERRITORIES IN THE INDEPENDENCE AND BULL RUN MOUNTAINS OF THE HUMBOLDT-TOIYABE NATIONAL FOREST IN NORTHEASTERN NEVADA AND THE CASSIA AND SUBLET DIVISIONS OF THE SAWTOOTH NATIONAL FOREST IN SOUTHERN IDAHO.

Years	N cases		Same bird		Different bird		Turnover %	
	Female	Male	Female	Male	Female	Male	Female	Male
Northern Nevada								
1992–1993	2	2	0	1	2	1	100.00	50.0
1993–1994	3	3	2	2	1	1	33.3	33.3
1994–1995	4	2	4	2	0	0	0.0	0.0
1995–1996	14	7	12	7	2	0	14.3	0.0
1996–1997	13	12	7	5	1	0	12.5	0.0
1997–1998	8	5	9	1	0	0	0.0	0.0
1998–1999	9	1	9	1	0	0	0.0	0.0
1999–2000	10	2	7	1	3	1	30.0	50.0
2000–2001	7	1	7	1	0	0	0.0	0.0
2001–2002	4	0	4	0	0	0	0.0	0.0
Southern Idaho								
2000–2001	3	0	2	–	1	–	25.0	–
2001–2002	5	3	3	3	2	0	40.0	0.0
2002–2003	4	4	3	3	1	1	25.0	25.0

was not significantly related to location (odds = 0.7661, P = 0.5874). Identities of both members of a breeding pair were determined at 26 nesting territories in two consecutive years. Of these, 17 (65.4%) were situations where the same two adults bred in both years, four (15.4%) involved a change in the female partner, three (11.5%) involved a change in the male partner, and two (7.7%) involved changes in both partners. In all cases where both partners were identified, neither member of a breeding pair was ever found breeding with a different partner in a subsequent year when its mate was still in the study area. We combined all mate turnover events for logistic regression analysis. The interaction between year and location was not significant, so the final model included year and location as the main effects without an interaction. The odds of breeding pairs experiencing turnover of a mate the following year did not change significantly over time (odds = 0.9489, P = 0.8952) and was not significantly related to location (odds = 0.6735, P = 0.5876).

During the 3-yr period in which we recorded the identities of breeding adults in southern Idaho, we identified 12 female and seven male breeding goshawks in two consecutive years (Table 3). Because of our limited sample, we did not analyze these data statistically. Female turnover occurred a total of four times for an average annual female turnover rate of 30%. Only one male turnover was recorded over the 3-yr period for an annual male turnover rate of only 12.5%. Here also, we did not record any incidences of mate infidelity.

DISPERSAL AND MOVEMENTS

Only seven goshawks (five females, two males) banded as nestlings in northeastern Nevada were ever found as breeding adults and five were banded as nestlings in 1992 (Table 4). One female banded as a nestling in 1992 returned to breed at 3 yr of age in a nesting territory 7.62 km west of its natal site in 1995 and bred there annually through 2002. A second female banded as a nestling in 1992 returned to breed as at 4 yr of age in 1996, 41.7 km north of its natal site. A third female banded in 1992 was found breeding as at 4 yr of age near Soldier Peak in the Ruby Mountain Wilderness of northeastern Nevada in 1996, 93.8 km south of its natal site. A fourth female banded in 1999 was found breeding at 1 yr of age in our study area in southern Idaho in 2002, 175.3 km northeast of its natal site. The fifth female was also banded in 1999 and was also found breeding as at 2 yr of age in the southern Idaho study area in 2001, 2002, and 2003,163.75 km northeast of its natal site. Overall female natal dispersal averaged 96.4 ± 73.6 km. There were only two observations for male natal dispersal in northeastern Nevada. One male banded in 1992 returned to breed in 1996 as a 4 yr of age, 23.99 km south of its natal site, and a second male also banded in 1992 returned to breed in 1996 as 4 yr of age, 14.17 km southwest of its natal site. Average male natal dispersal was 19.1 km. None of the nestlings banded in the southern Idaho study area were ever reencountered as breeding adults.

TABLE 4. NATAL DISPERSAL DISTANCES OF NORTHERN GOSHAWKS IN THE INDEPENDENCE AND BULL RUN MOUNTAINS OF THE HUMBOLDT-TOIYABE NATIONAL FOREST IN NORTHWESTERN NEVADA, 1992–2002.

Sex	Year banded	Year first breeding	Natal dispersal distance (km)
F	1992	1995	7.62
F	1992	1996	41.68
F	1992	1996	93.84
F	1999	2000	175.30
F	1999	2001	163.75
M	1992	1996	23.99
M	1992	1996	14.17

We recorded nine breeding dispersal events (eight female, one male) by eight different goshawks (seven females, one male) in northeastern Nevada and none in southern Idaho. Breeding dispersal distance in northeastern Nevada averaged 5.37 ± 3.93 km (N = 9). Female breeding dispersal distance ranged from 1.3–10.6 km ($\bar{x}$ = 5.78 ± 3.99, N = 8) and the only male breeding dispersal distance recorded was 2.1 km. None of the adult goshawks that we identified to be breeding in southern Idaho dispersed within the study area over the 3-yr period we made observations. As long as they remained in the study area, both males and females showed 100% fidelity to nesting territories and they were replaced at nesting territories only when they died or disappeared from the study area.

Three goshawks (one male, two females) banded as nestlings in our northeastern Nevada study area in 1996, 1999, and 2000 were captured in the Goshutes Mountains by HawkWatch International (J. Smith, pers. comm.) approximately 200 km east of their natal area as hatch year birds. In addition, two goshawks (one male, one female) banded at the Goshutes Mountains in the fall of 1991 and 1995, respectively, were found breeding at before 3 yr of age in the northern Nevada study area in 1992 and 1997, respectively. One hatch-year male goshawk captured at the Goshutes Mountains in 1997 was subsequently recaptured as a breeding male in the southern Idaho study area in 2002.

DISCUSSION

Overall occupancy of territories by breeding goshawks in the Independence and Bull Run Mountains of northeastern Nevada averaged 62% and 39.5% in the Sawtooth National Forest of southern Idaho. These averages were very similar to average nesting territory occupancies of 63% and 50% reported by Woodbridge and Detrich (1994) for the Klamath National Forest in northern California, by Patla (1997) for the Targee National Forest in southeastern Idaho, and Ingraldi (1998) for the Sitgreaves National Forest of east-central Arizona. Occupancy of nesting territories by goshawks in areas of the Tongass National Forest in southeast Alaska averaged much lower at only 33% (range = 13–62%; Flatten et al. 2001), but it was similar to the nesting territory occupancy of only 39.5% that we recorded in southern Idaho. Occupancy in neither of our study areas approached the average occupancy estimate of 81% reported by Reynolds and Joy (1998) for the Kaibab Plateau in Arizona.

Nesting territory occupancy declined significantly in northeastern Nevada from highs of >80% between 1992–1994 (Younk 1996) to a low of <30% in 2002. A less severe decline occurred in southern Idaho where occupancy decreased from 59% in 1995 to 32% in 2003. In situations where goshawks feed on one particular prey species, declining breeding populations of goshawks have been linked to declines in their preferred prey. For example, in interior Alaska where goshawks feed primarily on snowshoe hares which cycle every 10 yr, the breeding population of goshawks appears to fluctuate with changes in the hare population (McGowan 1975, Doyle and Smith 1994). In the Dixie National Forest of southern Utah, a decline in occupancy has been attributed to a widespread drought in the southwestern US (R. Rodriguez and C. White, pers. comm.). Goshawks in northeastern Nevada and southern Idaho feed mostly on ground squirrels, which can comprise between 50–90% of their diet (Younk and Bechard 1994a), but they also feed on several species of birds including American Robins (*Turdus migratorius*) and Northern Flickers (*Colaptes auratus*). Because the diet of these goshawks was variable from year to year, we felt it unlikely that the decline in the breeding population that we observed was related to a decline in ground squirrel populations. Rather, we feel that such a large scale, regional decline in the breeding population of goshawks in the northern Great Basin was more indicative of the effects of climate on goshawk breeding. We found a significant correlation between average March–April temperature and April–May precipitation in northern Nevada indicating that variations in climatic factors such as cold temperatures and high snowpack and rain in spring may play a major role in determining the number of goshawk pairs that breed annually (Fairhurst and Bechard 2005). Nesting territory occupancy may be related to severe weather (Squires and Reynolds 1997) and colder, wetter springs may negatively influence goshawk reproduction by increasing mortality through chilling of eggs and nestlings (Höglund 1964a, Zachel 1985, Kostrzewa and Kostrzewa 1990, 1991, Bloxton 2002). Cold weather may also affect foraging behavior of males (Zachel 1985) with poor food provisioning to pre-egg-laying females preempting egg laying entirely (Newton 1979a).

Our estimated average of 1.62 young/breeding pair for goshawks breeding in southern Idaho was similar to that reported for other goshawk populations but our estimate for the productivity of goshawks in northeastern Nevada was higher than reported elsewhere. Our mean productivity of 2.27 young/breeding pair in northeastern Nevada was higher than in northern California where breeding pairs average only 1.93 young/breeding pair (Woodbridge and Detrich 1994), in eastcentral Arizona where pairs average only 1.19 young/breeding pair (Ingraldi 1998), in the Kaibab Plateau in Arizona where pairs average only 1.55 young/breeding pair (Reynolds and Joy 1998), and in the Tongass National Forest in Alaska where pairs average only 1.9 young/breeding pair (Flatten et al. 2001). Most breeding pairs in northeastern Nevada that began breeding were successful in raising young to fledging age averaging only 13.5% annual failure of breeding attempts. This failure rate was similar to that reported by Woodbridge and Detrich (1994) who found 13% of breeding pairs failing in northern California, Flatten et al. (2001) who found 7% failing in Alaska, and Reynolds and Joy (1998) who found 18% failing in Arizona. Due to the decline in the number of breeding pairs in the population in northeastern Nevada, overall annual production of young fell from a high of 73 young in 1996 to a low of only 10 young in 2002. Likewise, in southern Idaho annual production of young varied from a high of 28 young in 2000 to a low of only two in 1998. With such marked variation in annual productivity, the recruitment of new breeders into these populations was undoubtedly highly variable over the 11 yr that we studied them. Despite this, two females dispersed nearly 200 km from their natal grounds

in northeastern Nevada and settled as breeders in southern Idaho indicating that, rather than settling into their natal areas as new breeders, young may disperse great distances, filling vacancies in remote breeding populations.

An average of 19.3 % and 20% of goshawk nesting territories in northeastern Nevada and southern Idaho, respectively, experienced turnover of at least one breeding adult during our study. Adult females were replaced at 18.7% and 40% of nesting territories, respectively. Adult males were replaced at 20.6% of the nesting territories in northeastern Nevada and only one of the males was replaced in 3 yr in southern Idaho. Squires and Reynolds (1997) have noted that fidelity to breeding territories is often difficult to determine because of the problems associated with finding all of the alternate nests in nesting territories. Nesting territories in northeastern Nevada and southern Idaho are relatively small and nest structures are built in aspen trees and lodgepole pines where they are fairly obvious. We thoroughly searched all territories and, although we cannot assume that our turnover estimates are entirely unbiased, we feel confident that when we did not find a bird on a territory it was because it no longer bred there. Furthermore, our estimate of annual turnover of breeders was similar to that found in the Kaibab Plateau in Arizona (16% for females and 25% for males, Reynolds and Joy 1998), northern California (28.6% for females and 23.5% for males, Detrich and Woodbridge 1994), and Alaska (35.7% for females, Flatten et al. 2001). In the 31 cases where we identified both members of a pair on the same nesting territory in northeastern Nevada and southern Idaho, only 57.5% were situations where both members of the pair remained together on the same territory that had been used in the previous year. Most mate turnovers involved female replacements, indicating that female mate turnover was higher in our study areas than elsewhere. Breeding goshawk pairs were found to retain the same mate at 72% of nesting territories in northern California (Detrich and Woodbridge 1994), 75.9% of the nesting territories in southeast Alaska (Flatten et al. 2001), and 98% of the nesting territories in the Kaibab Plateau (Reynolds and Joy 1998). Because we did not find a member of a breeding pair breeding with a different partner in a subsequent year when its mate was still in the study area, we felt that the occurrence of mate infidelity in this population was probably very low.

Natal-dispersal distance of goshawks in northeastern Nevada was sex-biased with females dispersing nearly five times farther than males (19 vs. 96 km for males and females). Reynolds and Joy (1998) reported a male natal dispersal of 15.9 km, which was similar to our estimate for male natal dispersal distance in northeastern Nevada. Nevertheless, their estimated female natal dispersal of 21.5 km was nearly five times less than our estimate for female natal dispersal in northeastern Nevada. Our estimate for breeding dispersal distance of adult goshawks in northeastern Nevada indicated that, once an adult began to breed in the population, it tended to breed in the same, or near to the same, territory from one year to the next. Our breeding dispersal distances of only 5.8 km for females and 2.1 km for males were much shorter than breeding dispersal distances in northern California where females disperse an average of 9.8 km and males disperse an average of 6.5 km between breeding territories (Detrich and Woodbridge 1994) and in Alaska where adults move 18.5 km between nesting territories in consecutive years (Flatten et al. 2001), but similar to Arizona where breeding females disperse an average of 5.2 km and males disperse an average of 2.8 km (Reynolds and Joy 1998).

Our results indicate that the northeastern Great Basin area of northeastern Nevada and southern Idaho supports a large metapopulation of Northern Goshawks that is comprised of several smaller, populations existing in isolated mountain ranges throughout the area. With their large natal dispersal distances, it appears that juvenile, female goshawks readily move between these isolated populations, which can be separated by hundreds of kilometers. However, once they settle into an area, females remain there and do not return to their natal areas. In view of these large dispersal distances, we feel that to accurately monitor the status of the breeding population of Northern Goshawks in the northeastern Great Basin, it is necessary to monitor all of the isolated populations that are distributed throughout the region including the Ruby and Santa Rosa Mountains and the Jarbidge Wilderness in northeastern Nevada.

We did not identify the cause for the decline in occupancy of goshawk nesting territories in our two study areas. Nevertheless, the fact that both areas experienced simultaneous declines in occupancy indicated that there was a large-scale factor that affected the metapopulation of goshawks in the northeastern Great Basin. While declines in breeding populations in the northern portion of the goshawk's North American range have been associated with 10-yr declines in snowshoe hares, this explanation cannot be used for goshawks in the northeastern Great Basin which feed mostly on ground squirrels which are not known to exhibit population cycles (Van Horne et al. 1997). We feel that other factors that operate on a landscape basis are probably the cause of the decline in goshawk breeding that we observed in the northeastern Great Basin. Kostrzewa and Kostrzewa (1990) and Fairhurst (2004) and Fairhurst and Bechard (2005) have found a significant relationship between goshawk occupancy and spring weather which may play a role in the breeding status of populations of goshawks distributed throughout the Great Basin. Apparently, warm, dry springs are most conducive to goshawk breeding and periods of cold and above average precipitation prevent goshawks from initiating breeding. Further work on the effect of weather on the breeding of goshawks in the Great Basin would increase our understanding of factors that influence populations of goshawks and the status of the species across its western North American range (Kennedy 1997, DeStephano 1998).

ACKNOWLEDGMENTS

We would like to thank James V. Younk, Michael S. Shipman, and Heath Smith who collected data in northern Nevada as part of their master's theses at Boise State University. Jon W. Beals and Charles E. Harris initiated the project in southern Idaho, and Kristin W. Hasselblad helped collect data. We would also like to express our gratitude to Pete Bradley, Nevada Department of Wildlife, Steve Anderson, John Warder, Will Amy, Portia Jelinek, and Bonnie Whalen, Humboldt-Toiyabe National Forest; Tom Bandolin and Robin Garwood, Sawtooth National Forest; and John Bokich, Kent McAdoo, Mike Jones, John Parks, Steve Lewis, Lynn Gionet-Sheffield, Gary Goodrich, and Jeff Campbell, Independence Mining Company and AngloGold-Meridian Jerritt Canyon Joint Venture Mining Company for all their assistance during this study. This study was funded by grants from the UDSA Forest Service Humboldt-Toiyabe and Sawtooth National Forests, Idaho Department of Fish and Game, Independence Mining Company, and AngloGold-Meridian Jerritt Canyon Joint Venture Mining Company.

ECOLOGY OF THE NORTHERN GOSHAWK IN THE NEW YORK-NEW JERSEY HIGHLANDS

THOMAS BOSAKOWSKI AND DWIGHT G. SMITH

Abstract. Evidence suggests that the Northern Goshawk (*Accipiter gentilis*) was once extirpated in the New York-New Jersey Highlands, but has recolonized the Highlands in the 1960s and 1970s following a dramatic reforestation in the 20th century. The reforestation produced large tracts of contiguous mature forest, which appear to be a primary habitat requirement of this species. Most goshawk nests in the Highlands were found deep in remote forest areas where nest sites are typically distant from human habitation and paved roads. Nest trees were almost always built in co-dominant or dominant trees of the stand, but were seldom built in the largest tree of the nesting stand. Canopy cover is very high (90%) and shrub cover is often reduced or nearly devoid (28.3%) at goshawk nest sites. Ruffed Grouse (*Bonasa umbellus*) appears to be the most common prey, but other predominant bird species in diets of Highlands goshawks included the Blue Jay (*Cyanocitta cristata*), Mourning Dove (*Zenaida macroura*), Rock Dove (*Columba livia*), and blackbirds. Sciurids, including eastern chipmunks (*Tamias striatus*), red squirrel (*Tamiasciurus hudsonicus*), and gray squirrel (*Sciurus carolinensis*) were also important components of goshawk diets from the Northeast. Highlands goshawks had a mean prey weight of 365.8 g, with bird prey averaging 332.3 g and mammal prey averaging 442.9 g. In the Highlands, productivity calculated from 36 nesting attempts averaged 1.4 young per nest, lower than found in two Connecticut studies (1.75 and 2.13). Although the goshawk is generally considered to be a permanent resident, dozens of northeastern hawk migration observation stations reveal a small, but distinct, fall migration during non-invasion years. Breeding bird atlas data confirm that the goshawk is rare in New Jersey, moderately rare in Pennsylvania (mostly northern), and numerous in New York. Various factors impacting Highlands goshawks are discussed including interspecific competition, lack of reserves, timber harvesting, tree diseases, and human disturbance factors.

Key Words: competition, food-niche overlap, forestry, habitat, New Jersey, New York, Northern Goshawk, productivity, migration, nest sites, site fidelity, prey.

ECOLOGÍA DEL GAVILÁN AZOR EN LAS TIERRAS ALTAS DE NUEVA YORK-NUEVA YERSEY

Resumen. La evidencia sugiere que el Gavilán Azor (*Accipiter gentilis*) fue alguna vez erradicado de las Tierras Altas de Nueva York-Nueva Yersey, pero recolonizó las Tierras altas durante los años 1960 y 1970, seguido de una drástica reforestación en el siglo 20. Dicha reforestación produjo largos espacios de bosque maduro contiguo, lo cual parece ser un requisito primordial de hábitat para esta especie. La mayoría de los nidos de gavilán en las Tierras Altas fueron encontrados hondo en áreas forestales remotas, donde los sitios de nidos estaban típicamente distantes de la población humana y de caminos pavimentados. Los nidos de los árboles estaban casi siempre construidos en árboles co-dominantes o dominantes del grupo de árboles, pero fueron raramente construidos en el árbol más grande del grupo de árboles en donde se encontraba el nido. La cobertura de copa es muy alta (90%) y la cubierta arbustiva es a menudo reducida o casi desprovista (28.3%) en los sitios de nidos de gavilán. El Grévol Engolado (*Bonasa umbellus*) parece ser la presa más común, pero otras especies de aves predominantes en la dieta de los Gavilanes Azor de las Tierras del Norte como la Charra azul (*Cyanocitta cristata*), Paloma huilota (*Zenaida macroura*), Paloma doméstica (*Columba livia*), y mirlos. Ardillas, incluyendo ardilla listada (*Tamias striatus*), ardilla roja (*Tamiasciurus hudsonicus*) y ardilla (*Sciurus carolinensis*), fueron componentes importantes de las dietas de los Gavilanes Azor. La media en el peso de las presas de los gavilanes de las Tierras Altas es de 365.8 g, con un promedio de 332.3 g para las presas aves y un promedio de 442.9 g para las presas mamífero. En las Tierras Altas, el promedio de la productividad calculada de 36 intentos de anidación fue de 1.4 joven por nido, más bajo que lo encontrado en dos estudios en Connecticut (1.72 y 2.13). Aunque el gavilán es considerado generalmente como residente permanente, docenas de estaciones de observación de migración de halcones del noreste revelan una pequeña, pero distinta, migración baja durante los años de no invasión. Datos del Atlas de Reproducción confirman que el gavilán es raro en Nueva Yersey, moderadamente raro en Pennsylvania (principalmente en el norte), y numeroso en Nueva York. Varios factores que impactan los gavilanes de la Tierras Altas son discutidos, incluyendo competencia interespecífica, falta de reservas, aprovechamiento de madera, enfermedades de árboles y factores humanos de disturbio.

Following a range extension in the late 1950s, the range of the Northern Goshawk (*Accipiter gentilis*, hereafter goshawk) has moved southward into Connecticut, New Jersey, and Maryland (Root and Root 1978, Speiser and Bosakowski 1984, Mosher 1989). Possibly, the goshawk was a resident throughout all northeastern states prior to colonization by European settlers and is only recently returning to reoccupy former habitat as these states undergo a dramatic reforestation. Similarly, reforestation has resulted in recolonization of goshawks (*Accipiter gentilis gentilis*) in Great Britain (Marquis and Newton 1982, Anonymous 1989). Despite extensive deforestation in the Northeast during the past several centuries, the goshawk has persisted in remote areas of Maine, Vermont, New Hampshire, Pennsylvania, Massachusetts, and the Adirondack Mountains of New York (Bent 1937). Investigations into the breeding ecology of goshawks in the New York-New Jersey Highlands were initiated in the late 1970s by Speiser (1981)

and continued with collaborative efforts throughout the 1980s by Speiser and Bosakowski (1984, 1987, 1989, 1991), Bosakowski et al. (1992), Bosakowski and Smith (1992), and Bosakowski and Speiser (1994). The Northern Goshawk is listed as threatened in New Jersey and as a species of concern in Rhode Island and Maryland (Mosher 1989), but has no special status in the remaining northeastern states.

STUDY AREA

Northern goshawk studies were conducted in the highlands physiographic region (Braun 1950) extending southwest to northeast across the New York-New Jersey border. The study area includes Passaic, Morris, Sussex, Warren, and Hunterdon counties in New Jersey, and Orange and Rockland counties in New York; this area is approximately 400,000 ha (Fig. 1) of which, approximately 192,000 ha is currently forested.

FIGURE 1. Map of the Highlands Study Area in New Jersey and New York (courtesy of USDA Forest Service).

History of Forests

Nearly all Highlands forests have been previously cut or burned within the last 200 yr (Ohmann and Buell 1968, Russell 1981). Early mining in the 1800s in the Highlands led to extensive clearcutting for charcoal production, fuelwood, and construction (Russell 1981). However, large-scale farming was never attempted in the Highlands because of thin rocky soil, and reforestation in the 20th century has progressed further in the Highlands than the surrounding lowlands and valleys (Speiser 1981). Extensive clearcutting, burning, and disease has resulted in second growth forest that is largely dominated by oaks (*Quercus* spp.) and other various sub-climax hardwood trees (Buell et al. 1966, Russell 1981). Overall, present forests contain dominant trees which are similar to the dominants of the 17th and 18th century forests, except that early forest had more chestnut (*Castanea dentata*) and hickory (*Carya* spp.) and less birch (*Betula* spp.) and maple (*Acer* spp.) than today (Russell 1981).

Present Forest Composition

The Highlands are part of the eastern deciduous forest biome (Shelford 1963). Chestnut oak (*Quercus prinus*) dominates ridgetops and upper xeric slopes, whereas white oak (*Quercus alba*), red oak (*Quercus rubra*), and tuliptree (*Lireodendron tulipera*) are common on lower slopes. Red maple (*Acer rubrum*), black birch (*Betula lenta*), and white ash (*Fraxinus americana*) are ubiquitous and common indicators of disturbance (Russell 1981). In areas with rich, moist soils, such as near wetlands, water courses, ravines, and broad lowland plateaus, eastern hemlock (*Tsuga canadensis*), white pine (*Pinus strobus*), sugar maple (*Acer saccharum*), American beech (*Fagus grandifolia*), and yellow birch (*Betula alleghaniensis*) dominate the forest. Braun (1950) considered the Highlands to be a transition zone between the oak-chestnut and white pine-hemlock-northern hardwoods region. However, due to chestnut blight, chestnut is now virtually absent except as an understory component. Wooded swamps are presently dominated by red maple, yellow birch, black gum (*Nyssa sylvatica*), white pine, hemlock, and occasionally Atlantic white cedar (*Chamaecyparis thyoides*) and black spruce (*Picea mariana*) (Russell 1981). Mature conifer plantations (planted circa 1920–1935) are sparsely distributed throughout reservoir watersheds and these are composed of various pine species including white pine, red pine (*Pinus resinosa*), Scotch pine (Pinus sylvestris), Norway spruce (*Picea abies*), and larch (*Larix* spp.). Overall, current forests are predominantly upland deciduous habitat (75%), except for limited areas of hemlock-white pine forests (20%) or mature conifer plantations (5%). Most areas are composed of a mosaic of submature (<40 yr) and mature second-growth forest (40–80 yr), older stands (>100 yr) are rare.

Overall, approximately 41% of the Highlands forests are considered potential, viable timberland available for harvesting (Michaels et al. 1992). However, the Highlands forests are rarely under much pressure for timber harvesting, because the current harvest level is only about 10% of the annual growth rate (Michaels et al. 1992). Most parcels of forest are small, 85% are <7.6 ha. Surveys have found that most landowners in the Highlands value their forestland more for its scenic value than for its timber, and no owner listed income from timber as the primary benefit (Michaels et al. 1992). Currently, thinning is the usual method of harvesting and clearcutting is rare, except for the purposes of new suburban development.

Current Land Cover Description

In 1985, forest was the predominant land cover (48%) in the Highlands, followed by residential/urban (29%) and agriculture (16%) (Michaels et al. 1992). Reservoirs and a few natural lakes account for most of the open water, although beaver (*Castor canadensis*) ponds and marshes are found in some sections. Other wetlands are typically a mix of forested wetland, brushy swamps (shrub-carr), and open marshes. Due to the higher elevations of the Highlands, temperatures are cooler and rainfall is slightly greater than the adjacent Piedmont and Kittatiny valley regions (Robichaud and Buell 1973). Public access to forests on military holdings and many private ownerships is restricted, but most city watersheds allow access with recreational permits. State and county lands are generally open to the public, as well as the few federal parks and refuges.

HABITAT ECOLOGY OF HIGHLANDS GOSHAWKS

Nest Tree Selection

In the Northeast, deciduous trees are usually favored by goshawks for nest building, even in mixed forests where conifers are abundant. Bent

(1937) reported that only 11 of 62 nests of eastern goshawks were built in conifers. In New York, Bull (1974) noted that only six of 40 goshawk nests were in conifers. In New York and New Jersey, Speiser and Bosakowski (1989) found that only five of 32 nests were in conifers and availability data indicated that the preference for deciduous trees (black birch and American beech) was significant. In deciduous trees in our study area, goshawk nests are almost always built in a primary crotch (Speiser and Bosakowski 1989). This often results placement of the nest in the lower one-third of the canopy layer (or crown height). Speiser and Bosakowski (1989) reported a mean relative nest height (nest height/nest tree height x 100) of 54.5% for the Highlands. Deciduous trees are likely preferred because they frequently provide a more stable triple or quadruple crotch for supporting the large nest (Speiser and Bosakowski 1989) with little overhead obstruction immediately above the nest platform. In contrast, conifers usually have thinner limb diameters and rarely have major crotch formations (especially low in the canopy) except in the case of deformities

Nest trees were almost always built in co-dominant or dominant trees of the stand, but were seldom built in the largest tree of the nesting stand. In the Highlands, only four of 32 nest trees had the largest diameter of trees in the nesting stand (Speiser and Bosakowski 1989). In older, taller forests, smaller sub-dominant trees are sometimes selected as nest trees probably because the goshawk prefers to nest low in the canopy.

NESTING HABITAT

Although goshawks nest in a variety of forest types throughout their range in North America, the vegetative structure and topography of nest sites remain relatively consistent (see review in Bosakowski 1999). Habitat selected for nesting in the Highlands is usually in forest stands with larger basal areas and larger tree diameters than random sites (Speiser and Bosakowski 1987) which supports the findings of many studies that mature and old-growth forest is preferred (Reynolds et al. 1982, 1992, Moore and Henny 1983, Iverson et al. 1996, Squires and Ruggiero 1996). If older, taller forests are not available, the goshawk will sometimes use younger and/or denser forests with smaller trees (Doyle and Smith 1994, Bosakowski 1999).

In the Northeast, deciduous forests, mixed conifer-deciduous forests, and monoculture pine plantations are all forest habitat types used for nesting (Speiser and Bosakowski 1987, Smith and Devine 1994,

Becker 2000), albeit pure coniferous forest is often scarce in the Highlands. In the Highlands, goshawk nest stands typically have a high degree of canopy cover ($\bar{x}$ = 90.0%) and shrub cover is often reduced or nearly devoid ($\bar{x}$ = 28.3%) (Bosakowski et al. 1992).

Generally, vegetation around nest sites usually appears to be similar in structure and size class to home ranges in the Highlands. Beier and Drennan (1997) found that goshawk foraging locations had significantly greater canopy closure, tree density, and large tree density, demonstrating that mature forests are not only necessary for nesting but also for foraging.

In the Highlands, nesting generally occurs on benches or bowl-like topography where the slope is generally slight to moderate, and several sites were flat with no aspect (Speiser and Bosakowski 1987). Slopes with southern aspects were avoided compared to random sites (Speiser and Bosakowski 1987).

Overall, we found goshawks to be relatively intolerant of human disturbance. They nested significantly further from human habitation and paved roads than random sites (Bosakowski and Speiser 1994), typically in the most remote forests available in the Highlands.

FEEDING ECOLOGY OF HIGHLANDS GOSHAWKS

Diets of goshawks in the Highlands were determined by examining prey remains found below goshawk nests and at prey-plucking posts following the methods outlined by Reynolds and Meslow (1984). Goshawk diets in the Highlands, as in other eastern forests, are comprised principally of birds (Meng 1959, Bosakowski et al. 1992, Bosakowski and Smith 1992; Becker et al., *this volume*). In an agricultural-woodland matrix, Meng (1959) found Common Crows (*Corvus brachyrhynchos*) to predominate the diet, whereas in contiguous forest, Bosakowski et al. (1992) found Ruffed Grouse to be the most common prey (Fig. 2). Other predominant bird species in diets of eastern goshawks included the Blue Jay, Mourning Dove, Rock Dove (*Columba livia*), and blackbirds. Sciurids, including eastern chipmunk (*Tamias striatus*), red squirrel (*Tamiasciurus hudsonicus*), and gray squirrel (*Sciurus carolinensis*), were also important components of eastern goshawk diets. All of these prey species appear to be most abundant in mature forest in the Highlands, although no field studies have been done to support this observation. Studies conducted in Minnesota (Eng and Gullion 1962) and

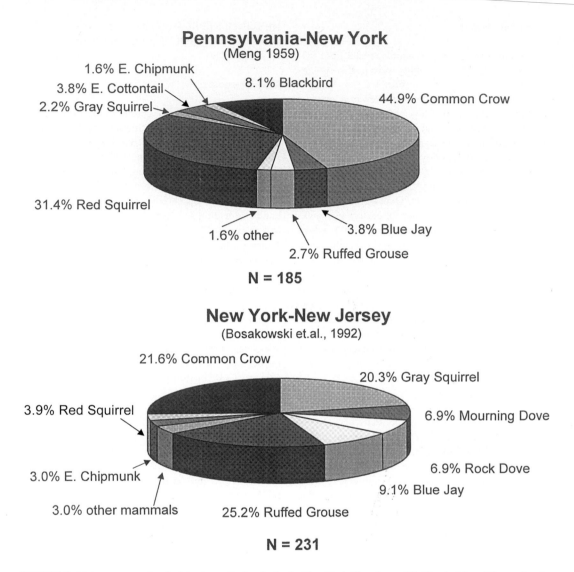

FIGURE 2. Major prey species for Northern Goshawks in the New York-New Jersey Highlands (a) and Pennsylvania-New York (b).

Sweden (Widen 1987) also showed a prevalence of grouse and tree squirrels in goshawk diets.

In comparison to other sympatric forest raptors, only the accipiters [goshawk and Cooper's Hawk (*Accipiter cooperii*)] had diets dominated by birds, whereas *Buteo* spp. diets were dominated by mammals (Bosakowski and Smith 1992). Mammals are generally less prevalent in the diet of eastern accipiters, however, goshawks took more than twice the proportion of mammals to birds (0.43) as compared to the smaller congener, Cooper's Hawk (0.17).

In western and boreal regions of North America, bird/mammal ratios differ from those in eastern populations with mammals representing a larger component of the goshawk diet. This difference can be attributed to the lack of ground squirrels and scarcity of lagomorphs (hares and rabbits) in eastern forests, prey that are more numerous in the more open western montane forests. Studies from northern Arizona, eastern Oregon and the Yukon Territories clearly show a preponderance of ground squirrels and lagomorphs in goshawk diets (Reynolds and Meslow 1984, Doyle and Smith 1992, Boal and Mannan 1994). However, in eastern Oregon (Reynolds and Meslow 1984) goshawks took a higher portion of birds compared to mammals.

MEAN PREY WEIGHT

In a study of five raptor assemblages, Jaksic (1983) found that raptor body weights were positively correlated with mean vertebrate prey weight. Analysis of prey weights for Highlands goshawks revealed a mean prey weight of 365.8 g, with bird prey averaging 332.3 g and mammal prey averaging 442.9 g (Bosakowski et al. 1992; plus errata—Bosakowski 1993). Reynolds and Meslow (1984) reported a mean prey weight of 306.6 grams for total prey with an average of 147.5 g for birds and 445.2 g for mammals in northeastern Oregon. Overall, average prey weight was significantly larger for eastern goshawks (Bosakowski et al. 1992, Bosakowski 1993) which correlates well with the larger body weight documented for eastern goshawks (Henny et al. 1985, Smith et al. 1990). For example, mean Oregon summer weights of males were significantly ($P < 0.001$) lower by 19.8% than fall weights from Wisconsin, and females were significantly ($P < 0.001$) lower by 15.6% (Henny et al. 1985). Not surprisingly, eastern and western goshawks were once considered different subspecies (Bent 1937).

INTERSPECIFIC COMPETITION

Schoener (1984) theorized that because of their elevated trophic position as terminal predators, *Accipiter* hawks should show competitively caused niche overdispersion. In comparing the goshawk with its closest North American relative, the Cooper's Hawk, Bosakowski et al. (1992) discovered that food-niche overlap by prey species was below competition levels (overlap <0.6) for New Jersey (0.47), Connecticut (0.45), and Oregon (0.47; data in Reynolds and Wight's [1984] recalculated using Schoener's overlap index). In all three cases, these results are consistent with niche overdispersion, which theoretically serves to reduce food-niche overlap. It is not known whether the niche overdispersion is the result of past or present competition levels between these two congeners (Connell 1980).

In the Highlands forests, goshawks frequently nest in close proximity to Red-shouldered Hawks (*Buteo lineatus*) and Barred Owls (*Strix varia*) as was also noted by Root and Root (1978) for northwest Connecticut. Bosakowski and Smith (1992) found that food overlap of the goshawk was very low with the Red-shouldered Hawk (*Buteo lineatus*; 0.307) and Barred Owl (*Strix varia*; 0.202), suggesting a reason for mutual tolerance of these sympatric forest raptors.

NESTING, REPRODUCTION, AND POPULATION BIOLOGY OF HIGHLANDS GOSHAWKS

NEST BUILDING

Nest building usually begins from late February to early March. However, Speiser and Bosakowski (1991) once observed nest building as early as 1 January at a New Jersey nest site during a mild winter. When the nest is completed, fresh sprigs of greenery (usually hemlock if available) are almost always present on active nests. Occasionally, goshawks re-use and re-furbish old nests of other raptors or crows (Bent 1937), and in northwestern New Jersey we have observed a Great Horned Owl (*Bubo virginianus*) using an old goshawk nest.

NESTING PHENOLOGY

In the Highlands, the majority of goshawks return to the nest site in late February as newly added sticks and fresh greenery were generally observed on the nest by mid-March. Incubation commenced primarily (80%) during the second through fourth week in April with a mean of 23 April (Speiser and Bosakowski 1991).

PRODUCTIVITY

Few data are available for productivity of goshawks in the eastern US. In the Highlands, productivity calculated from 36 attempts averaged 1.4 young per nest (Speiser 1992). In northwestern Connecticut, Root and Root (1978) conducted a study on 20 goshawk nests and reported the following reproductive statistics: mean clutch size = 2.82 (N = 17), mean brood size at 4 wk = 2.06 (N = 17), nesting success = 85.0%, mean young per nest attempt = 1.75 (N = 17), and nestling mortality = 27.5% (N = 14). A more recent Connecticut study (Becker 2000) revealed an average productivity of 2.13 young per nesting attempt for 15 nesting attempts (range one–four young). The reason for the apparently lower productivity in the Highlands is unknown, but might be a function of latitude because our study area is along the southern range limit for the species.

In the Highlands, females occasionally breed in immature plumage, but only two of 35 nesting attempts were by immature females, and all breeding males were in adult plumage (Speiser and Bosakowski 1991). Similar proportions of nesting by immature-plumaged females have been reported elsewhere (Henny et al. 1985, review by Palmer 1988).

NEST SITE FIDELITY

In the Highlands, nest areas were occupied from 1–8 yr with an average occupancy of 3.83 ± 3.05 (SD) yr (Speiser and Bosakowski 1991). Similar long-term fidelity has also been reported by Becker and Smith (2000) in Connecticut and in western North America by Reynolds and Wight (1978) and Woodbridge and Detrich (1994). During their occupancy, goshawks built one–five nests in the nest areas monitored in the Highlands (Speiser and Bosakowski 1991). The alternate nests in the Highlands were generally spaced within a few hundred meters of each other. However, a California study (Woodbridge and Detrich 1994) noted a maximum range of 2.1 km between alternate nests. In the Highlands, goshawks often used a new nest or different alternate nest in their nest area each year regardless of the nesting outcome of the previous year. Traditional nest site areas often remain unoccupied for many years after they are abandoned, suggesting that the goshawk population is well below saturation levels in the Highlands (Speiser and Bosakowski 1984, 1991).

BREEDING DENSITIES

No published information exists for breeding densities of goshawks in the Northeast. Speiser and Bosakowski (1984) speculated that goshawk densities in New Jersey appeared to be far below saturation levels, but systematic attempts to determine density were not made. In suitable goshawk habitat of the Highlands, nest areas were generally spaced at an average of approximately 8 km which is clearly below breeding densities reported elsewhere (Reynolds and Wight 1978, DeStefano et al. 1994a, Reynolds et al. 1994).

DISPERSAL, MIGRATION, AND POPULATION TRENDS

In the Highlands, Speiser and Bosakowski (1991) observed goshawks in mid-winter at or near several traditional nest sites (N = 6) and others were attracted near nest sites with broadcasts of various raptor calls (N = 5), suggesting that most goshawks in the Highlands are permanent residents. However, goshawks are also frequently among the many (15+) species of raptors observed during autumn hawk migration counts in the Northeast (Heintzelman 1976). During these flights, we observed goshawks

using the same migratory pathways as other hawks, flying southward along interior northeast–southwest ridgelines (i.e., flight direction is non-random). Fall migration for goshawks begins in late September and peaks by mid-October, and lasts into December in the Northeast (Heintzelman 1976). Most migrating goshawks are juveniles, except in irruption years, when large numbers of adults are observed (Bent 1937). The origin of these migrating birds remains unknown, but most are probably from the far northern boreal forest in Canada during invasion years (Doyle and Smith 1994).

A large number of hawk migration counting stations have been initiated in the Northeast, with peak numbers of observers and hawkwatches established in the late 1970s. Table 1 provides an example of the number of hawks counted during a typical non-invasion year for goshawks. The total of 297 goshawks indicates that the eastern goshawk population contains a small, but distinct, migratory component during non-invasion years. Geographically, the overall trend seems to indicate that larger numbers of goshawks appear to migrate through the interior higher ridges (Hawk Mountain, Wagoner's Gap, and Raccoon Ridge) of the Kittatiny Mountains than the lower elevation routes nearer to the coast (Skyline Ridge, Mt. Peter, and Hook Mountain) of the New York-New Jersey Highlands.

Using migration data from Hawk Mountain Sanctuary (Kempton, Pennsylvania), both Mosher (1989) and Bednarz et al. (1990) analyzed long-term trends for goshawk numbers. Mosher (1989) used a 3-yr moving average of data from 1934–1987 that showed a general increase in goshawk numbers. Bednarz et al. (1990) analyzed yearly counts from 1934–1987 and found that numbers of migrating goshawks increased during the DDT era, but no significant trend has occurred since the ban on DDT in 1973. Both studies note, however, that the periodic invasions of goshawks (Mueller et al. 1977) greatly confound the interpretation of migration data for this species. Overall, the general increase in counts of migrating hawks and the recent southern range extension provide evidence that goshawk populations may be increasing in the Northeast. Similar trends are apparent in Great Britain, where goshawk repopulation has paralleled reforestation (Marquis and Newton 1982, Anonymous 1989).

Another source of population data is the state breeding bird atlases which have been completed for most states in the Northeast. The New York state breeding bird atlas (Andrle and Carroll 1988) reported a total of 445 atlas blocks (5 × 5 km) with goshawk presence. A surprisingly large number of

TABLE 1. NORTHERN GOSHAWK MIGRATION COUNTS IN THE NORTHERN APPALACHIAN REGION FROM AUTUMN 1978 (HAWK MOUNTAIN NEWS, 1979). TABLE DOES NOT INCLUDE 13 STATIONS WITHOUT GOSHAWK SIGHTINGS.

Location	Days	Hours	N Goshawks
Bear Rocks, PA	44	270	
Belfrey Mountain, NY	5	5.5	2
Chimney Rock, NJ	14	53	1
Cornwall Fire Tower	36	127	2
Hawk Mountain, PA	89	670	63
Helderberg	22	44	7
Hook Mountain, NY	57	381	6
Huntingdon Ridge [a]	21	67	1
I-84 Port Jervis, NY	2	12	3
Kittatinny Mountain [a]	76	1,038	49
Little Gap [a]	35	241	9
Little Mountain	23	154	5
Mt. Peter, NY	45	280	3
Oneida, NY	28	71	2
Pulpit	96	719	33
Raccoon Ridge, NJ	77	388	35
Skyline Ridge, NJ	74	438	5
Sunrise Mountain, NJ	18	138	8
Wagoner's Gap, PA	73	414	42
Totals	835	5,512.5	297

[a] Indicates banding station.

goshawk detections were reported for a species that has the reputation of being so secretive. However, an impressive army of 4,300 atlas workers covered all but 12 of New York's 5,335 atlas blocks in a 6-yr period (Andrle and Carroll 1988). Blocks were surveyed from 1–6 yr, usually with a minimum of 16–20 hr of survey time per year. Although variability does exist among coverage and observers, the New York Atlas represents a monumental field effort and a unique source of complete census data for the goshawk which is currently unavailable for less populated western states and Canadian provinces.

In Pennsylvania, only 120 blocks (2% of all blocks surveyed) were reported with goshawks (Brauning 1992). Although this state had almost as much forest area as New York (68,000 km² versus 74,000 km²) goshawk detections were less numerous, as distribution was mostly limited to central and northern regions of the state. Atlas results from New Jersey revealed only 27 blocks positive for goshawks (Walsh et al. 1999) and were limited almost entirely to the northern half of the state with the exception of two nests found in the Pine Barrens region of southern New Jersey (Bosakowski and Smith 2002). Based on extensive fieldwork before the atlas began, it is interesting to note that Speiser and Bosakowski (1984) estimated that the state could only support about 20 pairs of goshawks.

POTENTIAL IMPACTS TO HIGHLANDS GOSHAWKS

LACK OF RESERVES

The Northern Goshawk has been recognized as an area-sensitive species in North America (Bosakowski and Speiser 1994), such that a future decrease in large, unfragmented, forested reserves could pose a threat to goshawk populations. Currently, only 6.9% of the northeast forests are on public lands, with another 3.7% classified as forest reserves, and 1.0% classified as nonproductive forest reserves (Brooks 1989). Public lands (state and national forests, state and national parks, county parks, and city watersheds) in the Northeast could be set aside for goshawk conservation, but clearly this action would not be enough protection because of the relatively small percentage of public ownership. In addition, incentives are also needed for private forest owners to ensure an adequate supply of older forests and goshawk habitat in the Northeast. Cline (1985) noted that wildlife managers have a variety of options for protecting raptors on private lands including voluntary agreements, management agreements and leases, conservation easements, acquisition of fee titles, and zoning and land-use regulations. In addition, managers could foster the adoption of changes in legislation and tax laws to increase incentives for private landowners (Cline 1985).

TIMBER HARVESTING

In New England, forest stands in mature size classes have recently increased 38% while sapling and seedling successional stages have decreased by a commensurate 40% (Brooks 1989). This forest maturation parallels the increasing numbers of migrating goshawks and breeding range expansion in the Northeast. Although the level of timber harvesting in the Highlands is presently low, Speiser and Bosakowski (1984, 1987) noted at least two goshawk nest sites which were lost to logging. As timber stocks continue to mature in the Northeast, industry pressure may mount to increase timber harvesting, thereby potentially impacting greater numbers of goshawks in the future. Nelson and Titus (1989) calculated that a forest growth period of 60–80 yr after clearcutting would be needed to provide suitable Red-shouldered Hawk habitat in Alleghany National Forest in Pennsylvania. We predict a similar time period would be required for goshawk habitat to regenerate owing to the close similarities in forest habitat used by goshawks and Red-shouldered Hawks.

Nelson and Titus (1989) suggested that tree cutting should not occur in goshawk nest sites, but suggested that selection cut, shelterwood (first cut only), and thinning could benefit the goshawk elsewhere in home ranges. However, Bryant (1986) noted that loss of canopy cover with a light selection harvest allowed Red-tailed Hawks (*Buteo jamaicensis*) to displace nesting Red-shouldered Hawks in Ontario. Selection harvesting is the primary method of timber harvesting in hardwood forests of the Northeast (Smith 1986), but its effect on goshawks in the Northeast is not known. Even so, Benzinger (1994) noted that if timber harvesting results in removal of >20% of the canopy, it would result in little or no reproduction of eastern hemlock, an important species in goshawk nest sites (Root and Root 1978, Speiser and Bosakowski 1987). Considering the above, the intensity and area of harvest within the home range should probably remain minor in the landscape to minimize impacts to goshawks. Studies of timber harvest impacts on goshawk populations are needed, especially including the wide variety of forest types found in the Northeast.

TREE DISEASES

In addition to losses of forest area to development, logging, and fires, disease may be an increasing problem in eastern forests. Benzinger (1994), Orwig

and Foster 2000), and others have reported a decline of eastern hemlock, characterized by dull foliage color, extensive needle drop, and sporadic mortality was probably due to the hemlock woolly adelgid (*Adelges tsugae*). Hemlocks are important trees in goshawk nest sites (Root and Root 1978, Speiser and Bosakowski 1987), and their loss could effect the habitat suitability and demography of goshawks in this region. Benzinger (1994) noted that the hemlock woolly adelgid and the elongate hemlock scale bug (*Fiorinia externae*) might be involved in the decline of hemlock. In addition, gypsy moth (*Lymantria dispar*) deforestation (Souto and Shields 2000) has occurred periodically throughout the Highlands in the last several decades and has resulted in some losses of large canopy trees (pers. obser.). While not a favored host, eastern hemlocks can suffer mortality up to 90% from a single gypsy moth defoliation episode (Benzinger 1994). Hemlock mortality from outbreaks of hemlock looper (*Lambdina fiscellaria* and *Lambdina. athasaria*) (Burns and Trail 2000) are currently limited to northern New England states (Benzinger 1994). In addition, acid rain threatens the stability of high elevation spruce-fir forests of the Adirondack Mountains and Vermont and New Hampshire, and may cause indirect mortality by weakening the immune system of trees.

HUMAN DISTURBANCE FACTORS

In the Northeast, reduction of human activity and disturbance may also help maintain existing breeding pairs. Recreational planners should temporarily or permanently re-route trails and activities away from traditional goshawk nests. One goshawk nest was found along the famous Appalachian Trail after hikers reported that they were attacked by a large hawk. Another goshawk nest was close to a trail in a county park, popular with joggers and walkers on a daily basis. These goshawks probably selected their nest sites during late winter–early spring when very few hikers were active and the area appeared to be free of human disturbance. Currently, the impacts of recreational activities on goshawk nesting and site fidelity in the Highlands remains unknown. However, with further encroachment of wild areas by suburban development, corrective actions could possibly improve the quality of existing goshawk territories for future nesting.

ACKNOWLEDGMENTS

We thank Michael L. Morrison and Richard T. Reynolds for inviting us to submit this paper and for reviewing several versions of the manuscript. John Squires and Douglass Boyce also provided critical reviews of an earlier version of the manuscript and we extend our thanks to them as well. Richard Kane and John Benzinger supplied information on breeding bird atlas data and regional information on goshawks for which we are grateful.

Studies in Avian Biology No. 31:119–125

HABITAT, FOOD HABITS, AND PRODUCTIVITY OF NORTHERN GOSHAWKS NESTING IN CONNECTICUT

Trevor E. Becker, Dwight G. Smith, and Thomas Bosakowski

Abstract. We documented active nests of the Northern Goshawk (*Accipiter gentilis*) at 16 different areas in Connecticut from 1997–1999. A total of 176 prey individuals were identified from remains found under goshawk nests and prey-plucking posts. Birds represented the dominant component of diets (70.5%) with a lower contribution from mammals (29.5%). Overall, Connecticut goshawk diets were dominated by sciurids and Ruffed Grouse (*Bonasa umbellus*). Productivity calculated from 15 known nesting attempts totaled 32 young for an average of 2.13 young per nesting attempt (range 1–4 young). Goshawks nested in large tracts of mature forests with high levels of canopy cover (82%). The nest site topography was consistent with previous studies finding that goshawks avoid southern slopes. Tree densities in the larger size classes and basal area were characteristic for mature forest. Goshawks constructed their nests in large diameter trees, which averaged 41.7 cm in diameter at breast height. Patch size of contiguous forests surrounding goshawk nests revealed a very high mean of 324.5 ha, thus suggesting that large forest patch size may be important for nesting by this forest interior species. Analysis of 202 ha circles centered on each nest revealed that total forest cover averaged 156.1 ha, which was comprised of 65.2 ha for conifer forest, 75.6 ha for deciduous forest, and 17.4 ha for mixed forest. Overall, the post-fledgling family areas for these nests were dominated by forest cover (>75%). Our results suggest that goshawks usually prefer isolation and little human disturbance at the nest site, but some exceptions were noted. Given the highly fragmented and urbanized landscape of Connecticut, we suggest that goshawk management should focus on providing large tracts of mature forest at least 300 ha in extent.

Key Words: *Accipiter*, Connecticut, forest, fragmentation, habitat, Northern Goshawk, nest sites, productivity, prey, site fidelity.

HABITAT, HÁBITOS ALIMENTICIOS Y PRODUCTIVIDAD DE ANIDACIÓN DEL GAVILÁN AZOR EN CONNECTICUT

Resumen. Documentamos nidos activos de Gavilán Azor (*Accipiter gentilis*) en 16 áreas distintas en Connecticut, de 1997–1999. Un total de 176 individuos de presas fueron identificados de los restos encontrados de bajo de los nidos de gavilán, y de los postes donde las aves despluman a sus presas. Las aves representaron el componente dominante de las dietas (70.5%) con una contribución menor de mamíferos (29.5%). Las dietas de los gavilanes de Connecticut estaban dominadas sobre todo por ardillas y Grévoles engolados (*Bonasa umbellus*). El total de la productividad calculada de 15 intentos de anidación conocidos fue de 32 jóvenes, de un promedio de 2.13 jóvenes por intento de anidación (rango 1–4 jóvenes). Los gavilanes anidaron en espacios grandes de bosques maduros con un alto grado de copa forestal (82%). La topografía del sitio del nido fue consistente con estudios previos, encontrando que los gavilanes evitan laderas sureñas. Las densidades de los árboles en las clases con los tamaños más grandes y área basal, fueron características de los bosques maduros. Los gavilanes construyeron sus nidos en árboles con mayor diámetro, con un promedio de 41.7 cm de diámetro a la altura del pecho. El tamaño del parche del bosque contiguo que envuelve los nidos de gavilán, reveló una media muy alta de 324.5 ha, sugiriendo que grandes tamaños de parches de bosque quizás sean importantes para la anidación de estas especies del interior de bosque. Análisis de 202 ha como punto central en cada nido, revelaron que el promedio del total de la cobertura forestal fue de 156.1 ha, el cual incluía 65.2% de bosque de coníferas, 75.6 ha de bosque deciduo, y 17.4 ha de bosque mixto. Sobre todo, los nidos en las áreas con familias de post-volantones fueron dominados por una cobertura forestal (>75%). Nuestros resultados sugieren que los gavilanes usualmente prefieren aislamiento y poco disturbio humano en el sitio del nido, pero algunas excepciones fueron encontradas. Dada la alta fragmentación y el paisaje urbanizado de Connecticut, sugerimos que el manejo del gavilán se debiese enfocar en la provisión de largos tramos de bosque maduro de al menos 300 ha de extensión.

The Northern Goshawk (*Accipiter gentilis*, hereafter goshawk) is an uncommon permanent resident and migrant in Connecticut. The Connecticut Breeding Bird Survey (Smith and Devine 1994), conducted between 1982–1988, found breeding evidence in 13.8% of all blocks surveyed in the state. Of these, 46.3% were confirmed breeding, 18.3% were listed as probable, and 35.4% were considered as possible.

Despite its occurrence, surprisingly little is known about the ecology and distributional status of this species within the state. The goshawk was considered a rare species in New England for most of the last century. Forbush (1925), for example, listed the goshawk as rare to casual in summer while, a decade later, Bagg and Eliot (1937) considered it to be exceptionally rare throughout New England. Similarly, Sage et al. (1913) reported only a single instance of goshawk breeding in Connecticut and further indicated that the species was a rare and irregular visitor in winter. The increased breeding population of the goshawk in the past 30 yr may be due to extensive reforestation, the growth of existing forest providing mature forest that they seem to prefer for nesting.

Most published studies on the nesting ecology and behavior of goshawks in the Northeast have been conducted in New Jersey and New York (Meng 1959, Speiser and Bosakowski 1987, Bosakowski et al. 1992, Bosakowski and Speiser 1994). However, Root and Root (1978) and Becker and Smith (2000) describe some aspects, mostly qualitative, of nesting ecology in Connecticut. The objectives of this study were to measure habitat and landscape features, describe food habits, and document productivity.

STUDY AREA

The study was conducted throughout much of the state of Connecticut in order to provide the most thorough coverage of goshawk nesting distribution and associated habitats. The landscape ecology of Connecticut is described in a number of books and articles (Devine and Smith 1996). Connecticut landscapes range from seashore habitats such as salt marshes that occur along the coast to hilly and wooded terrain in the interior, especially in the northwest and northeast sectors of the state.

Forests throughout the state are primarily deciduous or mixed conifer-deciduous that are dominated by northern red oak (*Quercus rubra*), sugar maple (*Acer saccharum*), birch (*Betula* spp.), ash (*Fraxinus* spp.), maples (*Acer* spp.), hickories (*Carya* spp.), and other hardwoods. Important understory and shrub layer components of these hardwood landscapes include witch hazel (*Hamamelis virginian*), flowering dogwood (*Cornus florida*), mountain laurel (*Kalmia latifolia*), spicebush (*Lindera benzoin*), blueberry (*Vaccinium* spp.), serviceberry (*Amelanchier* spp.), and seedlings and saplings of dominant tree species. Conifers such as white pine (*Pinus strobus*) are important components of these forests especially in the more northern sectors. Stands of red pine (*Pinus resinous*) and Norway spruce (*Picea abies*) can add

an element of evergreen variety to these habitats as well. In interior locales where conditions are wetter and cooler, such as rocky ravines or north facing slopes of steeper hills, hardwoods are replaced by eastern hemlock (*Tsuga canadensis*) groves which may also include smaller amounts of red maple (*Acer rubra*), yellow birch (*Betula lutea*), and white birch (*Betula papyrifera*).

Most Connecticut forest land suffers from varying degrees of fragmentation and development. Roadways, power lines, gas pipelines, and other intrusive features of development fragment existing forest into various smaller tracts. Similarly, residential development has made heavy inroads on Connecticut's otherwise extensive forested areas.

METHODS

LOCATING BREEDING PAIRS AND NESTS

A literature search and discussions with local birders and wildlife professionals provided information on past breeding territories and nest sites of goshawks in Connecticut. Follow-up searches were made of all of these known traditional nesting territories, beginning in February and continuing at monthly (or more frequent) intervals through June. Goshawks produce loud alarm calls, and will usually attack or mob human intruders that walk within 100 m of an active nest with young nestlings (Bosakowski 1999). By following-up reports of aggressive hawks that attacked hikers, joggers, and mountain bikers, we were able to locate many active nesting territories.

We also conducted extensive field searches of forests for new potential nest locations throughout much of rural Connecticut from 1997–1999. State parks and forests, wildlife management areas, public reservoirs, and private rural areas with extensive forest cover were surveyed on foot. Several tactics were employed during these searches. During each search, we stopped at periodic intervals to listen for communications between the members of a pair, which often occur as they establish and maintain a nesting territory. Survey efficiency was increased on days with multiple field observers. One territory was discovered during a vocal territorial dispute between a goshawk and Cooper's Hawk *(Accipiter cooperii)*.

If a pair was discovered occupying a breeding territory, it was kept under observation to ascertain evidence of breeding behavior. Identification of breeding behaviors was followed up by intensive and extensive searches for the nest site. Even with the large nests that goshawks build, nest searches were more productive before the leaf-out period in deciduous-dominated forest. At selected locations, tape-recorded calls were broadcast following the methods described in Bosakowski and Smith (1997), but no goshawks were found with this method. Field surveys become increasingly more difficult during incubation because both males and females tend to be quiet and secretive at this time. Active nests were confirmed by the presence of an incubating female on the nest and/or observations of young on the nest. Observations of productivity were made from the ground by observing the number of late stage nestlings in each of 15 nests. Diets of goshawks were determined by examining prey remains found below goshawk nests and at prey-plucking posts following the methods outlined by Reynolds and Meslow (1984).

Nest Site Measurements

Nest site parameters were measured using a 0.127 ha plot based on a 20-m radius centered on the nest tree. This plot size was chosen as representative after careful visual inspection of all located nest sites. This plot size is considerably larger than the standard 0.04-ha plot (James and Shugart 1970) which Speiser and Bosakowski (1987) considered to be too small to accurately assess habitat for a bird as large and mobile as the goshawk. All trees within the plot were identified by species and measured for diameter at breast height (dbh) using measuring tapes or calipers. Saplings <2 cm dbh were not recorded. From these measurements, the following nesting habitat variables were calculated: tree density (number/hectare) of live and dead trees, basal area of trees (meter^2/hectare), and tree densities by 10-cm size classes.

Basal area of the nest stand was taken using a plotless method by use of a ten-factor angle gauge to estimate basal area at five systematically-spaced points: at the base of the nest tree and at the four cardinal directions positioned 50 m away from the nest tree. During these tree tallies, the number of conifers was noted and percent of conifers was subsequently calculated. The presence of shrubs and canopy was measured along a compass line in each of the four cardinal directions from the nest tree. In each cardinal direction, five sampling points at 5-m intervals produced a total of 20 samples for both shrubs and canopy for each nest site. The canopy cover presence (+) or absence (-) was determined using an ocular sighting tube (James and Shugart 1970). Shrubs and saplings (<10 cm in dbh) were grouped together

because they are structurally similar (Collins et al. 1982). Shrubs and saplings were recorded as present if they were within arm's length of each sampling point (Collins et al. 1982).

Nest Tree Measurements

The nest tree was identified to species and the dbh was measured. Height measurements at the nest tree included canopy height of the nest tree, height of the nest from the ground, and the height of nest relative to the lower canopy. All height measurements of nests were made with a hand-held Accuscale altimeter. Geographic location of the nest tree was recorded using a hand-held global positioning system (GPS) unit.

Topography and Macrohabitat Features

These variables were centered at the nest site and included measurement of distances to edge, paved road, and human habitation. All measurements were taken from the nest site and measured with tape (<30 m) or paced (>30 m) from the nest tree. When distances to these variables were too great to be measured in the field, calculations were made from 1:1200 aerial photographs and USGS quadrangle maps. The variable of forest edge has been discussed by Giles (1978), Thomas (1979), and Forman and Gordon (1981) and is described as the juncture of two types of cover. Since coniferous and deciduous forest cover types are sometimes intermixed, the fragmented patches of deciduous and coniferous cover were grouped as representing the forest, and edges occurred where forest met a cover change, i.e., agricultural fields, residential-urban establishments, abandoned fields that have begun the succession process, large stretches of water bodies (lakes, rivers), human transportation corridors, and utility corridors. Patch size of contiguous forest was also calculated around each of the 16 nests.

Landscape Descriptors

Black-and-white low-altitude aerial photographs with a scale of 1:12,000 were obtained from Connecticut Department of Environmental Protection records. These photographs were taken in April 1996. We measured predominant land use patterns within a 202-ha plot circle centered at the nest tree. The 202-ha plot size was chosen to correspond with the post-fledgling family area estimated from telemetry data by Kennedy et al. (1994). Measures of land use within the 202-ha circular plot included total forest cover, amount of deciduous cover, coniferous cover, and mixed forest cover, area of residential-urban development, agricultural fields (pasture land, crop land, orchards), open water (lakes, rivers, reservoirs), wetlands, and recreational areas such as public open space, campgrounds, and picnic areas.

RESULTS AND DISCUSSION

During the study period, active nests of goshawks were documented at 16 different areas in Connecticut. Land use around nest sites showed that six of the 16 nesting territories were located on city water supply land, five were in state forests, one was in a state park, one was on town land, one was on a nature center, and two were located on private sanctuaries. Several factors probably effect the selection of most breeding locations in sanctuaries and state lands. First, logging and other disruptive activities are usually nonexistent, minimal or regulated, therefore, these locales support older and more extensive forests in which goshawk may nest. A second contributing factor is the relative degree of protection and isolation afforded goshawks nesting in these sanctuary forest lands. A third factor is that virtually all large contiguous forests (>200 ha) are on public lands, which cannot be subdivided for suburban housing developments. In a densely populated and heavily urbanized state like Connecticut, these sanctuaries provide island habitats set in a sea of urbanization.

FOOD HABITS

A total of 176 prey individuals were identified from remains found under goshawk nests and prey-plucking posts (Table 1). Birds represented the most frequent component of diets (70.5%) with a lower frequency of mammals (29.5%). No reptiles, amphibians, fish, or invertebrates were represented in the diet as was also the case for the New Jersey-New York Highlands (Bosakowski et al. 1992). In Connecticut, Ruffed Grouse (*Bonasa umbellus*) and Mourning Dove (*Zenaida macroura*) were most numerous among the 24 bird species taken, followed by Common Crow (*Corvus brachyrhynchos*), Blue Jay (*Cyanocitta cristata*), Mallard (*Anas platyrhynchos*), and Northern Bobwhite (*Collinus virginianus*). Among the nine species of mammals taken, tree squirrels were most numerous. Overall, frequency distributions of goshawk diets in this study were dominated by sciurids and Ruffed Grouse which is similar to that found in the New Jersey-New York Highlands (Bosakowski et al. 1992). Meng (1959)

found common crows to predominate the goshawk diet in New York and Pennsylvania, but the nesting habitat was in an agricultural-woodland matrix.

PRODUCTIVITY

In this study, productivity from 15 known nesting attempts in Connecticut totaled 32 young for an average of 2.13 young per nesting attempt (range 1–4 young). In northwestern Connecticut, Root and Root (1978) conducted a study on 20 goshawk nests and reported a mean of 1.75 young per nest attempt (N = 17). Both Connecticut studies revealed an apparently higher rate than reported by Speiser (1992) for 36 nesting attempts in the New Jersey-New York Highlands (1.4 young/nesting attempt). The present study compares well with higher productivity rates of 2.2 reported for several western localities in Arizona, Nevada, and Oregon (summarized in Bosakowski 1999). Factors that caused nesting failures in Connecticut included human interference and predation by Great Horned Owls (*Bubo virginianus*) on adults or young. Female goshawk are very vulnerable to attack when incubating eggs or brooding nestlings.

NESTING HABITAT

Field surveys yielded 16 goshawk nesting areas, all located in extensively forested habitats. Ten active territories were dominated by conifers; of these, eight stands were dominated by white pine and two by eastern hemlock. Four nesting areas were in mixed forest of eastern hemlock and hardwood species. Of these, one stand was predominantly eastern hemlock-red maple, and the remaining three were eastern hemlock-yellow birch stands. Two of the 16 nesting areas were located in pure deciduous forests. One of these sites was comprised mostly of yellow birch and white ash (*Fraxinus americana*), and the other site consisted primarily of red maple forest. In total, all but one nesting site were in stands of mature trees. The one exceptional nest was located in a young deciduous stand consisting of young (65%) and mature trees (35% of total trees). Overall, nest stands were dominated by conifers which averaged 66.1% (Table 2). The number of tree species within the majority of nest site plots was low ($\bar{x}$ = 7.9 species) but ranged between 5–14 tree species. The maximum tree species richness of 14 was the result of goshawks nesting in a young stand.

Overall, tree densities in the larger size classes and basal area were characteristic for mature forest (Table 2) and were consistent with forest structure

TABLE 1. PREY OF BREEDING NORTHERN GOSHAWKS IN CONNECTICUT.

Prey species		N individuals	Percent by number
Short-tailed shrew	*Blarina brevicauda*	1	0.6
Eastern chipmunk	*Tamias striatus*	13	7.4
Red squirrel	*Tamiasciurus hudsonicus*	10	5.7
Gray squirrel	*Sciurus carolinensis*	15	8.5
White-footed mouse	*Peromyscus leucopus*	5	2.8
Muskrat	*Ondatra zibethicus*	1	0.6
Woodchuck	*Marmota monax*	1	0.6
Eastern cottontail	*Sylvilagus floridanus*	4	2.3
Snowshoe hare	*S. transitionalis*	1	0.6
Unidentified rodent	—	1	0.6
Total mammals	—	52	29.5
Mallard	*Anas platyrhynchos*	6	3.4
Northern Pintail	*Anas acuta*	2	1.1
Wood Duck	*Aix sponsa*	1	0.6
Cooper's Hawk	*Accipiter cooperii*	2	1.1
Wild Turkey	*Meleagris gallopavo*	1	0.6
Ruffed Grouse	*Bonasa umbellus*	21	11.9
Northern Bobwhite	*Collinus virginianus*	6	3.4
Guinea Fowl (domestic)	*Numida meleagris*	2	1.1
Ring-necked Pheasant	*Phasianus colchicus*	4	2.3
Chicken (domestic)	*Gallus gallus*	5	2.8
Ring-billed Gull	*Larus delawarensis*	2	1.1
Rock Dove	*Columba livia*	5	2.8
Mourning Dove	*Zenaida macroura*	20	11.4
Northern Flicker	*Colaptes auratus*	3	1.7
Hairy Woodpecker	*Picoides villosus*	3	1.7
Downy Woodpecker	*Picoides pubescens*	1	0.6
Blue Jay	*Cyanocitta cristata*	7	4.0
Common Crow	*Corvus brachyrhynchos*	8	4.5
American Robin	*Turdus migratorius*	2	1.1
Thrush spp.	—	1	0.6
American Redstart	*Setophagia ruticilla*	1	0.6
House Sparrow	*Passer domesticus*	3	1.7
Red-winged Blackbird	*Agelaius phoeniceus*	1	0.6
Common Grackle	*Quiscalus quiscula*	2	1.1
Song Sparrow	*Melospiza melodia*	2	1.1
Unidentified small–medium Bird	—	13	7.4
Total birds	—	124	70.5
Grand total	—	176	100.0

found at nest sites across North America (see Table 1 in Bosakowski 1999). Canopy cover of nest stands in Connecticut averaged 82.1% and ranged from 65–100% (Table 2). Goshawks tended to select sites with a high canopy cover which is consistent with other regions (Bosakowski 1999). Canopy cover provides protection and concealment from aerial predators and may also provide cooler microclimates beneath the canopy to aid in thermoregulation of adults and to prevent desiccation of the nestlings. Shrub cover at northern goshawk sites averaged 52.8% which was moderately high. Bosakowski et al. (1992) found shrub cover ($\bar{x}$ = 28.3%) was significantly lower at

nest sites in the New Jersey-New York Highlands compared to random sites.

Most goshawk nest sites were located on gentle slopes (five) or relatively flat terrain (five), but the remaining six nests were on steep slopes. Of the 16 nest sites, eight were in uplands, four were in riverine settings, three were in or near wetlands, and one was located on a ridge-top plateau. In the New Jersey-New York Highlands, Speiser and Bosakowski (1987) noted that goshawk nests were generally situated on lower slopes and flat bench-like areas. In Connecticut, most of the goshawk nest plots (81.8%) sloped mainly to the north or east, and

TABLE 2. HABITAT VARIABLES AT NORTHERN GOSHAWK NESTS (N = 16) IN CONNECTICUT.

Variable	Mean	SD	Minimum	Maximum
Live trees (>10 cm/ha)	617.1	174.2	370.1	999.1
Total trees (>10 cm/ha)	716.5	219.4	456.7	1228.3
Live basal area (m²/ha)	47.3	12.1	25.9	71.4
Total basal area (m²/ha)	51.0	12.5	26.8	73.8
Live trees (<10 cm/ha)	630.9	596.3	189.0	2370.7
Live trees (10–19 cm/ha)	182.2	142.0	8.6	603.9
Live trees (20–29 cm/ha)	162.5	99.8	39.4	425.2
Live trees (30–39 cm/ha)	132.4	68.0	39.4	291.3
Live trees (40–49 cm/ha)	67.4	36.2	7.8	133.9
Live trees (50–59 cm/ha)	32.5	31.9	0	86.6
Live trees (60–69 cm/ha)	5.9	10.9	0	39.8
Live trees (70–79 cm/ha)	2.0	4.5	0	15.7
Live trees (80–89 cm/ha)	0.5	2.0	0	7.9
Nest stand basal area (m²/ha)	39.1	7.2	20.2	51.4
Decadence percent	7.2	5.0	1.4	16.7
Species richness index	7.9	2.3	5	14
Conifer trees percent	66.1	23.6	15.9	94.6
Shrub cover percent	52.8	26.7	0	95
Canopy cover percent	82.2	9.8	65	100
Distance to human habitation (m)	413.3	260.4	57.1	971.5
Distance to paved road (m)	399.0	314.5	59.7	1,142.9
Distance forest edge (m)	200.3	163.5	38.1	609.6
Forest patch size (ha)	324.5	298.4	27.9	1,180.9
Nest tree dbh (cm)	41.7	10.1	22.0	60.0
Nest tree height (m)	26.4	4.1	18.0	36.6
Nest height (m)	14.9	2.1	9.8	18.3
Percent nest height	56.6	4.8	48.3	65.9

southerly aspects were almost totally avoided (Fig. 1). Similarly, Speiser and Bosakowski (1987) noted that southern slopes were also avoided by goshawks nesting in the New Jersey-New York Highlands.

The distance to the nearest house or building averaged 413.3 m, but ranged between 57.1–971.5 m. Since most homes are built along paved roads, the distance to the nearest paved road was similar, averaging 399.3 m (range = 59.7–1,143 m). In the New Jersey-New York Highlands, Bosakowski and Speiser (1994) noted that goshawk nests were much further from paved roads ($\bar{x}$ = 1,171 m) and human habitation ($\bar{x}$ = 1,052 m) than Connecticut goshawk nests. This regional difference may be due to land use and forest fragmentation patterns, which tend to differ between the states.

Distance from the nest to the nearest edge such as residential areas, fields, power line cuts, highways, and open bodies of water averaged 200.3 m and ranged between 38.0–609.5 m in Connecticut. It is interesting to note that Bosakowski and Speiser (1994) reported a similar distance ($\bar{x}$ = 264 m) to forest openings (>1 ha) in the New Jersey-New York Highlands, which was not significantly different than that found for 70 random sites. Thus, the nearest forest edge is a function of the nature of available forest, and there has been no selection documented neither for nor against this variable.

LANDSCAPE AROUND NESTS

In light of the well documented effects of forest fragmentation on breeding bird declines (Galli et al. 1976, Robbins 1979), we determined patch size of contiguous forest around goshawk nest sites using aerial photographs. Patch size of forests surrounding goshawk nests revealed a very high mean of 324.5 ha (SD = 298.4, range 27.9–1,180.9), indicating that large forest patch size may be an important parameter for nesting by this forest interior species. Similarly, Bosakowski et al. (1999) reported that three goshawk nests in Washington were in a similar mean patch size of contiguous forest, averaging 396.7 ha (SD = 175, range 210–559). No other investigators have reported patch size for goshawks.

In another landscape comparison, we examined land use patterns within a 202-ha circle around the nest, which was hypothesized by Kennedy et al. (1994) to represent the post-fledgling family area (PFA). In this study, analysis of 202 ha circles

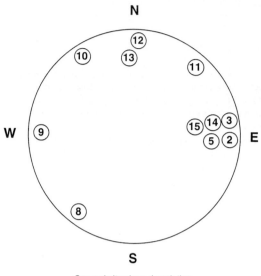

Directional slope of Northern Goshawk nest sites

General site slope description

Flat: 5
Gentle slope: 5
Steep slope: 6

FIGURE 1. Slope aspects of Northern Goshawk nest sites in Connecticut. Five of 16 nest sites had no discernible slope aspects and are not shown.

centered on each nest (N = 16) revealed that total forest cover averaged 156.1 ha (SD = 22.7), including 65.2 ha for conifer forest (SD = 46.6), 75.6 ha for deciduous forest (SD = 39.1), and 17.4 ha for mixed forest (SD = 13.9). Overall, the PFAs for these nests were dominated by forest cover (>75%). These results support previous observations from the New Jersey-New York Highlands (Speiser and Bosakowski 1987; Bosakowski and Speiser 1994) which noted that goshawks were restricted to extensive areas of contiguous forest. Given the highly fragmented and urbanized landscape of Connecticut, we suggest that goshawk management should focus on providing large tracts of mature forest at least 300 ha in extent. This recommendation is based on mean patch size, which also provides an adequate area for the inclusion of the hypothesized 202-ha PFA. In conclusion, this study corroborates that the goshawk is an area-sensitive species (Bosakowski and Speiser 1994), and should also be considered a forest-interior species as well.

ACKNOWLEDGMENTS

This research was part of an M.S. thesis (TEB) at Southern Connecticut State University under the advisement of DGS. Larry Fischer provided some of the nest locations and banding data, and assisted with some of the nest searches. Mike and Pat Redmond and Noble Proctor provided information on historic nest locations and other field information. Jeff Servino assisted with field work. Noble Proctor, Steve Burian, Vernon Nelson, and Leon Yacher provided information. Part of this research was funded by a grant from the Nature Conservancy.

Studies in Avian Biology No. 31:126–134

NORTHERN GOSHAWK ECOLOGY IN THE WESTERN GREAT LAKES REGION

CLINT W. BOAL, DAVID E. ANDERSEN, PATRICIA L. KENNEDY, AND AIMEE M. ROBERSON

Abstract. A substantial amount of research has been conducted on Northern Goshawks (*Accipiter gentilis*) in recent years, but the majority of this research has been conducted in western North America and Europe. Little information has been published concerning goshawks in the western Great Lakes region, including the states of Minnesota, Wisconsin, and Michigan, and the forested southern portion of the Canadian province of Ontario. We present an overview of the regional information available on Northern Goshawks in the western Great Lakes region which draws heavily on our recent studies in Minnesota, but also includes published and unpublished information from across the western Great Lakes region. Inclusion of this information on productivity, breeding-season food habits, breeding-season habitat use, residency status and migration patterns, and breeding season mortality provides a broader understanding of the ecology of goshawks in this region. Our recommendations for additional research needed to enhance management of western Great Lakes region goshawks include development of a collaborative sampling program to identify goshawk nest sites and monitor survival, mortality, and productivity at subsamples of nests across the region; identification of winter habitat and prey use; and monitoring of goshawks in silvicultural treatment areas to assess responses to forest management.

Key Words: Accipiter gentilis, ecology, food habits, foraging habitat, Minnesota, nesting habitat, western Great Lakes, Wisconsin.

ECOLOGÍA DEL GAVILÁN AZOR EN LA REGIÓN OCCIDENTAL DE LOS GRANDES LAGOS

Resumen. Una substancial cantidad de investigación acerca del Gavilán Azor (*Accipiter gentilis*) ha sido conducida en los últimos años, pero la mayor parte de esta investigación ha sido conducida hacia el oeste de Norte América y Europa. Poca información ha sido publicada acerca de los gavilanes en la región oeste de los Grandes Lagos, incluyendo los estados de Minnesota, Wisconsin, y Michigan, así como la porción sureña del área forestal de la Provincia Canadiense de Ontario. Presentamos una visión global de la información regional disponible acerca de Gavilanes Azor en la región occidental de los Grandes Lagos, la cual se basa fuertemente en nuestros recientes estudios en Minnesota, pero también incluye información publicada y no publicada a lo largo de la región occidental de los Lagos del Norte. La inclusión de la información en productividad, hábitos de alimentación durante la época de reproducción, hábitos de uso durante la época de reproducción, estado de residencia y patrones de migración, y mortandad en la época de reproducción, provee de un entendimiento más amplio de la ecología del gavilán en esta región. Nuestras recomendaciones acerca de la información adicional que se necesita para reforzar el manejo del gavilán de la región occidental de los Grandes Lagos, incluye el desarrollo de un programa de muestreo de colaboración, para identificar nidos de gavilán y monitorear supervivencia, mortandad, y productividad en submuestras de nidos a través de la región; identificación del hábitat de invierno y utilización de la presa; así como el monitoreo del gavilán en áreas con manejo de silvicultura, para evaluar respuestas al manejo forestal.

The Northern Goshawk (*Accipiter gentilis*) is a large raptor associated with mature deciduous, coniferous, or mixed forests (Bright-Smith and Mannan 1994, Siders and Kennedy 1996, Squires and Reynolds 1997). It breeds throughout northern temperate and boreal forests in northern North America, Europe, and Asia (Squires and Reynolds 1997). In North America, potential conflict between goshawk habitat requirements and timber harvest practices has led to concern for the status of the species (Kennedy 1997), which has been proposed for listing several times under the U.S. Endangered Species Act. The species' status continues to be the object of considerable litigation (Peck 2000; Squires and Kennedy, *this volume*) and as a result, over the last decade, numerous studies have addressed goshawk population ecology and status (see Block et al. 1994, Squires and Reynolds 1997; Squires and Kennedy, *this volume*). The vast majority of these studies, however, have been conducted in the western US and western Canada, with fewer studies in western Europe. Results of these studies have been incorporated into management plans designed to maintain goshawk populations in a variety of landscapes.

Existing goshawk management plans (Reynolds et al. 1992) generally focus on managing forest structure and landscapes to provide nest sites, foraging habitat, and prey species habitat. Such management plans, however, presuppose a thorough understanding of the species' habitat use and resource needs (Garshelis 2000). Even for western North America, an understanding of goshawk habitat preferences and resource requirements is often lacking or is very limited in scope and scale. Thus, existing data may not be relevant to the range of environmental conditions and forest management practices found across the species' distribution. Goshawks in western North America typically occupy areas of high elevation (1,200–3,900 m) and substantial topographic relief, with generally warm, dry summers and cool, wet winters (Kennedy et al. 1994, DeStefano and McClosky 1997, Keane 1999). In contrast, the western Great Lakes region (WGLR) of North America is of lower elevation (330–560 m), has relatively little topographic relief, and typically experiences cool, wet summers and cold, dry winters (Tester 1995). Forest-harvest practices in the western US typically focus on large tracts of land administered by a single public agency or landowner, whereas harvest practices in the midwestern and eastern US focus on smaller tracts of land under a mixture of public and private ownerships (Mannan et al. 1994). This has led to increased forest heterogeneity in midwestern and eastern deciduous forests and, in some cases, an increase in the extent of early-successional forest types, relative to pre-settlement landscapes (Whitcomb et al. 1981, Minnesota Forest Resources Council 2000, Reich et al. 2001). For these reasons, the existing information on goshawk habitat use and resource requirements, primarily from western North America and western Europe, may not directly apply to other regions of North America.

Here we provide an overview of the ecology of goshawks in the WGLR. Our emphasis is on Minnesota and draws extensively on our own research. Other areas within the WGLR are not as well represented because few published papers have been produced on goshawk populations outside of Minnesota. Roberson et al. (2003) recently reviewed the available published and unpublished literature for the WGLR and we rely heavily on this document for our summaries of the unpublished literature. We approach the interpretation of these unpublished data cautiously, but without including these forms of data, our overview would be almost entirely limited to our own work in Minnesota and a small number of published reports from Wisconsin and Michigan.

PRODUCTIVITY

Activities and behaviors associated with breeding goshawks typically occur between March and mid- to late August (Squires and Reynolds 1997). However, goshawks have been observed near their nesting areas in Minnesota as early as late February (Roberson 2001, Roberson et al., unpubl. data), possibly because their winter home ranges include their nesting areas (Boal et al. 2003). Initiation of incubation occurs from 31 March–23 April in Minnesota, with initial observations of nestlings from 8–15 May (Roberson 2001; Roberson et al., unpubl. data). Smithers et al. (2005) estimated mean hatch and fledging dates at goshawks nests in Minnesota in 2000–2002 as 28 May and 4 July, respectively.

In Minnesota, Boal et al. (2005a) reported 26 (62%) of 42 nesting attempts were successful, with 1.14 ± 1.07 (se) young fledged per nesting attempt and 1.85 ± 0.73 young fledged per successful nest. In Michigan, Lapinski (2000) reported goshawks fledged 1.14 and 1.71 young per active and successful nest, respectively, among 36 nesting attempts. Rosenfield et al. (1996) reported 11 (85%) of 13 goshawk nests in Wisconsin fledged at least one young, with a mean number of 1.7 fledged young per successful nest. Erdman et al. (1998) reported higher productivity in their study area in Wisconsin, with an average of 1.7 fledglings and 2.2 fledglings per nesting attempt. In general, productivity among successful nests in the WGLR fell slightly lower than the average, but within the range, of that reported in 16 studies from western North America (Squires and Kennedy, *this volume*).

NEST FAILURE AND NESTLING MORTALITY

In North America, the most common nest predator of goshawks appears to be the Great Horned Owl (*Bubo virginianus*; Moore and Henny 1983, Rohner and Doyle 1992). A wide variety of mammals are also known to prey upon goshawk nestlings (Squires and Kennedy, *this volume*). In Minnesota, inclement weather accounted for failure of 6 (13.9%) of 43 goshawk nesting attempts (Boal et al. 2005a). Another 21.0% of goshawk nesting failures were due to depredation by Great Horned Owls and mammalian predators (e.g., fishers [*Martes pennanti*], martens [*Martes americana*]). Elsewhere in the WGLR, Erdman et al. (1998) reported that predation by fishers was the primary cause of nesting failure among goshawks in Wisconsin, but did not provide details as to how they arrived at this conclusion or the number of nesting failures due to fisher depredation. This is not an exhaustive list of potential goshawk predators in the WGLR but it does suggest that, similar to other areas, goshawks in this region are subjected to both avian and mammalian predation.

FOOD HABITS

Goshawks are considered prey generalists with diets varying by region, season, and availability (Squires and Reynolds 1997; Squires and Kennedy, *this volume*). Local studies of food habits are necessary for developing management strategies for goshawk populations at regional and local levels (Reynolds et al. 1992).

A number of anecdotal records of prey items collected opportunistically at goshawk nests in the WGLR, provide a prey list rather than any quantitative assessment of food habits (Roberson et al. 2003). The video monitoring of prey deliveries to goshawk nests in Minnesota by Smithers et al. (2005) is the only quantitative food habits study conducted to date in the WGLR. Smithers et al. (2005) identified 576 (88.3%) of 652 prey items delivered to 13 goshawk nests in Minnesota as mammal or bird. Red squirrels (*Tamiasciuris hudsonicus*) accounted for 202 (42%) and eastern chipmunks (*Tamias striatus*) accounted for 95 (19.8%) of 479 prey deliveries identified to family or finer taxonomic resolution. This suggests sciurids are a key breeding-season prey species for goshawks in Minnesota. Other prey species accounting for ≥5% of identified prey included hares and rabbits (7.9%), American crows (*Corvus brachyrhynchos*, 7.7%) and Ruffed Grouse (*Bonasa umbellus*, 6.9%).

Mammals and birds accounted for 61% and 39% of biomass delivered, respectively, to goshawk nests in Minnesota (Smithers et al. 2005). Snowshoe hare (*Lepus americanus*, 25.5%), red squirrel (23.6%), and chipmunk (5.0%) accounted for 54% of mammalian biomass delivered to nests, while Ruffed Grouse (11.5%), crows (9.0%) and diving ducks (7.1%) accounted for 28% of avian biomass.

Several studies have documented red squirrels as important prey for goshawks (Squires and Kennedy, *this volume*) throughout their range, and they may be especially important during the winter when other prey are unavailable (Widén 1987). Squirrels dominated Swedish goshawk diets in terms of number (79%) and biomass (56%) during winters of both high and low squirrel abundance (Widén 1987). Winter food habits information for goshawks in the WGLR is not available, but the extensive use of red squirrels during the summer (Smithers et al. 2005)

and the patterns of squirrel use during winter in other areas (Widén 1987) suggest this species may be of year-round importance to goshawks in the region.

Rabbits and hares are also used extensively by goshawks throughout their range (Squires and Kennedy, *this volume*). In Minnesota, 25.5% of prey biomass delivered to nests was from snowshoe hares (Smithers et al. 2005). Ruffed Grouse comprised 5% of prey deliveries and 11.5% of biomass delivered to goshawk nests during a 3-yr period (2000–2002) of low grouse abundance (Smithers et al. 2005). There is some evidence that at least some goshawks in Minnesota may rely more heavily on Ruffed Grouse during some time periods (Eng and Gullion 1962, Apfelbaum and Haney 1984). Erdman et al. (1998) suggested that goshawk productivity was probably related to cyclic abundance of Ruffed Grouse and snowshoe hares in Wisconsin but it is unknown how he arrived at these conclusions since he did not describe goshawk diet. Eng and Gullion (1962) focused on Ruffed Grouse mortality, and did not assess proportional use of grouse in the diet of goshawks, and Apfelbaum and Haney (1984) reported on prey remains collected at only one nest in northern Minnesota. Because of the difficulties in accurately quantifying the extent of grouse predation by goshawks (Eng and Gullion 1962) and the biases associated with determining raptor diets based on prey remains (reviewed in Boal 1993), the results of these studies need to be interpreted cautiously. The importance of Ruffed Grouse in goshawk diets in the WGLR region through periods of varying grouse abundance is not known but they may be important prey item in the WGLR. Gallinaceous birds (primarily grouse and pheasants) are well documented as important prey of North American and European goshawks at northern latitudes. Fluctuations in these grouse populations have been shown to affect goshawk productivity, including number of nesting pairs, and number of young per active nest (Squires and Kennedy, *this volume*).

NESTING HABITAT

Nest Tree

Goshawks are thought to choose nest trees based on size and structure more than tree species (USDI Fish and Wildlife Service 1998a). Goshawks often nest in one of the largest trees in the nest stand, although height and diameter of nest trees vary geographically and with forest type (Reynolds et al. 1982, Hargis et al. 1994, Squires and Ruggiero 1996, Squires and Reynolds 1997). In Minnesota, goshawk nests were placed in the tallest and largest diameter at breast height (dbh) trees available in nest stands (Boal et al. 2001). However, height and dbh of goshawk nest trees in our study were among the lowest reported from 10 studies reviewed by Siders and Kennedy (1994). We suspect that available trees in northern Minnesota are smaller than those available in other study areas possibly due to shorter growing seasons (Tester 1995).

Using the North American Nest Card Program, Apfelbaum and Seelbach (1983) found that goshawks nested in 20 tree species or species groups, with deciduous trees reported twice as often as conifers throughout North America and nine to one over conifers in the Midwest. In a review of studies in the WGLR, the majority of known goshawk nests were placed in deciduous tree species (Roberson et al. 2003). In our research in Minnesota, we found 46 goshawk nests placed in aspen (*Populus* spp., 80%), birch (*Betula* spp., 19%), white pine (*Pinus strobes*, 4%), red pine (*Pinus resinosa*, 2%), and red oak (*Quercus borealis*, 2%) trees (Boal et al. 2001). Deciduous trees were clearly the dominant species (94%), even in conifer-dominated nest stands (Boal et al. 2001). Rosenfield et al. (1998) also found one of four goshawk nests in aspen trees within Wisconsin pine plantations. Thus, conservation of large deciduous trees in all stand types may be important for goshawk management in the WGLR.

Aspect and slope at nest sites may influence microclimate and goshawk habitat selection. Several studies have demonstrated clear associations between goshawk nest placement and slope, but slopes are highly variable (9–75%; Reynolds et al. 1982, Moore and Henny 1983, Hayward and Escano 1989, Siders and Kennedy 1996, Squires and Ruggiero 1996). Goshawk nests are also usually associated with a northerly aspect (Reynolds et al. 1982, Hayward and Escano 1989, Bosakowski and Speiser 1994). However, aspect and slope probably are inconsequential in Minnesota due to the lack of topographical relief on the landscape; most goshawk nests in Minnesota were on sites that were so level that slope and aspect could not be reliably determined (Boal et al. 2001).

NEST AREA

In a review of goshawk habitat studies, Daw et al. (1998) concluded that goshawks tend to select nest stands that are characterized by relatively large trees and relatively high canopy closure (>50–60%), regardless of region or forest type. Penteriani et al. (2001) also reported that high dbhs, high crown volumes, and flight space were significant predictors of goshawk nest site selection in France. These patterns were consistent with data from the few nest habitat studies conducted in the WGLR. Nest stands in Minnesota consisted of canopy trees that were both taller and greater in diameter than the average in stands where goshawks were foraging (Boal et al. 2001). Similarly, canopy closure at Minnesota and Wisconsin goshawk nests stands (Martell and Dick 1996, Rosenfield et al. 1998, Boal et al. 2001) were within the range (59.8–95.0%) reported by Siders and Kennedy (1994) for other areas.

Penteriani et al. (2001) suggested a distribution-wide commonality among goshawk nest stands is a variable, but typically low, stem density. In contrast, the 1,153 stems/ha (Martell and Dick 1996) and 1,196 stems/ha (Boal et al. 2001) observed at goshawk nest stands in Minnesota are among the highest reported for the species (Siders and Kennedy 1994, Penteriani et al. 2001). High stem density at goshawk nests in Minnesota was coupled with a multistoried canopy. However, there were distinct open layers between the foliage of the canopy and understory, and between the understory and shrub layers. We suspect these relatively unobstructed layers may be important as flight corridors for goshawks, particularly in stands with high stem densities.

In Minnesota (Boal et al. 2005b) we found goshawks nested primarily in early-successional upland deciduous stands (58%) and late-successional upland conifer stands (26%). Fewer nests were located in late-successional upland deciduous stands (12%) and early-successional upland conifer stands (5%). Elsewhere in Minnesota, Gullion (1981a) reported that three nests in the late 1970s near Cloquet were in hardwood trees in small stands dominated by jack pine (*Pinus banksiana*), red pine, and Scots pine (*Pinus sylvestris*), and surrounded by mixed conifer hardwood and young aspen stands. A goshawk nest in Itasca State Park was located in a jack pine-aspen forest (Apfelbaum and Haney 1984). Nests reported by Martell and Dick (1996) were found in aspen-balsam fir (*Abies balsamea*), red pine-aspen, mixed hardwood, and jack pine-aspen stands (Dick and Plumpton 1998).

Elsewhere in the WGLR, Ennis et al. (1993) reported nests on the Huron-Manistee National Forests were placed in red pine (35%), aspen (28%), oak (12%), northern-mixed hardwoods (10%), and other (15%) stand types. Postupalsky (1993) reported northern hardwood forest, aspen, or white pine stands as the most frequently used nest stand types in Michigan. Bowerman et al. (1988) reported most nests examined (62%, N = 45) in Michigan were located in early to mid-successional stage deciduous or mixed stands, with the remainder (38%) in red pine plantations. Peck and James (1983) described typical nest stands in Ontario as dense stands of deciduous, coniferous, and mixed forests. Rosenfield et al. (1998) reported that nest stands in Wisconsin varied in tree species composition and woodland age, including four nests in pine plantations. The proximity of some goshawk nests to pine plantations has been noted by researchers in Wisconsin (Rosenfield et al. 1996, 1998), Michigan (Bowerman et al. 1988), Minnesota (Dick and Plumpton 1998), and Ontario (Peck and James 1983).

BREEDING SEASON FORAGING HABITAT

The few studies on breeding-season foraging habitat of goshawks have been conducted in western North America (Austin 1993, Bright-Smith and Mannan 1994, Beier and Drennan 1997) and Europe (Kenward 1982, Widén 1989). Collectively, results from these studies suggest goshawks use a variety of forest types, and appear to select forests with a high density of large trees, high canopy cover and closure, high basal area, and relatively open understories (Kenward 1982, Widén 1989, Austin 1993, Bright-Smith and Mannan 1994, Hargis et al. 1994, Beier and Drennan 1997).

Until recently, information on goshawk foraging habitat during the breeding season in the WGLR was not available. Boal et al. (2005 b) assessed foraging habitat use relative to availability and found that breeding male goshawks in Minnesota preferentially used early-successional upland deciduous stands (aspen or birch) ≥50 yr old. Goshawks also used this stand type in the age range 25–49 yr old at least proportional to availability, but clearly avoided stands <25 yr old. Late-successional upland conifer stands (white pine and red pine) of all ages were also a clearly preferred stand type. Late-successional upland deciduous stands (maples and oaks) ≥50 yr old were used proportional to, or greater than, availability (depending on scale of assessment), whereas late-successional lowland deciduous stands (ash) were used proportional to availability. Late-successional lowland conifers (tamarack and lowland black spruce) were one of the most widely available stand types in goshawk home ranges, but were avoided. Wetlands and open and cut-over areas were also used less than was proportionally available. Elsewhere in the WGLR, Lapinski (2000) reported three female goshawks in the Upper Peninsula of Michigan foraged in mixed hardwood-conifer stands and jack pine, but avoided cedar, open, and swamp fir-swamp conifer cover types.

Similar to other parts of the goshawk's range, the landscape of north-central Minnesota has changed in the past several decades, with the ratio of forested land to non-forested land apparently declining from 1.72 in 1977 to 1.63 in 1990 and a shift from stands of white and red pines to stands of aspen (Minnesota Forest Resources Council 2000). It is clear that breeding male goshawks in Minnesota foraged in mature and old forested stands, especially upland conifer and upland deciduous stands (Boal et al. 2005b), but the influence the changes in vegetation communities may be having on goshawk populations is unknown.

The demonstrated preference for older age class stands by foraging male goshawks in Minnesota (Boal et al. 2005b) is consistent with reports on breeding-season foraging habitat use by goshawks in coniferous forests of the western US (Austin 1993, Bright-Smith and Mannan 1994, Beier and Drennan 1997), non-breeding goshawks in boreal forests of Sweden (Widén 1989) and Finland (Tornberg and Colpaert 2001), and year-round habitat use in coniferous forests of southeast Alaska (Iverson et al. 1996). However, even if goshawks do not typically venture into stand types that are used less than expected, the possible importance of those stand types to prey production in a goshawk's home range should not be overlooked (e.g., young aspen stands and Ruffed Grouse, Gullion and Alm 1983). Boal et al. (2005 b) also stressed that their data and assessments were limited to the breeding season and relative use of different stand types by goshawks may vary seasonally due to factors such as seasonal changes in prey availability or additional requirements for thermal or escape cover during the non-breeding season.

HOME RANGE

In a summary of goshawk studies in North America, (Squires and Reynolds 1997) found breeding-season home range sizes were between 570 and 3,500 ha. Their summary did not include information from the WGLR, although Eng and Gullion (1962) reported some of the first foraging area data collected for goshawks in North America. By examining the remains of marked grouse found at goshawk nest areas in northern Minnesota, they determined that nine banded male grouse were brought to the nests from drumming areas 1,097–2,514 m ($\bar{x}$ = 1,664 m) away. Also, in one of the first studies of goshawks using radio-telemetry, Davis (1979) found a nesting female goshawk in Minnesota with a home range size of 4,200 ha. In the Upper Pennisula of Michigan, Lapinski (2000) reported that breeding season home ranges of three female goshawks averaged 513 ha.

Recently, Boal et al. (2003) reported that mean breeding-season home range sizes for 17 male and 11 female goshawks in Minnesota were 2,593 ± 475 ha and 2,494 ± 631 ha, respectively. Although Hargis et al. (1994) and Kennedy et al. (1994) reported males' home ranges as larger than females', Boal et al. (2003) found negligible gender differences in home range sizes. However, even though gender differences were small, the combined home-range size of goshawk pairs (N = 10 pairs, $\bar{x}$ = 6,376 ± 1,554 ha) was on average 55 ± 5% greater than that of individual male and female members of pairs (Boal et al. 2003). Boal et al. (2003) speculated that a goshawk pair may exploit a larger area to meet the increasing food demands of growing nestlings. The combined home-range size of pairs may therefore be a better measure of the area required for successful brood rearing. This would suggest that management plans based on estimated home-range sizes of individual goshawks may underestimate the area actually required for successful nesting (Boal et al. 2003).

Variability in home range size estimates among studies may be partially explained by different estimation and data collection methods. Variability due to sex of goshawk and local environmental conditions, however, suggests home ranges need to be assessed at a local or regional scale. Home range size likely varies as a function of regional differences in forest conditions, spatial distribution of forest stands, climate, topography, and local prey availability.

RESIDENCY

The ecology of goshawks during the winter is one of the least understood aspects of the species ecology (Squires and Kennedy, *this volume*). Very little is known about winter movements or habitat requirements of goshawks in the WGLR (Dick and Plumpton 1998). In Minnesota, 26 (93%) of 28 radio-tagged goshawks remained within 7 km of their nest stands, one female moved 87 km, and one female was not relocated during the winter (Boal et al. 2003). With few exceptions, during the period 1999–2001 breeding adult goshawks in Minnesota appeared to be year-round residents, and remained close to their nest stands through the winter (Boal et al. 2003).

Elsewhere in the WGLR, Doolittle (1998) found that two radio-tagged goshawks remained in Wisconsin through the winter, and reported that the size of the male goshawk's use area was 32 km[2]

and the female's was 4 km[2]. Over 95% of the relocation points for the male were in the edges of conifer swamps; Doolittle (1998) speculated that conifer swamps may provide areas of thermal cover for prey during the Wisconsin winter. In the Upper Peninsula of Michigan, Lapinski (2000) reported that two females and a male selected hardwood-conifer mix and swamp fir-swamp conifer cover types and avoided aspen, cedar, hardwood, jack pine, and red-white pine cover types during the non-breeding season.

The pattern of winter residency among goshawks is variable across the species' distribution and this variability suggests goshawks are partial migrants where some individuals maintain year-round occupancy of breeding areas and breeding-season home ranges while other individuals in the population undergo seasonal movements to wintering areas. The proportion of individuals that migrate can vary from 0–100% depending on winter conditions (Dingle 1996). Winter ranges of 18 goshawks in California included nest stands from the previous breeding season (Keane 1999), whereas goshawks in Wyoming moved from their breeding areas (Squires and Ruggerio 1995). In Sweden, male goshawks radio-tagged in late summer and fall near their breeding area tended to remain in the area through the winter, while female goshawks tended to move away (Kenward et al. 1981b, Widén 1985b). It appears that goshawks in the WGLR tend to remain as year-round residents. Although data on winter ecology of goshawks is almost nonexistent in the region, breeding-season and winter habitat, and prey use may differ (Boal et al. 2001). Additional acquisition of region-specific winter data for goshawks remains an important missing component of our understanding of goshawk ecology in the WGLR and throughout the species distribution.

MIGRATION

Data on goshawk migration patterns is derived primarily from counts at migration stations, band returns, and radio-telemetry. These data also suggest goshawks are partial migrants. Sample sizes in migration studies to date, however, have been inadequate to fully understand patterns or routes for North American goshawk populations (Squires and Reynolds 1997, Hoffman et al. 2002). Hoffman et al. (2002) recently analyzed movement patterns of Northern Goshawks encountered at migration stations throughout the western US. Of the 722 goshawks captured from 1980–2001 at these sites only 2.3% of these birds (N = 17) were recaptured or resighted. This low resighting probability is one of the reasons researchers have doubted the utility of using migration counts to estimate goshawk population trends (Titus and Fuller 1990, Kennedy 1997, Kennedy 1998; but see Smallwood 1998 for an alternative view).

Given the caveats associated with migration counts, it is interesting to note that more goshawks are banded at Hawk Ridge in Duluth, Minnesota, than anywhere else in North America (Palmer 1988). Goshawks banded at Hawk Ridge have been recovered in northeastern British Columbia, Alberta, Saskatchewan, Ontario, and Minnesota (Evans 1981, Boal et al. 2003), and during potential irruption years in Missouri, Texas, Arkansas, and Louisiana (Evans and Sindelar 1974, Evans 1981). A female banded at Hawk Ridge in the fall of 1972 was recaptured in the fall of 1982 at Cedar Grove, Wisconsin (Evans 1983) and a male banded at Hawk Ridge in the fall of 1988 was re-captured as a breeding bird in north-central Minnesota in 1999 (Boal et al. 2001).

MORTALITY

The majority of information on causes of mortality among adult goshawks is anecdotal (Squires and Reynolds 1997). Furthermore, a large portion of annual mortality occurs outside the breeding season and therefore is not easily detected (Braun et al. 1996). Still, the primary cause of mortality among free-ranging goshawks appears to be depredation and starvation (Kennedy 2003). For example, Ward and Kennedy (1996) found radio-tagged juveniles goshawks in New Mexico succumbed to predation (50%), accidents and injuries (17%), and disease (8%). Conversely, Dewey and Kennedy (2001) found that most deaths of juvenile goshawks in a Utah population were from starvation or siblicide (a consequence of low food supplies).

Published mortality data for goshawks in the WGLR are based almost solely on females found killed at Wisconsin nests (Erdman et al. 1998) and relocated radio-tagged goshawks found throughout the year in Minnesota (Boal et al. 2005a). Five (56%; four females and one male) of nine (eight radio-tagged) goshawk mortalities in Minnesota occurred during the breeding season (Boal et al. 2005a). Three goshawks were depredated by avian predators and two were preyed upon by mammals (Boal et al. 2005a). Erdman et al. (1998) identified fishers as the cause of mortality for four nesting adult female goshawks in Wisconsin.

Of four winter mortalities documented in Minnesota, one goshawk had been shot, the recov-

ered radio of another had been obviously cut from the body of the goshawk, and the causes of mortality of the remaining two were not determined (Boal et al. 2005a). Furthermore, goshawk mortality in Minnesota occurred with equal frequency in the breeding and winter seasons and, although depredation appeared to be the most significant mortality factor, human persecution may still be a factor affecting goshawk survival despite legal protection (Boal et al. 2005a).

Discounting the single non-radio-marked female, the estimated annual survival rate (estimated using the modification by Pollock et al. [1989] of the Kaplan-Meier [Kaplan and Meier 1958] survival model) of 32 radio-marked goshawks was 74% ± 7.8% (SE) (Boal et al. 2005a). Although their sample size was relatively small for conducting survival analysis, the estimated annual survival rate is quite similar to mark-recapture estimates in California (61–69%; DeStefano et al. 1994b), New Mexico (60–96%; Kennedy 1997) and northern Arizona (69–87%; Reynolds and Joy 1998). All these authors indicate imprecision in their studies due to a variety of reasons, and Kennedy (1997) concluded that precise estimates of survival require large numbers of marked birds (>100), high re-sighting rates, and at least 5 yr of data. Such data have not been collected in the WGLR and are not likely to be collected in the future.

SUMMARY

When comparing goshawks in western North America to those in the WGLR, some differences are immediately apparent. The primary difference is in nesting habitat features due to the differences in landscapes. Goshawks in western North America primarily build nests in conifer trees situated in conifer stands on mountain slopes (Squires and Reynolds 1997). In the WGLR, goshawks typically build nests in deciduous trees in mixed or conifer dominated stands. Although exceptions occur, typically little or no slope exists at nests sites due to the generally level terrain of the region. Nest site canopy cover is similar between the regions, but nest trees in the WGLR appear to be smaller than in the West, probably due to regionally different patterns in species and growing seasons. However, similar to western North America, goshawks in the WGLR build their nests in the largest trees available in stands. In most other respects, the available information suggests little difference between the regions. Similar to western studies (Squires and Reynolds 1997), goshawks in the WGLR appear to remain reasonably close to their breeding areas year-round (Boal et al. 2003).

Productivity in Minnesota was also within the range of that reported for numerous studies in western North America (Squires and Reynolds 1997). Although very few data exist, that available suggests annual survival of goshawks in Minnesota (Boal et al. 2005a) is similar to the West (DeStefano et al. 1994b, Kennedy 1997, Reynolds and Joy 1998). Finally, similar to most other studies (Squires and Reynolds 1997), goshawks in the WGLR appear to have diets dominated by sciurids and leporids, especially red squirrels (Smithers et al. 2005).

RESEARCH NEEDS

A comprehensive report on research and monitoring needs for the Northern Goshawk in the WGLR was prepared by Kennedy and Andersen (1999). Information needs identified in that report have begun to be addressed through recent research, much of which has been summarized in this overview. Development of a more comprehensive understanding of goshawks in the WGLR would be facilitated by sharing results among investigators conducting current survey and monitoring efforts in the region. This would be further enhanced if standards for estimating habitat and demographic parameters were comparable across the region (Kennedy and Andersen 1999). However, as is evident from this paper and other information summaries on goshawks in the WGLR (Dick and Plumpton 1998, Kennedy and Andersen 1999), information on goshawk population dynamics, goshawk-habitat relations, and goshawk-prey interactions is sparse for the region. If this lack of information is to be addressed, research and monitoring priorities for goshawks in the WGLR should include:

1. A region-wide sampling program to locate goshawk nest sites and assess nesting and foraging habitat use. Survey methods developed by Roberson (2001, Roberson et al., unpubl. data) may facilitate nest detections. Radio-telemetry studies from other areas of the WGLR are needed to assess habitat use at local and regional scales. Habitat-use studies require stand-scale information across the region. Although some entities, such as the USDA Forest Service, possess stand age and structure data at a resolution relevant to understanding landscape-level patterns of goshawk habitat use, our study area was comprised of a myriad of land ownerships. The only available landscape data encompassing all ownerships are derived from remote sensing (e.g., LandSat Thematic Mapper). Thematic mapper data provide information only at the resolution of tree-species composition; this is inadequate for examining stand age and structure patterns of goshawk habitat in the WGLR. For example, a goshawk may be interpreted as avoiding a given stand type when, in reality, the hawk avoids it because it is available only at an unsuitable age class. Until stand age and structure data are available for the entire region, assessment of landscape patterns in habitat use will be possible for only a few goshawks, which might unpredictably bias inferences. Developing and compiling landscape level databases that detail stand structure and age should be a priority (Squires and Kennedy, *this volume*).

2. An emphasis on year-round management. Current evidence suggests goshawks are year-round residents in the WGLR (Boal et al. 2003). Thus, conservation plans for goshawks in the WGLR should not be limited to the breeding-season. However, regional winter habitat-use information is non-existent. We suggest radio-telemetry studies be initiated to identify stand characteristics of foraging goshawks year-round and to facilitate location of kill sites to determine winter prey use (Drennan and Beier 2003).

3. An experimental evaluation of the effects of forest management on goshawks (DeStefano 1998, Kennedy 1998). With some planning, we think silvicultural treatments in the vicinity of nests should be used as quasi-experiments (Penteriani and Faiver 2001). Radio telemetry could be used to monitor pre- and post-harvest movements and habitat use of goshawks. Monitoring could include multiple years following treatment to assess goshawk response to forest succession. Such an experimental examination would greatly enhance our ability to predict goshawk responses to silvicultural treatments than has thus far been provided by correlative studies (Kennedy 2003).

4. A collaborative, region-wide approach to monitoring demographics. Existing data are inadequate to determine if WGLR goshawk populations are declining, stationary, or increasing, or to identify habitat conditions that result in sources of goshawk recruitment or in population sinks (Dick and Plumpton 1998). Nest monitoring and methodologies used among projects and researchers have been inconsistent. We suggest that a collaborative effort using a consistent strategy for

monitoring samples of goshawk nests across the WGLR would facilitate an understanding of survival, mortality, and productivity in the region. Greater resolution of population dynamic assessments at the regional scale will require substantial research effort (Kennedy 1997, 1998). The applicability of suggestions by Hargis and Woodbridge (*this volume*) for monitoring goshawks at bioregional scales should be explored for the WGLR.

Studies in Avian Biology No. 31:135–140

GOSHAWKS IN CANADA: POPULATION RESPONSES TO HARVESTING AND THE APPROPRIATENESS OF USING STANDARD BIRD MONITORING TECHNIQUES TO ASSESS THEIR STATUS

FRANK I. DOYLE

Abstract. In this paper, I use the results from current research and from established bird monitoring techniques to highlight the inability of current techniques to establish the status of Northern Goshawk (*Accipiter gentilis atricapillus* and *A. g. laingi*) across Canada. At a national-scale monitoring of goshawks relies upon opportunistic goshawk sightings made during Breeding Bird Surveys (BBS), Christmas Bird Counts (CBC), or during migration counts. These sources indicate that the population trend is either stable (BBS and CBC), or possibly declining (migration counts over last 20–30 yr). However, recent goshawk population studies in western Canada have shown that individual subpopulations respond differently to harvesting of mature forest, with some showing a negative impact, while others appear to be thriving at the same rate of harvest. Work in the undisturbed boreal forests of the Yukon has linked goshawk density and productivity to prey abundance. Differences in the response of goshawk populations to timber harvest may therefore be primarily dependent on the prey available and the habitat used by the prey. Goshawks that are more reliant on prey associated with mature forests showed the greatest impact from harvesting. Across Canada, therefore, population responses to harvesting at the ecosystem level may vary, with the possibility that at the regional or local scale goshawk populations could be lost without this loss being detected by the present non-target monitoring techniques (CBC, BBS, and migration counts). Broad assessment of prey and prey habitat use will help managers to assess the risk to population persistence at regional and local scale.

Key Words: *Accipiter gentilis, laingi*, Canada, harvest, habitat, prey, status, threshold.

GAVILANES EN CANADÁ: RESPUESTAS POBLACIONALES AL APROVECHAMIENTO Y LO APROPIADO DEL USO DE TÉCNICAS ESTANDARIZADAS DE MONITOREO DE AVES PARA EVALUAR SU ESTADO.

Resumen. En este artículo utilizo los resultados de investigación actual, así como técnicas establecidas de monitoreo de aves, para resaltar la inhabilidad de las actuales técnicas para establecer el estado del Gavilán Azor (*Accipiter gentilis atricapillus* y *A. g. laingi*) en Canadá. A escala nacional, el monitoreo de los gavilanes reside en los avistamientos oportunos del gavilán, realizados durante Estudios de Aves Reproductoras (BBS), Conteos de Aves en Navidad (CBC) o durante los conteos de migración. Estos recursos indican que la tendencia de la población, es ya sea estable (BBS y CBC), o posiblemente decadente (conteos de migración durante los últimos 20–30 años). Sin embargo, estudios poblacionales recientes del gavilán en el oeste de Canadá, han mostrado que subpoblaciones individuales responden de forma distinta al cultivo del bosque maduro, algunas mostrando impacto negativo, mientras que otras parecen prosperar durante el cultivo. Trabajo realizado en el bosque boreal no perturbado del Yokon, ha vinculado la densidad y productividad del gavilán a la abundancia de la presa. Diferencias en la respuesta de las poblaciones del gavilán al aprovechamiento de la madera quizás se deban principalmente a la disponibilidad de la presa y al hábitat utilizado por la presa. Gavilanes que dependen más en presas asociadas con el bosque maduro, mostraron el gran impacto que causa el aprovechamiento. Es por esto que en Canadá, las respuestas al aprovechamiento a nivel de ecosistema quizás varíen, con la posibilidad de que las poblaciones de gavilán a escala regional o local se pierdan sin poder detectar dicha pérdida a través de las técnicas de monitoreo actuales de no-blanco (CBC, BBS y conteos de migración). Mayor valoración de la presa, así como de la utilización del hábitat por la presa, ayudarán a los administradores a evaluar el riesgo de la permanencia de la población a escala regional y local.

Goshawks in Canada are distributed throughout the entire forested portion of the landscape, from the US border to tree line in the Arctic, and thus potentially a large portion of the North American goshawk population is resident in Canada. My objective is to determine the status of goshawks across Canada based on all the available information on goshawk populations. In Canada, as in the US, large-scale harvesting of mature forests has taken place throughout the past century and up-to-date information on the present status of the goshawk is required to determine if this identified threat is influencing the status of goshawk population. However, recent long-term goshawk research in the west of Canada has highlighted how inappropriate the standard bird monitoring tools may be in establishing the population status of goshawks across Canada. In this paper I set out the problems associated with the present methodology, and focus on the differing responses of goshawk subpopulations to harvesting. Harvesting and its impact on prey, versus impacts at a nest stand or other factors such as depredation or climate, being identified by the Canadian research studies as likely to be the most critical factor influencing the status of goshawks in Canada. This impact on prey and the differences seen in the scale and type of this impact between forest types indicates that specific monitoring of goshawk populations may be the only accurate method for determining the overall status of this species.

In Canada raptor populations have been monitored by the Canadian Wildlife Service using trend information from breeding bird surveys (BBS), Christmas Bird Counts (CBC) and from migration counts (Hyslop 1995, Kirk and Hyslop 1998, Kennedy 2003). These counts indicate a range in Northern Goshawk (*Accipiter gentilis atricapillus* and *A. g. laingi*) population trends depending on the source with BBS and CBC indicating a relatively stable population, whereas the migration counts have shown a decreasing trend in the numbers of goshawks, which is significant at three of the eight migration stations. No discernible geographic trend was observed.

In contrast to this opportunistic count of goshawks, the last decade has seen several intensive long-term goshawk population studies (Table 1; Fig. 1) taking place in the Yukon, and in British Columbia (BC) (Doyle and Mahon 2001, Doyle 2003, McClaren 2003, Mahon and Doyle 2003a). These studies were designed to quantify the possible impacts to this raptor of harvesting mature forests and have show that goshawk populations react differently to that impact on an ecosystem specific basis. This variation in impacts could potentially result in the loss of goshawks at a local or regional level, an impact that may be unnoticed at a national level if relying on the opportunistic BBS, CBC, and migration counts to monitor population trends. This can occur because the negative responses by goshawks to harvesting in one forest type may be balanced by a positive response in another, such that the coarse opportunistic monitoring fails to detect any significant change. Consequently the habitat thresholds that may negatively impact goshawks may be exceeded in some landscapes, such that the goshawk population is lost without being noticed.

The work showing the potential weakness in relying of non-target species monitoring techniques to monitor goshawk populations has all taken place in western Canada over the past decade. No comparable studies have been conducted elsewhere in Canada. In BC this has included work on two island populations of the threatened goshawk sub-species, the Queen Charlotte goshawk (*A. g. laingi*), while those on mainland BC and in the Yukon are working with the larger *A. g. atricapillus*. The Yukon study took place within an undisturbed northern boreal forest

TABLE 1. LONG-TERM GOSHAWK STUDY AREA IN BRITISH COLUMBIA AND YUKON, CANADA.

Location	Number of goshawk nest areas located	Length of study	Forest type	Nest area spacing (km)
Haida Gwaii-Queen Charlotte islands [a]	9	1995–present	Rain-forest coastal western hemlock	9–15
Vancouver Island [b]	66	1995–present	Rain-forest coastal western hemlock	6–8
Interior BC (Lakes and Morice Forest Districts) [c]	40	1997–present	Sub-boreal spruce and pine	4–5
Interior BC (Kispiox Forest District) [d]	33	1995–present	Interior cedar hemlock	4–5
Yukon [e]	13	1986–1996	White spruce	3 (P)[f] 12 (L)[g]

[a] Doyle 2003.
[b] McClaren 2003.
[d] Mahon and Doyle 2003a, Doyle and Mahon 2001.
[e] Doyle and Smith 1994, Doyle 2000.
[f] P = Years with a peak in prey abundance,
[g] L = Years with low prey abundance.

FIGURE 1. Location of the long-term goshawk study areas in Canada.

ecosystem, while those in BC are all taking place within forest types associated with the southern boreal and coastal rain forest ecosystems that have all seen 30–40% of the mature forest harvested in the last 20–30 yr (Doyle 2003, McClaren and Pendergast 2003, Mahon et al. 2003). These BC studies show very different population responses to harvesting; the rain forest *laingi* may be possibly under threat with declining populations and reduced productivity while *atricapillus,* found in the drier mainland forests, may be benefiting from harvesting, at least in the short-term.

In the Yukon, the Northern Goshawk population was studied intensively at Kluane Lake as part of a long-term boreal forest ecosystem study (Krebs et al. 2001) in which all raptors, their prey, and the environment in which they lived were monitored to establish if and how these ecosystem components were linked together. This study established that goshawks were largely resident and that the number of nests and production of young (Fig. 2) was significantly linked to the abundance of their main prey the snowshoe hare (*Lepus americanus*) and possibly also to grouse, their secondary winter and early breeding

season prey. Rainfall and other factors such as nest depredation by wolverines (*Gulo gulo*; Doyle 1995) and Great Horned Owls (*Bubo virginianus*; Doyle 2000) influenced the breeding success of individual pairs; however, these impacts were insignificant compared to the density of snowshoe hares in winter. In addition, human impacts have also been cited in the past as possibly reducing breeding success at the nest stand level (Squires and Reynolds 1997), and certainly disturbance of any breeding birds can cause breeding attempts to fail. However, an ongoing long-term, adaptive-management experiment at the mainland study sites in BC (Mahon et al. 2003), has to date (3–5 yr post harvest, 73 nest areas) shown no significant impacts, with goshawks continuing to breed successfully even in highly fragmented nest stands. This does not mean a threshold fragmentation or disturbance threshold for some individuals at the nest-stand level does not exist, but it does indicate that this impact is not driving changes in population trends at this stage.

The critical role of prey in the breeding success and the subsequent status of individual goshawk populations may in part be explained by the fact

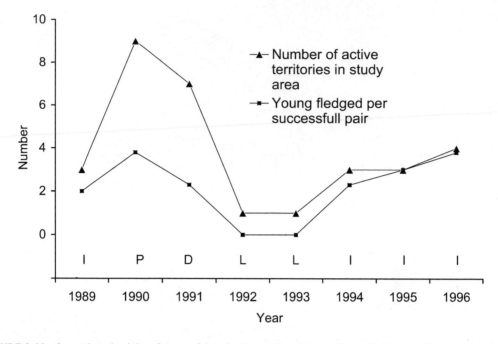

FIGURE 2. Number and productivity of successful goshawk nests in relation to the cyclic phases of the hare and grouse population at Kluane Lake, Yukon. (Doyle 2000). Phases in the abundance of hares and grouse over the period of the 10-yr snowshoe hare cycle: I = Increase, P = Peak, D = Decrease, L = Low.

that in BC as in the Yukon, populations appear to be largely resident. Birds' radio-tagged as breeding adults, and independent goshawk sightings indicate that some, and possibly all, adults and juveniles are resident in the breeding habitat during the winter months. Independent of these observations, birds in all the study locations began to breed in late winter (February–March; Doyle 2000, Mahon et al. 2003), 1–2 mo before spring or summer prey (migrant passerines, young prey or hibernating prey) were available. All birds, independent of their winter movements therefore appear to be largely dependent on the abundance and availability of winter prey to ensure their survival, body condition and subsequent ability to breed, if territories become vacant.

This likely dependence on winter prey has been identified as a possible driving factor in the observed differences in the resilience of goshawk subpopulations to habitat change (Doyle 2003). Within these same study areas in the winter months we see pronounced ecosystem differences in the species, abundance and habitat associations of the available prey (Fig. 3). In BC, two of the four long-term goshawk studies are being conducted on large islands (Haida Gwaii and Vancouver islands) off the west coast. On these islands the winter diet appears as though it may be dominated by

red squirrels (*Tamiasciurus hudsonicus*) and forest grouse, while the dominant winter prey on the mainland, the snowshoe hare, is absent, and other common mainland prey, ptarmigan and grouse, are at relatively low densities. When we then look at where these prey types are found within a landscape we can see clear differences in broad habitat types. Snowshoe hares, grouse, and ptarmigan are typically associated with openings of shrub-young forest (pole sapling), while red squirrels (Mahon and Doyle 2003b), and the island's forest grouse (Zwickle 1992) are most abundant in mature coniferous forest that once dominated the entire landscape (Canning and Canning 1996). Harvesting of the mature forests that dominate these landscapes will therefore likely have very different impacts on the resident goshawk population, depending on the habitat association of their prey in that ecosystem. On the mainland the harvested openings result in habitat (after a shrub layer has formed) in which snowshoe hare and grouse densities are higher than compared to the surrounding mature forest (Mahon and Doyle 2003b). In contrast, these same harvested habitats on Vancouver Island (Ethier 1999, McClaren 2003) and on Haida Gwaii (Doyle 2003) have few prey associated with them in winter and early in the breeding season.

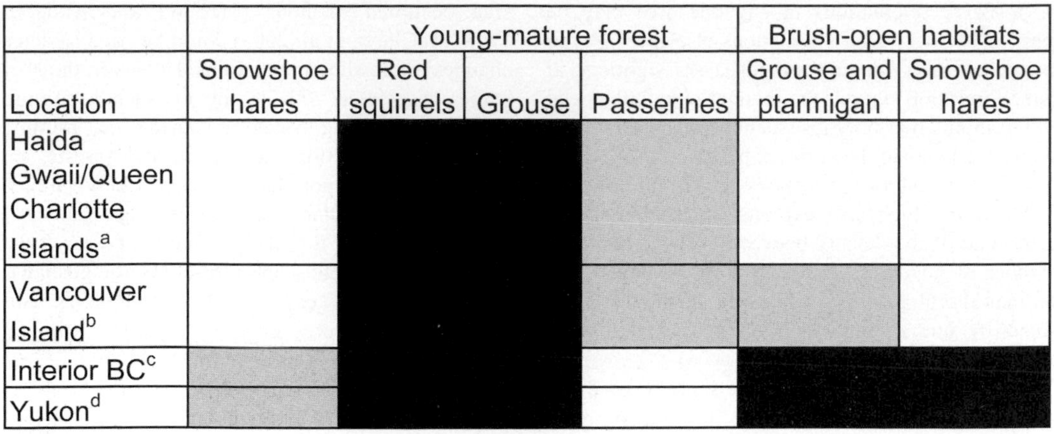

Location	Snowshoe hares	Young-mature forest			Brush-open habitats	
		Red squirrels	Grouse	Passerines	Grouse and ptarmigan	Snowshoe hares
Haida Gwaii/Queen Charlotte Islands[a]	white	black	black	gray	gray	white
Vancouver Island[b]	white	black	black	gray	gray	white
Interior BC[c]	gray	black	black	white	black	black
Yukon[d]	gray	black	black	white	black	black

[a] Doyle 2003.
[b] Ethier 1999.
[c] Mahon and Doyle 2003b.
[d] Doyle and Smith 1994, Doyle 2000.

FIGURE 3. Relationship between the location (ecosystem type), and the association of habitat and the main goshawk prey in late winter. Black = species abundant; gray = species occurs but less abundant; white = species absent.

In mainland versus island we also see different patterns in goshawk productivity and territory spacing which supports this observed link between habitat and prey (Table 1). The mainland territories are at around twice the density of their island counterparts and the annual productivity (both reoccupancy rates and young fledged per breeding attempt) is higher (Doyle 2003). In addition, at the territory scale, harvesting on the mainland has not been seen to reduce breeding success (Mahon et al. 2003), but on Haida Gwaii, in areas with >30% harvesting, no active nests have been located, and on Vancouver Island (McClaren and Pendergast 2003) landscapes with the highest rates of harvesting have significantly lower reoccupancy rates.

How these observed differences in available prey, habitat, and goshawk productivity vary across Canada have not been explored, but they provide the possibility that harvesting combined with individual ecosystem differences could lead to the loss of certain goshawk populations while other populations may remain stable or indeed increase in density. However, this does not mean that we can be complacent even for those populations that appear to be relatively robust. As was seen in the Yukon hare population, which predictably peaks and then crashes cyclically, we have to ensure that enough diversity of habitat types and their associated prey remains to support goshawk population through the low in hare numbers. In particular, sufficient areas of mature forest supporting populations of red squirrels or forest

grouse may be critical to the long-term persistence of goshawks and other predators. Both the Yukon study on goshawks and on another winter resident, the lynx (*Lynx canadensis*), showed a switch to prey typically associated with mature forests (red squirrels and forest grouse) during the low in hare numbers (Krebs et al. 2001). At present, the critical habitat and the threshold in habitat area required to maintain goshawk populations in landscapes in which they largely depend on cyclic prey is unknown. As we have seen the rate of timber harvesting in the goshawk study areas in BC has resulted in 30–40% of the mature forest being cut in the last 20–30 yr. In addition, this harvest has recently been spread across the landscape, such that out of the 73 or more goshawk territories located to date, none have no harvesting at a territory scale, if we assume that nest-area spacing in a landscape (Table 1) indicates the foraging area required by the birds in that landscape. If this rate and spatial arrangement of harvesting is taking place throughout the rest of the province or across large areas of Canada and a threshold in critical habitats does exist, will it allow for the retention of enough critical habitats to ensure the long-term persistence of goshawk populations across much of their range?

Finally, the possibility exists that this could all take place while information from migration stations fails to detect a notable population change at a time when action should be taking place to protect threatened populations at a regional or on a listed sub-species basis. This could occur because declines in goshawk populations in any one area may be masked by increasing populations elsewhere. As an example, large numbers of goshawks sightings at some migration stations are thought to be influenced by the abundance and subsequent population crash of snowshoe hares in the northern boreal forests, a prey species that we know is cyclic (9–11 yr cycle) (Doyle 2000), and which also exhibits a variation in the amplitude of the density between cycles. This large number of goshawks from the northern boreal forest may therefore effectively mask declines brought about by human influences on goshawk carrying capacity of landscapes.

Other broad-scale land-bird surveys methods such as BBS and CBC are likely to be inappropriate goshawk survey methods. BBSs are focused on detection of calling by songbirds, while CBCs are not stratified across regions or habitat types, because they are centered on communities. Most communities, and therefore count sites, are located in southern Canada. In addition they do not specifically target habitat types (forested landscapes in Canada) in which we may expect to locate goshawks in the winter months. As a consequence, the present survey methods may fail to detect any significant population change.

Therefore, we do not know the long-term resilience of individual goshawk populations to habitat change and changes in prey availability outside of few local studies conducted to date in western Canada. Furthermore, a possibility exists that the broad-scale monitoring methods that are being used to monitor goshawk populations across Canada may fail to detect local or regional population declines. Additionally, it may be too late by the time these broad-scale survey methods do detect a decline. If, for example, goshawk a population increases with timber harvesting until a critical threshold is reached and then that population (genetically or regionally) declines sharply, becoming extinct in the worst case scenario. In Canada, as in other areas of North America, standardized broadcast surveys using localized detection probability functions and area occupied methods (McLeod and Andersen 1998, McClaren et al. 2003) could be used to detect changes in breeding populations. However, the challenges associated with setting up such a comprehensive monitoring system in Canada, i.e., training, money, low-detection rates in coastal forests, and cyclic goshawk populations, will likely prevent such a strategic plan being put in place until it is too late. If this is the likely outcome, research that identifies broad landscape thresholds for goshawks within individual ecosystem types based on the habitat and available prey may be necessary. Although necessarily coarse in its assessment this will at least allow landscape managers to assess the risk of their actions to the goshawks population, both at a local and regional scale.

ACKNOWLEDGMENTS

The work on goshawks across Canada is indebted to the help of many organizations and volunteers at both at the provincial and federal level, whose dedication and commitment ensures the collection of the information that comprises the invaluable long-term databases that are provided by the BBS, CBC, and migration counts. In western Canada, the Yukon study on goshawks was funded by the Natural Sciences and Research Council of Canada, and was also indebted to the hard work of many researchers and students, both from Canada and abroad. In BC, the four long-term goshawk studies were supported by BC provincial funding (Forest Renewal, Forest Innovative Account, and the Habitat Conservation Trust Fund.) and through the support of licensees including Babine Forest Products, CANFOR, Huston Forest Products, Skeena Cellulose, Timber West, Western Forest Products, and Weyerhaeuser Ltd. I also thank Erica McClaren for reviewing this manuscript, and finally a special thanks both to her, and to Todd Mahon for sharing with me a passion to understand how we may successfully manage goshawks in harvested landscapes.

Studies in Avian Biology No. 31:141–157

ECOLOGY OF THE NORTHERN GOSHAWK IN FENNOSCANDIA

RISTO TORNBERG, ERKKI KORPIMÄKI, AND PATRIK BYHOLM

Abstract. We reviewed studies on the Northern Goshawk (*Accipiter gentilis*) carried out in northern Europe (Fennoscandia) since the 1950s concerning the following: diet composition, breeding performance, movements, home range, survival, and population trends. Goshawks feed mainly on forest grouse throughout the year in boreal forests but rely more on Ring-necked Pheasants (*Phasianus colchicus*) and hares (*Lepus* spp.) in mixed deciduous-coniferous forests in southern Fennoscandia. Breeding density of the goshawks varies from one–five pairs/100 km², on average three pairs/100 km². Mean clutch size (3.5), brood size (2.8), and productivity of fledglings (2) per occupied territory have remained stable over the decades irrespective of the decline of the forest grouse. Proportion of grouse in the diet as well as breeding output closely followed the density of grouse during the1950s–1970s with relatively dense grouse populations but this close connection has recently disappeared, probably due to a decline of grouse and disappearance of their multi-annual cycles. Goshawks are the most important cause of mortality among forest grouse, and grouse density, in turn, affects the dispersal distances of juvenile goshawks. Because of the narrower diet width of males compared to that of females, males tend to move over longer distances than females. Among adults, females move more than males, like in other raptors. Median distances moved by juveniles range from 50–100 km but some individuals can travel up to >1,000 km. After the dispersal phase, juveniles tend to establish more or less stable ranges before moving to the final breeding range. Not much is known about the site tenacity of breeders but in good conditions males, at least, likely remain on their territories throughout their life. Winter range size varies from 2,000–10,000 ha depending on sex, age, and the quality of the habitat or of the prey size. Juvenile males suffer from higher mortality than juvenile females but this difference disappears by the third year of life. Based on field studies and museum data, roughly one-third of juvenile hawks succumb because of starvation, one-third of trauma or trauma and starvation-disease, and one-fifth to one-third are killed by hunters. Productivity of goshawk populations has not changed during the years of declining trends found in many local studies, which may indicate an increased adult mortality. Annual mortality among the adults may likely not exceed 30% without a decline of the breeding population. The ultimate reason behind declining goshawk populations is likely the change in the forest bird community due to intensified forestry which has negatively affected the populations of main prey, forest grouse. Problems in nourishment of goshawks occur during the winter after migratory birds have moved to south.

Key Words: breeding, cause of death, diet, Fennoscandia, habitat choice, movements, Northern Goshawk, predation, survival.

ECOLOGÍA DEL GAVILÁN AZOR EN FENNOSCANDIA

Resumen. Revisamos estudios sobre el Gavilán Azor *(Accipiter gentilis)* llevados a cabo en el norte de Europa (Fennoscandia) desde 1950, relacionados a lo siguiente: dieta, composición, desempeño de reproducción, movimientos, rango del hogar, sobrevivencia, y tendencias de población. Los gavilanes se alimentaron principalmente de gallo del bosque *(Tetraonidae)* en bosques boreales, durante todo el año, pero dependían más en el Faisán de collar *(Phasianus colchicus)* y liebres *(Lepus spp.)* en bosques deciduos mixtos de coníferas, en el sur de Fennoscandia. La densidad de reproducción del azor varía de uno a cinco pares/100 km², en promedio tres pares /100 km². La media del tamaño de la puesta (3.5), el tamaño de la pollada (2.8) y la productividad de los volantones (2) por territorio ocupado, ha permanecido estable sobre los años, independientemente al decaimiento del gallo del bosque. La proporción del gallo del bosque en la dieta, así como la producción-rendimiento reproductivo, siguieron muy de cerca la densidad del gallo del bosque durante 1950s–1970s, con relativamente poblaciones densas de gallo del bosque, pero esta cercana conexión ha desaparecido recientemente, probablemente debido al decaimiento del gallo del bosque y a la desaparición de sus ciclos multi-anuales. Los Gavilanes son la causa más importante de la mortandad entre los gallos del bosque y de la densidad de los mismos, por lo tanto, influye en las distancias de dispersión de los gavilanes juveniles. Debido a la estrechez en la dieta de los machos, comparada con la de las hembras, los machos tienden a moverse sobre distancias más largas que las hembras. Entre los adultos, las hembras se mueven más que los machos, como en otros raptores. Las distancias medias en las que se mueven los juveniles van desde 50–100 km, pero algunos individuos pueden viajar por arriba de >1,000 km. Después de la fase de dispersión, los juveniles tienden a establecer rangos más o menos estables, antes de pasar al rango final reproductivo. No se conoce mucho acerca de la tenacidad de sitio de los reproductores, pero en buenas condiciones los machos al menos pueden permanecer en sus territorios por toda su vida. El tamaño del área de ocupación durante el invierno varía de

2,000–10,000 ha dependiendo del sexo, la edad y la calidad del hábitat, o del tamaño de la presa Los machos juveniles sufren de una mayor mortandad que las hembras juveniles, pero esta diferencia desaparece al tercer año de vida. Basado en estudios de campo y datos de museos, aproximadamente un tercio de halcones juveniles sucumben debido a inanición, un tercio por trauma o enfermedad de trauma e inanición, y de un quinto a un tercio son matados por cazadores. La productividad de las poblaciones de gavilán no ha cambiado durante los años de tendencias de declinación, encontradas en varios estudios locales, lo cual probablemente indique una incrementada mortandad adulta. La mortandad anual entre los adultos probablemente no exceda de 30%, sin un decaimiento en la población reproductiva. La última razón detrás del decaimiento de las poblaciones de gavilán, es probablemente el cambio en la comunidad de aves de bosque, debido a la intensa actividad forestal, la cual ha afectado negativamente a las poblaciones de la presa principal, gallo del bosque. Problemas en la alimentación del gavilán, ocurren durante el invierno, después de que las aves migratorias se han movido hacia el sur.

The Northern Goshawk (*Accipiter gentilis*) is one of the most numerous raptor species in northern Europe (hereafter Fennoscandia; Fig. 1). Due to its relatively high density and dietary preferences for small game species, especially forest grouse which are favored objects for sport hunting, the Northern Goshawk is probably the most hated species of bird of prey in much of Europe. It has been estimated that 5,000–6,000 goshawks were killed annually in Finland in the 1970s (Moilanen 1976) and 2,000 in the 1960s in Norway (Nygård et al. 1998). In spite that it has been now protected in all countries of North Europe—not until 1989 in Finland—it is still persecuted by humans. Research on Fennoscandian goshawks was initiated from diet investigations carried out in the 1950s in Finland and Sweden (Höglund 1964b, Sulkava 1964) and also in Norway (Hagen 1952). Since then, several studies on food habits during the breeding season have been carried out in Finland (Huhtala 1976, Wikman and Tarsa 1980, Lindén and Wikman 1983, Tornberg and Sulkava 1991, Tornberg 1997), Sweden (Widén 1987), and Norway (Selås 1989). Winter diet has been studied by stomach contents (Höglund 1964b)

FIGURE 1. Map of Fennoscandia showing main study sites of Northern Goshawks. 1. Sulkava (1964), 2. Höglund (1964a), 3. Huhtala (1976), 4. Lindén and Wikman (1983), 5. Kenward et al. (1981b), 6 Widén (1987), 7. Selås (1997a), 8. Kenward et al. (1999), 9. Tornberg (1997), 10. Nygård et al. (1998), 11. Byholm et al. 2003), and 12. R. Tornberg, E. Korpimäki, V. Reif, S. Jungell and S. Mykrä (unpubl. data).

and by radio tracking since the late 1970s in Sweden (Kenward et al. 1981, Widén 1987) and in Finland (Tornberg and Colpaert 2001). Breeding performance of goshawks is also well documented in all North European countries; most long-term studies have been carried out in Finland (Sulkava 1964, Lindén and Wikman 1980, Huhtala and Sulkava 1981, Lindén and Wikman 1983, Tornberg and Sulkava 1991, Sulkava et al. 1994, Byholm et al. 2002a) but also in Sweden (Widén 1985b, Kenward et al. 1999) and Norway (Selås 1997b). A countrywide survey of grouse was started in Finland in 1964, which enables a more accurate estimation of goshawk impact on grouse (Lindén and Wikman 1983, Tornberg 2001). In Sweden, an evaluation was done by Widén (1987). In farmland areas of Sweden, goshawks hunt pheasants more than grouse; Kenward et al. (1981b) estimated the impact of goshawk predation on released and wild pheasant stocks in central Sweden in the late 1970s.

Because goshawks use the same nesting territories year after year, they have become a popular species with bird banders. Around 2,000 goshawk nestlings are currently banded annually in Finland, mostly by volunteers. As a result, recovery rates of goshawks have been one of the highest among the banded birds (nearly 50,000 being banded since 1913 when bird banding was started in Finland; Valkama and Haapala 2002, Byholm et al. 2003). When shooting of goshawks was allowed, around 20% of banded goshawks were later recovered. These days recovery rates are around 10%. Total number of recoveries in Finland now exceeds 8,000 birds (Valkama and Haapala 2002) and similar situations prevail in Sweden and Norway. These large databases have enabled several analyses of movements, mortality, and causes of death of goshawks in all Fennoscandian countries (Haukioja and Haukioja 1971, Saurola 1976, Marcström and Kenward 1981a, Widén 1985b, Halley 1996, Byholm et al. 2003), as well as more specific studies on, e.g., sex allocation of goshawks in relation to varying environmental conditions (Byholm et al. 2002a, 2002b). As an easily trappable species, banded goshawks are often captured alive which has given more insight to their movements (Marcström and Kenward 1981b, Neideman and Schönebeck 1990). Large radio-tracking projects in central Sweden in 1970–1980 were also based on extensive live trapping that gave light to patterns of age- and condition-related movements (Kenward et al. 1981a). Pooling data from breeding performance, survival, and movements of an animal population facilitates building a population model. On the large Baltic Sea island of Gotland, Sweden, this was done

using productivity data of breeding goshawks combined with extensive radio-tagging of juvenile and adult goshawks (Kenward et al. 1991, 1999).

Goshawks have also been an ideal species for museum work due to large collections of specimens in zoological museums. Earliest studies were on taxonomic aspects (Voipio 1946) and later killed and naturally dying birds were studied in relation to changes in morphology (Tornberg et al. 1999), causes of death (Tornberg and Virtanen 1997), or body condition (Marcström and Kenward 1981a, Sunde 2002).

In this paper we summarize all noteworthy published papers on the ecology of Northern Goshawks in Finland, Sweden, and Norway. We attempt to document the goshawk's position in those areas based on past and current studies and to conclude and predict the future development of goshawk populations, as well as to outline future needs in research. We add also some previously unpublished data on diet, breeding, and home range size collected near Oulu in northern Finland during 1987–2003. For a description of this study area and the methods, see Tornberg (1997) and Tornberg and Colpaert (2001).

STUDY AREA

Fennoscandia is composed of three north European countries, Norway, Sweden, Finland, and parts of western Russia (Kola peninsula and Russian Karelia). Although situated between latitudes 55–70° N this area is mainly characterized by boreal forests (between latitudes 60–70° N) and mixed coniferous-deciduous forests in southern Sweden and Norway (between latitudes 55–60° N). The northernmost parts of Finland and the Scandinavian mountain range, Köli, belong to the arctic zone. All important goshawk studies carried out in the area are shown in Fig. 1.

CHARACTERS OF THE FENNOSCANDIAN GOSHAWK

Scandinavian goshawks belong to the nominate race *Accipiter gentilis gentilis*. Finland is a transition zone between the nominate race and the eastern paler and larger *A. g. buteoides* (Voipio 1946). Finnish goshawks are larger than Swedish ones based on both body mass and wing length indicating that Finnish goshawks belong to the larger *buteoides* race (Table 1). Winter weights in Sweden are derived from extensive trapping of goshawks in central and southern Sweden (Marcström and Kenward 1981b). Weights of Finnish hawks were obtained

TABLE 1. AVERAGE MEASUREMENTS TAKEN FROM SWEDISH AND FINNISH GOSHAWKS. DATA FROM SWEDEN BY MARCSTRÖM AND KENWARD (1981A) AND FROM FINLAND BY TORNBERG ET AL. (1999) AND TORNBERG (UNPUBL. DATA).

	Central Sweden				Northern Finland			
	Male	N	Female	N	Male	N	Female	N
Winter weight adult	866	52	1,328	60	933	12	1,485	18
Winter weight juvenile	839	289	1,229	215	828	11	1,384	21
Wing length adult	323	37	366	69	330	26	372	29
Wing length juvenile	323	308	363	197	327	79	367	86

from trapped birds in Oulu during 1990–1999. Wing lengths were measured from the flexed wrist to the end of longest primary with feathers flattened and straightened.

DIET

BREEDING SEASON

A major proportion of the diet of the goshawk was woodland grouse (*Tetraonidae*) in all food habit investigations in Fennoscandia (Höglund 1964b, Sulkava 1964, Huhtala 1976, Lindén and Wikman 1983, Widén 1987, Selås 1989, Tornberg 1997). Four grouse species are preyed upon by goshawks—Capercaillie (*Tetrao urogallus*), Black Grouse (*Tetrao terix*), Hazel Grouse (*Bonasa bonasia*), and Willow Grouse (*Lagopus lagopus*).

Grouse proportions in the goshawk diet are highest in western Finland declining to the west and south (Table 2). It must be remembered that proportions of grouse in diet studies based on the collection of prey remains may depend whether remains were collected only in the nest or also in the vicinity of the nest and whether the two groups are pooled (Sulkava 1964). Proportions of grouse in the diet at the beginning of the nesting season may be up to 80% but tend to decline later in the breeding season (Table 2). However, depending on the collection method, the proportion of soft and digestible grouse chicks might easily be underestimated in the diet (Höglund 1964b, Sulkava 1964, Grønnesby and Nygård 2000). Recently, with grouse numbers lower than in the 1950s, grouse proportions actually declined during the breeding season when more vulnerable prey, like juvenile corvids and smaller passerine birds,

TABLE 2. DIET COMPOSITION OF GOSHAWKS DURING THE BREEDING SEASON IN DIFFERENT LOCALITIES IN FENNOSCANDIA. UPPER ROW FOR EACH PREY SPECIES OR GROUP = DIET COMPOSITION DURING THE NEST-BUILDING AND INCUBATION PERIODS AND LOWER ROW = DIET DURING THE NESTLING PERIOD. GROUSE CHICKS ARE FOUND ONLY DURING THE NESTLING PERIOD.

	Locality[a]						
	1	2	3	4	5	6	7
Grouse adult	63.7		20.4	72.6	56.3	29.7	
	11.1	4.8	5.0	14.9	24.7	(14.5)[d]	14.0
Grouse juvenile	43.3	14.1		23.4	9.6		
Corvids	5.3		8.4		10.0	26.2	
	10.5	23.9	17.6	7.0	11.4	28.3	15.0
Other birds	9.0		49.5	(13.5)[b]	22.1	29.9	
	19.6	47.0	68.5	51.6	38.8	42.8	68.0
European red squirrel	15.2		12.5		4.7		
(*Sciurus vulgaris*)	10.2	7.9	5.1	0.8	6.3		
Other mammals	6.8		9.2	(14.0)[c]	6.9	(14.3)[c]	
	2.0	1.8	3.7	2.3	9.2	(14.5)	(3.0)[b]
Unidentified	3.2						
N	664		535	2101	557	462	
	342	772	641	128	649	442	367

[a] Location and source of data: 1. western Finland 1949–1959 (Sulkava 1964), 2. central Sweden. 1954–1959 (Höglund 1964b), 3. southern Finland 1977–1981 (Wikman and Tarsa 1980), 4. north-western Finland 1963–1976 (Huhtala 1976), 5. northern Finland 1965–1988 (Tornberg and Sulkava 1991), 6. central Sweden 1977–1981 (Widén 1985a), and 7. southern Norway 1983–1988 (Selås 1989).
[b] Includes corvids.
[c] Includes squirrels.
[d] Includes grouse chicks.

become available (Lindén and Wikman 1983, Selås 1989, Tornberg 1997). As grouse chicks grow, they become more and more profitable as prey and their proportion of the diet can increase up to 50% toward the autumn (Tornberg 1997).

The Black Grouse is generally the most important grouse species by number and biomass in the diet of goshawks (Huhtala 1976, Widén 1987, Selås 1989, Tornberg 1997). In Oulu (Fig. 1), its proportion during the breeding season was 25–30%. In more southern parts of the boreal forests, however, Hazel Grouse may be more important (Sulkava 1964, Lindén and Wikman 1983). When analyzing dietary proportions against availability in the field, the small grouse species, Willow Grouse and Hazel Grouse weighing 0.3–0.7 kg, may be preferred over the larger Black Grouse weighing 0.9–1.3 kg (Tornberg 1997). Large Capercaillies are relatively rare in goshawks' diet, limited to females weighing 2 kg during the breeding season. The proportion of mammals in the diet of goshawks varies between 10–20% in most studies. The most common mammal species is the European red squirrel (*Sciurus vulgaris*) whose proportion can sometimes reach 30%, particularly in poor grouse years (Sulkava 1964). Young mountain hares (*Lepus timidus*) are numerically the second most important mammalian prey but by biomass they can exceed red squirrels (Tornberg 1997). Interestingly, young

mountain hares were very rare prey specimens in the 1950s (Sulkava 1964).

The well-documented decline of forest grouse in Finland (Lindén and Rajala 1981, Väisänen et al. 1998) has affected prey choice of goshawks. Changes of grouse density in the province of Oulu in northern Finland and the corresponding proportion of grouse in the diet of goshawks are presented in Fig. 2. A second order polynomial gave the best fit for both the grouse density ($r^2 = 0.587$, $F = 24.870$, $P < 0.001$) and proportions of grouse in the diet in spring ($r^2 = 0.476$, $F = 11.353$, $P = 0.003$). It seems that grouse are slowly recovering from the long-term decline. Correspondingly, goshawks have quickly responded to this recovery. During grouse lows, goshawks attempt to switch to preying more on corvids, thrushes, and pigeons (Tornberg and Sulkava 1991, Sulkava 1999). Interestingly, these species form the main diet of the goshawk in central Europe (Opdam et al. 1977, Toyne 1997); grouse are usually not found in the diet there but *Phasianidae* can sometimes form a considerable proportion in the diet (Manosa 1994).

WINTER DIET

Systematically collected data on goshawk's winter diet are still scarce. Höglund (1964b) analyzed stomach contents in the 1950s–1960s in Sweden

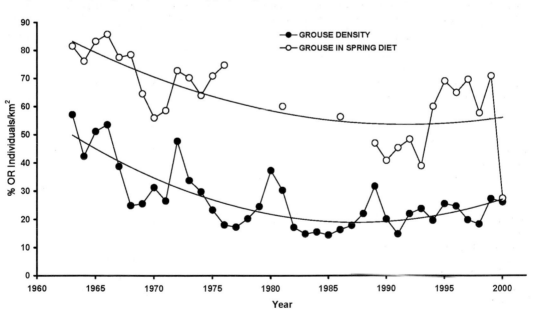

FIGURE 2. Density changes of forest grouse in the province of Oulu in northern Finland and corresponding proportions of grouse in the diet of the Northern Goshawk in spring. Density data for grouse were obtained from grouse censuses by the Finnish Game Research Institute and data for goshawk diets from the 1960s and 1970s are from Huhtala (1976) and for the 1980s and 1990s are from Tornberg and Sulkava (1991) and Tornberg (unpubl. data).

(N = 130), and found that the proportion of grouse was only 8%, i.e., less than half of that in the summer diet whereas the proportion of mammals increased from 10–35%. Later studies carried out by radio tracking in Sweden partly confirmed Höglund's findings. In the winters 1977–1981, red squirrels alone comprised 84% (N = 61) of goshawks' winter diet in central Sweden (Widén 1987). In agricultural areas of central Sweden, goshawks killed mainly red squirrels (33%), Ring-necked Pheasants (23%) and European hares (*Lepus europaeus*) (14%) that were killed only by females (Kenward et al. 1981b). Due to the large size of hares (3–3.5 kg), they accounted for 37% of the food intake by females, whereas males got 43% of their food from pheasants but females only 3%. Based on a radio-tracking study in northern Germany, goshawks killed mostly pheasants (41%) and rabbits (*Oryctolagus cuniculus*) (27%, N = 145) during winter (Ziesemer 1983). In northern Finland, a radio-tracking study during 1991–1995 revealed that dietary proportion by number of mountain hares and red squirrels was 55% (N = 55) and the biomass of hares alone was 70% (Tornberg and Colpaert 2001). Mountain hares were killed only by females. Correspondingly, as in farmlands, males hunted red squirrels and grouse more than females did. We present here the combined data of Tornberg and Colpaert

(2001) and new winter diet data from the vicinity of Oulu during 1999–2002. Excluding predation events near human settlements and a dump site where brown rats (*Rattus norvegicus*) were prey, the proportion of grouse was almost the same as in summer diet (37.6 % vs. 34.2%; Tornberg and Sulkava 1991; Table 3). Diet differed between the sexes in spite of few data being available for analysis. In farmland areas of central Sweden, an intersexual difference was found only for hares (Kenward et al. 1981b) but no difference was found in woodland areas (Widén 1987). During the breeding season, diets of the sexes were not found to differ substantially (Grønnesby and Nygård 2000).

FUNCTIONAL RESPONSE

When diet proportion or kill rate of a predator is plotted against the number of prey individuals, a functional response curve is obtained. Holling (1959) described three curve types: increase in the prey consumption of the predator may be linear (type I), convex (type II), or concave (type III) as a function of prey number. A type II curve is found when consumption in low prey density increases more rapidly than the number of prey and a type III curve occurs when consumption in low densities

TABLE 3. WINTER DIET OF GOSHAWKS IN THE OULU AREA, NORTHERN FINLAND. DATA ARE BASED ON PUBLISHED RESULTS BY TORNBERG AND COLPAERT (2001) DURING 1991–1995 AND TORNBERG (UNPUBL. DATA) DURING 1999–2002.

	Weight classes [a]	Male		Female		Total	
		N	%	N	%	N	%
Mountain hare adult	E			17	38.6	17	27.9
Capercaillie male (*Tetrao urogallus*)	E			2	4.5	2	3.3
Capercaillie female	D			1	2.3	1	1.6
Mountain hare juvenile	D	1	5.9			1	1.6
Black Grouse male (*Tetrao tetrix*)	D			6	13.6	6	9.8
Black Grouse female	C	3	17.6	2	4.5	5	8.2
Willow Grouse (*Lagopus lagopus*)	C			1	2.3	1	1.6
Hazel Grouse (*Bonasa bonasia*)	B	4	23.5	4	9.1	8	13.1
European red squirrel (*Sciurus vulgaris*)	B	6	35.3	9	20.5	15	24.6
Great Spotted Woodpecker (*Dendrocopos major*)	A	1	5.9			1	1.6
Crossbill (*Loxia curvirostra*)	A	1	5.9			1	1.6
Small passerine	A	1	5.9			1	1.6
Small mammals	A			2	4.5	2	3.3
Totals		17		44		61	

[a] Weight classes of prey: A = 0–100 g, B = 100–500 g, C = 500–1,000 g, D = 1,000–2,000 g, E = >2,000 g.

increases slower than number of prey. All curve types level off at high prey densities because the predator becomes satiated. Curve types predict different outcomes for the stability in the predator-prey interaction. Type II tends to destabilize and type III to stabilize prey population (Holling 1959, Begon et al. 1996).

Based on the existing studies in Finland and Sweden, goshawks' functional response may be concave (Lindén and Wikman 1983), convex (Wikman and Tarsa 1980, Tornberg and Sulkava 1991), or only a weak response (Widén 1985a, Tornberg 2001). It is likely that goshawks show a type III response for grouse in southern areas of Fennoscandia where they are less dependent on grouse as a stable food and where alternative prey is richly available. Whereas in the north, where grouse form the major part in the diet and alternative prey are scarce, a concave or no response is found.

BREEDING OUTPUT OF GOSHAWKS

Breeding Density and Quality of the Breeders

Because goshawks use the same breeding sites fairly regularly year after year, breeding densities in intensively studied areas can be reliably estimated. Reliability is also increased by the fact that breeding territories are very regularly spaced in a continuous woodland area (Widén 1985b, Selås 1997b). In southern Norway, mean distances during 1980–1990 varied from 4.5–5.4 km (Selås 1997b). In the vicinity of Oulu, distance between regularly occupied territories was around 4 km (Tornberg 2001). Studies carried out in western and southern Finland during the 1950–1970s show that goshawk density was around five pairs/100 km^2 when all nests studied were active (Huhtala and Sulkava 1981). In more restricted coastland areas of south Finland a breeding density of five–eight goshawk pairs/100 km^2 was reported during 1977–1983 (Forsman and Solonen 1984). Breeding density may have declined since the 1970s and is probably around three pairs/100 km^2 at present in large parts of Fennoscandia (Widén 1997). In the vicinity of Oulu, breeding density is, however, still around five territories/100 km^2 (Tornberg 2001), but due to a yearly average occupancy rate of about 80%, real breeding density falls to four pairs/100 km^2 and recently even lower (R. Tornberg, unpubl. data). For comparison, densities in central and southern Europe tend to be higher but varying considerably depending on the area, e.g., in northwest Germany from 3.6–7.4 pairs/100 km^2 (Krüger and Stefener 1996) and in central Poland from 9–13.9 pairs/km^2 (Olech 1998).

Physiologically, goshawks are able to breed as yearlings. In reality this takes place in females but not in males that likely can not provide enough food for the females during the courtship phase. On the island of Gotland, males and females entered the breeding population in the second year (Kenward et al. 1991). Their proportion among breeders was <10%. Females did not breed as yearlings due to a saturated breeding population but had to wait for vacancies in their second year of life. In western Finland and in the Oulu area, percentage of females breeding as yearlings was about 5–10% annually (P. Byholm and R. Tornberg, unpubl. data).

Clutch and Brood Sizes

Goshawks start breeding very early in spring; nest building can be initiated in mild winters and in good food conditions by late February (Huhtala and Sulkava 1981). Initiation of nesting is likely connected with the start of breeding by grouse, which is stimulated by high temperatures (Nielsen and Cade 1990). Start of egg laying takes place in western Finland around 20 April (Sulkava 1964, Huhtala and Sulkava 1981, Tornberg 1997, Byholm et al. 2002a). Yearly average clutch size can vary from 2–4 depending on food conditions, usually the availability of grouse (Byholm 2005). Based on extensive data from western Finland during good grouse years in 1960s–1970s mean clutch size was 3.51 (± 0.06, N = 164; Huhtala and Sulkava 1981). In the vicinity of Oulu, yearly clutch size during poor grouse years in 1988–2002 varied from 2.9–4.2, ($\bar{x} = 3.59 \pm 0.07$, N = 148). Consequently, grouse density seems not to strongly determine the mean clutch size, although high peaks or deep lows of grouse usually are reflected in the clutch size (Sulkava 1964, Huhtala and Sulkava 1981, Sulkava et al. 1994). Clutch size declines significantly with the postponing of the start of egg laying (Huhtala and Sulkava 1981, Sulkava et al. 1994, Byholm et al. 2002a). In lowland Britain, clutch size seem to higher than in Finland 3.96 (± 0.11, N = 47; Anonymous 1990), but is, on average, the same in central Poland (3.54, N = 143; Olech 1998).

Brood size in large data sets is always about 0.5–0.6 lower than clutch size due to partial brood loss (Byholm 2005) Hence, average brood size in western Finland has varied in the 1950–1970s in data collected in different localities, from 2.78–3.13 (Huhtala and Sulkava 1981). In the vicinity of Oulu, during 1988–2002, average brood size was 2.89 (± 0.12, N = 163). Mean brood size for whole Finland during 1989–1998 was 2.79 (± 0.05, N =

2,822; Byholm et al. 2002a). Hence, it seems that mean brood size has not declined since the 1950s in Finland although numbers of main prey, grouse, have decreased remarkably since then (Lindén and Rajala 1981). This is not necessarily surprising because alternative prey (migratory birds) is richly available during summer. Greatest mortality in goshawks' broods takes place soon after hatching when the youngest nestling in the brood usually dies or one egg does not hatch (Sulkava 1964, Huhtala and Sulkava 1981, Anonymous 1990, Byholm 2005). Mortality is higher in nests originally having four eggs than those having three eggs (Byholm 2005). Mortality is relatively low during the post-fledging dependence period. Interestingly, goshawk brood size is spatially well synchronized over large area up to over 300–400 km (Ranta et al. 2003). In England, brood size based on a small data set collected over several years was somewhat lower than in Finland 2.76 (± 0.16, N = 45; Anonymous 1990), but higher in central Poland 2.91 (N = 400; Olech 1998).

Goshawk nestlings leave the nest at the age of 44–46 d (Kenward et al. 1993a) and reach independence at the age of 75–82 d (Kenward et al. 1993b). In the vicinity of Oulu, where mean hatching date is 1 June, young goshawks leave their nesting territory around mid-August. Reaching independence means a jump in the mortality of young goshawks, which continues high during the first winter as illustrated by

the accumulation of dead goshawks to the Zoological Museum of the University of Oulu (Fig. 3). This has been verified by a large radio-tracking project on Gotland (Kenward et al. 1999). Adult mortality peaked in late winter-early spring (Haukioja and Haukioja 1971).

OCCUPANCY RATE AND PRODUCTIVITY

In birds of prey using serviceable breeding sites—old stick-nests, cliffs, or nest-boxes—occupancy rate counted as breeding sites used per sites available gives a reasonable estimate of size of the breeding population (Forsman and Solonen 1984). Populations of birds living in stable and predictable conditions can also be stable from year to year (Hunt 1998). Goshawks living in northern areas and having high winter mortality very seldom fill serviceable breeding sites for long periods. In southern Finland, mean occupancy rate was 68% in an 8-yr study of around 30 territories checked annually (Lindén and Wikman 1983). In a long-term study carried out in western Finland during 1979–1996, mean occupancy rate was 45% (Hakkarainen et al. 2004, Tornberg et al. 2005). In this study, the number of territories checked annually increased from 16 to 173 during the study. In the vicinity of Oulu, the corresponding figure was 83% during 1987–2003; number of territories annually checked increased from

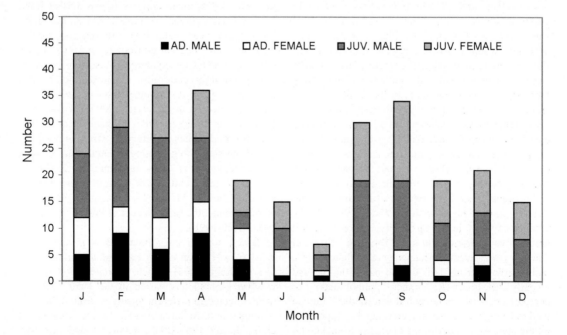

FIGURE 3. Number of Northern Goshawks accumulated monthly by the Zoological Museum of University of Oulu, 1964–2003.

10–32. In the study area at Oulu, occupancy rate declined strongly but remained stable in study area of western Finland (Hakkarainen et al. 2004) during the study years. Declining occupancy rates during a long study may depend on the improving familiarity of the research area in the course of investigation when less used territories are discovered. It is not surprising that in the western Finland study area the number of occasionally used territories increased during the study years (Hakkarainen et al. 2004).

Productivity is measured as young produced per breeding pair, i.e., per occupied territory (Steenhof 1987). Productivity in the previous studies varied from 1.8–2.1. Annual variation was substantial, being highest in southern Finland (C.V = 32.3%) and lowest in western Finland (C.V = 17.1%). In the vicinity of Oulu, C.V. was 22.6%. Productivity on Gotland during 1977–1981 was much lower at 1.36 young/occupied territory (Kenward et al. 1999). Even farther south in northwest Germany, Kruger and Stefener (1996) reported productivity to vary between 0.5–1.8. In central Poland, in a long-term study, it was fairly high at 2.25 (Olech 1998). Obviously, goshawks tend to compensate for higher mortality by man/natural causes or both in the north and east by higher productivity (see Kenward et al. 1991)

Numerical Response

It is not surprising that breeding output as estimated by average clutch and brood sizes follows the population density of grouse. Breeding attempts of goshawks failed almost totally after a very cold winter and poor grouse population in western Finland in 1956 (Linkola 1957, Sulkava 1964). No obvious differences were found in the mean clutch and brood sizes between good grouse years in 1950–1970s and relatively poor grouse years in the 1980–1990s. Yet, yearly clutch and brood sizes tend to follow grouse population fluctuations (Lindén and Wikman 1980), usually with a 1-yr time lag (Sulkava et al. 1994). Connection between grouse population density and goshawks' breeding output seems to be strongest in central and zone of the boreal forest (Lindén and Wikman 1980, Sulkava et al. 1994, Tornberg et al. 2005) while it seems to disappear in southern zone of boreal forest (Lindén and Wikman 1983). In Norway, breeding success of goshawks seems not to follow grouse fluctuations but may be indirectly linked with multi-annual vole cycles (Selås and Steel 1998).

Clutch and brood sizes may often poorly represent the dynamics of the whole goshawk population. We did not find any obvious correlation between brood size of goshawks and grouse density in Oulu area

during the 1990s. Better estimates in this sense may be population productivity and occupancy rate that also take into account the failed pairs (Steenhof 1987). In the Oulu area, population productivity closely followed the density variation of grouse until 1996 (r = 0.863, N = 10, P <0.001), but thereafter the connection disappeared (Fig. 4). Yet, the overall correlation during the whole study period was significant (r = 0.558, N = 17, P <0.05). In addition, a positive correlation (r = 0.549, N = 19, P<0.05) between grouse density and territory occupancy rate of goshawks with a 2-yr lag was found in western Finland in a long-term study during 1979–1996 (Tornberg et al. 2005). Similar relationship seems to prevail between winter censuses of goshawks and multi-annual fluctuations of forest grouse (Tornberg and Väisänen, unpubl. data). However, we found no correlation between occupancy rate of goshawks and density indices of grouse in the Oulu area with any time lags. A reason for these discrepancies in brood size and occupancy rates may be the decline of grouse populations and disappearance of the multi-annual cycles in grouse population fluctuation (see Fig. 2).

GOSHAWK PREDATION ON GROUSE—TOTAL RESPONSE

Pooling functional and numerical responses yields a total response or kill rate of the predator to varying densities of prey. Predation impact is defined as a function of kill rate to density of prey. Further, predation rate is obtained when predation impact is plotted against density of prey. (Keith et al. 1977, Lindén and Wikman 1983; Korpimäki and Norrdahl 1989, 1991). Three studies of the goshawk's predation impact on woodland grouse (Lindén and Wikman 1983, Widén 1987, Tornberg 2001) and one study on pheasants (Kenward 1977, Kenward et al. 1981a) have been carried out in Fennoscandia. Lindén and Wikman (1983) reported that goshawks took 12% of the adult Hazel Grouse in southern Finland during the 4-mo breeding season; on an annual basis predation impact would be 36%. In central Sweden, territorial goshawks killed 14% of Black Grouse males and 25% of females during the breeding season, but during winter, predation on grouse was negligible (Widén 1987). A grouse study carried out in the same area by radio-tagged birds gave almost the same mortality estimate (20%) for Black Grouse females during the breeding season (Angelstam 1984). In northern Finland, goshawks prey on all four available grouse species (Tornberg 2001). Based on a recent predation estimate for the breeding season, goshawks killed 22% of Willow

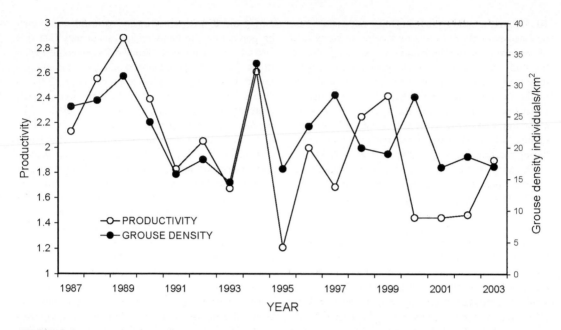

FIGURE 4. Productivity of the Northern Goshawk population and grouse density of the previous autumn in the Oulu area from 1987–2003.

Grouse, 16% of Hazel Grouse, 9% male Black Grouse, 14% of female Black Grouse, 4% female Capercaillies, and 7% of grouse chicks. On an annual basis, numbers for adult grouse were almost the same (Tornberg 2001). It seems that the goshawk is the most important predator of adult grouse during the breeding season accounting for 30–50% of adult grouse mortality excluding large Capercaillies (Widén 1987, Tornberg 2001). Impact of winter predation by the goshawks on woodland grouse is still unresolved due to incomplete and small data sets on winter diet, but in most years it might be as large as mortality during the breeding season.

Goshawks kill substantial numbers of pheasants in southern Fennoscandia, their predation impact being strongly density dependent. Where wild pheasant stocks prevail, loss by goshawk predation was 55% for females and 18% for males, but where captive-born pheasants were released, losses were substantially higher, goshawks were responsible for 90% of kills during the winter (Kenward 1977, Kenward et al. 1981b). Predation studies usually neglect the impact by non-breeders, which can be considerable in years of increasing and high predator populations (Rohner 1996). Healthy raptor populations should minimally contain around 30–40% non-breeders (Hunt 1998).

Elsewhere, we (Tornberg 2001, Tornberg et al. 2005) have suggested that goshawk predation may have a destabilizing effect on grouse population

due to obvious time lags in numerical response of goshawks to varying grouse densities and a high proportion of grouse in the diet also during poor grouse years (Fig. 5). In this sense, the predation impact of goshawks on forest grouse appears to be similar to the predation impact of Gyrfalcons (*Falco rusticolus*) on ptarmigans (*Lagopus* spp.) in Iceland (Nielsen 1999). The lagging numerical response of goshawks to varying densities of grouse is obviously different from numerical responses of various vole-eating owls and raptors to multi-annual vole cycles in Fennoscandia, because their numerical responses track varying vole densities without obvious time lags (Korpimäki 1985, 1994). In conditions more natural than the present in northern European boreal forests, goshawks may have had a remarkable role in driving grouse cycles.

MOVEMENTS OF GOSHAWKS

The goshawk is regarded as a resident raptor but individuals in their first year of life are mobile and some of them show directional movement southward in autumn and northward in spring (Marcström and Kenward 1981b). These movements can take young birds >1,000 km from their natal areas (Sulkava 1964, Saurola 1976, Halley 1996). However, most of the birds do not orient systematically southward but disperse randomly around their natal area (Sulkava 1964, Saurola 1976, Marcström and Kenward

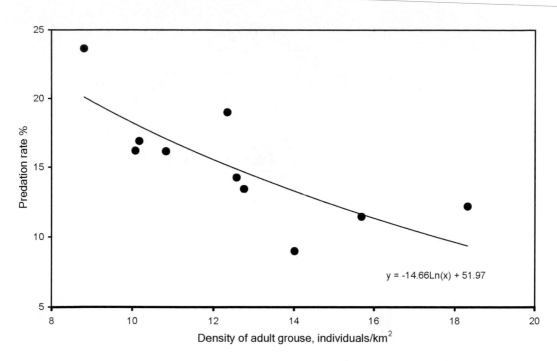

FIGURE 5. Predation rate by the Northern Goshawk on adult grouse in the Oulu area, 1989–1998 (redrawn from Tornberg 2001).

1981b, Halley 1996, Byholm et al. 2003). Sulkava (1964) showed that dispersal distances of the young goshawks were negatively related to abundance of grouse in the natal area. Byholm et al. (2003) confirmed this finding recently and also showed that birds in late broods dispersed farthest, especially males. Dispersal distances also seem to be related to sex and age. Juvenile males tend to be most mobile (Kenward et al. 1981b, Marcström and Kenward 1981, Neideman and Schönbeck 1990, Byholm et al. 2003, but see Halley 1996). Median distance for male hawks banded as nestlings and found dead during the first winter after reaching the independence was 80 km but only 34.5 km for females (N = 213; Byholm et al. 2003). In Norway, however, females moved more (median 109 km) than males (median 68.5 km, N = 77; Halley 1996). Hawks found dead in adult plumage had moved less far than those found as juveniles (Halley 1996, Byholm et al. 2003). Because birds could not be tracked, this may hint at return movements to the natal area after maturity (Halley 1996). Distance traveled by adults of both sexes tends to be the reverse of that found in juveniles. A similar tendency has been found also in radio-tracking studies (Kenward et al. 1981b) and when trapping and banding hawks after the breeding season (Marcström and Kenward 1981). Figure 6

illustrates the spread of juvenile goshawks banded as nestlings in the Oulu area. Most birds are found on the coastline of Bothnia Bay, Baltic Sea. Long-distance travelers seem to have moved in various directions.

Higher mobility of juvenile males than females is also apparent in trapping results from southern Sweden (Neidemen and Schönebeck 1990). A reason may be that food supply for males is lower than that for females. Tornberg (2000) estimated that food base of females is three times larger than that of males, mainly due to mountain hares (weighing 3–4 kg) and Capercaillie males (weighing 4 kg), prey that is nearly out of the males' hunting capacity. Kenward et al. (1993b) found that juvenile males moved further than females on Gotland when young rabbits reached full size. The food scarcity hypothesis is also supported by the trapping results in southern Sweden that showed an increase in proportion of males in years 1984–1987 when grouse population numbers were exceptionally low (Fig. 2). Juvenile males also starve more often than females (Tornberg et al. 1999, Sunde 2002). Southward migrations of goshawks in North America are related to food scarcity, especially during low phases of the 10-yr population cycles of snowshoe hares (*Lepus americanus*; Keith and Rusch 1989). There, however, differences between the

FIGURE 6. Finding sites of the juvenile Northern Goshawks banded as nestlings in the the Oulu area, 1962–2002. Data obtained from the Ringing Centre of the Natural History Museum of the University of Helsinki.

sexes in the length of migration, has not been documented.

In adult goshawks, males seem to be the more philopatric sex (Kenward et al. 1981b, Widén 1985b, Byholm et al. 2003), a fact common in many raptors (Newton 1979a, Korpimäki et al. 1987, Korpimäki 1993). Higher philopatry in males might be connected to their more active role in territory defense and brood rearing (Newton 1979a, Byholm et al. 2003). Also, males trapped as adults are less reluctant to leave their home ranges than females (Kenward et al. 1981a, Widén 1985b). In the Oulu area, one breeding radio-tagged female deserted her family during the fledging period of her young and shifted to nest in a different territory in the next year. The fledglings were then successfully reared by the male. Another female trying to nest near the city dump of Oulu in 1994 was found 2 yr later 100 km south eaten by an Eagle Owl (*Bubo bubo*). Fairly little is still known about site and mate tenacity in breeding goshawks in Europe and further study is badly needed.

One may argue that dispersers moving farther are in a poorer condition than those moving less. Investigating movements of trapped and either banded or radio-tagged hawks in Sweden did not explain the length of the movement or site tenacity of the trapped birds (Kenward et al. 1981a, Marcström and Kenward 1981b, Widén 1985b). In fact, males that were generally in poorer condition in late winter were more reluctant to leave the study area than females (Widén 1985b).

HOME RANGE

Juvenile goshawks are very mobile during their first year of life; post-fledging dispersal can take them >1,000 km from their natal areas but most of the young hawks settle within 100 km. Young hawks tend to maintain home ranges before settling in the final breeding territory (Halley et al. 2000). Those juvenile hawks that were radio-tracked during November–December usually stayed near the trapping site in central Sweden and northern Finland (Kenward et al. 1981b, Tornberg and Colpaert 2001). Winter ranges of different goshawk individuals can overlap extensively. This happens especially in areas with high food supply like near release pens of pheasants (Kenward 1977). So, wintering goshawks seem not to defend their home ranges. This was the

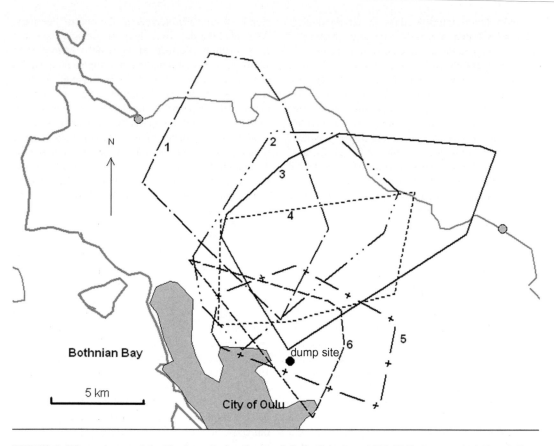

FIGURE 7. Winter ranges of the Northern Goshawks near Oulu in the winter 1992–1993. Ranges marked as follows: 1. adult female (breeding in the area), 2. adult male, 3. adult male (breeding in the area), 4. adult female (breeding 15 km southwest from the area), 5. adult female (breeding near dump site), and 6. juvenile female.

case also in Oulu (Fig. 7) where breeding birds did not try to displace visitors. Some observations of resident breeders hint that they know the core areas of their neighbors and avoid visits there.

Winter range sizes have been found to be related to landscape structure. In farmland areas of Sweden, range size correlated negatively with the amount of forest edge in the range (Kenward 1982). Because most of the kills took place near woodland edges, range size seems to relate negatively to the amount of good habitat, i.e., forest edge. Correspondingly, range size correlated negatively with the amount of mature forest, a preferred hunting habitat, in boreal forests of northern Finland (Tornberg and Colpaert 2001). Range size seems to respond flexibly either to the quantity or the quality of the food resource. Hawks that kill mostly large prey or live in areas with high food supply have the smallest ranges (Kenward 1982, Nygård et al. 1998). It is no wonder that juveniles being less experienced hunters than adults have larger ranges (Kenward et al. 1981b).

One might also expect larger winter home ranges for males that have a narrower food base than females. However, in boreal forests of central Sweden males' range size (5,110 ha, maximum polygon) was even slightly smaller than that of females' (6,179 ha). In this study, however, goshawks fed mainly on squirrels that might be more suitable prey for smaller males than larger, less agile females (Widén 1987). In the Oulu area, average winter range size (maximum polygon) was 7,091 ha ($\pm$ 3,935 ha, N = 9) for males and 5,710 ha ($\pm$ 664 ha, N = 15) for females, but the difference was not statistically significant.

HABITAT CHOICE

Goshawks are known to be old-forest specialists. This is, however, largely based on studies of the characteristics of the breeding habitats (Widén 1997, Penteriani 2002). Radio-tracking studies have shed light over the habitat use of goshawks outside and during the breeding season. As stated above, goshawks favored forest edges in farmland areas of central Sweden. Yet, in a more forest-dominated area radio-tagged birds thrived best in large patches, avoiding edges (Widén 1989). They preferred mature forests over younger stands. Correspondingly, goshawks also preferred mature forests in Oulu, but rather average sized patches that hint at favoring edges as hunting habitats. Goshawks used young forests proportionately to their availability but avoided open areas (Tornberg and Colpaert 2001). Because locating a goshawk is possible only when the bird is perched, it is impossible to know how much they fly over open terrain. Goshawks hunt with a short-stay, perched technique, perching 3–5 min and then flying 200–300m to a new perch (Widén 1984).

SURVIVAL AND CAUSES OF DEATH

A large number of banded hawks and good success at recapturing them have enabled reliable estimates of goshawk survival. Haukioja and Haukioja (1971) estimated the mortality of goshawks to be 63% in the first year assuming that 60% of the bands found were returned, 33% in the second year, 20% in the third, and stabilizing at around 10% in older age classes. Using a larger data set, Saurola (1976) estimated corresponding numbers as 64%, 35%, 18%, and 15%. It must be remembered that goshawks in Fennoscandia were under heavy persecution in 1960s–1970s with 5,000–6,000 goshawks, a remarkable proportion of the annual production, being killed annually by humans in Finland alone (Moilanen 1976). Analyses based on band recoveries may be biased, however, because young age classes are likely to be found easier than older specimens. Moreover, during the time when shooting was allowed, hawks killed by humans were likely to be overrepresented in total recoveries and young hawks prevailed among those being shot. Kenward et al. (1991, 1999) found in a large radio-tracking study on Gotland that 47% of the band recoveries were from killed hawks, whereas only 36% from radio-tagged birds. In addition, radio-tagged hawks showed an unbalanced mortality in young age classes in relation to sex—by 1 April, 46% of the males had died in their first year but only 31% of the females. In the second year, still more males (41%) than females (29%) died, but in older age classes mortality was balanced being 21% for both sexes.

Telemetry data collected in the Oulu area during 1991–1995 (N = 26; Tornberg and Colpaert 2001) were analyzed along with new data on eight tagged birds from the winters 1999–2003 (four adult males, one yearling male, two adult females, and one juvenile female) to get a survival estimate for winter months from 10 November to the end of February. We pooled the data over the years using a staggered entry method (Pollock et al. 1989). Mortality in adults (N = 26, males and females together) was 37% and for juveniles, 81% (N = 8). Because this method is very sensitive to small sample sizes, our estimate for juveniles is probably unreliable. The estimate for adults is very high compared to those obtained from band recoveries or telemetry data collected in more southern areas but is not necessarily unrealistic. Annual mortality may be a bit higher than estimated for winter months because natural mortality of adult hawks can still be high in March and April (Fig. 3).

Autopsies of naturally dying hawks on Gotland revealed that starvation was the most important cause of death (37%; Kenward et al. 1991), 33% of hawks died of trauma, and 22% of the combination of disease and starvation. Based on autopsies of goshawks brought to the Zoological Museum of the University of Oulu, 35% of hawks had died of starvation, 25% from collisions, 15% from a combination of trauma and starvation, and only 13% from shooting (N = 165; Tornberg and Virtanen 1997). Among banded hawks, the most important cause of death in the 1960s–1970s was killing by humans (83%; Saurola 1976). Similarly, shooting was the most common cause of death in Norway; before protection about 50% of birds found had been shot. After protection this cause of death fell to 5% (Halley 1996). After full protection of goshawks in 1989 in Finland, killing by humans declined but starvation may have increased due to intensified competition for food. Earlier, hawks prone to starve were often shot when they approached human settlements (Haukioja and Haukioja 1971). Hence, the cessation of shooting did not necessarily increase the number of young hawks because starvation among juveniles may have increased.

POPULATION STATUS AND TRENDS OF THE GOSHAWK IN FENNOSCANDIA

It is reasonable to argue that decline of a prey population induces a decline in the population of its predators. This typically concerns specialized predators (Begon et al. 1996) because generalists can switch to another prey if one prey type declines. The Northern Goshawk could be considered a generalist predator based on the wide spectrum of prey species in its diet. Because most diet studies have been performed during the breeding season when the greatest variety of suitable prey species, especially vulnerable juveniles, is available, food niche can be very wide. More focus should be directed to winter when availability of prey is more restricted.

Recent estimates show that goshawk still is one of the most common raptors in Fennoscandia. Several studies carried out in different localities in Fennoscandia, however, hint at a decline in breeding densities of goshawks. Widén (1997) reviewed nine studies and found a decline in eight of them. Selås (1998a) reported a decline in the breeding density in southern Norway from nine pairs/ 100 km^2 in the 1950s to three pairs to the 1980s but a slight increase to four pairs/100 km^2 in the mid-1990s. Recently, density has fallen back to the previous three pairs/100 km^2 (Selås 1998b, Selås, pers. comm.). In central Norway, breeding density in the 1990s was very low, only one pair/100 km^2 (Nygård et al. 1998). It is still difficult to evaluate whether declines reported in some studies indicate only local declines or whether they indicate a more general trend. A Finnish country-wide monitoring program of breeding populations of birds of prey which was initiated in1982 does not indicate declining density until the mid-1990s (Väisänen et al. 1998), even though during the 1990s a slight declining trend was detected (Björklund et al. 2002). The Swedish monitoring project from 1975 onward for winter and summer censuses show a 20% declining trend for winter but a slight increase for summer

densities (Svensson 2002). In Sweden and Norway, increasing numbers since the 1980s are, however, expected and obvious as Selås (1998a) has pointed out. This is due to a sarcoptic mange epidemic in red foxes (*Vulpes vulpes*) that caused fox numbers to crash and caused a corresponding increase in grouse numbers (Lindström et al. 1994). Hence, monitoring initiated in the 1970s–1980s does not necessarily reveal the long-term development of the goshawk population. Goshawk populations in central and south Europe seem to be more or less stable or even increasing (Kruger and Stefener 1996, Olech 1998)

In the Oulu area, occupancy rate of the goshawk population showed a strong negative trend during the 1990s (Fig. 8). We analyzed the population development by Moffat's equilibrium model (Hunt 1998) which assumes a fixed number of serviceable breeding sites. The model further assumes that juveniles start breeding in their second year. Simply by altering productivity of breeders and survival of juveniles, sub-adults, and adults, the model predicts future structure and development of the population. We used a series of survival values of 63% for adults (obtained from telemetry data), adjusting survival values for sub-adults (51%) and for juveniles

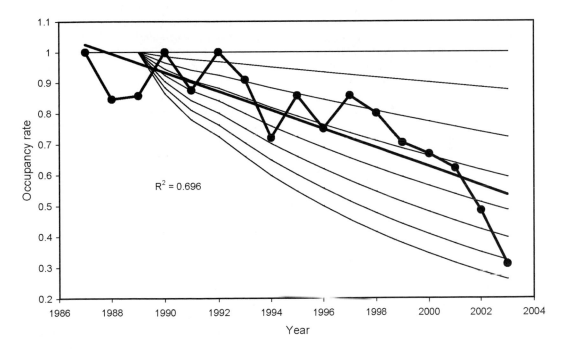

FIGURE 8. Occupancy of Northern Goshawk territories in the Oulu area (thick line) and simulations of the number of breeders with different survival rates by Moffat equilibrium model (Hunt 1998). Uppermost line denotes a survival value of 0 7 declining by 0.1 in each step.

(46%) according to estimates obtained from data by Kenward et al. (1999). We then modeled survival estimates by increasing each age category by 1%. We set population productivity at two fledglings/breeding pair. By the lowest series of values, the decline was steeper than observed which hints that the survival values used obtained from the telemetry study are too low. Using values 4% higher yielded a model that matches the observed line (Fig. 8). With these values, the population does not contain non-breeders which could explain the poor correlation between the occupancy rate of goshawk territories and grouse density because non-breeders are capable of responding quickly to changes in prey population. It seems that productivity is not a problem in a goshawk population but rather the poor survival of adults (Hunt 1998). Using values obtained from band recoveries in Finland (82%, 65%, and 36%) and productivity of two fledglings/pair gives a balanced breeding population containing 20% non-breeders. The goshawk population on Gotland remained stable, adjusted by lower proportion of the females breeding annually (40%) than the males (70%), which means that proportion of non-breeders of the breeders was around 40–50%.

CONCLUSIONS

Recently, a lot of debate has centered on reasons for changes in avian fauna of boreal forests in Fennoscandia (Haila and Järvinen 1990, Mönkkönen et al. 1999). The general conclusion derived from ornithological reports has been that old-forest species have declined and species living in young successional stages have increased or remained stable (Väisänen et al. 1986). This is considered to be due not only to the decline of the mature-forest stands but also to the fragmentation yielding patches too small to maintain meta-populations of certain old-forest specialists (Andrén 1994). The goshawk has been considered as an old-forest bird based on the nest-site selection (Penteriani 2002). Widén (1997) concluded that the goshawk has suffered from forestry because of the decrease of its main hunting habitat—old forests. Young successional stages of boreal forests, although basically maintaining higher grouse densities, are often too dense for successful hunting of the goshawk (Beier and Drennan 1997). Hence, Widén (1997) considers that habitat degradation is a more important reason for decline of goshawks than decline in the prey supply as such. It is, however, quite evident that the supply of the main prey, forest grouse, has declined.

In Finland, where grouse counts have been made since the mid-1960s, decline in all forest grouse species has been >50% (see Fig. 2). Modern forestry with extensive clear cuts, draining of the peat land bogs, and construction of a dense network of forest roads have had negative impacts on forest grouse (Kurki et al. 1997). Clear-cuts may have increased grasslands that maintain voles and their predators. During crashes of vole populations, small mammal predators switch to hunting grouse chicks and thus lower the productivity of grouse (Angelstam et al. 1984, Henttonen 1989). Removal experiments of mammalian predators have resulted in higher grouse populations or at least higher reproductive rate compared to control areas (Marcström et al. 1988, Kauhala et al. 2000). We conclude that shrinkage in the area of mature forests does not explain the observed negative trends in the goshawk population per se, but rather the availability of suitable sized prey during the non-breeding season. Goshawks are able to live in areas where forest cover is <20% of the area but where enough prey is accessible (Kenward 1982). In the Oulu area, goshawks preferred fairly small patches of forests. Surprisingly, the composition of the winter diet is close to that found in farmland areas of central Sweden with the difference that grouse replaced the pheasants (Kenward et al. 1981a; Table 2). Habitat of kill sites did not differ much from that of the habitat composition available (Tornberg and Colpaert 2001).

Forest fragmentation has caused a decline in forest grouse and perhaps also in red squirrels, whereas it may have increased mountain hare numbers. Comparisons of mountain hare densities between Finland and Russian Karelia show a three-fold higher hare population in Finland compared to Russian Karelia where forest stands are mostly at mature stage (Lindén et al. 2000). As found in winter diet studies, females can but male goshawks unlike cannot kill full-grown mountain hares. This has led to a curious situation where females may have benefited from forest fragmentation but males suffered. This appears to result in a higher starvation risk and poorer winter condition in male goshawks (Widén 1985b, Tornberg et al. 1999, Sunde 2002). It may also explain why breeding output expressed as clutch and brood sizes do not match well with the density fluctuations of grouse. Females in good condition in spring can lay eggs with a minimal aid from the males. Therefore, recent changes in forest structure may have even affected their morphology. Tornberg et al. (1999) found, based on museum material from the last 40 yr, that adult males have become smaller and females larger. This change was more on the outer morphology (body, wing, tail, and tarsus length) than bone length. This might be explained by dietary changes caused by a general decline of grouse populations—females have found larger alternative prey than males. Another interesting adaptation that probably originates from a tighter dependence of males on grouse, appears as a changing sex ratio in goshawk broods as a function of grouse density (Byholm 2003). Goshawk pairs produce significantly more males in good grouse years compared to poor years. This might be a compensative response for higher juvenile mortality of males induced by natural selection.

When evaluating the conservation needs for a declining raptor species, focus should not be on only one apparently important fact, but on a wider scale, e.g., how the change in habitat has affected the food supply. One must also realize when the food supply is a limiting factor, it is not likely to be limiting during the breeding season at northern latitudes. Kenward (1996) presumes that problems faced by the goshawks in the sub-boreal region of North America might be due to poor food supply in winter. Protection of the goshawks has not increased goshawk numbers. It can be possible that nowadays, when more young probably are entering the winter than during the years when many juveniles were killed by humans, intra-specific competition for food in goshawk populations has intensified. This may lead to more starving young birds but also a weaker winter supply for adults and poorer breeding performance in the next spring (Haukioja and Haukioja 1971). In a specialist predator-prey interaction, a decline of the predator may lead to an increase in prey population. In goshawk-grouse systems, this does not necessarily happen these days because increased impact by mammalian predators harvests grouse populations independently of their density (Angelstam et al. 1984, Marcström et al. 1988, Korpimäki and Norrdahl 1997). In fact, mammalian

predators and goshawks are competing for a common resource, grouse, which is of vital importance for the goshawks but not necessarily for mammalian predators (Selås 1998a). Modern forestry improves the conditions of mammalian predators and at the same time harms forest grouse and the predators dependent on them. All in all, habitat restoration is the ultimate solution for the sustainable populations of forest grouse and goshawks.

Future research effort should be directed to winter ecology of goshawks. Topics like: (1) winter food supply, (2) predation rates on the most important prey species, (3) hunting habitats with precise data on kill sites, (4) movements, survival, and causes of death of different age classes, and (5) relationships to competitors, should be investigated with modern field techniques. In addition, we badly need individual-level studies on goshawks during both the breeding and non-breeding seasons in boreal forests. For example, it could be important to know how the reproductive effort of individual pairs and members of pairs varies in relation to temporal and spatial density fluctuations of main prey, and how sexual differences in the main food supply induced by modern forestry practices (beneficial for females, costly for males) affects reproductive effort, division of duties during the breeding season, and reproductive success of individual goshawks.

ACKNOWLEDGMENTS

This paper is dedicated to the pioneer investigator of goshawks and other Fennoscandian raptors and owls, S. Sulkava, Department of Zoology, University of Oulu. We are grateful for valuable comments that V. Selås, V. Penteriani, and S. Sulkava made on the manuscript. We further thank the Finnish Game Research Institute and Ringing Centre of Finnish Museum of Natural History for data on grouse densities and ringed goshawks.

Studies in Avian Biology No. 31:158–197

POPULATION LIMITATION IN THE NORTHERN GOSHAWK IN EUROPE: A REVIEW WITH CASE STUDIES

Christian Rutz, Rob G. Bijlsma, Mick Marquiss, and Robert E. Kenward

Abstract. This paper investigates factors limiting breeding densities in populations of Northern Goshawk (*Accipiter gentilis gentilis*) in western, central, and southern Europe. We review the current status of the species and describe major population trends during the last century. Large-scale trends in numbers coincided with marked changes in the external environment (early 20th century—extensive human persecution; 1950s—maturation of forests providing new nesting habitat; 1960s—organochlorine pesticide use in agriculture). We present four lines of evidence suggesting that goshawk breeding numbers in Europe are indeed limited by extrinsic factors, rather than fluctuating at random: (1) temporal stability of breeding numbers, (2) existence of non-breeders in stable populations, (3) growth dynamics of newly-founded and recovering populations, and (4) regular spacing of territories in continuously suitable nesting habitat. We evaluate the published literature to assess the relative importance of seven potentially limiting factors. Consistent with other raptor species, we identify nest-site availability and food supply as the two principal factors limiting breeding numbers in the goshawk. Importantly, their relative influence appears to be affected by the degree of illegal killing. Currently in Europe, killing by humans rarely has direct effects on breeding population levels. However, even moderate levels of killing may limit goshawks indirectly, by preventing their full use of habitats in close proximity to human activity. In the absence of illegal killing, goshawks in western Europe are highly adaptable to intense human activities. They readily occupy a wide range of nesting habitats, including small woodlots in highly fragmented rural landscapes and even urban parks in metropolitan areas. In such settings, goshawks show extraordinary degrees of tolerance of human activities, and enjoy comparatively high productivity, indicating that these habitats offer good living conditions. Hence, the nest-site preferences reported for European populations may not always or entirely represent natural ecological needs, but partly reflect choices imposed on the species by human activities. Populations subject to little illegal killing in areas where nesting sites are freely available seem to be limited mainly by food supply. In some areas, goshawks appear to suffer from nest-site competition with the dominant Eurasian Eagle-Owl (*Bubo bubo*). Weather conditions may account for some of the year-to-year variation in breeding density, probably acting through an effect on spring food supplies, but they do not generally limit goshawks in temperate Europe. Circumstantial evidence suggests that pesticide use negatively affected goshawk populations in the 1960s. However, present-day levels of organochlorines and other environmental pollutants generally seem to be too low to have significant population-level consequences. The role of parasites and diseases in limiting goshawks is unknown, but likely to be negligible according to work on other species. We put our findings into context by contrasting goshawk ecology between Europe and North America. Goshawks in North America (*Accipiter gentilis atricapillus* and *A. g. laingi*): (1) live at lower densities than in Europe, (2) make less use of artificial habitats (small woodlots, towns, and parks) for foraging and breeding, (3) use mammalian foods more often, and (4) produce fewer young per pair. Differences in goshawk ecology between continents are probably due to some underlying extrinsic factor, such as prey availability, rather than a discrete subspecific difference attributable to particular morphology or intrinsic behavior. Field methods and the format for reporting results should be further standardized to obtain comparable data. We encourage researchers to pool existing data sets for reanalysis, as such large-scale approaches with appropriate independent replication at the population-level are needed to produce statistically robust insights into goshawk population biology. Gaps in our knowledge on the species include: (1) biology of non-breeders, (2) the effect of food shortage on population dynamics, and (3) habitat use during breeding season and winter. We propose several lines of future research; for virtually all areas of goshawk biology, there is a particular need for carefully-designed experiments.

Key Words: *Accipiter gentilis*, avian population limitation, competition, density dependence, Eurasian Eagle-Owl, habitat use, intra-guild competition, meta analysis, Northern Goshawk, pesticides and environmental pollutants, urban ecology, wildlife management and conservation.

LIMITANTES EN LAS POBLACIONES DE GAVILÁN AZOR EN EUROPA: UNA REVISIÓN CON CASOS DE STUDIO

Resumen. El presente artículo investiga factores que limitan las densidades reproductivas del Gavilán Azor (*Accipiter gentilis gentilis*) en el occidente, centro y sur de Europa. Revisamos el estatus actual de la especie y describimos las principales tendencias de la población durante el último siglo. Tendencias de larga escala en números coincidieron con cambios marcados en el medio ambiente externo (principios del siglo

20—persecución extensiva por humanos; en la década de los cincuenta—maduración de bosques, proveyendo hábitat nuevo para anidación; en la década de los sesenta—uso del pesticida organoclorin en la agricultura). Presentamos cuatro líneas de evidencia que sugieren que los números reproductores del gavilán en Europa están de hecho limitados por factores extrínsecos, en vez de fluctuaciones al azar: (1) estabilidad temporal de números reproductores, (2) existencia de no-reproductores en poblaciones estables, (3) dinámica de crecimiento de poblaciones recién encontradas y en poblaciones en recuperación, y (4) espaciamiento regular de territorios en hábitat susceptible para anidación. Evaluamos la literatura publicada para estimar la importancia relativa de siete factores potencialmente limitantes. Consistente con otras especies de raptor, identificamos que la disponibilidad de sitio de anidación y el suministro de alimento son los dos factores principales los cuales limitan el número reproductivo en el gavilán. Significativamente, su influencia relativa parece ser afectada por el grado de caza ilegal. Actualmente en Europa, la cacería por humanos raramente tiene efectos directos en los niveles de las poblaciones reproductoras. Sin embargo, niveles moderados de cacería quizás limiten a los gavilanes indirectamente, al impedir la plena utilización del hábitat en proximidad a la actividad humana. Con la ausencia de caza ilegal, los gavilanes son altamente adaptables a actividades humanas intensas en Europa occidental. Ellos fácilmente ocupan un amplio rango de hábitats de anidación, incluyendo pequeños sitios forestales en paisajes rurales altamente fragmentados, e incluso en parques urbanos en áreas metropolitanas. En dichos escenarios, los gavilanes muestran un extraordinario grado de tolerancia a las actividades humanas, y gozan comparativamente de una productividad alta, indicando que estos hábitats ofrecen condiciones buenas para vivir. Por lo tanto, las preferencias de sitios de nido reportadas para poblaciones Europeas quizás no siempre o completamente representen necesidades ecológicas naturales, pero en parte reflejan opciones impuestas en la especie por actividades humanas. Las poblaciones sujetas a por lo menos un poco de caza ilegal en áreas en donde los sitios de anidación están libremente disponibles, parecen estar limitadas principalmente por la disponibilidad de alimento. En algunas áreas, los gavilanes parece que sufren por competencia del sitio de nido con el dominante Búho-Águila de Euroasia (*Bubo bubo*). Las condiciones climáticas quizás influyan para algunas de las variaciones de año tras año en la densidad de reproducción, probablemente actuando a través de un efecto en el abastecimiento de alimento en primavera, pero estos generalmente no limitan a los gavilanes en la Europa templada. Evidencia circunstancial sugiere que el uso de pesticidas afectó negativamente a las poblaciones de gavilán en la década de los sesenta. Sin embargo, los niveles actuales de organoclorines y otros contaminantes para el medio ambiente generalmente parecen ser muy bajos como para tener consecuencias significativas a nivel de población. El papel de los parásitos y enfermedades en la limitación de gavilanes se desconoce, pero parece ser insignificante de acuerdo al trabajo realizado con otras especies. Pusimos nuestros hallazgos en contexto, contrastando la ecología del gavilán entre Europa y Norte América. Los gavilanes en Norte América (subespecie: *Accipiter gentilis atricapillus* y *A. g. laingi*): (1) viven en menores densidades que en Europa, (2) hacen menor uso de hábitats artificiales (pequeños lotes arbolados, pueblos y parques) para forrajeo y reproducción, (3) utilizan más a menudo a mamíferos como alimento, y (4) producen menos juveniles por pareja . Las diferencias en la ecología de los gavilanes entre continentes quizás se deban a algunos factores fundamentales extrínsecos, tales como la disponibilidad de la presa; en vez de una diferencia discreta subespecífica la cual puede ser atribuida a morfología particular o a comportamiento intrínseco. Tanto métodos de campo, como el formato para reportar resultados deberían ser más estandarizados para obtener datos comparables. Alentamos a los investigadores para mancomunar el conjunto de datos existentes para reanalizar, por ejemplo, aproximaciones de larga escala con replicación independiente apropiada al nivel de población las cuales son necesarias para producir penetraciones estadísticas robustas en la biología de las poblaciones de gavilán. Los huecos en nuestro conocimiento sobre la especie incluyen: (1) biología de no reproductores, (2) efectos en la escasez de alimento en las dinámicas poblacionales, y (3) utilización del hábitat durante la época reproductiva y el invierno. Proponemos varias líneas de investigación para el futuro, virtualmente para todas las áreas de la biología del gavilán existe una necesidad particular para experimentos diseñados cuidadosamente.

In this review, we attempt to identify major factors limiting breeding numbers of Northern Goshawks (*Accipiter gentilis gentilis*, hereafter goshawk) in western, central, and southern Europe. Populations in northern Europe differ in their biology, associated with cyclic prey populations (Tornberg et al., *this volume*), so we only occasionally refer to Scandinavian studies to highlight important points or to present additional support for some lines of argument.

The ecological processes underlying population limitation in birds have been reviewed by Newton (1998). Following his terminology, we distinguish between extrinsic (environmental) and intrinsic (demographic) factors influencing breeding numbers. Extrinsic factors are features of the external environment, including food and nest sites, competitors, humans, natural predators, and parasites, and are generally defined as ultimate causes of population limitation. Their effect is mediated by intrinsic factors—the rates of births, deaths, immigration, and emigration. Changes in these demographic features affect population density at the proximate level. External factors that act in a density-dependent manner are said to regulate breeding numbers.

Apart from its heuristic value, an understanding of the causes of population limitation is crucial for conserving and/or managing animal populations (Newton 1991, 1998). Our main focus is the ultimate level of density limitation, but we also review demographic responses (productivity and mortality), where this elucidates the relative importance of a particular factor, or when nothing more is available in the published literature. Earlier reviews identified food supplies and nest sites as the main ultimate factors limiting breeding numbers of raptors (Newton 1979a, 1991, 2003a). We shall concentrate on these aspects, but in the goshawk, human-related factors such as deliberate killing and pesticide impact also deserve scrutiny.

The goshawk has been studied extensively in Europe. This is in part due to its charismatic appearance and behavior, but mainly because it is an avian top predator that is particularly time and cost effective to study (Bijlsma 1997, Rutz 2003a). The goshawk is often used as a model organism for addressing fundamental ecological questions (Kenward 1978a, b; Dietrich 1982, Ziesemer 1983, Kenward and Marcström 1988, Bijlsma 1993, Rutz 2001, Drachmann and Nielsen 2002, Krüger and Lindström 2001, Nielsen and Drachmann 2003, Rutz 2005b, Rutz et al. 2006), or as a bio-indicator for monitoring pollution levels in terrestrial ecosystems (Ellenberg and Dietrich 1981, Hahn et al. 1989, Kenntner et al. 2003, Mañosa et al. 2003). Moreover, some European goshawk populations prey on game species (Kenward et al. 1981a, Ziesemer 1983, Mañosa 1994, Nielsen 2003), domestic poultry (Ivanovsky 1998), and/or racing pigeons (*Columba livia*, Opdam et al. 1977, Bühler et al. 1987, Bijlsma 1993, Nielsen 1998, Nielsen and Drachmann 1999b, Shawyer et al. 2000), so applied studies have addressed stakeholder conflict and the issue of predator control (Kenward and Marcström 1981; Kenward 1986, 2000; Galbraith et al. 2003); as management has moved on from past persecution to eradicate predators, we use the terms culling, selective removal and illegal killing for contemporary human impacts on goshawks (REGHAB 2002).

As a consequence of this general interest, a large body of literature on European goshawk populations has accumulated, including reviews of the species' general biology (Kramer 1972, Glutz von Blotzheim et al. 1971, Cramp and Simmons 1980, Kenward and Lindsay 1981, Fischer 1995) and detailed reports on local population ecology (Holstein 1942, Opdam 1978, Looft 1981, Ziesemer 1983, Brüll 1984, Link 1986, Jørgensen 1989, Bijlsma 1993, Drachmann and Nielsen 2002).

Here, we critically review published information within the context of population limitation. We start with a reassessment of the species' status in western and central Europe and a description of the major population trends during the last century, updating Bijlsma (1991a), and Bijlsma and Sulkava (1997). We show that large-scale trends in numbers coincided with marked changes in the external environment. We then: (1) summarize evidence that population densities are indeed limited, rather than fluctuating at random, (2) explore a selection of putative limiting factors and assess their relative importance, and (3) use results from urban study areas, which differ markedly from natural or rural breeding habitats, to evaluate our account of non-urban populations. Our review enables a comparison of patterns of population limitation in the European goshawk with those suggested for the North American subspecies (*Accipiter gentilis atricapillus* and *A. g. laingi*). We close the paper by identifying gaps in our knowledge on goshawk biology and by proposing several lines of future research.

METHODOLOGICAL NOTES

LITERATURE REVIEW AND DATA HANDLING

We made every possible effort to locate relevant information on the species, which has been published from about 1950 onward (for population trends, from about 1900 onward). We mainly focused on peer-reviewed material, which we compiled by standard bibliographic searching techniques, but also considered results in academic theses, technical reports, or non-refereed journals if the presentation of the data allowed us to evaluate the validity of the authors' conclusions. We might have missed some publications from southern and especially central Europe, mainly because they appeared in non-indexed journals. The apparent bias towards German and Dutch studies might partly be the result of our own familiarity with this literature, but it also reflects the greater research intensity in these countries compared to elsewhere in Europe.

Throughout this paper, we support important arguments by giving reference to studies which produced conclusive evidence. In the case of more trivial statements, we quote one or two key references, which will guide the reader to related publications. In addition to the critical review of the literature, we will illustrate important points with detailed case studies, mainly based on our own research and including hitherto unpublished material.

For several sections of this review, we compiled data from the original literature for meta-investigations, which treat individual studies or goshawk populations as the unit of observation. Quantitative analyses of this material will be presented elsewhere (Rutz 2005b, C. Rutz et al., unpubl. data). In some cases, we asked authors to provide unpublished information or original data for (re-)analysis. Time constraints prevented us from sampling such material at a scale which would have produced an exhaustive data set, leaving much scope for future collaborative work.

To give as complete a summary of the current knowledge on the species as possible, we had to consider studies which differ markedly in their field methods as well as in their statistical analyses. In two cases, we decided to tag studies to draw the reader's attention to methodological aspects that we consider important for evaluating the presented data. Firstly, we indicate whether a study estimated brood size by observation from the ground (OFG) or by climbing nest trees, because the former method is known to underestimate nestling numbers (Bijlsma 1997, Goszczyński 1997, Altenkamp 2002). Secondly, we note when we felt that multiple statistical testing (MT), without correcting probability values appropriately, might have led to spurious conclusions (Rice 1989).

The population levels of some forest raptors can be reasonably indexed using mean nearest-neighbor distances (NND) in continuously suitable woodland habitat (Newton et al. 1977). An advantage of the NND-method is that it is comparatively robust to the arbitrary delineation of study areas; on the other hand it overestimates actual population density— particularly where suitable nesting habitat is limited relative to foraging habitat. Because few studies reported NND values, we were constrained to using overall density estimates (pairs/100 km^2) in most contexts. Estimates of goshawk breeding densities are significantly affected by the size of the study plot (Fig. 3 in Gedeon 1994). We acknowledged this problem by restricting our analyses to density values obtained for plots >50 km^2 in size (the largest variation has been found for plots <50 km^2), or even >100 km^2 in some cases, and by controlling for plot size in all statistical models.

General(ized) linear (mixed) modeling (GL[M]M) was carried out in GenStat 6.0 and Minitab 12.0, using standard procedures (Crawley 1993, Grafen and Hails 2002).

Cross-continental Comparison

When comparing goshawk biology between Europe and North America, we were aiming to highlight marked differences between continents that are unlikely to be artifacts of fieldmethod variations. A more quantitative cross-continental comparison, employing statistical models that can control for confounding factors, is in preparation (C. Rutz et al., unpubl. data).

We made an attempt to build exhaustive databases of key demographics and life-history traits for goshawks on both continents. Our European database was created, using sources and searching techniques described above. For the North American database, we used recent literature reviews (Block et al. 1994, Kennedy 1997, Squires and Reynolds 1997, USDI Fish and Wildlife Service 1998a, Kennedy 2003, Andersen et al. 2004; Squires and Kennedy, *this volume*) as a starting point, and subsequently filled in gaps by standard searching techniques. Studies were entered more than once, if they reported data for two or more distinct study plots. At the time of writing, our European and North American databases contained 225 and 99 entries, respectively.

We omitted all studies that had been completed before 1975 because goshawk populations in Europe were subject to much illegal killing and pesticides before that time. For breeding density estimates, we only used studies, where study plots were between 100–2,500 km^2 in size, did not contain 100% woodland cover, and were surveyed for at least 3 yr. In this way, we aimed to exclude studies that had actively selected optimal goshawk habitat, which inadvertently results in density overestimation. Our criterion for minimum plot size was more stringent than in other analyses in this review, because we could not easily control for percentage woodland cover in this comparison (most American studies do not give quantitative estimates of forest cover) Areas >2,500 km^2 overcome problems of biased habitat composition but are difficult to search reliably—see Smallwood (1998) for the relationship of breeding density *vs.* study area size in North American studies. We used maximum breeding density (the maximum annual number of active nests) if given in the original source, and mean breeding density otherwise.

In the case of diet composition, we only used studies that were based on direct observations at nests, collection of prey remains around nests, radio tracking, or any combination of these techniques. These methods typically provide a unique record for each prey individual. We omitted pellet only data because this method represents hair or feathers from one prey in several pellets while unique identifiers like particular bones are often digested by hawks. Reliance on pellet analysis has been shown to produce severely biased diet descriptions (Goszczyński and Piłatowski 1986, Mañosa 1994, Padial et al. 1998, Lewis et al. 2004). Parameters of breeding performance (nest success, clutch size, brood size, and productivity) were only used for studies that had investigated at least five nests. In this exploratory analysis, we pooled studies where nest trees were climbed for nestling banding with those where observations were made from the ground.

Applying the above filtering criteria to our data bases and excluding data from duplicate publications to avoid pseudo-replication resulted in a data set containing material reported in a total of 117 sources (plus four unpublished data sets) from Europe and 57 from North America (Table 5). For Europe, we had access to almost all original sources (96%) for data extraction; whereas for North America, we had to compile values from other review articles for about 39% of all studies. We do not think that this additional source of error led to serious misinterpretations, although we discovered several inconsistencies in values given in three review articles (USDI Fish and Wildlife Service 1998a, Kennedy 2003, Andersen et al. 2004). Data for comparison between areas are presented as ranges of values, with medians if they come from four or more areas.

CURRENT STATUS AND POPULATION TRENDS

The goshawk is a widespread inhabitant of coniferous and deciduous forests in western and central Europe (Fig. 1). Regional densities generally vary between 0.5–6.2 pairs/100 km² of land (Table 1), but local densities can reach values of well over 10 pairs/100 km² (Poland—13.9 pairs/100 km², Olech 1998; Germany—15.6 pairs/100 km², Mammen 1999; The Netherlands—15.0–52.5 pairs/100 km², Bijlsma et al. 2001). The altitudinal distribution of nesting sites ranges from below sea level (Müskens 2002, Busche and Looft 2003) up to the tree line (Gamauf 1991, Oggier and Bühler 1998). The population in Britain is small, because it is only recently established from loss and deliberate release by falconers, and is still in the early stages of colonization (Petty 1996a, *Case study 3*). Large gaps in distribution, such as in northwest France, western Belgium, and the floodplain of the River Po in northern Italy, coincide with agriculture in lowlands and a lack of woodlands (Bijlsma and Sulkava 1997).

The total population in central and western Europe—Poland through France—was estimated at 29,000–44,000 breeding pairs in the early 1990s (Bijlsma and Sulkava 1997). Despite further increases in range and numbers, these figures are probably still valid. Mebs and Schmidt (unpubl. data) estimate the total breeding population of the western Palearctic to be 159,000 pairs (range = 135,000–183,000).

Goshawks were much reduced in density and distribution in the first half of the 20th century by intensive human persecution. From the start of World War II, human persecution abated in many parts of Europe due to legal protection of the species, declining numbers of gamekeepers, or changes in forestry and hunting practices. In western and central Europe, the large-scale planting of Norway spruce (*Picea abies*) and Scots pine (*Pinus sylvestris*) on heaths, moors and otherwise unproductive habitats, and the conversion of deciduous into non-native coniferous woodland reached its peak between the mid-1800s and the early 1900s. These new forests gradually matured in the first half of the 20th century, providing new habitat for goshawks on a large scale (*Case studies 1, 3*). Similarly, though starting somewhat later, extensive planting of conifers also took place in Great Britain (Petty 1996b, *Case study 3*). The combination of reduced persecution and increased acreage of coniferous forest resulted in goshawk population increases over much of Europe through the mid-1950s.

The subsequent population crash between 1956 and 1971 (Table 2) paralleled the massive application of persistent organochlorine and mercurial pesticides and seed dressings in farmland areas, presumably via impaired reproduction and adult survival (Conrad 1977, Thissen et al. 1981). Populations away from intensive farming, such as in the central Alps, remained unaffected by pesticides and showed stable numbers throughout the 1960s and 1970s (Bühler and Oggier 1987). The recovery and expansion of remaining populations in various regions started more or less synchronously in the 1970s, coinciding with successive bans in the uses of organochlorines, and numbers leveled off in the 1980s or 1990s (Tables 1, 2).

Regional variations in intensity of killing by humans, food availability and possibly nest-site competition with Eurasian Eagle-Owls (*Bubo bubo*) were responsible for sometimes curtailed expansion or localized declines. Nevertheless, by the late 20th century, abundance and distribution of goshawks in much of Europe had reached unprecedented levels compared to the past century, despite continued

FIGURE 1. Breeding distribution of the Northern Goshawk in Europe from Clark (1999), reproduced with permission of Oxford University Press.

killing. This was not only due to the increased area of coniferous woodland, but also habitat fragmentation, eutrophication (*Case study 1*), and the novel tendency exhibited by the species to exploit human-dominated environments.

EVIDENCE FOR DENSITY LIMITATION

Four inter-related lines of evidence suggest that breeding densities in European goshawk populations are limited, rather than fluctuating at random. The data for goshawks presented here are consistent with results from other raptor studies (Eurasian Sparrowhawk [*Accipiter nisus*], Newton 1989; Eurasian Kestrel [*Falco tinnunculus*], Village 1990; Golden Eagle [*Aquila chrysaetos*], Watson 1997), and with conclusions from a comparative study, reviewing patterns observed in various diurnal raptors (Newton 1979a, 1991, 2003a)

STABILITY OF BREEDING NUMBERS

Local breeding densities often remain fairly stable over periods of several years in the absence of significant perturbations, e.g., deliberate killing, and pesticides, or environmental changes, e.g., change in

TABLE 1. OVERVIEW OF DISTRIBUTION AND ABUNDANCE OF GOSHAWKS IN WESTERN AND CENTRAL EUROPE IN THE SECOND HALF OF THE 20TH CENTURY.

Country/period	Occupied squares	N pairs/territories	Sources
Britain (except Northern Ireland: 244,000 km², 9.4%)			
1968–1972	35	(<35)	Marquiss (1993).
1988–1991	236	200	Marquiss (1993).
mid-1990s	?	400	Petty (1996a).
Denmark (43,000 km², 10.8%)			
1950–1960	?	100	Grell (1998).
1971–1974	299	150–200	Grell (1998).
1985	?	650	Jørgensen (1998).
1993–1996	796	700	Grell (1998).
Germany (356,750 km², 31%)			
1970	?	2125	Kostrzewa and Speer (2001).
1978–1982	?	5,150–6,950	Kostrzewa and Speer (2001).
1998–1999	?	8,500	Kostrzewa and Speer (2001), cf. Mammen (1999).
The Netherlands (42,318 km², 7.2%)			
1950	?	400	Bijlsma (1989).
1969	?	75–100	Bijlsma (1989).
1973–1977	210	500–600	Bijlsma (1989).
1979–1983	?	1,200–1,400	Bijlsma (1989).
1986	?	1,300–1,700	Bijlsma (1989).
1988	594	1,500–1,800	Bijlsma (1993).
1989–1994	770	1,800–2,000	Bijlsma et al. (2001).
1995–1999	928	1,800	Bijlsma et al. (2001).
1998–2000	959	1,800–2,000	Müskens (2002).
Belgium (Flanders: 13,672 km², 10.8%)			
1973–1977	7	(<10)	Devillers et al. (1988).
1985–1988	?	110–160	G. Vermeersch and A. Anselin, pers. comm.
2000–2003	>100	300–400	Gabriëls (2004), J. G. Vermeersch and A. Anselin, pers. comm.
Belgium (Wallonia: 16,844 km², 31.4%)			
1973–1977	107	130–200	Devillers et al. (1988).
2001–2003	?	430–440	J.-P. Jacob, pers. comm.
Luxembourg (2,586 km², 31.7%)			
1976–1980	97	50–60	Melchior et al. (1987).
France (547,030 km², 27%)			
1970–1975	369	(400)	Yeatman (1976).
1979–1982	?	3,000–4,500	Thiollay and Terrasse (1984).
1985–1990	688	2,200–3,100	Joubert (1994).
2000	?	4,600–6,500	Dronneau and Wassmer (2004).
Switzerland (41,293 km², 30%)			
1972–1974	238	600	Oggier (1980).
1985	?	1,300	Bühler and Oggier (1987).
1993–1996	376	1,400–1,600	Oggier and Bühler (1998), Winkler (1999).
Austria (83,849 km², 39%)			
1981–1985	435	2,300	Gamauf (1991), Dvorak et al. (1993).
Czech Republic (78,641 km², 33.3%)			
1973–1977	707	?	Šťastný et al. (1987).
1985–1989	577	2,000–2,800	Šťastný et al. (1996).
1990	?	2,000–2,500	Danko et al. (1994).
Slovakia (48,845 km², 41%)			
1973–1977	282	1,700	Šťastný et al. (1987).
1985–1989	378	1,600–1,800	Danko et al. (2002).
Poland (312,683 km², 29%)			
1990	?	3,500–5,000	Heath et al. (2000).
2000	?	5,000–6,000	Tomiałojć and Stawarczyk (2003).

Notes: For each country, total area and percentage woodland cover are given in brackets. Distribution is expressed as number of 10-km squares occupied (square size 24 × 27 km in France, 8 × 10 km in Belgium in 1973–1977, 5 × 5 km in The Netherlands and Luxemburg, and 12 × 11.1 km in Czech Republic and Slovakia in 1985–1989) and abundance as the number of pairs/territories. Note that some estimates or mappings were considered inaccurate by later sources. T. Mebs and D. Schmidt (unpubl. data) estimate the total breeding population of the western Palearctic to be 159,000 pairs (range 135,000–183,000) based on recent estimates including unpublished data.

TABLE 2. TRENDS OF GOSHAWKS IN WESTERN AND CENTRAL EUROPE IN THE SECOND HALF OF THE 20TH CENTURY AT THE POPULATION (P) AND RANGE (R) LEVEL.

Country	1950–1970		1970–1990		1990–2000		Sources
	P	R	P	R	P	R	
Britain	a	a	2	2	2	2	Marquiss (1993), Petty (1996a), Petty et al. (2003b).
Denmark	-2	-	2	2	0	0	Grell (1998), Jørgensen (1998), Nielsen and Drachmann (1999a).
Germany	-2	-	2	1	0/-	0	Kostrzewa and Speer (2001), Mebs (2002).
Schleswig-Holstein	-	-	+/0	+	0/-	0	Looft (2000), Berndt et al. (2002), Busche and Looft (2003).
Niedersachsen	-2	-	+	+	0	0	Kostrzewa and Speer (2001).
Nordrhein-Westfalen	-2	-	+	+	0	0	Kostrzewa et al. (2000), Arbeitsgruppe Greifvögel NWO (2002).
Hessen	-	-	1	+1/0	0/-	0	Hausch (1997).
Baden-Württemberg	-2	-	+	+	0	0	Hölzinger (1987).
Bayern	-2	-	+	+	0/-	0	Link (1986), Bezzel et al. (1997a).
The Netherlands	-2	-2	2	2	0	2	Bijlsma et al. (2001), Müskens (2002).
East	-2	-2	2	2	0/-1	0	Bijlsma et al. (2001), Müskens (2002).
West	a	a	2	2	2	2	Bijlsma et al. (2001), Müskens (2002).
Belgium	-2	-	2	2	2	2	Devillers et al. (1988).
Flanders	-2	-	2	2	2	2	Geuens (1994), De Fraine and Verboven (1997), Gabriëls (2004).
Wallonia	-2	-	2	2	0	0	Heath et al. (2000).
Luxembourg	-	-	+	+	0	0	Heath et al. (2000).
France	-2	0	1	1	0	0	Yeatman (1976), Thiollay and Terrasse (1984), Joubert (1994), Dronneau and Wassmer (2004).
Switzerland	-2	-	2	2	1	0	Oggier and Bühler (1998), Winkler (1999).
Austria	-	-	1	1	0	0	Dvorak et al. (1993), Gamauf (1991).
Czech Republic	-	-	1	1	-	0	Kren (2000), Šťastný et al. (1996).
Slovakia	-	-	1	0	0	0	Danko et al. (2002).
Poland	-2	-	1	1	1	1	Drazny and Adamski (1996), Tomiałojć and Stawarczyk (2003).

Notes: a = absent; + = increase (1 = <50%, 2 = >50%); - = decline (1 = <50%, 2 = >50%); 0 = stable/fluctuating; +/0/- = various trends in different regions.

prey abundance, deforestation, and habitat succession (Table 2). Examples of populations, for which breeding numbers fluctuated on average by no more than 15% of the mean over at least 15 yr, are shown in Fig. 2a. On the other hand, when numbers change systematically, and are not indicative of the recovery of formerly depleted populations, trends often coincide with obvious alterations in the environment. This observation suggests causal relationships between extrinsic factors and breeding numbers, and we explore these potential links in detail later.

We are aware of the fact that the investigation of numerical population stability is problematic, because the choice of time frame over which counts are assessed and the definition of stability are arbitrary (Newton 1998). Further, populations should ideally be monitored together with quantitative estimates of various environmental key factors but no study on goshawks has yet accomplished this difficult task satisfactorily. We therefore simply note

that most long-term data sets on population trends we examined fit qualitatively into the general picture described above.

More importantly, some evidence suggests that year-to-year stability in numbers, exhibited by several goshawk populations, is due to density-dependent processes. For example, the percentage of change in numbers of territorial pairs appears to correlate negatively with the number of pairs in the previous year (Fig. 2b); in other words, years of lowest densities are followed by the greatest proportional increases, whereas years of highest densities are followed by the greatest declines (Newton and Marquiss 1986, Newton 1998). This finding should be interpreted with care, however, because such a pattern could also be found in a non-regulated population that exhibits random fluctuations (Newton 1998). Statistical investigation of density dependence is still an area of hot debate (Turchin 2003), and clearly beyond the scope of our review.

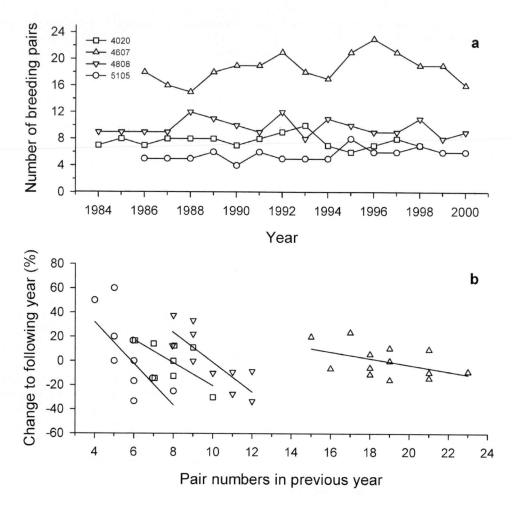

FIGURE 2. Long-term dynamics of four undisturbed goshawk populations in Nordrhein-Westfalen, Germany (numbers are Gauss-Krüger coordinates of study plots; see Arbeitsgruppe Greifvögel NWO 2002). (a) Population trends. (b) Graphic test for density dependence (percentage of change in population, y, in relation to population level, x, in previous year). Best-fit lines in (b) are shown for illustration purposes only (Newton and Marquiss 1986, Newton 1998). Note that some points in (b) overlap. Stability of breeding numbers and density-dependent population regulation can be found in many other stable populations. Unpublished trend data were collected by E. and B. Baierl, D. Becker, G. Müller, U. Siewers, and G. Speer, and communicated by E. Guthmann.

Krüger and Lindström (2001) failed to find a direct link between the per capita growth rate of their study population and the breeding pair density of the preceding season. Interestingly, population growth was significantly related to an interaction between density and autumn weather conditions, suggesting a coupling between density-dependent regulation and density-independent limitation.

Further support for the existence of density-dependent population regulation comes from the growth patterns of increasing populations, and the observation that productivity falls as breeding density increases (Looft 1981, Link 1986, Möckel and

Günther 1987, Bijlsma 1993, Krüger and Stefener 1996 [OFG], Altenkamp 2002). The latter result, however, seems not very robust, as some studies have documented the converse pattern. An increase in productivity with density was reported for a population in central Poland (Olech 1998), and three populations in southern Germany (Bezzel et al. 1997a [OFG]). Olech (1998) interpreted her finding as an artifact of killing by humans, which affected the age-structure of the breeding population which in turn may have caused changes in productivity. Likewise, Bezzel et al. (1997a) hypothesized that their results were probably attributable to the effects of persistent illegal killing and habitat destruction which held breeding numbers well below carrying capacity. An increase in breeding performance with density could also occur as a response to a substantial change in food supply, as discussed later.

Non-breeding Population

Several studies demonstrated that breeders are replaced soon—often within a few days—after their disappearance due to death or breeding dispersal (Looft 1981, Link 1986, Bijlsma 1991b). Further, some authors reported that extra birds visit active nests (Kollinger 1974, Bednarek 1975, Link 1986) or hold singleton-territories (Bezzel et al. 1997a, Penteriani et al. 2002b) during the breeding season. Both observations suggest the existence of a surplus population (Newton 1979a, 1991; Kenward et al. 1999, 2000) of non-breeders (also called floaters), which are physiologically capable of breeding, but will not do so until a breeding place becomes available.

Conclusive evidence that some individuals are excluded from breeding can only be produced by controlled removal experiments in populations with identifiable individuals (Village 1990, Newton and Marquiss 1991), or by following cohorts of radio-tagged hawks through their early life (Kenward et al. 1999, 2000). In goshawks, individuals can also be identified by comparing length, shape, coloration, and pigment patterning of molted primaries (Opdam and Müskens 1976, Ziesemer 1983, Kühnapfel and Brune 1995, Rust and Kechele 1996, Bijlsma 1997). Three investigators compared shed feathers of replacement birds to those sampled from known breeders in the study population in an attempt to estimate the extent of breeding dispersal. Ziesemer (1983) reported that only five (3.3%) of 151 new female breeders (N = 463 female years) had bred at another territory in the study area before. This is in close agreement with results by Link (1986) in his Erlangen study plot, who found that only four females (2%, N = 268 female years) and two males had bred previously in another territory. In an urban population in the city of Hamburg, not a single case of breeding dispersal was found (C. Rutz, unpubl. data; cf. Bezzel et al. 1997a). Because so few breeders within large study areas change territories, we can assume that most new breeders are unlikely to have previously bred elsewhere. In other words, the majority of new recruits appear to have been floaters, despite already having adult plumage.

Due to their elusive behavior, non-breeders are difficult to study, and little is known about this crucial component of goshawk populations. So far,

the only quantitative estimate of the proportion of non-breeders in a goshawk population comes from a large-scale radio-tagging study on the Baltic island of Gotland (N = 318 tagged hawks; Kenward et al. 1999). It was estimated that in this stable population each year about 30% of males and 60% of females did not breed (for use of molted feathers, see Link 1986).

Theory suggests that there is a tight coupling between breeder and non-breeder dynamics (Newton 1988a, 2003b; Hunt 1998). As non-breeders do not depend on habitat with suitable nest sites, they can potentially exploit areas and prey resources denied to breeders. However, the floating sector of a population is inevitably limited by the numbers and productivity of breeders; the total number of non-breeding hawks is likely to be set at an equilibrium point, where annual additions match the annual substractions (Hunt 1998). On the other hand, non-breeding numbers could directly affect breeding numbers, as it is the floater pool that provides new breeding recruits that fill vacant territories. If the non-breeding sector has collapsed, for example, breeders that died or emigrated can no longer be replaced (*Case study 2*). Generally, non-breeders will form a small proportion of depleted or increasing populations and a large proportion of stable populations at capacity level (Newton 2003b). This intriguing model of population regulation has not yet been tested in goshawks but our current knowledge of goshawk population biology is largely consistent with these ideas.

Dynamics of Expanding Populations

When established populations experienced a marked decline in density, breeding numbers often returned to the original level at the end of the recovery phase (Bezzel et al. 1997a, Olech 1998, Looft 2000, Krüger and Lindström 2001, Arbeitsgruppe Greifvögel NWO 2002). However, this is not invariably the case, as populations in some areas increased well beyond their original density in recent decades (*Case study 1*).

More convincing evidence of density limitation comes from the growth trajectories of newly founded populations, which generally exhibit a logistic pattern, characterized by three phases—establishment, expansion, and saturation (Shigesada and Kawasaki 1997). The observation that numbers do not grow indefinitely but level off toward the end of the colonization process indicates that the populations are limited by some external factor (Newton 1998). Examples, which we shall describe in detail, include the expansion of the Dutch goshawk population during the 1980s and 1990s (Bijlsma 1993, Lensink

1997, *Case study 1*), the spread of goshawks in several areas of Great Britain (Petty et al. 2003a; P. Toyne, unpubl. data, *Case study 3*) and the recent establishment of urban populations (Würfels 1999, Rutz 2001, Altenkamp 2002). Similar patterns of spatial and numerical expansion have been described for other populations (Geuens 1994, Albig and Schreiber 1996, De Fraine and Verboven 1997, Nielsen and Drachmann 1999a, Greifvögel NWO 2002; G. Vermeersch and A. Anselin, pers. comm.).

REGULAR SPACING OF TERRITORIES

In well-forested areas, nest sites often show a pattern of regular spacing (Fig. 3; Bednarek 1975, Waardenburg 1976, Link 1986, Bühler and Oggier 1987, Jørgensen 1989, Bijlsma 1993, Mañosa 1994, Penteriani 1997, Kostrzewa et al. 2000, Krüger and Lindström 2001). Most probably, this is the result of a spacing mechanism that maintains the minimum distance between adjacent nesting territories, despite increasing numbers of birds of breeding age, and which ultimately obliges some individuals to delay breeding until a vacancy occurs. For goshawks in Norway, Selås (1997a) could show that the removal of breeders by hunters led to an increase in goshawk breeding density in periods with increasing food supplies, but not in periods in which prey density remained unchanged. This observation strongly suggests that the territoriality of established breeders can hold breeding densities below levels that would otherwise be permitted by the available food supply. Similar experimental evidence for the operation of a spacing mechanism in goshawks does not exist for western, central or southern Europe, but its key components—territorial behavior of breeders and exclusion of potential breeders—are well-documented.

The existence of territorial behavior in the goshawk has been shown by direct observation at nest sites (Holstein 1942, Brüll 1984, Link 1986, Norgall 1988, Bijlsma 1993, Penteriani 2001) and more recently by monitoring radio-tagged individuals (Ziesemer 1983, 1999; Rutz 2001, 2005a). In The Netherlands, the probability of nest failure tended to increase with decreasing NND values, possibly as a result of increased levels of aggressive interactions (re-analysis of data from Appendix 26 in Bijlsma 1993; GLM [binomial error, logit link-function], Δ deviance = $[\chi^2]$ = 3.06, df = 1, P = 0.083; *cf.* Link 1986). Territorial behavior leads to the exclusion of some individuals from the breeding population which is best illustrated by the observation that the age of first-breeding varies with the degree of intraspecific competition in a population (Olech 1998).

FIGURE 3. Breeding dispersion of goshawks in a Dutch study area (SW-Veluwe; R. G. Bijlsma, unpubl. data), illustrating the regular spacing of territories, characteristic of established populations at capacity level (hatched = woodland; unhatched = heaths, farmland, built-up; scale bar = 1 km). The figure depicts the situation in 1990, in which the following nest numbers of other raptor species were recorded in the same area: 54 *Accipiter nisus*, 74 *Buteo buteo*, 32 *Falco subbuteo*, 9 *Falco tinnunculus*, 19 *Pernis apivorus*.

In comparatively undisturbed goshawk populations, new breeding recruits are usually ≥2 yr of age (Bednarek 1975, Ziesemer 1983, Link 1986, Bijlsma 1993). Both male and female hawks can be sexually mature in their first year of life, but circumstantial evidence suggests that they are generally forced to delay breeding because of dominance by older individuals which occupy all the available territories (Newton 1979a, Fischer 1995, Kenward et al. 1999, Nielsen and Drachmann 2003). However, in situations where competition is relaxed, because a large proportion of breeding hawks is killed by man (Kollinger 1974, Bednarek 1975, Looft 1981, Grünhagen 1983, Link 1986; Bijlsma 1991b, 1993; Bezzel et al. 1997a, Rust and Mischler 2001), or hitherto uncolonized habitat becomes available for (re-)colonization (Waardenburg 1976, Thissen et al. 1981; Würfels 1994, 1999; Rutz et al. 2006), birds will breed in their first year of life.

In the absence of extensive illegal killing or habitat destruction, the regular spacing of nesting territories in continuously suitable woodland habitat changes little from year to year (Bednarek 1975, Bühler and Oggier 1987, Selås 1997a), because of the species' strong fidelity to prime nesting territories (Kostrzewa 1996, Krüger and Lindström 2001, Krüger 2002a). Territories are often used over long periods of time, despite the turnover of occupants (Ziesemer 1983, Ortlieb 1990, Bijlsma 2003).

FACTORS LIMITING BREEDING NUMBERS

NEST-SITE AVAILABILITY

The goshawk is a prime example of a forest-dwelling raptor species. Its close association with woodland habitat is strikingly illustrated by its breeding distribution, which mirrors the availability of forests at both global (Cramp and Simmons 1980) and European scales (Fig. 1). In this section, we focus on potential nest-site limitation in areas that provide at least some forested habitat. Specifically, we ask whether evidence suggests that a shortage of suitable nesting sites can hold goshawk breeding densities below levels that would otherwise be permitted by available food supplies.

A major difficulty in addressing this question arises from the fact that goshawks use forests not only for nesting but also for foraging (Gamauf 1988a, Kenward and Widén 1989, Ziesemer 1999); hence, goshawk numbers in areas with low woodland cover may be limited by a shortage of suitable nest sites, forest-dwelling prey, and/or structural habitat features necessary for nesting and efficient hunting. We attempt to separate these effects by employing a two-step approach. Firstly, we review current knowledge of typical goshawk nesting and hunting habitats. We then proceed to quantify the species' dependence on forest habitat, looking for both spatial and temporal correlations between forest availability and breeding densities.

During the past two decades or so, much goshawk research in western Europe has focused on describing features of nesting habitat (Penteriani 2002). Studies were conducted at different ecological scales (nest tree, nest stand, landscape level, and cross-scale approach) and varied considerably regarding the robustness of the study design (e.g., use of appropriate controls) and the sophistication of the data analyses (quantitative descriptions Dietzen 1978, Looft 1981, Link 1986, Anonymous 1989, Dobler 1990, Bijlsma 1993, Mañosa 1993, Toyne 1997, Steiner 1998, Weber 2001; multivariate modelling—Kostrzewa 1987a, Gamauf 1988a, Penteriani and Faivre 1997, Penteriani et al. 2001; Krüger 2002a, b).

Despite marked regional differences in nest stand characteristics (Penteriani 2002), the goshawk generally shows a strong preference for nesting in large, mature forests with a low degree of disturbance by humans. Pairs typically nest some distance away from the forest edge (Looft 1981, Link 1986, Gamauf 1988a, Bijlsma 1993) within the most mature parts of the forest (Penteriani 2002). The nest stand is often characterized by a dense canopy and good flight-accessibility, and the nest is built in one of the largest trees within the stand (Penteriani 2002). Goshawks seem to avoid proximity to human settlements and areas of high human activity (Kostrzewa 1987a, Gamauf 1988a, Krüger 2002a; but see Dietzen 1978, Dietrich 1982). Some of the above characteristics were shown to be significant predictors for patterns of territory occupancy and productivity (Möckel and Günther 1987, Bijlsma 1993, Kostrzewa 1996 [MT], Krüger and Lindström 2001, Krüger 2002a), indicating that nest-site choice had fitness consequences for breeding pairs. An alternative interpretation is that the nest site contributes little to fitness, the statistical association arising mainly from the best quality birds occupying nest sites with favored characteristics.

It is tempting to conclude from these data that goshawks can be limited by the availability of suitable nest sites in areas where forests do not offer mature stands that fulfill the above criteria. However, detailed studies in The Netherlands and Germany have shown that goshawks exhibit a surprising plasticity in nest-site choice. Where few hawks are killed by humans, they occupy a wide range of forests, including woodlots of <0.5 ha, lanes of broad-leaved trees along roads in open polders (*Case study 1*), and even nest successfully in small city parks completely surrounded by buildings and with extraordinary high levels of human activity. We therefore suggest that any remaining preference for nesting in large mature forests could be an artifact of differences in killing by humans. Avoidance of humans could reflect shyness selected by decades of persecution. Deliberate killing would have been most common in fragmented habitats with a high proportion of farmland, because nests are easily detected in small woodlots (Bijlsma 1993, Olech 1998), private landowners often resented predation by raptors, particularly goshawks, and law enforcement was commonly absent or successfully frustrated.

To clarify, goshawks may not require mature woodland for successful nesting in the absence of killing by humans, but they may still prefer this habitat type, and their use of resources will often be dictated by environmental habitat availability. In areas with abundant prey supplies, goshawks may use less preferred nest sites if good ones are not available. This may be the situation in parts of western Europe.

Comparatively little is known about goshawk foraging habitats in Europe, particularly in the western, central, and southern parts. Only few radio-tracking studies have been conducted, and the majority of them investigated ranging behavior during the winter time (Kenward 1979, 1982; Dietrich 1982, Ziesemer 1983, Kluth 1984, Straaß 1984; Rutz 2001, 2003b; Meier 2002, Lechner 2003; C. Rutz et al., unpubl. data). Habitat-use and home-range data based on chance observations of unmarked individuals (Gamauf 1988a, Krüger 1996, Lõhmus 2001) or collections of molted feathers or pluckings (Brüll 1984, Link 1986, Krüger and Stefener 1996) are clearly biased and must be interpreted cautiously (Altenkamp 1997).

For foraging, goshawks generally seem to prefer richly-structured habitats, probably because the success of their principal hunting techniques—short-stay-perch hunting and contour-hugging flight (Rudebeck 1950–51, Hantge 1980, Fox 1981, Kenward 1982, Widén 1984)—depends chiefly on cover for self concealment. Usually, this cover is provided by forested habitat. Near Oxford, England, most of the 60 winter kills registered with four radio-tagged males were made in woodland (58%) or within 100 m of woodland (25%; Kenward 1982). Some evidence shows that goshawks inhabiting well-forested habitats make extensive use of forest-edge zones (Kenward 1982, 1996), but foraging in very open parts of agricultural landscapes has also been observed (Dietrich 1982, Ziesemer 1983, Meier 2002; C. Rutz et al., unpubl. data). Chance observations from Austria showed that goshawks spent more time in forests during the breeding season (65% of observations) than in winter (47%; Gamauf 1988a; cf. Dietrich 1982). Kenward (1996) reviews how the ecology of the main prey species affects ranging behavior in Scandinavian goshawks.

Despite doubts about the species' need of forests when food is abundant elsewhere (Kenward and Widén 1989), the literature almost unequivocally emphasizes the overriding importance of this habitat type. However, goshawks can hunt efficiently in terrain that lacks forest cover. As Olech (1997) pointed out, this can be inferred indirectly from prey lists, which often contain a considerable amount of species thriving in open habitats (Zawadzka and Zawadzki 1998). Goshawks readily use anthropogenic elements for cover during low and fast prey-searching flights and even adopt alternative hunting strategies that do not rely on concealment at all. Two such techniques closely resemble hunting behavior typically shown by Peregrine Falcons (*Falco peregrinus*), namely exposed perched hunting and high soaring and stooping (Erzepky 1977, Grünhagen 1981, Alerstam 1987, Rutz 2001). In conclusion, thanks to its remarkable behavioral plasticity, the goshawk can forage efficiently in a wide range of habitats, including forests, woodland-farmland mosaics and even metropolitan areas, provided they offer sufficient prey. Nevertheless, in the light of the insights produced by a review on goshawk-habitat interactions in Fennoscandia (Widén 1997), we stress the need for more data on goshawk ranging and hunting behaviour. Widén (1997) warns that the species might only need a small patch of suitable habitat for nesting, but that it can be seriously affected by forest fragmentation where this can potentially decrease foraging efficiency on certain kinds of prey.

We will now try to quantify the goshawk's dependence on forested habitat. At a regional scale, we found no relationship between the estimated countrywide breeding density per 100 km^2 of area, and per 100 km^2 of woodland, respectively and the country's percentage woodland cover (Fig. 4; Table 1). This is not surprising, because we were unable to control for various confounding factors and because the accuracy of density estimates varies substantially across countries. However, when we restricted the analysis to areas where several adjacent populations could be compared directly, local breeding density increased significantly with the amount of forested habitat (Fig. 4b; GLMM, P <0.001). Importantly, study plots with high forest cover held higher absolute numbers of pairs (Fig. 4b), but fewer pairs per unit of woodland area (Fig. 4d; GLMM, P <0.001; cf. Goszczyński 1997). This implies that spacing of nests in heavily forested areas is wider. Because of the inevitable circularity of this analysis (the x variable is part of the y variable), we tried to confirm this finding with an additional index of population density—mean NND. In a cross-study analysis, mean NND was not related to forest availability (Fig. 5; GLM, P >0.05), and the same result was obtained when we re-analyzed data from Bühler and Oggier (1987) for ten Swiss populations (GLM [normal error, identity link function, controlled for plot size], $F_{1,7} = 1.98$, P = 0.203) (Bednarek 1975, Link 1986). An obvious need exists for more data to understand

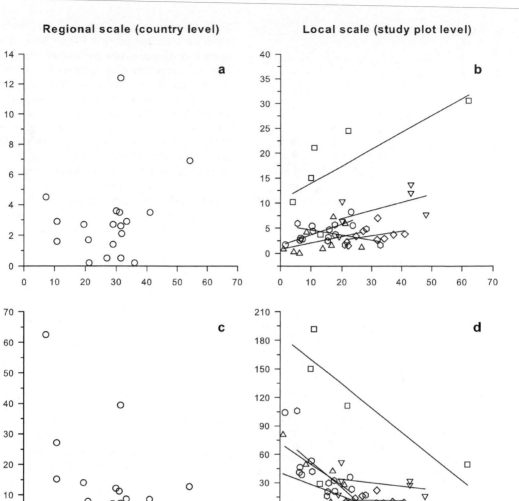

FIGURE 4. Goshawk breeding density (pairs/100 km² area, or pairs/100 km² woodland) in relation to woodland cover. (a) and (c): Regional scale; data from19 European countries (Table 1). No relationship (GLM [normal error, identity link function] on square-root-transformed data) was found between the estimated countrywide breeding density and the country's percentage woodland cover (pairs/100 km² area, $F_{1,17} = 0.69$, $P = 0.417$; pairs/100 km² woodland, $F_{1,17} = 3.32$, $P = 0.086$). Conclusions were not altered by controlling for country size (pairs/100 km² area, $F_{1,16} = 1.06$, $P = 0.319$; pairs/100km² woodland, $F_{1,16} = 3.94$, $P = 0.065$). (b) and (d): Local scale; data from studies that investigated ≥6 nearby sub-populations (total: N = 47; Switzerland, N = 9, Bühler and Oggier 1987 [diamonds]; Denmark, N = 8, Nielsen and Drachmann 1999a [circles]; The Netherlands, N = 6, Bijlsma et al. 2001 [squares]; Germany, N = 6, Link 1986 [inverse triangle], two sets, each N = 9, Weber 2001 [triangle, hexagon]; all plots <50 km² excluded). Here, GLMMs were built with study-identity modeled as a random effect (six levels), and plot size (covariate) and percentage forest cover (covariate) as fixed effects. This approach ensured that: the influence of plot size was eliminated, and conclusions could be generalized beyond the study areas investigated. Maximum breeding density increased significantly with forest cover (b) (Wald statistic = [χ^2] = 16.86, df = 1, P < 0.001), whereas maximum breeding density per unit of woodland decreased significantly with the amount of forest in the plot (d) (Wald statistic = [χ^2] = 18.01, df = 1, P < 0.001). Note that *y*-axes have different scales and that for illustration purposes, all figures show raw data with best fit-lines produced by linear regression.

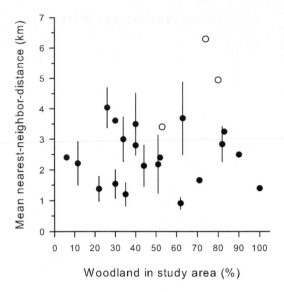

FIGURE 5. Nest spacing of goshawks (nearest-neighbor-distance, NND, mean ± SD) in relation to woodland cover of the study area; data are from western, central and southern Europe (filled), and from northern Europe (open). Sources: Pielowski (1968), Dietzen (1978), Dietrich (1982), Widén (1985b), Bühler and Oggier (1987) combined with Bühler et al. (1987), Gamauf (1988a), Anonymous (1990), Mañosa et al. (1990), Dobler (1991), Mañosa (1994), Penteriani (1997), Selås (1997a), Jędrzejewska and Jędrzejewski (1998), Olech (1998), Zawadzka and Zawadzki (1998), Kostrzewa et al. (2000), Weber (2001), Penteriani et al. (2002b), R. G. Bijlsma, unpubl. data, R. E. Kenward et al., unpubl. data. The association (GLM [normal error, identity link function]) was non-significant for western, central, and southern European data (N = 20, $F_{1,18}$ = 0.11, P = 0.744), and for western, central, southern, and northern European data (N = 23, $F_{1,21}$ = 0.66, P = 0.425).

goshawk nest spacing in relation to habitat composition at various spatial scales.

The experimental manipulation of nest-site abundance is impractical in this species. However, in some regions, the availability of suitable woodland habitat changed significantly in the course of time, as a result of forestry activities (Hölzinger 1987) or natural processes, and we can ask whether goshawk numbers changed correspondingly. Without doubt, large-scale logging of forests can have devastating effects on goshawk populations. The widespread destruction of woodland across Europe during the Middle Ages until the beginning of the 19th century may have caused dramatic population declines (Bijleveld 1974). Nowadays, forestry practices may still affect local populations (Bezzel et al. 1997a, Widén 1997, Ivanovsky 1998), but moderate timber harvesting appears to have no effect on population

levels, as long as cover reduction does not exceed about 30% (Penteriani and Faivre 2001). Forestry operations during incubation and the early nestling stage may cause breeding failures (Toyne 1997), but are unlikely to cause reduction of breeding density, unless substantial areas are clear felled. The felling of active nest trees—intentional or accidental (Bijlsma 1993, Bezzel et al. 1997a, Kostrzewa et al. 2000)—seems to be infrequent and thus unimportant. So far, the only attempt to assess the impact of forestry operations on goshawk populations on a countrywide scale was made in The Netherlands. Bijlsma (1999a, b) estimated, based on a representative sample of 559 goshawk nests out of a total population of about 1,800 pairs, that forestry operations caused the loss of 45 goshawk broods (8%) in 1998 (see also Drachmann and Nielsen 2002).

Another cause of habitat deterioration in Europe is forest dieback, e.g., the widespread tree mortality due to acid rain (Hölzinger 1987, Flousek et al. 1993). Such wide-scale phenomena could potentially affect goshawk populations across Europe (Kostrzewa 1986, Hölzinger 1987, Gamauf 1988b), but as yet remain speculative. Afforestation can provide new nesting habitat when stands are allowed to mature and enter the stage at which they become attractive for Goshawks. We illustrate the positive effects of such habitat alterations in detail in *Case studies 1* and *3* (Risch et al. 1996, Olech 1998).

In conclusion, the nest-site preferences reported for most European areas probably only partly reflect essential ecological needs, as has been proposed repeatedly (Penteriani 2002). Rather, they almost certainly evidence behavior selected partly by past human persecution (Krüger 2002a). Impressive examples of the species' behavioral and ecological plasticity occur mainly in areas without deliberate killing.

In areas with extensive woodland cover and negligible human disturbance, territorial behavior of breeding pairs probably renders structurally suitable nesting habitat unavailable for other prospective breeders, as suggested from the regular spacing of nests discussed above (Newton et al. 1977, 1986). Further, hunting conditions in large forest stands without farmland nearby might be less profitable than hunting in open woodland-mosaics with greater abundance of suitable prey (Kenward 1982, Krüger 2002a, but see Widén 1997).

An interesting feature of many stable undisturbed goshawk populations is that, despite the presence of non-breeders, some suitable nest sites remain vacant (Ziesemer 1983, Bühler et al. 1987, Kostrzewa 1996, Nielsen and Drachmann 1999a, Krüger and

Lindström 2001). Nest territories apparently vary in quality, as some are used every year, others intermittently, or only occasionally (Krüger and Lindström 2001). This suggests that breeding numbers may be limited by factors other than nest-site availability, e.g., the supply of potential prey.

Case study 1. The Netherlands—the effect of habitat alteration

The changes in numbers, distribution and behavior of goshawks living in a rapidly altering landscape can be illustrated by studies in The Netherlands. This small country in western Europe, situated in the floodplains of the rivers Rhine, Meuse, and Waal, reached an average human density of 462 inhabitants/km^2 in the early 2000s, at least two–three times as many as in any other western European country except Belgium. During the 20th century, the human population trebled, the number of houses increased sevenfold and the number of cars exploded from zero to >7,000,000. In less than a century, a mainly rural society transformed itself into a high-tech society where farming is industrialized and natural habitats are all but lost (<4% of surface by 1996); each square meter nowadays feels the stamp of human impact (Bijlsma et al. 2001). Nevertheless, goshawk densities are higher than anywhere else in Europe, showing a 40-fold increase in the past century (Fig. 6).

In the early 20th century, three important developments triggered the initial population growth. Firstly, widespread planting of coniferous forests in the late 19th and early 20th century on sandy heaths and moors in the eastern and southern Netherlands enlarged the potential breeding area substantially. By the late 20th century, almost 10% of the Dutch land surface was covered with woodland, including regions where woodland had been previously scarce or even absent. These forests became attractive breeding sites 10–15 yr or 40–50 yr after planting, depending on soil type and tree species. Secondly, goshawks received legal protection in 1936. Until then, goshawks were relentlessly persecuted (Bijleveld 1974, Bijlsma 1993). Although some legal killing continues to the present, its impact rarely suppresses density, and, if so, only locally and temporarily. Conversely, systematic persecution in the past has been shown to reduce nesting success, increase the turnover of breeding birds and reduce their mean lifespan (Bijlsma 1993). Thirdly, the availability and density of major prey species (pigeons, thrushes, and corvids; Table 3) increased markedly from the 1940s through the 1980s (Thissen et al. 1981, Bijlsma et al. 2001) due to

significant changes in land use and farming practice, and the maturation of woodland habitat.

The combination of these three factors resulted in an expanding goshawk population, from an estimated 50 pairs at the start of the 20th century to 1,800–2,000 pairs in 1998–2000 (Fig. 6; Bijlsma 1989, 1993; Müskens 2002). This growth was briefly interrupted in the late 1950s and 1960s (Fig. 6b), when massive application of persistent organochlorine pesticides in farmland led to excessive adult mortality and impaired breeding success (Thissen et al. 1981, Bijlsma 1993). Since the early 1970s, after DDT, aldrin, dieldrin, and mercury in seed dressings had been successively banned, goshawks recovered quickly. The first stage of recovery took place exclusively in the coniferous woodlands of the eastern Netherlands, which, though largely depleted of goshawks during the 1960s, still held sparse populations.

After reaching saturation levels in the core breeding range in the 1980s (mainly coniferous forests in the eastern and central Netherlands), goshawks started to colonize hitherto unoccupied habitats between the large forests, and spread into marshes and newly created deciduous forests of the central and western Netherlands, outside the main range of coniferous woodland (Fig. 6a). This westward trend into the agricultural, industrial and densely populated lowlands of The Netherlands continues. Now goshawks nest in previously unoccupied habitats: small woodlots (<0.5 ha) and tree lanes in open farmland, duck decoys, thickets, suburbs, city parks and recreational sites; in 2001, even a failed breeding attempt on an electricity pylon was discovered. Consequently, breeding goshawks occupied >1,000 5-km squares by the year 2000, covering some 60% of the total land surface, compared to only 214 in 1973–1977 (471% increase). Whereas the goshawk is still spreading, breeding density started to decline in parts of the eastern Netherlands since about the early 1990s, following precipitous declines in major prey species (*Case study 2*).

FOOD SUPPLIES

It is intuitively obvious that goshawk breeding density must be related to the availability of food resources. In areas where profitable prey is scarce, hawks face an energetic bottleneck and may cease breeding altogether. A powerful test of whether food limits density would be to increase its supply over a large area experimentally and monitor the subsequent numerical response of the local goshawk population (Boutin 1990, Newton 1998). When breeding numbers increase, we may conclude that

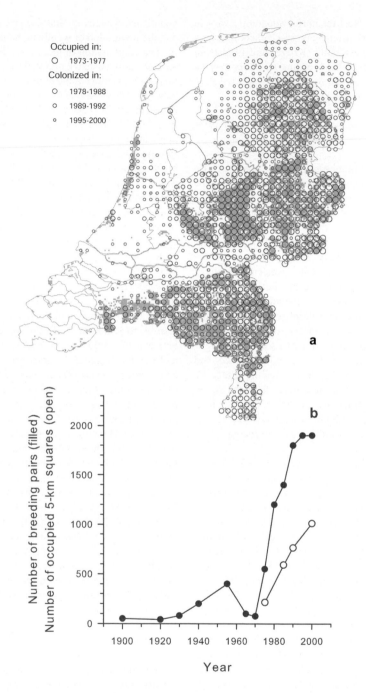

FIGURE 6. Population trend and breeding distribution of the goshawk in The Netherlands (a and b). In (a), distribution is shown as 5-km squares occupied in 1973–1977; smaller symbols show further colonization of 5-km squares in respectively 1978–1988, 1989–1992, and 1995–2000 (Bijlsma 1989, 1993; Bijlsma et al. 2001, Müskens 2002). The distribution of coniferous forest is shaded. Note the marked drop in breeding numbers in the late 1950s and 1960s in (b); the scale and timing of the decline and the subsequent recovery were consistent with an effect of pesticides, probably dieldrin and DDT. Whereas goshawks in the 1970s were largely confined to squares with a high proportion of coniferous forest, the west and northward spread in the 1980s and 1990s involved habitats never before occupied by this species in The Netherlands (a). For further details, see *Case study 1*.

TABLE 3. BREEDING SEASON DIET COMPOSITION OF THE GOSHAWK IN VARIOUS AREAS IN WESTERN, CENTRAL, AND SOUTHERN EUROPE.

Country	Area	Plot size (km²)	Forest area (%)	Study period	Prey items (N)	GD	Ra	Ow	Ga	RC	Wa	GT	PD	Wo	Th	Co	St	OP	Ma	Re	Sources
Portugal	Littoral center	220	70	2001	153	0.0	0.0	0.0	0.0	0.7	0.0	0.0	69.3	2.0	7.8	13.1	0.0	2.0	0.7	4.6	Petronilho and Vingada (2002).[a]
Poland	SW	600	23	1982–1994	1,167	0.6	1.1	2.4	4.6	0.5	0.2	0.2	50.8	4.7	12.0	10.3	3.8	5.0	3.3	0.2	Drazny and Adamski (1996).[a]
Poland	Central	?	71	1982–1993	803	(1.2)	2.0						(50.2)	6.1	7.1	8.9			(2.9)		Olech (1997).[c]
Britain	Kielder Forest	620	81	1973–1996	5,445	4.5		(11.4)					(49.8)			18.0			6.4		Petty et al. (2003a).[c]
Germany	City of Berlin, W	?	?	1982–1986	606	1.8	0.8	0.5	0.0	0.7	0.7	5.4	48.7	5.3	5.4	15.3	9.9	2.3	2.8	0.3	Jacob and Witt (1986).[a]
Germany	City of Hamburg	(3 pairs)	-	1997–1998	306	0.3	0.7	0.0	0.0	0.3	0.7	0.3	43.1	1.0	13.1	24.8	5.9	1.0	8.8	0.0	Rutz (2004).[a,d]
Netherlands	E (sand)	14,110	19	1997–2002	4,653	1.4	2.3	2.2	1.3	0.4	2.3	0.8	42.7	5.1	6.0	21.7	7.1	1.6	5.0	0.2	Bijlsma (1998–2003).[a]
Slovakia	Central	959	54	1991–1997	282	0.7	5.3	2.5	3.9	0.0	0.0	0.0	41.1	6.7	12.4	11.7	0.7	7.1	7.8	0.0	Šotnár (2000).[a]
Germany	City of Cologne	200	?	1989–1996	5,511	0.8	1.3	0.9	(5.0)	0.5	1.5	5.0	(40.0)	0.9	9.9	(26.3)	5.3		(11.4)		Würfels (1994, 1999).[c]
Denmark	Vendsyssel	2,417	8	1977–1997	19,670	0.6	1.7	1.7	4.9	1.3	3.1	3.4	37.2	0.8	17.6	13.9	3.3	12.6	4.0		Nielsen and Drachmann (1999b).[c]
Denmark	Sydjylland	10,720	?	1973–1981	4,472								(35.4)	(4.7)	(4.8)				1.0		Storgård and Birkholm-Clausen (1983).[c]
Poland	Central	10	21	1982–1985	1,054								34.1	0.8		7.4	1.9		8.8		Goszczyński and Piłatowski (1986).[b]
Germany	City of Berlin, E	?	?	1999–2001	2,083				5.4				33.4	(4.5)	(9.7)	(15.5)	15.9	1.7	2.8		Altenkamp and Herold (2001).[b]
Netherlands	N+W (peat, clay)	11,000	4	1997–2002	1,618	8.3	3.0	2.9	1.6	1.2	8.2	1.1	32.3	1.9	9.3	15.0	7.9	1.7	3.8	0.7	Bijlsma (1998–2003).[a]
Germany	N, two plots	-	-	1970–1975	2,845	0.6	2.2	4.4	4.7	0.6	5.7	1.5	30.4	1.1	18.6	9.7	4.9	3.5	3.1	7.1	Looft (1981).[a,e]
Wales		3,250	50	1991–1993	2,230	0.1	1.0	0.6	0.0	0.0	1.2	0.1	30.4	0.3	14.6	36.0	0.4	1.7	13.0	0.6	Toyne (1998).[a,f]
France	Alsace	(19 pairs)	?	1979–1998	727	1.5	2.2	0.6	4.5	1.0	0.4	0.4	28.1	4.3		23.0		3.6	12.6		Kayser (1993).[b]
Britain	several plots	-	-	1974–1980	848	0.9	0.8	0.1	33.1	0.4	1.4	0.5	26.3	0.2	5.0	5.8	1.3	0.8	22.8	0.6	Marquiss and Newton (1982).[a]
Austria	Alp foothills	250	?	1990–1998	712	(1.0)			(10.2)	(0.0)			25.7	(1.7)	(24.1)	(8.6)	5.8		(3.6)		Steiner (1998).[b]
Germany	Bayern	6,690	?	1969–1996	13,498	0.6	0.7	5.4	0.8	0.4	0.1	0.2	25.1	1.0	46.5	9.7	1.8	5.7	1.9	0.1	Bezzel et al. (1997b).[a,g]
Belarus	N	800	~35	1973–1994	639	3.9	1.4	1.1	17.4	(0.0)	2.7	(0.0)	23.2	1.8	1.9	31.7		2.3	4.0	8.6	Ivanovsky (1998).[a]
Estonia	mainly N, SE	?	?	1987–1992	988	2.5	1.6	1.1	9.9	0.0	5.0	0.0	19.4	2.1	16.8	27.2	2.7	8.1	2.9	0.7	Löhmus (1993).[a]
Spain	Granada	(8 pairs)	?	1994	410		0.5	0.5	9.0				19.3	1.7	4.1	20.7			22.0		Padial et al. (1998).[a,h]
Poland	NE	96	63	1989–1997	1,539	0.6	0.6	0.4	4.8	0.1	1.3	1.5	17.5	6.0	10.4	23.7	0.9		5.7		Zawadzka and Zawadzki (1998).[a,i]
Spain	Catalonia	176	≤30	1985–1989	1,636				19.3				(12.8)			13.5			(19.4)		Mañosa (1994).[c]
Italy	Abbruzzi region	318	?	1984–1993	782			1.7					(8.5)	(2.2)	22.4	26.9	0.0		26.2		Penteriani (1997).[b,j]
France	Lorraine	148	35	1965–1966	233	1.7	6.0	0.9	0.9	1.7	0.4	0.4	7.3	6.9	22.7	12.4	26.6	7.7	1.7	2.6	Thiollay (1967).[a]

Notes: This is not an exhaustive list of goshawk diet studies from Europe. In cases where two or more studies described the diet of Goshawks in a certain area, the most recent, or the one based on the largest sample size was included. The definition of breeding season varies slightly between studies, and the reader is referred to the original sources for further details. All studies estimated diet composition from pluckings, which had been collected at or near nest sites. Note that this method has been shown to underestimate the contribution of small (Ziesemer 1981) and large prey species (Rutz 2003a). Values in brackets are minimum estimates, as the original source gives only data for the most important species in the taxonomic group (e.g., Blackbird [*Turdus merula*] in case of thrushes), and other species may have been included in the other birds category. A missing entry means that the relevant information could not be extracted from the original source; it does not mean, however, that a certain prey group had zero contribution to total diet. Studies are arranged according to the dominance of pigeons and doves in the diet. Abbreviations for prey groups: GD = grebes, ducks and geese; Ra = raptors; Ow = owls; Ga = galliformes; RC = rails and coots; Wa = waders; GT = gulls and terns; PD = pigeons and doves; Wo = woodpeckers; Th = thrushes; Co = corvids; St = European Starling; OP = other passerines; Ma = mammals; Re = rest.

[a] Complete prey list given in original source.

[b] Only main prey species and groups listed (for details, see original source).

[c] Only major taxonomic groups listed.

this resource had indeed been acting as a limiting factor. Because of the obvious practical difficulties, no such study has been carried out with goshawks. However, sometimes humans unwittingly provide goshawks with extra food in the form of managed game, domestic poultry, or racing pigeons. These cases are not properly controlled and replicated experiments, so care must be taken in interpreting any associated response in goshawk numbers (or the lack of it)—the increase in food supply may be coupled with an increase in killing of hawks by humans (Kenward 2000, Nielsen 2003).

If food supplies limit goshawk numbers we expect to find two major correlations: (1) at the regional scale, differences in goshawk density match differences in food supplies (spatial correlation), and (2) at the level of the local population, breeding numbers track changes in local food supplies over time (temporal correlation). Before investigating the published information for concordance with these predictions, however, we need to understand the general feeding ecology of the species.

The goshawk is a versatile predator, focusing on prey species which are abundant, profitable, and sufficiently vulnerable to an attack (Dietrich 1982, Kenward 1996, Tornberg 1997, Bijlsma 1998). There are marked regional differences in goshawk diet across Europe, as illustrated by the selection of studies presented in Table 3.

A significant functional response to temporal variation in prey abundance has been demonstrated for populations in Fennoscandia (Kenward 1977, 1986; Kenward et al. 1981a, Wikman and Lindén 1981, Lindén and Wikman 1983, Tornberg and Sulkava 1991, Selås and Steel 1998, Tornberg 2001, but see Widén et al. 1987), but comparable data for goshawks in western, central, and southern Europe are scarce (Mañosa 1994; Olech 1997; Rutz and Bijlsma, in press). However, in cases where dietary studies were either carried out for a long period of time (Bezzel et al. 1997b, Nielsen and Drachmann 1999b, Nielsen 2003) or replicated in the same area after several decades (Tinbergen 1936, Pielowski 1961, Opdam et al. 1977, Brüll 1984, Haerder in Holzapfel et al. 1984; Bijlsma 1993, 1998–2003; Olech 1997; C. Rutz et al., unpubl. data) the observed changes in goshawk diet composition correlated well with obvious changes in the availability of prey species in the environment.

The ability of the goshawk to adjust its feeding ecology in response to changes in the availability of different prey species is further illustrated by marked dietary shifts in the course of the breeding season (Opdam et al. 1977, Brüll 1984, Bijlsma 1993,

TABLE 3. CONTINUED.

[a] A total of 18 unidentified prey items, which had been recorded by radio telemetry, were excluded.
[e] List contains 187 unidentified prey of various sizes.
[f] List contains 12 unidentified prey items.
[g] Sample size reported by authors (N = 13,342) is incorrect.
[h] List contains 52 unidentified birds of various sizes.
[i] List contains 358 unidentified birds of various sizes.
[j] List contains 61 unidentified birds of various sizes.

Mañosa 1994, Toyne 1998). We note, however, that it remains to be established whether predation by goshawks is indeed opportunistic, according to the technical definition of optimal foraging theory (Stephens and Krebs 1986). First results (Dietrich and Ellenberg 1981, Dietrich 1982, Ziesemer 1983, Tornberg 1997) suggest that prey vulnerability is an important determinant of goshawk diet composition (*cf.* Götmark and Post 1996).

It is inherently difficult to test for a spatial correlation between goshawk density and food supplies, because local populations differ markedly in their feeding ecology, and data on prey abundance and/or proportional availability have rarely been collected in the course of goshawk diet studies. These problems can be circumvented by using diet composition as a proxy measure of environmental prey availability (Rutz 2005b), and a cross-study meta-analysis employing this approach has recently been conducted (Rutz 2005b, C. Rutz et al., unpubl. data). Here, we will focus on material from just two studies, which each related goshawk breeding density in several sub-populations to an index of local land productivity (Bühler and Oggier 1987, Weber 2001). We reanalyzed the data sets provided in the original publications by means of robust GLMs (normal error, identity link function, controlled for plot size and forest availability in plot) and found no significant relationship for the German sample (N = 18 local populations, analysis on square-root-transformed data: $F_{1,14} = 0.92$, P = 0.355), but a significant negative association for the Swiss sample (nine local populations, analysis on $\log_{10}$-transformed data: $F_{1,5} = 7.01$, P = 0.046). It is questionable, however, whether the two productivity indices used (yield of winter corn and subjective rank scale, respectively) described goshawk prey abundance adequately. Areas in Sweden and Germany with the most abundant free-living Ring-necked Pheasants (*Phasianus colchicus*) were most attractive to goshawks, leading to higher winter densities than in a control area (Kenward 1986, *cf.* Mrlík and Koubek 1992), but this did not subsequently translate into differences in goshawk breeding densities. However, abundance of European rabbits (*Oryctolagus cuniculus*) in one area reduced dispersal tendencies and was associated with increased breeding density (Kenward et al. 1993a)

Temporal correlations between goshawk density and prey abundance have rarely been studied. In a long-term study (25 yr) in Germany, population growth rate did not vary significantly with food supplies, but the authors admitted that the indices used to describe food abundance were crude and probably biased (Ziesemer 1983, Krüger and Lindström 2001).

Krüger and Lindström (2001) did not test the interaction between food supply and population density in the previous year, because they excluded a priori the possibility of a numerical response. In fact, even in Fennoscandia, where hawks primarily prey upon several species of woodland grouse (Tornberg et al., *this volume*), which show cyclic fluctuations in numbers, goshawk densities have rarely been found to correlate with prey abundance (Selås 1997a, 1998a; but see Lindén and Wikman 1983, Tornberg 2001, Ranta et al. 2003). In Denmark, a strong increase in released Ring-necked Pheasants since the early 1990s was not correlated with local goshawk trends (Nielsen 2003), but a numerical response might have been masked by increased hunting pressure on hawks (Mikkelsen 1986). Using data presented in Goszczyński (1997, 2001), we did not find a correlation between average number of prey found in goshawk nests during control visits and the number of successful broods in the study area (N = 6 yr, Spearman rank correlation, $r_s = 0.41$, P = 0.419).

Goshawk breeding density can remain stable after a crash in prey populations, providing that alternative prey are available (Ziesemer 1983, Mañosa 1994, Olech 1997). If, however, populations of several or all important prey species crash simultaneously, goshawk breeding density may decline. This is illustrated by *Case study 2*, which is the first attempt to quantify the effect of temporal changes in food supply on breeding density and demographic key parameters in western European goshawks. Recent survey work shows that European farmland bird populations are in precipitous decline (Pain and Pienkowski 1997, Newton 1998, Krebs et al. 1999, Donald et al. 2001), but, at present no evidence suggests that this shortage of food supply affects goshawk numbers on a continental scale. This is not surprising as most of the affected farmland bird species are small-bodied passerines that play only a minor role in goshawk diets (Table 3); in fact, some favored goshawk prey species (Woodpigeons [*Columba palumbus*] and corvids) show increasing trends in farmland-dominated landscapes, at least in parts of Europe.

Apparently, goshawks easily switch to an alternative prey if one of their principal prey species becomes scarce. Hence, scope for density limitation seems limited. So far, however, we have only been concerned with breeding season food supply. The availability of food during the winter may also limit breeding numbers (Newton 1998), if it negatively affects the survival of potential breeders or their physiological condition. In farmland-dominated areas in western Europe, breeding season and winter diets show similar species composition (Opdam et al. 1977, Ziesemer 1983, Brüll 1984, Nielsen 2003), suggesting that winter food does not form a significant bottleneck for the populations concerned. In more natural areas in central and eastern Europe, however, the situation may be quite different. In east Poland, for example, goshawks mainly depend on thrushes, woodpeckers, and Jays (*Garrulus glandarius*) during the breeding season, and face rapid depletion of food supplies when thrushes emigrate in autumn (Jędrzejewska and Jędrzejewski 1998, van Manen 2004). Poor food supply during winter and the pre-laying stage probably causes low goshawk breeding densities in this region (van Manen 2004) despite high food abundance during summer (Wesołowski et al. 2003).

Finally, circumstantial evidence demonstrates that various aspects of goshawk biology vary with food supply in a way consistent with theoretical expectations. This is probably best illustrated by studies that compare urban and rural-breeding goshawk populations, which differ significantly in their access to food resources; we will describe these findings in detail later. Much of the other work has been conducted in Scandinavia, but in this case we consider it reasonable to generalize the conclusions to hawks, living in other parts of Europe: (1) home-range size is a decreasing function of food availability (Kenward 1982, 1996; Ziesemer 1983), (2) daily activity patterns are related to hunting success (Widén 1981, 1984), (3) juveniles, which have been raised under good food conditions, disperse later (Kenward et al. 1993a, b) and are more likely to return to the vicinity of their natal nest site (Byholm et al. 2003), (4) productivity increases in relation to food availability (Lindén and Wikman 1980, Tornberg 2001, Byholm et al. 2002b, Ranta et al. 2003), and (5) during winter, juvenile hawks congregate in areas of high food supply (Kenward et al. 1981a).

Case study 2: The Netherlands—the effect of food shortage

In *Case study 1*, we described changes in goshawk breeding numbers in The Netherlands during the 20th century. Despite a continuing increase in geographic range (Fig. 6a), numbers stabilized from about the early 1990s (Fig. 6b). For example, between 1990 and 2000 the number of occupied 5-km squares increased by 30%, but breeding numbers remained stable at 1,900–2,000 pairs. This discrepancy can partly be explained by a substantial reduction in number and availability of main prey species in core breeding areas of goshawks in the last two decades of the 20th century.

The impact of food supply on density and reproductive output has been investigated in the central Netherlands (Bijlsma 2003, unpubl. data). The 20 km² large plot of Planken Wambuis (52°03'N, 5°48'E) is typical of coniferous forests planted on poor soil in the eastern Netherlands in the late 19th and early 20th centuries. Every 5 yr, the breeding bird fauna has been surveyed, using a low-intensity variety of the combined mapping method (Tomiałojć 1980). The recorded densities in large sampling plots are a relative measure of abundance, and useful in assessing changes in breeding bird composition and numbers. Annually since 1973, all nests of raptors, including goshawks, have been located and checked to determine clutch and brood size, and weigh and measure nestlings; molted feathers, for individual recognition, and prey remains were also routinely collected.

Avian biomass in spring and early summer declined by 80% between 1975 and 2000, especially in the weight categories of 51–250 g (pigeons, doves, thrushes, corvids, European Starling [*Sturnus vulgaris*]) and 251–500 g (pigeons), i.e. the major prey base of goshawks (Fig. 7a). Racing pigeons, weighing 250–300 g and an important male goshawk prey during the breeding season, declined dramatically, as demonstrated by data from regular counts of homing pigeons. And finally, the rabbit population crashed by >95% between the mid-1970s and early 2000s as a result of severe winters, the outbreak of viral hemorrhagic disease in 1990–1991, and dominance of *Deschampsia flexuosa* in the undergrowth caused by increased nitrogen deposition (Fig. 7a; Heij and Schneider 1991, Bijlsma 2004a).

In the early 1970s, the local goshawk population steeply increased, a recovery from the pesticide-induced decline in the 1960s, reaching stable numbers (six–seven pairs) in 1976–1986, then declining to three–five pairs in the 1990s and early 2000s (Fig. 7b). Several lines of evidence suggested that, over the years, floaters also disappeared from the area. In recent years, lost breeders have not been replaced, and territories remain vacant.

The declines in numbers of breeding pairs and non-breeders as well as in reproductive output closely mirror the changes in prey availability. Although circumstantial, this suggests a limiting effect of food supply, while other extrinsic factors apparently remained unchanged. The overriding impact of food supply is also visible in changes in predatory behavior, with increasing goshawk predation on raptors, owls and corvids, resulting in the local demise of Eurasian Kestrel, Eurasian Hobby (*Falco subbuteo*), Eurasian Sparrowhawk, Long-eared Owl (*Asio otus*),

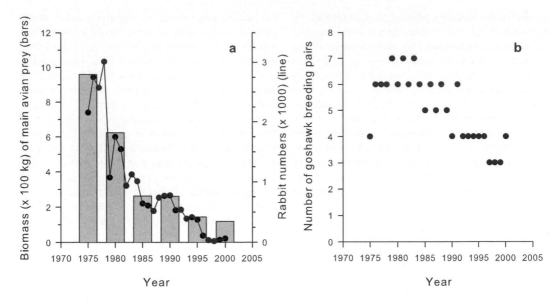

FIGURE 7. The effect of food shortage on goshawks at Planken Wambuis (20 km²), central Netherlands, 1975–2000. (a) Collapse of goshawk prey populations in the study area. Bars show estimated total biomass of birds in the body size category 51–500 g in 5-yr periods; figures were calculated on the basis of standardized breeding bird counts (combined mapping) and number of pairs in spring (×2 to include both pair members, but excluding young); line is local rabbit numbers. (b) Change in number of goshawk breeding pairs. For further details, see *Case study 2*.

and the increased frequency with which unprofitable prey—larks, tits, and finches—are captured. A full report of this study has been presented elsewhere (Rutz and Bijlsma, in press).

KILLING BY HUMANS

Because goshawks are predators of medium-sized mammals and birds, racing pigeons, and domestic poultry, they have a long history of being controlled. Moreover, their populations have also been harvested to provide captive birds for falconry—initially for food but subsequently for sport. The extensive literature describes past persecution and harvest but impact has rarely been quantified, mainly because goshawk populations were not monitored with precision during the periods when such activities were at their peak. Population monitoring is relatively recent, commencing broad scale from the 1970s following the large reduction in raptor populations in the 1950s and 1960s which was associated with widespread environmental pollution. Human persecution of raptors in Europe has been reviewed by Bijleveld (1974) and Newton (1979a, b). The case of the goshawk is probably best illustrated in a historical context, by comparing time periods with different levels of killing.

The killing of raptors was encouraged from the 16th century onward, with the payment of bounties

to reduce predation of domestic stock. The numbers of goshawks killed must have been large, but there is no documented impact on wild populations, and breeding populations remained extant across Europe with no recorded national extinctions at that time. In the 19th century, game preservation became important as pheasant game shooting was enhanced with reared birds. Game preservers were employed to kill predators, including goshawks, which can be a problem particularly at pheasant release sites (Kenward 1977, Nielsen 2003). Moreover during the 19th century, raptors were commonly viewed as potential pests, so large numbers were killed (Braaksma et al. 1959, Richmond 1959, Bijleveld 1974), and it was not until some populations were clearly in decline, even to extinction in some places, that legal protection was initiated.

Goshawk populations were resilient where large areas of forest remained because game preservation was less intensive within forests and breeding production was sufficient to buffer the losses due to persecution. Recent work from Scandinavia shows that goshawk populations can, under some circumstances, withstand considerable levels of killing. For example, it was estimated from the recoveries of banded birds that 14% of the Fennoscandian goshawk population was killed annually by man (Haukioja and Haukioja 1970), with no apparent decline in the breeding population. Calculations by Kenward et al. (1991), based upon Swedish banding returns and supplemented by radio-telemetry data, suggest that a loss to persecution of up to 35% of young birds might be sustained without leading to population decline. Birds in their first year are more likely to be killed than are older birds, so persecution falls heaviest on non-breeders. We note, however, that the situation in Fennoscandia contrasts markedly with that in western and central Europe, where breeders and their broods have been the main targets. Such losses are likely to be additive to other sources of mortality, and hence have greater potential impact on breeding numbers than the destruction of non-breeders.

Irrespective of general population resilience, goshawks did decline at the end of the 19th century, mainly in countries with poor forest cover such as Denmark (Jørgensen 1989) and Britain (Marquiss and Newton 1982). Where forests are fragmented, goshawks are particularly vulnerable as few breeding pairs are remote from intensive human persecution. Goshawks can have large overlapping home ranges, both during and outside the breeding season (Kenward et al. 1981a, Kenward and Walls 1994); areas of food abundance, such as pheasant release pens, attract many individuals (Kenward et al. 1991, Nielsen 2003) so that a substantial proportion of the population can be at risk.

From the mid-20th century, at least partially in response to the pollutant-associated steep declines of the 1960s, goshawks became legally protected in many countries, and populations increased in a few areas. In conservation terms, the species is now considered secure though sufficiently vulnerable to be listed in the Bern Convention as a species requiring international coordination for its conservation (Tucker and Heath 1994). At present the goshawk has legal protection in the breeding season across Europe, though birds can be legally killed in some countries outside of the breeding season (Finland) or in special circumstances where they are considered damaging to game (Hungary, Czech Republic, some regions of Germany, and Sweden) or wildlife conservation interest (in several parts of Germany, after the re-introduction of Black Grouse [*Tetrao tetrix*]; Dobler and Siedle 1993, 1994; Busche and Looft 2003).

Despite protection, illegal killing continues throughout Europe, as documented by numerous anecdotal reports in the literature. We now focus on results from long-term studies that provide data sets sufficiently robust to assess the effects of past persecution on local populations. Human persecution

has indeed been shown to negatively affect demographics and density of local breeding populations. Several studies demonstrated how persistent killing of adult birds at nests changed the age-composition of the breeding population (Link 1986, Bijlsma 1993, Bezzel et al. 1997a, Olech 1998, Rust and Mischler 2001), ultimately leading to reduced population productivity through age-dependent reproduction (Drachmann 2003, Risch et al. 2004). For populations in the northern Netherlands (Bijlsma 1993) and in Denmark (Drachmann and Nielsen 2002), it was possible to establish the complete causal chain where killing by humans (ultimate level) leads to demographic effects (proximate level) which in turn leads to changes in breeding density (*cf.* Rust and Mischler 2001). The aim of the Danish study was to identify the causes of a pronounced decline in breeding numbers between 1994–2000 in the Vendsyssel area (Drachmann and Nielsen 2002). In this period, illegal killing significantly reduced fecundity and survival of 1- and 2-yr-old females, which in turn appeared to reduce population growth rate (*cf.* Noer and Secher 1990). In a long-term study in northern Germany, a marked drop in breeding numbers coincided with a change in hunting law, legalizing the killing of goshawks; after legal protection was re-established, numbers increased again to their previous level (Looft 2000). Further examples of correlations between the intensity of hunting pressure and goshawk population trend are given in Bijlsma (1991a).

In conclusion, there is evidence that killing by humans can directly limit goshawk breeding density, but nowadays, it seems rarely substantial enough to cause widespread decline (Bijlsma 1991a). For any population, killing of adult territory holders during the breeding season has greater significance than the destruction of broods, or of immature birds during winter (Newton 1998). Even if direct effects seem generally negligible, moderate culling could have a substantial indirect impact by continuing to constrain goshawks in their choice of nesting sites. In many parts of Europe, remote habitats with low degrees of human activity are apparently preferred, such as in large mature forest—a limited resource in modern, human-altered landscapes. We explore this idea further in a later section.

Case study 3: Great Britain—the effect of killing by humans

In Britain, the goshawk population declined following reductions in forest, which fell to <5% of land cover by 1900 (Petty 1996a). Goshawks were widely persecuted for game preservation and were already rare by the early 19th century. Amongst the last records were nests robbed of eggs or young, and possibly the last breeding females were those killed in 1864 and 1893. There was sporadic breeding in southwest England from the 1920s but these birds were persecuted and did not persist (Meinertzhagen 1950).

During the 1960s and 1970s, goshawks started breeding in at least 13 widely separated regions of Britain, and five breeding populations subsequently established (Marquiss and Newton 1982). They probably all arose from birds imported from central Europe in the 1960s and from Finland in the 1970s, which had escaped from captivity or had been deliberately released. Kenward et al. (1981b) estimated that in the period 1970–1980, an average of 20 goshawks per year escaped from captivity, and a further 30–40 were released. These birds clearly had a major impact on the distribution of colonists and their establishment, because the number of new areas and the overall population trajectory were proportionately enhanced following years of high importation (Marquiss 1981).

By 1980, about 60 pairs probably existed but then importation was restricted and subsequent population growth varied according to annual productivity and deliberate killing (Marquiss et al. 2003). In some areas, breeding production was reduced by half due to the destruction of breeders or the removal of their eggs and young (Marquiss and Newton 1982). The impact of the illegal killing away from breeding sites was difficult to quantify but a potential effect was inferred from a comparison of population growth in two regions, Scottish borders where goshawks lived in a large area of state-owned forest remote from game interests, compared with northeast Scotland where many of the birds used privately owned woodlands close to pheasant rearing sites (Marquiss et al. 2003). In both areas, breeding performance was little affected by the killing, and production was similarly good at 2.45 young per breeding pair. However in the Northeast, goshawks were said to be a problem at pheasant release sites (Harradine et al. 1997) with ample evidence of birds shot and trapped.

The population growth in the Northeast was less than half of that in the Borders. Three types of evidence suggested that lack of potential recruits constrained the growth of the breeding population in the Northeast. Firstly, on average only 70% of breeding sites were occupied each year compared with virtually complete occupancy each year in the Borders. Secondly, breeding numbers increased or decreased from one year to the next correlated with the production of fledged young 2 yr earlier. Finally, the birds bred in the Northeast at a younger mean age. In the

state forest of the Borders area, no birds were found breeding in their first year of life, whereas in the Northeast yearling birds comprised 13% of breeding females. The long-term consequence of poor population growth was pronounced. The two populations started simultaneously in the early 1970s, but by 1996, the Borders held 87 pairs compared with 17 in the Northeast.

The number of breeding pairs has increased slowly but steadily in Britain, and they are now widespread, though still absent from Ireland and the far North of Scotland (Marquiss 1993). By the mid-1990s, the population was possibly about 400 pairs (Petty 1996a), and has increased since then. Nevertheless, illegal killing is common and widespread, accounting for at least 42% of banded bird recoveries (Petty 2002). Some goshawks are poisoned or shot, and many are caught in cage traps set with live decoys for corvids. These traps are operated legally, providing that non-target species are released, but this does not always happen (Dick and Stronach 1999).

However, a substantial decline in the number of professional gamekeepers has occurred in Britain (Tapper 1992), and attitudes have changed at least in southern Britain (Kenward 2004). Thus, although some gamekeepers kill individual raptors that cause problems at pheasant pens, they no longer persecute them in the sense of seeking local eradication. The more enlightened approach has enabled rapid recolonization by Common Buzzards (*Buteo buteo*), but unfortunately, the much larger home ranges and greater predatory competence of goshawks makes them more vulnerable at pheasant pens (Kenward et al. 2000, 2001). However, secluded nesting habitat for goshawks has increased substantially as conifer plantations from the 1960s and 1970s have matured. State-owned forest, in particular, harbors relatively unmolested breeding goshawk populations, whose production fuels further increase despite killing by humans elsewhere.

ENVIRONMENTAL POLLUTION

The evidence for pollution effects on goshawks is largely indirect and circumstantial. They did not experience the sudden widespread regional extinction suffered by other bird-eating raptors (Hickey 1969), so investigative research was limited. In retrospect, had goshawks been severely affected in Europe, we would have expected four sorts of evidence (Newton 1979b). (1) a steep population decline in the 1960s, followed by slow increase as pesticide levels fell from the mid-1970s, (2) impaired breeding with many eggs broken, thin-shelled or failing to hatch, and small brood sizes in successful nests, (3) elevated levels of pesticide residues in unhatched eggs and in the tissues of full-grown birds, and (4) a spatial correspondence with these symptoms occurring in areas of greatest pesticide use.

Widespread population declines in goshawks happened in parts of Europe (Bijlsma 1991a), including a precipitous decline in The Netherlands (*Case study 1*). The scale and timing of that decline and subsequent recovery were consistent with an effect of pesticides, probably dieldrin and DDT (Thissen et al. 1981). Bijleveld (1974) reported cases of impaired breeding with failure of eggs to hatch in four of 20 clutches, but shell thinning was not pronounced. Samples from northwest Europe showed shells were 8% thinner than pre-pesticide levels (Anderson and Hickey 1974, Nygård 1991), which is insufficient to cause widespread egg breakage (Newton 1979a), and this apparently did not happen (G. Müskens, pers. comm.). In Germany, some shell thinning occurred and its extent was correlated with the concentrations of DDE in the egg contents (Conrad 1977, 1981). In Belgium, shells were at their thinnest (12.8% of pre-pesticide shell thickness) in the 1950s and less so (10%) in the 1960s (Joiris and Delbeke 1985).

In a few instances, the levels of pesticide residues in eggs and body tissues were sufficient to cause death (Koeman and van Genderen 1965), but median values in eggs from Germany, Britain, Norway, and Bohemia were usually much lower than in Eurasian Sparrowhawks from the same region (Bednarek et al. 1975, Conrad 1978, Marquiss and Newton 1982, Frøslie et al. 1986, Diviš 1990). The samples of goshawk material were small, pesticide levels often low, and the residues from DDT and DDE, the cyclodienes (HEOD), PCBs, and mercury were often correlated (Delbeke et al. 1984, Frøslie et al. 1986), so it was difficult to attribute effects to specific pollutants. However, the precipitous population decline in The Netherlands in the near-absence of egg breakage suggests the main causal factor was cyclodienes rather than DDT (Newton 1988b).

Lastly, the symptoms of pesticide poisoning were most apparent in regions of intense agriculture, such as The Netherlands, Belgium and Germany (Ellenberg 1981). However, because the monitoring of goshawk populations and breeding performance is so labor-intensive and goshawk populations are fairly tolerant of additive mortality (Kenward et al. 1991), it is likely that symptoms might have been overlooked elsewhere. Moreover, poor breeding success and some population decline can also be symptomatic of deliberate killing which occurred simultaneously with organochlorine use in some regions (Bednarek et al. 1975, Link 1981, Terrasse 1969, van Lent 2004).

Taken together, this evidence was sufficient to suggest that goshawks were affected by organochlorine pesticide pollution in Europe, though major population decline probably occurred only in regions of heavy application. Where affected, goshawks probably acquired most of their pollutant burden through their consumption of pigeons, a major food in agricultural landscapes (Table 3). Pigeons feed on newly-sown grain which, in the late 1950s and 1960s, was usually dressed with aldrin or dieldrin to protect it against insect attack. Populations remote from such regions seem to have been little affected, presumably because most goshawks, and much of their herbivorous prey (non-grain eating species accumulated only low levels of organochlorines) are relatively sedentary (Bühler and Oggier 1987, Mañosa et al. 2003). This, together with the fact that goshawks are widely distributed, means that they can be used as model bioindicator species (Ellenberg and Dietrich 1981). Such work continues with particular emphasis on PCBs (Herzke et al. 2002, Wiesmüller et al. 2002, Kenntner et al. 2003, Mañosa et al. 2003, Scharenberg and Looft 2004), although to date detrimental effects of these chemicals on goshawk populations are not established.

INTERSPECIFIC COMPETITION AND PREDATION

The goshawk is a powerful raptor, and throughout its European breeding range, it belongs to the upper segment of regional raptor guilds (Glutz von Blotzheim et al. 1971, Cramp and Simmons 1980). Goshawks seem unlikely to suffer much from interference competition, as most sympatric large raptors differ markedly in their habitat preferences and feeding ecology. The notable exception is the Eurasian Eagle-Owl.

Some competition for avian prey might be expected with the smaller Eurasian Sparrowhawk (van Beusekom 1972, Opdam 1975, Brüll 1984, Bijlsma 1993, Overskaug et al. 2000). Moreover, in large parts of Europe, goshawks share their preferred nesting habitat with four similar-sized species—Common Buzzard, European Honey-buzzard (*Pernis apivorus*), Red Kite (*Milvus milvus*), and Black Kite (*Milvus migrans*) (Kostrzewa 1987a, b; Gamauf 1988a; Dobler 1990; Kostrzewa 1996; Selås 1997b; Krüger 2002a, b; Weber 2001), and goshawks may compete with them for prime nesting territories. However, little doubt exists that competition within this species complex is highly asymmetric in favor of the goshawk. Goshawks have been shown to regularly kill adults as well as nestlings of the aforementioned species (Table 3; Uttendörfer 1952), take over their territories (Newton 1986, Kostrzewa 1991, Fischer 1995, Risch et al. 1996), and defend successfully their own nest sites against interspecific intruders (Kostrzewa 1991, Fischer 1995). Cases where goshawks fall victim to members of the other species are exceptional (Uttendörfer 1952, Krüger 2002b).

It is not surprising therefore that the few studies explicitly addressing the question of interspecific competition between goshawks and other raptor species, assumed a priori that the goshawk is dominant over its sympatric competitors (Kostrzewa 1991, Krüger 2002a; but see Dobler 1990). Indeed, goshawks were found to affect nest dispersion (Newton 1986, Kostrzewa 1987a, Gamauf 1988a, Toyne 1994) and density (Risch et al. 1996; but see Gedeon 1994) in various co-existing raptors, and to reduce their nest success and/or productivity (Kostrzewa 1991, Krüger 2002b, see also Petty et al. 2003a, Bijlsma 2004b). Only two studies took the opposite perspective and investigated whether goshawks themselves, despite their apparent dominance, suffer from the presence of another species. Dobler (1990) found no effect of the distance to the next Red Kite nest site on goshawk productivity (OFG). Likewise, Kostrzewa (1987b) observed no impact of Common Buzzards or Honey Buzzards on patterns of nest occupancy in goshawk. Stubbe (quoted in Gedeon 1994) found a significant increase in Red Kite density coincident with a drop in goshawk numbers, but this association on its own is insufficient evidence of interspecific competition.

In some parts of The Netherlands, goshawks have to compete for nests with the highly territorial Egyptian Goose (*Alopochen aegyptiacus*). Absent in the early 1970s, this species increased dramatically during the past two decades, reaching >5,000 pairs by 2000 (Lensink 2002). Egyptian Geese readily take over goshawk and Common Buzzard nests, whether unused or occupied. In an area of 45 km² in the northern Netherlands, all 24 nests of Egyptian Geese in 2002 were thus situated, and egg dumping took place in two of ten occupied goshawk nests in 2003 (R. G. Bijlsma, unpubl. data). So far, the geese have had no obvious impact on goshawk breeding numbers, but they presumably influence the raptor's nest-site choice in some regions.

Goshawks may also compete with mammalian predators where important food resources are shared. This is the case in southern Norway, where the red fox (*Vulpes vulpes*) seems to depress goshawk breeding numbers by limiting grouse abundance

(Selås 1998a). Similar effects of resource exploitation could exist in western and central Europe, as suggested for the dunes in the western Netherlands (Koning and Baeyens 1990). Of course, extensive hunting of game by humans could act in the same way, depleting food supplies to a level where goshawks show a numerical response. This has not yet been investigated, probably because researchers have traditionally focused on the opposite effect, i.e., the potential impact of goshawks on game populations (REGHAB 2002).

The Eurasian Eagle-Owl is the largest owl species in the world with adult birds in western and northern Europe weighing about 2–3 kg (Mikkola 1983). Its breeding range in Europe largely overlaps with that of the goshawk (Cramp and Simmons 1980). Occasionally, eagle-owls kill other large raptors, including goshawks (Mikkola 1983, Brüll 1984, Tella and Mañosa 1993, Serrano 2000, Busche et al. 2004). Raptors typically make up about 5% of the diet of eagle-owls (Mikkola 1983, Penteriani 1996), but values as high as 21% have been recorded (Grünkorn 2000). For a goshawk study population in northeast Spain, Tella and Mañosa (1993) estimated that about 9% of all successful broods (N = 44) were affected by eagle-owl predation. However, predation on nestlings by eagle-owls has probably little effect on goshawk breeding numbers, because these losses are not necessarily additive to other sources of mortality. The same holds true for predation of nestlings or eggs by any other predator, e.g., pine marten (*Martes martes*; Sperber 1970, Möckel and Günther 1987). Losses of adult hawks are theoretically more relevant, but seem to occur too infrequently to have a significant impact on stable breeding populations at capacity level.

Of greater importance is the fact that eagle-owls compete with goshawks for nest sites in areas where suitable cliff ledges are scarce. In such habitats, eagle-owls may breed on the ground, but they seem to prefer tree nests built by diurnal raptor species, especially Common Buzzards and goshawks (Grünkorn 2000; C. Rutz et al., unpubl. data). In fact, evidence is accumulating that the large-scale reintroduction of the eagle-owl into parts of northern Germany, which is virtually cliff-free, had a substantial effect on the density and productivity of several local goshawk populations (Busche et al. 2004, C. Rutz et al., unpubl. data). Similar impacts of eagle-owls on Black Kites have been documented in the Italian Alps (Sergio et al. 2003). Following extensive conservation measures for about 20 yr, eagle-owls are thriving in Germany (Mädlow and Mayr 1996, Berndt et al. 2002, Dalbeck 2003) and elsewhere in Europe (Penteriani 1996, Mebs and Scherzinger 2000); some recovering populations have increased well beyond previous densities, and are now entering hitherto unoccupied areas (Doucet 1989a, Berndt et al. 2002, Wassink 2003). Competition with other diurnal raptors appears to have little effect on goshawk numbers, but as eagle-owls spread, they might well reduce sympatric goshawk populations.

WEATHER CONDITIONS

Potential weather effects on goshawk population dynamics were investigated by Krüger and Lindström (2001), using data from 25-yr population monitoring in eastern Westphalia, Germany. Per capita growth rate of their study population was best explained by a model including the variables annual mean habitat quality, weather during nestling rearing, autumn weather, and density which explained 63% of the variance. In particular, population growth was reduced in association with more rainfall during nestling rearing and in autumn, but increased with higher temperatures during these periods (especially in July and August). Although nest-site quality appeared to be the principal factor in shaping population dynamics, its effect was significantly modified by weather conditions. It is unclear whether this finding represents a direct influence of weather on goshawks or impacts of weather on the productivity of prey.

Being large, goshawks can withstand several days of fasting (Kenward et al. 1981a, Marcström and Kenward 1981a) which must help them survive through inclement weather that would kill smaller birds. In the harsh environment of Fennoscandia, however, severe weather conditions during winter have been shown to cause substantial losses among juvenile and adult goshawks (Sulkava 1964, Sunde 2002), probably through food shortage. To our knowledge, band recovery data from western and central Europe have not yet been examined for the potential effects of winter weather on adult mortality and subsequent breeding numbers. Pooling recovery data across years did not reveal a pronounced mortality peak during the winter months (Bijlsma 1993, Kostrzewa and Speer 2001).

Kostrzewa and Kostrzewa (1991) failed to find relationships between winter weather and breeding density or the proportion of pairs laying in the following season, but see Huhtala and Sulkava (1981). In The Netherlands, the severity of the preceding winter affected mean laying date, but had no obvious impact on clutch size or nest success (Bijlsma 1993). Goshawk mortality might be higher in particularly

severe winters but it seems unlikely that winter weather is an annual bottleneck for populations in Europe's temperate regions. In contrast to their Scandinavian counterparts, goshawks in western and central Europe do not rely on the availability of a few prey species and can more easily switch to alternative prey as necessary. This fundamental difference in feeding ecology and hence, vulnerability to winter food shortage is reflected in differing migratory patterns—goshawks in Fennoscandia are partial migrants, whereas those in western and central Europe are sedentary (Glutz von Blotzheim et al. 1971, Cramp and Simmons 1980).

In a German area, heavy rainfall in the pre-laying period had no effect on the density of territorial pairs but appeared to influence the proportion of territorial pairs that laid eggs (Kostrzewa and Kostrzewa 1990 [MT]; see also Bezzel et al. 1997a). Favorable weather conditions in March are associated with early egg laying (Looft 1981, Bijlsma 1993, Drachmann and Nielsen 2002; V. Looft and M. Risch, unpubl. data), which in turn could positively affect productivity (Huhtala and Sulkava 1981, Bijlsma 1993, Penteriani 1997 [OFG], Drachmann and Nielsen 2002; V. Looft and M. Risch, unpubl. data; C. Rutz, unpubl. data), assuming a causal relationship between the two factors (Meijer 1988). In some cases, a direct correlation between rainfall and temperature in spring and reproductive performance of goshawk pairs has been found (Kostrzewa and Kostrzewa 1990 [OFG, MT], Bijlsma 1993, Penteriani 1997 [OFG, MT], Kostrzewa et al. 2000 [OFG, MT], Drachmann and Nielsen 2002; but see Goszczyński 2001, Altenkamp 2002). Dobler (1991) reported an effect of elevation on breeding density and laying date (OFG) and argued that elevation is most probably correlated with weather parameters, such as average temperature and precipitation (cf. Bühler and Oggier 1987).

Some anecdotal reports show that prolonged periods of rain or low temperatures can cause mortality among goshawk nestlings (Looft 1981, Link 1986, Anonymous 1990, Kostrzewa and Kostrzewa 1990), but the effects of such losses on population trends are likely to be small or non-existent.

The impact of a catastrophic weather event, a gale, on local goshawk populations was investigated in northeastern Switzerland and northern France (Schlosser 2000, Penteriani et al. 2002b). Despite the windstorm's devastating effect on forest-stand structure, no differences in subsequent breeding density, nest-stand choice, and productivity were found (Penteriani et al. 2002b [OFG]), suggesting a considerable tolerance of the species to sudden habitat changes caused by such drastic weather events—but see Kos (1980) and Bezzel et al. (1997a) for the possible impact of clear-felling of large forest tracts by humans.

It is difficult to interpret the available data on potential effects of weather factors on goshawk populations, because the topic does not lend itself to experimentation, and observational studies are often statistically compromised: some studies involved multiple-testing without correction of P-values, and most had insufficient data to control for confounding variables or for non-independence of data points. Weather conditions may account for some of the year-to-year variation in density (Newton 1986), probably acting through an effect on spring food supplies, but they do not generally seem to limit goshawk breeding numbers in temperate Europe.

PARASITES

To our knowledge, large-scale reductions in goshawk numbers due to epizootics have not been documented. Goshawks are hosts to a range of parasites, including various blood and other endo-parasites (Krone 1998, Krone et al. 2001). Lists of parasite species sampled from goshawks, however complete, tell us little about the potential impact of infections on goshawk populations. A crucial issue is whether parasites hold breeding numbers below the level that would otherwise occur, for example by causing substantial additive mortality among mature birds or by significantly reducing productivity (Newton 1998). We know of only three systematic studies that attempted to assess the potential importance of parasites for local goshawk populations in Europe.

Trichomonosis is an infectious disease in birds, which is caused by the protozoan flagellate *Trichomonas gallinae*. It is particularly common in the Columbiformes, which typically form a substantial part of the goshawk's breeding season diet (Table 3). This together with incidental cases of fatal trichomonosis infection in nestling goshawks, led several authors to hypothesize that the disease might be a significant mortality factor (Trommer 1964, Sperber 1970, Looft 1981, Link 1986, Cooper and Petty 1988). Recently, Krone et al. (2005, unpubl. data) investigated the prevalence of *T. gallinae* in an urban population of goshawks in the city of Berlin, Germany. In 80% of all investigated broods at least one nestling was infected (N = 90 broods, containing 269 nestlings, at 37 different territories). From necropsies of 46 adult hawks, 22% tested positive for *T. gallinae*. The authors conclude that trichomonosis is the most important infectious disease in their study

population, but it remains to be established whether it acts as a population limiting factor. A similar result was obtained in a study in southwest Poland in which all surviving 35–40-d-old nestlings were found to be infected with *T. gallinae* (N = 11 broods, containing 28 nestlings; Wieliczko et al. 2003). In another study in Wales, Great Britain, the impact of the blood parasite *Leucozytozoon toddi* on nestling goshawks was investigated (Toyne and Ashford 1997). A total of 35% of 23 broods were infected, but the parasite had no detectable effects on nestling mass or mortality (*cf.* Wieliczko et al. 2003).

From this material, we cannot judge the impact of parasite infections on breeding numbers in goshawk, but, on basis of what is known from other bird species (Newton 1998), it is probably small or non-existent. Under extreme environmental conditions, such as food scarcity or in adverse weather, high parasite loads might contribute to the mortality of adult hawks, but this is not necessarily additive to other forms of mortality.

URBAN POPULATIONS AS NATURAL EXPERIMENTS

Most goshawks breed in natural or rural habitats with extensive patches of mature woodland and little human disturbance. However, during the last 30 yr, the species has colonized urban environments throughout Europe (Table 4). Now goshawks breed in metropolitan habitats, ranging from suburban districts to the centers of large cities with >9,000,000 inhabitants. Some urban populations have apparently already reached stable breeding numbers, whereas others are still expanding or have only a few pioneer pairs.

In the context of this review, these urban populations resemble natural experiments, offering valuable opportunities to assess our ideas on the dynamics of goshawk populations in semi-natural habitats or in rural areas. Regarding their biotic and abiotic properties, urbanized areas differ markedly from other environments generally inhabited by goshawks. In particular, cities are characterized by high levels of human activity, a comparatively small amount of woodland, and a high abundance of avian prey species.

MUCH HUMAN ACTIVITY BUT NO DELIBERATE KILLING

In most metropolitan environments, levels of human activity are high, but at the same time, deliberate killing of goshawks is virtually absent—a situation rarely encountered in other landscapes.

TABLE 4. URBAN BREEDING POPULATIONS OF GOSHAWK.

Country	City	Habitat type	Study area (km²)	Remark	Year of first colonization	Pairs in [year][a]	Density (pairs/ 100 km²)[a]	Trend[b]	Sources
Germany	Saarbrücken	suburban	315		unknown	≥14 bp (80)	≥4.4 bp	?	Dietrich (1982),
	Cologne	urban	200	western part of city	1988 (87?)	≥22 bp (98)	≥11.0 bp	0	Würfels (1994, 1999).
	Hamburg	urban	300	city north of river Elbe	1985	17 bp (00)	5.7 bp	0	Rutz (2001), and unpubl. data.
		urban, suburban	701	eastern part of city + periphery	unknown[c]	42 terr. (01)	6.0 terr.	+	Altenkamp (2002).
	Berlin	urban	486	western part of city	unknown[c]	35 terr. (97)	7.2 terr.	+	Altenkamp and Herold (2001).
Netherlands	Amsterdam	(sub-)urban	?[d]		probably 1990s	5 bp (03)	?	?	Zijlmans (1995), Müskens (2002), P. Marcus, pers. comm.
	Groningen	(sub-)urban	50	whole town	1996	6 bp (00)	12.0 bp	0	Dekker et al. (2004).
Russia	Moscow	urban	?[d]	whole city	end of 19th century	~35 bp (00)	?	+	Samoilov and Morozova (2001), I. Aparova, pers. comm.

Note: Anecdotal reports of goshawks breeding in or near cities; Germany—Münster, Billerbeck, Dülmen (Bednarek 1975), Wuppertal (Richter 1994), Leipzig, Coburg, Nürnberg (Fischer 1995), Kiel (Berndt et al. 2002), Leverkusen (P. Wegner, pers. comm.), Russia—Perm (Kazakov 2003), Ukrania—Kiev (Domashevskiy 2003), Latvia—Riga (U. Bergmanis, quoted in Altenkamp 2002), Czech Republic—Prague (Danko et al. 1994).

[a] bp = breeding pair; terr. = breeding territory.
[b] Use of symbols same as in Table 2.
[c] For a detailed discussion, see Altenkamp (2002).
[d] As yet, no systematic survey work.

The fact that goshawks successfully colonized large cities is an impressive demonstration that the mere presence of humans is not sufficiently disturbing for the species to prevent successful breeding. This finding contrasts strikingly with the conclusions reached by studies on nest-site characteristics of goshawks in semi-natural or rural landscapes, which we have reviewed above.

Urban-breeding goshawks are remarkably tolerant of human activity (Würfels 1994, 1999; Rutz 2001, 2003a, b, 2004; Altenkamp and Herold 2001, Altenkamp 2002, Aparova 2003, Kazakov 2003). In highly urbanized settings, the flushing distance for perched hawks is typically as low as 10–20 m (Würfels 1994, 1999; Rutz 2001, 2003b; R. Altenkamp, pers. comm.); birds can often be approached even closer, as long as the observer shows no particular interest in them and behaves like other nearby humans (Rutz 2001, 2003b, 2004). The degree of tolerance presented by breeding adults appears to increase with the average stress level they are exposed to at their nest sites (Altenkamp 2002; C. Rutz, pers. obs.). Deviating from footpaths in parks rarely provokes alarm calls from nesting hawks, and mobbing attacks during nestling banding are exceptional (Altenkamp 2002; C. Rutz, pers. obs.). Brooding females generally do not flush from the nest when approached even when the nest tree is struck with a stick (Altenkamp 2002, Aparova 2003; C. Rutz, pers. obs.). A similar degree of tolerance of human activity at nest sites has been described for breeders in rural areas, but only exceptionally.

Hawks regularly perch in single trees beside busy streets or in back yards in residential areas (Rutz 2001, 2003b, 2004). More surprisingly, this forest-dwelling raptor often sits completely exposed on anthropogenic structures, including roofs of buildings, television aerials, electricity pylons (Lessow 2001, Rutz 2004), and even parked cars (Wittenberg 1985) and garden furniture (P. Wegner, pers. comm.). In Hamburg, at least five male and two female territory holders regularly used prominent man-made structures to engage in peregrine-like perched hunting (Rutz 2001, 2004). In several cities, goshawks pluck prey on roofs, chimneys, and balconies (Tauchnitz 1991, Würfels 1994; Rutz 2001, 2003b, 2004). Three radio-tagged males used buildings and parked cars for cover while hunting in low-quartering flight (Rutz 2001, 2003b) and plucked their prey in back yards (Rutz 2001, 2004; C. Rutz et al., unpubl. data). Several foraging trips were recorded after sunset under artificial light conditions (Dietrich 1982).

Despite their extraordinary tameness, urban goshawks still present obvious stress responses in certain situations. They seem to become nervous when aware of being watched and fly off immediately when an observer raises a pair of binoculars (C. Rutz, pers. obs.). Urban-breeding goshawks appear to be unaffected by human activity but could pay a price for living in this novel environment if, for example, they had lowered reproductive performance due to high stress levels or increased mortality risk due to anthropogenic obstacles in their hunting habitat (Sweeney et al. 1997). Nothing indicates that this is the case; in fact, all closely monitored urban populations in Europe had higher productivity even after breeding numbers stabilized toward the end of the colonization process than did rural populations (Table 5), and the observed adult and juvenile mortality rates are low (C. Rutz, unpubl. data; but see Rutz et al. 2004). Detailed color-banding studies in Hamburg show that a considerable proportion of new recruits had fledged in the city (Rutz 2005b, unpubl. data).

ALMOST COMPLETE ABSENCE OF MATURE WOODS

If, for this raptor, mature woodland per se were necessary for nesting, we would expect comparatively low breeding densities in highly urbanized areas. Quite the opposite is true: where detailed census data are available, densities in metropolitan habitats exceed those found in nearby rural areas with more woodland (Table 5). For example, Altenkamp and Herold (2001) reported a density of 6.0 territories/100 km² for a study plot in urban Berlin and a density of 3.8–4.1 territories/100 km² in surrounding rural areas of the federal state of Brandenburg. Likewise, the high density of 11.6 pairs/100 km² in urban Cologne (Würfels 1999) compares with only 4–5 territories/100 km² in a rural plot west of the city boundary (Kostrzewa et al. 2000). The same applies to Hamburg and its rural surroundings (C. Rutz et al., unpubl. data).

Urban goshawks use various types of green space for nesting. Some public parks, cemeteries and hospital grounds resemble non-urban nesting sites. Examples are large parks at the periphery of the cities of Cologne (Würfels 1994, 1999) and Moscow (Aparova 2003), inner-city park complexes with extensive patches of mature trees in Berlin (Altenkamp and Herold 2001, Altenkamp 2002), or a well-forested cemetery in the city of Hamburg (Rutz 2001). In the same cities, however, successful broods in private gardens and small parks (1–20 ha in size), which are completely surrounded by built-up habitat and present high levels of human activity compared with rural nest sites, are not unusual (Fig. 8; Zijlmans 1995, Würfels 1999, Rutz 2001, Altenkamp 2002). In Hamburg, one pair successfully fledged young from a nest in a solitary tree, situated in a residential area. Nests are often located close to or even above extensively used footpaths and in close proximity to buildings (Würfels 1994, 1999; Aparova 2003, R. Altenkamp, pers. comm.; C. Rutz, unpubl. data); in Hamburg, a successful nest was only 10 m from a five-story building (C. Rutz, unpubl. data).

Above we emphasized that woodland provides not only nest sites for goshawks, but also important food supplies. In fact, provisioning males in

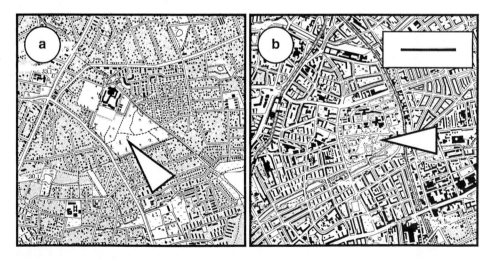

FIGURE 8. Examples of typical goshawk breeding sites (nest near arrow head) in a metropolitan setting (city of Hamburg, Germany; C. Rutz, unpubl. data). (a) Territory in small public park in residential area. (b) Territory in hospital park. Scale bar (for both maps) is 500 m.

TABLE 5. COMPARISON OF GOSHAWK KEY DEMOGRAPHICS BETWEEN EUROPE AND NORTH AMERICA.[a]

	Europe					North America				
	North	West	Central	South	(Sub-)Urban	North-west	West coast	West-central	North-central	East coast
Forest cover in study area (%)	53 (20–80)	30 (4–82)	44 (8–90)	55 (30–83)	5, 16, 40	50, 85	25, 86	95	62	48
Breeding density (pairs/100 km²)	4.0 (1.4–5.6) [9]	4.8 (0.8–31.6) [30]	8.8 (1.9–20.0) [11]	5.0 (0.2–15.3) [4]	8.8 (5.9–12.0) [3]	4.0, 10.0 [2]	4.8 (1.0–8.2) [2]	4.8, 12.5 [1]	1.8 [1]	1.2 [1]
Nearest-neighbor distance (km)	3.4, 5.0, 6.3 [9]	2.6 (1.2–4.0) [39]	1.7, 3.7 [11]	3.4 (1.5–5.0) [5]	2.8 [4]	NA [2]	3.3 [7]	3.9 [2]	NA [1]	8.0 [1]
Nest success (%)	74 (57–86) [3]	77 (33–91) [8]	69 (63–100) [2]	72 (57–81) [4]	84 (69–93) [1]	75, 84, 95 [3]	83 (77–91) [1]	79 (47–91) [9]	70 (62–85) [5]	83, 85, 94 [3]
Brood size (juvs/succ. brood)	2.7 (2.2–3.1) [8]	2.5 (1.5–3.4) [44]	2.7 (1.8–3.0) [9]	2.5 (2.3–2.8) [4]	2.9 (2.0–3.1) [4]	2.0, 2.3, 2.9 [3]	1.9 (1.8–2.2) [4]	2.1 (1.7–2.6) [9]	1.8 (1.6–2.2) [5]	1.8, 2.1, 2.1 [3]
Productivity (juvs/started brood)	1.8 (1.3–2.5) [12]	1.8 (0.5–2.6) [50]	1.8 (1.1–3.0) [12]	1.4, 1.7, 1.8 [4]	1.7, 2.5, 2.9 [4]	1.8 (1.6–2.4) [3]	1.6 (1.4–1.9) [4]	1.6 (0.9–2.4) [11]	1.4 (1.1–2.2) [5]	1.5, 1.8, 2.0 [3]
Clutch size (eggs/clutch)	3.3 (2.8–3.6) [5]	3.4 (2.2–4.0) [41]	3.4 (2.9–3.6) [9]	3.2, 3.3, 3.4 [3]	3.4 [3]	NA [4]	NA [4]	NA [13]	NA [6]	2.8 [3]
Adult breeder mortality (%)	21, 37 [4]	29 (20–36) [14]	NA [8]	NA [3]	NA [1]	36 (59) [2]	26 [1]	21 (14–29) [4]	20, 26 [2]	NA [1]
Mammals in summer diet (%)	14 (1–18) [8]	5 (0–23) [4]	6 (3–10) [10]	20 (1–33) [8]	3 (0–11) [7]	65 (22–78) [5]	51 (8–79) [12]	67 (21–91) [9]	70 [2]	47 (30–73) [4]

Notes: This table is a raw summary of data from a detailed cross-continental meta-investigation of goshawk key demographics (C. Rutz et al., unpubl. data). Each cell gives median (for N >3), range of values (in brackets), and sample size (in square brackets) (NA = no data available). Note that studies vary considerably in methodology, e.g., climbing of nest trees vs. observation from the ground, size of the study plot, duration of study.

[a] *Sources:* The following are the sources used to compute summary statistics, organized by geographical region and country or state for Europe and North America, respectively (study plots that covered territory of two countries/states are listed only once—N = 5). Note that the number of sources does not necessarily match sample sizes given in table cells, as some papers reported data for several distinct study sites, whereas in a few other cases, data from several papers had to be combined to yield a single datapoint.

Europe—north: Estonia (Lelov 1991; Lõhmus 1993, 2004); Finland (Huhtala and Sulkava 1976, Wikman and Tarsa 1980, Huhtala and Sulkava 1981, Wikman and Lindén 1981, Tornberg and Sulkava 1991, Sulkava et al. 1994, Tornberg 2000, Tornberg and Colpaert 2001, Byholm et al. 2002a, Byholm 2003; Tornberg et al., *this volume;* R. Tornberg et al., unpubl. manuscript); Latvia (Weber 2001); Norway (Myrberget 1989, Selås 1997a, Grønnesby and Nygård 2000, Steen 2004); Sweden (Widén 1985b, 1987; Kenward et al. 1999, Ryttman 2001, R. E. Kenward et al., unpubl. data).

TABLE 5. CONTINUED.

Europe—west: Belgium (Draulans 1984, Doucet 1987, Draulars 1988, Doucet 1989b, De Fraine and Verboven 1997); Denmark (Storgård and Birkholm-Clausen 1983, Rassmussen and Storgård 1989; Nielsen and Drachmann 1999a, b); France (Nore 1979, Joubert and Margerit 1986, Kayser 1993, Joubert 1994, Penteriani et al. 2002b); Germany (Dietzen 1978, Hillerich 1978, Kos 1980, Knüwer 1981, Looft 1981, Oelke 1984, Looft 1984, Heise 1986, Link 1986, Schneider et al. 1985, Möckel and Günther 1987, Saude 1987, Zang 1989, Dobler 1991, Schönbrodt and Tauchnitz 1991, Stubbe et al. 1991, Kehl and Zerning 1993, Albig and Schreiber 1996; Bezzel et al. 1997a, b; Hausch 1997, Raddatz 1997, Arntz 1993, Kostrzewa et al. 2000, Krüger and Stefener 2000, Altenkamp and Herold 2001, Weber 2001, Arbeitsgruppe Greifvögel NWO 2002, Ehring 2004); Switzerland (Bühler et al. 1987); The Netherlands (Thissen et al. 1981, Erkens and Hendrix 1984, Bijlsma 1989, Rosendaal 1990, Bijlsma 1993, Bakker 1996; Bijlsma 1998-2003; Woets 1998, Dekker et al. 2004); United Kingdom (Marquiss and Newton 1982, Anonymous 1990, Toyne and Ashforc 1997, Toyne 1998. Marquiss et al. 2003, Petty et al. 2003a).

Europe—central: Austria (Steirer 1995, A. Gamauf, unpubl. data); Belarus (Ivanovsky 1998); Czech Republic (Diviš 2003); Hungary (Varga et al. 2000); Poland (Król 1985, Goszczyński and Pilatowski 1986, Czuchnowski 1993, Drazny and Adamski 1996, Pugacewicz 1996, Goszczyński 1997, Olech 1997, Jędrzejewska and Jędrzejewski 1998, Olech 1998, Zawadzka and Zawadzki 1998, Goszczyński 2001, Wieliczko et al. 2003, van Manen 2004); Romania (Kalabér 1984); Serbia/Macedonia (Grubač 1983; Slovakia (Šotnár 2000).

Europe—south: Italy (Perco and Benussi 1981, Penteriani 1997); Portugal (Petronilho and Vingada 2002); Spain (Morillo and Lalanda 1972, Veiga 1982, Mañosa et al. 1990; Mañosa 1991, 1994; Verdejo 1994, Padial et al. 1998).

Europe—(sub-)turban: Berlin (Deppe 1976, Jacob and Witt 1936, Altenkamp and Herold 2001, Altenkamp 2002); Cologne (Würfels 1994, 1999); Groningen (Dekker et al. 2004); Hamburg (C. Rutz, unpubl. data); Saarbrücken (Dietrich 1982).

Nearctic—north-west: Alaska (Zachel 1985, Titus et al. 1997, Flatten et al. 2001, Lewis 2001, Lewis et al. 2004); Alberta (Schaffter 1998); British Columbia (McClaren et al. 2002, Mahon et al. 2003); Yukon (Doyle and Smith 1994, Doyle 2000).

Nearctic—west coast: California (Bloom et al 1986, Woodbridge et al. 1988, Austin 1993, Woodbridge and Detrich 1994, Keane 1999, McCoy 1999, Maurer 2000, Keane et al., *this volume*); Oregon (DeStefano et al. 1994b, Thrailkill et al. 2000); Washington (Watson et al. 1998, Bosakowski et al. 1999).

Nearctic—west-central: Arizona (Crocker-Bedford 1990, Zinn and Tibbitts 1990, Dargan 1991, Boal and Mannan 1994, Reynolds et al. 1994, Snyder 1995, Crocker-Bedford 1998, Reynolds and Joy 1998; Reynolds and Joy, *this volume*; Rogers et al., *this volume*); Idaho (Patla 1997, Hanauska-Brown et al. 2003; Bechard et al., *this volume*); Nevada (Oakleaf 1975, Herron et al. 1985, Younk and Bechard 1994a; Bechard, *this volume*); New Mexico (Kennedy 1991, 1997; McClaren et al. 2002); Utah (Lee 1981, Kennedy 1997, Stephens 2001, McClaren et al. 2002); Wyoming (Good et al. 2001).

Nearctic—north-central: Michigan (La Sorte et al. 2004); Minnesota (Gullion 1981a, Smithers 2003; Boal et al., *this volume*); South Dakota (Bartelt 1977); Wisconsin (Rosenfield et al. 1996, Erdman et al. 1998).

Nearctic—east coast: Connecticut (Root and Root 1978, M. Root and P. DeSimone, unpubl. data; Becker et al., *this volume*); New York/New Jersey (Allen 1978, Bosakowski and Smith 1992, Speiser 1992; Bosakowski and Smith, *this volume*); Pennsylvania (J. T. Kimmel and R. H. Yahner, unpubl. data).

Hamburg spent 88% of daylight hours in forested patches (N = 3 radio-tagged birds; Rutz 2001). However, almost half of all 143 recorded kills were made during short hunting excursions into the matrix of built-up habitat, indicating that urbanized areas enabled more efficient hunting.

These examples demonstrate that the goshawk is much more flexible in its choice of nesting and foraging habitat than previously thought. Large stands of mature forest, usually considered to be of paramount importance for the species, are not obligate requirements for successful breeding, provided that food is readily available, some trees are present for nesting, environmental contaminants are not at poisonous levels, and there is little or no deliberate killing by humans. In most cities, the degree of nest-site competition with other raptor species is probably small, but in the presence of urban-living eagle-owls, intra-guild conflicts may arise. In Hamburg, for example, eagle-owls have recently started colonizing parts of the city, and have taken over traditional goshawk breeding territories in urban parks (C. Rutz, unpubl. data).

For two urban populations, well documented colonization histories are available with detailed information on all stages of the invasion process—first settlement, rapid expansion, and saturation (Fig. 9).

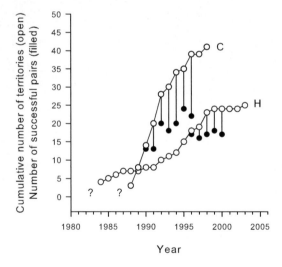

FIGURE 9. Expansion of two urban populations of goshawk in the cities of Hamburg (H) and Cologne (C), Germany. Cumulative number of established territories (open symbols) and number of successful pairs (filled) investigated in the course of monitoring studies are shown (Würfels 1999, C. Rutz, unpubl. data). The trajectory for Hamburg includes some pairs in the suburban periphery of the city; for a full description of the colonization process, see Rutz (2005b).

Toward the end of the expansion processes, the number of successful breeding attempts stabilized, whereas new territories were still being established in the respective study plots, i.e., the cumulative number of territories increased further (Fig. 9). Nest attempts in these newly founded territories were often successful, confirming that the sites were suitable for breeding. This observation suggests that goshawk breeding numbers in urban settings are not generally limited by the availability of nest sites.

ABUNDANT FOOD SUPPLY

In many of the larger German cities, including Berlin, Cologne, and Hamburg, profitable goshawk prey (Table 3), such as feral pigeons, European Starlings, corvids, and thrushes are abundant. For example, 10,600 pairs of feral pigeons were counted in urban Hamburg (area = 747 km²; Mitschke and Baumung 2001), which is more than twice the estimated number (4,300) for the whole federal state of Schleswig-Holstein north of the city (area = 15,763 km²; Berndt et al. 2002). As detailed above, breeding densities of urban goshawk populations are comparatively high, associated with the rich food supply.

Consistent with the idea of favorable food conditions in cities, urban goshawks start egg laying about 10–14 d earlier, and have greater reproductive output, than their rural counterparts (Altenkamp 2002; C. Rutz, unpubl. data). In Berlin, nest success was 87.2% (N = 391 broods), and successful pairs fledged on average 2.85 juveniles (N = 302 broods; Altenkamp 2002). Breeding pairs in nearby rural areas showed lower productivity (Altenkamp and Herold 2001). The same holds true for a comparison of urban vs. rural pairs in the city of Hamburg and its exurban periphery (C. Rutz, unpubl. data). In fact, Altenkamp (2002) demonstrated that productivity of goshawk pairs was positively related to the degree of urbanization within individual territories, as measured by the proportion of built-up habitat around nests. Moreover, by comparing series of molted primaries found at nest sites, the longer time sequences for feathers from urban individuals suggested that the annual loss of breeders was lower for the Hamburg than for rural populations (C. Rutz, unpubl. data). When data on breeding performance and demographics are compared between an urban area and a rural control plot, both study populations should ideally be at capacity level to avoid artificial results (Newton 1998). In most studies, urban populations were still increasing during data collection, at least in the early years of the investigation. However, snapshot analyses in Hamburg, carried out several years after goshawk numbers had stabilized, indicated the generality of the above findings (C. Rutz, unpubl. data; Würfels 1999 and Altenkamp 2002 continued their studies well into the saturation phase).

Further, radio monitoring demonstrated (Rutz 2001) that, home-range size was smaller, time spent in active flight was shorter, and hunting success was higher for three urban-breeding males than for their rural counterparts (Hantge 1980, Kenward 1982, Ziesemer 1983, Widén 1981, 1984; Kennedy 1991). Taken together, these data provide compelling evidence that urban environments offer excellent foraging conditions for goshawks.

On basis of the available information, it is difficult to evaluate the relative importance of food and nest sites in limiting urban goshawk populations. Considering the extremely heterogenous spatial dispersion of resources in most metropolitan environments, it is possible that breeding numbers in different areas within the same city are ultimately checked by different extrinsic factors. In Hamburg, for example, breeding density is comparatively low in the western part of the city center despite high pigeon abundance, possibly because of a lack of suitable nest sites. On the other hand, in suburban parts in the northeast, parks suitable for nesting are still plentiful but food resources apparently are insufficient to permit settling of additional pairs.

COMPARISON WITH NORTH AMERICA

This section reviews evidence for differences in goshawk biology between Europe and North America. Whereas our focus remains on populations from western and central Europe as in previous sections of this paper, this part also considers all available studies from northern Europe (Tornberg et al., *this volume*). We look first at demographic parameters, then at densities and breeding habitats, and finally at movements and diets. We re-assess ideas from a preliminary comparison (Kenward 1996) that suggested goshawks in North America might be limited by intra-guild effects, primarily from Great Horned Owls (*Bubo virginianus*) and Red-tailed Hawks (*Buteo jamaicensis*), and/or by poor food supplies in winter. Our key findings are presented in Table 5.

DEMOGRAPHY

Variation in breeding performance parameters within and between regions of Europe and North America seem as great as between the continents

(Table 5). Nevertheless, brood size and productivity seem generally larger in Europe than in North America. Nest success, on the other hand, is similar between continents with a tendency for low values in central and southern parts of Europe and northwestern North America. High variability within regions presumably reflects findings that clutch and brood sizes are influenced by food supply and the effects of weather conditions (Tornberg et al., *this volume*; Keane et al., *this volume*). Data on occupancy are not compared because this varies with length of study, declining initially as the infrequently used nesting places are discovered and then more gradually as tree stands change and new nesting sites become more attractive than some previous ones. Occupancy needs to be standardized with respect to search effort, and landscape change (Kennedy 1997; Reynolds and Joy, *this volume*).

Survival rates of adult goshawks have been estimated on both continents, using systematic banding of nestlings, mark-recapture of adult birds, cross comparison of molted feathers found at nests, and quantitative radio-tagging. Annual turnover rates for adults at nests in western central America are quite variable (14–29%; Table 5), but the median value of 21% is similar to the 20% and 23% of two studies in western Europe (Bühler et al. 1987, Drachman and Nielsen 2002; other estimates are probably inflated due to illegal killing), and 21% from 133 radio-tagged hawks on the Swedish island of Gotland (Kenward et al. 1999). The climate of this southern Baltic island is more typical of central Europe than the north, where adult mortality estimates of 37% for northern Finland (Tornberg et al., *this volume*) suggest higher mortality in the more extreme winters (Sulkava 1964, Sunde 2002). In Alaska, an adult mortality estimate was similar at 36% (Flatten et al. 2001); on basis of new data, adult male breeder mortality is as high as 59% (K. Titus et al., unpubl. data).

Data from banding tends to overestimate juvenile mortality of raptors (Kenward et al. 1999, 2000), and juvenile survival through the first year of life has been studied by radio tagging in only a few areas. In North America, three deaths were recorded when 39 young were tracked for 4–6 mo post-fledging during 2 yr in New Mexico (Ward and Kennedy 1996), giving a weighted annualized estimate of mortality of only 20%. In Utah, where a study did not extend beyond dispersal, only one death was recorded among 59 fledged hawks (Dewey and Kennedy 2001). Annualized estimates of 84% for 14 young hawks in Alaska (Titus et al. 1994) and 81% for eight in Finland (Tornberg and Colpaert 2001) were much higher which may reflect poor conditions in the north. Differences might be less if annualizing of mortality rates and analytic treatment through dispersal were comparable in all studies, but might well still indicate higher juvenile mortality at higher latitudes. The mortality rate was 42% for 185 radio-tagged juveniles tracked for 9–12 mo on Gotland (Kenward et al. 1999). Interestingly, life-table analyses for hawks banded as nestlings in The Netherlands similarly produced a first-year mortality estimate of only 41% (Bijlsma 1993), suggesting even better overall survival prospects in this more southerly country.

Although Goshawk mortality rates seem similar for Europe and North America, there may be differences in causes of death. Thus, natural predation accounted for five of nine deaths recorded for radio-tagged goshawks in Minnesota (Boal et al., *this volume*), compared with only two of 63 on Gotland, where other goshawks caused both deaths (Kenward et al. 1999). Analyses of extensive data sets of band recoveries also indicate that non-human predation accounts for only a small proportion of deaths in Europe (2.4%, Bijlsma 1993; 1.5%, Nielsen and Drachmann 1999c). Squires and Kennedy (*this volume*) speculate that Great Horned Owls are the dominant predator of goshawks due to their wide distribution, abundance, and capacity to prey on large raptors. Kenward (1996) noted that the Great Horned Owl is much smaller and nests more frequently in trees than the Eurasian Eagle-Owl, and hypothesized that goshawks in sub-boreal forests in North America may suffer from nest-site competition with the Red-tailed Hawk, a widely abundant North American Buteo (Crocker-Bedford 1990, La Sorte et al. 2004). Red-tailed Hawks are larger than their European counterpart, the Common Buzzard, and they tend to nest earlier in the season than goshawks (Craighead and Craighead 1956). Levels of intra-guild predation might increase in western European regions, as eagle-owl populations expand.

NESTING DENSITIES AND HABITATS

Whereas many studies in Europe have searched systematically for nests in well-defined areas that do not focus on a particular habitat, North American researchers have mostly concentrated on large areas of forest. This complicates a landscape-based comparison of breeding densities between continents. Some researchers may also have selected areas perceived as good for the species and hence for obtaining large samples of nests.

A cross-regional median nest density for Europe of 5.0 pairs/100 km² (N = 5 regions; Table 5) compares with a median of 4.8 pairs/100 km² for North America (N = 7 values). A tendency for lower nearest-neighbor distances between nests in Europe (Table 5; Fig. 5) may reflect clumping in areas with more fragmented forest in Europe. We note that breeding densities in parts of western Europe, notably The Netherlands (Bijlsma 1993) and Germany (Mammen 1999), are generally higher than those found in northern and central areas of the European breeding range, and also clearly exceed those found in any part of North America. Study areas in Europe contained less woodland cover (median = 44%, N = 5 regions; Table 5) than those in North America (median = 62%, N = 7 studies; Rutz et al., unpubl. data).

Direct comparison of sites chosen for nesting is constrained by differences in the emphasis of studies in Europe as opposed to North America: European studies have tended to focus on fine details of predation and productivity, whereas North American studies have traditionally focused on habitat use (Kenward, *this volume*). Nevertheless, Penteriani (2002) has recently contrasted goshawk nesting habitat in 15 European studies with 28 in North America across three spatial scales: nest tree, nest stand, and landscape. The review failed to detect significant differences in goshawk habitat use between the two continents (Penteriani 2002 [MT]) Here, we briefly discuss the three most important nest-stand characteristics, updating and amending Siders and Kennedy (1994), and Penteriani (2002) (Table 6).

The range in diameter at breast height (dbh) of trees in nest stands from four western-European study areas (Anonymous 1989, Mañosa 1993, Penteriani and Faivre 1997, Penteriani et al. 2001) was 17–46 cm, similar to the 15–59 cm in North American studies. With nests in conifers, mixed, and deciduous woodland on both continents, and mature deciduous trees generally spaced more widely than conifers, tree density in nest stands is hard to compare. A highly variable stand density in five European studies, of 223, 300, 550, and 1,716 stems/ha, compared with a median of 757 stems/ha (range 387–1,345) in North America. Canopy closure is high in North American nest areas at a median 76% (31–95) in 26 studies of which only two were <60% (Hargis et al. 1994, Lang 1994). High canopy closure might indicate a tendency to hide from over-flying large raptors. Although only four European teams have measured this parameter, it is clear from use of trees in narrow rows or even standing alone in towns that goshawks in some parts of Europe can tolerate low canopy cover and tree density for nesting. To our knowledge, goshawks have not been found breeding in urbanized environments in their North American range.

TABLE 6. COMPARISON OF GOSHAWK NEST-STAND CHARACTERISTICS BETWEEN EUROPE AND NORTH AMERICA.[a]

Variable	Europe	North America	Mann-Whitney U-test
Diameter at breast height	26	32	U = 18.5
(cm)	(17–46)	(15–59)	P = 0.327
	[4]	[14]	
Tree density	550	757	U = 38.0
(stems/ha)	(223–1,716)	(387–1,345)	P = 0.447
	[5]	[20]	
Canopy closure	84	76	U = 32.5
(%)	(73–92)	(31–95)	P = 0.245
	[4]	[26]	

Notes: Each cell gives median, range of values (in brackets), and sample size (in square brackets).

[a] *Sources*:

Diameter at breast height: Europe (Anonymous 1989, Mañosa 1993, Penteriani and Faivre 1997, Penteriani et al. 2002b); North America (Reynolds et al. 1982, Saunders 1982, Moore and Henny 1983, Hall 1984, Fischer 1986, Fleming 1987, Ingraldi and MacVean 1994, Siders and Kennedy 1994, Rosenfield et al. 1998, Finn et al. 2002b, McGrath et al. 2003, La Sorte et al. 2004; Becker et al., *this volume*; S. B. Lewis et al., unpubl. data).

Tree density: Europe (Gamauf 1988a, Anonymous 1989, Mañosa 1993, Penteriani and Faivre 1997, Selås 1997b); North America (Reynolds et al. 1982, Saunders 1982, Moore and Henny 1983, Hall 1984, Fischer 1986, Hayward and Escano 1989, Bosakowski et al. 1992, Ingraldi and MacVean 1994, Lang 1994, Siders and Kennedy 1994, Martell and Dick 1996, Squires and Ruggiero 1996, Patla 1997, Rosenfield et al. 1998, Bosakowski et al. 1999, Boal et al. 2001, Finn et al. 2002b, McGrath et al. 2003; Becker et al., *this volume*).

Canopy closure: Europe (Gamauf 1988a, Zanghellini and Fasola 1991, Penteriani and Faivre 1997, Penteriani et al. 2002b); North America (Reynolds et al. 1982, Saunders 1982, Moore and Henny 1983, Hall 1984, Fischer 1986, Crocker-Bedford and Chaney 1988, Hayward and Escano 1989, Joy 1990, Bosakowski et al. 1992, Bull and Hohmann 1994, Hargis et al. 1994, Ingraldi and MacVean 1994, Lang 1994, Siders and Kennedy 1994, Kimmel 1995, Squires and Ruggiero 1996, Titus et al. 1996, Patla 1997, Rosenfield et al. 1998, Bosakowski et al. 1999, Daw and DeStefano 2001, Finn et al. 2002b, McGrath et al. 2003, La Sorte et al. 2004; Becker et al., *this volume*).

Future comparisons of habitat characteristics between continents should make an attempt to include data from European studies that investigated goshawk populations in human-altered landscapes; these data are not yet available, but once they have been published their inclusion will probably reveal significant cross-continental differences in the above habitat measures.

MOVEMENTS AND DIET

Juvenile goshawks can disperse long distances in both Europe and North America, associated with food shortage (Byholm et al. 2003; Bechard et al., *this volume*; Sonsthagen et al., *this volume*; Tornberg et al., *this volume*; Underwood et al., *this volume*). However, throughout Europe south of Fennoscandia, dispersal distances are remarkably short—the majority of recoveries of banded hawks were typically made within 20 km of the nest (Unger 1971, Looft 1981, Link 1986, Bühler and Klaus 1987).

Goshawks in North America tend to favor woodland habitats for hunting, though some individuals use edge zones where woodland is fragmented (Boal et al., *this volume*; Sonsthagen et al., *this volume*; Squires and Kennedy, *this volume*). The same is true of northern Europe, though hunting in edge zones may prevail further south (Kenward and Widén 1989; C. Rutz et al., unpubl. data). The size of goshawk home ranges varies with habitat and food supply (Kenward 1982, 1996; Ziesemer 1983; C. Rutz

et al., unpubl. data), so a standardization of recording and estimation techniques would be needed for rigorous comparison of resource use in Europe and North America.

The majority of diet studies are based on prey remains collected at nests, often late in the nestling period. The number of studies employing video-monitoring, caging of young in the nest, and stomach analysis (Rutz 2003a) is too small for systematic comparisons across regions. In most European goshawk populations, mammals form a relatively small proportion of items in the breeding season diet (Table 3). Cross-regional medians for Europe and North America are 6% (N = 5) and 65% (N = 5), respectively; the largest values reported for individual study populations in Europe are close to the lowest estimates from the Nearctic (Table 5). With lagomorphs being an important part of the mammalian prey in many areas, the difference in terms of prey biomass is even more dramatic. Breeding goshawks in North America are more dependent on mammals than in Europe.

Some of this difference may reflect availability of suitable prey. In North America, the lowest proportions of mammals were from the coast range of western Oregon (16%; Thrailkill et al. 2000) and Alaskan islands (22%; Lewis et al. 2004), while other values below the median were from coastal states of California, Connecticut, and New York or New Jersey (Table 5). In terms of distance from coasts with their more equitable climate and diversity of habitats for birds, most European study areas would qualify as coastal states in North America. European goshawks took most mammals in areas with abundant rabbits; the importance of this smallest European lagomorph for European goshawks is summarized elsewhere (Kenward 1996).

Differences in diet choice between continents seem more likely to be due to habitat, and/or prey availability rather than greater active selection of avian prey by goshawks in Europe as a result of either learning or being innately more prone to hunt birds. Several detailed radio-tracking studies militate against a greater innate tendency to hunt birds in Europe than in North America. They demonstrated that, at least in northern parts of Europe, winter diet contains more mammals than breeding season diet (71% vs. 20%, Tornberg 1997, Tornberg and Colpaert 2001; 82% vs. 14%, Widén 1987; 72% vs. 18%, R. E. Kenward et al., unpubl. data). Indeed, female European goshawks are adapted to subduing mammals by having relatively more powerful legs than males (Marcström and Kenward 1981), and in northern Europe they obtain more than half their biomass intake from mammals in winter (Kenward et al. 1981a; Tornberg et al., *this volume*). Tornberg et al. (1999) demonstrated that long-term changes in the foraging ecology, probably reflecting prey availability, of Finnish goshawks (1960s–1990s) were associated with significant morphological shifts—females increased in size with an increasing proportion of mountain hares in their diet. The proportion and biomass of mammals in the winter diet of European goshawks is smaller overall for males than for females, because females surpass males in being able to subdue full-grown lagomorphs; European red squirrels (*Sciurus vulgaris*) were killed by male goshawks at least as frequently as by females (Kenward et al. 1981a; Tornberg et al., *this volume*).

Noting that mass of snowshoe hares (*Lepus americanus*) makes them suitable for both male and female goshawks, Kenward (1996) speculated that the widespread nature of this prey may explain why male and female goshawks are less dimorphic in North America than in Europe. Further studies could show whether morphology of North American male goshawks is as adapted to subdue mammals as that of European females, or whether winter diet may give males mammal-hunting skills that influence diet at nests. In some areas, however, North American goshawks kill birds extensively (Table 5). It therefore seems most likely that, despite any possible adaptation for killing mammals among male goshawks in North America, greater tendency to kill mammals than in Europe reflects constrained availability of birds, perhaps reinforced by learning in winter.

In this context, it is interesting that productivity was lowest, and the proportion of mammalian prey highest, in the central North America region (Table 5). Perhaps it is only in regions with the most continental climate that goshawks may be constrained to large forests by persistence there of mammalian prey in winter. In this case, goshawks might be most likely to colonize woodland fragments in farmland of North America in mid-latitude coastal areas of the east, and that is where competitive or predatory constraints of Great Horned Owls and Red-tailed Hawks might best be sought.

CONCLUDING REMARKS

From preliminary screening of our databases and a raw summary of data presented in Table 5, it seems that goshawk ecology differs between North America and Europe in the use of some habitats, in diet, and in breeding density and productivity. Goshawks in North America apparently make little use of human-altered habitats for foraging and breeding. They live at lower densities than in Europe, and produce fewer young per pair. They also use mammalian foods more often than do hawks in Europe and, perhaps associated with this, North American goshawks exhibit less pronounced sexual-size dimorphism.

The differences in goshawk ecology between continents seem to be due to some underlying factor such as prey availability, rather than a discrete subspecific difference attributable to particular morphology or intrinsic behavior. Compared with Europe, in interior North America, fewer species of birds are resident—many more of them are summer breeding migrants (Newton 2003c). We do not know their relative abundances but it is possible that, compared with Europe, avian prey is less available in North America during the winter and spring. If this were true across a range of habitats in North America, it is one potential explanation for the greater use of mammalian prey, lower breeding densities, the lack of use of urban environments, and the overall lower breeding performance. Moreover, it could be argued that the greater use of mammalian prey is a sufficient explanation for reduced sexual-size dimorphism.

However, other major differences exist between the continents; two important confounding variables are the presence in North America of more predators such as Great Horned Owls and competitors such as Red-tailed Hawks and Cooper's Hawks (*Accipiter cooperii*). Both predation risk and competition might influence habitat use by goshawks, their diet, breeding density, and performance. On present evidence it is difficult to distinguish between the influences of food availability, predation and competition.

CONCLUSIONS AND MANAGEMENT IMPLICATIONS

The goshawk is one of the best-studied raptor species in Europe. Much research remains to be done but taken together, the available information enables a qualitative assessment of the relative importance of various extrinsic factors in limiting breeding densities. Consistent with findings from other raptors, we identify nest-site availability and food supply as the two principal factors limiting goshawk populations. Importantly, given adequate food supply, nest-site availability appears to be heavily influenced by the level of killing by humans. The greater the killing, the more restricted is the range of nesting habitats acceptable to goshawks.

Currently, deliberate killing by humans only rarely has direct effects on goshawk population levels. However, even moderate levels of killing may have pronounced indirect consequences for both breeding density and breeding range. In some parts of Europe, goshawks nest in remote, mature forests, which are a limited resource in modern landscapes. In North America, such avoidance of human-altered habitats is even stronger, and may reflect more an avoidance of other raptors, notably Great Horned Owls and Red-tailed Hawks, than of humans. Natural selection among goshawks for avoidance of humans seems to be stronger in Europe than in North America, where researchers visiting goshawk nests routinely wear protective clothing because of attacks by hawks (Speiser and Bosakowski 1991). In Europe, goshawks typically hide or at least keep out of shotgun range, except for occasional attacks in the far north (T. Nygård, pers. comm.) and some western areas (M. Marquiss, pers. obs.; R. G. Bijlsma, pers. obs.).

Whether or not this avoidance of human-altered habitats is a response to past persecution or to other raptors, certain types of illegal killing may still critically affect goshawk populations by altering the species' tolerance of human activity and proximity, and hence, the suitability of habitat for nesting and foraging. For Europe, we deduced the above relationship mainly from the observation that, when deliberate killing ceased, goshawks in western Europe became highly tolerant of intense human activity. It would be wrong, however, to conclude that such an increase

in stress tolerance is sufficient to trigger the invasion of urban habitats. A comparative analysis of all known urban goshawk populations (Table 4) shows that other factors often play a role, such as the availability of potential recruits from rural populations at capacity level (Rutz 2005b).

For populations that inhabit areas where nest sites are freely available and killing by humans is rare or absent, numbers are mainly limited by food resources. We have argued for the goshawk's strong dependence on forested habitat for nesting and hunting, but in the light of the above findings, it seems that the importance of certain nest-stand characteristics may be much overstated in the literature.

Case study 2 illustrates how goshawks can be affected by a shortage of food. Many farmland bird populations are in precipitous decline on a continental scale, but recent trend data give no evidence of widespread decline in European goshawk populations in agricultural areas. However, in order to efficiently evaluate the potential effects of changes in prey abundance on goshawks in the future, we need to learn more about how goshawks use prey resources: this involves careful monitoring of the avifauna in study plots and robust use-availability analyses (Tornberg 1997).

In some parts of Europe, goshawks appear to suffer from nest-site competition with re-introduced eagle-owls. At present, only a few local goshawk populations seem to be affected, but regional impact could accompany the current range expansion of eagle-owls. In Europe we are approaching the situation pertaining in North America, where lower levels of raptor persecution have permitted Great Horned Owls to remain common.

Other extrinsic factors appear to be of minor importance under most circumstances. Weather conditions may account for some of the year-to-year variation in nesting density, probably acting through an effect on spring food supplies, but they are not a principal limiting factor in temperate Europe. Circumstantial evidence suggests that pesticide use negatively affected European goshawk populations in the 1960s. Nowadays, however, levels of organochlorine pesticides and other environmental pollutants generally seem to be too low to have significant population-level consequences. The role of parasites and diseases in limiting goshawk breeding densities is unknown, but perhaps negligible by analogy with work on other species.

The insights produced by our review have implications for future conservation. A step toward conserving goshawk numbers in Europe would be to minimize activities (such as shooting) that enhance the avoidance of humans. If goshawk predation is to be managed for socio-economic or conservation reasons, this should be by live trapping, which enables release of non-target species and relocation of hawks. It is best done with traps set on fresh kills to selectively remove specific individuals (Kenward 2000). In contrast, illegal nest destruction should be discouraged because it has demographic impact on non-target individuals.

We predict that, once freed from selective or learned impacts of human antipathy, the species will begin to display its full behavioral plasticity, allowing it to use hitherto unexploited resources. Stress tolerance and relaxed nest-site preferences, as observed in The Netherlands and some European cities will no longer be the curious exception. Additionally, goshawk conservation should focus on important prey populations (Table 3) as well as breeding and hunting habitats. This will provide opportunity for cooperation for incentive-driven conservation with other stakeholders, including land-managers and hunters. Considering the good recovery of eagle-owl populations across Europe, we recommend that further releases of this top-predator be restricted until issues concerning their impact on raptor-guilds have been adequately addressed.

FUTURE RESEARCH

Most scientific research on goshawks in Europe involves the monitoring of local populations over long time periods. Such studies are extremely important, should be continued, and new ones will hopefully be launched in the future. Ideally, all population studies should simultaneously monitor a selection of extrinsic factors—use of habitat and food by goshawks can only be investigated appropriately if their availability in the environment has been quantified. It is evident from our review that a handful of long-term projects contributed disproportionately to our understanding of goshawk biology. We note, however, that most studies on the species, including those presenting large data sets, suffer from either or both of the following shortcomings—data are correlational and hence not ideal for establishing causal relationships, and/or they lack independent replication. We propose two standard approaches of scientific inference—controlled experiments to establish cause-and-effect relationships, and meta-analyses to indicate generality (Rutz 2005b).

Carefully designed field experiments are particularly needed in goshawk research; pioneering attempts in this direction have recently been undertaken (Kenward et al. 1993a, Dewey and Kennedy 2001, Krüger 2002b, Kennedy and Ward 2003). Such work benefits from being strictly hypothesis driven, but inevitably requires innovative approaches to overcome apparent practical constraints. We believe, however, that efforts will pay off by producing robust biological insight. For some aspects of goshawk biology, enough data have been gathered to conduct meta-analyses (Kennedy 1997, Rutz 2005b). We encourage researchers to embark on joint collaborative projects, as such large-scale work will give insight that cannot come from single-site studies.

New material needs to be gathered on: (1) the biology and dynamics of the non-breeding segment of goshawk populations, (2) year-round habitat use using radio telemetry, (3) the role of winter food and/or weather conditions for limiting local goshawk populations, (4) the effect of declining farmland bird populations and habitat fragmentation on rural-breeding goshawks, (5) the effect of humans and other predators on urban and rural-breeding goshawks, (6) nest spacing in relation to forest availability at various spatial scales, (7) goshawk prey choice in relation to prey availability, and, perhaps most importantly, (8) the direct and indirect influences of food availability on population dynamics and other aspects of goshawk biology. In addition, basic monitoring data are needed for some geographic regions, as illustrated by Table 5; the main gaps that need filling are: breeder mortality estimates for parts of Europe, and clutch-size data for the entire American breeding range. Our Table 5 may indeed serve as a good orientation to guide future research efforts at a regional and/or geographic scale, and, in 10–20 yr, a substantial update may enable an even better understanding of goshawk biology.

Finally, we suggest that goshawk researchers further standardize their field methodology—delineation of study areas, measurement of nesting habitat parameters, estimation of occupancy and productivity, description of ranging behavior, and resource use—and adopt a standard format for reporting key features of their study area and population, including information on the size of the study plot, its percentage woodland cover, breeding density (mean and maximum), and mean NND in continuously suitable woodland habitat. At present, cross-continental comparisons are hampered by substantial technique variations between areas (C. Rutz et al., unpubl. data). Bijlsma (1997) produced a manual describing field methods for raptor research, which succeeded in standardizing the work of Dutch field workers, yielding large, comparable data sets. It would be desirable if a similar manual could be compiled for international use. Taken together, these measures will ensure that data collected with much fieldwork effort can be efficiently used in collaborative analyses.

ACKNOWLEDGMENTS

We are most grateful for the invitation to contribute to this goshawk monograph. We thank A. Kacelnik and I. Newton for stimulating discussions of ideas presented in this paper; and I. Newton, V. Penteriani, W. van Manen, and F. Ziesemer for their in-depth review of the manuscript and many helpful comments. Thanks to C. Marti for his editing work, and for being so patient during the final stages of manuscript preparation. The following colleagues kindly communicated unpublished manuscripts and/or data: D. E. Andersen, I. Aparova, A. Dekker, A. Gamauf, E. Guthmann, S. Kluth, O. Krone, W. van Manen, P. Marcus, T. Mebs, A. Mitschke, J. T. Nielsen, V. Penteriani, M. Risch, W. Scharenberg, H. Sevink, H. Steiner, M. Weber, and H. Wirth. Our cross-continental comparison of goshawk demographics greatly benefited from having access to draft manuscripts of other articles in this volume. Dirk Zoetebier (SOVON Vogelonderzoek Nederland) prepared Fig. 6a, and the map shown in Fig. 1 was reproduced with permission from Oxford University Press. During the preparation of this review, CR was holding a Rhodes Scholarship and a Senior Scholarship of St. Catherine's College, Oxford.

Studies in Avian Biology No. 31:198–218

NORTHERN GOSHAWK FOOD HABITS AND GOSHAWK PREY SPECIES HABITATS

Joseph E. Drennan

Abstract. Food habits of Northern Goshawk (*Accipiter gentilis*) were reviewed and evaluated to characterize diet across the species ranges and within the southwestern US. The eleven prey most frequently observed in southwest diet studies are the Abert squirrel (*Sciurus aberti*), red squirrel (*Tamiasciurus hudsonicus*), rock squirrel (*Spermophilus variegatus*), golden-mantled ground squirrel (*Spermophilus lateralis*), cliff chipmunk (*Eutamias dorsalis*), gray-collared chipmunk (*Eutamias cinereicollis*), mountain cottontail (*Sylvilagus nuttallii*), desert cottontail (*Sylvilagus audubonii*), and eastern cottontail (*Sylvilagus floridanus*), Steller's Jay (*Cyanocitta stelleri*), and Northern Flicker (*Colaptes auratus*). Habitat characteristics and natural history information regarding these species were reviewed and compared to descriptions of goshawk habitat. Goshawks consume a wide variety of prey species across their range including medium-sized birds and small mammals. Percentage of mammals in goshawk diet is generally greater than avian prey. In certain areas, and during certain periods of the year, goshawks may consume only one or two prey species. While goshawks appear to be opportunistic in their feeding behavior, low diet breadth in some areas, particularly during winter months, is likely caused by the migration or hibernation of certain prey species. Both goshawks and their prey prefer habitats with relatively high canopy closure and large diameter trees, suggesting a habitat management strategy to benefit goshawks.

Key Words: *Accipiter gentilis*, diet, food habits, habitat requirements, Northern Goshawk.

HÁBITOS ALIMENTICIOS DEL GAVILÁN AZOR Y HÁBITATS DE LAS ESPECIES DE LAS PRESAS DEL GAVILÁN

Resumen. Los hábitos alimenticios del Gavilán Azor (*Accipiter gentilis*) fueron revisados y evaluados para caracterizar la dieta a lo largo de la especie, dentro del suroeste de Estados Unidos. Las once presas observadas más frecuentemente en estudios de dieta del suroeste son la ardilla (*Sciurus aberti*), ardilla roja (*Tamiasciurus hudsonicus*), ardilla (*Spermophilus variegatus*), ardilla terrestre de manto dorado (*Spermophilus lateralis*), ardilla listada (*Eutamias dorsalis*), ardilla (*Eutamias cinereicollis*), conejo de montaña, desierto y de pascua (*Sylvilagus* spp.), charra copetona (*Cyanocitta stelleri*) y carpintero de pechera (*Colaptes auratus*). Las características del hábitat y la información histórica natural relacionadas a esta especie fueron revisadas y comparadas para describir el hábitat del gavilán. Los gavilanes consumen una amplia variedad de especies de presas que están a su alcance, incluyendo aves de tamaño mediano y mamíferos pequeños. El porcentaje de mamíferos en la dieta del gavilán es generalmente mayor que las presas aves. En ciertas áreas, y durante ciertos períodos del año, los gavilanes quizás consumen solamente una o dos especies de presas. Mientras los gavilanes parecen ser oportunísticos en sus hábitos alimenticios, una baja amplitud de dieta en algunas áreas, particularmente durante los meses de invierno, es probablemente causada por migración o hibernación de ciertas especies de presa. Tanto gavilanes, como sus presas, prefieren hábitats con copas relativamente cerradas y árboles con mayor diámetro, sugiriendo una estrategia del manejo del hábitat para beneficiar a los gavilanes.

The Northern Goshawk (*Accipiter gentilis*, hereafter called goshawk) has been a key species in decisions regarding forest management across its range, especially in the southwestern US (Reynolds et al. 1992), the Rocky Mountain Region (Kennedy 2003), and Alaska (Iverson et al. 1996). Despite protection of nest stands (≥8 ha), Crocker-Bedford (1990) found that goshawk reproduction on the Kaibab Plateau declined following timber harvest in adjacent areas. Crocker-Bedford's (1990) study and several lawsuits that followed led to the formation of the Goshawk Scientific Committee (GSC) with a charter to develop a credible management

strategy for the goshawk in the southwestern US (Reynolds et al. 1992). The resulting *Management Recommendations for the Northern Goshawk in the Southwestern United States* (MRNG) recommended managing goshawk habitats not only for the nest stand but also for goshawk prey species abundance (Reynolds et al. 1992). However, the Arizona Game and Fish Department (1993) and the USDI Fish and Wildlife Service (Spear 1993) argued that prey availability (as determined by forest structure) is more important than prey abundance because accipiter hawks are morphologically adapted to hunt in forests. Prey availability is a function of prey abundance and forest structure (tree spacing, canopy closure, and ground cover) whereas prey abundance refers only to the quantity of prey. Despite these disagreements, most agree that nest-stand management alone is insufficient to maintain goshawk populations. Researchers and managers need to consider protecting and enhancing not only the nesting habitat of goshawks but also their foraging habitat and prey populations.

The purpose of my review is to characterize the diet of the goshawk across its range and in the southwestern US, to describe the habitat requirements of the primary prey species in the Southwest; and to identify the overlap between the goshawk's habitat and that of its primary prey.

GOSHAWK DIET STUDIES

Goshawk food habits have been described throughout its Holarctic boreal-forest range, including northern Europe (Widén 1987), the Mediterranean region (Mañosa 1994) and North America (Reynolds and Meslow 1984, Bosakowski and Smith 1992). These studies report a wide variety of prey items consumed by goshawks over their entire range (Table 1) and show goshawks to be opportunistic foragers with diets that reflect the diversity of available prey species (Opdam 1975, Widén 1987, Kenward and Widén 1989, Kennedy 1991). In western North America, the dietary diversity of goshawks ranked fourth highest out of 30 raptor species; continent-wide, goshawk dietary diversity ranked second highest out of 34 species (Marti et al. 1993).

Although goshawk diets are diverse, studies suggest that sometimes only one or two prey species represent the bulk of goshawk diet, at least seasonally (Palmer 1988, Stephens 2001, Drennan and Beier 2003). In New York and Pennsylvania, Meng (1959) reported American Crows (*Corvus brachyrhynchos*) and red squirrels (*Tamiasciurus hudsonicus*) accounted for 45% and 31% of the total diet, respectively. In Minnesota, Eng and Gullion (1962) reported goshawk predation was the single most important cause of mortality to Ruffed Grouse (*Bonasa umbellus*), accounting for 30% of known losses to banded birds. On the North Kaibab Plateau, Boal and Mannan (1994) found that goshawks consumed golden-mantled ground squirrels (*Spermophilus lateralis*) more than twice as often as any other species.

Such a dependence on a single prey species could lead to a decline in predator populations if that prey species declined (Craighead and Craighead 1956,

Newton 1979a). However, this is unlikely in the Southwest, where goshawks preyed on 34 different prey species in New Mexico (Kennedy 1991) and between 19 (Boal and Mannan 1994) and 22 (Reynolds et al. 1994) in Arizona. A high number of prey species may buffer the effects of fluctuations in individual prey species populations (Boal and Mannan 1994). Goshawks in Nevada shifted their diet during the breeding season when nestling birds became more abundant and ground squirrels began to estivate (Younk and Bechard 1994a). The wide variety of prey consumed by goshawks in the western US is listed in Appendix 1.

METHODS TO STUDY RAPTOR FOOD HABITS

Goshawk diets are studied using several different methods, including pellet analysis, stomach contents, uneaten prey remains, direct observation, photographic recording, the confined nestlings technique, and combinations of these methods. Some early studies described the diet of nesting goshawks anecdotally without quantification (Sutton 1925, Gromme 1935, Dixon and Dixon 1938). Comparisons between studies are often subjective and, in some cases, not possible due to differences in methods used and the objectives of the study. Some studies can be compared at various levels with minor modifications and an understanding of the techniques. Marti (1987) described all of the techniques used in the studies analyzed here and suggested improvements for future raptor food-habit study methodology.

Relative percentages of birds and mammals comprising the goshawk diet vary according to the technique used to collect diet information. Of the techniques used to evaluate diet, direct observation at the nest is considered the least biased and most accurate to determine diurnal raptor diets (Errington 1930, 1932; Marti 1987). However, direct observation is seldom used because it is time consuming (Errington 1932, Marti 1987), the probability of identifying different prey item types is not always equal, and no information on items consumed away from the nest can be obtained.

Diet analyses from prey remains and pellets tend to underestimate small mammals (Marti 1987). Bloom et al. (1986) suggested that collecting castings at nests might fail to detect nestling birds because they lack developed bones and feathers. Collopy (1983) found that his collection of prey remains accurately reflected the species composition of Golden Eagle (*Aquila chrysaetos*) diets but

TABLE 1. FREQUENCY OF PREY ITEMS OF SELECTED GOSHAWK DIETS ACROSS THEIR RANGE.

Species	N.E. Spain Mañosa (1994)	Central Sweden Widén (1987)	Oregon Reynolds and Meslow (1984)	New York Bosakowski and Smith (1992)
Class Mammalia				
Blarina brevicauda				1
Marmota monax				1
Sylvilagus spp.			3	7
Lepus spp.		6	24	1
Oryctolagus vulgaris	333			
Sciurus spp.	86	124	4	60
Glaucomys sabrinus			15	
Tamiasciurus spp.			13	19
Tamias striatus				18
Spermophilus spp			23	
Microtus sp.				1
Peromyscus leucopus				7
Neotoma spp.			3	
Ondatra zibethicus				2
Class Aves				
Anas platyrhynchos	24		2	1
Anas acuta				1
Aythya fuligula	3			
Bucephala clangula	6			
Aix sponsa				3
Meleagris gallopavo				1
Dendrogapus obscurus			5	
Tetrao spp.	176			
Bonasa spp.	25		3	7
Collinus virginianus				6
Phasianus colchicus				4
Oreotyx pictus			10	
Zenaida macroura			7	21
Alectoris rufa	362			
Coturnix coturnix	21			
Columba spp.	248	141		17
Vanellus vanellus		4		
Scolopax rusticola		5		
Larus spp.		4		
Streptopelia turtur	28			
Bubo virginianus			1	
Asio spp.		1		
Otus spp.	27		1	
Athene noctua	18			
Aegolius acadicus			1	
Picus viridus	31			
Colaptes auratus			15	1
Melanerpes lewis			1	
Sphyrapicus spp.			2	
Picoides spp.	15	2	2	
Dendrocopus major		3		
Dryocopus pileatus			1	
Garrulus glandarius	184	99		
Corvus spp.		110		5
Perisoreus canadensis			5	
Cyanocitta spp.			30	21
Sturnus vulgaris	79			

TABLE 1. CONTINUED.

Species	N.E. Spain Mañosa (1994)	Central Sweden Widén (1987)	Oregon Reynolds and Meslow (1984)	New York Bosakowski and Smith (1992)
Pica spp.	54	37	1	
Turdus spp.	197	113	20	4
Ixoreus naevius			4	
Sialia sialis				1
Parus major		7		
Setophagia ruticella				1
Passer domesticus				3
Quiscalus quiscula				6
Piranga spp.				2
Melospiza melodia				4
Pheuticus melanocephalus		1		
Junco hyemalis		2		
Sturnella neglecta		2		
Carpodacus spp.		2		
Fringilla coelebs	23	12		

seriously underestimated the relative biomass of prey eaten compared to the direct observation method.

Diet studies typically report the frequency of occurrence for each prey species observed either through direct observation of prey deliveries at the nest or through analysis of pellets and prey remains. Some studies also include a conversion of the observed numbers of prey items to biomass estimated from published body weights. Where frequency and biomass are reported simultaneously, biomass figures show a larger percentage for mammals and a lower percentage for birds (Tables 2–5), because of the larger mean mass of mammals relative to birds.

Analyses of pellets and prey remains must determine the minimum number of prey items per sample (Reynolds and Meslow 1984); however, most studies are vague concerning techniques used. For example, if 10 pellets containing cottontail (*Sylvilagus* spp.) fur are examined does this mean that 10 cottontails were consumed or one just cottontail? A sample of goshawk pellets from Wyoming (N = 793) found that only 14% had remains exclusively from mammals while 79% contained both mammal and bird remains (Squires 2000). Some studies reported the percentage of prey items in a random sample of several pellets from multiple nests, treating each pellet as an independent sample, rather than each nest (Bloom et al. 1986, Kennedy 1991). Due to the variety of techniques used in goshawk diet studies for obtaining, analyzing, interpreting, and reporting data, cross-study comparison of results requires careful thought and understanding of the methods to provide meaning.

SOUTHWESTERN US DIET STUDIES

Goshawk diet studies in the Southwest are limited to the Kaibab and Coconino National Forests in Arizona (Boal and Mannan 1994, Reynolds et al. 1994, Drennan and Beier 2003) and the Jemez Mountains in New Mexico (Kennedy 1991). Three of these studies were conducted in the breeding season either using pellets and prey remains alone (Reynolds et al. 1994) or in combination with the direct observation of prey deliveries (Kennedy 1991, Boal and Mannan 1994) and one study was conducted during the winter (December–March) using direct observation of radio-tagged goshawks (Drennan and Beier 2003). Because of the variation in the techniques used in these studies and their limited geographic extent, the results may not be applicable to other areas in the Southwest.

The Boal and Mannan (1994) study, based on direct observation of prey deliveries (1,539 hr), is the most accurate quantification of goshawk prey selection in the Southwest. In the other two southwestern studies conducted during the breeding season, Reynolds et al. (1994) used pellets and prey remains and likely underestimated the percentage of small mammals in the diet, and Kennedy (1991) took a random sample (N = 63) of pellets from eight nests over five breeding seasons supplemented by 160 hr of direct observations. Boal and Mannan (1994) found a higher percentage of small mammals compared to other studies: 76% mammals versus 24% birds by frequency (Table 2). Kennedy's (1991) analysis, using both direct observation and analysis of prey remains and pellets demonstrated the bias

TABLE 2. PERCENT BIRDS AND MAMMALS IN GOSHAWK DIET BY FREQUENCY (BIOMASS) FOR DIRECT OBSERVATION STUDIES ONLY.

Study	State/region	Percent birds	Percent mammals
Boal and Mannan (1994)[a]	Arizona	24 (6)	76 (94)
Drennan and Beier (2003)[a,c]	Arizona	0	100
Kennedy (1991) [a,b]	New Mexico	33	67
Schnell (1958)	California	69 (54)	31 (46)
McCoy (1999)	California	21 (24)	79 (76)
Younk and Bechard (1994a)	Nevada	32	67
Bloxton (2002)	Washington	75	25
Lewis (2001)	Southeast Alaska	27 (26)	73 (74)
Schaeffer (1998)[d]	Alberta, Canada	24 (11)	76 (89)
Rutz (2003a)	Germany	91	9

[a] Southwestern US study.
[b] Kennedy (1991) reported results from three different techniques—direct observation, pellets and prey remains, and prey remains only.
[c] Winter study.
[d] Schaeffer (1998) provided results of two methods—direct observation and pellets and prey remains.

TABLE 3. PERCENT BIRDS AND MAMMALS IN GOSHAWK DIET BY FREQUENCY (BIOMASS) FOR STUDIES UTILIZING PELLETS AND PREY REMAINS.

Study	State/region	Percent birds	Percent mammals
Reynolds et al. (1994)[a]	Arizona	38	62
Kennedy (1991)[a,b]	New Mexico	51	49
Bloom et al. (1986)	California	48 (32)	52 (68)
Bull and Hohmann (1994)	Oregon	58	42
DeStephano et al. (1994)	Oregon	51 (37)	49 (63)
Reynolds and Meslow (1984)	Oregon	55	45
Thraikill et al. (2000)	Oregon	84	16
Watson et al. (1998)	Washington	50 (49)	50 (51)
Zachel (1985)	Alaska	21 (10)	78 (90)
Grzybowski and Eaton (1976)	New York	61	39
Meng 1959	New York, Pennsylvania	61	39
Bosakowski and Smith (1992)	New Jersey, New York, Connecticut	66	34
Penteriani (1997)	Italy	75 (71)	25 (29)
Lõhmus (1993)	Estonia	97	3
Schaeffer (1998)[c]	Alberta, Canada	47 (38)	53 (62)

[a] Southwestern US study.
[b] Kennedy (1991) reported results from three different techniques—direct observation, pellets and prey remains, and prey remains only.
[c] Schaeffer (1998) provided results of two methods—direct observation and pellets and prey.

TABLE 4. PERCENT BIRDS AND MAMMALS IN GOSHAWK DIET BY FREQUENCY FOR STOMACH ANALYSIS.

Study	State/region	Percent birds	Percent mammals
Storer (1966)[a]	North Dakota; Ontario, Canada	40	60
Sutton (1931)	Pennsylvania	67	33

[a] Winter study.

TABLE 5. PERCENT BIRDS AND MAMMALS IN GOSHAWK DIET BY FREQUENCY (BIOMASS) FOR PREY REMAINS TECHNIQUE.

Study	State/region	Percent birds	Percent mammals
Kennedy (1991)[a,b]	New Mexico	52	48
Stephens (2001)[c]	Utah	9	91
Doyle and Smith (1994)	Yukon, Canada	22 (14)	78 (86)

[a] Southwestern US study.
[b] Kennedy (1991) reported results from three different techniques—direct observation, pellets and prey remains, and prey remains only.
[c] Winter study.

of prey remains and pellet analysis towards birds. Using the direct observation technique she found a diet of 67% mammals to 33% birds (Table 2), whereas using pellet and prey remains analyses she found a diet of 51% birds and 49% mammals (Table 3). In contrast, Drennan and Beier (2003) observed winter diets of eight radio-tagged goshawks and found a diet of 100% mammals. In that study, not only were goshawks strictly consuming mammals but also they only took two species—cottontails and Abert squirrels (*Sciurus aberti*) and no individual goshawk consumed both.

COMPARISON OF GOSHAWK DIETS

This review summarizes the findings of 27 studies with quantitative information on goshawk diets as well as studies that provide only qualitative or anecdotal information. The four studies mentioned above were conducted within the Southwest and eleven of the studies were conducted in Washington, Oregon, California, Nevada, and Utah (Schnell 1958, Reynolds and Meslow 1984, Dixon and Dixon 1938, Bloom et al. 1986, Bull and Hohmann 1994, DeStephano et al. 1994, Younk and Bechard 1994b, Watson et al. 1998, McCoy 1999, Thraikill et al. 2000, Stephens 2001). The remaining studies are from the eastern US (Sutton 1925, 1931; Gromme 1935, Meng 1959, Storer 1966, Grzybowski and Eaton 1976, Bosakowski and Smith 1992), Alaska (Zachel 1985, Lewis 2001), Canada (Doyle and Smith 1994, Schaeffer 1998), and Europe (Opdam 1975, Lindén and Wikman 1983, Goszycynski and Pilatowski 1986, Widén 1987, Lõhmus 1993, Mañosa 1994, Penteriani 1997, Rutz 2003a). The percentages of small mammals and birds from quantitative goshawk diet studies conducted in North America are compared by study methods in Tables 2–5.

As reported above, studies in the Southwest each report a higher percentage of small mammals compared to avian prey in the diet. For the 27 papers I reviewed that represent goshawk diet studies across their range, 14 reported >50% mammals by frequency and 10 out of 11 papers reported >50% mammals by biomass (not all papers reported prey biomass). Although mammals appear to be more important in goshawk diet overall, avian prey may be important in certain study areas and during certain times of the year. At Donner Lake, California, 56% of prey items delivered to a single goshawk nest were nestling and fledgling American Robin (*Turdus migratorius*) and Steller's Jay (*Cyanocitta stelleri*; Schnell 1958). In northern

Nevada, goshawks consumed Belding's ground squirrel (*Spermophilus beldingi*) primarily but increased their consumption of American Robins and Northern Flickers (*Colaptes auratus*) after 1 July (Younk and Bechard 1994a), probably as a response to ground squirrels estivating in combination with an increase in the abundance of nestling and fledgling birds.

The percentage of birds and mammals in goshawk diet varies by region. Studies conducted in the northeastern US (Grzybowski and Eaton 1976, New York; Meng 1959, New York and New Jersey; Bosakowski and Smith 1992, New York, New Jersey, Connecticut; Sutton 1931, Pennsylvania) each reported a higher percentage of birds than mammals and each had similar values (i.e., 61–67% birds and 33–39% mammals) despite the relatively long period between studies. Seven of the nine studies conducted in California (Schnell 1958, Bloom et al. 1986, McCoy 1999), Oregon (Reynolds and Meslow 1984, Bull and Hohmann 1994, DeStephano et al. 1994, Thraikill et al. 2000) and Washington (Watson et al. 1998, Bloxton 2002) reported ≥50% birds by frequency. European studies in Italy (Penteriani 1997), Estonia (Lõhmus 1993), and Germany (Rutz 2003a) each reported very high percentages of birds (75–97%) compared to mammals (3–25%) by frequency. All of the studies conducted in Canada and Alaska that were reviewed, reported much higher percentages of mammals compared to birds.

One limitation of goshawk food-habit studies is that most have been conducted exclusively during the breeding season. One exception is Storer (1966) who collected data in the fall and winter from the north-central US and found a diet of 60% mammals and 40% birds from stomach analyses (Table 4). Other studies reporting on winter diet found nearly exclusive consumption of mammals during winter months in northern Arizona (Drennan and Beier 2003) and Utah (Stephens 2001). In southeast Alaska, the relative abundance of goshawk prey shifted during winter, with many common prey items absent or rare during that period (Iverson et al. 1996). The tendency for a higher percentage of mammals consumed in the winter would also be expected in the Southwest, due to the unavailability of many bird species in the ponderosa pine (*Pinus ponderosa*) forest type during the winter months (Table 6). Only three of seven mammal species present in this habitat type during summer remain active throughout winter. Other species are either intermittently present in winter or completely absent due to hibernation or migration.

TABLE 6. SEASONAL ABUNDANCE OF SELECTED GOSHAWK PREY SPECIES IN PONDEROSA PINE FOREST HABITAT IN THE SOUTHWESTERN US. X = PRESENT, - = INTERMITTENTLY PRESENT (I.E., DURING WARM, DRY PERIODS), BLANK = ABSENT DUE TO HIBERNATION OR MIGRATION. NUMBERS INDICATE TIMING OF PARTURITION AND THE NUMBER OF YOUNG.

Species	Jan	Feb	Mar	Apr	May	Jun	Jul	Aug	Sept	Oct	Nov	Dec
Abert squirrel	x	x	x	x	x	2–5	x	x	x	x	x	x
Red squirrel	x	x	x	3.3	x	x	x	3.3	x	x	x	x
Golden-mantled ground squirrel		-	x	x	5.4	x	x	x	x			
Cliff chipmunk	-	-	x	x	x	4–5	x	4–5	x	x	x	-
Gray-collared chipmunk	-	-	x	x	x	4.9	x	x	x	x	x	-
Rock squirrel	-	-	x	x	5.6	x	x	5.6	x	x	-	-
Sylvilagus spp.	x	x	x	4–7	x	x	x	4.7	x	x	x	x
Red-naped Sapsucker	x	x	x	x	x	4–5	x	x	x	x	x	x
Williamson's Sapsucker	-	-	-	x	x	5–6	x	x	x	x	-	-
Northern Flicker	-	x	x	x	x	5–8	x	x	x	x	-	-
Hairy Woodpecker	x	x	x	x	x	4	x	x	x	x	x	x
Steller's Jay	x	x	x	x	x	4	x	x	x	x	x	x
American Robin	x	x	x	x	x	4	x	x	x	x	x	-
Mourning Dove	-	-	-	-	2	x	x	2	4	2	-	-
Blue Grouse	x	x	x	x	x	7–10	x	x	x	x	x	x
Band-tailed Pigeon	-	-	-	x	1	x	1	x	1	x	-	-
Total species present	8	9	12	15	16	16	16	16	16	16	10	7

Migratory patterns of goshawks vary across their range. In northern latitudes, goshawks respond to the cycles of prey species such as Ruffed Grouse and snowshoe hare (*Lepus americanus*), migrating south in large numbers in years when prey populations decline. In the lower 48 states, they are partial migrants in some areas (Squires and Ruggiero 1995, Stephens 2001) and permanent residents in other areas (Boal et al. 2003, Drennan and Beier 2003). Other researchers have noted that at least some goshawks in the Southwest winter in their breeding home range territory (P. Kennedy, unpubl. data; R. Reynolds, unpubl. data). If goshawks remain within their breeding territories during winter, the reduction in prey species diversity (Table 6) alone, or in combination with increased energetic requirements, may create a period of peak stress.

Few studies have investigated the relationship between winter caloric requirements, energy expenditures, prey availability and subsequent reproductive success for resident goshawks. Keane et al. (*this volume*) found that annual goshawk reproduction was greatest in years following winters with mild temperatures, high cone-crop production, and abundant populations of Douglas's squirrel (*Tamiasciurus douglasii*). Supplementary feeding at goshawk nests during the breeding season caused a demographic response in some years but not others (Ward and Kennedy 1994), suggesting that prey availability is not the only factor limiting goshawk productivity. J.M. Ward (unpubl. data) also speculated, based on preliminary data, that supplementary feeding at goshawk nests would not influence fitness in terms of the clutch size, timing of nesting, or the size of nestling goshawks, but that increased survival rates of nestling and fledgling goshawks was due to the greater time available, i.e., because they were not foraging, to nesting females for defending against predators.

Several studies have identified unusual prey items in goshawk diets. In Wyoming, Squires (2000) discovered mule deer (*Odocoileus hemionus*) and American marten (*Martes americana*) hair in five pellets regurgitated by goshawks but could not discern if these prey were killed or scavenged. Also in Wyoming, Squires (2000) documented carrion in the diet of goshawk, apparently a rare behavior for goshawks. In southeast Alaska, Lewis (2003) reported the first record of goshawks preying on Pigeon Guillemot (*Cepphus columba*), a seabird that has relatively little overlap with goshawk nesting territories. Cat (*Felis* sp.) was identified in the prey remains of a goshawk nesting in New Mexico (Kennedy 1991).

KEY PREY SPECIES

This comparison of goshawk food habits identifies three characteristics of goshawk diets in the Southwest: a preference for small mammals (Tables 2 and 3), a significant decrease in prey diversity during winter months (Table 6), and nine species of small mammals and two bird species which occurred most frequently in Southwest prey studies (Table 7). Based on these studies, the highest ranking mammal groups (N = 6) and bird species (N = 2) in the Southwest studies were selected for consideration in this report. The total number of mammal species was nine because two mammal groups had more than one species. The chipmunk group included two species because they were ranked in the top eight by two of the three studies (Kennedy 1991, Boal and Mannan 1994). I also included three cottontail species because these were rarely identified to species by any of the studies.

These 11 species were also selected by the GSC (Reynolds et al. 1992). However, the MRNG also included American Robin, Band-tailed Pigeon (*Columba fasciata*), Blue Grouse (*Dendrogapus obscurus*), Hairy Woodpecker (*Picoides villosus*), Mourning Dove (*Zenaida macroura*), Red-naped Sapsucker (*Sphyrapicus nuchalis*)), and Williamson's Sapsucker (*Sphyrapicus thyroideus*). While these species were present in goshawk diets in other regions (Schnell 1958, Meng 1959, Reynolds and Meslow 1984, Bloxton 2002), they represented <5% of the goshawk diet in the Southwest (Kennedy 1991, Boal and Mannan 1994, Reynolds et al. 1994).

HABITAT REQUIREMENTS AND NATURAL HISTORY OF SELECTED GOSHAWK PREY SPECIES

The 11 prey items most frequently observed in Southwest food habit studies were Abert squirrel, red squirrel, rock squirrel (*Spermophilus variegatus*), golden-mantled ground squirrel, cliff chipmunk, gray-collared chipmunk (*Eutamias cinereicollis*), mountain cottontail (*Sylvilagus nuttalli*), desert cottontail (*Sylvilagus auduboni)*, eastern cottontail (*Sylvilagus floridanus*), Steller's Jay, and Northern Flicker. Most of these species or their ecological equivalents are also important prey throughout the goshawks' geographic range.

Natural history and habitat requirements for the 11 prey species were researched in the literature and are presented in the following order: distribution, habitat, density, reproduction and development,

TABLE 7. IMPORTANT GOSHAWK PREY IN THE WESTERN US RANKED HIGHEST TO LOWEST BY FREQUENCY (BIOMASS). THE SYMBOL - INDICATES THE SPECIES WAS NOTED IN THE DIET BUT WAS NOT IN THE TOP EIGHT RANKS.

Species	Boal Mannan 1994[a]	Reynolds et al. 1994[a]	Kennedy 1991[b]	Bull and Hohmann 1994[b]	Reynolds and Meslow 1984[c]	McCoy 1999[d]	Bloom et al. 1986[d]	Schnell 1958[d]	Younk and Bechard 1994[e]
Golden-mantled-ground squirrel	1 (3)	7	4		4 (3)	2 (1)	3 (4)	3 (3)	4
Belding's ground squirrel	7 (4)	8	5					7 (5)	1
Rock squirrel					-	-			3
Spermophilus sp.				3					
Abert squirrel	6 (2)	3	1	-					
Gray squirrel					- (2)	- (6)			
Douglas squirrel					- (4)	1 (2)	1 (2)	4 (4)	
Northern flying squirrel					4 (5)				
Red squirrel	5 (5)	4	5	4					
Chipmunks	3 (7)	-	4	-	-	3 (5)		5 (-)	
Lagomorphs							- (1)		
Cottontail	2 (1)	1	3		-	8 (5)			
Lepus spp.	-	4	-	2	2 (1)				
Steller's Jay	4 (6)	2	3	-	1 (6)	-	2 (-)	2 (1)	
Gray Jay						4 (6)			
Common Raven	-		-			- (3)			
Mountain Quail		-	-		- (7)				
Ring-billed Gull						6 (4)			
Clark's Nutcracker	-		-		-	-			
Woodpeckers	-	5	-	-	-				
American Robin	-	-	5	1	-	5 (7)		1 (2)	5
Grouse	-	-			-	- (7)	- (3)		
Northern Flicker	8 (8)	4	2	5	4 (8)		4 (-)		2

[a] Arizona.
[b] New Mexico.
[c] Oregon.
[d] California.
[e] Nevada.

home range, nest, and diet. While an effort was made to obtain research conducted in the Southwest, much pertinent information on these species was collected outside the area of interest. In some cases, information from closely related species was used to fill gaps in the knowledge base.

ABERT SQUIRREL

Distribution and habitat

The Abert squirrel is a resident of ponderosa pine forests ranging from south-central Wyoming, through the southwestern US and into Durango, Mexico (McKee 1941). North of the Grand Canyon on the Kaibab Plateau, a subspecies is known as the Kaibab squirrel *(Sciurus aberti kaibabensis)*.

The Abert squirrel is apparently dependent on ponderosa pine forests (Keith 1965, States et al. 1988, Snyder 1993), although it has been known to occur occasionally in pinyon-juniper *(Pinus edulis-Juniperus* spp.) woodlands, Douglas-fir *(Pseudotsuga menziesii)*, and spruce *(Picea* spp.)-fir forests (Rassmussen 1941, Keith 1965, Patton and Green 1970, Patton 1975b, Ratcliff et al. 1975, Hall 1981, Hoffmeister 1986). The best cover conditions are uneven-aged ponderosa pine stands with small even-aged groups within these stands (Patton 1975b). Average tree diameter for ideal stands is between 28 and 33 cm diameter at breast height (dbh); however, small groups of larger trees generally are present in the stand, resulting in a mosaic of diameter and height groups (Patton 1975b). Ratcliff et al. (1975) found that basal area and volume per hectare were significantly correlated with squirrel abundance but number of trees per hectare was not. Gambel oak *(Quercus gambeli)* were found in optimal stands at densities of 2.5–5 trees per ha in the 30–36 cm dbh class (Patton 1975b). Trees used for feeding averaged 48 cm dbh and nest trees averaged 43 cm dbh (Patton and Green 1970). Interlocking tree crowns are an essential component of both nesting and feeding stands (Patton 1975b, Hall 1981).

Densities

Population densities of Abert squirrel vary seasonally and annually (Pearson 1950, Keith 1965, Farentinos 1972, Hall 1981); however, statistics on squirrel harvests collected by the Arizona Game and Fish Commission suggest that populations are stable over long time periods. For example, for the 15-yr period from 1966–1981, hunters harvested

between 1.2–2.4 squirrels per hunting trip, but for 10 of these years, the harvests varied only from 1.4–1.8 squirrels per hunting trip (Hoffmeister 1986; Appendix A.10).

Patton (1984) created a habitat capability model to evaluate Abert squirrel habitat quality and estimate population densities. The model used data on tree size, tree density, tree grouping, cone production, and squirrel densities to construct five habitat quality rankings and found from 0.05 squirrels per hectare in the lowest ranked habitat to 2.48 squirrels per hectare in the highest ranked habitat. On a 72-ha study area in Colorado, Farentinos (1972) found that population density varied from 0.3 squirrels per hectare in spring (N = 24) to 0.6 squirrels per hectare in the fall (N = 40). Trowbridge and Lawson (1941, as cited in Keith 1965) reported population density ranged from 0.3–1.3 squirrels per hectare in uncut stands. Population density on stands where timber harvesting had previously occurred was 0.03 squirrels per hectare for two consecutive years (Trowbridge and Lawson 1941, as cited in Keith 1965).

Reproduction and development

On the Mogollon Plateau, Keith (1965) reported mating in late April and May. Young were born between 10 June and 12 July. Litter size varied between two and five. The mean litter size was 3.4. Stephenson (1974) reported a mean litter size of 2.9 in northern Arizona.

Home range

Several authors have reported spatial overlap in Abert squirrel home ranges (Farentinos 1979, Patton 1975a, Pederson et al. 1976, Hall 1981). In Colorado, Farentinos (1979) reported the mean home range size for males as 20.7 ha in the breeding season and 7.5 ha in the non-breeding season. Home range size for females was 7.4 ha in the breeding season and 5.8 ha in the non-breeding season. Near Flagstaff, Arizona, Keith (1965) reported that adults have a home range of 2 ha in winter and 7.3 ha in summer. On the Beaver Creek watershed, 50 km south of Flagstaff, Patton (1975a) radio-tagged two males and one female Abert squirrels and calculated home ranges of 12.1, 34.4, and 4.0 ha, respectively. On the Kaibab Plateau, Hall (1981) found that three males had a mean home range size of 4.4 ha in the summer and a single female had a home range size of 14 ha. In Utah, Pederson et al. (1976) reported the mean home range size to be 2.5 ha (N = 7).

Nest

Abert squirrels appear to have two types of nests—summer (day) nests and nursery nests (Hall 1981). Generally, summer nests are poorly maintained and often lack a roof, whereas nursery nests are usually roofed and well maintained with fresh green clippings of ponderosa pine (Hall 1981). Nests are typically located in a fork of the main trunk or in the angle formed by the trunk and one or more limbs, and, on average, 15 m above ground in a 50 cm dbh ponderosa pine within an interlocking forest canopy (Hall 1981). Other researchers have reported average nest heights from 14 m above ground in southern Utah (Pederson et al. 1976), to 10.7 m in northern Colorado (Farentinos 1972). Pederson et al. (1976) found that squirrel nest boxes placed anywhere between 7.6 and 14 m in ponderosa pines were occupied by Abert squirrels in >50% of the cases. Hollow Gambel oak trees have been used as dens (Patton and Green 1970, Patton 1975b), but nesting attempts were not documented. Patton (1975a) followed three squirrels with radio transmitters, and found that each squirrel used multiple nests. Two males and one female used two, six, and five nests, respectively ($\bar{x}$ = 4.3).

Diet

The Abert squirrel diet consists almost exclusively of ponderosa pine and associated fungi (Hall 1981); however, Reynolds (1966) reported Abert squirrels using pinyon pine in the same way they use ponderosa pine (i.e., eating the cambium of the subterminal branches) near Silver City, New Mexico. Cambium from subterminal twigs is taken throughout the year, but apical buds are a major item in winter diets of Abert squirrels in Arizona (Keith 1965, Hall 1981, Stephenson 1974). Staminate cones are eaten in late June when mature. Ovulate cones, the most nutritious part of ponderosa pine, are eaten to the degree available during late spring and summer. Hypogeous fungi is eaten in all seasons (Stephenson 1974), but is the major part of the diet in the summer (Hall 1981). Carrion, in small amounts, also has been noted in the diet (Coughlin 1938, Keith 1965). Acorns are taken when available and constitute as much as 40% of the fall diet during years of good cone crops (Stephenson 1974).

Abert squirrels are dependent on currently available food because they typically do not cache food (Keith 1965, Stephenson 1974). However, Hall (1981) observed three types of food storing behavior: burying cones in duff, storing mushrooms at a limb joint in a tree, and storing mushroom parts in terminal needle clusters. The first two types of storage may be for a period of days or weeks, while the terminal needle clusters are used for a few hours or 2 d at most.

RED SQUIRREL

Distribution and habitat

The red squirrel ranges from Alaska through most of Canada and the northern portions of the midwestern, northeastern, and Appalachian states. This squirrel inhabits coniferous forests throughout most of the Rocky Mountains and south into the higher elevation plateaus of Arizona and New Mexico (Hoffmeister 1986).

On the Mogollon Plateau, red squirrels are found only where firs and spruce are present (Burnett and Dickermann 1956). In the San Francisco Peaks, red squirrels are found mostly above 2,600 m elevation in Engelmann spruce (*Picea engelmannii*), corkbark fir (*Abies lasiocarpa*), bristlecone pine (*Pinus aristata*), and Douglas-fir (Hoffmeiester 1986).

Spruce-fir, Douglas-fir, and lodgepole pine (*Pinus contorta*) forests types are preferred by red squirrels. In the Southwest, Engelmann spruce and a mixture of spruce and Douglas-fir are the most important habitats (Vahle 1978). The three most important overstory variables controlling red squirrel habitat in southwest mixed-conifer forests are size, density, and grouping of trees (Vahle and Patton 1983). Vahle and Patton (1983) reported that the best habitat consists of multi-storied stands of mixed conifer with trees from 30–36 cm dbh in dense groups of 0.4 ha or less. Generally, at least one 45 cm dbh tree is present in this cluster and is typically a Douglas-fir. A 50 cm dbh or greater live tree, snag, or downed log, was universally present at the center of the food cache.

Densities

In central Alberta, Kemp and Keith (1970) reported densities of 0.06 adult squirrels per hectare on one study area and 0.1 squirrels per hectare on another study area; however, they acknowledged that their estimates were probably low. In the same area, Rusch and Reeder (1978) compared densities of red squirrels between stands of mixed spruce (*Picea* spp.), aspen (*Populus tremuloides*) and jack pine (*Pinus banksiana*). Mixed spruce stands supported the highest densities with 1.6–7.0 squirrels per hectare. Densities in jack pine were intermediate with 1–2.6 squirrels per hectare. Aspen stands had the lowest densities with 0–1.0 squirrels per hectare. The numbers given by Rusch and Reeder (1978) are substantially larger than those Kemp and Keith (1970) reported due in part to the different methods and units of measurement. Rusch and Reeder (1978) used live-trapping, mark-recapture methods and estimated the entire population, while Kemp and Keith (1970) used an observation method and estimated only the adult portion of the total population.

In mixed conifer habitat in eastern Arizona, Vahle and Patton (1983) inventoried 141 squirrel caches to determine population densities. Despite finding one squirrel with eight caches, they confirmed the relationship of one squirrel per cache in fall and winter. Based on the number of caches they estimated population density in the range of 1–2.5 squirrels per hectare.

Sullivan and Moses (1986) compared red squirrel densities in thinned and unthinned lodgepole pine stands in British Columbia. Squirrels were more abundant in the unthinned stands with average densities during May and August of 1.2 squirrels per hectare compared to 0.2/ha in thinned stands. The authors suggested that young stands might provide a dispersal sink for juvenile and yearling squirrels.

Thompson et al. (1989) used track station transects to index red squirrel populations in Ontario. They compared their indices of abundance for uncut stands and stands of less than 5, 10, 20, and 30 yr old. The highest track counts were in the uncut stands ($\bar{x} = 30$). The <5-, 10-, and 30-yr-old stands all had low scores (<4) but the 20-yr-old stand had a moderate population index (10).

Reproduction and development

Red squirrels may have one or two litters per year. Hoffmeister (1986) gives evidence for two litters in Arizona based on examination of dentition in juveniles on the Kaibab Plateau and in the Graham Mountains. The annual reproductive rate expressed as the number of young per female varied from 2.4–4.4 over a 4-yr study period in Rochester, Alberta (Rusch and Reeder 1978). Kemp and Keith (1970) also in Rochester, reported mean litter sizes of 3.4 and 4.3 for the years 1967 and 1968, respectively. Layne (1954) summarized litter sizes from several authors and reported a mean of 4.9 (range = 2–8). This figure is higher than the means of 3.9 for the study by Rusch and Reeder (1978), 4.0 by Wood (1967) and 3.3 by Smith (1968). In Colorado, Dolbeer (1973) found an average embryo count of 3.3 (range = 2–5).

Home range

Because red squirrels are notorious for their strong territorial behavior, most authors report the size of a defended territory and not the home range size. Rusch and Reeder (1978) estimated territory size of red squirrels at 0.2–0.7 ha. Kemp and Keith (1970) estimated territory size from observations in a variety of habitats and found territories ranging from 0.4–0.8 ha. Gurnell (1984) estimated territory size to be approximately 60–100% of the home-range size. Burt and Grossenheider (1980) report that home ranges are <3.4 ha in size.

Nest

Nest height is between 4.6 and 9.1 m above ground regardless of tree size (Vahle and Patton 1983). Nest tree measurements for 186 nest trees in eastern Arizona ranged as follows: tree dbh from 33.5–38.1 cm; tree height from 14.3–16 m; tree distance from center of cache from 4.0–4.7 m; number of trees with crowns interlocking nest tree crowns 2.3–2.7 (Vahle and Patton 1983). In Colorado, Hatt (1943) reported a horizontal diameter of 28–46 cm for nests and an inside diameter of 10–13 cm. The inside of the nest is generally composed of grasses. Nests are often placed in cavities within trees; if outside the bole, they are firmly supported and protected (Hoffmeister 1986).

Diet

The red squirrel feeds on a variety of seeds, nuts, eggs, and fungi (Burt and Grossenheider 1980). Layne (1954) divided food items into six categories based on stomach analyses of 145 stomachs collected in Ithaca, New York: mast, fleshy fruits, green plant matter, fungus, flesh, and insects. Mast was consumed every month of the year and represented almost 75% of the annual diet. Fleshy fruits and green plant matter each comprised nearly one-quarter of annual diets. Fungus was 7% of the annual diet despite only being consumed in July and August as 12% and 26% of the monthly diets, respectively.

In Alberta, Rusch and Reeder (1978) calculated that a single red squirrel consumed an average of 639 meristematic buds and the seeds from 35 pine cones each day. At the same study site, Rusch and Reeder (1978) noted that almost all species of fleshy mushrooms were consumed. In an outdoor enclosure at the University of Alaska, red squirrels were fed nothing but white spruce (*Picea glauca*) seeds for 3 wk and consumed about 144 cones per squirrel, per day (Brink and Dean 1966).

ROCK SQUIRREL

Distribution and habitat

The rock squirrel is found in southern Nevada and most of Utah, Colorado, New Mexico, and Arizona (Burt and Grossenheider 1980). They are primarily found in or among rocks, on slopes, canyon walls, or rock piles (Hoffmeister 1986). In Arizona, they occur from as low as 490 m elevation in Yuma County to >3,350 m in Coconino County on the San Francisco Peaks.

Densities

Rock squirrels are less abundant in the winter, but whether they hibernate is unknown (Hoffmeister 1986).

Reproduction and development

Hoffmeister (1971) found a nest containing six young on 20 May in the Grand Canyon. Rock squirrels may have two litters in southern Arizona but only one in northern Arizona (Hoffmeister 1986).

Home range

Findley et al. (1975) referenced the work of W. Stalheim studying rock squirrels near Albuquerque, New Mexico, and reported squirrels having overlapping home ranges, which averaged about 14 ha per squirrel (N = 16).

Nest

Burrows and nests are placed in rock piles, making excavation and research difficult (Hoffmeister 1986).

Diet

In Arizona, rock squirrels have been observed eating the buds and seeds of mesquite (*Prosopis juliflora*), cactus (*Opuntia* spp.) fruit, juniper berries (*Juniperus* spp.), blooms of *Agave*, seeds of *Ephedra*, ripe fruits of western red currant *(Ribes cereum)*, ripe berries of gray thorn (*Acacia* spp.), bulbs of mariposa lilies (*Lilium* spp.), serviceberry (*Amelianchier* sp.), skunkbush (*Rhus* sp.), and lupine (*Lupinus* sp.) seeds, apricots and peaches, acorns (*Quercus* spp.), hackberry (*Celtis reticulata*), grapes (*Vitas* spp.), walnuts (*Juglans* spp.), cultivated corn (*Zea mays*) and wheat (*Triticum*

spp.) (Hoffmeister 1986). Rock squirrels prefer leaves (Hart 1976).

GOLDEN-MANTLED GROUND SQUIRREL

Distribution and habitat

The golden-mantled ground squirrel is common throughout the mountains of the western US, southern British Columbia, and Alberta (McKeever 1964). It is usually found from the mid-transition zone up to the Hudsonian zone (Mullally 1953). In the Southwest, the golden-mantled ground squirrel occurs along the Mogollon Plateau from the San Francisco Peaks to the White Mountains, on the Kaibab Plateau, in the Chuska Mountains (Hoffmeister 1986), and in woodlands to above timberline in northern New Mexico (Findley et al. 1975).

A study conducted on the Beaver Creek watershed, 50 km south of Flagstaff, Arizona, found golden-mantled ground squirrels preferred dense, mature forest on a silviculturally treated watershed (Goodwin and Hungerford 1979). Only at higher elevations were the squirrels observed in more open stands (Goodwin and Hungerford 1979). Lowe (1975) found this species abundant in both dense and open forests above 2,256 m. In the Trinity Mountains of northern California, golden-mantled ground squirrels invaded cut areas within virgin forest after timber harvesting (Tevis 1956).

Densities

On the Beaver Creek watershed, Goodwin and Hungerford (1979) estimated densities of golden-mantled ground squirrels at 0.6 squirrels per hectare in denser forests and 0.1 squirrels per hectare in more open stands. In northeastern California, squirrels were more abundant in ponderosa pine forests than they were in either lodgepole pine, red fir (*Abies magnifica*), or white fir (*Abies concolor*) forest types (McKeever 1964).

In Arizona, golden-mantled ground squirrels hibernate from October or November until April or May, depending on elevation and seasonal variations (Hoffmeister 1986). McKeever (1964) found adults hibernating from mid-March to late May. Juveniles did not appear until mid-May to early June. Mullally (1953) reported hibernation dates from October or November until mid-March or April in southern California. Captive squirrels from the same study population hibernated from 25 December to early March, but were intermittently awake and active for short periods in all cases (Mullally 1953).

Reproduction and development

McKeever (1964) reported that almost all males emerged from hibernation in breeding condition, but females did not enter breeding condition until 2–3 wk after emerging from hibernation. The gestation period in captivity was about 27 d (McKeever 1964). Mean litter size in Lassen County, California was 5.0 (range = 3–8) for pregnant females (N = 36; McKeever 1964), and 5.1 embryos for Plumas County, California (Tevis 1955).

Home range

No information on home range size was found in the literature. However, based on body size, golden-mantled ground squirrels are expected to have a home range size intermediate between the smaller chipmunks (0.8 ha) and the larger Abert squirrel (2.0–21.0 ha).

Nest

Burrows are either dug into the ground near a large surface object, dug into a partially decomposed log or stump, or result from taking over a gopher hole (Mullally 1953). Fourteen burrows excavated by Mullally (1953) had an average depth of 46 cm and an average length of 112 cm. Seldom is more than one entrance present (Mullally 1953).

Diet

McKeever (1964) reported eight categories of food items from analyses of 561 stomachs collected throughout the year. Fungi were the most important item for the entire year, representing 57% of the stomach contents. Leaves were the second most important item, at 30% of the annual diet. Seeds, flowers, arthropods, mammals, fruit, and bulbs each represented <5% of the annual average diet. Seeds were especially important in fall, representing 30% of the diet for the month of October. Bulbs were taken only in fall and represented 30% of the diet for November. Carrion represented 10% of the diet for November; however, this figure is probably exaggerated in this study because of an abundance of dead animals caught in traps on the study area.

The diet of golden-mantled ground squirrels changes throughout the year. After emerging from hibernation in spring, the diet was 56% (by volume) leaf material (Tevis 1953). In summer and fall, intake of leafy material declined and fungi dominated the diet at 65% and 90%, respectively (Tevis 1953).

Tevis (1952, 1953) studied eating habits of golden-mantled ground squirrels during a food shortage caused by a failure in the conifer seed crop in the fall of 1950 and during a late frost in spring 1951 which killed many flowers of spring-blooming shrubs. The diet of golden-mantled ground squirrels for the year following the food shortage was marked by an increased consumption of fungi. Of the several populations studied, Tevis (1952) concluded that where hypogeous fungi flourished, it offset the deleterious effects of the failure of the seeds crops. In Colorado, the common dandelion (*Taraxacum officinale*) provided >80% of the diet between June and August (Carlton 1966). The stems were preferred and the seeds and flowers were rarely eaten (Carlton 1966).

GREY-COLLARED CHIPMUNK

Distribution and habitat

The grey-collared chipmunk ranges from Bill Williams Mountain and the San Francisco Peaks to the White Mountains in Arizona (Hoffmeister 1986). In New Mexico, the grey-collared chipmunk occurs on several mountains in the southern portion of the state including the Mogollon, Organ, Mimbres, Magdalena, San Mateo, and Elk mountains (Findley et al. 1975).

In Arizona, grey-collared chipmunks prefer mature forests above 2,225 m (Goodwin and Hungerford 1979). Lowe (1975) reported that grey-collared chipmunks were abundant in mature ponderosa pine forests west of Flagstaff at elevations between 2,250 and 2,440 m.

Densities

Clothier (1969) reported population densities as 5.0/ha in May and 12.5/ha in August in southeast Coconino County.

Reproduction and development

Young are born in the first 2 wk of June and the gestation period is at least 30 d (Clothier 1969). One litter per summer is produced. Mean litter size is 4.9 (range = 4–6). Young emerge from underground burrows in July (Clothier 1969).

Home range

No information on home range was found in the literature for grey-collared chipmunks. However, eastern chipmunks (*Tamias striatus*) home range size is usually <0.8 ha (Burt and Grossenheider 1980).

Nest

Nests are located under logs, stumps, and roots or in tree cavities (Hoffmeister 1986).

Diet

No information on diet was found in the literature. However, based on information from similar species they likely consume an array of food items including seeds, berries, and fungi.

CLIFF CHIPMUNK

Distribution and habitat

The cliff chipmunk is distributed from central Nevada through Utah, Arizona, and parts of western New Mexico (Burt and Grossenheider 1980). In Arizona, the cliff chipmunk is found from the Arizona Strip southeastward through the Mogollon Plateau to the White Mountains and on various isolated mountain ranges (Hoffmeister 1986).

Cliff chipmunks are found in a wide variety of habitats, especially where there are large rocks or cliffs (Hoffmeister 1986). In Arizona, they range from as low as 975 m in the Grand Canyon to as high as 2,865 m in the Graham Mountains (Hoffmeister 1986). In Nevada, Brown (1971) found that cliff chipmunks were restricted to stands of small diameter trees that were well spaced. In Arizona, cliff chipmunks are found along rock cliffs and in thinned pine stands (Goodwin and Hungerford 1979).

Densities

Goodwin and Hungerford (1979) found wide variations in population densities from 0.1 squirrel per hectare in dense pine stands to about 1.3 squirrels per hectare in thinned pine stands and along rock ledges. Density increased as thinning increased, but cliff chipmunks were not found in clearcuts (Goodwin and Hungerford 1979). Cliff chipmunks apparently do not hibernate, but they may become inactive during periods of extreme winter cold (Hoffmeister 1986).

Reproduction and development

Cliff chipmunks may have two litters a year in Arizona (Hoffmeister 1986). The closely related least chipmunk (*Eutamias minimus*), which also has eight mammae, has 2–6 young per litter and possibly two litters per year (Burt and Grossenheider 1980).

Home range

No information on home range was found in the literature for cliff chipmunks. However, home range size for eastern chipmunks is usually <0.8 ha (Burt and Grossenheider 1980).

Nest

No information on nesting habits of the cliff chipmunk was found in the literature. The least chipmunk excavates its own burrows beneath stumps and rocks (Burt and Grossenheider 1980).

Diet

Cliff chipmunks feed on the fruits and seeds of most of the trees and shrubs, as well as the seeds of grasses and forbs (Hoffmeister 1986). Stems and blossoms of plants are preferred over other parts (Hart 1976).

COTTONTAILS

Distribution and habitat

Three species of cottontails occur in the Southwest—eastern cottontail, mountain cottontail, and desert cottontail. The eastern cottontail is most often found in mountains and adjacent slopes but it has never been found at elevations as high as those inhabited by the mountain cottontail (Hoffmeister 1986). Mountain and eastern cottontails are not known to overlap in their distribution anywhere in Arizona, but come within 10 km of each other in the White Mountains (Hoffmeister 1986). Mountain cottontails preferred habitats dominated by sagebrush (*Artemisia tridentata*) in southern British Columbia (Sullivan et al. 1989). In Colorado, Cayot (1978) found that mountain cottontails decreased in abundance as elevation increased from 2,070–2,710 m. At higher elevations, Cayot (1978) found a negative association between mountain cottontail abundance and bare ground, downed trees, and common juniper (*Juniperus communis*). Mountain cottontail abundance was greater on southeast aspects where ponderosa pine was more common and bitterbrush (*Purshia tridentata*) reached 50% cover. Mountain cottontails are typically high-mountain residents in Arizona, inhabiting grassy and rocky areas near or among spruce-fir or on the sagebrush flats and gullies near ponderosa pine or spruce-fir forests (Hoffmeister 1986). The desert cottontail is found throughout the Southwest (Burt and Grossenheider 1980) but mostly inhabits deserts and semiarid grasslands at elevations below coniferous forest (Hoffmeister 1986).

Densities

Densities of eastern cottontail vary from one/ 2 ha to several times higher in winter concentrations (Burt and Grossenheider 1980). Trent and Rongstad (1974) estimated fall densities of eastern cottontails in a 6-ha woodlot in Wisconsin as 9/ha. McKay and Verts (1978) reported densities at monthly intervals over a 20-mo period in Oregon. Population densities ranged from 0.07–2.54/ha (McKay and Verts 1978). Population density peaked in August and was lowest in April over the 20-mo study period (McKay and Verts 1978). Scribner and Warren (1990) reported densities of eastern cottontails ranging from 8–28/ha in playa basins in Texas.

Reproduction and development

Reproduction occurs later at higher latitudes and higher elevations (Conaway et al. 1963). Mountain cottontails in Oregon averaged four litters in 1972 and only three litters in 1973 (McKay and Verts 1978). In Missouri, eastern cottontails had seven–eight litters per year each with four–six viable embryos resulting in approximately 35 young produced annually (Conaway et al. 1963). Powers and Verts (1971) reported 4.3 viable embryos per adult female mountain cottontail, which is lower than for the eastern cottontail but considerably greater than previously expected for mountain cottontails. The gestation period for six timed pregnancies of eastern cottontails was between 26 and 28 d (Marsden and Conaway 1963).

Home range

Home range size varies between species. Eastern cottontail home range size ranges from 1.2–8.0 ha and desert cottontail home range size from 0.4–6.0 ha (Burt and Grossenheider 1980). In southwestern Wisconsin, adult male home range size varied from 2.8 ha in spring to 4.0 ha in summer to 1.5 ha in late summer (Trent and Rongstad 1974). Adult female home range size varied from 1.7 ha in the spring to 0.8 ha throughout the summer and fall and did not overlap in the summer (Trent and Rongstad 1974).

In Oregon, male eastern cottontails dispersed greater distances than females and juvenile males dispersed more than adult males (Chapman and Trethewey 1972).

Nest

The desert cottontail nest is a grass-lined depression in the ground (Burt and Grossenheider 1980). Eastern cottontail nests were located most often within dense brush, grass cover, and downed logs (Allen 1984). No information was found on the mountain cottontail nest.

Diet

The eastern cottontail feeds on green vegetation in the summer and bark and twigs in the winter (Burt and Grossenheider 1980). In California, mountain cottontails consumed mainly sagebrush and juniper in the fall and grasses in the spring and summer (Orr, 1940 as cited in Hoffmeister 1986).

STELLER'S JAY

Distribution and habitat

The Steller's Jay is a permanent resident of coniferous forest from southern Alaska, west through British Columbia and Alberta, and south through the western states into Mexico (Terres 1991). Coons (1984) found Steller's Jays present on the San Francisco Peaks during all months of the year. The mean elevation where birds were detected during the spring, summer, and fall was between 2,680 m and 2,900 m, but dropped to between 2,560 and 2,590 m during the period from November–February (Coons 1984).

Densities

Haldeman (1968) reported the number of breeding pairs in three study areas. Ponderosa pine, burned ponderosa pine, and a mixed-stand composed of fir, pine, and aspen, supported 8, 7, and 10 pairs of birds per 40 ha, respectively (Haldeman 1968). Breeding densities during a 3-yr study in five different forest treatments ranged from zero pairs per 40 ha in the cleared plot to nine pairs per 40 ha on the control plot. The number of birds seen per hour in the winter was 0.1 both in a mixed-stand of fir, pine, and aspen, and in a pure ponderosa pine stand (Haldeman 1968). In west-central Colorado, the density of Steller's Jays in an aspen-conifer forest ranged from four/40 ha in the

78% aspen overstory forest to one/40 ha in both 98% and 1% aspen overstory forests (Scott and Crouch 1988).

Reproduction and development

Females incubate for 16 d and the young are altricial. Both sexes help raising young (Erlich et al. 1988).

Home range

Brown (1963) reported that Steller's Jays maintained non-overlapping areas of dominance around their nests ranging in size from 0.02–0.4 ha in size. However, larger home ranges adjacent to each other did overlap and were from 0.9–1.4 ha in size. In Arizona, Vander Wall and Balda (1981, 1983) reported Steller's Jays flying as far as 3.2 km daily to forage on pine seeds, acorns, berries, and other seasonally abundant food.

Nest

Steller's Jays build cup nests with a bulky foundation of large sticks cemented together with mud (Bent 1946). The inside of the cup is lined with rootlets or pine needles (Bent 1946). Nests are built on horizontal limbs or in the crotch of trees (Erlich et al. 1988).

Diet

Based on two stomachs collected in northern California, Coleoptera accounted for 92% and Lepidoptera 4% of the diet (Otvos and Stark 1985). During December and January the diet was between 90 and 99% acorns or pine seeds (Erlich et al. 1988).

Northern Flicker

Distribution and habitat

The Northern Flicker ranges from treeline in Alaska and across northern Canada, south through most of the lower 48 states (Terres 1991). In Arizona, Northern Flickers have a widely scattered elevational distribution. On the San Francisco Peaks from June–September, mean elevation ranged between 2,590 m and 2,835 m (Coons 1984). Northern Flickers were not recorded during November, December, or January anywhere on the San Francisco Peaks study area including a site as low as 2,440 m (Coons 1984).

Densities

Haldeman (1968) recorded densities in three different forest stands—ponderosa pine, burned ponderosa pine, and a mixed-stand of fir, pine, and aspen. The number of breeding pairs per 40 ha was 9, 17, and 7, respectively. Breeding densities during a three year study in five different forest treatments ranged from zero pairs per 40 ha in cleared plots, to four pairs per 40 ha on strip cut plots (Szaro and Balda 1979). Densities of Northern Flickers in the Santa Catalina Mountains north of Tucson, averaged two/40 ha (Horton and Mannan 1988). At the same study area, Horton and Mannan (1988) recorded a decrease in density on plots that were control burned. Prior to burning in 1984, the density was 2.6/40 ha and in 1985, after the burn, the numbers dropped to 2.1/40 ha (Horton and Mannan 1988).

In winter the number of birds seen per hour was 0.2 in a mixed stand of fir, pine, and aspen and 0.9 in a pure ponderosa pine stand (Haldeman 1968). Flicker densities were positively correlated with aspen overstory density (Scott and Crouch 1988).

Reproduction and development

Northern Flickers are monogamous and the average clutch is five–eight eggs (range 3–12) (Erlich et al. 1988). They have one brood per year over most of their range but two broods is common in the south (Erlich et al. 1988). Both sexes share incubation of the eggs for 11–14 d when young are born altricial. The young fledge from 25–28 d after hatching (Erlich et al. 1988).

Home range

Home range and territory are likely the same size but no specific figures are available (Moore 1995). A territory of 16 ha was estimated for a breeding pair in a conifer forest in Ontario (Lawrence 1967)

Nest

The Northern Flicker is a primary cavity nester and excavates nest holes preferentially in snags but sometimes in live trees, typically cottonwood (*Populus* spp.), willow (*Salix* spp.), sycamore (*Platanus* spp.), or juniper (Bent 1939). Scott and Patton (1975) recorded 10 nests in the White Mountains of Arizona, five in dead ponderosa pine, two in dead aspen, and three in live aspen. The average height of these 10 nests was 13 m above ground level (Scott and Patton 1975). Preston and Norris

(1947) reported two nests at 6 m above ground level. On the Mogollon rim in central Arizona, Li and Martin (1991) found average nest height to be 16 m above ground level. In the Sierra Nevada Mountains, mean height of nest trees was 13 m and mean nest height was 8 m (N = 68; Rafael and White 1984).

Mean nest tree dbh was 45 cm in Arizona (Li and Martin 1991). In the Sierra Nevada, mean dbh of nest trees was 60 cm. The majority of nests (97%) were in aspen trees and the remainder was in conifers (N = 37; Li and Martin 1991). Northern Flickers selected snags 57% of the time; 14% of Northern Flicker nests were found in dead portions of live trees and 30% in live trees (Li and Martin 1991). In the Sierra Nevada, Northern Flickers used snags, dead portions of live trees and live trees 78%, 20%, and 3% of the time, respectively (N = 20; Rafael and White 1984).

Diet

The Northern Flicker feeds chiefly on the ground but occasionally may capture flying insects and glean bark (Erlich et al. 1988). The preferred food is ants, more than any other North American bird (Erlich et al. 1988). In addition to ants, some beetles, caterpillars, crickets, spiders, and codling moths are eaten (Bent 1939). Acorns are the main plant item in the diet (Bent 1939). Otvos and Stark (1985) reported the stomach contents of nine Northern Flickers collected between 1962 and 1968 in northern California. Formicids (Hymenoptera) composed nearly 90% of the diet with *Liometopum* spp., *Prenolepis imparis*, *Formica* spp., and *Lasius* spp. each contributing about 20% to the total diet. Plant material comprised 3% of the diet (Otvos and Stark 1985). Scott et al. (1977) reported that animal matter comprised 60% of the Northern Flickers diet and of this, 75% was ants. Plant material in Northern Flicker diets includes seeds of annuals, cultivated grains, and the fruits of shrubs and trees (Scott et al. 1977).

PREY SPECIES HABITAT

The habitats used by the primary prey of the goshawk in the Southwest vary from small (<1 ha) stands of large, mature Douglas-fir with high canopy closure for red squirrels, to areas with relatively low canopy cover and high grass-forb cover for golden-mantled ground squirrels. All of the prey species occur in ponderosa pine forest except red squirrels, which are restricted to spruce-fir forest. The desert cottontail, cliff chipmunk, rock squirrel, and Northern Flicker are found in more than three different habitat types on the Coconino National Forest

(Anonymous 1991a, 1991b). The Abert squirrel is the only species restricted to ponderosa pine forest.

Home range size of goshawk prey species is variable but always much smaller than the home range size of any individual goshawk. Home ranges of prey species varies from less than 1 ha for chipmunks to >20 ha for Abert squirrel. By contrast, goshawk home ranges in North America are estimated to range from 570–3,500 ha depending on sex and habitat characteristics (Squires and Reynolds 1997).

Goshawks and their prey may respond differently to silvicultural treatments. For example, golden-mantled ground squirrels preferred dense, mature forest over open stands on silviculturally treated forest in Arizona (Goodwin and Hungerford 1979), but they increased in numbers in northern California following clear-cut timber harvest (Tevis 1956). On the Kaibab National Forest in northern Arizona, Crocker-Bedford (1990) estimated that the number of Northern Goshawk pairs declined by >50% following timber harvest. This contrast in the type of response to a forest treatment illustrates the complexity of forest management and suggests that decisions cannot be based on the needs of a single prey species alone.

This review summarizes several goshawk dietary studies to identify the primary prey of the goshawk in the Southwest and the habitats of these species. However, knowledge of the habitats used by goshawk prey must be associated to the habitats used by goshawks, because many of the prey species occupy habitats where goshawks are unlikely to encounter them (e.g., Northern Flicker in Mojave desert scrub). Life-history traits of goshawk prey are variable. Most of these species produce young during the goshawk nesting season (May–July) but many hibernate or migrate to lower elevations during the winter months (Table 6). Population dynamics of these species is variable with some species cyclic and others relatively stable year to year.

GOSHAWK HABITAT

Several studies have characterized goshawk nesting habitat across its range. Despite highly variable tree species composition both within a region and across the subspecies' range, these studies generally agree that goshawk nest sites have large trees, dense canopies, and, in the southern portion of the hawk's range, are typically on slopes with northerly aspects (Bartlelt 1977, Moore and Henny 1983, Speiser and Bosakowski 1987, Crocker-Bedford and Chaney 1988, Kennedy 1988, Hayward and Escano 1989). Whereas nest stands have been studied extensively, little is known about the structure and composition of goshawk foraging habitat.

Only eight studies have described goshawk foraging habitats. In North America, four studies found that goshawks preferred stands with average tree diameter ≥52 cm dbh (Austin 1993), greater canopy cover, basal area, and tree densities than at random sites (Hargis et al. 1994), areas with high canopy closure as determined from LANDSAT imagery (Bright-Smith and Mannan 1994), and greater density of large trees (>40 cm dbh), higher canopy closure, and higher tree density than paired comparison sites (Beier and Drennan 1997). In Europe, Widén (1989) found that goshawks preferred mature conifers over younger stands in a Swedish boreal forest. In three Swedish and one British study area, Kenward (1982) reported that goshawks spent 50% of their time in woodlands which comprised only 12% of their habitat. In the same study, goshawks avoided open country and had a preference for woodland edge or forested areas within 200 m of an opening. Despite the preference for mature forest conditions reported in these studies which were conducted in the breeding season, goshawks used all available habitats for foraging including dense stands of small diameter trees, meadows, seedling and sapling stands, and clearcuts. During winter, goshawks in Arizona used habitats with more medium-sized trees and denser canopy closure than paired reference sites, but indices of prey abundance did not differ between used and reference sites, suggesting that goshawks are habitat specialists even during winter (Drennan and Beier 2003). In Utah, wintering goshawks used habitats with greater canopy closure and greater tree density than random locations (Stephens 2001).

OVERLAP BETWEEN GOSHAWK HABITAT AND PREY SPECIES HABITAT

The habitats used by goshawks and their prey vary throughout the year. In summer, habitats used by goshawks and their primary prey appear to overlap entirely for some individuals, as expected. In winter, goshawks may remain on their breeding territories in ponderosa pine forest, descend to lower elevation pinyon-juniper woodland and grassland, or ascend to spruce-fir forests. Goshawks wintering in ponderosa pine forest overlap with Abert squirrels and some bird species, a relatively narrow prey base compared to goshawks wintering in pinyon-juniper where a greater diversity of prey species are available. In the spruce-fir zone, red squirrel is the only prey species available to goshawks. Although no studies in the Southwest have shown goshawk winter

movements in response to low populations of prey species, this pattern has been documented for studies areas at more northern latitudes (Doyle and Smith 1994, Yukon, Canada, 60° N). If goshawk movements at lower latitudes are driven by prey abundance, the most sensitive habitat would be spruce-fir where only a single prey species is expected present during winter months.

Habitats used by goshawks and their primary prey share several similar attributes. At the coarsest scale, both goshawks and their prey require forested habitats for at least part of the year. At a finer scale, most prey species reach their highest densities in habitats with high canopy closure, high numbers of large trees per hectare, and presence of downed woody material, and snags, habitats that are also preferred by goshawks. Although habitats used by goshawks and their prey have many similarities, they also have many differences. The biggest difference across all prey species is related to the area of habitat used; goshawks use relatively large areas compared to most prey species. During the breeding season goshawks typically range over areas >500 ha whereas most prey species have small home ranges (<20 ha). Because goshawk habitat covers large areas, it is inherently more diverse than the habitats used by individual prey species. As a result, goshawks probably respond to the composition of habitat types across the landscape more so than prey species.

CONCLUSION

Goshawks consume a wide variety of prey across their range. In the Southwest, goshawks consume a greater percentage of mammalian prey compared to avian prey. This preference for mammals is also evident in diet studies conducted in Canada and Alaska. However, in the Pacific Northwest and the northeastern US, goshawk diet studies report greater percentages of avian prey in goshawk diet compared to mammals (Tables 2–5).

Although this review focused mainly on goshawk prey and prey habitats in the Southwest, diets of goshawk in the western US are highly similar (Table 7) with many of the same prey species or their ecological equivalents present in diets throughout this region. Cottontails, golden-mantled ground squirrel, chipmunks, Steller's Jay, Northern Flicker, and American Robin are common prey throughout the western US, and in other regions where they occur. In California and Oregon, the ponderosa pine-dependent Abert squirrel of the Southwest is replaced by the mixed-conifer dwelling Douglas squirrel and northern flying squirrel (*Glaucomys sabrinus*).

Although the forest types used by these species are different, the general requirements are similar (mature forest with relatively high canopy closure, groups of closely spaced trees, and hypogeous fungi) suggesting that successful habitat management approaches might be similar for these regions.

Goshawk diet has been reported from >30 studies across their range but is relatively limited in the Southwest. Southwest diet studies are limited to two studies on the Kaibab Plateau in Arizona (Boal and Mannan 1994, Reynolds et al. 1994) and one study in the Jemez Mountains of New Mexico (Kennedy 1991). Results of these studies may not be applicable to other areas within the Southwest. Further, all three studies were conducted in the breeding season when prey populations were at their peak. Winter diet of goshawks is poorly known; however, this may be the period of greatest stress on goshawks in terms of food availability and weather conditions. Two studies suggest an extremely narrow diet breadth during winter (Stephens 2001, Drennan and Beier 2003). Further research on the wintering diet of goshawks, both in ponderosa pine forest and pinyon-juniper woodlands, should be a priority. Ideally, this research should be directed at the relationship of winter prey availability and goshawk fitness.

Basic natural history information on many of the primary prey species of goshawks in the Southwest is lacking, especially for rock squirrels, chipmunks, and cottontails. This review identifies many of the gaps in knowledge on these prey species. In addition, comparisons between prey studies and goshawk studies are often difficult because different variables were measured or different scales of habitat were evaluated. For example, prey species habitat might be described only for a small area such as a nest site, whereas, goshawk habitat studies are generally focused on larger areas that include the nest area and in some cases, winter habitat and foraging habitat. Future studies on goshawk foraging and prey ecology should carefully select habitat variables for measurement and consider the appropriate scale to allow for better comparisons between preferences of predator and prey.

The wide range of habitats used by the goshawks' primary prey species in the Southwest reflects the diversity of habitats used by goshawks. Because goshawk prey species occur in a wide range of habitats, forest managers should consider maintaining habitat components essential for goshawk nesting and foraging while maintaining habitat elements of preferred prey in areas that may not meet the criteria of documented habitat characteristics for goshawks. This approach suggests managing for a mosaic of habitat types across the landscape that provide habitat that meets the requirements of goshawk prey species and goshawks. The practice of managing landscapes in a more holistic manner, considering areas beyond the traditionally recognized limits of a species, will benefit not only goshawks but their prey species as well.

ACKNOWLEDGMENTS

I thank W. Block and P. Beier for coordinating funding and reviewing earlier drafts of this manuscript. D. Patton offered ideas and provided access to his extensive collection of journals, which indulged my curiosity and saved me many trips to the library. I thank R. Jackman and M. Morrison for reviewing this manuscript. I also thank K. Bickert for her generous gift of time and patience allowing me to complete this project. This research was partially funded by a challenge cost share agreement between the USDA Forest Service and Northern Arizona University (order number-43-82FT-4-1657).

APPENDIX 1. List of species observed in goshawk diets in western North America. Based on Schnell 1958, Bloom et al. 1986, Kennedy 1991, Boal and Mannan 1994, Bull and Hohmann 1994, and Reynolds et al. 1994.

Mammals
  Black-tailed jackrabbit (*Lepus californicus*)
  White-tailed jackrabbit (*Lepus. townsendii*)
  Snowshoe hare (*Lepus americanus*)
  Cottontail (*Sylvilagus* spp.)
  Golden-mantled ground squirrel (*Spermophilus lateralis*)
  Belding's ground squirrel (*Spermophilu beldingi*)
  California ground squirrel (*Spermophilubeecheyi*)
  Rock squirrel (*Spermophilus variegatus*)
  Douglas' squirrel (*Tamiasciurus douglasii*)
  Red squirrel (*Tamiasciurus hudsonicus*)
  Northern flying squirrel (*Glaucomys sabrinus*)
  Western gray squirrel (*Sciurus griseus*)
  Abert squirrel (*Sciurus* aberti)
  Cliff chipmunk (*Eutamias dorsalis*)
  Uinta chipmunk (*Eutamias umbrinus*)
  Yellow pine chipmunk (*Eutamias amoenus*)
  Broad-footed mole (*Scapanus latimus*)
  Woodrat (*Neotoma* spp.)
  Weasel (*Mustela* spp.)
  Unidentified microtine
  Cat (*Felis* spp.)
Birds
  Mallard (*Anas platyrhynchos*)
  Gadwall (*Anas strepera*)
  Cooper's Hawk (*Accipiter cooperii*)
  Northern Goshawk (*Accipiter gentilis*)
  American Kestrel (*Falco sparverius*)
  Prairie Falcon (*Falco mexicanus*)
  Blue Grouse (*Dendrogapus obscurus*)
  Ruffed Grouse (*Bonasa umbellus*)
  Mountain Quail (*Oreortyx pictus*)
  Band-tailed Pigeon (*Columba fasciata*)
  Rock Pigeon (*Columba livia*)
  Mourning Dove (*Zenaida macroura*)

Birds (continued)
  Long-eared Owl (*Asio otus*)
  Spotted Owl (*Strix occidentalis*)
  Western Screech-owl (*Otus kennicottii*)
  Northern Pygmy Owl (*Glaucidium gnoma*)
  Belted Kingfisher (*Ceryle alcyon*)
  Northern Flicker (*Colaptes auratus*)
  White-headed Woodpecker (*Picoides albolarvatus*)
  Red-breasted Sapsucker (*Sphyrapicus ruber*)
  Williamson's Sapsucker (*Sphyrapicus thyroideus*)
  Red-naped Sapsucker (*Sphyrapicus nuchalis*)
  Hairy Woodpecker (*Picoides villosus*)
  Nuttall's Woodpecker (*Picoides nuttallii*)
  Pileated Woodpecker (*Dryocopus pileatus*)
  Western Scrub Jay (*Aphelocoma coerulescens*)
  Gray Jay (*Aphelocoma ultramarina*)
  Steller's Jay (*Cyanocitta stelleri*)
  Clark's Nutcracker (*Nucifraga columbiana*)
  Common Raven (*Corvus corax*)
  American Crow (*Corvus brachyrhnchos*)
  Pygmy Nuthatch (*Sitta pygmaea*)
  Western Bluebird (*Sialia mexicana*)
  Mountain Bluebird (*Sialia currucoides*)
  Hermit Thrush (*Catharus guttatus*)
  American Robin (*Turdus migratorius*)
  European Starling (*Sternus vulgaris*)
  Yellow-rumped Warbler (*Dendroica coronata*)
  Black-headed Grosbeak (*Pheucticus melanocephalus*)
  Eastern Towhee (*Pipilo erythrophthalmus*)
  Dark-eyed Junco (*Junco hyemalis*)
  Western Meadowlark (*Sturnella neglecta*)
  Western Tanager (*Piranga ludoviciana*)
  Unidentified finch (*Carpodacus* spp.)
  Evening Grosbeak (*Coccothraustes vespertinus*)

DIET, PREY DELIVERY RATES, AND PREY BIOMASS OF NORTHERN GOSHAWKS IN EAST-CENTRAL ARIZONA

Andi S. Rogers, Stephen DeStefano, and Michael F. Ingraldi

Abstract. Recent concern over persistence of Northern Goshawk (*Accipiter gentilis*) populations in Arizona has stemmed from two long-term demography studies that report substantial yearly fluctuations in productivity and evidence of a declining population. Although many factors could be involved in changes in productivity and population declines, availability of food is one such factor. As part of a demography study on the Sitgreaves portion of the Apache-Sitgreaves National Forest in Arizona, we used remote cameras to assess diets of goshawks. Northern Goshawks preyed upon 22 species during two nesting seasons. Adult pairs tended to specialize on particular species of prey. Prey delivery rates decreased throughout the nesting season with a corresponding increase in biomass in the latter stages of the nestling and fledgling periods. Adults appeared to take larger prey as nestlings increased in age.

Key Words: *Accipiter gentilis,* Arizona, diet, food habits, Northern Goshawk, remote cameras, video surveillance.

DIETA, TASA DE ENTREGA DE PRESA Y BIOMASA DE LA PRESA DEL GAVILÁN AZOR EN ARIZONA DEL ESTE CENTRAL

Resumen. La reciente preocupación acerca de las poblaciones del Gavilán Azor (*Accipiter gentilis*) en Arizona, ha sido estancada en dos estudios demográficos de largo plazo, los cuales reportan substanciales fluctuaciones anuales en la productividad y evidencia en la disminución en la población. A pesar de que muchos factores podrían estar involucrados en los cambios en la productividad y en la disminución de la población, la disponibilidad de alimento es uno de ellos. Como parte del estudio demográfico en la porción Sitgreaves del Bosque Nacional Apache-Sitgreaves en Arizona, utilizamos cámaras remotas para evaluar las dietas de los gavilanes. Gavilanes Azor cazaron 22 especies durante dos temporadas de anidación. Las parejas adultas tendieron a especializarse en particulares especies de presa La tasa de entrega de presa disminuyó durante la temporada de anidación, con un incremento correspondiente a la biomasa en los estados tardíos en los períodos de crecimiento y volanteo. Al parecer los adultos tomaron presas más grandes, conforme los polluelos crecían.

Concern and controversy exist over the persistence of Northern Goshawk (*Accipiter gentilis*) populations in the western US (Reynolds et al. 1982, Crocker-Bedford 1990). A long-term demographic study conducted on the Apache-Sitgreaves National Forest reported substantial yearly fluctuations in productivity of goshawks, and equivocal evidence of a declining local population (Ingraldi 1999). Probable causes of decline have been linked to habitat alterations that include timber harvesting, fire suppression, and grazing, some of which have reduced numbers of large diameter trees and increased the density of smaller diameter trees (Kochert et al. 1987, Lehman and Allendorf 1987, Moir and Detericch 1988).

In Arizona, Northern Goshawks are found in mature ponderosa pine (*Pinus ponderosa*) and mixed conifer forests in the northern and central parts of the state, with the southernmost edge of the sub-species *Accipiter gentilis atricapillus* range reaching the rim of the Mogollon Plateau. The changing structure of mature forests may decrease habitat for goshawks by limiting nest sites and reducing the availability

of certain prey (Beier and Drennan 1997, DeStefano and McCloskey 1997). Some important prey species in the Southwest include eastern cottontail (*Sylvilagus floridanus*), Steller's Jay (*Cyanocitta stelleri*), Northern Flicker (*Colates auratus*), and Abert's squirrel (*Sciurus aberti*) (Kennedy 1991, Reynolds et al. 1992, Boal and Mannan 1994). To better understand goshawk-prey relationships in central Arizona, we examined prey delivery by adult goshawks to their nests. Studying raptor diets allows a better understanding of raptor niches and may provide information on prey distribution (Marti 1987). In addition, information on raptor diet is important for understanding ecological aspects such as diet overlap between and among species, predation, and prey availability (Hutto 1990, Rosenberg and Cooper 1990, Redpath et. al 2001).

Diet is most commonly measured through indirect methods, such as examination of pellets and prey remains, and direct methods, such as observations from blinds. These methods are not only time intensive, but evidence suggests that they can be subject to bias (Duffy and Jackson 1986, Bielefeldt et al. 1992, González-Solís et al. 1997). We chose video monitoring as a primary method to quantify goshawk diet. We investigated diet, prey delivery rates, and prey biomass of nesting Northern Goshawks during the breeding seasons of 1999 and 2000 in east-central Arizona. Our objectives were to assess patterns related to prey consumption by breeding goshawks by (1) identifying and quantifying prey items, delivery rates, and biomass of prey brought to nests by adult goshawks, and (2) assessing the effect of nestling age, brood size, and time of day on prey delivery rates and biomass.

METHODS

STUDY AREA

Our study took place on the Sitgreaves portion of the Apache-Sitgreaves National Forest in east-central Arizona. The Sitgreaves Forest encompasses about 330,300 ha and is located on the Mogollon Plateau, a large glacial escarpment stretching east across central Arizona and into New Mexico. The rim of the plateau formed the southern boundary of our study area (Rogers 2001). A wide variety of vegetation communities occur within the study area (Brown 1982). The Mogollon Rim edge has deep drainages with mixed-conifer communities of Douglas-fir (*Pseudotsuga menziesii*), white fir (*Abies concolor*), aspen (*Populus tremuloides*), ponderosa pine, New Mexico locust (*Robinia neomexicana*), and Gambel oak (*Quercus gambelii*). Ridgetops are commonly dominated by ponderosa pine forest. Elevations range from 1,800–2,400 m and decrease going north as ponderosa pine and juniper-pinyon forest transitions to a pinyon-juniper woodland dominated by alligator juniper (*Juniper deppeana*), Utah juniper (*Juniper osteosperma*), and Rocky Mountain pinyon pine (*Pinus edulis*). Lowest elevations are comprised of a grassland community with blue grama (*Bouteloua gracilis*), sand dropseed (*Sprobus crytandrus*), and fourwing saltbush (*Atriplex canescens*). Goshawk nest stands were located within or near major drainage systems, dominated by mature ponderosa or mixed conifer vegetation cover, and spread throughout the study area.

OBSERVATIONS

We recorded nest activities at four nests in 1999 and six nests in 2000. No nests were observed for more than one breeding season. When Northern Goshawk young were between 4–7 d old we climbed nest trees and mounted weatherproof remote cameras (Electro-optics EOD-1000 remote camera, St. Louis, MO; mention of trade names does not imply endorsement by the U.S. Government) (Rogers 2001). Cameras were equipped with 3.6 mm lenses, had a resolution of 380 lines, a 1 lux digital color system, and measured 3.5 x 12 cm in size. Once positioned, we secured cameras on the trunk of the tree or an overhanging branch. To minimize nestling stress we shaded them with towels during camera installation. Cameras were connected to 75 m of telephone power cord and coaxial video cable, which were tacked along the trunk of the tree. Located away from the base of the nest tree was a 12-volt time-lapse video-cassette recorder (VCR) (Panasonic AG-1070 DC, Secaucus, NJ and Sony SVT-DL224, Park Ridge, NJ), which provided 24 hr of recording per videotape. VCRs were housed in military ammunition cans for weatherproofing and powered by one 12-volt, 64 amp-hour lead acid battery. After camera set-up was complete we locked ammunition cans, attached all ground equipment to trees with cables, and covered equipment with forest litter for shade and camouflage.

We collected video 6 d of each week from 22 June–18 July 1999, and 6 June–31 July 2000. We recorded activity at each nest in a 2-d sequence (12 hr/day) with video recorded from 0450–1650 H on day one and 0800–2000 H on day two. Batteries and tapes were changed at the end of day two, usually at night to reduce disturbance. We continued to record until no prey deliveries were seen on video footage for two consecutive days.

Video was viewed by one person (ASR) to minimize observer bias. We quantified total number and type of prey items delivered (class, genus, or species) and portion size of prey items both delivered and consumed. We aged nestlings (Boal 1994) and assigned each nest a single age value by averaging each nestling's estimated age. We recorded brood size and documented nestling and adult mortality.

PREY DELIVERIES

We calculated prey delivery rate as the total number of prey items delivered per hour. Cached or questionable prey items were those that were identified as the same species and portion re-delivered within a half-hour of the initial delivery. Goshawks may consume a portion of a prey item and then cache the remainder to re-deliver to the nest. Therefore, in order to limit inflated prey delivery rates due to caches, we excluded all questionable prey items delivered to nests (e.g., five items delivered to the nest before dark, followed by the same items delivered within 2–3 hr the next morning were likely cached items). In addition, we could monitor cached prey delivered to nests more accurately with longer hours of taped observation; therefore, we excluded videotapes in which the sampling day was ≤6 hr.

BIOMASS

We estimated biomass of prey in two ways: (1) total biomass delivered to the nest by adults, and (2) total biomass consumed at the nest by adults and nestlings. Biomass rate was estimated as grams/ hour. Total biomass was estimated based on portions delivered, whereas values for consumed biomass were calculated by taking the difference of portion delivered and portion not consumed. As we did with prey delivery rate, we excluded videotapes in which the sampling period was ≤6 hr.

Biomass calculations for whole animals

Whole mass of mammals was assigned from Cockrum and Petryszyn (1992), birds from Dunning (1993), and reptile mass (short-horned lizards [*Phrynosoma hernadesi*]) was calculated from specimens (N = 5) from the University of Arizona's herpetology museum. Within the genus *Eutamius* we were unable to distinguish between the grey-collared chipmunk *(Eutamius cinereicollis)* and cliff chipmunk *(Eutamius dorsalis),* which co-occur on the Sitgreaves Forest (Hoffmeister 1986). We assigned mass for *Eutamius* by averaging mass of both species calculated from specimens in the University of Arizona mammal collection (N = 50).

Prey items described to class only were characterized a priori as small (50–200 g), medium (200–600 g), or large (>600 g) for mammals, and small (<40 g), medium (60–150 g), and large (>150 g) for birds (Cockrum and Petryszyn 1992, Dunning 1993). No size category was used for lizards because all individuals were identified to species. Whole prey items not recognizable to genus or species were assigned biomass values of the mean mass for the size class to which they belonged (Table 1). If prey was not recognizable to class, genus, or species, it was usually small in size. These items were categorized as unknown and given the mass value of the smallest overall prey item delivered to nests (10 g). We estimated whole mass for juvenile birds based on Bielefeldt et al. (1992), and juvenile mammal whole mass from minimum mass from ranges found in Wilson and Ruff (1999).

Biomass calculations for partial animals

Prey delivered in pieces were given proportional mass values, with pieces categorized as minus head, three-quarters, half, two legs and thighs, legs only, and one leg. We calculated partial prey mass for items identified to species by collecting and dissecting one individual of each species (hereafter referred to as reference specimens) represented in the diet of Northern Goshawks on the Apache-Sitgreaves National Forest. When we were unable to collect an individual species we substituted an individual from the same genus or an individual of comparable size. We used the reference specimens to estimate proportional mass of prey pieces by dividing the reference piece weight (half, minus head, etc.) by the total mass of the reference animal, then multiplying that proportion times the animal's mean mass from the literature (Rogers 2001).

Partial prey items not recognizable to species were given proportional values based on mean prey mass of partial prey pieces across the size class to which it belonged. For example, a half of a medium sciurid would receive a mass value from averaging half a golden-mantled ground squirrel (*Spermophilus lateralis*) and half a red squirrel (*Tamiasciurus hudsonicus*).

ANALYSES

All prey delivery rate and biomass data were truncated at fledgling age (40 d). Forty days is a combined estimate for average fledging dates for male and female goshawk young. We calculated diet composition by class, genus, and species and expressed values as percentages. We summarized total species in goshawk diet, which included videotapes with <6 hr of daily footage, and videos collected after fledging (40 d). To reflect the percentage of total grams consumed, we expressed delivered biomass and consumed biomass as percentages. We also determined the percentage of time that goshawks consumed entire prey portions rather than leaving the nest with an item to be cached. Lastly, we looked at percent representation of most common prey items for each individual nest.

Daily biomass and prey delivery data were pooled for all 10 nests after determining no difference in rates at age increments of 5 d (analysis of variance [ANOVA]). We used multiple linear regression to assess relationships of brood size and nestling age on biomass and prey delivery rates. For multiple regression analysis we used estimates of consumed biomass instead of total biomass. We transformed

TABLE 1. SIZE CLASSES AND WEIGHTS USED TO CALCULATE BIOMASS OF PREY DELIVERED TO 10 NORTHERN GOSHAWK NESTS ON THE APACHE-SITGREAVES NATIONAL FOREST IN EAST-CENTRAL ARIZONA, 1999 AND 2000.

Prey types		Mass (g)[a]
Small mammal (50–200 g)		
Chipmunk[b]	*Eutamius* spp.	63
White-throated wood rat	*Neotoma albigula*	180
Average small mammal		121.5
Medium mammal (200–600 g)		
Golden-mantled ground squirrel	*Spermophilus lateralis*	200
Red squirrel	*Tamiasciurus hudsonicus*	230
Average medium mammal		215
Large mammal (>600 g)		
Abert's squirrel	*Sciurus aberti*	680
Rock squirrel	*Sciurus variegatus*	760
Eastern cottontail	*Sylvilagus floridanus*	1,500
Black-tailed jackrabbit	*Lepus californicus*	2,100
Average large mammal		1,260
Small bird (<40 g)		
Dark-eyed Junco	*Junco hyemalis*	20
White-breasted Nuthatch	*Sitta carolinensis*	21
Western Bluebird	*Sialia mexicana*	28
Townsend's Solitaire	*Myadestes townsendi*	34
Average small bird		25.8
Medium bird (60–150 g)		
Hairy Woodpecker	*Picoides villosus*	66
American Robin	*Turdus migratorius*	77
Northern Flicker	*Colaptes auratus*	111
American Kestrel	*Falco sparverius*	116
Mourning Dove	*Zenaida macroura*	119
Steller's Jay	*Cyanocitta stelleri*	128
Average medium bird		102.8
Large bird (>150 g)		
Band-tailed Pigeon	*Patagioenas fasciata*	342
Rock Dove	*Columba livia*	354
Cooper's Hawk	*Accipiter cooperii*	439
Average large bird		378.3
Short-horned lizard	*Phrynosoma hernadesi*	40

[a] Mass calculated by averaging adult male and female mean mass for each species; mass across size classes was calculated from all species within the size class, e.g., average small mammal = mass of chipmunk + mass of wood rat/2.
[b] Mass for chipmunks was calculated by averaging mass of *Eutamius dorsalis* and *Eutamius cineriecollis*.

biomass data using a natural log transformation. We used simple linear regression to assess (1) time of day (morning = 0450–1050 H, afternoon = 1050–1550 H, evening = 1550–2000 H) for the number of prey items delivered, and (2) the effect of nestling age on average daily prey mass brought in by adults.

RESULTS

We had no nest abandonment due to camera presence, and eight of ten goshawk nests were successful (i.e., fledged ≥1 young). Of 23 nestlings from 10 nests, 19 survived to fledging, and brood size varied from two (seven nests) to three (three nests) individuals. The two failed nests were due to an adult

female choking on a piece of rabbit (Bloxton et al. 2002) and nestling mortality by a Great Horned Owl (*Bubo virginianus*). We collected 2,458 hr of usable video from videotapes (i.e., ≥6 hr for each tape).

PREY DELIVERIES

We documented 670 prey deliveries and observed a mean delivery rate of 0.30 (SE = 0.01, range = 0.00–0.67) prey items/hour. Goshawk diet was composed of 73% mammals, 18% birds, 2% reptiles, and 7% unknown prey items. We successfully identified 627 (93%) prey items to class and were able to identify, at least to genus, 422 (62%) of all prey items. Goshawk diet was comprised of 22 different species (Table 2). Five mammal and one bird genera contributed 78% of all prey. Mammals contributing >5% each to goshawk diet were eastern cottontails, chipmunks, golden-mantled ground squirrels, red squirrels, and Abert's squirrels. Steller's Jays were the only bird species that contributed >5% to diet (Table 2). Lastly, these six most common prey items were not taken equally among individual nests, with some nests showing possible specialization for particular prey items (Table 3).

Nestling age and time of day affected daily prey delivery rates, but brood size did not (Rogers 2001). Mean prey delivery rates decreased overall, but with a peak in delivery rate near 18 d of age (Fig. 1).

TABLE 2. TOTAL NUMBER OR PREY SPECIES AND BIOMASS DELIVERED AND CONSUMED AT 10 NORTHERN GOSHAWK NESTS ON THE APACHE-SITGREAVES NATIONAL FOREST IN EAST-CENTRAL ARIZONA, 1999 AND 2000.

Prey species		N	Percent number	Percent biomass
Abert's squirrel	*Sciurus aberti*	62	9.25	18.48
Golden-mantled ground squirrel	*Spermophilus lateralis*	63	9.40	7.06
Eastern cottontail	*Sylvilagus floridanus*	89	13.3	42.31
Red squirrel	*Tamiasciurus hudsonicus*	53	7.92	7.66
Chipmunk	*Eutamius* spp.	67	10.1	2.51
Rock squirrel	*Spermophilus variegatus*	8	1.19	3.25
White-throated wood rat[a]	*Neotoma albigula*	–	–	–
Black-tailed jackrabbit[1]	*Lepus californicus*	–	–	–
Unknown mammals		144	21.5	7.42
Northern Flicker	*Colaptes auratus*	10	1.49	0.65
Steller's Jay	*Cyanocitta stelleri*	34	5.08	2.42
Band-tailed Pigeon	*Patagioenas fasciata*	1	0.15	0.18
Mourning Dove	*Zenaida macroura*	3	0.46	0.16
Rock Dove	*Columba livia*	4	0.61	0.39
Hairy Woodpecker	*Picoides villosus*	1	0.15	0.25
American Robin	*Turdus migratorius*	3	0.46	0.10
Dark eyed Junco	*Junco hyemalis*	1	0.15	0.03
American Kestrel	*Falco sparverius*	1	0.15	0.03
Townsend's Solitaire[a]	*Myadestes townsendi*	–	–	–
Cooper's Hawk[a]	*Accipiter cooperii*	–	–	–
Western Bluebird[1]	*Sialia mexicana*	–	–	–
White-breasted Nuthatch[1]	*Sitta carolinensis*	–	–	–
Unknown birds		61	9.10	2.74
Short-horned lizard	*Phrynosoma hernadesi*	16	2.39	0.77
Unknown prey items		49	7.31	0.54
TOTAL		670	100	100

[a] Prey items delivered after fledging of Northern Goshawks, or delivered but not consumed by birds at the nest. Items are not quantified into total prey item or biomass estimates.

TABLE 3. PERCENT OF SIX COMMON PREY SPECIES BROUGHT TO 10 NORTHERN GOSHAWK NESTS ON THE SITGREAVES FOREST, ARIZONA, 1999 AND 2000.

Nest	Eastern cottontail	Golden-mantled ground squirrel	Abert's squirrel	Red squirrel	Chipmunk spp.	Steller's Jay	Total[a]
1	30	3	15	0	6	14	68
2	4	21	26	4	18	2	75
3	11	0	16	0	0	0	27
4	9	21	7	16	10	12	75
5	0	6	0	32	17	4	59
6	2	21	0	0	9	7	39
7	16	2	9	2	6	43	78
8	6	13	0	14	10	6	49
9	23	4	32	0	0	7	66
10	0	11	9	33	25	6	84

[a] Percentages do not total to 100 because of other prey species, not listed here, that were brought to the nest.

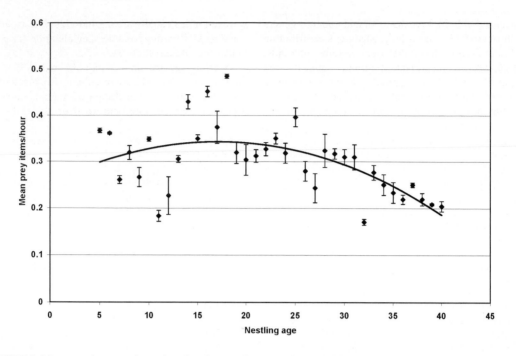

FIGURE 1. Mean prey items per hour plotted against nestling age at 10 Northern Goshawk nests on the Sitgreaves Forest, Arizona, 1999 and 2000.

Daily delivery rates decreased by a factor 0.3% as nestlings aged (t = -2.73, df = 162, P = 0.007). Time of day affected mean prey delivery rates with highest rates during the morning (mean delivery rate = 2.2 items per hr, SE = 1.2, N = 81) and decreasing rates throughout the day (afternoon = 1.4 items per hr, SE = 0.9, N = 151; evening = 1.3, SE = 0.9, N = 76). Prey delivery rates decreased by a factor of 0.46 prey items/interval (t = -5.68, df = 307, P < 0.001) from morning to afternoon to evening.

PREY BIOMASS

Daily mean biomass rate was 42.4 g/hr (SE = 2.75, range 0.00–238.8). Mammals and birds accounted for 92% and 6.9% of the biomass consumed, respectively. Lizards contributed 0.8%, and 0.5% of biomass was attributed to unknown prey items. Four species of mammals (eastern cottontails, red squirrels, golden-mantled squirrels, Abert's squirrels) contributed 75% of the total biomass consumed (Table 2). No bird species contributed >5% biomass consumed.

Of 102,078 total grams of prey delivered, goshawks consumed 79,958 grams (78%) at the nest. Goshawks consumed the entire prey item brought in 73% of the time. Nestling age and time of day affected biomass rates, but brood size did not (P =

0.14). Mean biomass consumed by nestlings at age five was 5.64 g/hr and increased linearly to 51.09 g/hr at 40 d (Fig. 2). Daily biomass rates increased by 1.03 g/hr as nestlings grew older (t = 4.20, df = 158, P < 0.001). Lastly, average prey mass increased by a factor of 46.53 g/d as nestlings aged (t = 4.40, df = 161, P < 0.001). Average prey mass brought to nests with five-day-old chicks was 63.25 g and increased to 792 g by fledging date (Fig. 3).

DISCUSSION

In 1992, the USDA Forest Service (USFS) developed guidelines for Northern Goshawks and forest management that are currently being implemented on some national forests across the southwestern US (Reynolds et al. 1992). These management recommendations recognized 14 consistently abundant and important prey species, out of a total of 66 potential prey species from various goshawk diet studies (Schnell 1958, Meng 1959, Reynolds and Meslow 1984, Kennedy 1991, Boal and Mannan 1994) and suggested managing habitat for all prey species. Among the 14 prey species listed in the guidelines, we observed that six species contributed >5% each to goshawk diet on the Sitgreaves Forest. Our study supports the idea that managing habitat for these consistently hunted prey items is important.

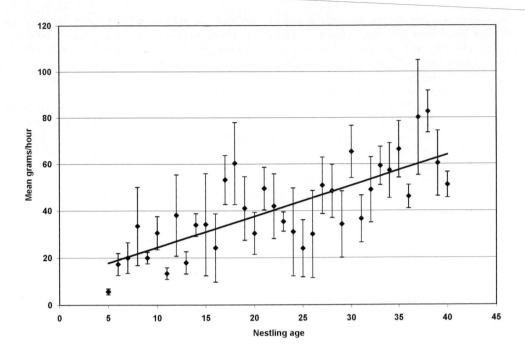

FIGURE 2. Mean biomass of consumed prey plotted against nestling age for 10 Northern Goshawk nests on the Sitgreaves Forest, Arizona, 1999 and 2000.

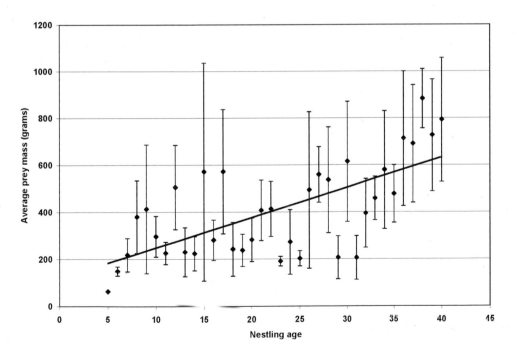

FIGURE 3. Average mass of prey items plotted against nestling age for 10 Northern Goshawk nests on the Sitgreaves Forest, Arizona, 1999 and 2000.

Most goshawk diet studies conclude that goshawks are generalists and opportunistic foragers, with diet reflecting prey availability (Widén 1987, Kennedy 1991). Our study on the Sitgreaves Forest supports the idea that Northern Goshawks as a population are diet generalists, due to the high number of prey species fed upon (22 species). When we looked at diet composition at each nest, however, we saw that one or two prey species often dominated the diet. For example, we reported 21% cottontails by number and 42% by total biomass consumed; however, of the total eastern cottontails consumed, over half (58%) came from only two nests (Table 3). We saw this pattern more dramatically with Steller's Jays: >40% of all Steller's Jays came from one nest. Similarly, goshawks preyed upon red squirrels unequally among nests, with 30% of nests comprising 83% of total red squirrels.

Two reasons may explain why individual goshawks took prey unequally: adult goshawks exhibited preference for particular prey items, or goshawks took the prey within the foraging area that was most available. It is likely that increased proportions of a particular prey species at a nest were due to the habitat requirements of that prey within an individual goshawk foraging area. For example, we only detected red squirrels at nests close to areas of high elevation mixed conifers. Hoffmeister (1986) reported that on the Mogollon Rim, red squirrels are rarely found below 2,400 m in elevation, and rely heavily on Engelmann spruce (*Picea engelmanni*) and Douglas-fir cones. Currently, USFS guidelines in the Southwest recognize three vegetation cover types as important for management of goshawks: ponderosa pine, mixed species, and spruce-fir cover types (Reynolds et al. 1992). Because certain prey appeared frequently in goshawk diet on the Sitgreaves National Forest, it may be important to continue to focus management in these various vegetative cover types where these prey could occur in high numbers.

Seasonal shifts in diet of goshawks may be due to reproductive timing, hibernation, and/or migration of prey species (Squires and Reynolds 1997). Also, initially abundant juvenile prey (e.g., rabbits) become more scarce as they are preyed upon by entire guilds of predators during the year. It is also plausible, however, that a diet shift may occur in order to meet the energetic needs of growing nestlings. One solution for meeting energetic needs of aging nestlings would be to either capture prey more frequently, or increase the size of prey items delivered to nests. Our results provide some evidence of an increase in average mass of prey items delivered to nests as the nestlings increase in age. In addition, prey delivery rates decreased overall as the nesting season progressed. By bringing fewer but larger prey, adult goshawks may meet the increasing energetic needs of nestlings and simultaneously reduce the number of prey items brought to the nest.

Prey delivery rates lend information on hunting efficiency of adults, frequency and timing of feeding bouts, and correlation with food density (Zammuto et al. 1981). The average daily prey delivery rate we observed was 0.30 prey items/hr, with the rate decreasing as nestlings aged (i.e., one less prey item about every 2 wk). When looking at mean delivery rate versus age, we saw a slight increasing trend around the age of 18–20 d. We speculate that this increase could be due to additional items brought to the nest by the adult female. During this time (18–20 d), females begin to spend greater time off the nest and could be hunting more frequently.

Problems associated with using delivery rates as a measure of availability include (1) differences in efficiency of capturing prey in various vegetative cover (Buchanen 1996), (2) the physiological condition of the hawk, and (3) age of the hawk (Bennetts and McClelland 1997). Part of the explanation regarding decreased delivery rates could be due to the increase in average biomass delivered to nests in the latter part of the nestling season, and the ability of nestlings to consume and manipulate prey more efficiently as they get older (Schnell 1958). However, this speculation would require further research.

Sutton (1925) reported that Northern Goshawks are inclined to take avian prey more frequently than mammalian prey. In a review of diet studies from across the US, Squires and Reynolds (1997) reported that southern populations of goshawks may depend less on mammals than northern populations, with the exception of Boal and Mannan's (1994) study in northern Arizona, where they found that mammals and birds comprised 76% and 24% frequency of occurrence, respectively. DeStefano et al. (*this volume*) reported a possible trend in increasing proportions of birds to mammals in prey taken by nesting goshawks as one moves from south to north in eastern Oregon. Reynolds et al. (1994) reported 62% mammals and 38% birds on the Kaibab National Forest, Arizona, and Kennedy (1991) observed similar proportions of mammalian and avian prey items contributed to goshawk diet in the Jemez Mountains, New Mexico. Similarly, in our study on the Sitgreaves Forest in Arizona, mammals, birds, reptiles, and unknowns contributed 73%, 18%, 2%, and 7%, respectively, to goshawk diet. In summary, evidence suggests that goshawks in the Southwest are taking mammals more frequently than previous studies have suggested. In general, however, it is likely that the goshawk's role as a diet generalist allows them to exploit prey based on prey availability. Prey availability, in turn, is at least partly dictated by forest vegetation type and structure, as well as other local habitat variables.

Past discrepancies among studies with respect to proportions of mammalian and avian prey items might be attributable to the method used to quantify diet. Most studies that reported a higher percent of birds than mammals in goshawk diet used indirect methods such as analysis of pellets or prey remains to assess dietary components. These methods have been scrutinized because they can overestimate bird species due to the relative ease in locating feathers over small pieces of mammal fur and bones (Simmons et al. 1991, Bielefeldt et al. 1992). Goshawks on the Sitgreaves National Forest regularly pluck feathers and discard them outside the nest bowl, whereas bits of mammal fur and bones are usually consumed. Goshawks in our study consumed entire prey items (excluding feathers) most of the time (73%) which meant that entire prey items were consumed, including the feet, tails, and bones of mammals and birds. Thus, in order to locate mammalian prey items, we would have been restricted mainly to pellet analysis. It seems likely, based on our observations of goshawks consuming entire prey items, that collecting prey remains alone would have overestimated avian prey. We conclude that through the use of remote cameras, we minimized the bias toward avian prey and furthered evidence suggesting indirect methods of diet assessment are skewed toward birds (Rogers 2001).

ACKNOWLEDGMENTS

Funding was provided by the Arizona Game and Fish Department, with logistic support from the USGS Arizona Cooperative Fish and Wildlife Research Unit and the School of Natural Resources, University of Arizona. We thank G. Andrejko, S. Blackman, J. de Vos, L. Holmquist, R. W. Mannan, E. Rogan, G. Shaffer, the staff of the Pinetop Game and Fish office, and several field assistants for their help in various ways.

Studies in Avian Biology No. 31:228–238

WINTER MOVEMENT AND HABITAT USE OF NORTHERN GOSHAWKS BREEDING IN UTAH

Jared Underwood, Clayton M. White, and Ronald L. Rodriguez

Abstract. Few studies detail population-wide winter movements of Northern Goshawks (*Accipiter gentilis*) in North America or examine their winter ecology and habitat associations. Using satellite-telemetry transmitters, landscape-habitat models, aerial photos, and field sampling, we assessed movements and wintering habitats of goshawks breeding in Utah. In our study, 42 adult females were fitted with 30 g or 32 g platform transmitter terminals (PTT) between 2000 and 2003. Our data suggest that females in the populations studied were either migrants or semi-migrants that moved randomly throughout the state or residents. Resident birds remained in the general area around the breeding territory but used a wider variety of habitat cover types and commonly moved downward in elevation during winter. In contrast, birds that migrated or semi-migrated from their breeding territories for the winter generally used the pinyon-juniper habitat cover type. This pinyon-juniper habitat tended to be a mosaic of fairly open pinyon-juniper forest and sagebrush ecotones. The wintering areas for each bird were analyzed using vegetative sampling methods in order to determine correlations between habitat structure and goshawk use. Vegetative structure in the winter areas varied widely, but all goshawks used areas of forest-non-forest edge throughout the winter. Many of the selected winter sites showed signs of human manipulation (tree harvest, tree and brush removal by chaining, or fire). These findings increase our understanding of what constitutes goshawk wintering habitat and place new priority on understanding the use of various habitat cover types by wintering Northern Goshawks.

Key Words: *Accipiter gentilis,* diet, habitat, movement, Northern Goshawk, Utah, winter.

MOVIMIENTOS DURANTE EL INVIERNO Y USO DEL HABITAT DEL GAVILÁN AZOR REPROCUCTOR EN UTAH

Resumen. Pocos estudios detallan los movimientos a nivel poblacional del Gavilán Azor (*Accipiter gentilis*) en Norte América, o examinan su ecología durante el invierno y sus asociaciones del hábitat. Utilizando transmisores de telemetría satelital, modelos de hábitat-paisaje, fotografías aéreas, y muestreo de campo, evaluamos movimientos y hábitats de invierno de gavilanes reproductores en Utah. En nuestro estudio, 42 hembras adultas fueron adaptadas con terminales transmisoras de plataforma (PTT) de 30 g ó 32 g, entre 2000 y 2003. Nuestros datos sugieren que las hembras en las poblaciones estudiadas fueron ya sea migrantes o semi-migrantes, las cuales se movieron aleatoriamente por todo el estado, o bien, residentes. Las aves residenciaron en el área general alrededor del territorio de reproducción, pero utilizaron una variedad más amplia de tipos de hábitat de cobertura, y comúnmente se movieron a una elevación más baja durante el invierno. En contraste, las aves que migraron o semi-migraron de sus territorios de reproducción durante el invierno, generalmente utilizaron el hábitat de tipo de cobertura piñón-junípero. Este hábitat de piñón-junípero tendió a ser un mosaico de bosques de piñón-junípero substancialmente abierto y de ecotonos de Artemisa. Las áreas utilizadas durante el invierno de cada ave fueron analizadas, utilizando métodos de muestreo vegetativo, con el fin de determinar correlaciones entre estructura del hábitat y uso del gavilán. La estructura vegetativa en las áreas utilizadas durante el invierno variaron ampliamente, pero todos los gavilanes utilizaron áreas de bordes forestales y no forestales durante todo el invierno. Muchos de los sitios de invierno seleccionados, mostraron señales de manipulación humana (cultivo de árboles, remoción de árboles y arbustos por corta o fuego). Estos hallazgos incrementan nuestro entendimiento sobre qué es lo que constituye el hábitat del gavilán invernando y pone en nueva prioridad el entendimiento en la utilización de hábitats con varios tipos de cobertura por los Gavilanes Azor.

The Northern Goshawk (*Accipiter gentilis*) inhabits mature and old-growth forested regions (Palmer 1988, Squires and Reynolds 1997). It is a predator of small- to medium-sized mammals and birds, and tends to hunt over large ranges (Palmer 1988, Squires and Reynolds 1997). Three putative subspecies breed in North America: the widespread *Accipiter gentilis atricapillus*, and the more geographically isolated *A. g. apache* and *A. g. laingi* (Squires and Reynolds 1997). Goshawks are said to prefer mature to old-growth forest stands with dense canopy cover in which to nest (Squires and Reynolds 1997), consequently their nesting habitat and therefore population numbers may be negatively affected by timber harvest (Crocker-Bedford 1990). Because of this, much like the Spotted Owl (*Strix occidentalis*), the Northern Goshawk has become a flagship animal in the last 15 yr for the preservation of old-growth and mature forests. Although the goshawk remains unlisted under the Endangered Species Act (ESA) it has been designated a sensitive species by many regions of the USDA Forest Service (USFS). This designation generated an increased interest in their biology and habitat requirements in an attempt to protect the goshawk, and prevent the need for listing it under the ESA.

Many studies have attempted to understand the breeding habitat requirements of Northern Goshawks (Bosakowski 1999). Other authors such as Reynolds et al. (1992) and Graham et al. (1999b) have integrated findings of various studies into forest-management recommendations that manage for healthy, sustainable forested landscapes that also benefit the goshawk and their prey. However, to effectively protect a species we must understand its biology not only in the breeding season but also in the non-breeding or winter season (Squires and Ruggiero 1995, Beier and Drennan 1997, Squires and Reynolds 1997). For this study, the winter and the wintering habitat were defined as any area or areas that a goshawk used between mid-September and mid-March, corresponding to the time between dispersal of the current year's young and commencement of a new breeding season (Palmer 1988, Squires and Reynolds 1997).

The few winter studies conducted on the behavior, migration patterns, and wintering habitat of the goshawk in North America have produced limited information (Doerr and Enderson 1965, Squires and Ruggiero 1995, Stephens 2001, Sonsthagen et al. 2002, Boal et al. 2003, Drennan and Beier 2003). It has been difficult to understand migration patterns of the goshawk through these studies because they relied on radio telemetry, which often failed to track goshawks that migrate >25 km from the area they were trapped (Stephens 2001, Drennan and Beier 2003). Winter habitat studies have looked only at winter habitat selection by resident birds (Drennan and Beier 2003) or by birds trapped in a small area (Stephens 2001). Relatively small sample sizes of goshawks (N = 4–12; Squires and Ruggiero 1995, Stephens 2001, Drennan and Beier 2003) also limited the ability to extrapolate these findings to larger population.

We hoped to examine goshawk winter biology and habitat use on a population-wide scale to better evaluate the necessity of incorporating winter biology into goshawk protection and management. The objectives of this study were to: (1) more fully understand the duration, distance, and patterns of winter migration, (2) use geographic information systems (GIS) and other computer tools to identify wintering sites, ascertain winter site fidelity, determine habitat cover types most frequently used, and assess landscape-level habitat selection, and (3) collect data to determine winter diet and importance of vegetative structure (Beier and Drennan 1997) in the selection of wintering areas.

METHODS

STUDY SITE

The study area included six national forests in the state of Utah. The six national forests cover 3,200,000 ha and range from the northern to southern and eastern to western borders of Utah. The elevation of these forests ranges from 1,200–3,300 m with a variety of habitat cover types distributed along an elevational and latitudinal gradient. The most common forest cover types include ponderosa pine (*Pinus ponderosa*), lodgepole pine (*Pinus contorta*), conifer-quaking aspen (*Abies-Picea-Populus tremuloides*), spruce-fir (*Picea-Abies*), pinyon-juniper (*Pinus edulis-Juniperus* spp.), and mixed-forest areas where all forest varieties intermingle. The Northern Goshawk is known to breed throughout the study area in all habitat cover types except pinyon-juniper (Graham et al. 1999b). However, most of the nests occur between 1,800–3,000 m in the conifer-quaking aspen cover type (Johansson et al. 1994, Graham et al. 1999b).

TRAPPING AND TRACKING

During the months of June through August, 2000–2002, adult female goshawks (N = 42) were trapped at their nests using a live Great Horned Owl (*Bubo virginianus*) to lure the goshawks into a modified dho-gaza net trap (Clark 1981). Britten et al. (1999) suggested a maximum transmitter load of 3–5% of the bird's mass in Peregrine Falcons (*Falco peregrinus*). We assumed this same maximum load would apply to goshawks, another medium-sized raptor, and therefore excluded males from this study because the weight of the transmitters. Goshawks were selected from known territories on various forests corresponding to different regions of the state. This was done to see if winter migration was dependent on location in the state. After the goshawks were trapped, they were fitted with satellite platform terminal transmitters (PTT) manufactured by North Star Science and Technology (Columbia, MD), attached with a backpack harness (Snyder et al. 1989).

The transmitter-marked goshawks were tracked throughout the life of the transmitter, approximately 1 yr, but seven of the transmitters lasted nearly 2 yr. In order to conserve battery life the transmitters were placed on a rotational pattern that consisted of transmitting for 6 hr followed by 68 hr of dormancy. This duty cycle was selected based on extending the life of the transmitter for the desired study length. During the period of transmitter activity it emitted a location signal every 60 sec. These location signals were then processed by the ARGOS satellite company and sent to the USFS with a confidence interval of their accuracy.

The accuracy associated with location estimates varies widely, for this study we only used location estimates (LC: 3, 2) with an associated accuracy buffer of 250 m or 500 m respectively (Argos, pers. comm.). This level of accuracy is similar to that received by aerial tracking of radio-marked raptors and other animals (Marzluff et al. 1994, Samuel and Fuller 1996, Carral et al. 1997, DeVault et al. 2003) and to other published satellite-telemetry studies on raptors (McGrady et al. 2002). The data points received from the PTTs were input into Arc View version 3.3 (ESRI 1996), a GIS computer program, in order to view migration and wintering areas of the goshawks. If a goshawk traveled >100 km and stayed, the length of stay in the wintering area and winter site fidelity between years were recorded. Winter site fidelity was determined for the transmitter-marked goshawks in which the transmitter lasted for two winters. Fidelity was assumed if the bird returned to the same winter area on consecutive winters. The sizes of the winter territories for 2000 and 2001 were analyzed by calculating the kernel home range (95% probability polygons) as described in Sonsthagen (2002).

To determine whether goshawk migration corresponded with inclement weather patterns (Squires and Ruggiero 1995), goshawk movements were compared to the time of the first major winter storm. This was accomplished using storm data (NOAA 2003a) collected statewide on a county basis and individual readings from the closest NOAA weather station to the nest site (NOAA 2003b). The date of the first major winter snow storm for the area in which the bird nested was compared to the date that the bird migrated. Movements that occurred subsequent to the first winter storm were evaluated in relation to the closest preceding major winter storm.

GIS HABITAT ANALYSIS

To determine the most frequently used habitat cover types, after each wintering area was identified, we used GIS landscape habitat layers (Utah, Arizona, Nevada, and Wyoming), GAP analysis vegetation layers (USGS GAP Analysis Program 2000), aerial photos (State of Utah 2001), and USGS 1:24 k topographic maps, to assign each location estimate to a habitat cover type. Since finer-scale habitat associations were not permitted due to the accuracy buffer surrounding the location estimates, the vegetative cover associated with each location point was placed in one of four major habitat cover types: ponderosa pine (areas dominated by ponderosa pine but also including in lesser amounts quaking aspen, fir, Gambel oak [*Quercus gambelii*], pinyon, Utah juniper [*Juniperus utahensis*], and rocky mountain juniper [*Juniperus scopulorum*]), pinyon-juniper forests (areas dominated by pinyon, juniper or any combination thereof but also including limited amounts of ponderosa pine, fir, Gambel oak, and big-tooth maple [*Acer grandidentatum*]), grassland-shrubland (any grassland, shrubland, burn, chaining, logged area, or combination thereof), and montane forest (consisting of any areas dominated by a combination of quaking aspen, fir, spruce, and pine). GIS landscape habitat layers and GAP vegetative layers were verified using the aerial photos and field observations. Since each location point was coupled with an accuracy buffer of 250 m or 500 m, multiple habitat cover types were sometimes associated with a particular location estimate. All habitat cover types found within the accuracy buffer were used to label the estimate.

The use of satellite telemetry has inherent flaws. While the specific location for a bird is generally found within the associated accuracy buffer, in some cases the true location of the bird is outside of the reported buffer zone (Britten et al. 1999, McGrady et al. 2002). We occasionally received a location estimate an impossible distance for the bird to have traveled based on estimates received both before and after said estimate. Points such as these were excluded from all analyses.

FIELD HABITAT ANALYSIS

To investigate the importance of vegetative structure in the selection of wintering areas each habitat cover type was also sampled in the field for certain vegetative characteristics: the percent canopy cover of the tree layer, the shrub layer, and the herbaceous-ground layer. These vegetative characteristics were chosen for their connection with prey availability to goshawks (Beier and Drennan 1997). At each site data were also collected on amount of litter and bare ground, elevation, and possible prey species (Squires and Reynolds 1997, Bosakowski 1999) in order to obtain a more complete picture of the winter habitat.

Because of the inaccuracy associated with location estimates we field sampled from areas where clusters of estimates occurred. This approach was taken to mitigate the problem of estimates whose true location might be outside of the associated buffer. By sampling in areas where many location estimate buffers overlapped we hoped to increase the likelihood that a goshawk had actually been using the area sampled. A cluster was defined as a geographically isolated collection of location estimates. The degree of isolation, the number of location estimates, and the geographic area included in a location estimate cluster varied for each bird. Uniform metrics used to define a cluster could not be created due to the variety in the spatial distribution of each bird's location estimates, and total number of location estimates received for each bird. Rather than eliminate some birds from the analysis, these three metrics were used to assess the location estimate data for each bird at the individual's appropriate relative scale.

Many goshawks ranged over a large area, and because we received up to one hundred plus location estimates for each bird, time and personnel constraints did not allow us to examine all clusters in the field. Since only a limited number of clusters for each bird could be sampled, clusters were rated for importance. The process of rating the clusters is described as follows. Clusters with a high density of location estimates when compared to other equally sized geographic areas for the same bird were given highest priority. Of these clusters, those that contained location estimates from varied times during the winter months received higher priority than clusters where estimates spanned only a limited time period. Lastly, clusters situated in the most heavily used habitat cover types were rated more important than those appearing in habitat cover types used only infrequently.

Since the accuracy of our location estimates would not allow fine-scale, micro-habitat data collection, the field data collected only give a general idea of the habitat features found in the wintering areas. After the top-rated clusters for each bird were identified, they were assessed in the field for vegetative structure and other previously mentioned habitat characteristics by establishing a transect within the cluster. Transects were established either between several location estimates or around a particular

location estimate within the cluster. This was based on the density and distribution of the location estimates in the cluster. If the location estimates of a cluster were within 0.5 km of each other, transects started at one estimate and ended at another. If the estimates within the cluster were >0.5 km apart, transects were set in a random direction around a central location estimate within the cluster. Approximately every 150 m along the transect line, habitat structure surrounding the transect was surveyed using a modified Daubenmire classification scheme in which each layer of vegetation within a 15-m radius of the sampling point was assigned a value from one–seven (Table 1) corresponding to an ocular estimation of the range of canopy cover (Daubenmire 1952). This sampling allowed the general vegetative structuring of the wintering areas to be described.

Detections of each possible prey species, based on Squires and Reynolds (1997) and Bosakowski (1999), were assigned into one of four categories: (1) sign, meaning that tracks or droppings of the animal were found or its calls were heard, (2) observation, in which the prey item was actually sighted, (3) prey remains found, which referred to prey remains encountered that we could attribute to goshawks, and (4) kill sites, where we actually observed a goshawk take a prey item, or flushed a goshawk from a recent kill. These data were collected opportunistically along the vegetative transects during winter and spring months in which the habitat was sampled.

FIELD HABITAT DATA ANALYSIS

To further ameliorate the problem of location estimate accuracy buffers and to allow comparison across individuals, all analyses of the field data were done using 3-km radius sampling areas. Each bird's wintering area was divided in a systematic fashion into these uniform sized sampling areas. The first, and highest rated, sampling area generated for each bird had the greatest possible number of location

TABLE 1. MODIFIED DAUBENMIRE CLASSIFICATION SCHEME, USED IN THE DISCUSSION OF COVER THROUGHOUT THE ANALYSIS.

Classification number	Corresponding % canopy/ground cover
1	0–1
2	1–5
3	5–25
4	25–50
5	50–75
6	75–95
7	95–100

estimates and highly rated clusters. This continued in a systematic fashion until all wintering location estimates and clusters were included in a sampling area. Only the top three rated sampling areas were used in analysis. These top three sampling areas generally contained the majority of the winter location estimates and all of the highest rated clusters. The number of location estimates contained in each sampling area was divided by the total number of winter location estimates received for that goshawk, giving a percentage of winter spent in each sampling area.

Cover data collected for each of the three main vegetative layers (tree, shrub, and herbaceous) were placed by habitat cover type (pinyon-juniper, ponderosa pine, montane forest, and non-forest) in a table showing the number of transect points in which the cover data collected corresponded to each of the seven Daubenmire cover categories. This was done to describe the general vegetative characteristics of the areas in which the goshawks wintered.

To determine if goshawks spent more time in areas with certain vegetative characteristics the data were further analyzed by regression analysis of the percentage of winter spent in a sampling area with the average vegetative cover characteristics of that sampling area. Cover data collected for all transect points within a particular habitat cover type were averaged by sampling area to give a mean cover percentage for each vegetative layer. The average vegetative cover percentage for each sampling area was then regressed against the amount of time a bird spent in each sampling area.

To assess possible preference for specific cover characteristics, the vegetative cover averages for each sampling area and the corresponding time spent in each sampling area were compared with the cover available in each habitat cover type. A line of preference was incorporated into each graph. Preference for a specific cover characteristic was implied if most of the averages for a vegetative characteristic were found to be above this preference line and an avoidance of certain cover characteristics was implied if most of the sampling area averages were found to be below this line. Cover availability was calculated by taking the percentage of all data points found in each cover class (Table 1), for each vegetative layer in a particular habitat cover type.

RESULTS

SATELLITE TELEMETRY AND MIGRATION

Of the 42 goshawks fitted with PTTs, some winter data were collected on 38 and complete winter data

(September–March) on 21; seven birds were tracked for more than one winter. A total of 2,639 location estimates were analyzed for this study (LC 3: N = 946, LC 2: N = 1,693). PTTs did not all perform equally well and some variation existed in the total number of winter location estimates collected for each bird (approximately normally distributed, with a range of N = 11–214, mean of N = 68). Several winter movement patterns were observed. Birds were considered migratory (Squires and Ruggiero 1995) if they flew >100 km from the nest site and then stayed in that area without returning to the nest territory (N = 7). We chose movement of 100 km or greater as the definition of migration for two reasons. First this definition corresponded well with the study of Squires and Ruggiero (1995) which deemed migratory movements as those of >65 km. Second, a natural break appeared in the movement patterns of the goshawks at around 100 km. Birds that flew >100 km from the nest site did so in a couple of days and then stayed in that area without returning to the nest site. We defined goshawks as semi-migratory if they moved within 100 km of the nest site, did so in small bouts of 20 or 30 km, and stayed in each area for several weeks before moving to another area 20 or 30 km away. Resident birds were those that stayed within 25 km surrounding the nest stand throughout the winter.

Of the seven goshawks tracked for >1 yr, five of them were considered migratory—one of these did not migrate the first year but did migrate the second winter. Three birds that migrated the first year migrated to the same location the second winter. The fifth goshawk stopped briefly in the area it used the previous winter and then continued 360 km further south to a new wintering location. Seven other birds migrated to an area >100 km away but were not tracked the entire winter. The total distance traveled to reach the wintering site varied from just over 100 km to >600 km (Fig. 1). The direction of migration was usually to the south or southwest, however, one bird migrated to the northeast.

Semi-migratory birds dispersed over an area of up to 100 km from the nest territory, staying in one area for several weeks and then moving to another (N = 4). Four other birds appeared to start following this pattern but were not tracked the entire winter.

Goshawks considered residents simply expanded their nesting territory by incorporating 5–25 km of the surrounding habitat (N = 10). See Sonsthagen et al. (2002) for a description of nesting and wintering territory size. Of the seven goshawks tracked for >1 yr, two were in this category. These two birds never left the area surrounding their nest territory during

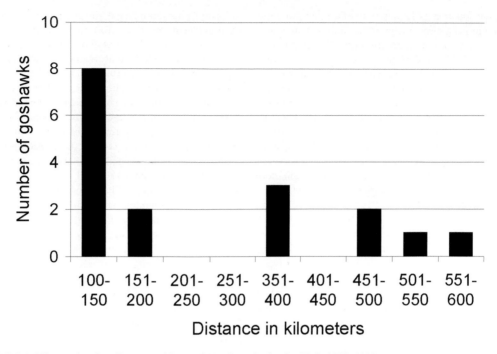

FIGURE 1. Winter migration distances of (N = 17) Northern Goshawks, Utah, 2000–2003.

winter. Six other birds appeared to be residents but were not tracked the entire winter. In summary, of the goshawks in this study 41% were considered resident, 43% were considered migratory, and 16% were considered semi-migratory.

Goshawks that migrated left nesting areas between August and December. Of these goshawks one migrated in August, six in September, two in October, six in November, and four in December. Most of the goshawks returned in March (N = 7) and one returned in February. The length of stay in the wintering area varied from 60–204 d, with an average of 138 d (N = 8). Of the seven birds for which we had multiple years of data, five exhibited winter-site fidelity while the other two wintered in different places on consecutive years but in the same habitat cover type.

We found no association between the time of the first major winter storm and migration. Sixty percent of goshawks that migrated or semi-migrated began before the first major storm of the year. Only two goshawks left within a week after the first major winter storm. The remaining goshawks (32%) moved within 1 wk of a major storm, but this may be an artifact of increased storminess throughout the winter. All four migratory goshawks tracked for multiple years left within 10 d of the date on which they left the first year regardless of the weather.

GIS HABITAT ANALYSIS

Seventy-nine percent of the goshawks in this winter habitat study spent time in pinyon-juniper habitat cover type. In areas where no pinyon-juniper habitat exists, they used mountain shrub habitat cover type dominated by maple and Gambel oak. Most goshawks (N = 15) that migrated or semi-migrated, moved exclusively to pinyon-juniper habitat cover type. Those that stayed around their breeding territories used habitat similar to their breeding habitat, which consisted of ponderosa pine or montane forest habitat cover types.

FIELD HABITAT ANALYSIS

The field data collected consisted of 821 transect points spread over all 38 wintering areas. For each bird up to three sampling areas were evaluated for vegetative components. The percent of total location estimates within each sampling area varied according to its rank. The densest sampling areas contained from 17.4–100% of all winter location estimates for a bird with the average being 37.4%. For the second and third ranked sampling areas the average percent of total winter location estimates included was 18.3% and 9.1%, respectively. For some birds only one sampling area was necessary since nearly all their location estimates fell within that sampling area. For each bird a mean of 2.5 sampling areas and 9.6 clusters (approximately normally distributed, range = 3–22) within those sampling areas were analyzed in the field. The data summarized from all transect points included the canopy cover of the tree, shrub, and herbaceous layers, as well as litter cover and the percentage of ground left bare. The percentage of vegetative cover for each of the vegetative layers varied widely within each of the four habitat cover types (Table 2).

Regression analysis found no significant correlation between the time spent in an area and its corresponding vegetative cover. P-values for these relationships ranged from $P = 0.100–0.965$.

The scale and manner of our data collection did not allow us to statistically demonstrate habitat selection; however, possible preference in all habitat cover types was shown for areas with higher herbaceous cover. In the non-forest habitat cover type possible preference was also shown towards areas that had 5–25% tree cover. In all habitat cover types possible preference was shown towards areas that had some degree of shrub cover (5–75%) but were not densely covered (over 75%). Preference for other vegetative cover characteristics sampled could not be shown.

Although winter diet was not empirically assessed, observations of possible prey were recorded in each of the winter areas. We noted common prey observed in winter territories and the number of winter areas in which each prey was found (Fig. 2). Observed winter foraging behavior was similar to hunting tactics observed during the breeding season. Goshawk hunting behavior was observed at multiple kill sites. All of these sites were on the edge of the pinyon-juniper woodlands and sagebrush-grassland openings, or in areas of the pinyon-juniper woodlands that had been thinned by humans and brush piles left on the ground. All kills appeared to be cottontail rabbits (*Sylvilagus* spp.).

Finally, all goshawks exhibited an altitudinal migration during some part of the winter. They either migrated to a lower elevation or simply expanded upon their nesting areas to include surrounding lower elevations. Sonsthagen (2002) found that there was a statistically supported difference between the elevation of the summer habitat and the winter habitat.

DISCUSSION

Migration

The winter movement patterns we observed throughout this study show that goshawks within the same population have various alternative winter movement strategies. To answer the question of why some goshawks migrated or semi-migrated and others did not we looked at weather as suggested by Squires and Ruggiero (1995) and found that it did not appear to drive migration in Utah. Other reasons for winter migration have been suggested by Newton (1986) who stated that the biggest factors in raptor migration patterns appeared to be prey availability and interaction with conspecifics. Additionally Harmata and Stahlecker (1993) suggested that raptor winter movement was based on wintering area fidelity at a location established where the individual survived its first winter. Although our study was not able to empirically assess any of these hypotheses, several observations made throughout the study and certain observed trends in the data are congruent with these statements and would lead us to suggest that the same factors are driving the winter movements of goshawks in Utah.

In agreement with the hypothesis of Harmata and Stahlecker (1993), wintering area fidelity has been observed in Alaskan goshawks (McGowan 1975). In our study many goshawks that migrated passed over habitat similar to that where they eventually wintered. Five of seven goshawks tracked for multiple years showed winter site fidelity both years. Four other goshawks in this study wintered around known breeding territories far from their own. These goshawks may have passed their first winter around their natal nest territory (Tornberg and Colpaert 2001) and then dispersed to find a breeding territory in spring. By returning in subsequent winters to their natal site they too exhibit winter site fidelity. If this conclusion is valid then these four birds provide further support that goshawk wintering areas and migration depend upon the wintering location of the first year.

Our study also seemed to support the hypothesis of Newton (1979a, 1986) that competition or other interaction with conspecifics also may lead to migration. In our study one goshawk did not migrate the first year but did the second year. During the second year, the area it had previously used during winter was occupied by at least one other goshawk; competition with this goshawk may have led to our goshawk's migration. As an additional support for this hypothesis, we observed that when two birds were trapped within several kilometers of each other, one would often migrate or semi-migrate and the other would incorporate both territories into its winter range. This pattern was observed for five pairs.

Finally, although our study did not empirically assess numbers of prey in the wintering territories or in the breeding areas, we would agree with Newton's

TABLE 2. VEGETATIVE AND GROUND COVER PERCENTAGES OF 38 NORTHERN GOSHAWK WINTERING AREAS BY HABITAT COVER TYPE, UTAH, 2000–2003.

Vegetative/ground cover layer	Daubenmire classification category (0–7) and corresponding percent canopy cover							
	0 (0%)	1 (0–1%)	2 (1–5%)	3 (5–25%)	4 (25–50%)	5 (50–75%)	6 (75–95%)	7 (95–100%)
	Percent of transect points where vegetative/ground cover matched each Daubenmire category							
Pinyon-juniper tree layer	0	0	1.21	31.17	53.85	13.77	0	0
Pinyon-juniper herbaceous layer	0	10.12	31.98	40.89	10.93	6.07	0	0
Pinyon-juniper shrub layer	0	8.91	23.48	43.32	22.27	2.02	0	0
Pinyon-juniper litter cover	3.64	0	8.10	47.77	31.17	6.07	2.83	0.40
Pinyon-juniper bare ground	3.64	0.40	1.62	12.55	38.06	37.25	6.48	0
Ponderosa tree layer	0	0	2.20	18.68	30.77	43.96	4.40	0
Ponderosa herbaceous layer	0	1.10	21.98	34.07	29.67	12.09	1.10	0
Ponderosa shrub layer	0	5.49	25.27	37.36	27.47	4.40	0	0
Ponderosa litter cover	0	0	1.10	14.29	13.19	19.78	42.86	8.79
Ponderosa bare ground	13.19	57.14	9.89	8.79	6.59	4.40	0	0
Montane forest tree layer	0	0	0	5.53	30.15	52.76	10.55	1.01
Montane forest herbaceous layer	4.52	3.02	10.55	17.59	25.63	26.13	12.56	0
Montane forest shrub layer	7.04	2.51	16.58	32.16	23.12	15.08	3.52	0
Montane forest litter cover	2.51	0	5.53	19.10	27.14	25.63	16.08	4.02
Montane forest bare ground	26.13	42.71	17.09	10.05	3.52	0.50	0	0
Non-forest tree layer	24.30	38.73	23.94	6.69	2.82	1.76	1.41	0.35
Non-forest herbaceous layer	1.06	3.17	7.04	17.96	25.70	23.59	19.72	1.76
Non-forest shrub layer	3.52	1.41	3.52	19.01	42.25	24.30	5.99	0
Non-forest litter cover	0.35	3.87	17.61	58.10	16.20	3.17	0.70	0
Non-forest bare ground	6.34	9.15	14.08	23.94	30.28	16.20	0	0

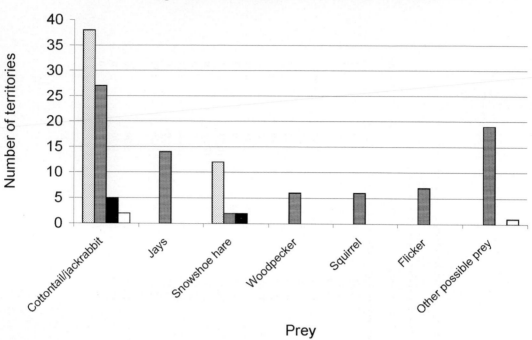

FIGURE 2. Number of Northern Goshawk winter territories in which each possible prey species was observed. Utah, 2000–2003.

(1979a) hypothesis that the most important factor motivating the migration of all raptors was prey availability. This would seem to explain several of the observed winter movement patterns. In our study the length of the stay in winter areas varied by bird, possibly due to the prey abundance in the breeding/nesting area. Variety in prey abundance, or accessibility also may explain the difference in date of departure for the goshawks that migrated. If there were abundant and vulnerable prey then goshawks seemingly would be less inclined to migrate. But as the winter set in, the disappearance of more prey species due to mortality, hibernation, or migration may have prompted the goshawks to move as suggested by Newton (1979a). The differences in movement of goshawks in our study would indicate a behavioral plasticity so that migration occurred when of survival value.

HABITAT ANALYSIS

The vegetative analysis of these winter areas showed that goshawks were capable of using a broad variety of habitat cover types and that vegetative cover within those habitats cover types varied widely. These finding are similar to Hargis et al.

(1994) and Kenward and Widén (1989). However, possible preference in all habitat cover types was shown toward areas with a high degree of herbaceous cover relative to the available habitat and areas where the shrub cover was neither too dense (>75%) nor too sparse (<1–5%). In the non-forest habitat cover type, areas with some degree of tree cover (5–25%) were preferred over areas with little or no tree cover. Preference toward these areas was probably driven by prey availability and abundance; however this was not empirically assessed. Herbaceous plants such as forbs and grasses act as the most important food resource (Fitzgerald et al. 1994) for cottontail rabbits and other prey commonly taken by wintering goshawks. Protective escape cover, usually in the form of shrubs, is another essential habitat component for these prey items (Chapman and Flux 1990, Fitzgerald et al. 1994). If the shrub cover is too dense, prey availability is limited (Beier and Drennan 1997) and if too sparse, prey abundance would be limited (Chapman and Flux 1990, Fitzgerald et al. 1994). In the non-forest habitat, a preference for areas with higher tree density is probably due to the goshawk's method of hunting (Palmer 1988, Beier and Drennan 1997, Bosakowski 1999). This method consists of the perch-and-wait tactic in which the hawk waits at a perch for a prey to come into sight. Numerous perches would increase the area available for hunting.

Because of the use of the pinyon-juniper habitat cover type by most of the wintering goshawks, a description of this habitat is given based on observations collected at the wintering sites. On a landscape scale, the areas selected generally consisted of a mosaic of pinyon-juniper forest habitat and non-forested openings. Most of the pinyon-juniper areas used had been altered by humans. Anthropogenic modification of these sites commonly included old chained areas, burn areas, or zones of selectively logged trees. Although we do not know what percentage of the total pinyon-juniper habitat cover type in Utah has been altered, human disturbance was found in at nearly all pinyon-juniper wintering areas surveyed. The type and degree of disturbance in the pinyon-juniper habitat varied but most was concentrated on thinning or removing stands of pinyon and juniper trees to open up habitat. Goshawks appeared to stay away from areas where pinyon and juniper trees had grown too dense (>75% cover) or where most of the trees were young and bushy, instead preferring the thinned areas where tall trees provided roost sites (Palmer 1988). As previously discussed, winter foraging areas in this habitat cover type usually consisted of non-forested openings that were surrounded by pinyon-juniper woodlands. Areas used for foraging also consisted of chained mesa tops with pinyon-juniper habitat left in the steep ravines. These steep, tree-covered ravines possibly served as night roost sites.

Results of winter-diet observations are similar to the findings of Drennan and Beier (2003) and Stephens (2001), who found a significant use of cottontails by wintering goshawks. Goshawks that stayed at higher elevations might have been using snowshoe hares (*Lepus americanus*) for food as Palmer (1988), Doyle and Smith (1994), Squires and Reynolds (1997) found. Snowshoe hare prey remains were found but no goshawks were observed in the act of hunting. With cottontail densities higher in edge habitat and disturbed areas and more common in pinyon-juniper woodlands than in montane forest or ponderosa pine habitat (Chapman and Flux 1990, Fitzgerald et al. 1994), use of this prey may explain goshawk migration to pinyon-juniper woodlands.

Some reviewers have expressed concern over the accuracy of the buffers used for analyzing the data. We used values supplied by Argos and the makers of the PTTs, North Star (McGradey et al. 2002). Many times we were able to use the location estimates we received to locate live birds in the field, or to locate

birds that had died. In most cases these birds were located within 250–500 m of where the location estimates had placed them. Furthermore, although it is unrealistic to reanalyze all location estimates with larger buffers for the GIS habitat analysis, when a random selection of estimates was reanalyzed and assigned to a habitat cover type using the suggested increase in buffered distance (1 and 3 km) it did not alter in any biological or interpretive manner the results of our findings. If anything, a larger buffer appeared to strengthen our finding that goshawks use a mosaic pattern of habitat during the winter months because more of the location estimates and their associated buffers incorporated a forest and a non-forest habitat type. Finally, because we were only trying to develop a broad definition of the habitat characteristics in the goshawk wintering areas the field sampling data were analyzed using 3-km radius sampling areas, a scale similar to that suggested by the reviewers.

Management Implications

Although management of goshawk breeding areas mandates an absence of human disturbance (Reynolds et al. 1992, Graham et al. 1999b), most wintering areas showed signs of human alteration. Disturbance may contribute to an increase in prey densities or ability for the goshawks to sustain mobility within the forest stand (Kenward and Widén 1989). Therefore, preventing alteration of habitat is probably not as important in the wintering areas used by goshawks as it has been found to be in summer territories (Kenward and Widén 1989); it may even be beneficial by increasing prey densities and availability (Palmer 1988, Chapman and Flux 1990) and creating edge habitat in which goshawks prefer to hunt (Palmer 1988).

When incorporating goshawk winter biology and habitat use into future management plans it would therefore be important to include measures that benefit important goshawk prey species (lagomorphs), a concept similar to that proposed by Reynolds et al. (1992) and Graham et al. (1999b). It would also be important to include all vegetative types used by wintering goshawks in the management plan.

ACKNOWLEDGMENTS

We thank the many USDA Forest Service biologists and wildlife technicians, especially K. Paulin, K. Hartman, K. Rasmussen, M. Madsen, A. Alvidrez, S. Dewey, and T. Hollingshead whose support facilitated many aspects of this project and to V. J. Anderson whose insights and direction made the project possible. Special thanks are also due to those brave souls who worked as field assistants B. Shaheen, L. Bardo, C. Riding, and R. P. Corson and to M.B. Lee and D. B. for making countless maps and managing the satellite data. Lastly we thank S. Sonsthagen for all her advice and help in carrying out the project and the anonymous reviewers who helped better this paper. Funding for this project was provided by the USDA Forest Service.

Studies in Avian Biology No. 31:239–251

SATELLITE TELEMETRY OF NORTHERN GOSHAWKS BREEDING IN UTAH—I. ANNUAL MOVEMENTS

Sarah A. Sonsthagen, Ronald L. Rodriguez, and Clayton M. White

Abstract. Irruptive movements exhibited by Northern Goshawks (*Accipiter gentilis*) can make determining year-round movements of these birds difficult. Recent advancements in satellite telemetry have made these units useful in assessing movements of various raptor species. Studies documenting individual winter movements of Northern Goshawks in North America are limited and detailed studies examining winter ecology of Northern Goshawks have been largely restricted to the European subspecies (*A. g. gentilis*). Adult females (N = 36) were fitted with platform transmitter terminals (30 g in 2000 and 32 g in 2001) within the six national forests throughout Utah. Our data indicate that females breeding in Utah are partially migratory and are capable of extensive movements. Migratory birds traveled distances of 100–613 km. Smaller movements were observed by dispersing birds traveling between 49 and 85 km. We suggest that yearly variants such as prey availability and local weather conditions influence the degree of movement as indicated by a previous study.

Key Words: *Accipiter gentilis*, migration, Northern Goshawk, satellite telemetry.

TELEMETRÍA SATELITAL DE GAVILANES AZOR REPRODUCTORES EN UTAH—I. MOVIMIENTOS ANUALES

Resumen. Movimientos interrumpidos presentes en el Gavilán Azor (*Accipiter gentilis*), pueden dificultar la determinación de los movimientos anuales. Avances recientes en telemetría satelital han hecho útiles estas unidades para estimar los movimientos de varias especies rapaces. Estudios los cuales documenten movimientos individuales de inverno del Gavilán Azor en América del Norte son limitados, y estudios detallados que examinen la ecología en el invierno del Gavilán Azor han sido restringidos en gran parte a las subspecies de Europa (*A. g. gentilis*). Hembras adultas (N = 36) fueron adaptadas con terminales transmisoras de plataforma en el 2002 de 30 g y en el 2001 de 32 g, dentro de seis bosques nacionales a lo largo de Utah. Nuestros datos indican que las hembras reproductoras en Utah son parcialmente migratorias y son capaces de realizar amplios movimientos. Aves migratorias viajaron distancias de 100–613 Km. Movimientos más pequeños fueron observados por aves dispersas viajando entre 49 y 85 Km. Sugerimos que variantes anuales, tales como disponibilidad de presa, y condiciones locales del clima, influyen el grado de movimiento como lo indica un estudio previo.

Fragmentation of forests throughout North America has been perceived as detrimental to Northern Goshawk (*Accipiter gentilis*) populations because forest corridors may no longer be able to facilitate movement of goshawks over broad regions. Additionally, fragmentation is thought to inhibit goshawk movement between forest patches, as birds are unable to travel over non-forested landscapes (Kennedy 1997, Graham et al. 1999b). Breeding adults are relatively sedentary in summer, whereas in winter, they need to forage over large areas in search of prey (Palmer 1988). Studies documenting individual winter movements of Northern Goshawks in North America are limited (Squires and Ruggiero 1995, Stephens 2001). To date, detailed studies examining winter ecology of Northern Goshawks have been restricted to the European subspecies (*A. g. gentilis*, Kenward et al. 1981b, Widén 1984, 1985b, 1987, and 1989, Tornberg and Colpaert 2001). These studies indicated that Northern Goshawks in Sweden can be highly migratory, partially migratory (a population that is composed of migratory and resident individuals), or resident (Kenward et al. 1981b, Widén 1985b). In Finland, goshawks exhibit dispersal patterns similar to those in Sweden (Tornberg and Colpaert 2001). Within the Swedish population, adult females typically migrated longer distances to wintering grounds than adult males. Additionally, adult females migrated more often than adult males (Kenward et al. 1981b, Widén 1985b).

Within North America, Northern Goshawks exhibit a wide variety of movement types in winter or are resident (Evans and Sindelar 1974, Squires and Ruggiero 1995, Squires and Reynolds 1997, Stephens 2001, Sonsthagen 2002). Squires and Ruggiero (1995) studied winter movements of Northern Goshawks breeding in south-central Wyoming using radio telemetry. Their data indicated that Northern Goshawks (N = 4) breeding in Wyoming were migratory (traveling 65–185 km), and inclement weather may have initiated these movements, although a larger sample would be required to confirm that pattern. Stephens (2001) monitored movements of Northern Goshawks breeding in the Ashley National Forest, Utah, using radio telemetry during winters of 1998–1999 and 1999–2000. His data suggest that this population is composed of partial migrants. Of the seven individuals trapped in 1998, six were considered migratory (traveling 14 to >100 km). The remaining bird stayed on its breeding territory. In 1999, 14 individuals were monitored. Eight migrated with distances ranging from 8–100 km, three were considered residents, and no data were collected for the remaining individuals.

Irruptive movements exhibited by Northern Goshawks (Mueller et al. 1977, Kennedy 1998) can make determining year-round movements difficult. Satellite telemetry, however, has become useful in assessing movements in migratory birds (Brodeur et al. 1996, Fuller et al. 1998, Ueta et al. 1998, 2000; McGrady et al. 2000, 2002). However, Britten et al. (1999) warned that satellite telemetry units were not suitable for describing movements on small scales (<35 km). Using satellite telemetry, we describe the year-round movements of Northern Goshawks breeding in Utah in 2000 and 2001 and address the concern that current levels of habitat fragmentation inhibit goshawk movement between forest patches. We hypothesized that Northern Goshawks breeding throughout Utah would exhibit movement patterns similar to those observed by Squires and Ruggerio (1995) and Stephens (2001), because our study area is in close proximity to these previous studies, with some individuals migrating long distances in winter months while others being resident.

METHODS

FIELD TECHNIQUES

Thirty-eight adult female and six adult male Northern Goshawks were captured at nest sites during the breeding seasons of 2000–2001; Ashley National Forest (N = 14), Dixie National Forest (N = 12), Fishlake National Forest (N = 7), Manti LaSal National Forest (N = 6), Wasatch-Cache National Forest (N = 4), and Uinta National Forest (N = 1). A live Great Horned Owl (*Bubo virginianus*) was used to lure breeding Northern Goshawks (Rosenfield and Bielefeldt 1993) into a modified dho-gaza net trap (Clark 1981), which was set according to McCloskey and Dewey (1999).

Birds were banded with USGS Bird Banding Laboratory aluminum bands and plastic alphanumeric violet color bands. Standard measurements including mass, flattened wing length from the wrist to wing tip, tail length (central retrix), tarsus length, and hallux length were recorded to the nearest 0.1 millimeter, along with eye color. Body mass was important to ensure that the transmitters did not exceed 4.5% of the mass of a bird and measurements might provide additional insight into migration patterns, e.g., birds with longer wings relative to body mass may be more likely to migrate. Nests were revisited to determine number of fledglings and observe behavior of the transmitter-equipped female.

SATELLITE TELEMETRY DATA

Adult females (N = 36) were fitted with a 30 or 32 g platform transmitter terminals (PTT) manufactured by North Star Science and Technology, Columbia, Maryland. Only adult females were fitted with PTT units, because of transmitter weight and high first-year mortality observed in juveniles (Kenward et al. 1999, Kenward 2002). The units were attached with a backpack harness constructed with Teflon ribbon (Snyder et al. 1989). The PTT units were programmed to have a duty cycle of 6 hr of transmission followed by 68 hr without transmission, which allows the transmitters to transmit for approximately 1 yr.

Data were sent to the USDA Forest Service District Station, Cedar City, Utah, by Argos satellite systems, along with a corresponding accuracy estimate for each location. Data points were input into ArcView version 3.2, a geographic information system (GIS) computer program (ESRI 1996). Only data points with accuracy estimates of 3, 2, or 1, which is based on the position of the PTT unit relative to the satellite as it passes over the transmitter to estimate the location (Fuller et al. 1998). These estimates represent an actual transmitter location within 150, 350, or 1,000 m, respectively, of the estimated location. Location estimates with an accuracy estimate of 3, 2, or 1 were removed when distances between successive location estimates were greater than a flight speed of 80 km/hr, which is based on the maximum flight speed observed in the Peregrine Falcon (*Falco peregrinus*; Cochran and Applegate 1986, Chavez-Ramierez et al. 1994).

Based on our observations in this study, young fledged between mid-July and early-August and birds that migrated returned to their territories between mid-March and late-April (Appendix 1). Thus, we used a two-season designation consisting of breeding and non-breeding seasons. Data points received from 1 May–31 August were considered as breeding season. To ensure all birds had returned to their breeding territories, we classified all points received from 1 September–30 April as non-breeding.

Kernel home range and distances between points were calculated using an ArcView extension, Animal Movement Analysis version 1.1 (Hooge et al. 1999). Home-range was calculated using a least squares cross validation kernel estimate (Silverman 1986) as modified by Hooge et al. (1999) using smoothing parameters provided. Area was calculated for 95% probability polygons. Because Northern Goshawks are highly mobile, we defined females as migratory if they traveled >100 km from their nest site, dispersive if they moved to a different area that was distinct from their breeding territory but was <100 km from their nest site, and resident if their winter range extended out from their nest site with no distinct foraging areas. These definitions differ from those used by Stephens (2001). We describe an additional movement pattern for dispersing birds, which, based on what we observed, better fit the movement types utilized by Northern Goshawks in our study.

Along with location estimates, transmitters also provided temperature readings, which we used to assess the status of the transmitter and bird. When transmitters gave warm temperature readings (>25°C), we knew the transmitter was still attached to a live bird. However, when the transmitter gave cold temperature readings (<25°C), the transmitter may have malfunctioned or come off of the bird, or the bird had died. While we do not have data to demonstrate the fate of all goshawks carrying transmitters that went cold, we know some of those hawks died because we found goshawk remains when we recovered transmitters (42%, N = 8). Harnesses were constructed and attached so that they would remain on the bird and would likely not be lost. Therefore we assume the 12 remaining transmitters that sent cold temperatures and were not recovered were likely attached to dead birds.

STATISTICAL ANALYSIS

Data were analyzed in SAS, version 9.1 (SAS 2004) and Minitab version 13.2 (Minitab 2000). Home-range data were natural-log transformed to achieve normality. A general linear model (GLM, $\alpha = 0.05$) was used to compare home-range areas (the 95% probability polygons) and morphological characteristics (mass, tail length, and wing length) between individuals that dispersed or migrated and individuals that were residents. A GLM was also used to compare morphological characteristics (mass, tail length, and wing length) between individuals with transmitters that sent warm temperature readings throughout the course of the study and those that lost their transmitters or died. A regression was

used to test if a significant ($\alpha = 0.05$) increase in home-range size occurred throughout the course of the study. In addition, a chi-square test was used to determine if a difference occurred in the number of migrants between years.

RESULTS

Female Northern Goshawks breeding in Utah exhibited a variety of movement patterns in winter (Appendix 1). Of the 36 females tagged during the course of the study, 13 females exhibited movements >100 km (N = 8 in 2000; N = 5 in 2001). In 2000, 10 of 25 (40%) of the females migrated or dispersed and nine of 14 (64%) migrated or dispersed in 2001, which was not a significant difference ($\chi^2 = 2.11$, df = 1, P = 0.2).

In 2000, eight birds migrated. Two females (Ashley 1 and Ashley 7) from the Ashley National Forest migrated to wintering areas approximately 100 and 191 km from their breeding territories (Fig. 1). Female Ashley 1 continued to provide data through winter 2001. She used the same winter range as in 2000, approximately 191 km from her nest site. Dixie 7 was assumed to be a migrant. No data were received prior to her transmitter sending cold readings approximately 115 km south of her breeding site (Appendix 1). Fishlake National Forest females 1 and 2 migrated 104 and 174 km to their winter ranges (Fig. 2). Fishlake 2 continued to send data through the winter of 2001. She wintered in the same area as in 2000, approximately 174 km from her nest site. One female (Manti 3) from the Manti LaSal National Forest migrated 180 km to her wintering area in 2000 (Fig. 3). Two transmitters (Manti 3 and Manti 4) continued to send data through winter 2001. Both females migrated in 2001, traveling 156 (resident in 2000) and 544 km to their winter ranges (Fig. 3). Manti 3 and Manti 4 did not winter in the same area in 2001 as they did in 2000. One female was studied on the Wasatch National Forest in 2000; she traveled 527 km to her wintering area (Fig. 3).

In 2001, five birds migrated. Ashley 11 moved to a winter range approximately 144 km from her nest site (Fig. 4). On the Dixie National Forest, all females (Dixie 8, Dixie 9, and Dixie 10) migrated, traveling 114, 277, and 384 km to their winter ranges (Fig. 4). Of the two females studied on the Wasatch National Forest, one (Wasatch 3) migrated 613 km to her winter range (Fig. 5); the other transmitter sent unusable data.

Three females dispersed from breeding territories throughout the course of the study. In 2000, Dixie National Forest 4 and 6 moved to wintering areas

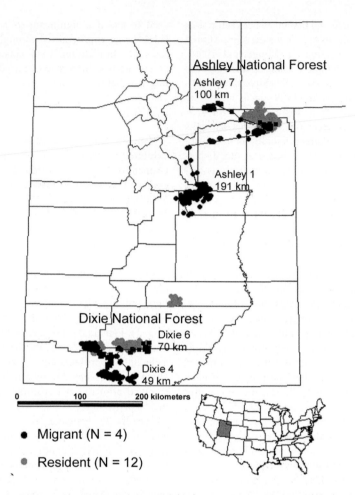

FIGURE 1. Map of Northern Goshawks breeding on the Ashley and Dixie National Forests in 2000. Resident females (Ashley 2, 3, 4, 5, 6, 8, and 9, Dixie 1, 2, 3, and 5) are shown in gray. Migratory females (Ashley 1 and 7, Dixie 4 and 6) are shown in black, with the flight path from their breeding territory to wintering area denoted with a black line. Distances for migratory birds are shown at their wintering areas.

approximately 49 and 67 km from their nest sites (Fig. 1). In 2001, one female dispersed from the Manti LaSal National Forest (Manti 5) 85 km to her wintering range (Fig. 5). The remaining 20 birds studied were residents in 2000 and 2001; Ashley National Forest (Fig. 1; N = 7 in 2000; Fig. 4, N = 2 in 2001), Dixie National Forest (Fig. 1; N = 5 in 2000), Fishlake National Forest (Fig. 5; N = 2 in 2001), Manti LaSal National Forest (Fig. 3; N = 3 in 2000), and Uinta National Forest (Fig. 2; N = 1 in 2000). Two transmitters sent unusable data (accuracy estimates other than 3, 2, or 1). Additionally, 21 of the 36 transmitters did not move and sent cold temperatures prior to the completion of the study.

Home-ranges of female goshawks across all national forests significantly increased throughout the course of the study (R^2 [adj.] = 30.8%, P < 0.000;

Table 1). In summer 2001, only nine of 19 females bred and two of those breeding attempts failed during incubation, resulting in an overall high average size of home-range. During non-breeding months, females that migrated or dispersed had larger kernel home-range 95% probability polygons than resident females, though they were not statistically significant (Table 2). Also, females that migrated had a slightly larger wing length (6.9 mm, F = 2.98, df = 1, P = 0.09) than residents (Table 3). No significant differences in morphological measurements were found between individuals that had warm transmitters and those who had cold transmitters when data were averaged across years (Table 4). Nonetheless, a significant difference occurred in tail length between individuals that were trapped in 2000 that had warm transmitters versus those that had cold transmitters

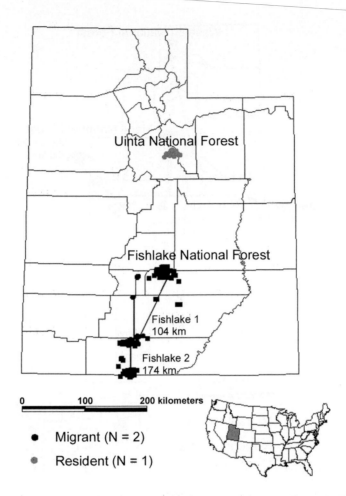

FIGURE 2. Map of Northern Goshawks breeding on the Fishlake and Uinta National Forests in 2000. Resident females (Uinta 1) are shown in gray. Migratory females (Fishlake 1 and 2) are shown in black, with the flight path from their breeding territory to wintering area denoted with a black line. Distances for migratory birds are shown at their wintering areas.

TABLE 1. COMPARISON OF THE AVERAGE KERNEL HOME RANGE (KM²) 95% PROBABILITY POLYGONS (SILVERMAN 1986) AS MODIFIED BY HOOGE ET AL. (1999) FOR FEMALE NORTHERN GOSHAWKS RESIDING IN EACH OF UTAH'S NATIONAL FORESTS.

National forest	Breeding 2000 Home range (km²)	Non-breeding 2000 Home range (km²)	Breeding 2001 Home range (km²)	Non-breeding 2001 Home-range (km²)
Ashley	91.7 (N = 9)	204.5 (N = 9)	158.4 (N = 7)	265.9 (N = 6)
Dixie	151.7 (N = 6)	297.2 (N = 6)	270.7 (N = 4)	368.2 (N = 5)
Fishlake	-	75.3 (N = 2)	299.5 (N = 3)	570.2 (N = 3)
Manti LaSal	149.0 (N = 3)	216.9 (N = 4)	215.4 (N = 5)	487.6 (N = 5)
Uinta	96.6 (N = 1)	106.0 (N = 1)	-	-
Wasatch	48.3 (N = 1)	262.5 (N = 1)	293.5 (N = 1)	1,088.6 (N = 1)
Overall average home range (km²)	116.4	217.9	223.0	433.7

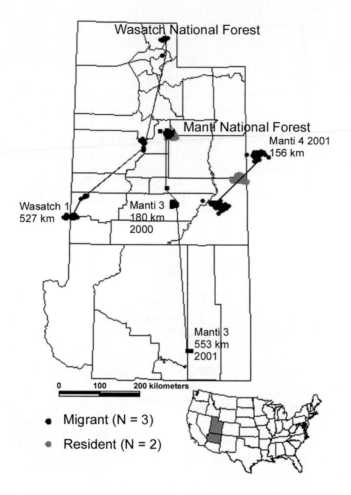

FIGURE 3. Map of Northern Goshawks breeding on the Manti and Wasatch National Forests in 2000. Resident females (Manti 1 and 2) are shown in gray. Migratory females (Manti 3 and 4, Wasatch 1) are shown in black, with the flight path from their breeding territory to wintering area denoted with a black line. Distances for migratory birds are shown at their wintering areas.

TABLE 2. COMPARISON OF THE MEAN KERNEL HOME RANGE 95% PROBABILITY POLYGONS (SILVERMAN 1986), AS MODIFIED BY HOOGE ET AL. (1999), MEAN STANDARD ERROR (SE), AND P-VALUES BETWEEN INDIVIDUALS THAT MIGRATED AND THOSE THAT WERE RESIDENTS ACROSS YEARS USING A GLM ($\alpha = 0.05$).

	Breeding	SE	Non-breeding	SE
Mean area (km²) for migrants	176.5 (N = 16)	35.5	303.0 (N = 14)	75.9
Mean area (km²) for residents	101.4 (N = 16)	20.4	149.7 (N = 18)	33.1
P-value	0.24	-	0.18	-

(11.8 mm, $F = 5.77$, df = 1, $P = 0.03$; Table 5). This pattern was not observed in 2001.

DISCUSSION

Our data indicate that female Northern Goshawks breeding in Utah are partially migratory, i.e., the population is composed of migratory and non-migratory individuals, and are capable of extensive movements over broad regions of non-forested landscape, as we have observed several instances where females have migrated over non-forested areas. Dixie 7 migrated 115 km from her natal site on the Kaibab Plateau, Arizona, to breed on the Dixie National

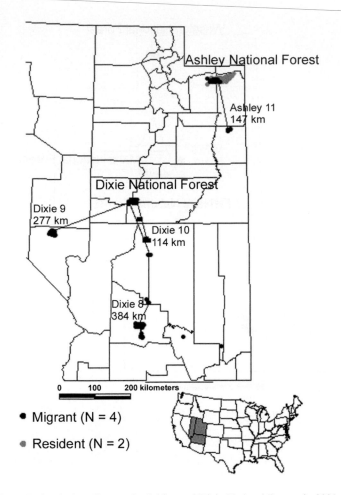

FIGURE 4. Map of Northern Goshawks breeding on the Ashley and Dixie National Forests in 2001. Resident females (Ashley 10 and 12) are shown in gray. Migratory females (Ashley 11, Dixie 8, 9, and 10) are shown in black, with the flight path from their breeding territory to wintering area denoted with a black line. Distances for migratory birds are shown at their wintering areas.

TABLE 3. COMPARISON OF MEAN, MEAN STANDARD ERROR (SE), AND P-VALUE OF MORPHOLOGICAL CHARACTERS OF FEMALE NORTHERN GOSHAWKS SAMPLED IN 2000 AND 2001 BETWEEN INDIVIDUALS THAT MIGRATED (N = 16) AND THOSE THAT WERE RESIDENTS (N = 18) USING A GLM (α = 0.05).

	Mean	SE	P-value
Mass			
migrant	951.5 g	18	
resident	982.2 g	14	0.18
Tail length			
migrant	267.2 mm	3.3	
resident	262.6 mm	2.9	0.31
Wing length			
migrant	368.6 mm	3.3	
resident	361.7 mm	2.3	0.09

Forest, Utah, over a large non-forested patch of land between the two forests. Additionally, she returned to that area in winter 2000. Manti La Sal 3 made a similar migration as Dixie 7 over the non-forested habitat between the Dixie National Forest and Kaibab Plateau. She continued on with her migration to central Arizona. Two females from the Wasatach National Forest (females 1 and 3) migrated long distances, 527 and 613 km respectively, over non-forested areas to their winter ranges in Nevada (Appendix 1).

Annual variables such as prey availability and local weather conditions, likely influenced the degree of movement, as indicated by Squires and Ruggiero (1995). We had four individuals (Ashley 1, Fishlake 2, Manti 3, and Manti 4) with successive years of data; two of them wintered in the same

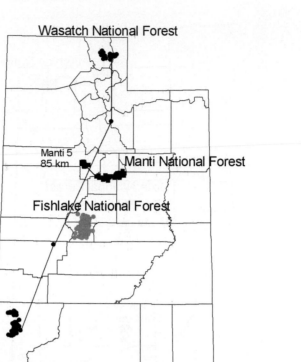

FIGURE 5. Map of Northern Goshawks breeding on the Fishlake, Manti, and Wasatch National Forests in 2001. Resident females (Fishlake 4 and 5) are shown in gray. Migratory females (Manti 5 and Wasatch 3) are shown in black, with the flight path from their breeding territory to wintering area denoted with a black line. Distances for migratory birds are shown at their wintering areas.

TABLE 4. COMPARISON OF MEAN, MEAN STANDARD ERROR (SE), AND P-VALUE OF MORPHOLOGICAL CHARACTERS OF FEMALE NORTHERN GOSHAWKS SAMPLED IN 2000 AND 2001 BETWEEN INDIVIDUALS WITH TRANSMITTERS SENDING WARM TEMPERATURES (N = 15) AND TRANSMITTERS SENDING COLD TEMPERATURES (N = 19) USING A GLM (α = 0.05).

	Mean	SE	P-value
Tail length			
cold transmitters	261.6 mm	2.6	
warm transmitters	268.7 mm	3.5	0.16
Wing length			
cold transmitters	364.4 mm	3.2	
warm transmitters	365.6 mm	2.4	0.77
Mass			
cold transmitters	968.1 g	14	
warm transmitters	967.3 g	19	0.58

TABLE 5. COMPARISON OF MEAN, MEAN STANDARD ERROR (SE), AND P-VALUE OF MORPHOLOGICAL CHARACTERS OF FEMALE NORTHERN GOSHAWKS TRAPPED IN 2000 BETWEEN INDIVIDUALS WITH TRANSMITTERS SENDING WARM TEMPERATURES (N = 12) AND THOSE SENDING COLD TEMPERATURES (N = 11) USING A GLM (α = 0.05).

	Mean	SE	P-value
Tail length			
cold transmitters	259.9 mm	4.1	
warm transmitters	271.7 mm	3.4	0.03[a]
Wing length			
cold transmitters	367.3 mm	4.7	
warm transmitters	363.8 mm	2.7	0.56
Mass			
cold transmitters	957.2 g	18	
warm transmitters	975.8 g	23	0.50

[a] Denotes a significant P-value.

winter range both years and two moved to different wintering areas. This differs from the findings of Stephens (2001), who suggested that Northern Goshawks utilize the same areas each winter (N = 3). In addition, 10 of 25 (40%) females migrated in 2000 and nine of 14 (64%) migrated in 2001, indicating a non-significant year-to-year difference (χ^2 = 2.11, df = 1, P = 0.2). The idea of an annual effect on winter movements is supported by observations of periodic invasions of Northern Goshawks, which are correlated with 10-yr population declines in Ruffed Grouse (*Bonasa umbellus*) and snowshoe hare (*Lepus americanus*) (Mueller et al. 1977, Palmer 1988).

The increase in kernel home-ranges between seasons was expected, because during summer females primarily guard nests while males hunt. The significant increase in kernel home ranges throughout the course of the 2-yr study, however, was unexpected. Some potential explanations for this steady increase of home-range sizes may be attributed to a drought occurring throughout the West that started in about 1999 and continued throughout our study. The severity of the drought increased annually, potentially reducing prey abundances and resulting in larger foraging areas. Newton (1986) and Kenward (1982) reported that range size of accipiters is inversely dependent on prey abundance. In addition, we observed reduced nesting activity within our study areas (>50% of known nest territories occupied in 2000 to <10% occupied in 2001). Reynolds et al. (1998) reported that annual fluctuation in Northern Goshawk demography and nesting density are related to abundances of main prey species, mainly the red squirrel (*Tamiasciurus hudsonicus*). Birds trapped in 2001 were in poor body condition as indicated by lack of pectoral muscle mass, which we attributed to poor conditions of the range and its affect on prey availability.

We hypothesize that food plays a part in the process of migration (sensu, Squires and Reynolds 1997). Females that migrated or dispersed had larger home-ranges in winter (Table 2) than individuals that remained on breeding territories. We suggest a larger home range reflects a less rich or less dense local prey base causing the hawks to range farther, which has been noted in several raptor species involved in predator-prey cycles (Newton 1979a). We had 11 birds with successive breeding season data. Only two of these birds attempted to nest the following year and both were resident birds the previous winter (Appendix 1). Since studies indicate that winter food supply affects subsequent breeding densities (Newton 1998), we speculate that migratory females did not nest as a result of lower prey availability on the winter range, relative to resident birds, as indicated by significantly larger home ranges and its effect on their breeding condition. Additionally, females may migrate to reduce competition for resources. A study conducted in Michigan monitored a mixed-species community of raptors during two winters of differing prey densities in a 96 km² farmland (Craighead and Craighead 1956). Craighead and Craighead (1956) results indicate that prey availability influenced the number of individuals and species present in a particular area and interactions between them. Degree of winter territoriality may be related to prey numbers such that high prey densities reflect lower incidence of aggressive behavior (Eurasian Kestrel [*Falco tinnunculus*], Cavé 1968). Although the increase in the number of migrants was not significant across years, more females are likely migrating or forced to migrate as a result of increased territoriality between wintering raptors thus reducing local competition.

Females that migrated had slightly longer wings (Table 3) than those that did not. Migratory populations of many birds (Horned Larks [*Eremophila alpertris*], Behle 1942; Cooper's Hawks [*Accipiter cooperii*], R. Rosenfield, pers. comm.) have longer, more attenuated wings than non-migratory populations of the same species. If wing length is an inherited trait, female goshawks that make successful migrations year after year may pass onto offspring the behavioral tendency to migrate and the morphological traits associated with that behavior. Whether such a difference has genetic underpinnings is unknown.

Lastly, an important characteristic that comes from our data dealt with tail length. Although, we do not have data to demonstrate the fate of all goshawks carrying transmitters that sent cold temperature readings, we know some of those hawks died because we recovered transmitters (N = 8). In 2000, all hawks that carried transmitters that sent cold temperature readings had a statistically shorter tail by an average of 11.8 mm than hawks whose transmitters continued to send warm readings (Table 5). Based on continual yearly trapping and measuring of individual birds, tails become shorter annually (B. Woodbridge, pers. comm.). Perhaps the added weight of transmitters was enough of a factor to cause already old goshawks to die. Although, not all territories of females that had cold reading transmitters were reoccupied, we do not believe unoccupied territories were a result of mortality observed in our study. New females reoccupied territories that were occupied by females whose transmitters sent cold readings the previous year (N = 3) and territories that were not used in this study and active in 2000 were not reoccupied in 2001. In addition, by providing extra winter food, studies have indicated that winter food supply may affect subsequent breeding densities (Newton 1998). Therefore, we hypothesize that unoccupied territories reinforce the notion that prey densities were low due to drought conditions and the low nesting density or re-occupancy rate was an artifact of this and not an artifact of mortality observed in our study.

Female Northern Goshawks observed in our study were capable of extensive movements (613 km), despite concerns that current levels of forest fragmentation maybe limiting Northern Goshawk migrations (Kennedy 1997, Graham et al. 1999a). Our data suggest that forest fragmentation does not have a detrimental effect on goshawk movement and notions that current levels of fragmentation are inhibiting goshawk movements are likely overstated as indicated by our four birds that dispersed and migrated over non-forested areas to breeding and wintering areas (Appendix 1). Additionally, partial migratory behavior observed in Northern Goshawks presents a need for researchers to examine breeding territories as potential wintering sites and determine what characteristics provide suitable winter range conditions. Although forest fragmentation does not appear to limit female Northern Goshawk movement, it is important to keep in mind that fragmentation may reduce goshawk numbers by limiting breeding and wintering habitat. This is especially important since raptors are already at lower densities than other birds (goshawks, 3.6–10.7 pairs/ 100 km^2, Squires and Reynolds 1997) without added pressure of contending with habitat fragmentation (Newton 1998).

ACKNOWLEDGMENTS

Funding for this project was provided by the USDA Forest Service, Intermountain Region, and Brigham Young University. We thank all of the Forest Service biologists and technicians working on the Northern Goshawk project in Utah for their time and energy, especially; S. Blatt, S. Dewey, K. Hartman, D. Jauregui, J. Jewks, M. Lee, L. Parry, K. Paulin, R. Player, K. Rasumussen, B. Smith, and C. Staab and also the field technicians, S. Gericke and I. Mariotto. T. Maechtle, North Star Science and Technology, showed us how to attach satellite telemetry units and provided his expertise. We would also like to thank, D. Turner, USDAS Forest Service, for statistical analysis, T. Bowyer, K. Crandall, S. Peck, and R. Rader for their comments on earlier drafts of this manuscript.

APPENDIX 1. DESCRIPTION OF FEMALE NORTHERN GOSHAWK MOVEMENT THAT WERE TRAPPED ON UTAH'S NATIONAL FORESTS IN 2000 AND 2001. HAWKS ARE LISTED BY FOREST WITH A NUMERICAL IDENTIFICATION.

Individual	Year	Description
Ashley 1	2000	Bird migrated. Data were received from 15 June 2000–25 April 2002. She remained near her breeding territory in a 90.3 km^2 area until 9 September 2000. She traveled 191 km southwest to a 943 km^2 area near Price, Utah, 21 September 2000–16 April 2001, 28 April 2001–25 October 2001, and 18 November 2001–9 April 2002. She returned to her breeding territory 19 April 2001, 3 November 2001, and 12 April 2002–25 April 2002. She traveled the same route between territories. She did not attempt to breed in 2001.
Ashley 2	2000	Bird was a resident. Data were received 16 June 2000–20 July 2001. She remained near her breeding territory in a 38.0 km^2 home-range. She attempted to breed in 2001 in the same territory, nest failed during incubation.
Ashley 3	2000	Bird was a resident. Data were received 8 August 2000–9 October 2000. She remained near her breeding territory in a 22.0 km^2 area until 12 September 2000. On 18 September 2000, she traveled 28 km northwest to an 11.0 km^2 area. Her transmitter stopped moving and sent cold temperatures after 9 October 2000.
Ashley 4	2000	Bird was a resident. Data were received 16 June 2000–12 January 2001. She remained near her breeding territory in a 252.4 km^2 area until 12 November 2000. She traveled 14 km northeast to a 2.7 km^2 area 14 November 2000–24 November 2000. On 27 November 2000, she returned to her breeding territory until 6 January 2001. She traveled to a 24.7 km^2 area 12.5 km south of her nest site 9 January 2001. Her transmitter stopped moving and sent cold temperatures after 12 January 2001.
Ashley 5	2000	Bird was a resident. Data were received 14 June 2000–4 March 2001. She remained near her breeding territory in a 124.6 km^2 area. Her transmitter stopped moving and sent cold temperatures after 4 March 2001.
Ashley 6	2000	Bird was a resident. Data were received 20 June 2000–17 September 2001. She remained near her breeding territory in a 235.4 km^2 area. She did not attempt to breed in 2001.
Ashley 7	2000	Bird migrated. Data were received 15 June 2000–7 November 2000. She remained near her breeding territory in a 102.9 km^2 area until 4 October 2000. She traveled 100 km west to a 290.5 km^2 area near Robertson, Wyoming, 10 October 2000–4 November 2000. Her transmitter stopped moving and sent cold temperatures after 7 November 2000, 36 km east of winter area 1.
Ashley 8	2000	Bird was a resident. Data were received 20 June 2000–9 October 2000. She remained near her breeding territory in a 104.6 km^2 area. Her transmitter stopped moving and sent cold temperatures after 9 October 2000.
Ashley 9	2000	Bird was a resident. Data were received 16 June 2000–22 October 2001. She remained near her breeding territory in a 240.0 km^2 area. She did not attempt to breed in 2001.
Ashley 10	2001	Bird was a resident. Data were received 6 August 2001–10 April 2002. She remained near her territory in a 287.6 km^2 area.
Ashley 11	2001	Bird was a migrant. Data were received 8 August 2001–15 November 2001. She remained near her breeding territory in a 205.2 km^2 home-range until 5 November 2001. She traveled 147 km southeast to a 115.0 km^2 area. Her transmitter stopped moving and sent cold temperatures after 15 November 2001.
Ashley 12	2001	Bird was a resident. Data were received 8 August 2001–9 March 2002. She remained near her breeding territory in a 341.8 km^2 area. Her transmitter stopped moving and sent cold temperatures after 9 March 2002.
Dixie 1	2000	Bird was a resident. Data were received from 3 September 2000–28 October 2001. She remained in her breeding territory in a 68.9 km^2 home-range until 10 November 2000. She moved frequently between her breeding territory and an adjacent 349.4 km^2 area 22.6 km west. She did not attempt to breed in 2001.
Dixie 2	2000	Bird was a resident. Data were received 2 September 2000–24 November 2000. She remained near her breeding territory in a 204.9 km^2 area. Her transmitter stopped moving and sent cold temperatures after 24 November 2000.
Dixie 3	2000	Bird was a resident. Data were received 5 September 2000–18 September 2000. She remained near her breeding territory in a 9.5 km^2 area. Her transmitter stopped moving and sent cold temperatures after 18 September 2000.
Dixie 4	2000	Bird was dispersive. Data were received 3 September 2000–27 September 2001. She remained near her breeding territory in a 191.7 km^2 area until 25 September 2000 and 18 July 2001–20 September 2001. She foraged in a 341.3 km^2 area, 49 km north of Kanab, Utah. She moved between these two areas 15 times. From 22 October 2000–10 November 2000, she was in a 117.4 km^2 area 39 km east of winter area 1. She did not attempt to breed in 2001.

APPENDIX 1. Continued.

Individual	Year	Description
Dixie 5	2000	Bird was a resident. Data were received 12 September 2000–1 January 2001. She remained near her breeding territory in a 92.1 km² area. Her transmitter stopped moving and sent cold temperatures after 1 January 2001.
Dixie 6	2000	Bird dispersed. Data were received 2 September 2000–10 January 2001. She foraged in a 308.3 km² area near her breeding territory until 12 November 2000 and 7 December 2000–19 December 2000. She traveled 67 km west to a 106.6 km2 area 18 November 2000–1 December 2001 and 26 December 2000–4 January 2001. From 22 December 2000–23 December 2000 and 7 January 2001–10 January 2001, she foraged in a 96.6 km² area 67 km west of her nest site and 22 km east of winter area 1. Her transmitter stopped moving and sent cold temperatures after 10 January 2001.
Dixie 7	2000	Bird was assumed to migrate. No data were collected before her transmitter stopped moving and sent cold temperatures after 30 September 2000, 115 km south of her nest site near Jacob Lake, Arizona. She was banded as a nestling on the Kaibab Plateau, Arizona.
Dixie 8	2001	Bird migrated. Data were received 8 August 2001–28 April 2002. She remained near her breeding territory in a 238.5 km² area until 9 October 2001, 25 February 2002–28 February 2002, and 22 March 2002–28 April 2002. She traveled 354 km south to a 201.6 km² area near Prescott, Arizona, from 21 October 2001–16 December 2001, 7 January 2002–31 January 2002, 6 February 2002–13 February 2002. She traveled to a 61.9 km² area 30 km south of winter area 1 22 December 2001–3 January 2002 and 3 February 2002.
Dixie 9	2001	Bird migrated. Data were received 6 August 2001–10 February 2002. She remained in a 197.5 km² area, 277 km west of her nest site in the Sheep Mountain Range, Nevada.
Dixie 10	2001	Bird migrated. Data were received 24 August 2001–18 October 2001. She remained near her breeding territory in a 242.3 km² area until 18 September 2001. She traveled 114 km south to a 153.3 km² area near Jacob Lake, Arizona. Her transmitter stopped moving and sent cold temperatures after 18 October 2001.
Fishlake 1	2000	Bird migrated. Data were received 5 September 2000–28 October 2000. She remained near her breeding territory in a 15.9 km² area until 8 September 2000. She traveled 104 km south to a 221.6 km² area near Tropic, Utah, 18 September 2000–28 October 2000. Her transmitter stopped moving and sent cold temperatures after 28 October 2000.
Fishlake 2	2000	Bird migrated. Data were received 1 September 2000–21 December 2001. She remained near her breeding territory in a 182.2 km² area until 5 November 2000 and 30 March 2001–19 September 2001. On 8 November 2000, she was 124 km south near Cannonville, Utah. She traveled 49 km south to a 51.1 km² area 11 November 2000–24 March 2001. She returned to her breeding site twice during this time. She returned to winter area 1 25 September 2001–23 October 2001 in a 192.9 km² area. She traveled to a second winter area 1 November 2001–21 December 2001. She did not attempt to breed in 2001.
Fishlake 3	2000	Bird was assumed to be a resident. No data were collected due to poor signals. Transmitter stopped moving and sent cold temperatures after 1 March 2001. Transmitter was found near her breeding territory.
Fishlake 4	2001	Bird was a resident. Data were received 12 September 2001–4 January 2002. She remained near her breeding territory in a 364.2 km² area. Transmitter stopped moving and sent cold temperatures after 4 January 2002.
Fishlake 5	2001	Bird was a resident. Data were received 7 August 2001–24 January 2002. She remained near her breeding territory in a 663.9 km² area. After 24 January 2002, her transmitter stopped moving and sent cold temperatures.
Manti 1	2000	Bird was a resident. Data were received 18 July 2000–24 October 2001. She remained near her breeding territory in a 88.1 km² home-range. She attempted to breed in 2001, her nest failed during incubation.
Manti 2	2000	Bird was a resident. Data were received 10 July 2000–22 November 2001. She remained near her breeding territory in a 366.4 km² home-range. She did not attempt to breed in 2001.
Manti 3	2000	Bird migrated. Data were received 22 July 2000–26 February 2002. She remained near her breeding territory in a 99.4 km² area until 1 November 2000. She traveled 179 km south to a 59.0 km² area east of Boulder, Utah, 10 November 2000–13 March 2001. She returned to her breeding territory 25 March 2001–12 October 2001 foraging in a 257.4 km² area. From 1 December 2001–16 February 2002, she migrated to a 35.9 km² area 544 km south near Winslow, Apache Sitgreaves National Forest, Arizona. She did not attempt to breed in 2001.

APPENDIX 1. CONTINUED.

Individual	Year	Description
Manti 4	2000	Bird migrated. Data were received 5 September 2000–24 April 2002. She remained near her breeding territory in a 373.4 km^2 area until 15 April 2001, 24 April 2001–14 October 2001, and 27 March 2002–24 April 2002. From 18 April 2001–21 April 2001 and 23 October 2001–24 March 2002, she traveled 156 km northeast to a 116.6 km^2 area near Glade Park, Colorado National Monument, Colorado. She did not attempt to breed in 2001.
Manti 5	2001	Bird dispersed. Data were received 12 July 2001–4 January 2002. She remained near her nest site in a 235.9 km^2 area until 11/22/01. She traveled 30 km west to 412.6 km^2 winter area near Ephraim, Utah, 25 November 2001–11 December 2001. From 14 December 2001–4 January 2002, she foraged in a 113.7 km^2 area near Levan, Utah, 55 km west of winter area 1. After 7 January 2002, her transmitter stopped moving and sent cold temperatures.
Uinta 1	2000	Bird was a resident. Data were received 10 July 2000–11 March 2001. She remained near her breeding territory in a 102.2 km^2 area.
Wasatch 1	2000	Bird migrated. Data were received 17 July 2000–20 March 2001. She remained near her breeding territory in an 82.7 km^2 area until 29 September 2000. She traveled to a 31.1 km^2 area 261 km south near Scipio, Utah, 1 November 2000–26 November 2000. From 2 December 2000–8 March 2001, she wintered in a 65.8 km^2 area 258 km southwest of winter area 1 near Enterprise, Utah. She traveled to a 75.1 km^2 area 20 km west in Nevada 11 March 2001. Her transmitter stopped moving and sent cold temperatures after 20 March 2001.
Wasatch 2	2001	Too few data points collected to determine movement type. Two data points were collected on 20 Sept 2001 and 3 December 2001 located 30 km apart within 22 km of nest location. Bird Banding Lab recovered her band after 3 December 2001.
Wasatch 3	2001	Bird migrated. Data were received 3 August 2001–13 January 2002. She remained near her nest site in a 392.8 km^2 area until 31 October 2001. She traveled to a 499.1 km^2 area 613 km south near Mt. Trumbull, Arizona, 9 November 2001–28 November 2001. She traveled to a 147.2 km^2 area 36 km north to winter area 2 near Wolf Hole, Arizona, 1 December 2001–7 December 2001. She returned to winter area 1 10 December 2001–7 January 2002. She returned to winter area 2 10 January 2002. After 13 January 2002, her transmitter stopped moving and sent cold temperatures.

Studies in Avian Biology No. 31:252–259

SATELLITE TELEMETRY OF NORTHERN GOSHAWKS BREEDING IN UTAH—II. ANNUAL HABITATS

SARAH A. SONSTHAGEN, RONALD L. RODRIGUEZ, AND CLAYTON M. WHITE

Abstract. Irruptive movements exhibited by Northern Goshawks (*Accipiter gentilis*) can make determining year-round habitats of these birds difficult. Recent advancements in satellite-received transmitters and habitat modeling of landscapes have become useful in assessing movements and habitats of Northern Goshawks breeding in Utah. Studies documenting individual winter movements of Northern Goshawks in North America are limited, and detailed studies examining winter ecology have been largely restricted to the European subspecies. Adult females (N = 36) were fitted with 30 or 32 g platform transmitter terminals in 2000 and 2001 within the six national forests throughout Utah. Resident birds used forest habitat types and elevations similar to their breeding areas throughout winter. In contrast, birds that migrated or dispersed used pinyon-juniper habitat and lower elevations. In addition, migratory individuals had significantly larger home range sizes, suggesting lower prey availability within pinyon-juniper forests for Northern Goshawks.

Key Words: *Accipiter gentilis*, habitat, Northern Goshawk, satellite telemetry.

TELEMETRÍA SATELITAL DE GAVILANES AZOR REPRODUCTORES EN UTAH—II. MOVIMIENTOS ANUALES

Resumen. Movimientos interrumpidos presentes en el Gavilán Azor, pueden dificultar la determinación de sus hábitats, que utilizan durante todo el año. Avances recientes en transmisores de recepción satelital y en modelación del hábitat del paisaje, se han vuelto útiles para la estimación de los movimientos y hábitats del Gavilán Azor reproductor en Utah. Estudios los cuales documenten movimientos individuales de inverno del Gavilán Azor en América del Norte son limitados, y estudios detallados que examinen la ecología en el invierno del Gavilán Azor han sido restringidos en gran parte a las subespecies de Europa. Hembras adultas (N = 36) fueron adaptadas con terminales transmisoras de plataforma (en el 2002 de 30 g y en el 2001 de 32 g) dentro de seis bosques nacionales a lo largo de Utah. Aves residentes utilizaron tipos de hábitat forestal y elevaciones similares a sus áreas de reproducción a través del invierno. En contraste, aves que migraron o se dispersaron, utilizaron hábitat de piñón-junípero y elevaciones más bajas. Además, individuos migratorios tuvieron un rango en el tamaño del hogar significativamente más amplio, sugiriendo que existe menor disponibilidad de presa para el Gavilán Azor dentro del bosque de piñón-junípero.

Population viability of Northern Goshawks (*Accipiter gentilis*) is a concern because habitat fragmentation is thought to reduce overall habitat quality for goshawks (Kennedy 1997, Graham et al. 1999a). Knowledge of breeding habitat alone is not adequate to understand biological requirements of goshawks, therefore non-breeding habitats need to be defined to determine relationships between habitat types and goshawk abundance (Kennedy 1997). Breeding habitat for Northern Goshawks has been well defined in the literature (Reynolds et al. 1982, Moore and Henny 1983, Hayward and Escano 1989, Hargis et al. 1994), but the winter ecology of Northern Goshawks is well known only in Europe (Kenward et al. 1981b, Kenward 1982, Widén 1987, Tornberg and Colpaert 2001). Few studies have examined winter habitats of Northern Goshawks in North America (Squires and Ruggiero 1995, Stephens 2001). Squires and Ruggiero (1995) studied four migratory individuals in southeastern Wyoming, where

winter ranges contained quaking aspen (*Populus tremuloides*) with mixed conifer, Engelmann spruce-subalpine fir (*Picea engelmannii-Abies lasiocarpa*), lodgepole pine (*Pinus contorta*), and cottonwood (*Populus* spp.) groves surrounded by sagebrush (*Artemisia* spp.). Stephens (2001) reported goshawks using three main habitat types in the Ashley National Forest, Utah, including mixed lodgepole pine, subalpine fir, and Douglas-fir (*Pseudotsuga menzieseii*) stands, pinyon-juniper (*Pinus edulis, Juniperus osteosperma,* and *Juniperus scopulorum*) stands, and lowland riparian areas. Although these studies provided valuable information about winter habitat use of Northern Goshawks near their breeding grounds, more data on goshawks that moved greater distances are needed to adequately assess habitat use.

In this study, we used satellite telemetry to assess annual habitat use by Northern Goshawks breeding in southwestern North America. Satellite telemetry had been used successfully to assess movements of various raptors (Brodeur et al. 1996, Fuller et al. 1998, Ueta et al. 1998, Ueta et al. 2000, McGrady et al. 2002), but none of these studies expanded the use of satellite technology to determine habitat types. Earlier studies (Britten et al. 1999) warned against using satellite telemetry for small-scale movements (<35 km) because actual locations may be several hundred meters from the recorded location. Though we understand the potential limitations in the accuracy of satellite telemetry locations estimates when considering small-scale movements, given the limited amount of data describing annual habitat use by Northern Goshawks, we feel it is important to broaden our understanding of annual habitat types used by goshawks at a landscape scale.

Using satellite telemetry, we determined the year-round habitats of Northern Goshawks breeding throughout Utah at a landscape scale. We hypothesized that Northern Goshawks would use habitats consistent with those described in previous studies during breeding months with birds breeding in mature to over-mature forest stands (Reynolds et al. 1982, Speiser and Bosakowski 1987, Hayward and Escano 1989). During winter, however, individuals would exploit a variety of habitat types, as described by Squires and Ruggiero (1995) and Stephens (2001), including those used during the breeding season.

METHODS

FIELD TECHNIQUES

Adult female Northern Goshawks (N = 36) were trapped at their nest sites in six national forests (Ashley, Dixie, Fishlake, Manti LaSal, Uinta, and Wasatch national forests) in Utah. These forests span about 720 km from north (Wasatch National Forest, ca. 41° 45' N) to south (Dixie National Forest, ca. 37° 25' N) and 540 km east (Manti LaSal National Forest, ca. 109° W) to west (Dixie National Forest, ca. 113° W). We used a live Great Horned Owl (*Bubo virginianus*) to lure birds into a modified dho-gaza net trap (Clark 1981), which was set according to McCloskey and Dewey (1999). Birds were banded with USGS Bird Banding Laboratory aluminum bands and plastic violet alphanumeric color bands. Females were fitted with a 30 or 32 g platform terminal transmitter (PTT) manufactured by North Star Science and Technology, Columbia, Maryland. We used a backpack harness made with Teflon ribbon (Snyder et al. 1989) to attach PTTs. We recorded standard measurements including mass, wing chord, tail length (central retrix), tarsus length, and hallux length to the nearest 0.1 mm along with eye color to assess bird's age. To limit potential transmitter effects, PTT units did not exceed 4.5% of the bird's body mass.

SATELLITE TELEMETRY DATA

North Star Science and Technology programmed PTTs with a duty cycle of 6 hr of transmission followed by 68 hr without transmission. Data were sent to the USDA Forest Service District Station, Cedar City, Utah, by Argos satellite systems along with a corresponding location class for each location. Data points were input into ArcView version 3.2, a geographic information system (GIS) (ESRI 1996). We only used data points with location classes 3, 2, and 1, which is based on the position of the PTT unit relative to the satellite as it passes over the transmitter to estimate the location (Fuller et al. 1998). These estimates represent an actual transmitter location within 150, 350, or 1,000 m of the estimated location, respectively (McGrady et al. 2002). Estimated locations with a class of 3, 2, or 1 were removed when distances between successive location estimates were greater than a flight speed of 80 km/hr, which is based on maximum flight speed observed in the Peregrine Falcon (*Falco peregrinus*; Cochran and Applegate 1986, Chavez-Ramierez et al. 1994).

Location estimates were characterized as day or night to determine potential differences between day and roost habitats. Data were considered daytime at sunrise through 1 hr before sunset at 40° latitude (U.S. Naval Observatory 1999). Times were rounded to the nearest 5 min. Data received 1 March–30 April were considered spring, 1 May–31 August as summer, 1 September–30 November as autumn, and 1 December–28 February as winter.

Habitat type and elevation for each point were determined in ArcView with Utah Forest Inventory and Analysis (USDA Forest Service 1988a), Arizona, Nevada, Utah, and Wyoming GAP analysis vegetation layers (USGS GAP Analysis Program 2000), Utah Contours (State of Utah 2000), Arizona 90 meter Digital Elevation Model (USGS 2000), and Wyoming 90 meter Digital Elevation Model (USGS 1997) elevation layers. Buffers were placed around each estimated location according to its accuracy estimate because the actual location of the transmitters would be within 150–1,000 m (radius) of estimated location. We assessed and recorded all habitat types within each buffer. Buffers containing multiple habitat types were categorized as conifer, conifer-aspen, non-forest, and non-forest-forest. We defined conifer as a buffer containing any combination of alpine fir, Douglas-fir, Engelmann spruce, lodgepole pine, pinyon-juniper, ponderosa pine, or white fir (*Abies concolor*); conifer-aspen as any combination of previously mentioned conifer types with aspen; non-forest as any combination of a non-forest habitat such as perennial grass and sagebrush; and non-forest-forest as any combination of non-forest habitat types and forest habitat types. Assuming birds are relatively sedentary at night, data received during the same night were considered one estimate. If night locations had more than one elevation or habitat type for a particular night, each estimate was weighted proportional to its occurrence that night. Total weighted values for each night summed to one. No habitat data were available for Colorado (3.2% of points) and no elevation data were available for Colorado and Nevada (4.3% of points). Location estimates along with their corresponding buffer will be referred to as location estimates throughout the rest of this manuscript.

Some researchers have indicated at error distances for location estimates provided by Argos underestimate the actual error associated with a given location estimate (Craighead and Smith 2003). In an attempt to address these concerns, we characterized habitat within use areas for individual goshawks for each season. Use areas were defined by a kernel home range 95% polygon calculated in ArcView version 3.2 using extension Animal Movement (Hooge et al. 1999). Habitats were categorized as described above.

STATISTICAL ANALYSIS

Habitat and elevation data collected from summer 2000 through summer 2001 were analyzed in SAS release 8.2 (SAS Institute, Inc. 2001). Habitat types were categorized as conifer, deciduous, non-forest, pinyon-juniper, or any combination of these categories, using definitions described above. Data were not stratified based on day or night locations. Data were normally distributed and had equal variances. A logistic regression was used to determine potential differences in habitat categories among seasons in 2000, accounting for bird and breeding location. A regression with repeated measures (PROC MIXED) was used to determine potential differences in elevation among seasons in 2000, accounting for bird and breeding location. Buffers categorized as conifer-deciduous-non-forest-pinyon-juniper, conifer-non-forest-pinyon-juniper, conifer-pinyon-juniper, deciduous-non-forest-pinyon-juniper, and deciduous-pinyon-juniper were removed from the regression because of low sample size.

RESULTS

We received 5,557 (LC3 N = 940, LC2 N = 1,665, LC3 N = 2,952) location estimates from units attached to the 35 birds used in this study. Habitats used varied with national forest and migratory behavior. Detailed descriptions of habitats exploited by individual birds are described in Sonsthagen (2002). On the northern national forests (Ashley, Uinta, and Wasatch national forests), five of 15 individuals migrated, whereas, on the southern national forests (Dixie, Fishlake, and Manti LaSal national forests) 11 of 20 females migrated. Most individuals (79%) that migrated or dispersed used primarily pinyon-juniper and non-forest habitat in winter, whereas, most residents (93%) used alpine fir, Douglas-fir, Engelmann spruce, lodgepole pine, ponderosa pine, quaking aspen, white fir, or any combination of these in winter. Proportion of location estimates in each habitat type and elevation varied between day and night. No distinct habitat use pattern was found due to high variability between locality, seasons, and years.

Females breeding in the northern national forests used the same habitat types throughout most of the year, but percent of use varied between breeding and non-breeding periods (Table 1). In summer, autumn, and spring, females used mainly Douglas-fir (0–16.3%), Douglas-fir-aspen (2.5–25.0%), Engelmann spruce-lodgepole pine (4.7–20.6%), lodgepole pine (0–14.4%), lodgepole pine-aspen (6.4–25.2%), and quaking aspen (5.1–25.0%). In winter, females used habitat types similar to those in other months but in differing frequencies. Females increased their use of pinyon-juniper habitat from an average of 2.6% in all other seasons to 15.4% in winter 2000 and 20.6% in winter 2001 (Table 1). Two females from the Wasatch National Forest used pinyon-juniper habitat almost exclusively in winter and migrated 527 km and 613 km to their winter ranges. In autumn and spring, birds used a wider range of habitats. In general, more points were in non-forest and non-forest-forest habitats in non-breeding months. Additionally, in 2001, only three of seven females bred, which may have affected our results.

Females breeding on the southern national forests used a variety of habitat types with frequency of use varying between seasons and years (Table 2). In summer 2000, females used mainly alpine fir (27.8%) and quaking aspen (56.9%). In 2001, however, birds used alpine fir (13.3%), pinyon-juniper (10.5%), quaking aspen (21.6%) and non-forested (11.1%) habitats. Only one-half of the females studied in summer 2001 bred, which may have affected our results. In autumn, females used similar habitat

TABLE 1. PERCENT OF LOCATION ESTIMATES THAT OCCURRED BY HABITAT TYPE FOR FEMALE GOSHAWKS BREEDING IN THE NORTHERN NATIONAL FORESTS (ASHLEY, UINTA, AND WASATCH NATIONAL FORESTS), UTAH, BY YEAR AND SEASON FROM 2000–2001. NIGHT LOCATIONS WERE WEIGHTED PROPORTIONAL TO THEIR OCCURRENCE SO THAT EACH NIGHT'S ESTIMATES SUMMED TO ONE.

Habitat type	Summer 2000	Autumn 2000	Winter 2000	Spring 2001	Summer 2001	Autumn 2001	Winter 2001	Spring 2002
Alpine fir	0.2	0.1	0.2	-	-	-	-	4.8
Alpine-aspen	-	-	0.1	-	-	-	0.1	-
Douglas-fir	14.4	11.0	6.3	16.3	14.1	12.6	0.7	-
Douglas-fir-aspen	2.5	4.0	4.5	5.8	5.0	12.6	13.2	25.0
Engelmann spruce	-	-	-	-	-	-	-	-
Engelmann-lodgepole	8.2	9.4	10.1	16.5	20.6	4.7	7.0	7.1
Lodgepole pine	14.4	12.2	9.8	4.9	8.6	1.5	-	-
Lodgepole-aspen	25.2	14.2	15.4	6.4	12.7	23.1	18.2	7.1
Pinyon-juniper	0.4	3.6	15.4	3.0	5.9	2.9	20.6	-
Ponderosa pine	0.4	0.5	0.1	0.2	-	0.8	-	-
Quaking aspen	8.9	10.6	8.5	5.1	14.1	10.9	19.8	25.0
White fir	5.0	6.5	6.5	5.1	-	-	-	-
Conifer	0.4	-	0.3	0.6	1.3	3.1	0.2	4.8
Conifer-aspen	9.7	8.6	5.9	8.0	7.9	6.7	2.4	-
Non-forest	4.1	7.2	8.0	16.1	5.1	8.8	6.9	14.3
Non-forest-forest	6.4	12.1	8.9	11.8	9.7	12.0	10.3	11.9
N locations	278	367	400	177	330	191	145	42
N individuals	11	11	8	7	8	7	4	3

TABLE 2. PERCENT OF LOCATION ESTIMATES THAT OCCURRED BY HABITAT TYPE FOR FEMALE GOSHAWKS BREEDING IN THE SOUTHERN NATIONAL FORESTS (DIXIE, FISHLAKE, AND MANTI LASAL NATIONAL FORESTS), UTAH, BY YEAR AND SEASON FROM 2000–2001. NIGHT LOCATIONS WERE WEIGHTED PROPORTIONAL TO THEIR OCCURRENCE SO THAT EACH NIGHT'S ESTIMATES SUMMED TO ONE.

Habitat type	Summer 2000	Autumn 2000	Winter 2000	Spring 2001	Summer 2001	Autumn 2001	Winter 2001	Spring 2002
Alpine fir	27.8	9.9	2.6	12.3	13.3	28.5	25.3	2.3
Alpine-aspen	6.9	1.6	2.0	3.6	4.1	4.4	4.7	-
Douglas-fir	-	1.5	1.2	3.1	1.6	2.1	-	-
Douglas-fir-aspen	2.8	0.5	1.3	0.7	-	-	-	-
Engelmann spruce	-	4.3	1.1	6.2	6.8	5.1	-	8.0
Engelmann-lodgepole	-	-	-	-	0.2	-	-	-
Lodgepole pine	-	-	-	-	-	-	-	-
Lodgepole-aspen	-	-	-	-	-	-	-	-
Pinyon-juniper	2.8	19.2	46.1	25.6	10.5	10.2	17.7	-
Ponderosa pine	-	12.2	5.3	3.8	6.6	5.4	13.2	47.7
Quaking aspen	56.9	12.2	12.1	12.1	21.6	11.8	-	-
White fir	-	8.5	8.8	4.7	6.9	7.9	0.5	2.3
Conifer	2.8	9.3	3.6	3.4	6.5	6.7	4.3	30.7
Conifer-aspen	-	0.3	1.7	0.4	2.5	1.3	0.9	2.3
Non-forest	-	9.4	7.3	11.4	11.1	6.3	17.5	4.5
Non-forest-forest	-	11.1	7.7	12.5	8.1	10.8	15.8	2.2
N locations	36	361	355	222	368	319	108	44
N individuals	3	12	9	7	11	12	7	2

types between years with an increase in the percent of points occurring in alpine fir (9.9% in 2000 to 28.5% in 2001; Table 2). In winter 2000, birds used mainly pinyon-juniper (46.1%) and quaking aspen (12.1%). Conversely, in winter 2001, females used a wider range of habitat types; alpine fir (25.3%), pinyon-juniper (17.7%), ponderosa pine (13.2%), non-forest (17.5%), and non-forest-forest (15.8%) habitat types. In spring 2000, birds used a wider range of habitats with pinyon-juniper (25.6%), quaking aspen (12.1%) and non-forest-forest (12.5%) habitats having the highest frequency of use, whereas, in spring 2001 goshawks used ponderosa pine (47.7%) and conifer (30.7%) habitats almost exclusively. In general, a higher percentage of locations were in pinyon-juniper, non-forest, and non-forest-forest habitat types in the non-breeding period.

Though we received data for approximately 1 yr from most of our transmitters, four transmitters continued to send data for 2 yr. From the northern national forests, Ashley 1 was migratory and wintered in the same location each year using mainly Douglas-fir and quaking aspen habitat (Sonsthagen 2002). We had three birds with 2 yr of data from the southern forests (Fishlake 2, Manti 3, and Manti 4; Sonsthagen 2002). Fishlake 2 wintered in the same area each year and also used pinyon-juniper habitat almost exclusively with frequencies ranging between 83.3–92.9%. Manti 3 and Manti 4 did not winter in the same area in 2001 as they did in 2000, but both used pinyon-juniper habitat almost exclusively (70.6–100%) each winter. Manti 4 migrated 156 km in 2001 to Colorado National Monument, her winter range was composed of pinyon-juniper with corridors of sagebrush (J. Underwood, pers. comm.). No vegetation layers are available for Colorado, so we were unable to determine the percentage of points in each habitat type. Habitats within each use area, as determined by kernel home range 95% polygons, did not differ from those described above for location estimates in a given season and year.

We detected significant differences in habitat use among seasons (Table 3). Logistic regression indicated significant differences in the number of locations among seasons in conifer, deciduous, non-forest, pinyon-juniper, conifer-deciduous, and non-forest-pinyon-juniper for the 2000 habitat data after accounting for individuals and breeding locality. Significant differences in the number of locations that occurred in conifer habitat were detected among all seasons except autumn–winter, where summer had highest number of estimates in conifer and spring the lowest. Of location estimates in deciduous habitat, significant differences occurred between spring-summer, spring-autumn, and spring-winter. We found lower numbers of location estimates in spring in deciduous habitats than in all other months. Non-forested locations differed significantly among all seasons except summer-autumn. Summer had the highest number of estimates and winter the lowest. Pinyon-juniper locations differed significantly among all seasons except spring-winter, where spring had the highest number and summer the lowest number of locations. Significant differences in the number of locations

TABLE 3. PAIRWISE SEASON COMPARISON AMONG HABITAT TYPES FOR DATA COLLECTED IN SUMMER 2000 TO SPRING 2001 IRRESPECTIVE OF NATIONAL FOREST USING A LOGISTIC REGRESSION ($\alpha = 0.05$) WITH SLOPES FOR EACH SEASONAL COMPARISON.

Pairwise season comparison	Conifer slope	Deciduous slope	Pinyon-juniper slope	Non-forest slope	Conifer/ deciduous slope	Conifer/ pinyon-juniper slope	Conifer/ Non-forest slope	Deciduous/ pinyon-juniper slope	Deciduous/ Non-forest slope	pinyon-juniper / Non-forest slope
Spring-summer	-1.0[a]	-0.6[a]	2.6[a]	-1.1[a]	0.2	0.4	0.5	-18.7	1.0	-0.2
Spring-autumn	-0.5[a]	-0.4[a]	1.7[a]	-0.9[a]	0.4[a]	-0.2	0.2	-19.9	0.4	-1.3[a]
Spring-winter	-0.4[a]	-0.6[a]	0.2	0.7[a]	-0.1	18.8	27.4	-4.1	9.7	-1.7[a]
Summer-autumn	0.5[a]	0.1	-0.9[a]	0.2[a]	0.2	-0.6	-0.3	-1.2	-0.6	-1.1[a]
Summer-winter	0.6[a]	-0.1	-2.4[a]	1.8[a]	-0.3	18.4	27.0	14.6	8.7	-1.5[a]
Autumn-winter	0.1	-0.2	-1.5[a]	1.6	-0.5[a]	19.0	27.2	15.8	9.3	-0.4

[a] Significant slopes ($\alpha = 0.05$).

that occurred in conifer-deciduous habitat were among spring-autumn and autumn-winter. Spring had more estimates than autumn and autumn less than winter. Of the locations in non-forest-pinyon-juniper, significant differences occurred among all seasons except spring–summer and autumn-winter. Autumn and winter had more locations than spring and summer.

Individuals were observed at elevations ranging from 1,525–3,505 m. Elevation ranges used by Northern Goshawks varied with locality, but two general trends existed (Tables 4, 5). Birds from the northern forests remained at relatively the same elevation range throughout the year (Table 4). Birds from the southern forests used a wide range of elevations in autumn and spring and dropped to lower elevations in winter (Table 5). Birds residing on the same forest did not exhibit the same trends each year, which may be attributed to movement type (migratory versus resident) exhibited by individuals. In general, migratory individuals moved to lower elevations and residents remained at elevations similar to their breeding territory. We found a significant difference (P = 0.044) among elevations that individuals occurred at and season in the 2000 data, after accounting for the region in which the birds were located. Elevations used in summer were higher than in winter.

DISCUSSION

These habitat data provide information on the common habitat types used throughout the year. Two general trends characterized habitat types and elevations exploited by goshawks. Northern Goshawks that migrated or dispersed from their nest sites used pinyon-juniper and non-forest habitat types and lower elevation ranges than representative of their breeding site. In contrast, individuals that remained residents used habitats common to their breeding territory and remained at relatively the same elevation throughout the year. Not all individuals, however, displayed these trends. Females breeding on the Ashley National Forest used habitats similar to their breeding sites across all movement types. One female on the Manti LaSal National Forest (Manti 4, 2000) used pinyon-juniper habitat and lower elevations while remaining near her nest site. Additionally, we had four birds (Ashley 1, Fishlake 2, Manti 3, and Manti 4) with 2 yr of data. Although, not all of these individuals wintered in the same area each year, they used the same habitats as the previous winter.

We are aware of potential limitations in accurately estimating satellite telemetry locations (Britten et al. 1999, Craighead and Smith 2003) and do not suggest that these values presented here are absolute. Rather, we present these data heuristically to illustrate

TABLE 4. PERCENT OF LOCATION ESTIMATES THAT OCCURRED BY ELEVATION FOR FEMALE GOSHAWKS BREEDING IN THE NORTHERN NATIONAL FORESTS (ASHLEY, UINTA, AND WASATCH NATIONAL FORESTS), UTAH, BY YEAR AND SEASON FROM 2000–2001. NIGHT LOCATIONS WERE WEIGHTED PROPORTIONAL TO THEIR OCCURRENCE SO THAT EACH NIGHT'S ESTIMATES SUMMED TO ONE.

Elevation (meters)	Summer 2000	Autumn 2000	Winter 2000	Spring 2001	Summer 2001	Autumn 2001	Winter 2001	Spring 2002
1,525	-	0.1	-	-	-	0.9	4.2	-
1,675	0.4	1.2	0.6	-	-	1.9	3.6	-
1,830	0.2	2.7	15.4	-	-	2.6	13.2	-
1,980	0.9	3.1	4.0	5.6	0.4	0.3	3.7	2.2
2,135	4.3	4.3	5.4	7.7	1.0	2.1	2.1	13.0
2,285	7.3	4.7	8.2	11.5	2.9	8.6	7.3	13.0
2,440	13.1	15.0	19.8	34.9	20.1	14.7	5.8	10.9
2,590	31.2	34.5	24.9	27.7	37.9	21.2	17.4	38.0
2,745	21.3	25.2	16.9	10.5	21.8	25.5	26.1	14.1
2,895	18.3	7.9	4.0	0.2	11.1	15.7	9.8	4.3
3,050	2.6	1.3	0.7	1.2	4.5	4.8	6.6	4.3
3,200	0.3	0.2	0.2	0.7	0.3	0.9	0.2	-
3,355	-	-	-	-	-	0.6	-	-
3,505	-	-	-	-	-	-	-	-
3,660	-	-	-	-	-	-	-	-
3,810	-	-	-	-	-	-	-	-
3,965	-	-	-	-	-	-	-	-
N estimates	278	373	402	162	313	164	143	46
N individuals	11	11	8	7	8	7	4	3

TABLE 5. PERCENT OF LOCATION ESTIMATES THAT OCCURRED BY ELEVATION FOR FEMALE GOSHAWKS BREEDING IN THE SOUTHERN NATIONAL FORESTS (DIXIE, FISHLAKE, AND MANIT LASAL NATIONAL FOREST), UTAH, BY YEAR AND SEASON FROM 2000–2001. NIGHT LOCATIONS WERE WEIGHTED PROPORTIONAL TO THEIR OCCURRENCE SO THAT EACH NIGHT'S ESTIMATES SUMMED TO ONE.

Elevation (meters)	Summer 2000	Autumn 2000	Winter 2000	Spring 2001	Summer 2001	Autumn 2001	Winter 2001	Spring 2002
1,525	-	-	-	-	-	0.4	4.8	-
1,675	-	5.8	7.8	10.1	3.5	2.8	18.0	2.2
1,830	-	11.1	21.5	8.9	10.6	9.4	22.8	-
1,980	2.6	10.4	26.1	11.0	7.6	10.4	10.2	11.4
2,135	2.6	10.7	12.6	15.7	3.7	8.8	10.7	15.9
2,285	5.1	10.5	6.0	3.8	7.0	8.3	7.3	20.5
2,440	3.1	10.4	3.4	6.4	10.5	14.6	3.4	18.2
2,590	9.0	15.7	2.6	8.8	15.2	14.0	3.5	29.5
2,745	32.9	7.1	5.4	5.4	12.3	14.8	12.2	-
2,895	16.2	9.8	5.5	7.9	15.8	8.7	4.3	2.3
3,050	11.1	5.4	5.6	15.1	8.6	5.6	2.7	-
3,200	14.1	1.8	2.2	4.3	3.2	1.6	-	-
3,355	2.6	0.8	0.5	1.7	0.7	0.6	-	-
3,505	2.6	0.3	0.4	0.9	1.1	0.1	-	-
3,660	-	-	0.3	-	-	-	-	-
3,810	-	-	0.2	-	-	-	-	-
3,965	-	-	-	-	-	-	-	-
N estimates	39	359	358	219	351	319	110	44
N individuals	3	12	9	7	11	12	7	2

habitat use of goshawks on an annual basis. While researchers have expressed concern about the error estimates we used in this study, we used current published error distances for the location estimates provided by Argos (McGrady et al. 2002). In addition, habitats within each use area did not differ from those described for location estimates. Underwood et al. (*this volume*) increased buffers (1 and 3 km) around location estimates and did not detect any biological difference in their results. Finally, in several instances we used location estimates to locate live birds or retrieve transmitters from birds that had died. In these cases we were able to locate birds and transmitters within 500 m of where the location estimates placed the transmitters. Therefore, the error estimates that we used in this study do not appear to alter the biological or interpretive significance of our findings.

We hypothesize that prey availability may be a driving factor in Northern Goshawks using an area. Availability of prey depends on prey abundance, but also habitat characteristics that influence accessibility of prey (Widén 1994). In Sweden and Northern Finland, goshawks in boreal forests hunted in mature forests (Widén 1987, Tornberg and Colpaert 2001). Conversely, goshawks studied in the farmland-forest mosaics of Sweden appeared to favor foraging on forest-edge zones (Kenward 1982). In both landscapes, suitable prey abundances were greater

in areas exploited by goshawks. Additionally, large tracts of land may not be used by raptors because of the lack of perch availability. Widén (1994) suggested perch availability is the limiting factor for the exploitation of clearcuts by pause-travel-foraging raptors, like Northern Goshawks. Habitat fragmentation, therefore, may affect the ability of individuals to use an area rather than reduce habitat quality for potential prey.

Finally, winter home ranges of individuals that migrated were larger than residents and main habitat utilized by migratory individuals was pinyon-juniper (Sonsthagen 2002). Because home-range size in accipiters is inversely proportional to prey abundance (Kenward 1982, Newton 1986), this outcome indicates that individuals wintering in pinyon-juniper and non-forest habitats are moving to areas with lower prey abundance. Winter density and territoriality of raptors vary according to prey availability (Craighead and Craighead 1956, Cavé 1968). Therefore, females may be moving to reduce local competition or females that are more aggressive secured territories forcing birds to migrate to areas with lower prey availability.

The nature of our data clearly defined wintering habitat currently used by Northern Goshawks and highlighted two completely different landscapes, one similar to that used during breeding and the other pinyon-juniper habitat. Because of the spatial scale of our data, we could not further address the finer points of the habitats nor did it allow us to speculate on the effects that increased habitat fragmentation might have on Northern Goshawks. Additionally, effects of fragmentation on population numbers are difficult to assess because effects of habitat loss depend on the quality of the area lost (Newton 1998). In migrant populations, breeding and non-breeding habitat loss may have different effects on population levels depending on the strength of density-dependence in the two areas (Sutherland 1996, Newton 1998). The strength of density-dependence in winter ranges is measured by the rate of increased mortality with increased population size or habitat loss, whereas, the strength of breeding area density-dependence is measured by the rate of decreased reproduction in relation to increased population size or habitat loss. Therefore, habitat loss will have a larger impact on population size in the range with the larger slope (Newton 1998). Also, size of the remaining patches may influence bird density (Newton 1998). This is especially important because goshawks normally exist at a low density (3.6–10.7 pairs/100 km^2; Squires and Reynolds 1997). So the question of habitat loss or fragmentation becomes circular reasoning because while small patches may facilitate prey capture, prey are usually present at lower densities (Tornberg and Colpaert 2001) requiring greater risk to the goshawk in trying to fulfill nutritional needs.

ACKNOWLEDGMENTS

Funding for this project was provided by the USDA Forest Service, Intermountain Region and Brigham Young University. We thank all of the Forest Service biologists and technicians working on the Northern Goshawk project in Utah for their time and energy, especially; S. Blatt, S. Dewey, K. Hartman, D. Jauregui, J. Jewks, M. Lee, L. Parry, K. Paulin, R. Player, K. Rasumussen, B. Smith, and C. Staab and also the field technicians, S. Gericke and I. Mariotto. T. Maechtle, North Star Science and Technology, showed us how to attach satellite telemetry units and provided his expertise. We thank K. Peine and D. Eggett, Brigham Young University, for their help in analyzing the satellite telemetry habitat data. We would also like to thank T. Bowyer, K. Crandall, S. Peck, and R. Rader for their comments on earlier drafts of this manuscript.

Studies in Avian Biology No. 31:260–273

A REVIEW AND EVALUATION OF FACTORS LIMITING NORTHERN GOSHAWK POPULATIONS

RICHARD T. REYNOLDS, J. DAVID WIENS, AND SUSAN R. SALAFSKY

Abstract. Northern Goshawk (*Accipiter gentilis*) populations are suspected of declining due to forest-management treatments that alter the range of environmental conditions beneficial to their reproduction and survival. To develop effective goshawk conservation strategies, information on intrinsic and extrinsic factors that influence goshawk fitness is required. We reviewed the literature for information on factors that commonly limit avian populations, and were, therefore, potentially limiting goshawk populations. We evaluated the relative importance of these factors, and discussed how and at what scale these factors operate to constrain goshawk populations. Food availability and forest structure appeared to be the most ubiquitous factors limiting goshawks, but the degree to which these factors affected goshawks appeared to depend on interactions with other limiting factors such as weather, predation, competition, and disease, each of which operates at multiple spatial and temporal scales. Goshawks occur primarily in forests and woodlands, but the degree to which they are limited by forest composition and structure is difficult to determine because goshawks, at both the individual and population levels, use a wide variety of structural conditions while foraging. Much of the diversity in habitats used by hunting goshawks appears to result from their entry into the diverse habitats of their prey. Our review suggested that the availability of suitable nest sites influences goshawk site occupancy and reproduction, but that forest structural conditions beyond nest sites have a larger effect on goshawk reproduction and survival by affecting both the abundance and accessibility of their prey. This highlights the importance of conservation strategies that address a range of ecosystem needs by integrating the diverse habitat requirements of the goshawk prey community with the forest structural components of goshawk nest sites and foraging areas.

Key Words: *Accipiter gentilis*, competition, disease, food abundance and availability, forest composition and structure, Northern Goshawk, population limitation, predation, weather.

REVISIÓN Y EVALUACIÓN DE LOS FACTORES QUE LIMITAN A LAS POBLACIONES DE GAVILÁN AZOR

Resumen. Se sospecha que las poblaciones del Gavilán Azor (*Accipiter gentilis*) están disminuyendo debido a los tratamientos de manejo forestal, los cuales alteran el rango de las condiciones ambientales benéficas para su reproducción y sobrevivencia. Para desarrollar estrategias de conservación efectivas del gavilán, se requiere información de factores intrínsecos y extrínsecos los cuales influencien la buena salud del gavilán. Revisamos la literatura para informarnos de los factores que comúnmente limitan a las poblaciones de aves, y fueron por consiguiente, potencialmente limitantes poblaciones de gavilán. Evaluamos la importancia relativa de estos factores y discutimos cómo y a qué escala estos factores operan para limitar las poblaciones de gavilán. La disponibilidad de alimento y la estructura del bosque parecen ser los factores más omnipresentes que limitan al gavilán, pero el grado en el que dichos factores afectaron a las poblaciones de gavilán, también parece depender de sus interacciones con otros factores, tales como el clima, depredación, competencia y enfermedades, las cuales operan cada una a múltiples escalas espaciales y temporales. Mientras los gavilanes aparecen principalmente en bosques y tierras forestales, el grado en el cual ellos están limitados a la composición y a la estructura del bosque es equívoco, ya que los gavilanes, tanto a nivel individual como a nivel de población, utilizan una amplia variedad de condiciones estructurales mientras forrajean, mucho de lo cual parece estar relacionado a la diversidad de los hábitats ocupados por sus presas. Nuestra revisión sugirió que la disponibilidad de sitios de nidos adecuadamente boscosos, influye fuertemente el sitio de ocupación y de reproducción del gavilán, pero dichas condiciones estructurales del bosque, más allá del sitio del nido, quizás influencien más la reproducción y la sobrevivencia del gavilán, al afectar la abundancia y la accesibilidad de su presa. Esto resalta la importancia de las estrategias de conservación, las cuales dirijan un rango de necesidades del ecosistema, y que integren los requerimientos de la comunidad presa del gavilán, con los componentes estructurales del bosque de los sitios de los nidos del gavilán y los hábitats de forrajeo.

Many questions relevant to wildlife conservation involve factors that limit the distribution and abundance of a species. Such factors include biotic and abiotic features of an organism's environment that affect individual fitness and important population processes. While raptor populations are normally regulated by interactions between resource levels and density-dependent factors, human impacts such as disturbance, pollutants, and resource management may accentuate these factors and lead to reduced viability (Newton 1991). Goshawk populations in both North America (*Accipiter gentilis atricapillus*) and in Eurasia (*A. g. gentilis*) are thought to be declining due to changes in forest conditions caused by management activities, especially tree harvests (Reynolds et al. 1982, Kenward and Widén 1989, Crocker-Bedford 1990, Kennedy 1997, Kennedy 2003). As a result, the status of goshawk populations in North America has been the object of considerable conservation interest (Reynolds et al. 1992, Kennedy 1997, Crocker-Bedford 1998, DeStefano 1998, Kennedy 1998, Smallwood 1998, Andersen et al. 2004) and litigation (Silver et al. 1991, Martin 1998, Peck 2000). Although a variety of factors may contribute to the stability of goshawk populations, a negative cause-effect linkage is often implied between forest management (e.g., loss of old forests) and goshawk viability.

Stability in raptor numbers is often attributed to density-dependent factors, such as food and breeding sites, that affect populations through a negative feedback process between population size and growth rates arising from increased competition for critical resources. Instability in raptor numbers is often attributed to density-independent factors, such as weather and habitat disturbance, that alter the range of environmental conditions required for survival and reproduction (Newton 1991). Disturbance, whether natural or human-induced, can also affect raptor populations by changing the abundance and availability of resources which in turn, may influence other ecological relationships such as competition, predation, or disease. Developing effective conservation strategies requires an understanding of the life history of goshawks as well as the relative importance of factors that limit their populations.

We reviewed the literature for information on factors limiting goshawk populations, and evaluated the evidence for how and at what scale these factors acted on goshawk vital rates. We define a factor as limiting if changes in the factor result in a new probability distribution of population densities due to its affect on survival or reproduction (Williams et al. 2002). Our review focused on factors that commonly limit avian populations, and therefore potentially limit goshawk populations. These factors included food, vegetation composition and structure, predators, competitors, disease, and weather. We view these factors as important components of goshawk habitat, i.e., the collection of biotic and abiotic factors that allow occupancy by goshawks (Hall et al. 1997, Andersen et al. 2004). Our literature review was mostly limited to factors affecting goshawk reproduction and survival. This was because little information exists on goshawk emigration and immigration, two processes that can affect goshawk population dynamics. We did not view this lack of information fatal to our objective because changes in reproduction and survival often have the greatest impact on population dynamics in raptors, and because individuals must be born and survive to emigrate (Noon and Biles 1990, Boyce 1994, Sæther and Bakke 2000). Our review focused on goshawks in North America, but because Eurasian goshawks have similar habitat requirements, hunting techniques, and prey species, we included information on Eurasian goshawk ecology and demographics where pertinent.

POTENTIAL LIMITING FACTORS

Territoriality and Intraspecific Competition

Territoriality is an intrinsic mechanism that reduces intraspecific competition for resources and operates to adjust breeding densities to local resource abundance (Newton 1979a). Territoriality constrains breeding densities by setting an upper limit to the number of breeding individuals that can occupy a habitat patch (Newton 1991). Because territorial interactions occur within the defended part of a home range, territoriality operates to limit goshawks at a scale between the nest area and the home range (Fig. 1). However, the expression of territoriality can affect the numbers of breeding goshawks at spatial scales up to the population level. For example, competition for a limited number of breeding sites can result in a surplus of non-territorial hawks. If a local breeding area is saturated with territorial hawks, individuals without territories are forced into non-breeding status where they must either wait for a breeding vacancy or emigrate. Thus, non-territorial individuals can stabilize goshawk populations by either replacing mortalities on local territories or emigrating to other populations. Where strong competition occurs for territories and non-breeders are abundant, newly recruited individuals are often of an advanced age. Hence, age at first breeding has

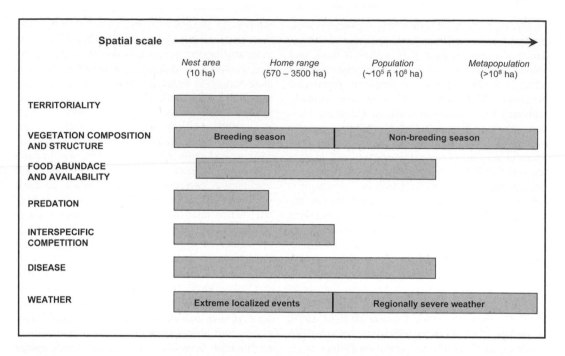

FIGURE 1. Range of spatial scales at which various physical and biotic factors usually operate to limit Northern Goshawk reproduction and survival. Note that the effects of each factor, summed over individuals and pairs of goshawk, can affect their density, reproduction, and survival at the population or even metapopulation levels. Temporal scales at which these factors may operate are not shown.

been proposed as an indicator of population stability (Kenward et al. 1999, Balbontín et al. 2003).

A regular spacing of breeding territories (Reynolds et al. 1994, Woodbridge and Detrich 1994, Reynolds et al. 2005; Reynolds and Joy, *this volume*), stability in territory distribution over time (Reynolds et al. 2005), a surplus of non-breeders (Widén 1985b, Hunt 1997), and a delayed age at first breeding (Wiens and Reynolds 2005) suggest that goshawk breeding density can be limited by territoriality. For example, in Arizona, a high density of regularly spaced goshawk territories (8.6/100 km²), a temporally constant survival rate of breeding adults (75%), a high territory fidelity rate (94%), and delayed age at first breeding ($\bar{x}$ = 4.2 yr), suggested a high level of competition for a limited number of breeding sites (Reynolds et al. 1994, Reich et al. 2004, Reynolds et al. 2004, Wiens et al. 2006b; Reynolds and Joy, *this volume*). However, while territoriality may set upper limits to the number of breeding goshawks, other factors may determine whether territorial pairs actually breed. Moreover, not all forests are likely to have equal carrying capacities of breeders because the size of goshawk territories within and among landscapes may vary in

relation to the demographic structure of populations, variation in local forest conditions, or spatial and temporal variations in resource abundance.

VEGETATION COMPOSITION AND STRUCTURE IN THE BREEDING SEASON

Our review showed that the composition and structure of vegetation used by goshawks during the breeding and non-breeding seasons often differed. Therefore, we reviewed the literature for vegetation effects on goshawk vital rates during the breeding as well as the non-breeding seasons. During breeding, goshawk movements are energetically limited to a finite space around their nest (Krebs et al. 1987); the used space defines the breeding home range. A restricted use of space by breeding goshawk suggests that vegetation composition and structure limits goshawk reproduction and survival at the home range scale (Fig. 1). Estimated sizes of goshawk breeding season home ranges varied from 570–10,823 ha, depending on gender, landscape configuration and availability of forests, and data collection and estimation method (Titus et al. 1994, Squires and Reynolds 1997, Boal et al. 2003).

Goshawks nest in most of the forests and woodlands that occur within their geographic breeding range. The principal forest types occupied by goshawks in North America include coniferous forests, deciduous forests, and mixed coniferous-deciduous forests (Marshall 1957, McGowan 1975, Reynolds et al. 1982, Speiser and Bosakowski 1987, Doyle and Smith 1994, Lang 1994, Reynolds et al. 1994, Woodbridge and Detrich 1994, Beier and Drennan 1997, Squires and Reynolds 1997, Daw and DeStefano 2001). The horizontal and vertical structure of these forests and woodlands vary widely with some types lacking tall trees or continuous canopies (Franklin and Dyrness 1973, Eyre 1980, Barbour and Billings 1988). Tall trees and continuous canopies are characteristics often thought to be necessary for successful goshawk breeding. However, in far northern regions where trees are not available, goshawks have been known to nest on rocks or the ground (Dement'ev et al. 1966, Wattel 1973). Studies of vegetation used by breeding North American goshawks showed that mature and old forests with relatively closed canopies are used most often (Austin 1993, Bright-Smith and Mannan 1994, Hargis et al. 1994, Beier and Drennen1997, Drennen and Beier 2003), but that mid-aged and younger forests (Fischer 1986, Austin 1993, Bright-Smith and Mannan 1994, Hargis et al. 1994), forests adjacent to meadows (Hargis et al. 1994), and open shrub or tundra areas containing scattered patches of trees were also used (Bent 1938, White et al. 1965, Swem and Adams 1992, Younk and Bechard 1994a). Nonetheless, annually consistent higher breeding densities in tall, canopied forests suggest that contiguous forests composed of tall trees provide better habitat for goshawks (Reynolds and Meslow 1984, DeStefano et al. 1994a, Woodbridge and Detrich 1994, Reynolds et al. 1994; Reynolds and Joy, *this volume*; but see Younk and Bechard 1994a, b).

Goshawks typically place their nests in forest patches comprised of large trees. Because nest areas are a small fraction of the home range, they typically have a lower diversity of vegetation types and seral stages then the remainder of the home range, much of which used for hunting (Reynolds et al. 1992, Hargis et al. 1994, McGrath et al. 2003). We therefore partitioned our assessment of breeding season vegetation as a goshawk limiting factor into the nest and foraging areas (Reynolds et al. 1992). These two areas are consistent with the spatial scales used in most investigations of goshawk habitat (Andersen et al. 2004).

Nest Area

Availability of nest sites often limits bird populations as shown by increases in their populations after the placement of artificial nests in areas that otherwise appeared suitable (Cavé 1968, Reese 1970, Rhodes 1972, Hammerstrom and Hammerstrom 1973, Newton and Marquiss 1983, Village 1983, Newton 1991). Goshawk nest habitat has been variously partitioned into the nest site, habitat immediately surrounding the nest (Reynolds et al. 1982, Squires and Reynolds 1997), the nest area, a 8–10 ha area surrounding a nest that includes the hawk's roosts and prey plucking sites (Newton 1979a, Reynolds et al. 1992), and the nest stand, and the stand of trees homogenous in vegetation composition and structure that contains a nest (Reynolds et al. 1982, Woodbridge and Detrich 1994). The size of nest stands can be highly variable and their frequency of use by breeding goshawks has been shown to increase with nest stand size. In California, where nest-stand boundaries were defined by edges of forest-management treatments, lava flows, and meadows, nests in small forest stands (<20 ha) were only occasionally occupied, whereas nests in larger stands (>60 ha; maximum = 115 ha) were occupied more often (Woodbridge and Detrich 1994). However, while we believe that it is likely that a minimum forest patch size for sustaining goshawk nesting exists, we question whether the relationship identified by Woodbridge and Detrich (1994) might simply reflect the fact that most alternate nests of goshawks tend to be near the center of their territories (Reynolds et al. 2005; Reynolds and Joy, *this volume*) and that, as stand size increases, the alternate nests are included within the stand. Because of the large reported variability in sizes of nest stands and because a nest site does not encompass a pair's roosts and prey handling areas, we believe that the nest area is the best scale at which to describe goshawk nest habitat.

While the variety of forest types occupied by goshawks is suggestive of their adaptability to diverse forest compositions, goshawks demonstrate considerable specificity in choice of vegetation structure in nest areas. Nest area vegetation structure consistently includes a relatively high density of mature or old trees, high canopy cover, and an open understory (Squires and Reynolds 1997). High tree density and canopy closure within a nest area has been associated with increased territory occupancy and nesting rates (Keane 1999, Finn et al. 2002b). Because of the consistency of these nest area vegetation structures, and because tree species composition is so highly variable, structure appears to be more important than species composition in goshawk choice of nest areas (Erickson 1987, Reynolds et al. 1992, Rissler 1995).

Uniformity in vegetation structure among goshawk nest areas is also evident in comparisons of nest area vegetation to vegetation within the home range. Hargis et al. (1994), Daw 1997) and McGrath et al. (2003) found that the diversity of vegetation characteristics (e.g., forest age classes, canopy closures, basal areas, and openings) surrounding goshawk nests increased with distance from nests. Not surprisingly, difference between nest area and home range vegetation is greatest where goshawks nest in small stands of trees in non-forested landscapes (Bond 1940, White et al. 1965, Dement'ev et al. 1966, Swem and Adams 1992; Younk and Bechard 1994a, b).

While nest areas with large trees and dense canopies appear to be preferred by goshawks, the extent to which they are required for successful nesting is uncertain because goshawks tolerate some reduction in these structural conditions. For example, Penteriani and Faivre (2001) and Penteriani et al. (2002b) reported continued use of nest areas by European goshawks when up to 30% of trees within 50 m of the nest tree were lost by windstorm damage or logging. Nonetheless, identifying the effects of nest area disturbance on goshawk occupancy can be confounded by: (1) individual goshawk variability in among-year fidelity to a nest (R. Reynolds, unpubl data), (2) the difficulty of determining whether the lack of suitable alternate nests constrained goshawk movement among nests, and (3) a potentially high natural (irrespective of disturbance) frequency of movement among alternate nests (55–76% of egg-laying goshawks annually moved to alternate nests in Arizona; Reynolds et al. 2005; Reynolds and Joy, *this volume*).

FORAGING AREA

Foraging habitat is where goshawks search, pursue, and capture prey. Our review showed that relatively little is known about how and which vegetation types and seral stages outside of nest areas are used by hunting goshawks (Schnell 1958). This limited understanding stems from the difficulty of observing goshawks due to their elusive behavior, the density of the forest vegetation they occupy, and their rapid movements through large home ranges resulting from their short-perch-short-flight hunting behavior (Kenward 1982, Widén 1985b). Because of these difficulties, most observations of goshawk behavior and movements comes from radio-telemetry stud-

ies. Nonetheless, the usefulness of radio telemetry for understanding goshawk behavior can be limited. First, numbers of goshawks included in most radio-telemetry studies were small, thereby limiting inferences to populations. Second, the limited range over which a transmitter's signal can be received (especially in forests and mountainous terrain) can result in a hawk being out of range during periods of a study, potentially biasing estimates of home range size, behavior, and vegetation use. Third, the elusiveness of goshawks often makes it necessary to triangulate using ≥2 observers or use radio signal strength to estimate a goshawk's location, potentially resulting in large location errors (Bright-Smith and Mannan 1994, Titus et al. 1994, Boal et al. 2003). Finally, because radio-tagged goshawks are seldom observed directly, their behavior is usually unknown (Bright-Smith and Mannan 1994). In spite of these shortcomings, radio telemetry remains the best tool to study the behavior and habitat use by goshawks.

As the number of telemetry studies increases, it is increasingly evident that within and among the geographically varied regions and forest types occupied by goshawks, the diversity of vegetation structural and seral stages used by individuals is strikingly broad. Vegetation types used by individuals ranged from young to old forests, from early seral to late-seral forests, from closed-canopied to open forests, woodlands, and shrub-steppe with highly fragmented tree patches, and from forest interiors to edges and openings. Nonetheless, when individual goshawks were pooled within studies (excluding studies in which goshawks hunted in shrub-steppe), typically a preference was observed for mature and old forests (Kenward 1982, Widén 1985b, Austin 1993, Bright-Smith and Mannan 1994, Hargis et al. 1994, Titus et al. 1996, Younk 1996, Beier and Drennan 1997, Good 1998, Lapinski 2000, Boal et al. 2000, Bloxton 2002, Stephens 2001, Drennan and Beier 2003). Goshawk use of such a broad diversity of vegetation structures shows a level of behavioral adaptability that suggests that if nest sites and foods were not limiting, goshawks could breed in most if not all forests and woodlands within their range. Where goshawks occur in more canopied forests their selection for mature and old forest age appears to be in accordance with the vegetation structure best suited to their morphology and hunting behavior and where many of their prey are more abundant (Reynolds et al. *this volume*).

A number of non-telemetry studies compared vegetation in plots of increasing radii from nests to determine if goshawks preferentially nested in landscapes with vegetation conditions different from those around random points, and whether different home range vegetation conditions affected goshawk breeding performance. Allison (1996), Daw and DeStefano (2001), Joy (2002), and McGrath et al. (2003) found that differences in vegetation in goshawk nest plots and random plots were greatest in plots with short radii (≤250 m), but the differences diminished with increasing distance from plot centers. These studies demonstrated the importance of older forests in goshawk nest areas, but that beyond nest areas forest composition and structure began to resemble random landscapes. Hall (1984), Joy (2002), and McGrath et al. (2003) found that landscapes surrounding goshawk nests had greater diversity and intermixture of different forest age-classes and vegetation types than landscapes around random points. In contrast, Finn et al. (2002a) reported that historical goshawk nest sites containing a higher proportion of late-seral forests in surrounding landscapes were occupied more often by breeding goshawks than historical nest sites with a lower proportion of late-seral forests in surrounding landscapes.

While these landscape studies implicitly or explicitly tested the hypothesis that mature and old forests are important to goshawk occupancy and reproduction, none determined whether or how goshawks actually used any of the vegetation types or seral stages within plots. While telemetry studies showed that goshawks preferentially used mature and old forests, many showed goshawks using young forests, edges and openings (Bright-Smith and Mannan 1994, Hargis et al. 1994, Good 1998). Use of vegetation types are also likely to shift seasonally and yearly due to changes in seasonal or annual food abundance among the types. As well, temporally changing parental requirements at nests may cause adults to expand their foraging areas (Hargis et al. 1994), which could change the availabilities, and therefore use, of vegetation types. Thus, non-telemetry landscape studies add little to our understanding of how, when, and why goshawks use habitat. A further potential limitation of studies of the relationship between landscape vegetation conditions and frequency of goshawk breeding (Finn et al. 2000) is that they require some level of confidence that the territories are or are not occupied by breeding goshawks. High confidence is difficult to attain, however, because goshawks do not lay eggs every year, and when they do, they more often than not move to an alternate nest. Correctly classifying territories as having breeders can be achieved only by conducting extensive searches for active nests over large areas and several years (Reynolds et al. 2005; Reynolds and Joy, *this volume*).

Much of the diversity of vegetation types and seral stages used by goshawks appears to stem from their entry into the diverse habitats of their prey. In Sweden and Norway, goshawks in boreal forests hunted in mature forests, the habitat of their main prey (tree squirrels; Widén 1989, Tornberg and Colpaert 2001). In farmland and forest mosaics in Sweden, goshawks favored forest edge, the habitat of their main prey there (rabbits and pheasants; Kenward 1977). In both areas, prey abundance was greater in the habitats used by goshawks. In Nevada, goshawks hunted in open shrub-steppe vegetation where their main prey, Belding's ground squirrel (*Spermophilis beldingi*), was abundant in openings (Younk and Bechard 1994a). Belding's ground squirrels were also important in Oregon (Reynolds and Meslow 1984, Daw and DeStefano 1994) where the goshawks likely entered meadows to hunt them. Another important prey in western North America is the golden-mantled ground squirrel (*Spermophilis lateralis*; Reynolds and Meslow 1984, Boal and Mannan 1994, Reynolds et al. 1994, Woodbridge and Detrich 1994). This ground squirrel occurs in open forests, meadows, and associated edges, where they were presumably hunted by goshawks. In Sweden, wintering goshawk habitat use (preferred mature forests, avoided younger forests and used agricultural lands, wetlands, and clearcuts proportional to the availability) was associated with higher prey density and vegetation features that influenced a goshawk's ability to successfully hunt (Widén 1989).

Evidence contrary to the supposition that goshawks select foraging habitat based on prey abundance comes from sites where radio-tagged goshawks were assumed but not directly observed to have been foraging, where they presumably killed prey based on changes in transmitter pulse rates, where goshawks were observed feeding, and where the remains of their prey were found. Beier and Drennan (1997) investigated the relative importance of vegetation structure versus prey abundance on goshawk choice of foraging habitat by comparing vegetation attributes and indices of prey abundance at locations where radio-tagged goshawks were assumed to have hunted to vegetation and prey abundance at randomly located plots. They argued that forest structure was more important than prey abundance because goshawk hunting plots had more large trees with higher canopy closure than random plots and there was no significant differences in prey indices at foraging sites and random plots (Beier and Drennan 1997). Good (1998) also characterized forest structure and relative prey abundance at sites where radio-tagged goshawks killed prey. He suggested that, on average, forest structure had a greater influence on the repeated use of kill sites than prey abundance because goshawks returned more often to kill sites with greater densities of large trees and less shrub cover than to kill sites with higher prey abundances (Good 1998). We believe, however, that inferences about a goshawk's choice of hunting habitat based on foraging or kill sites are equivocal for several reasons. First, we find that judging whether or not goshawks were hunting based on telemetry signals, or even when directly observed, to be problematic. Second, we question the validity of the assumption that kill sites (as judged by prey remains or observations of feeding goshawks) are necessarily the same sites where the prey was first detected by goshawks. This assumption requires that the bird and mammal prey did not attempt to escape and thereby leave the detection site before being captured. Furthermore, goshawks often move their prey to denser hiding cover while feeding, and, during the breeding season when they deliver food to nests, they sometimes stop to pluck their prey on the way (R. Reynolds, pers. obs.). Misidentifying plucking or feeding sites as kill sites in these situations could introduce a systematic bias towards denser vegetation. Finally, studies using indices of prey abundance fail to account for variation in bird and mammal detection probabilities due to among-plot differences in vegetation structure. Failure to account for variable detection probabilities can lead to unreliable estimates of animal abundance (Buckland et al. 2001).

Reynolds et al. (1992) developed management recommendations for forests in the southwestern US by combining existing information on (1) the structural components of goshawk nest areas with (2) vegetation structures thought suited for goshawk foraging given their morphology and behavior with (3) the structural and seral stages of vegetation that provides the habitats of the community of goshawk prey species (Reynolds et al., *this volume*). Short wings, long tail, and a short-perch, short-flight hunting tactic (Kenward 1982, Widén 1985a) are morphological and behavioral adaptations of goshawks for hunting in forests where prey searching fields are obscured by tall and dense vegetation. Because many prey species occur in the lower vegetation column, goshawk prey searching is focused toward the ground and lower forest layers (Reynolds and Meslow 1984). The size of the search field around a hunting perch depends on the height and density of surrounding trees, density and composition of understory vegetation, prey location, and goshawk perch height (Janes 1985a, b). Presumably, goshawks change their perching time, height, and location in accordance with these structural characteristics to increase encounters with prey (Schipper et al. 1975, Baker and Brooks 1981, Bechard 1982). In the Southwest, older forest with tall trees and lifted crowns were recommended because goshawks need flight space below the forest canopy and open understories enhance the detection and capture of prey (Reynolds et al. 1992). The idealized home range also contained a diversity of vegetation types and seral stages, including small openings, to provide the habitats of the goshawk's diverse suite of prey (Reynolds et al. 1992).

VEGETATION COMPOSITION AND STRUCTURE IN THE NON-BREEDING SEASON

Goshawks are typically year-round residents, especially during winters when prey is abundant (Speiser and Bosakowski 1991, Doyle and Smith 1994, Boal et al. 2003). However, some adult goshawks regularly winter outside of their breeding areas (Squires and Ruggiero 1995, Squires and Reynolds 1997). Squires and Reynolds (1997) reported that adult goshawks in Wyoming wintered as far as 346 km from their nests, and Wiens et al. (2006b) reported that the majority of juvenile goshawks left their conifer forest habitat for low elevation woodlands and shrub-steppe shortly after dispersing from their natal area, and that some of these made movements as far as 442 km in their first fall. Estimates of home-range size for goshawks that stay on or close to their breeding home range during the non-breeding season (October–February) are typically much more variable (1,000–8,000 ha) than breeding home ranges (Boal et al. 2003; Sonsthagen et al., *this volume*; Underwood et al., *this volume*). Winter expansion of space use suggests that the vegetation component of goshawk habitat during the non-breeding season may operate to affect goshawk survival at larger spatial scales then during breeding (Fig. 1). In North America, the vegetation component of goshawk winter habitats has been studied far less than their breeding habitats, making it difficult to assess the importance of vegetation as a factor limiting goshawks during the non-breeding season. Wiens et al. (2006b) reported increased mortality of radio-marked juvenile goshawks following dispersal from their natal territories and movement into pinyon-juniper woodlands and shrub-steppe. Squires and Ruggiero (1995) reported predation by eagles on adult goshawks that had also moved into shrub-steppe. These studies suggest that movements to vegetation types that provide little cover increases mortality, particularly of inexperienced juveniles (Squires and Ruggiero 1995, Wiens 2004).

The composition and structure of vegetation used by wintering goshawks varies within and among regions and probably depends to some extent on the degree of landscape heterogeneity in the vicinity of breeding habitat. In western North America where montane forest habitats are surrounded by lower elevation woodland, shrub-steppe, and desert, winter home ranges include a higher diversity of vegetation types then breeding areas (Squires and Ruggiero 1995, Stephens 2001). While it is unknown why some adult goshawks move from forests to open woodlands, shrublands, desert scrub, and agricultural areas during the non-breeding season, some of this movement could be in response to extreme weather or low winter prey abundance in montane forest habitat (Doyle and Smith 1994, Reynolds et al. 1994, Squires and Ruggiero 1995, Stephens 2001, Drennan and Beier 2003; Underwood et al., *this volume*). Radio-telemetry studies show that adult goshawks often stayed on their breeding areas in winter (Reynolds et al. 1994, Doyle and Smith 1994, Boal et al. 2003).

Studies in Europe suggest that food may be a more important limiting factor than vegetation structure during the non-breeding season (Widén 1989, Kenward et al. 1999, Sunde 2002). Contrarily, some evidence shows that wintering goshawks selected habitat based on structure rather than prey abundance. Drennan and Beier (2003), studying radio-tagged goshawks in Arizona, found that canopy closure and density of medium-sized trees (20–40 cm dbh) were higher at foraging sites than randomly-located sites and there were no difference in indices of prey abundance at kill and random sites. These authors hypothesized that goshawks probably do respond to prey abundance when locating a home range, but that they select older forest conditions within the home range where they can best use their maneuverability to capture prey (Drennan and Beier 2003). Stephens (2001) investigated whether vegetation characteristics at winter kill sites of radio-tagged goshawks in Utah differed from random locations. Differences were detected only in tree diameter and canopy closure, which were higher at kill sites. Potential problems with using foraging sites for determining non-breeding foraging habitat use are similar to those discussed above.

FOOD AVAILABILITY

Food availability is a function of both food abundance and a consumer's access to the food.

Goshawks typically eat a variety of prey species including ground and tree squirrels, rabbits and hares, medium to large passerines, woodpeckers, and grouse (Squires and Reynolds 1997; Reynolds et al., *this volume*). The diet of a local goshawk population depends in part on the composition of the local bird and mammal fauna which typically varies among vegetation types. Prey availability can vary seasonally and annually according to the extent to which their populations undergo annual fluctuations or seasonal changes in abundance due to the timing of their reproduction, migration, aestivation, or hibernation. In addition to a vegetation influence on prey availability, differences in size, color, age, and behavior also influence prey's availability to goshawks. Thus, based on goshawk foraging behavior, differences in suites of prey among vegetation types, and effects of local and region-wide weather patterns on prey populations, we believe that food availability limits goshawks at the home range to metapopulation scales (Fig. 1).

Food supply affects the distribution and abundance of raptors, the sizes of their territories or home ranges, the proportion of pairs breeding, nest success, and number of young produced (Schoener 1968; Southern 1970; Galushin 1974; Baker and Brooks 1981; Salafsky 2004, 2005). In goshawks, many of these demographic parameters vary considerably among years (Squires and Reynolds 1997, McClaren et al. 2002, Reynolds et al. 2005; Keane et al., *this volume*). Several studies of goshawks in North America and Europe identified a close association between annual fluctuations in goshawk reproduction (proportion of pairs breeding, timing of egg laying, clutch size, and fledgling production) and annual fluctuations in prey abundance (McGowan 1975; Sollien 1979; Lindén and Wikman 1980; Huhtala and Sulkava 1981; Doyle and Smith 1994; Keane 1999; Salafsky 2004, 2005). However, in Germany, prey abundance was not a major limit to goshawk population growth rate, presumably because the local prey base was diverse (>60 prey species) and prey populations remained relatively stable over time (Krüger and Lindström 2001). Because female raptors must accumulate body fat and protein reserves to produce eggs, low prey abundance early in the breeding season may result in a failure to lay eggs, delayed egg laying, smaller clutches, or nest failures (Newton 1979a, 1991). This also appears to be the case in goshawks, as indicated by close associations between goshawk reproduction and the relative abundance (Keane et al., *this volume*) and density (Salafsky et al. 2005) of prey in the spring.

Density, physiological condition, and survival of goshawk fledglings, juveniles, and adults also appear to be directly related to food availability. Decreases in goshawk numbers were attributed to the rarity of rabbits in Spain (Cramp and Simmons 1980), and goshawks wintering in Sweden were more abundant and had greater body mass in areas with higher pheasant availability (Kenward et al. 1981b). In Norway, likelihood of starvation in goshawks, particularly juvenile males, increased with latitudinal gradient in the northernmost range of the species, perhaps due to a gradient in prey availability or biomass (Sunde 2002). Large annual differences in the density of primary bird and mammal prey species on the Kaibab Plateau, Arizona explained 86% of annual variation in juvenile survival through the first 3.5 mo post-fledging, and starvation was identified as the leading cause of mortality in years when prey was relatively scarce (Wiens et al. 2006a). In New Mexico and Utah, supplemental feeding experiments showed that surplus food during the nestling and fledgling-dependency periods increased fledging success, and that food appeared to interact with parental care and sibling competition to regulate post-fledgling survival (Ward and Kennedy 1996, Dewey and Kennedy 2001). The many instances of food limitation in the literature suggested to us that food is a important and ubiquitous factor limiting goshawk reproduction and survival.

Predation

Goshawk reproduction and survival rates may depend on the abundance of predators and the frequency of exposure to them. Predators of goshawks include Great Horned Owls (*Bubo virginianus*; Rohner and Doyle 1992), eagles (Squires and Ruggiero 1995), Red-tailed Hawks (*Buteo jamaicensis*; Wiens 2004), and mammals such as martens (*Martes americana*; Doyle 1995) and wolverines (*Gulo gulo*; Paragi and Wholecheese 1994,), and perhaps foxes (*Vulpes, urocyon*), coyotes (*Canis latrans*), bobcats (*Lynx rufus*), and raccoons.(*Procyon lotor*). Of these, Great Horned Owls may be the most important because of their killing capacity and their abundance in the North American range of goshawks (Orians and Kuhlman 1956, Luttich et al. 1970, McInvaille and Keith 1974, Houston 1975). For goshawks, exposure to predation can be high because goshawks and several species of large forest owls often nest in close proximity (Rohner and Doyle 1992, but see Gilmer et al. 1983). Because other large raptors occupy more open habitats, some authors suggested that tree-cutting may not only increase the

numbers of goshawk predators but increase goshawk predation risk by diminishing hiding cover (Crocker-Bedford 1990, La Sorte et al. 2004).

Young goshawks are more susceptible to predation than adults due to their inexperience and poor flight skills. Indeed, most reports of predation are on nestlings, fledglings, and juvenile goshawks. Nonetheless, Great Horned Owls occasionally kill adult goshawks (Rohner and Doyle 1992) but the extent of such losses is unclear. Squires and Ruggiero (1995) reported a likely case of raptor predation on an adult male goshawk that had migrated to open sagebrush during winter. Survival of adult goshawks on the Kaibab Plateau in northern Arizona, an area with abundant Great Horned Owls (R. Reynolds, pers.obs.), was 75% for both females and males (Reynolds et al. 2004). In view of combined but unknown losses to other mortality sources (e.g., age, starvation, accident, and disease), it seems unlikely that predation was a significant mortality factor of adult goshawks on the Kaibab Plateau. Newton (1986) found that predation on Eurasian Sparrowhawks (*Accipiter nisus*), a smaller species with potentially more predators, was of little direct consequence to its population dynamics. Reports of predation on goshawks are typically incidental, and we found no studies that specifically addressed the effects of predation on goshawk vital rates. Because predation appears to occur primarily at or in the vicinity of, nests where whole families of goshawks are susceptible to predation, the scale at which predation is most likely to operate to limit goshawk populations is the nest area (Fig. 1). However, predation can also act at much broader spatial scales by affecting adult survival in wintering areas and the number of dispersing juveniles. An example of this was a doubling of the risk of predation for radio-marked juveniles after they dispersed from natal areas in Arizona (Wiens et al. 2006a).

Inter-Specific Competition

Inter-specific competition is the use of a resource by two or more species such that the combined use limits individual fitness or population size of the competing species (Birch 1957, Emlen 1973). A necessary condition of competition is that a resource must be short of the demand for it. Without knowing if resources are in short supply, or whether competitors are consuming resources from the same area, we can only assume that species with similar geographic ranges, habitats, and diets are potential competitors (Wiens 1989). Different habitat and food preferences among raptor species has been widely noted and often attributed to competition (Janes 1985a, b). Competition among goshawks and other species is likely to be strongest for nest sites and food. Thus, inter-specific competition operates primarily at the nest-site and home-range scales, but it can affect goshawk fecundity and survival at all spatial scales (Fig. 1).

The extent to which goshawk behavior, reproduction, and survival are affected by inter-specific competition is unknown. Goshawks and other raptors often nest in close proximity (Reynolds and Meslow 1984), and Great Horned Owls, Spotted Owls (*Strix occidentalis*), and Great Gray Owls (*Strix nebulosa*) often lay eggs in goshawks nests (Forsman et al. 1984). However, goshawks displaced from nests by owls may simply move to an alternate nest within their territory, so long as alternate nest areas are available. It is unlikely that breeding goshawks could be completely excluded from a forest area by other raptors because territoriality in these other raptors results in wide dispersions of their nests (McInvaille and Keith 1974). Sharp-shinned Hawks (*Accipiter striatus*) and Cooper's Hawks (*Accipiter cooperii*) are potential competitors with goshawks for nest sites and food because their ranges overlap and they occupy similar habitats. However, these smaller hawks are not likely to be strong competitors with goshawks for nests sites because they not likely to be able to exclude goshawks (Reynolds et al. 1982, Moore and Henny 1983, Siders and Kennedy 1994). Red-tailed Hawks are another species sympatric with goshawks that nest in similar forests. However, Red-tailed Hawks more often nest adjacent to forest openings, high on ridges, and in relatively open sites (La Sorte et al. 2004, Titus and Mosher 1981, Speiser and Bosakowski 1988), whereas goshawks typically nest on slopes or in drainage bottoms in relatively denser forest sites (Reynolds et al. 1982, LaSorte et al. 2004). Competition between these species is likely to be low except in naturally open forests or forests fragmented by meadows, burns, or clear-cuts (La Sorte et al. 2004).

Several species of hawks and owls potentially compete for food with goshawks. Cooper's Hawks nest and hunt in the same vegetation conditions and feed on some of the same prey as goshawks (Storer 1966, Reynolds and Meslow 1984). Red-tailed Hawks and Great Horned Owls have significant diet overlap with goshawks, but neither typically eats as many birds as goshawks (Fitch et al. 1946, Smith and Murphy 1973, Janes 1984, Bosakowski and Smith 1992). In Arizona, 48% of Red-tailed Hawk diets consisted of species that occurred in goshawk diets (Gatto et al. 2005). Because Red-tailed Hawks are typically more abundant in open habitats (Howell et

al. 1978, Speiser and Bosakowski 1988), the extent to which they compete for food probably varies by the openness of forest type or the extent of forest fragmentation. In most North American forests, a variety of mammalian carnivores including foxes, coyotes, bobcats, lynx (*Lynx canadensis*), weasels (*Mustela* spp.), and martens co-occur in forests with goshawks and feed on many of the same prey species. While the combined effects of food depletion by these competitors on the abundance and distribution of goshawks is unknown, competition for food among these species may be high when prey populations are low. For example, numerous co-occurring species of mammalian carnivores, owls, and hawks in Sweden consumed large numbers of small vertebrate prey, and their combined consumption resulted in food limitations for several of them (Erlinge et al. 1982).

DISEASE AND PARASITISM

Although many diseases and parasites have been reported in raptors, information on the distribution of disease organisms, and on individual and species-specific raptor differences in susceptibility to infections is limited. Because few studies have addressed diseases in wild goshawks, much of our evaluation of disease as a goshawk limiting factor was inferred from the incidence and effects of disease in other raptors. Some common raptor diseases are erysipelas, salmonellosis, botulism, aspergillosis, avian leucosis, Newcastle disease, bronchitis, laryngotracheitis, pox, herpesvirus hepatitus, miliaria, coccidia, trichonomonas, a variety of intestinal round worms (*Capillaria* and *Serratospiculun*), myiasis, and mallophaga (Newton 1979a). The distribution and abundance of these disease organisms vary by season, habitat, and region. Susceptibility to disease is dependent on raptor behavior, diet, body condition, age, genetic predisposition, and chance (Alverson and Noblet 1977, Schröder 1981, Newton 1986, Phalen et al. 1995, Newton 1991). Schröder (1981) reported that 68 of 105 eagles and hawks had infectious and parasitic diseases compared to 19 of 45 falcons. Schröder (1981) and Delannoy and Cruz (1991) found that 14% of captive eagles and hawks died from tuberculosis and 21% were affected with mycoses, suggesting that among raptor diseases caused by pathogens, bacterial infections are of the greatest importance. Disease and parasites have been associated with abnormal behavior, nest desertions, and reduced mating success, clutch sizes, hatching success, and nestling growth and survival of juveniles (Newton 1991). For example, female Boreal Owls (*Aegolius funereus*) with higher levels of blood parasites had smaller clutch sizes than females with fewer blood parasites (Korpimäki et al. 1993). Infestations of the warble fly (*Philornis* spp.) on Puerto Rican Sharp-shinned Hawk nestlings accounted for 69% of nest failures (Delannoy and Cruz 1991), and trichomoniasis killed 22% of Cooper's Hawk nestlings in the urban area where the hawks fed on doves, a presumed carrier of the protozoan *Trichomonas gallinas* (Boal and Mannan 1999, 2000).

Among *Accipiter*, Newton (1986) found disease practically non-existent in a population of Eurasian Sparrowhawks he studied for 14 yr in Scotland. However, five of 10 goshawks had blood parasites in Britain (Peirce and Cooper 1977) and 22 of 31 goshawks had parasites in Alaska (McGowan 1975). Redig et al. (1980) reported aspergillosus (*Aspergillus fumigatus*) in 26 of 49 (53%) and three of 45 (7%) wild goshawks trapped in Minnesota in 1972 and 1973, respectively. In New Mexico, Ward and Kennedy (1996) reported that one of 12 juvenile goshawks died of disease, as determined by necropsy. Cooper and Petty (1988) found an approximate 15% reduction in goshawk productivity due to nestling deaths from blood parasites. However, in many birds, parasitism is responsible for fewer nestling deaths than predation (Newton 1991).

A number of new epizootics may threaten raptor populations, one of which is West Nile virus (WNV; Daszak et al. 2000). Factors such as the distribution and population size of susceptible hosts, the size and distribution of vector populations, and the presence of suitable habitat characteristics all contribute to the transmission of WNV (Deubel et al. 2001, Petersen and Roehrig 2001). Anecdotal evidence indicates that captive goshawks suffer high mortality when exposed to WNV (J. Scherpelz, Rocky Mountain Raptor Program, pers. comm.), but some raptors appear capable of developing resistance to WNV; mortality of rehabilitated and wild owls declined during their second year of exposure WNV (Caffrey and Peterson 2003). Although the effect of WNV on wild goshawks is uncertain, we suspect that a concern will continue because of its known effect on many bird species. While disease appears most commonly to effect goshawks at the individual level (home-range scale), disease may affect goshawk fecundity and survival at the population scale. The spread of disease beyond the population scale is likely to be restricted by the distances between metapopulations (Fig. 1).

The importance of disease as a goshawk limiting factor is unknown because disease often predispose individual raptors to other mortality agents (Esch 1975), and food shortages may predispose goshawks to disease. Hence, it is not often clear whether mortality due to disease is additive or compensatory (Robinson and Holmes 1982). However, when compared to starvation and trauma, disease was not a significant cause of mortality in eagle and hawk populations studied by Keymer et al. (1981) and Redrobe (1997). On the Baltic island of Gotland, only 3% of goshawk deaths were caused by disease as compared to 15% from starvation and 10% from trauma (Kenward et al. 1993a). Although disease has been identified in captive and wild goshawks, no strong evidence indicates that disease is a significant factor limiting their populations (USDI Fish and Wildlife Service 1998a, Kennedy 2003).

WEATHER

Weather can affect bird populations in two ways: within-year effects, reflecting sudden, extreme, and episodic events; and among-year effects, reflecting weather variation over larger temporal and spatial scales (Rotenberry and Wiens 1991). Extreme weather events such as hail storms and wind storms can cause direct mortality of eggs, nestlings, juveniles and adults, or indirect mortality by damaging vegetation structure and food supplies. Prolonged periods of regionally severe weather such as droughts or winters with heavy snow may have strong indirect effects on goshawk reproduction and survival by reducing food availability. Weather can act as a goshawk limiting factor at multiple spatial scales, from a single individual or nest by a localized event, e.g., hail, wind, to populations and metapopulations during region-wide severe weather such as drought (Fig. 1).

Inter-annual variation in raptor reproduction has been closely tied to variation in local weather conditions (Franklin et al. 2000, Dreitz et al. 2001, Krüger and Lindström 2001, Bloxton 2002, Seamans et al. 2002). Snowy winters can reduce prey availability during courtship, a period when females need energy for egg laying, leading to lowered numbers of breeding goshawks (Kostrzewa and Kostrezewa 1990). Cold and wet springs can lead to delayed egg laying, and prolonged rain periods can affect brood sizes, presumably by reducing the hunting activity of adults and by lowering prey availability (Newton 1986, Kostrzewa and Kostrzewa 1990, Patla 1997, Penteriani 1997). Several goshawk studies showed that heavy spring precipitation lowered nesting success and that mild spring temperatures favored increased goshawk reproduction (Kostrzewa and Kostrzewa 1990, Patla 1997, Penteriani 1997,

Krüger and Lindström 2001; Keane et al., *this volume*), but see Ingraldi (1998) for a positive relationship between spring precipitation and productivity). Kostrezewa and Kostrzewa (1990) found that variations in spring rainfall and temperature affected breeding success in goshawks more than any other factor, and Krüger and Lindström (2001) found that increased precipitation during the nestling phase and autumn periods had a strong negative effect on goshawk population growth rate. Demographic studies of Spotted Owls found that nearly all of the temporal process variation in reproductive output was explained by weather (Franklin et al. 2000, Seamans et al. 2002, LaHaye et al. 2004), and we predict that a large proportion of temporal process variation in goshawk reproduction also will be explained by weather.

Goshawk nestlings are poor at regulating their body temperature in the first 10–15 d after hatching, making them more vulnerable to weather extremes than juveniles or adults. However, even late-term nestlings are susceptible. In Arizona, for example, increased mortality of late-term nestlings was observed during 10-d of continuous rain in 1998 (R. Reynolds, pers. obs.). However, in the same study population and in the same year, Wiens et al. (2006a) found no indication that continuous, heavy rainfall affected the survival of radio-tagged juvenile goshawks once they had fledged. Sunde (2002) also found no effects of temperature or precipitation on relative starvation risk or body condition of juvenile or adult goshawks recovered dead in Norway.

SYNTHESIS AND CONCLUSIONS

We reviewed information on the biology of goshawks relative to several well-known avian population limiting factors including food, vegetation compositions and structure, predation, competition, disease, and weather. While we found numerous sources of information on how some of these factors limited goshawk reproduction, many uncertainties remain regarding how these factors affect survival, particularly of adults. Adding to this uncertainty is the inadequacy of demographic data on goshawks to properly assess population trends irrespective of limiting factors (Andersen et al. 2004; Squires and Kennedy, *this volume*). This inadequacy precluded a quantitative evaluation of how these limiting factors influence goshawk population dynamics. The great variability in habitats occupied by goshawks combined with methodological differences among studies in data collection and analyses restricted our assessment of the relative importance of the different

limiting factors as well. Nevertheless, several important patterns emerged from our review.

A number of studies identified a tie between vegetation characteristics around goshawk nests and territory occupancy and reproduction (Crocker-Bedford 1990, Woodbridge and Detrich 1994, Keane 1999; Finn et al. 2002a, b; Joy 2002, Penteriani et al. 2002a). However, no study to our knowledge quantified a direct relationship between goshawk survival and vegetation composition and structure, either in breeding habitats or in winter habitats, although some evidence suggests that predation on goshawks may be higher in non-forested habitats. Several studies established an association between food abundance and goshawk reproduction (McGowan 1975; Sollien 1979; Lindén and Wikman 1980; Huhtala and Sulkava 1981; Doyle and Smith 1994; Keane 1999; Salafsky 2004, 2005), and survival (Kenward et al. 1981b, Ward and Kennedy 1996, Dewey and Kennedy 2001, Wiens et al. 2006a). Nearly all long-term goshawk studies reported predation of nestlings and a few reported predation on adults, but none provided evidence suggesting that predation was a primary factor limiting goshawk populations. Little direct information is available regarding the effect of inter-specific competition on goshawks, but at least two studies suggested that competition might have an increasingly negatively affect on goshawks with increasing forest fragmentation and loss of mature forest structure (La Sorte et al. 2004; Gatto et al. 2005). No study found disease to be a major threat to goshawk populations, although there is concern over the arrival of WNV in the goshawk's North American range. In contrast, several studies indicate that goshawk reproduction was influenced by weather (Kostrzewa and Kostrzewa 1990, Patla 1997, Penteriani 1997, Ingraldi 1998, Krüger and Lindström 2001; Keane et al., *this volume*), but evidence of weather effects on goshawk survival were mainly anecdotal, and studies of the direct effects of weather on juvenile and adult survival failed to detect an effect (Sunde 2002, Wiens et al. 2006a).

While lack of evidence is not proof that any of these factors did not significantly affect goshawk populations, considerable evidence suggested that vegetation structure at nest sites and foraging sites, and the abundance and availability of food were the primary factors limiting goshawk reproduction and survival. This is in agreement with Widén (1989), who argued that, based on higher goshawk breeding densities in areas richer in prey, and extremely high goshawk breeding densities in areas with only 12–15% woodland but extremely rich in prey, goshawks were limited more often by food availability than by nesting habitat. The evidence was not clear, however, whether food, nest sites, or vegetation structure at foraging sites were more important in limiting breeding goshawks because vegetation structure appears to affect goshawks both directly and indirectly. Goshawks may be affected directly because they prefer older forest structures for nest sites, perhaps for protection from weather and predators, and a forest structure of tall trees and open understories that increases access to prey, and indirectly by affecting the distribution and abundance of prey.

INTERACTIONS AMONG FACTORS

Essential to understanding how the factors reviewed here might limit goshawk populations is recognizing that these factors interact in complex ways at multiple spatial and temporal scales. We developed a schematic representation of the various pathways through which the limiting factors reviewed in this paper are likely to affect goshawk reproduction and survival (Fig. 2). Among-year variation in regional weather conditions leads to among-year fluctuations in forest productivity and, in turn, among-year

fluctuations in goshawk prey populations. Among-year fluctuations in food abundance interact with forest structural conditions and weather, ultimately affecting prey availability and goshawk reproduction. The strength of these interactions are likely to depend on factors such as the number of species within the prey base, whether or not prey populations fluctuate in synchrony, spatial variation in the composition and structure of vegetation, and abundances of predators and competitors. Extreme weather events and disease can interfere with this flow of energy through the goshawk's food web by directly or indirectly affecting the physiological condition of goshawks, which, in turn, affects their reproduction and survival. The magnitude of competition, predation, and disease can also vary spatially or temporally depending on differences in food abundance, forest structure, and weather. The resulting changes in goshawk reproduction and survival contribute to the persistence of local populations, which in turn are regulated by dispersal within and among regional populations. When considered within the context of forest management (see Fig. 3 in Squires and Kennedy, *this volume*), our schematic provides a conceptual framework for understanding the causal pathways between these potential population limiting factors and goshawk viability.

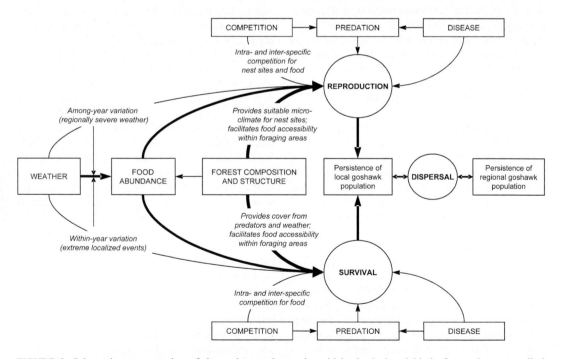

FIGURE 2. Schematic representation of the various pathways by which physical and biotic factors interact to limit Northern Goshawk vital rates and, ultimately, the persistence of local and regional breeding populations. Thicker lines indicate pathways with relatively stronger effects.

We propose that the additive effects of food abundance, forest composition and structure, and weather are much stronger than their individual effects on goshawk reproduction and survival. For example, if prey abundance is reduced by a period of environmental stress, goshawks may be unable to attain sufficient food to lay eggs. Alternatively, if prey abundance is high but goshawks cannot see or capture their prey because of unsuitable forest structure, they may have to change their hunting habitat, expand their foraging movements, alter their hunting behavior, or switch to alternate prey. Each of these changes could lower goshawk hunting efficiency. Lowered hunting efficiency, whether caused by low prey abundance or availability, can have an additional negetive effect on goshawk reproduction by causing females to leave their nests to help with hunting, thereby increasing the exposure of eggs or nestlings to predators (Newton 1986, Dewey and Kennedy 2001). Weather, predation, and competition may also play a even larger role when habitat is lost or degraded through natural or human disturbance. Finally, low food abundance or availability in forests may force adult goshawks in winter to leave for more open habitat where predation risks may be higher. Because of all the above, we argue that food abundance, vegetation structure and composition, and weather are likely to be the most ubiquitous factors limiting goshawk populations. We also argue that these factors, which often act in concert, are likely to mask the direct effects of forest management on goshawk vital rates in short-term studies.

Population Limitation and Natural Variation

Population limitation refers to a process that sets the equilibrium point (Sinclair 1989), or, more generally, a process that determines the stationary probability distribution of a population's density (Williams et al. 2002). Temporal and spatial variation in the operation of limiting factors may cause goshawk population densities to move around an average value. Some goshawk demographic parameters such as the proportion of pairs breeding, fecundity, juvenile survival, and recruitment appear to vary among years more than other parameters such as territory distribution, territory occupancy, and adult survival (Squires and Reynolds 1997,

Andersen et al. 2004, Reynolds et al. 2004, Wiens et al. 2006a; Reynolds and Joy, *this volume*). Goshawk vital rates are closely tied to their food resources. Therefore, temporal variation in food abundance superimposed on spatial variation in food availability can be expected to generate substantial spatial and temporal variation in goshawk vital rates. Because short-term studies are not likely to detect the full range of natural variability in goshawk vital rates, and because an understanding of the extent and source of this variation is needed to tease-out the effects of forest management on the interactions among limiting factors, identifying the cause-effect responses of goshawks to management is necessarily a long-term endeavor.

Concluding Comments

We believe that the extent to which food, forest vegetation, predation, competition, disease, and weather affects goshawk populations can be mediated by providing suitable forest structure for goshawk nesting and foraging, as well as the habitats of a local suite of goshawk prey. Forest landscapes that include the habitats of the goshawk's prey (Reynolds et al. 1992; Drennan et al., *this volume*), forest structures that protect goshawks from weather and predators at nest sites (Reynolds et al., *this volume*), and forest structures that enhance the availability of prey to goshawks are more likely to sustain viable goshawk populations than forests lacking these features. An underlying issue in the debate over the status of the Northern Goshawk is the management of remaining old-growth forests (Peck 2000). However, we believe that the issue is broader than this and that a full understanding and recognition of the various natural factors that result in variation of goshawk demographic performance is the key to developing sound management strategies for goshawks and the forest ecosystems that they are dependent upon.

ACKNOWLEDGMENTS

Support for this manuscript was provided by the USDA Forest Service Rocky Mountain Research Station. We thank M. L. Morrison, C. D. Marti, and two anonymous reviewers for their helpful comments on a draft of the manuscript.

Studies in Avian Biology No. 31:274–287

A DESIGN FOR MONITORING NORTHERN GOSHAWKS AT THE BIOREGIONAL SCALE

CHRISTINA D. HARGIS AND BRIAN WOODBRIDGE

Abstract. Information on Northern Goshawk (*Accipiter gentilis*) populations is generally obtained by studying nesting activity at local scales. Although this approach provides breeding information for specific territories, it can not be used to track changes in the abundance of goshawks over broader spatial extents. To address the need for broad-scale monitoring, the USDA Forest Service (USFS) assembled a working group to develop a design for monitoring goshawk population trends at a bioregional scale (i.e., northern Rockies or Intermountain Great Basin). The working group consisted of statisticians, wildlife biologists, and goshawk researchers within and outside of the USFS. The group was chartered to create a monitoring design to be implemented on national forest lands, but the USFS invites collaboration with other landowners and state natural resource agencies in order to provide a more complete picture of goshawk status across land ownerships. The objectives of the monitoring design are: (1) to estimate the frequency of occurrence of territorial adult goshawks within a bioregion, (2) to assess changes in frequency of occurrence over time, and (3) to determine whether changes in frequency of occurrence, if any, are associated with changes in habitat. The sample population for each bioregion is a grid of 600 ha primary sampling units (PSUs) across all potential goshawk habitats on national forest lands and on lands owned or managed by collaborating parties of each bioregional monitoring program. The sampling frame is stratified to increase efficiency under a fixed monitoring budget. The indicator used to determine the frequency of occurrence of goshawks is the proportion of PSUs with goshawk presence, based on response to broadcast acoustical surveys in a sample of PSUs. Sampled PSUs are surveyed two times (nestling and fledgling periods) to obtain one estimate of goshawk presence per breeding season. Frequency of goshawk presence within the bioregion is estimated using a maximum likelihood estimator. Changes in frequency of goshawk presence will be assessed after a minimum of 5 yr, using a logistic model with habitat parameters entered as covariates. Information from bioregional monitoring will help determine the status of goshawk populations and their habitats over a spatial extent that is meaningful for goshawk conservation.

Key Words: *Accipiter gentilis*, broadcast surveys, maximum likelihood estimation, monitoring, Northern Goshawk, presence-absence data.

DISEÑO PARA MONITOREAR EL GAVILÁN AZOR A ESCALA BIOREGIONAL

Resumen. La información en poblaciones de Gavilán Azor (*Accipiter gentilis*), es generalmente obtenida a través del estudio de la actividad de anidación a escalas locales. Aunque este enfoque proporciona información de reproducción para territorios específicos, no puede ser utilizada para rastrear cambios en la abundancia del gavilán sobre extensiones espaciales mas amplias. Para dirigir la necesidad de monitoreo de mayor escala, el Servicio Forestal USDA (USFS) formó un grupo, con la finalidad de desarrollar un diseño para monitorear las tendencias de las poblaciones de gavilán a escala bioregional (ej. norte de las Rocallosas o las Intermontañas de la Gran Cuenca). El grupo de trabajo consistió en estadistas, biólogos de vida silvestre y de investigadores de gavilán dentro y fuera del USFS. El grupo fue contratado para crear un diseño de monitoreo para ser implementado en tierras del sistema de bosques nacionales, pero el USFS invitó a otros propietarios de terrenos y a agencias estatales de recursos naturales, con el fin de proporcionar un cuadro más amplio del estado del gavilán, el cual incluyera los distintos tipos de tenencia de la tierra. Los objetivos del diseño de monitoreo son: (1) Estimar la frecuencia de ocurrencia de gavilanes territoriales adultos dentro de una bioregión, (2) Evaluar los cambios en la frecuencia de la ocurrencia a través de los años, y (3) determinar si los cambios en la frecuencia de ocurrencia, si los hay, están asociados con cambios en el hábitat. La muestra de la población para cada bioregión consta de una red de unidades de muestreo preliminar de 600 ha (PSUs) con todos los hábitats potenciales del gavilán, en las tierras de bosques nacionales y en tierras que pertenecen o son manejadas por partidos en colaboración, por cada programa de monitoreo bioregional. El marco de muestreo está estratificado, para incrementar la eficiencia bajo un presupuesto de monitoreo mixto. El indicador utilizado para determinar la frecuencia de ocurrencia de los gavilanes, es la proporción de PSUs con la presencia de gavilán, basado en respuesta a estudios de emisiones acústicas en una muestra de PSUs. Los PSUs muestreados son estudiados dos veces (períodos de crecimiento y volanteo, para obtener un estimado de la presencia de gavilán por temporada de reproducción. La frecuencia de la presencia del gavilán dentro de la bioregión es estimada usando un estimador de probabilidad máxima. Los cambios en la frecuencia de la presencia del gavilán serán apreciados después de un mínimo de 5 años, utilizando un modelo logístico con parámetros de hábitat introducidos como covariables. La información del monitoreo bioregional ayudará a determinar el estado de las poblaciones de gavilán y sus hábitats sobre una extensión espacial, la cual es muy importante para la conservación del gavilán.

Information on Northern Goshawk (*Accipiter gentilis*) populations is generally obtained by tracking nesting activity at local scales. Although this approach provides breeding information for specific territories, it does not provide information on population status or trend. Local occupancy and breeding information is important to assess the effects of local management actions, but population trends must be estimated at scales that reflect the size and spatial extent of goshawk populations. Current information suggests that goshawk populations and metapopulations exist over extensive geographic areas, with genetic mixing facilitated by the species' potentially long dispersal distances and use of a broad range of forest habitats. However, insufficient information on genetics or movements prohibits the delineation of discrete biological populations.

In the absence of specific information that would enable us to delineate goshawk populations, we based the monitoring design on a bioregion concept, using geographic and ecological scales appropriate for goshawks as a surrogate for biological populations. We use the term bioregion to mean a geographically extensive area characterized by coarse-scale similarity in ecological conditions. Generally speaking, climatic, physiographic, and ecological factors are more similar within a bioregion than between bioregions. We selected the bioregion as the appropriate spatial extent for analysis of goshawk population data, after considering both smaller and larger spatial extents: individual national forests and the entire range of the goshawk.

We consider individual national forests too small for evaluating goshawk population trends, both for ecological and sampling reasons. Goshawks within a specific national forest are not isolated from goshawks on adjacent forests and other neighboring lands, so population trends for a given forest are likely not meaningful. Also, because of the inherent variability in population estimates, the sample size required to detect a significant change in abundance at the forest scale would be unaffordable for most individual forests.

The entire range of the goshawk was considered too large for aggregating and interpreting population and habitat data due to the wide variation in goshawk habitat relations across the species' range. Differences in ecological conditions between bioregions could result in different trends in goshawk populations over time. If all bioregions closely follow the bioregional survey protocol, however, it will be possible to compare trends across bioregions and assess the status of the goshawk across much of its range in the US.

The USDA Forest Service (USFS) assembled a working group to design an approach for monitoring goshawks at a bioregional scale. The working group consisted of statisticians, wildlife biologists, and goshawk researchers from within and outside of the USFS. This chapter describes the monitoring design so that each bioregion can identify interested collaborators and begin monitoring at the earliest opportunity.

The goal of bioregional monitoring is to determine the relative abundance of goshawks and their habitats, and to track broad scale changes in population status and habitat over time. The objectives are: (1) to estimate the frequency of occurrence of territorial adult goshawks within each area defined as a bioregion, (2) to assess changes in goshawk frequency of occurrence over time, and (3) to determine whether changes in frequency of occurrence, if any, are associated with changes in habitat. The targeted precision is to be within 10% of the actual frequency of goshawk occurrence with 90% confidence. The degree to which we are able to detect change in goshawk occurrence over time is unknown, but given our current understanding of detection rates and goshawk persistence at the scale of the sample unit, sample sizes are designed to detect at least a 20% change in the frequency of occurrence over a 5-yr monitoring period.

Although the design described in this chapter was originally intended for use on USFS lands, a complete picture of goshawk population status can only be obtained if monitoring is extended across all potential goshawk habitats, regardless of ownership. The USFS invites collaboration with other agencies and conservation groups to implement this monitoring design as broadly as possible.

The potential contributions and inherent limitations of bioregional monitoring must be clearly recognized. Currently no monitoring program in place throughout the range of the Northern Goshawk provides information on population trends or broad-scale changes in habitat, and the bioregional monitoring design fills this gap in a way that is practical and cost effective. However, this design is not structured to investigate the effects of management treatments. We suggest ways to seek potential correlations between observed population trends and environmental factors, but any correlations cannot be assumed to be causative. Bioregional monitoring is not research and should not be viewed as a substitute. Trends obtained through bioregional monitoring could, however, be used to motivate research and to provide justification for funding such research.

PLANNING AND DESIGN

We recommend that each bioregion identify a bioregional coordinator to oversee the goshawk monitoring program, because the success of the program rests on having a central entity to carry out the necessary planning activities, ensure that data are collected in a consistent and rigorous way, conduct data analysis, prepare annual reports, and administer the budget. The bioregional coordinator will communicate frequently with other bioregional coordinators to promote consistency across bioregions in all aspects of design, data collection, and analysis. The coordinator can be affiliated with any agency, research facility, or university.

DESCRIPTION OF THE INDICATOR

The selected indicator of goshawk frequency of occurrence is P, the proportion of primary sampling units (PSUs) (Levy and Lemeshow 1999) with goshawk presence, which is estimated ($\hat{P}$) using a sample of PSUs. Each PSU is approximately 600 ha and the sampling frame is a grid of PSUs laid over all potential goshawk habitat on all lands of collaborators in the bioregion. Goshawk presence is estimated for each sampled PSU based on whether at least one detection is made within the PSU using the field protocol described in the data collection section below. The data are binary because each PSU survey can have one of two possible outcomes—presence or absence.

If $\hat{P}$ is expressed as a simple summary proportion of PSUs with observed presence, it will tend to underestimate the true P because of surveys where absence was observed even though a goshawk was present. To reduce this bias, many of the PSUs are visited twice to allow the estimation of the detection probability (the conditional probability that presence will be observed given that the PSU has actual presence). The detection probability is used as a multiplicative adjustment to the simple summary proportion , thereby reducing the negative bias of $\hat{P}$ (MacKenzie et al. 2002, 2003).

DELINEATION OF BIOREGIONS

To aid in delineating bioregional boundaries, we evaluated current information on goshawk distribution, dispersal and movement patterns. An assessment of the distribution of known goshawk territories in the western US (USDI Fish and Wildlife Service 1998a) suggests that populations and metapopulations exist over extensive geographic areas, encompassing a broad range of forest habitats. Natal dispersal distances of 101 km (B. Woodbridge, unpubl. data), and 60–106 km (Wiens 2004) have been reported in the western US, although shorter distances have been reported (14.4–32.0 km; Reynolds and Joy 1998). These likely are underestimations because survey efforts in mark-recapture studies are typically limited to specific study areas, whereas birds dispersing outside of the study area are unlikely to be detected. In northern Arizona, >80% of juveniles radio marked over 4 yr dispersed beyond the 15,000 km² principal aircraft monitoring area around the natal territories (Wiens 2004). This high potential for movement suggests that monitoring for population trend should occur over spatial extents of several thousand square kilometers.

We delineated 10 bioregions (Table 1, Fig. 1) by overlaying the geographic range of the Northern Goshawk (Squires and Reynolds 1997) with the Forest Service National Hierarchical Framework of Ecological Units (Bailey 1980, McNab and Avers 1994). In the absence of data on any differences in goshawk abundance between geographic areas, the boundaries of each bioregion were established by simply aggregating neighboring polygons of similar adjacent ecological provinces. If a relatively small polygon of one ecological province was completely or nearly enclosed within a larger polygon of a different ecological province, it was included in the bioregion of the larger polygon (Fig. 2). Boundaries

TABLE 1. BIOREGIONS FOR MONITORING NORTHERN GOSHAWKS.

Goshawk bioregion	Area (km²)
West Coast	121,590
Cascade Sierra	1,181,072
Central Rocky Mountains	317,891
Colorado Plateau and southwest mountains	514,700
Great Lakes	490,500
Intermountain Great Basin	620,861
Northern Rockies-Blue Mountains	480,028
Northeast and central Appalachian Mountains	517,225
Coastal Alaska	173,700
Interior Alaskan forests	697,545

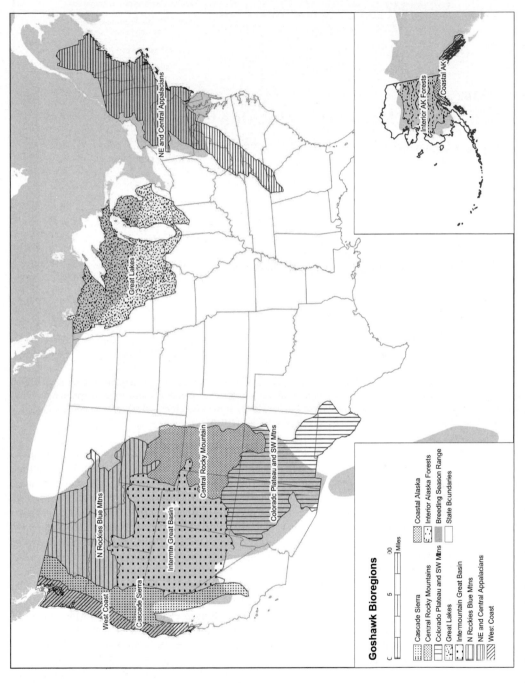

FIGURE 1. Bioregions for monitoring Northern Goshawks.

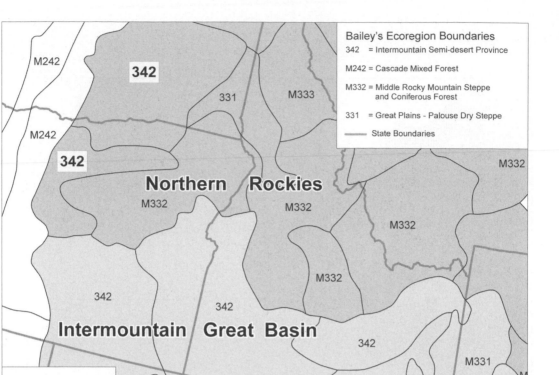

FIGURE 2. Bioregional boundaries were formed by aggregating polygons of one or more ecoregional provinces, except where these polygons were surrounded by a dissimilar province. In this example, polygons of the Intermountain semi-desert province (342, highlighted in white) were placed in the Northern Rockies bioregion rather than being included in the Intermountain Great Basin bioregion with other polygons of this province.

were also influenced by the configuration of national forests, so that no national forest would be split between two bioregions. Exceptions to this rule occurred with the Toiyabe and Inyo National Forests, both of which occur in the Cascade-Sierra and Intermountain Great Basin bioregions (Fig. 3). The striking difference in biotic and abiotic conditions between these two provinces provides strong rationale for splitting each of these national forests. Consequently, these national forests will need to report separate goshawk data for each of the two bioregions.

Goshawk movement between bioregions will occur, but bioregional boundaries often represent major physiographic features and/or changes in vegetation types that act to reduce connectivity of goshawk habitat among bioregions. In addition, bioregional boundaries reflect different ecological factors that affect goshawks such as climate, disturbance regimes, prey populations, and forest cover

types. For example, a large proportion of goshawks within the Intermountain-Great Basin bioregion are migratory, occupy landscapes with little forest cover, and are strongly influenced by population dynamics of prey species associated with nonforested habitats such as Belding's ground squirrel (*Spermophilus beldingi*; Younk and Bechard 1994a). These conditions contrast with the ecology of goshawks in the adjacent Cascade-Sierra Nevada bioregion, where goshawks are largely nonmigratory, associated with coniferous forest habitats, and strongly influenced by forest-dwelling prey species such as Douglas squirrels (*Tamiasciurus douglasii*; Keane 1999).

The bioregions are truncated at the Canadian border (with the possible exception of bi-national collaboration in the Great Lakes bioregion), and we acknowledge the artificial nature of these boundaries. Trans-national movement of goshawks will be considered when population trends are reported for bioregions that border Canada.

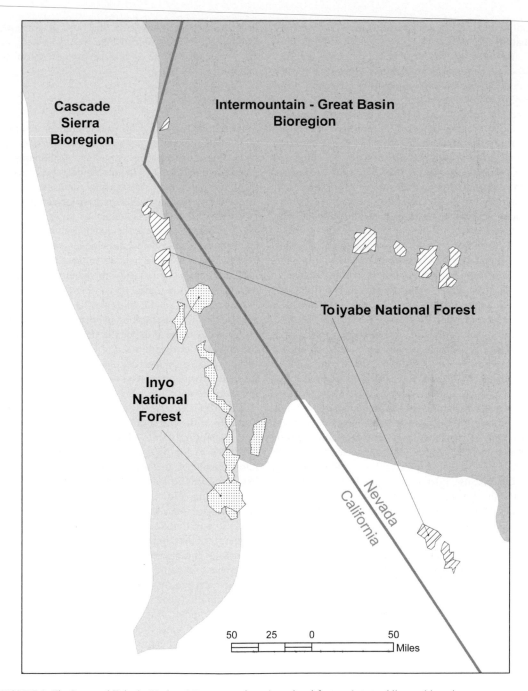

FIGURE 3. The Inyo and Toiyabe National Forests are the only national forests that straddle two bioregions.

SAMPLING UNITS

The PSU is the scale of resolution at which goshawk presence is determined, and the total number of PSUs that are surveyed represent the sample size. Secondary sampling units (SSUs) are call points within a PSU where goshawk vocalizations are played, and each PSU has up to 120 call points, depending on the amount of available habitat. The area between call points is considered part of the survey because any detections of goshawks, nests, or molted feathers that are made while walking between call points contribute to the outcome of presence for that PSU.

PSU size of 600 ha is based on ecological factors and sampling considerations. Ideally, PSU size should be large enough to obtain a reasonable probability of detecting a goshawk, while maintaining a size that reflects the spacing of goshawk breeding sites, so that an outcome of presence represents no more than one nesting pair and their offspring. To determine optimum PSU size, we compared the spacing of goshawk breeding sites (geometric centroid of all known alternate nests) in three geographical areas. Mean nearest-neighbor distances among goshawk nesting areas on the Kaibab Plateau of Arizona (Reynolds et al. 2005), southern Cascade Mountains (Woodbridge and Dietrich 1994), and Modoc Plateau are remarkably similar, ranging from 3–4 km. One-half of this distance, a radius of 1.5–2 km, yields an area of 706–1,257 ha, which approximates territory size. We tested a range of potential PSU sizes from 405–1,214 ha at 202.3 ha increments, by overlaying each size with several maps of goshawk nest sites at known density and spacing. As expected, the greater the size of the PSU, the greater the proportion of PSUs that contained the core area of a goshawk territory (Table 2), which translates to an increased probability of detecting a goshawk. At a PSU size of 607 ha, however, 0.3% of the PSUs contained core areas of two adjacent territories. This suggested that a PSU size >607 ha could potentially confound survey results because a detection in the PSU could represent either one or two family groups. By selecting a PSU size of approximately 600 ha, the PSUs would generally contain only one territory, and would also fit proportionally within the sampling design of the forest inventory analysis (FIA) program, which collects vegetation data across the US on all land ownerships at a scale of one monitoring point per 2,402 ha. The USFS is moving toward a strategy whereby wildlife monitoring data are collected in concordance with the FIA sampling design. If the

PSU were exactly 600.7 ha, the ratio of goshawk PSU area to FIA grid cell size would be 4:1; we have selected 600 ha as a close approximation to that size.

SAMPLING FRAME AND STRATIFICATION

The sampling frame for each bioregion includes all habitats potentially occupied by goshawks on all lands owned or managed by parties collaborating in goshawk monitoring. The bioregional coordinator identifies potential habitat using published literature and knowledge of existing nest locations in the bioregion. All habitats suitable for breeding (nesting and foraging) are considered primary habitat. Habitats with little or no prior documented use by goshawks are marginal habitat. Unforested areas are not considered habitat and are therefore excluded from the sampling frame.

A base map for the bioregion is constructed or acquired using vegetation cover types, structural stages, slope, aspect, elevation, landform, and land-ownership. A grid comprised of 600 ha square PSUs is automated over the base map, using a randomly selected universal transverse mercator (UTM) coordinate as the initial anchor.

Each bioregion will need to determine whether grid cells with split land ownership will be included in the sampling frame. Ideally, only grid cells with ≥90% ownership by one of the monitoring collaborators should be included, to ensure that surveyors have access to all suitable habitats within each PSU for sampling. However, in some bioregions with checkerboard land ownership, this standard could result in substantial removal of potential goshawk habitat from the sampling frame, reducing the effectiveness of the monitoring design. In such case it is preferable to obtain permission from land owners to conduct surveys for goshawks so that these mixed ownership PSUs can be included.

The sampling frame is stratified to provide a reasonable estimate of goshawk frequency of occurrence with an efficient use of funds. Stratification is needed because systematic or simple random sampling would result in a large commitment of monitoring funds in areas that are likely not used by goshawks, with the inherent risk that little would be learned about goshawk population status. The stratified design uses knowledge of currently occupied habitat coupled with information on road access to target areas that can be easily sampled and have a reasonable expectation of goshawk presence, while ensuring that marginal and less accessible habitats are included in the sample.

TABLE 2. PRIMARY SAMPLING UNITS (PSU) SIZE IN RELATION TO NUMBER OF TERRITORIES WITHIN THEM.

PSU size (hectares)	Number of PSUs (N)	Percentage of PSUs with 0, 1, or 2 territories		
		0	1	2
405	429	85.3	14.7	0
607	292	78.8	20.9	0.3
809	229	73.4	25.8	0.9
1,012	182	67.6	30.2	2.2
1,214	158	64.6	31.6	3.2

The sample design consisted of four strata:

1. Primary habitat, easy to access.
2. Primary habitat, difficult to access.
3. Marginal habitat, easy to access.
4. Marginal habitat, difficult to access.

Bioregional coordinators can use any procedure to assign PSUs to the four strata. Errors in assignment are to be expected, especially if goshawk habitat is poorly understood in a bioregion and/or if accessibility is unknown. Nevertheless, even crude stratification can provide a more efficient design than simple random sampling. A bioregion might contain several thousand PSUs, and in the absence of stratification, the survey effort is likely to overemphasize the more abundant marginal habitats and provide little new information about goshawk presence.

The following procedure (S. Joy, R. Reich, and V. Thomas, unpubl. report) was used to stratify PSUs on the San Juan and Rio Grande National Forests into primary and marginal habitat for a field test of the monitoring design. A geographic information system (GIS) layer was created for each national forest, consisting of goshawk nests known to be active in at least one of the past 10 yr. This layer was used in conjunction with a vegetation layer obtained from common vegetation unit polygons that provided several variables of forest composition and structure. A GIS analyst then centered a square on each nest that was 600 ha so that it was comparable to the size of a PSU, and obtained the following habitat attributes from each square: percent cover of trees, shrubs, grass, bare soil, and water, percent cover of the first, second, and third dominant tree species, the structural stage, tree species diversity, elevation, slope, aspect, and presence or absence of aspen. To sample the range of topographic and vegetative variability on each forest, the analyst also generated a number of random points, commensurate with the number of nests on each national forest, centered a 600 ha square on each, and collected the same set of habitat attributes. The attribute coverages for nest squares and random squares were merged (but were separate for each national forest), with nest squares assigned a value of one and random squares a value of zero. A logistic regression was used to determine which habitat attributes contributed most to distinguishing nest squares from random squares. For the San Juan National Forest, the most significant variables were mean elevation, mean slope, tree cover, aspect, and land contour. For the Rio Grande National Forest, the most significant variables were elevation and low amounts of grass cover, with high grass likely being a surrogate for non-forested areas. The results of the model were then applied to the actual grid of PSUs for each forest. The analysis generated a probability surface using the coefficient of the logistic regression model, and selected threshold probability values for each habitat attribute that maximized the overall accuracy of correctly classifying a PSU as primary habitat. The logistic model for each forest was then applied to the PSU grid, identifying which PSUs were primary habitat. Marginal habitat was any forested habitat that did not meet the model criteria of primary habitat.

Accessibility categories were not formally assigned during the goshawk test. We recommend that these categories be based on roads, wilderness areas, and travel distances from field offices. The accessibility layer is laid over the primary-marginal habitat layer to produce the four strata listed above.

Before leaving the topic of stratification, we add the caveat that the map of primary and marginal habitat is not intended to be used for management decisions and conservation measures. Stratification is based on our best, current understanding of goshawk habitat use, but this understanding could be biased by a previous emphasis of goshawk surveys in areas with roads and proposed timber sale areas. The purpose of the map is to provide better efficiency in goshawk surveys, but the results of the surveys could greatly change our understanding of habitats used by goshawks. Certain habitats that are initially classified as marginal will gain importance if surveys yield detections in these habitats.

Sample Size

The number of sampled PSUs must be sufficiently large to meet the objectives for this monitoring design with the desired precision and confidence. Each of the three objectives has a different sample size requirement, but the bioregional coordinator should choose the largest sample size needed to meet all three objectives. The largest sample size will likely be needed for the third objective, to assess changes in the relative abundance of goshawks in relation to changes in habitat or other environmental factors. Unfortunately, this sample size is the most difficult to calculate because it requires not only within-year variance but also between-year variance, as well as variance associated with different habitat variables. It is easiest to estimate the sample size needed for a single year estimate of P. We recommend that bioregional coordinators begin by estimating this sample size, and then increase this sample size by a safety margin, perhaps 10–15%, to meet the sample size needs for the other objectives.

The sample size needed for a single year estimate of P will vary by bioregion, depending on the representation of total PSUs in each of the four strata, the average cost of sampling a PSU in each stratum, and the probability of goshawk presence in each stratum. Pilot data specific to the bioregion are needed in order to provide an estimate of cost and the probability of goshawk presence.

The sample size is allocated among the four strata to minimize, for a fixed total cost, the standard error of $\hat{P}$ (the estimate of the actual frequency of occurrence of territorial adult goshawks, P). This procedure begins by using pilot data to calculate coefficients for probabilities of presence and for cost factors for each of the four strata. The coefficients are used to derive a variance for the maximum likelihood estimator of overall goshawk presence. The formula for sample size estimation and allocation is based on the sample size estimation algorithm for a binomial distribution, but the variance is larger by an additive term than the usual variance associated with a binomial distribution because detection probabilities are less than one. The procedure also uses information on the total number of PSUs in each stratum to provide a weighted average for sample size allocation. Although the weighted averages account for differences in PSU representation among the four strata, they do not result in proportional sampling because of the influence of the coefficients for goshawk presence, detectability, and cost. The procedure also assumes that a fixed cost is to be allocated among the four strata.

An interactive spreadsheet for sample size calculation and allocation has been developed by Jim Baldwin (USDA Forest Service, Pacific Southwest Research Station). Bioregional coordinators can obtain a copy of the spreadsheet by contacting us.

DATA COLLECTION

Annual Schedule

The design calls for two surveys per sampled PSU. Survey 1 occurs when goshawks are tending nestlings and survey 2 occurs during late nestling and post-fledging periods. The dates of the two survey periods are determined from local information on nesting phenology, but generally, the nestling phase occurs from late May through late June or early July, and the late nestling and post-fledging periods occur from late June through late August. Surveys can be conducted any time from dawn to dusk.

Multi-year Schedule

The design employs a 100% annual re-measurement schedule wherein a fixed number of PSUs are repeatedly sampled each year. We considered a design that samples a portion of the total sample annually, known as the serial alternating panel design (Urquhart and Kincaid 1999), because it enables a bioregion to obtain a larger sample size over a multi-year sampling period. That approach, however, could result in higher variance for $\hat{P}$ because each annual sample is smaller than if 100% annual re-measurement took place. Moreover, sampling only part of the total each year requires stable funding for each annual increment in order to stay on schedule for the entire sample to be surveyed. Furthermore, from a logistical perspective, 100% annual re-measurement allows for increased efficiency as the sample territories become well known over a period of years. In contrast, the serial alternating panel design creates new logistical challenges each year, as new PSUs are initiated into the sample.

Survey Method

Each PSU is surveyed using the broadcast acoustical survey method (Kennedy and Stahlecker 1993, Joy et al. 1994, USDA Forest Service 2000a) The sampling grid in each PSU is comprised of call stations located on 10 transects that are 250 m apart, with 12 call stations per transect. Call stations along each transect are 200 m apart, and adjacent transect stations are offset 100 m to maximize coverage. This spacing ensures that each call point is within auditory detection distance (roughly 150 m) of the next adjacent call point within the stand (Woodbridge, unpubl. data). If the entire PSU consists of potential goshawk habitat, there will be 120 call points, but points that fall >150 meters from potential habitat are not surveyed. Areas considered to be non-habitat are cliffs, talus slopes, non-forested areas, and water bodies. The actual number of call points will therefore vary for each PSU. Transect lines and call points are permanently marked and/or recorded with a global positioning system instrument (GPS).

Field tests indicate that a two-visit survey with the recommended transect and call point spacing results in a detection rate >90% for actively breeding goshawks and >80% for non-breeding adults during the nesting season (Woodbridge and Keane, unpubl. data; Table 3). This rate is higher than that reported by Kennedy and Stahlecker (1993) and by Watson et al. (1999). However, neither of these studies used the full complement of transects and call stations in the protocol to obtain detection rates.

The procedure is to survey the PSU until a detection is made or until all potential habitat within the

TABLE 3. COMPARISON OF DETECTION RATES OF TWO SURVEY METHODS FOR NORTHERN GOSHAWKS (KEANE AND WOODBRIDGE, UNPUBL. DATA).

		Territory plot status	
Method	Nesting	Occupied non-nesting	Unoccupied-old nests[a]
Broadcast acoustical survey protocol			
One visit	0.90	0.64	0.36
Two visits	0.94	0.87	0.59
Three visits[b]	1.00	0.96	0.73
Stand search survey protocol			
One visit	0.97	0.74	0.43
Two visits	1.00	0.93	0.67
Three visits	1.00	0.98	0.81

[a] Rate is for detection of old nests at unoccupied territory plots.
[b] Three-visit probability calculated using binomial expansion of 1-visit detection P.

PSU is completely surveyed. We anticipate 10–30 hr to survey each PSU. For efficiency, surveyors start in areas of the PSU with the highest likelihood of goshawk presence. Transect lines and call points can be established with GIS prior to field work, and surveyors can use GPS units to obtain the most efficient and economical survey coverage rather than run transect lines systematically. However, surveyors should avoid using roads to walk or drive between call points, because part of the survey method is looking and listening for goshawk or any goshawk sign, such as nests, plucking posts, molted feathers, and whitewash, between call points.

This protocol calls for two surveyors working together. Most time is spent walking between stations, so it is important to be alert for goshawks approaching, often silently, to investigate the surveyors. Use of two observers enhances the probability of visual detections of goshawks or molted feathers, because one person can focus upward to look for nests or silently approaching goshawks while the other can focus downward to look for feathers and whitewash.

If a detection occurs, the PSU is recorded as having goshawk presence and the survey is ended. If a detection does not occur, the surveyors continue on to call points with increasingly less likelihood of goshawk presence. The detection of an unused nest is not considered presence. The detection of a molted goshawk feather results in a present outcome for a PSU, but we encourage surveyors to continue to survey the PSU with broadcast calls because of the additional information associated with an aural response or visual detection.

Following Kennedy and Stahlecker (1993), the surveyors conduct two, three-call sequences in a circle centered on the call point, for a minimum of 3 min spent at each call point. Each sequence begins with broadcasting a call at 60° from the transect line for 10 sec, then listening and watching for 30 sec. This is repeated two more times, each time rotating 120° from the last broadcast. After the second sequence of three broadcasts, the surveyors move to the next call point, walking at an easy pace while listening and watching carefully for goshawk calls and sign.

Surveyors do not survey under conditions such as winds >15 mph or rain that may reduce ability to detect goshawk responses. To avoid misidentifying broadcasts of co-workers, simultaneous surveys are conducted no closer than two transect widths apart. To ensure accurate identification of feathers, feathers are compared to known samples or to pictures of feathers. A useful resource is *Feathers of Western Forest Raptors and Look-alikes*, a CD with color images of raptor feathers created by B. Woodbridge and produced by E. Frost. A companion CD created by B. Woodbridge, *Voices of Forest Raptors and Sound-alikes*, is useful for broadcast surveys as well as identification of response calls. Both CDs are available through an email request to C. Vojta (cvojta@fs.fed.us).

During the nestling period, surveyors broadcast the adult alarm call. During the late nestling and post-fledging period, the wail or juvenile food-begging call is broadcast because it is more likely to elicit responses from juvenile goshawks. Effective coverage of a survey area is dependent on the surveyors' ability to broadcast sound that can be detected at least 200 m from the source.

Kennedy and Stahlecker (1993) and Fuller and Mosher (1987) recommend using equipment producing at least 80–110 dB output at 1 m from the source. Until recently, the most commonly used broadcast equipment has been a small personal cassette player connected to a small megaphone. Recent developments include compact disk and MP3 players as storage media and improved digital amplifiers that store goshawk calls on internal chips. Other equipment required for surveys include compass, binoculars, flagging or other station markers, and plastic baggies and labels for feathers and prey remains. GPS units are highly recommended, because they provide the surveyors with greater flexibility in traveling between call points.

When the surveyors hear a response, they record the type of response, compass bearing, station number and distance from transect. Response types fall into one of three categories as defined by Joy et al. (1994): vocal non-approach, silent approach, and vocal approach. Surveyors attempt to locate the goshawk visually and determine the sex and age (adult versus juvenile or fledgling) of the responding individual.

HABITAT DATA

The monitoring design uses two sources of habitat data: landscape variables associated with each sampled PSU, and data from all forest inventory analysis (FIA) points within the bioregional sampling frame. This section describes the purpose and acquisition of each type of data. Because the bioregional monitoring plan is in its infancy, we anticipate the need for numerous discussions among land managers, the academic community, and bioregional coordinators to identify specific habitat components and other environmental factors that might influence goshawk abundance. We view this section on habitat data to be the starting point for those discussions.

Data collected from each sampled PSU are used to compare forest composition, forest structure, and landscape pattern of PSUs with and without goshawk detections. These data can be used in habitat relationship models to predict goshawk presence and to inform management decisions, especially when the data are supported with research studies that have investigated the underlying mechanisms of the observed relationships. They can also be used to assess changes in landscape pattern and structure over time, in relation to changes in goshawk occurrence.

The bioregional coordinator acquires habitat information from all sampled PSUs, regardless of survey outcome, using the best available vegetation coverage with pixel resolution between 20–30 m. The variables for which data are collected are: (1) number of vegetation patches, (2) number of vegetation cover types, (3) size of largest vegetation patch

(including patch area that extends beyond the PSU boundary), (4) percent of PSU in primary, marginal, and non habitat as defined by the initial PSU stratification process, (5) proportion of PSU in each structural stage (using structural stage classes standard within the bioregion), (6) estimated proportion of PSU that has been thinned and/or burned under prescription in the last 20 yr, (7) estimated proportion of PSU that has been harvested in the last 20 yr (from commercial thinning, overstory removal or clearcutting), and (8) straight-line distances from the PSU center to the nearest permanent water including springs, road (regardless of use status), trail, and meadow edge.

The second source of habitat data is from the FIA program, which is the national forest inventory that has been in existence since 1930. The FIA program consists of a coast-to-coast hexagonal grid, each hexagon 2,403 ha in size, with one point per hexagon, and a set of plots at each point. Forest composition and structure data are obtained from each set of plots to enable the FIA program to report on status and trends of forest area, species composition, tree growth and mortality, and other aspects of forest lands. Data from individual FIA points cannot explain goshawk presence at any given detection point, but the summary of FIA information across a bioregion can be used to assess overall habitat availability and to observe changes in habitat availability over time.

The bioregional coordinator acquires data from all FIA plots within the bioregional sampling frame by making a request through the appropriate FIA regional office, which is associated with the Forest Service Research and Development branch (see http://fia.fs.fed.us). The bioregional coordinator can request FIA personnel to provide summary information on stand structural variables that characterize overall habitat condition, e.g., basal area, stand density, and dbh. These data are available after each period of FIA data collection (usually annually). The coordinator uses the summary information to assess changes in habitat condition over time, and to look for possible correlations between changes in the bioregional estimate of goshawk occurrence and changes in habitat.

The bioregional coordinator should acquire additional information to aid in interpreting the annual bioregional estimate of goshawk occurrence. For example, climatic data, especially measures of precipitation and temperature could prove useful because climatic factors are likely to have a direct influence on the timing and success of nesting efforts, and on prey availability. Prey availability is a significant factor affecting goshawk reproduction and abundance (Lindén and Wikman 1983, Doyle and Smith 1994). Where red squirrels (*Tamiasciurus hudsonicus*) and Douglas squirrels are known primary prey of goshawks, cone crop data can be a useful surrogate for prey availability (Keane 1999).

We also recommend acquiring data on land management activities for the bioregion, such as an estimated areal extent of hazardous fuel reduction activities. In many cases, these data might already be collected by other entities and might be available at little or no cost to the bioregional monitoring effort.

DATA ANALYSIS

ESTIMATING THE RELATIVE ABUNDANCE OF GOSHAWKS

The parameter of interest is P, the proportion of all PSUs in a bioregion with goshawk presence. P is estimated from the proportion of all PSUs with goshawk presence in each of the four strata, or:

$$P = \frac{\text{Total number of sites with presence}}{\text{Total number of sites}}$$

$$= \frac{N_1 P_1 + N_2 P_2 + N_3 P_3 + N_4 P_4}{N_1 + N_2 + N_3 + N_4}$$

where N_1, N_2, N_3, and N_4 are, respectively, the total number of PSUs in each of the four strata and P_1, P_2, P_3, and P_4 are, respectively, the proportion of PSUs with presence in each of the four strata.

Data from each sampled PSU are independent because the sampled PSUs were randomly selected within each stratum. Moreover, data from each visit are independent because the outcome of the first visit does not change the probability of detecting presence during the second visit, assuming that the presence status remains constant throughout each year's sampling season.

Each visit has a constant probability of missing presence when a goshawk is present but those probabilities (q_n and q_f) differ between surveys because of differences in goshawk behavior between the nestling and fledging periods. The detection probability is $1 - q_n$ for the nestling period and $1 - q_f$ for the fledging period.

In order to estimate P, the bioregional coordinator must first estimate 6 parameters: the proportion of PSUs with goshawk presence for each of the four strata, P_1, P_2, P_3, and P_4, and the two probabilities of missing presence, q_n and q_f. These parameters are derived from the particular sequence of presence/absence data recorded for up to two surveys at each site, which can be one of the following sequences:

00, 01, 1•, 10, or 11. The sequence labeled 1• denotes where just one survey was made.

In order to provide data for sequences 11 and 10, a proportion, r, of all PSUs with detections during survey 1 must be randomly selected and visited a second time. The bioregional coordinator may choose to include all PSUs (*i.e*, $r = 1$) with detections rather than a proportion of them. If not all PSUs have two surveys, then r needs to be selected to provide a minimum of 30 PSUs that are surveyed a second time.

The probability that selected PSU j in stratum i will have a particular sequence of presence status (x_{ij}) follows (ignoring any adjustments related to sampling without replacement from a finite population) (J. Baldwin, pers. comm., MacKenzie et al. 2002):

$$
\begin{aligned}
f(x_{ij}) &= (1 - P_i) + P_i q_n q_f & \text{for } x_{ij} = 00 \\
&= P_i (1 - q_n) q_f \, r & \text{for } x_{ij} = 10 \\
&= P_i q_n (1 - q_f) & \text{for } x_{ij} = 01 \\
&= P_i (1 - q_n)(1 - q_f) r & \text{for } x_{ij} = 11 \\
&= P_i (1 - q_n)(1 - r) & \text{for } x_{ij} = 1\bullet
\end{aligned}
$$

The likelihood function will be the product of all of the individual probabilities

$$L = \prod_{i=1}^{4} \prod_{j=1}^{n_i} f(x_{ij})$$

with the log of the likelihood equal to

$$\log L = \sum_{i=1}^{4} \sum_{j=1}^{n_i} \log f(x_{ij})$$

The estimation procedure results in values for P_1, P_2, P_3, P_4, q_f, and q_n that maximize $\log L$.

Maximizing either the likelihood function or the log of the likelihood results in the same values of the parameter estimates, but it is numerically more convenient to use the log of the likelihood function. Standard errors will be estimated using a bootstrap process. The sample size of each bootstrap sample is the same as the original sample for each stratum, but the bootstrap samples are created by random sampling with replacement.

Missing values will almost certainly occur because of weather, snowpack, fire, or lack of available crews, and some PSUs might receive additional surveys. Adjustments can be made to the definition of $f(x_{ij})$ (the probability of observing sequence x_{ij}) to allow for such occurrences. For now the above formulas are adequate for planning purposes.

ASSESSING CHANGE IN GOSHAWK RELATIVE ABUNDANCE OVER TIME

The bioregional coordinator can begin to assess change in the relative abundance of goshawks after 5 yr. By graphing $\hat{P}$ and the associated confidence interval for each year, the coordinator can visually assess the pattern prior to conducting a statistical analysis. We anticipate that the data will show upward or downward spikes in $\hat{P}$ rather than a smooth trend, and that a model other than a simple linear model will be needed to test whether a change has occurred in the proportion of PSUs with goshawk presence.

The ability to detect changes in P across years will depend on the values of P for each year relative to 0.5. It is more difficult to detect absolute changes in P when values approach 0.5 than when values are at either end of the continuum (e.g., <0.3, >0.7), as the variance of $\hat{P}$ will tend to be largest when P is around 0.5. We anticipate that values of P (and therefore also of $\hat{P}$) will fall in the lower range of potential values for marginal habitat, and could likely fall in the higher range of potential values for primary habitat.

The observed history of presence for each PSU is needed in order to evaluate whether a change in P has occurred (MacKenzie et al. 2003). If a PSU is observed to have goshawks present in 1 out of 5 yr, its likelihood contribution for use in the maximum likelihood estimation process is different than a PSU with no observed goshawks in all 5 yr. In the second example (no observed presence), the probability that the PSU has a goshawk present is weighted by the average of the probabilities that the PSU truly contains no goshawks, or that goshawks were present but not observed.

MacKenzie et al. (2003) illustrate how detection history is used to estimate changes in occupancy status of potential Northern Spotted Owl (*Strix occidentalis caurinus*) territories after 5 yr. The authors first used the detection history to estimate the probability that a territory was occupied in any given year. They then developed a set of models in which colonization and extinction rates were year-specific or were held constant, and chose the best model with respect to Akaike's information criterion (AIC; Akaike 1974). The authors concluded that the best model suggested a fairly static average level of occupancy over 5 yr. The process for estimating change in the relative abundance of goshawks would be similar, but PSUs rather than territories would be the sampling unit for which change would be measured.

EVALUATING THE ROLE OF HABITAT AND ENVIRONMENTAL FACTORS IN GOSHAWK POPULATION TRENDS

Habitat and other environmental data provide opportunities to look for patterns between population change and environmental factors such as habitat structure, precipitation, prey abundance, or management actions. To look for possible correlations, we recommend using environmental variables as covariates in a series of logistic models, and information theoretics as a means of model comparison. (Akaike 1974, Burnham and Anderson 2002). Relevant variables to use in model development are discussed in the data collection section above.

Simple correlations between goshawk population trends and environmental changes are insufficient, however, for developing meaningful conservation strategies. We need knowledge of the mechanisms that affect population size in order to make recommendations for management. Therefore, status and trend monitoring should be accompanied by research aimed at understanding causal relationships. Although the bioregion is an appropriate spatial scale for monitoring goshawk populations, it is not necessarily the best scale for investigating the mechanisms driving population change (Keane and Morrison 1994), so research will likely occur separately from bioregional monitoring. Correlations observed during population monitoring can suggest fruitful directions for research, but research studies do not necessarily have to wait for results from population monitoring in order to test meaningful hypotheses. There is currently enough knowledge of goshawk ecology to establish research studies concomitant with population monitoring, so that research results can be used to interpret monitoring trends during the same time frame.

COORDINATION AMONG BIOREGIONS

The bioregional monitoring plan provides an opportunity to aggregate information if data are collected in a consistent fashion between bioregions. In particular, consistency is needed in carrying out the broadcast acoustical survey method. Detection probabilities could be affected if the spacing of call points and transect lines is altered or if the number of visits to a PSU is increased. Training should be coordinated between bioregions to ensure that surveyors move at similar paces and have similar identification skills.

Consistency is also needed in classifying goshawk habitat. Although each bioregion will likely differ in habitats used by goshawks, there may be important similarities at coarse scales. For example, geographic differences in vegetation associations can be aggregated into similar physiognomic classes. In order to build consistency in landscape variables such as the number of vegetation types and the number of structural stages in each PSU, it is important to first agree on what is meant by a vegetation type and a structural stage. Without coordination and agreement, bioregions will differ in how finely these classifications are made.

SUMMARY

We recognize the ambitious scope of this monitoring plan and acknowledge that adequate and consistent funding is necessary for it to succeed. We are encouraged, however, by the success of several monitoring programs and survey designs that have occurred at a scale comparable to our proposed bioregions. Most notable are several land-bird-monitoring programs (Howe et al. 1997, Hutto and Young 2002, Robbins et al. 1986), and monitoring of the Northern Spotted Owl (Lint et al. 1999) and the Marbled Murrelet (*Brachyramphus marmoratus*; Madsen et al. 1999). Commonalities shared by these programs are a well-stated objective, clear statistical design, data-collection protocol, centralization for data analysis and reporting, and adequate funding. We have built from these examples in developing this monitoring plan for goshawks.

ACKNOWLEDGMENTS

Funding for development and testing of this monitoring plan was provided by the USDA Forest Service, through Ecosystem Management Coordination and the Terrestrial Wildlife Ecology Unit. Members of the working group were B. Woodbridge (leader), C. D. Hargis, R. T. Reynolds, J. Baldwin, A. Franklin, C. Schultz, G. Hayward, A. Williamson, K. Titus, S. Dewey, P. Janiga, and D. A. Boyce. We are grateful to J. Baldwin for statistical consultation and for preparation of the statistical equations used in the text. We are grateful to D. LaPlante for GIS evaluation of PSU size, and B. Allison for preparation of the figures. We greatly appreciate the willingness of C. L. Ferland to test this monitoring design, and thank D. Gomez, M. Ball, and L. Wiley for their logistic support. We thank D. E. Andersen, P. H. Geissler, T. Max, A. R. Olsen, M. G. Raphael, L. F. Ruggiero, T. Schreuder, and R. King for valuable comments on earlier drafts.

Studies in Avian Biology No. 31:288–298

RESOURCE SELECTION FUNCTION MODELS AS TOOLS FOR REGIONAL CONSERVATION PLANNING FOR NORTHERN GOSHAWK IN UTAH

Carlos Carroll, Ronald L. Rodriguez, Clinton McCarthy, And Kathleen M. Paulin

Abstract. Because the Northern Goshawk (*Accipiter gentiles*) has a relatively large home range size and low density, data on regional-scale habitat configuration is a critical element of conservation planning for the species. We built a resource-selection-function model to predict goshawk occurrence based on 565 nest-site locations surveyed from 1992–2002 on USDA Forest Service lands throughout Utah. Potential explanatory variables included regional-scale geographic information system (GIS) data on vegetation type, MODIS satellite imagery metrics, topography, climate, and road density. The final model included variables for the tasseled-cap indices of brightness, greenness, and wetness derived from satellite imagery, elevation, slope, aspect, and coefficients for eight vegetation classes. Habitat variables show greater predictive power at the scale of a core or post-fledgling area (~ 1.7 km²) scale than at stand or home range scales. The model had an area under the receiver-operator-characteristic curve (ROC) of 0.874, indicating a useful to highly accurate model. Comparison using a separate validation data set of the performance of the RSF model and an expert-based ranking of the habitat value of potential vegetation types showed that both models were significant predictors of goshawk distribution, with a slight advantage to the RSF model. We compared predicted goshawk habitat distribution with that of other biodiversity targets incorporated in an ecoregional plan for the Utah high plateaus region. RSF values for goshawk were positively correlated with habitat value for wolf (*Canis lupus*) and black bear (*Ursus americanus*) but negatively correlated with rare plant locations. Use of these modeling techniques may strengthen currently planned national goshawk surveys by allowing assessment of regional habitat distribution and stratification of primary and secondary habitat across multiple land ownerships and jurisdictions.

Key Words: *Accipiter gentilis*, conservation planning, focal species, habitat model, resource selection function, spatial analysis.

MODELOS DE SELECCIÓN DE FUNCIÓN DE RECURSO, COMO HERRAMIENTAS PARA LA PLANEACIÓN DE LA CONSERVACIÓN DEL GAVILÁN AZOR EN UTAH.

Resumen. Debido a que el Gavilán Azor (*Accipiter gentilis*) tiene un rango en el tamaño del hogar relativamente grande y una baja densidad, información sobre la configuración del hábitat a escala regional es un elemento crítico en la planeación para la conservación de la especie. Construimos un modelo de selección de función de recurso para predecir la ocurrencia del gavilán, basado en 565 localidades de sitios de nidos, estudiadas de 1992–2002, en tierras del USDA Servicio Forestal por todo Utah. Potenciales variables explicativas incluyeron datos de tipo de vegetación en sistemas de información geográfica (SIG) de escala regional, imágenes de satélite métricas MODIS, topografía, clima y densidad de caminos. El modelo final incluyó variables para los índices de brillo, verdor y humedad derivados de la imagen satelital, elevación, pendiente, aspecto y coeficientes para ocho clases de vegetación. Variables del hábitat muestran mayor poder de predicción a la escala del centro o en el área de post-volantón (~ 1.7 km²), que en el grupo de árboles o en escalas de los rangos de hogar. El modelo tuvo un área bajo la curva recibidor-operador-característica (ROC) de 0.874, indicando que este modelo es útil y altamente preciso. La comparación, utilizando un grupo de datos de validación distinta del desempeño del modelo RSF y una clasificación basada-en-experiencia del valor del hábitat de los valores potenciales de la vegetación, mostró que ambos modelos fueron pronósticos significativos de la distribución del gavilán, con una pequeña ventaja en el modelo RSF. Comparamos la distribución pronosticada del hábitat del gavilán con la de otros blancos de biodiversidad incorporados en un plan ecoregional para la región alta de la meseta de Utah. Los valores RSF para el gavilán fueron positivamente correlacionados con el valor del hábitat para el lobo (*Canis lupus*) y el oso negro (*Ursus americanus*), pero negativamente correlacionados con localidades de plantas raras. La utilización de este tipo de técnicas de modelación podría fortalecer estudios nacionales sobre el gavilán actualmente planeados, permitiendo la evaluación de la distribución del hábitat regional y la estratificación del hábitat primario y secundario a través de múltiples propietarios y jurisdicciones.

Until recently, conservation planning in the US has been species-based, due to the prevalent interpretation of the Endangered Species Act (USDI Fish and Wildlife Service 1997, 1998a) and other legal mandates. Because knowledge and resources are insufficient to manage for all species individually, land-management agencies increasingly have advocated ecosystem-level regional planning (USDA and USDI 1994). Although the concept of management indicator species, as often applied, has been questioned (Landres et al. 1988, Noss 1990), the broader notion that the population status of a species can be used to assess ecological integrity in conjunction with landscape or ecosystem-level metrics remains useful. Population viability analysis of well-selected focal species allows us to evaluate the effectiveness of conservation strategies in a way not possible with composite indicators of ecosystem function (Carroll et al. 2003a). Lambeck (1997) suggested linking conservation of species and ecosystems by focusing on a few focal species that are most sensitive to changes in key landscape processes (e.g., fire). The Northern Goshawk (*Accipiter gentilis*) may fall into two of four categories of focal species (Lambeck 1997)—it is area-limited, with a home range size that may be >20 km², and may be resource-limited by its association with large trees that are used for nesting or to facilitate hunting (Reynolds et al. 1992, Beier and Drennan 1997, Squires and Reynolds 1997).

Many potential focal species occur at low densities due to their high trophic position. This makes collecting accurate survey data difficult and expensive. Although planning for the goshawk benefits from the availability of long-term demographic data in a few portions of the species' range (Reynolds and Joy 1998, Ingraldi 1999), population parameters from intensive demographic studies may provide ambiguous information on declining viability without information on regional-scale trends in habitat (Doak 1995). Coordinated planning across multiple ownerships is necessary for insuring viability of area-limited or wide-ranging species. Although legal mandates have resulted in more complete data on goshawk distribution than is available for most species (Graham et al. 1999b, USDA Forest Service, unpubl. data), data collection is primarily focused on federal lands with timber or other development activities. Our knowledge of goshawk distribution and abundance on other public and private lands is still relatively poor. In order to develop an estimate of goshawk habitat value across the entire region of interest (the Utah high plateaus (UHP) ecoregion (Fig. 1), we developed a resource selection function

(RSF; see Appendix 1 for definitions of terminology) (Manly et al. 1993, Boyce and McDonald 1999) based on a multivariate analysis of correlations between known goshawk nest locations and regional-scale habitat variables. We then compared RSF model results with those from an expert-based assessment of goshawk habitat quality (Graham et al. 1999b).

The use of particular focal species in developing regional conservation plans (Carroll et al. 2001) complements two other major tracks of conservation planning; special elements and ecosystem representation (Noss and Cooperrider 1994, Noss et al. 2002). The special elements approach concentrates on occurrences of imperiled species, rare plant communities, and other rare natural features, as are found in the databases of the conservation data center (CDC) network maintained by state and non-governmental organizations (Groves et al. 2003). The level of threat to, and hence the conservation attention merited by a species, is based on the heritage ranking system developed by the CDCs rather than on federal or agency mandates (such as endangered or sensitive species; Groves et al. 2003). Focal species are distinct from special elements in that they are meant to be a representative subset of those species whose persistence is dependent on broader-scale habitat configuration and thus would be inadequately protected by managing only those sites with recorded occurrences. The representation approach seeks to capture examples of all geoclimatic or vegetation types in a network of protected areas. These vegetation types occur at a broader scale than those localized plant communities evaluated as special elements (Groves et al. 2003).

We used model predictions to assess the degree of overlap between areas of high priority for goshawk conservation and for conservation of other focal species and the broader special element conservation goals. For this step, we used habitat models and special elements data developed in a cooperative federal and non-governmental organization (USDA Forest Service (USFS) and Nature Conservancy (TNC)) planning process for the UHP ecoregion, which covers approximately 46,000 km² in the states of Utah and Colorado (Tuhy et al. 2004; Fig. 1). The UHP ecoregion is a series of plateaus that rise steeply from the north-south trending valleys that separate them. Common vegetation types include conifer forests of spruce (*Picea* spp.), fir (*Abies* spp.), pine (*Pinus* spp.), and Douglas fir (*Pseudotsuga menziesii*), as well as aspen (*Populus tremuloides*), grassland, montane shrubs, and big sagebrush (*Artemisia*

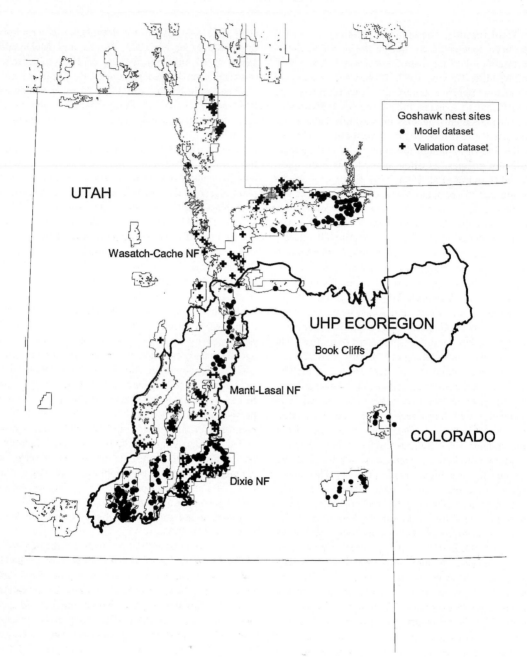

FIGURE 1. Locations of Northern Goshawk nest sites on USDA Forest Service lands in Utah. Dots mark nest locations used in development of the resource selection function (RSF) model. Crosses mark nest locations used for model validation.

tridentata). Precipitation ranges from 375–900 mm annually and annual temperature averages 0–8 C (USDA Forest Service, unpubl. data). The ecoregion encompasses portions of four national forests, several Bureau of Land Management (BLM) field offices, Ute tribal land, and state and private lands. The UHP ecoregional planning process combines methods for ecological assessments used by the USFS with the ecoregional planning methods developed by TNC (Tuhy et al. 2004). Because the ecoregional plan is intended as a decision support tool rather than as a management decision as defined under the National

Environmental Policy Act (NEPA), the plan and its associated data may be applied independently by the USFS and TNC. But because the process uses information on the distribution of biodiversity on all land ownerships within the ecoregion, it will allow public land management decisions such as forest plan revisions to better include information on the biological context of public lands.

Work groups composed of agency biologists and other experts chose three species for in-depth analysis as the focal species component of the UHP plan: the gray wolf (*Canis lupus*), black bear (*Ursus americanus*), and Northern Goshawk. The wolf has recently dispersed into Utah from adjacent populations in Wyoming and Idaho, and has been the focus of a recent state management planning process designed to anticipate and reduce conflicts with livestock and sport hunting (Utah Division of Wildlife Resources 2005). The black bear was selected due to its association with semi-arid vegetation communities and the hypothesized sensitivity of populations in portions of the UHP ecoregion to high rates of sport harvest and control associated with livestock depredation. Due to their relatively large area requirements, these three species may all be expected to be dependent on habitat configuration at regional scales. It was hypothesized that habitat and population viability requirements differ between the species in such a way as to provide contrasting and complementary information to the planning process. Although the impact of factors such as regional habitat connectivity on goshawk populations is poorly known in comparison to the two terrestrial species, field data suggests that a significant proportion of dispersal distances exceed 100 km (Wiens et al. 2006b) and thus a regional-scale perspective on habitat distribution is informative.

The objectives of the goshawk analysis thus spanned multiple spatial scales and management contexts to include the following goals:

1. Provide a multi-ownership assessment of goshawk distribution for use in ecoregional planning.
2. Subsequently inform decisions at the national forest and project level as to the relative importance of a project area for goshawks.
3. Provide initial estimates of regional habitat distribution and potential sampling strata (primary and secondary habitat) for potential use in broad-scale regional surveys (Hargis and Woodbridge, *this volume*).
4. Suggest general hypotheses concerning factors and spatial scales of habitat influencing goshawk distribution that could be tested by future surveys.

METHODS

Resource Selection Function Model

An RSF model (Manly et al. 1993) was constructed to predict goshawk nest site occurrence based on regional-scale GIS data such as vegetation type, satellite imagery metrics, topography, climate, and road density variables (Table 1). Satellite imagery was transformed into the tasseled-cap indices of brightness, greenness, and wetness (Crist and Cicone 1984), a standardized means of representing the three principal axes of variation in the values of the six moderate resolution imaging spectrometer (MODIS) spectral bands that are equivalent to those in the older thematic mapper (TM) imagery (Appendix 1; Wharton and Myers 1997). Pseudo-habitat variables that are derived directly from unclassified satellite imagery are correlated to varying degrees with ecological factors such as net primary productivity and thus abundance of prey species and have proved useful in modeling wildlife distributions (Mace et al. 1999, Carroll et al. 2001). However, interpretation of changes in these metrics is complex. The cover type class (e.g., forest versus grassland) and topographic position of a site will affect the manner in which the metric changes in response to changes in ecological attributes such as productivity. Forest stands may first increase and then decrease along the tasseled-cap axes as they age (Cohen et al. 1995). Closed hardwood-conifer forest typically has higher greenness than pure conifer stands. Brightness often corresponds to the amount and reflectivity of exposed soil. Greenness, as its name suggests, is often a correlate of primary productivity. Wetness, however, does not necessarily reflect the presence of water. Wetness is often highest in young conifer stands, with hardwoods and older conifers having lower wetness (Cohen et al. 1995). We also assessed whether we could improve the model by addition of variables representing expert-based habitat rankings for nesting, foraging, or overall habitat value based on potential vegetation type for the state of Utah (Graham et al. 1999b).

Three moving-window sizes were used to approximate hypothesized scales of goshawk habitat selection: 1 km^2 nest site or stand, 1.7 km^2 core or post-fledging area, and 22 km^2 breeding-season home range (Graham et al. 1994, 1999b). Imagery from two seasonal dates in 2001 was used—May to represent nest establishment and July to represent height of the growing season. The following number of nest-site locations from USFS lands throughout Utah, dating from 1991–2002, were used in model

TABLE 1. DATA LAYERS EVALUATED IN THE DEVELOPMENT OF THE RESOURCE SELECTION FUNCTION MODEL FOR NORTHERN GOSHAWK IN UTAH.

Data layer	Resolution	References
Vegetation variables		
Potential vegetation type	>5 ha MMU	Graham et al. 1999b
Existing vegetation type—GAP	5 ha MMU	Edwards et al. 1995
Satellite imagery metrics		
July leaf area index (LAI)	1 km	Wharton and Myers 1997
July enhanced vegetation index (EVI)	1 km	Wharton and Myers 1997
May brightness	1 km	Crist and Cicone 1984
May greenness	1 km	Crist and Cicone 1984
May wetness	1 km	Crist and Cicone 1984
July brightness	1 km	Crist and Cicone 1984
July greenness	1km	Crist and Cicone 1984
July wetness	1 km	Crist and Cicone 1984
Topographic variables		
Elevation	90 m	USGS unpubl.
Slope	90 m	USGS unpubl.
Aspect (transformed)	90 m	Beers et al. 1966
Climatic variables		
Average annual snowfall	2 km	Daly et al. 1994
Average annual precipitation	2 km	Daly et al. 1994
May precipitation (mean, min., max., range)	2 km	Daly et al. 1994
July precipitation (mean, min., max., range)	2 km	Daly et al. 1994
Average annual temperature	2 km	Daly et al. 1994
May temperature (mean, min., max., range)	2 km	Daly et al. 1994
July temperature (mean, min, max, range)	2 km	Daly et al. 1994
Human-impact associated variables		
Road density	1:100,000	USGS unpubl.

development: Dixie National Forest (excluding the Escalante Ranger District)—208, Manti-Lasal National Forest—70, Ashley National Forest—138, for a total of 416. Because nest-site data spanning 11 yr were compared with a single year of satellite imagery, we cannot represent the inter-annual variability in the environment at nest sites, e.g., due to drought. The 416 nest locations comprised 199 territories. Although nests were assigned to territories by field personnel based on proximity, territory membership is not known with certainty. To avoid bias due to uneven survey effort over time, nest locations were weighted in the model-fitting by the inverse of the number of nest sites in the territory. These used locations were compared with 1,687 available locations randomly selected from within the boundaries of the forests listed above. All habitats within USFS lands were included as available habitat, including vegetation types that might have been classified as unsuitable by an expert-based model. Our goal was to evaluate goshawk occurrence probability over a geographic region, rather within specific habitat types. Extrapolation of our model to adjacent ownerships for which little survey data exists can be expected to be more problematic than its application on USFS

lands. However, because ecoregions are delineated based on similarities in biological, edaphic and climatic characteristics (Groves et al. 2003), and our results were intended for use in multi-ownership eco-regional planning, we expanded our scope of inference to the eco-region as a whole.

Model predictions, especially on non-USFS lands, should therefore be seen as map-based hypotheses to be validated with new field data (Murphy and Noon 1992, Carroll et al. 1999). The model predictions should also be seen as hypotheses because the multiple logistic regression analysis was not restricted to a limited set of a priori models. Comprehensive sets of candidate models are difficult to construct a priori when evaluating variables such as satellite imagery metrics whose functional relationship to biological processes is poorly known. Alternate models were compared using AIC and BIC (Appendix 1), diagnostic statistics that penalize for overfitting (Akaike 1973, Schwarz 1978). AUC, the area under the receiver operating curve (ROC), was used as a measure of model performance. AUC is similar to but more informative than alternate model diagnostics such as correct classification rate or confusion matrices (Manel et al. 2001).

One hundred and forty-nine nest locations from areas not included in the original data set (Fishlake National Forest—40, Dixie National Forest Escalante Ranger District—40, Uinta National Forest—34, and Wasatch-Cache National Forest—35) were withheld for use in model validation and compared in this step with 1,516 random points distributed throughout these validation areas. We compared our RSF model results with the habitat value predicted by an expert-based ranking of goshawk habitat for the state of Utah (Graham et al. 1999b) by comparing the AIC of two univariate models predicting validation data class (nest or random) from either RSF or expert-based habitat values, and by a t-test for significant difference in means in predicted habitat values between nest and random sites in the validation area. Categorical class values from Graham et al. (1999b), which integrate expert-based rankings of nesting and foraging habitat, were assigned a numerical value as follows:

6. Optimum—nest value and all prey values are high.
5. High—nest value and at least one prey value are high.
4. Medium—at least one of nest and three prey values are high.
3. Medium-low—nest value and at least one prey value are medium.
2. Low—all values are medium or low.
1. Non-habitat.

Although the expert-based model (Graham et al. 1999b) was limited to Utah, summary figures for the final RSF model encompass the entire UHP eco-region lying within both Utah and Colorado.

COMPARISON OF GOSHAWK HABITAT WITH OTHER ECO-REGIONAL PLANNING TARGETS

The planning process for the UHP eco-region identified special element targets by considering species with heritage ranks of G1 (critically imperiled globally) to G3 (vulnerable globally), and then added other species of concern due to factors including declining populations or status as an endemic, disjunct, or vulnerable population (Tuhy et al. 2004). The goals for special elements sought to include a set proportion of the known occurrences of each species or community type within priority areas identified in the eco-regional plan. All occurrences of the rarest elements were targeted. For more common species, the goal was the proportion of the known occurrences thought to be sufficient to insure viability of the population (Groves et al. 2003).

We assessed the degree of spatial overlap between goshawk habitat and other elements of biodiversity by comparing the RSF model results for the goshawk with predicted habitat value for the remaining two UHP focal species (wolf and black bear) and with the rare plant special element data. We focused the latter comparison on rare plants because that category forms the majority of special element data in the UHP ecoregion (1,438 of 2,299 locations; Tuhy et al. 2004). The wolf model was a RSF model developed from wolf territory data for the Yellowstone region (Wyoming) and extrapolated to Utah and Colorado (Carroll et al. 2003b). The black bear model was an expert-based ranking of the habitat value of vegetation types in Utah for black bear (UDWR 2000), which we then extrapolated to western Colorado. Further details of the RSF model for wolf (Carroll et al. 2003b) and the expert-based model for black bear (Utah Division of Wildlife Resources 2000), as well as analysis of concordance between this species-based data and ecosystem representation goals are treated in the UHP eco-regional plan (Tuhy et al. 2004).

We measured the value of the goshawk-, wolf-, and black bear-predicted habitat models at 1,438 rare plant locations and 5,859 random locations within the UHP eco-region. The resulting data were then analyzed with Spearman rank correlations and principal components analysis (PCA; Insightful Corp. 2001, McCune et al. 2002). Although the taxa evaluated here can be expected to show contrasting spatial scales of habitat selection that is not depicted in the PCA, PCA biplots remain useful for visual assessment of patterns of habitat similarity between species that aids interpretation of the correlation coefficients (Carroll et al. 2001). We also evaluated spatial overlap between conservation targets by assessing the proportion of rare plant locations that would be included within the 20% of the eco-region with highest RSF values for goshawk.

RESULTS

RESOURCE SELECTION FUNCTION MODEL

The resource selection function took the form:

$$w(x) = \exp(-42.60564 + (0.3779376 \times \text{JULGRN}) + (-0.02276473 \times \text{JULGRN}^2) + (0.175529 \times \text{JULWET}) + (-0.03550869 \times \text{MAYBRT}) + (0.02652771 \times \text{ELEVLAT}) + (-0.000004058102 \times \text{ELEVLAT}^2) + (-0.1311468 \times \text{SLOPE}) + (6.678469 \times \text{TRANSASP}) + (-0.1057033 \times \text{VCLASS1}) + (0.9648604 \times \text{VCLASS2}) + (-1.63612 \times \text{VCLASS3}) + (1.74222 \times \text{VCLASS4}) +$$

$(0.7659255 \times VCLASS5) + (0.4041541 \times VCLASS6) + (-0.3272406 \times VCLASS7) + (-0.5334307 \times VCLASS8) + (-0.0006313316 \times JULGRN \times JULWET) + (-0.001929468 \times TRANSASP \times ELEVLAT) + (-2.077283 \times RDDEN))$

where JULGRN is July MODIS greenness, JULWET is July MODIS wetness, MAYBRT is May MODIS brightness, ELEVLAT is latitude-adjusted elevation (m), SLOPE is slope in degrees, TRANSASP is transformed aspect, and the eight vegetation classes (VCLASS) are 0 (base class)—barren, 1—true fir, 2—Douglas-fir, 3—pinyon-juniper, 4—lodgepole pine, 5—ponderosa pine, 6—aspen, 7—grassland and sagebrush, and 8—montane shrub. As elevation and greenness show convex quadratic functions in the RSF, their effect is highest at moderate values. RDDEN is a variable derived from road density for which road density values less than 0.6 km/km² are assigned a value equal to $((-1 \times \text{road density}) + 0.6)$. This is interpreted as a nuisance parameter reflecting survey bias against areas of difficult access, and therefore is set to zero when predicting actual goshawk distribution (Carroll et al. 2001). All variables were as averaged by a moving window of 1.7 km² in size, except for the MODIS variables, which due to their coarser original resolution (1 km²) were averaged over 3 km². Deviance (-2LL) equaled 899, with $\chi^2 = 372$, df = 19, and P <0.001. Pseudo-r² equaled 0.441, while a pseudo-r² corrected through cross-validation equaled 0.416. The area under the ROC curve equaled 0.874, indicating a useful model (AUC >0.7), and nearly reaching the highly accurate class (AUC >0.9 [Swets 1988]). Excluding the vegetation types, all individual variables were significant at P <0.001, except for ELEVLAT (0.74), JULGRN × JULWET (0.01), and TRANSASP × ELEVLAT (0.01). ELEVLAT is retained because of the significance of its quadratic term. Only two of the eight vegetation variables (pinyon-juniper and lodgepole pine) showed individual significance of P ≤ 0.05. However, the vegetation type factor as a whole was highly significant and improved AIC and model generality; therefore, it was retained in the model.

Comparison of the performance of the RSF model and expert-based model (Graham et al. 1999b) using the validation data showed that both models were highly significant predictors of goshawk distribution, but the RSF model performed somewhat better in terms of its AIC value (940.3) than did the expert-based model (946.9). For a t-test of significant difference in means between nest and random sites for the RSF model, t = 10.47, df = 1,663, P <0.001, for nest sites $\bar{x} = 0.077$ (SD = 0.094), for random sites 0.026 (0.052). For a t-test of significant difference in means for the expert-based model, t = 7.69 (df = 1,663, P <0.001), for nest sites $\bar{x} = 2.283$ (SD = 0.901), and for random sites $\bar{x} = 1.529$ (SD = 1.161).

Although both models showed similar predictive power for the validation data set, they showed strong contrasts in predicted habitat value in several areas of Utah (Fig. 2). The RSF model undervalued habitat in comparison to the expert-based model on the Wasatch-Cache National Forest and northern Manti-La Sal National Forest, while overvaluing habitat in comparison to the expert-based model on the Dixie National Forest, Escalante Ranger District, in the western Book Cliffs, and in extreme northcentral Utah (Fig. 2). The areas overvalued by the RSF model appear to be generally more xeric than those it undervalues. Based on the RSF model, and subject to the uncertainties attendant on model extrapolation beyond USFS lands, general public lands in the UHP eco-region have 80% higher habitat value than do private lands. Within the Utah portion of the UHP eco-region, general public lands have 26% higher expert-based habitat value (Graham et al. 1999b) than do private lands.

RSF values for goshawk were positively correlated with habitat value for wolf and black bear (Spearman's correlation coefficient or rho = 0.39 and 0.41, respectively, with P <0.001, df = 8,156 for both), but negatively correlated with rare plant locations (rho = -0.10, P <0.001, df = 8,156). Goshawk nest locations were found at higher elevations than rare plants (mean elevation 2,704 vs. 2,269 m, t = -16.71, P <0.001, df = 1,798; mean elevation of the UHP eco-region is 2,277 m). Protection of the 20% of the UHP eco-region with highest goshawk RSF values would protect 15.11% of rare plant locations. Results of the principal components analysis show that on the first two axes, which account for 64.54% of total variation in the data, the distribution of goshawk habitat is most similar to that of wolf habitat, slightly less similar to that of black bear habitat, and most dissimilar to the distribution of rare plants (Fig. 3).

DISCUSSION

Empirical distribution models such as those developed here are an important initial stage in development of a multi-ownership monitoring program (Hargis and Woodbridge, *this volume*) that can place local habitat and population trends within the context of the regional metapopulation (Carroll et al. 2001). However, initial models must be seen as

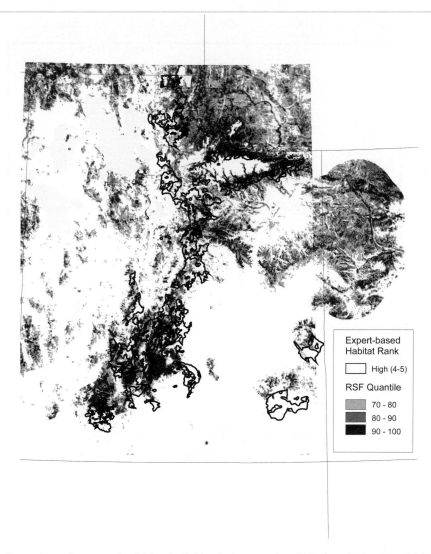

FIGURE 2. Comparison of areas rated as high value habitat in the expert-based Northern Goshawk model (Graham et al. 1999b) and the resource selection function (RSF) model.

map-based hypotheses which can refined with new field data (Murphy and Noon 1992, Carroll et al. 1999). While ideally the geographically extensive data necessary for building such models are collected through standardized surveys, such efforts only have recently been proposed as part of agency monitoring programs (Hargis and Woodbridge, *this volume*). The goshawk distribution data used here, although greatly superior to non-verifiable occurrence data such as sightings, nevertheless may show sampling bias that must be evaluated during the analysis process. Although we might expect the distribution of survey effort would bias goshawk occurrence towards more productive, low-elevation

forests, Daw et al. (1998) found that goshawk habitat was characterized similarly by both non-systematic and systematic datasets. However, Daw et al. (1998) compared habitat at a finer spatial scale (0.4 ha) than considered here. Our habitat evaluation is similar to most goshawk studies in that it ignores winter habitat distribution, which may be distant from breeding season habitat. The combination of multiple explanatory variables (e.g., vegetation) with varying levels of error in a GIS also leads to spatial error propagation and increased levels of uncertainty (Heuvelink 1998). Despite problems of survey bias, regional habitat models built from the non-systematic survey data can provide initial estimates of species

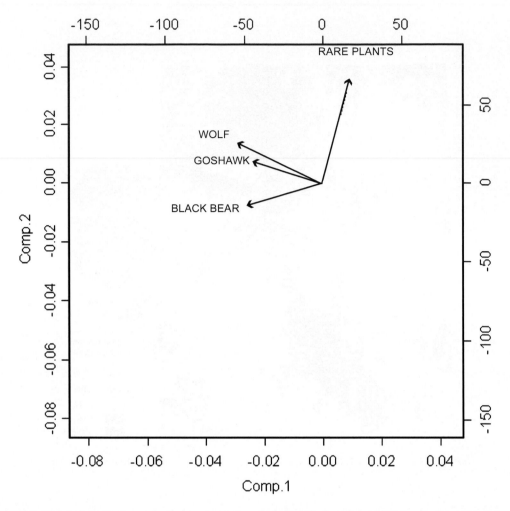

FIGURE 3. Biplot of results from principal components analysis (PCA) of predicted habitat value for goshawk (RSF model), wolf, and black bear at 1,438 rare plant locations and 5,859 random locations within the Utah high plateaus (UHP) eco-region. The biplot shows the first and second PCA axes, which together encompass 64.5% of the total variation in the data.

distribution and abundance as averaged over coarse spatial and temporal scales (Carroll et al. 2001).

INTERPRETATION OF COEFFICIENTS OF THE RSF MODEL

Interpretation of individual coefficients in regression models must be done with caution due to correlation between coefficients, but may be informative in suggesting new hypotheses as to important habitat factors. Goshawk occurrence peaks in vegetation of moderate greenness, which may indicate avoidance of both non-forested areas with low greenness and young forest or other forest types with high greenness. Areas of high brightness (low cover) are avoided. The positive association with July wetness

may indicate association with mesic forest types. The inclusion of the July tasseled-cap indices suggest that summer vegetation characteristics may the best seasonal coarse-scale predictors of goshawk occurrence. However, the negative coefficient for May brightness suggests avoidance of areas with late season snow cover. The coefficients of the topographic variables (elevation, slope, and aspect) suggest association with mid-elevation areas (adjusted for latitude), areas of low slope, and areas with northeast aspects. As elevation increases, there is less selection for mesic aspects, as would be expected due to the effect of elevation on temperature and precipitation. Although no climatic variables entered into the model, spatial variation in climate may be partially represented by factors included within the effects of elevation and the tasseled-cap indices. Among the vegetation classes, avoidance of pinyon-juniper and association with lodgepole pine were significant in the RSF model. This agrees with vegetation cover type associations found in earlier analyses (Graham et al. 1999b). A model without vegetation type variables tended to overpredict occurrence in pinyon-juniper due to that vegetation type's high greenness. Habitat variables show greater predictive power at the scale of a core or post-fledgling area (~ 1.7 km²) scale than at stand or home range scales. This agrees with results from other habitat models for other birds with high trophic positions (e.g., California Spotted Owl [*Strix occidentalis occidentalis*]; Carroll 1999), but is a finer spatial scale than that identified in habitat models for mammalian carnivores (Carroll et al. 1999). This could suggest contrasts in scale of habitat selection between the taxa, but could also arise from use of nest sites (birds) versus the less informative foraging sites (mammals) in the models, or from contrasts in underlying landscape heterogeneity between study regions.

VALUE AND LIMITATIONS OF NON-SYSTEMATIC SURVEY DATA

Due to sampling bias, we might expect the RSF model to accurately predict goshawk distribution within the extent of the survey data used in model creation but to have low generality outside that region. However, the validation results suggest that the RSF model performs slightly better than the expert-based model when tested with new data. The habitat estimates provided by both types of models are essential complements to the original nest site location data in that they allow conservation planning to occur across multiple jurisdictions that differ in survey effort. However, validation with new data from non-USFS ownerships would be a useful test of the level of extrapolation error that might be expected in multi-ownership planning. The variables used in the RSF model, such as the tasseled-cap indices, are somewhat more difficult to interpret in terms of the biological requirements of the species than are the potential vegetation types used to build the expert model (Graham et al. 1999b). Therefore the RSF results might best be used in combination with more conceptual (expert-based) models to suggest new factors that may influence goshawk distribution. RSF model development is potentially more rapid than expert-based habitat assessment over large regions, which may be useful for broad-scale monitoring programs that need an initial rapid assessment of habitat

distribution to delineate sampling strata (primary and secondary habitat) and semi-discrete populations or management units (Hargis and Woodbridge, *this volume*). Because the variables in RSF models may be more easily updated and replicable than expert-based models, they may also help in assessing whether changes in frequency of goshawk occurrence are linked to changes in habitat. At a finer scale than that of the bioregional surveys, the models were successful in providing a multi-ownership assessment of goshawk distribution for use in the UHP ecoregional plan (Tuhy et al. 2004) and providing data that can inform forest and project-level management decisions as to the relative importance of project areas for goshawks. Basing such decisions on known nest site locations alone not only sacrifices habitat in poorly-surveyed jurisdictions but also ignores the importance of unoccupied but suitable habitat for metapopulation persistence (Lande 1987).

INTEGRATING GOSHAWK CONSERVATION PRIORITIES WITH OTHER BIODIVERSITY GOALS

Land managers increasingly need information on how to combine conservation measures for well-studied, high-profile species with a broader mandate for protection of large numbers of poorly known taxa (Groves et al. 2003). The Utah high plateaus eco-regional planning process allowed us to assess this question in the context of a mountainous region with strong physical gradients in aridity and vegetation type. In this environment, we see some overlap within our mammalian and avian focal species but little overlap between this group and broader biodiversity targets such as rare plants. Amongst the three focal species analyzed in the UHP ecoregional plan, goshawk and wolf appear closest in habitat associations in the principal components analysis (Fig. 3). Both species select mesic, high productivity forest types that occur at moderate to high elevations in the region. In contrast, the black bear, an omnivore, is found at high densities in more xeric, lower elevation woodlands that contain mast-producing species such as Gambel oak (*Quercus gambelii*). Because rare plant locations occur in dissimilar habitats to all three of the focal species (Fig. 3), it appears that conservation measures focused on protecting high-value habitat for goshawk and other focal species would be poor at protecting rare plants. This effect is likely in part an artifact of the tendency of special element databases to be biased towards more easily surveyed areas with high human access (Carroll et al. 2003a). However, much of the contrast between rare plants and wide-ranging focal species in the UHP ecoregion is due to the association of rare plants with barren substrates whose low tree cover is due to edaphic or erosional processes (Tuhy et al. 2004).

Although not a surrogate for broader biodiversity goals, inclusion of wide-ranging species such as goshawk in regional conservation planning efforts addresses factors that would be missed in a plan based exclusively on special-element data (Carroll et al. 2003a). In addition to showing contrasting site-level habitat associations (Fig. 3), the three focal species may also respond to habitat availability at contrasting spatial scales. In the context of Utah and the larger Great Basin, the UHP eco-region has a disproportionate importance for terrestrial species such as the wolf because it is predominantly higher-elevation, productive habitat and connects the mainland of widespread montane habitat in the northern Rocky Mountains with more isolated habitat patches to the south (Carroll et al. 2006), forcing the planning process to address this species in an interregional context (Tuhy et al. 2004). Demographics of the goshawk, as well as the wolf and black bear, show the effect of the high environmental stochasticity (year-to-year variation) in fecundity in the semi-arid ecosystems typical of the Utah study area (Reynolds and Joy 1998, Costello et al. 2001).

Levels of interpopulation connectivity may strongly influence persistence of metapopulations characterized by high environmental stochasticity (Lande et al. 2003). Although we know little as to what constitutes population connectivity in goshawks as compared to terrestrial mammals, the species' long-distance dispersal ability (Wiens et al. 2006b) suggests that development of regional-scale distribution models, as well as broad-scale monitoring programs (Hargis and Woodbridge, *this volume*), are necessary initial steps in the development of effective conservation strategies.

ACKNOWLEDGMENTS

This work was supported by the USDA Forest Service Region 4 and The Nature Conservancy, Utah. We thank the following forest biologists for generously sharing goshawk field data and GIS data: A. Heap, R. Player, C. Staab, J. Waters, and R. Williams. We thank the participants in the UHP ecoregional regional planning process, especially P. Comer and J. Tuhy, for advice and data. M. Morrison, D. Turner, and two anonymous reviewers provided helpful reviews of the manuscript.

APPENDIX 1. DEFINITION OF TERMS.

AUC—a measure of model performance based on the area under a receiver-operating characteristics (ROC) curve. Because the ROC curve measures model sensitivity and specificity across the full range of probabilities, the AUC statistic, unlike the correct classification rate, is independent of any arbitrary threshold for classifying a species as present or absent.

AIC—Akaike information criterion, a model-fitting statistic that incorporates penalties for the addition of variables

BIC—Bayesian information criterion, a model-fitting statistic that is similar to AIC but with larger penalties for overfitting

Eco-regional plan—A plan consisting of documents and spatial data, usually developed by a land management agency or conservation organization, that seeks to evaluate the relative importance of areas for conservation of biological diversity at the scale of an eco-region. Importance is often evaluated in terms of special elements, ecosystem representation, and focal species viability. Eco-regions are defined by shared environmental and biogeographical factors.

Focal species—Species subject to in-depth habitat or viability analysis in eco-regional planning. They may be especially sensitive to key ecosystem processes and are meant to be a representative subset of those species whose persistence is dependent on broader-scale habitat configuration and thus would be inadequately protected by managing only those sites with recorded occurrences (i.e., as special elements).

MODIS—Moderate resolution imaging spectrometer, a satellite-based sensor launched on the Terra satellite that provides multispectral images of the earth at low spatial but high temporal and spectral resolution.

RSF—resource selection function, a function that is proportional to the probability that a resource unit, such as an area of habitat, will be used by an animal.

Special element—Rare and localized species and communities and other ecological features that are evaluated in eco-regional planning based on records of their occurrence at specific sites that are generally small in size.

Tasseled-cap transformation—A transformation of the six of the reflectance bands of satellite imagery (e.g., TM or MODIS) into three indices—brightness, greenness, and wetness—that represent the major axes of variation in TM data. This transformation is similar to a principal components transformation except that the axes are fixed for all data rather than dependent on a particular data set.

TM—Thematic mapper, a sensor on the Landsat series of satellites that records seven spectral bands at high spatial but low temporal resolution.

AN ECOSYSTEM-BASED CONSERVATION STRATEGY FOR THE NORTHERN GOSHAWK

RICHARD T. REYNOLDS, RUSSELL T. GRAHAM, AND DOUGLAS A. BOYCE, JR.

Abstract. The Northern Goshawk (*Accipiter gentilis*) is a large forest-dwelling raptor whose viability is in question because of habitat changes resulting from tree cutting, fire exclusion, and livestock grazing. We describe an approach for developing a goshawk habitat conservation strategy, first used in the southwestern US in 1992, that can be applied throughout the range of the species. The strategy described sets of desired habitats based on existing knowledge of the life history and habitats of goshawks, the life histories and habitats of their prey, and the ecology of overstory and understory vegetation in forests occupied by goshawks. These habitats included components such as overstory and understory compositions and structures, snags, logs, woody debris, openings, and size and arrangement of plant aggregations. The strategy incorporated the dynamic nature of forest ecosystems by developing desired landscapes consisting of temporally shifting mosaics of vegetation structural stages that comprised the habitats of goshawks and their prey. This multi-species, ecosystem-based strategy will benefit goshawks because their populations are limited by food and habitat and because the desired landscape will contain goshawk and their prey habitats through time. The approach used in this conservation strategy should be appropriate for other forests occupied by goshawks. However, because the species of prey, and the composition, structure, and dynamics of the vegetation vary among forest types, the approach is likely to result in unique desired habitats and landscapes as well as forest management prescriptions to develop them.

Key Words: *Accipiter gentilis*, conservation strategy, food webs, forest management, habitat, landscapes, prey, structural stage.

UNA ESTRATEGIA DE CONSERVACIÓN PARA EL GAVILÁN AZOR BASADA EN EL ECOSISTEMA

Resumen. El gavilán Azor (*Accipiter gentilis*) es un raptor grande que habita en el bosque, el cual su viabilidad está en duda debido a los cambios del hábitat, los cuales son resultado de la corta de árboles, exclusión del fuego y del pastoreo para ganado. Describimos un enfoque para desarrollar una estrategia de conservación del hábitat del gavilán, utilizada por primera vez en el suroeste de los Estados Unidos en 1992, la cual puede ser utilizada en todo el rango de la especie. La estrategia describió grupos de hábitats deseados, basada en información existente de la historia de la vida y de los hábitats del gavilán, las historias de las vidas de sus presas y la ecología de la vegetación de dosel y sotobosque, en bosques ocupados por gavilanes. Estos hábitats incluyeron componentes tales como, composición y estructura del dosel y sotobosque, árboles muertos en pie, troncos, madera de desecho, aberturas y el tamaño, edad y yuxtaposición de agregaciones de plantas. La estrategia incorporó la dinámica natural de los ecosistemas del bosque, a través del desarrollo de paisajes deseados, que consistían en mosaicos cambiantes temporales de fases estructurales de vegetación, los cuales abarcaban los hábitats del gavilán y sus presas. Esta estrategia basada en el ecosistema, multi-especie, debiese de beneficiar al gavilán, ya que sus poblaciones parecen estar limitadas por el alimento y el hábitat, y porque el paisaje deseado contendrá gavilán y hábitat de su presa en todo momento. El enfoque utilizado en esta estrategia de conservación debería de ser apropiado para otros bosques ocupados por el gavilán .Sin embargo, ya que la presa de la especie, así como la composición y dinámica de la vegetación varía en los tipos de bosque, el enfoque podría resultar en hábitats y paisajes únicos deseados, así como en prescripciones de manejo forestal para desarrollarlos.

Considerable effort has been directed towards developing conservation strategies that protect forest species. Many conservation strategies prompted by recovery goals in the Endangered Species Act are autecological, spatially and temporally limited, and typically use habitat reserve designs (Everett and Lehmkuhl 1996, but see Della Sala et al. 1996, MacCracken 1996, Noss 1996, and Everett and Lehmkuhl 1997 for discussions on the merits of reserves). These strategies often fail to recognize important ecological relationships and linkages that support a species (e.g., food webs) and they often view habitats as static. Although reserves may protect species that are sensitive to human activities, their very design shifts resource extraction pressures to unprotected areas, which may diminish the ecological values of reserves by limiting dispersal (gene flow) of focal species among reserves (Suzuki 2003). Conservation strategies that address all stages of a species' life history, the physical and biological factors that limit its populations, the members of its ecological community, and the spatial and temporal dynamics of the ecosystems it occupies, should be robust to failure. Implementing such strategies in landscapes increases the probability of sustaining whole ecosystems on which a species may depend, and eliminates the difficult tasks of specifying the sizes, numbers, dispersion, and connectivity of reserves or protected areas needed to sustain a species.

Apex predators, because they are often sensitive to changes in their habitats (Belovsky 1987, Melián and Bascompte 2002), are prime candidates for conservation strategies. Population viability of the Northern Goshawk (*Accipiter gentilis*), an apex predator that occurs primarily in forests and woodlands throughout the Holarctic (Squires and Reynolds 1997), is in question because of habitat changes resulting from tree cutting, fire exclusion, and livestock grazing (Herron et al. 1985, Crocker-Bedford 1990, Reynolds et al. 1992, Widén 1997, but see Kennedy 1998). As a result, goshawks have been the object of considerable litigation and the species was considered for listing under the Endangered Species Act (Boyce et al., *this volume*). To protect the habitats of goshawks, conservation strategies were developed for three forest types in the southwestern US in 1992 (Reynolds et al. 1992). These southwestern goshawk conservation strategies (SWGS) accounted for the requisite resources (vegetation structure and food) and ecological relationships (competition, predation, and disease) of goshawks and their prey. Further, because forests change through the dynamic processes of plant establishment, growth, succession, and natural and anthropogenic disturbances, the SWGS identified and incorporated the spatial and temporal scales encompassing these dynamics. The SWGS described sets of desired forest conditions that included habitat components such as tree species composition, structure, landscape pattern, snags, woody debris, tree sizes and densities, and the sizes, ages, and arrangement of tree groups. To account for forest dynamics, the desired forest conditions consisted of temporally shifting mosaics of vegetation structural stages intended to sustain the habitats of both goshawks and their prey in large landscapes for centuries.

The SWGS was incorporated into all USDA Forest Service southwestern national forest management plans in 1996 (USDA Forest Service 1996; Boyce et al., *this volume*). Shortly thereafter, the SWGS was reviewed by animal and forest scientists (Braun et al. 1996, Squires et al. 1998, Long and Smith 2000, Peck 2000, Beier and Maschinski 2003,

Andersen et al. 2004). Here we provide an overview of the approach, components, and processes used in the SWGS, particularly those applicable to southwestern ponderosa pine (*Pinus ponderosa*) forests, not only to correct misunderstandings evident in some of the reviews, but to demonstrate how the process can be used to develop similar conservation strategies in other forests. We conclude with a discussion of problems that may hinder tests of the effectiveness of the SWGS for sustaining goshawks and identify some unintended, additional values resulting from implementation of the SWGS.

ESSENTIAL INFORMATION

Information on the life history, ecology, and habitat of the goshawk, the biological and physical factors (food, habitat, predators, competitors, disease, and weather) that potentially limit goshawk populations, the life histories and populations of important goshawk prey species, and the ecology (e.g., composition, structure, pattern, and dynamics) of a forest ecosystem, is essential for developing desired forest conditions in this ecosystem-based conservation strategy.

GOSHAWK LIFE HISTORY

Goshawks are relatively long-lived, solitary breeders with large home ranges, and that breed in a broad range of forest and woodland types (Squires and Reynolds 1997) where they feed on a variety of birds and mammals (Reynolds and Meslow 1984, Boal and Mannan 1994, Reynolds et al. 1994). Goshawks exhibit high levels of year-to-year fidelity to breeding territories and to mates (Doyle and Smith 1994, Woodbridge and Detrich 1994, Squires and Ruggiero 1995, Reynolds et al. 1994), and often lay eggs in numerous alternate nests within their territories (Reynolds et al. 1992, Woodbridge and Detrich 1994; Reynolds and Joy, *this volume*). Studies have shown that where forests have suitable structures for nests and hunting, and where food is abundant, goshawks are more abundant, breed more often, have heavier body masses, and smaller home ranges (McGowan 1975, Bednarek et al. 1975, Sollien 1979, Lindén and Wikman 1980, Cramp and Simmons 1980, Sulkava et al. 1994, Salafsky 2005; Reynolds et al., *this volume*).

GOSHAWK LIMITING FACTORS

A fundamental step in developing conservation strategies is to identify the environmental factors that limit a goshawk population's ability to grow. These factors typically affect goshawk birth, death, emigration, and immigration rates. Sources of information for these factors include the published literature, unpublished reports, and expert opinion. Information on factors that may limit goshawk populations is often scarce or absent. In these cases, information on how factors influence other raptor populations may offer indications on how they might influence goshawks. A recent review of the goshawk and other raptor literature identified factors that may limit goshawk populations—the abundance and availability of habitats and foods, the types and abundances of predators and competitors, diseases, and weather (Reynolds et al., *this volume*). The review also showed that in studies of goshawk breeding density and reproduction, the availabilities of nest sites, foods, and suitable foraging sites appeared to be the most common factors affecting goshawk populations, and that predation, competition, disease, and weather would be less likely to affect goshawks negatively if foods and vegetation structures were not limiting (Reynolds et al., *this volume*). For example, when prey are abundant, competition for food might be reduced, food stress would less likely predispose goshawks to disease, weather effects on prey availability might be reduced, and, when high quality nest sites are available, predation at goshawk nests might be reduced (Reynolds et al. 1992). The conservation problem was then to identify and develop the habitats of sufficient quality to support goshawks and their prey populations. The variation among habitats in the composite availabilities of nest sites, foraging sites, foods, escape cover, and abundances of predators and competitors determines habitat quality. The approach used in SWGS assumes that if quality habitats are available in landscapes then the above limiting factors would less likely constrain the growth of goshawk populations.

GOSHAWK HABITAT

North American goshawks nest and hunt in a wide variety of forest and woodland types within their geographic range (Squires and Reynolds 1997). Based on the use of space around goshawk nests by adults and fledglings, the SWGS identified three components of the breeding home range: the nest area (approximately 12 ha), the post-fledging family area (PFA; approximately 170 ha exclusive of nest area) surrounding the nest area, and the foraging area (approximately 2,190 ha exclusive of PFA) surrounding the PFA (Reynolds et al. 1992). We know more about the composition and structure of vegeta-

tion in nest areas than in the other areas because of their small size, readily defined boundaries, and the numerous studies that described nest site and nest area vegetation. Forest structure within nest areas provide protected nest, roost, and prey handling sites (Reynolds et al. 1982). Little foraging occurs within nest areas (Schnell 1958) and nest area sizes and shapes can vary by landform, forest setting, and method used to quantify them (Reynolds 1983, Kennedy 1989, Kennedy 1990, Boal et al. 2003). Goshawk nest areas typically have relatively high densities of large trees and high canopy cover, inherent to the forest type and biophysical setting, open understories, and are typically on shallow slopes or in drainages protected by slopes (Squires and Reynolds 1997). While most nest areas are embedded within extensive forests or woodlands, some goshawk individuals and populations nest in small patches of trees within open shrub, tundra, or riparian habitats (Bond 1940, White et al. 1965, Swem and Adams 1992, Younk and Bechard 1994a, b). Despite the disparate species compositions of forests types used by breeding goshawks, the structure of forests within nest areas is surprisingly consistent suggesting that structure is more important than species composition in their choice of nest habitat.

The PFA, defined in the SWGS as the adult female core area including the nest (Kennedy 1989), is used by the adult female for foraging and by her fledglings during the post-fledging dependency period (Reynolds et al. 1992). Because PFAs are larger than nest areas, they typically include a wider diversity of forest conditions—species composition, age classes, openings, and landforms. Because goshawk fledglings spend much of the post-fledging dependency period near the center of a PFA where they may require additional hiding cover from predators, the desired PFA habitat condition is a transition from the denser forests in nest areas to more open foraging habitat in the outer portions (Reynolds et al. 1992).

The foraging area surrounds the PFA and comprises the remainder of the home range of breeding goshawks (Reynolds et al. 1992). The foraging area is used by adult goshawks for hunting, and, like the PFA, should comprise suitably structured foraging habitat and a mix of prey habitats (Reynolds et al. 1992). A number of radio-telemetry studies determined the use of habitats by goshawks (Kenward et al. 1981b, Widén 1985b, Kenward and Widén 1989, Bright-Smith and Mannan 1994, Hargis et al. 1994, Squires and Ruggiero 1995, Beier and Drennan 1997, Good 1998, Drennan and Beier 2003), but their elusive behavior and rapid movements through large home ranges make goshawks difficult to observe and to unequivocally determine whether or not they were actually hunting in the habitats they were detected using. Nonetheless, these studies suggested that breeding goshawks hunted primarily in mature and old forests, but that they also hunted in a variety of other forest age classes, structures, and compositions, and into openings and along forest edges (White et al. 1965, Widén 1989, Bright-Smith and Mannan 1994, Hargis et al. 1994, Younk and Bechard 1994a, b; Bosakowski et al. 1999, Daw and DeStefano 2001). The diversity of habitats used by hunting goshawks often expands during winter when many juveniles and some adults move to lower elevation woodland and shrub communities (Reynolds et al. 1994, Squires and Ruggiero 1995, Stephens 2001, Sonsthagen 2002). Whether these goshawks leave their forest habitats in response to reduced food availability or weather changes is unknown. The year-round diversity of habitat use by goshawks is often reflected in their diets; goshawks eat birds and mammals that occur in mature forests, but frequently eat species whose main habitats are in open forests, along forest edges, and in openings (Reynolds and Meslow 1984, Widén 1989, Boal and Mannan 1994, Daw and DeStefano 2001). Nonetheless, at least within forest situations, goshawks spend much of their time in areas with large trees (Bright-Smith and Mannan 1994, Hargis et al. 1994), areas with high-crown base heights (open understories), allowing goshawks to fly beneath the forest canopy. Older forests also contain abundant tree perches from which goshawks search for prey, and are the prime habitat of many goshawk prey species (Reynolds et al. 1992).

GOSHAWK PREY

Goshawks feed on birds and small mammals (Squires and Reynolds 1997), and the composition of a local goshawk diet depends on the composition of the bird and mammal fauna in a particular forest, the relative abundances and availabilities of the species that goshawks are able to capture, and the dietary preferences of the goshawks. Goshawk diets comprise a limited range of prey sizes (Storer 1966, Snyder and Wiley 1976, Reynolds and Meslow 1984, Bosakowski et al. 1992). The upper prey-size limit appears to be determined by the goshawk's ability to kill with a minimum risk of injury to itself, and the lower size limit is likely determined by a goshawk's ability to capture smaller prey. Small prey are more maneuverable and escape goshawks more readily and return less energy per capture than larger prey (Reynolds 1972,

Andersson and Norberg 1981, Temeles 1985). These limits result in goshawk diets composed of robin-to-grouse-sized birds and chipmunk-to-hare-sized mammals (Reynolds et al. 1992).

Goshawks are morphologically and behaviorally suited to hunt in forests. Both their maneuverability for capturing agile prey, provided by short wings and long tail, and their short-perch-short-flight foraging tactic (Kenward 1982), are suited for environments where flight and vision is impaired by tall, dense vegetation (Reynolds et al. 1992). Because of these adaptations it is often assumed that goshawks are limited to old-growth forests and that habitat availability is the main factor limiting goshawk populations. However, even within the forests, goshawk reproduction and survival can be highly variable among years (Reynolds et al. 2005; Keane et al., *this volume*; Reynolds and Joy, *this volume*), and this variation has been associated with inter-annual variations in prey abundance (McGowan 1975, Lindén and Wikman 1980, Doyle and Smith 1994, Selås 1997b, Keane 1999, Salafsky 2004). Furthermore, Widén (1989) reported higher breeding densities in areas richer in foods, and Bednarek et al. (1975) reported extremely high goshawk breeding densities in areas with only 12–15 % of woodland but very rich in food. Widén (1989) suggested that goshawks are more often limited by food than by nesting habitat.

GEOGRAPHIC AND ANNUAL VARIATION IN DIETS

Goshawk diets differ among forest types, among regions, and both seasonally and annually. Reynolds and Meslow (1984), Kennedy (1991), and Boal and Mannan (1994) reported between 14 and 37 different prey species in goshawk diets in a variety of western American conifer forests, while in eastern American deciduous forests, 23 different prey species were reported (Bosakowski and Smith 1992, Bosakowski et al. 1992). Much of the among-forest and regional differences in diets disappears, however, when prey are grouped at the genus level because prey species are often regionally replaced by congeners. For example, red squirrels (*Tamiasciurus hudsonicus*) in western Oregon are replaced by Douglas squirrels (*Tamiasciurus douglasi*) in eastern Oregon and Nuttall's cottontail (*Sylvilagus nuttalli*) in western North America is replaced by the eastern cottontail (*Sylvilagus floridanus*) in eastern North American (Hall 1981). Due to such replacements, goshawk diets can be generalized to include rabbits, tree squirrels, ground squirrels, woodpeckers, jays, thrushes, doves, pigeons, and grouse. However, goshawks frequently supplement these prey with as many as 20 other incidental bird and mammal species (Schnell 1958, Reynolds and Meslow 1984).

Annual variation in local goshawk diets may stem from annual variation in prey abundances associated with eruptive or inter-annual fluctuations in species such as snowshoe hare (*Lepus americanus*), red squirrel, and grouse (McGowan 1975, Doyle and Smith 1994). Although little winter goshawk diet information is available, diets are likely to vary seasonally due to habitat differences among prey, differential sampling of habitats by foraging goshawks, and the timing of estivation, hibernation, or migration of some prey. The abundance of non-migratory prey (tree squirrels, hares, grouse, and woodpeckers) during winter may affect whether goshawks stay on breeding territories or move to non-forest habitats in winter.

DETERMINING DIETS

Because the SWGS approach for developing conservation strategies requires the identification of a suite of important goshawk prey in a focal forest type, we review methods for estimating goshawk diets and a process that can be used to reduce a complete list of prey in a forest type to a reduced list of important prey. Most of our understanding of goshawk diets comes from the breeding period when prey is delivered to nests by adults. Breeding season diets have been estimated with several methods, each with a characteristic bias. A prey-remains method takes advantage of the fact that goshawks regurgitate pellets and pluck feathers and fur from prey in their nest areas (Reynolds and Meslow 1984, Martin 1987). A bias associated with this method is inaccurate counts of individuals or species due to species-specific differences in detectability of remains when they are being collected (Reynolds and Meslow 1984, Bielefeldt et al. 1992). A direct-observation method involves identifying and counting prey delivered to nests from adjacent blinds or with cameras (Schnell 1958, Boal and Mannan 1994, Grønnesby and Nygård 2000). Problems with direct observations are that the number of nests that can be observed is typically limited and difficulty of identifying prey whose diagnostic parts (feathers and fur) have been removed by the goshawks. Schnell (1958) identified 14 prey species from observations at a single nest in California, whereas Reynolds and Meslow (1984) identified 37 different species from prey remains collected at 58 goshawk nests in Oregon. Diet studies that combine these two methods are likely to result in more precise estimates of goshawk diets, but neither method accounts for prey eaten away from nests (Lewis et al. 2004).

What little we know about non-breeding season diets comes mostly from radio-telemetry study of wintering goshawks (Kenward 1979, Widén 1987, Stephens 2001, Drennan and Beier 2003, Tornberg and Colpaert 2001). Diets of goshawks that remain in forests during winter are not likely to differ greatly from the breeding diets, except prey that hibernate or migrate will be missing, and diets of goshawks that move to open habitats are more likely to include non-forest prey. Of course, diets should be determined from an adequate sample of goshawks within a forest type to reduce sampling error (e.g., a goshawk taking aquatic birds from a lake), and should be determined over an adequate number of years to include inter-annual fluctuations in prey species.

SUITES OF IMPORTANT PREY

Reducing a complete list of goshawk prey in a forest to a subset of important goshawk prey may be necessary because some species are taken only incidentally and their inclusion might dilute the forest habitats needed by more commonly captured prey. Goshawk diets are rarely dominated by a few species. In California, six of a total 14 prey species contributed about 80% of the numbers of prey in the diet of a single goshawk pair (Schnell 1958), 18 of 37 species contributed 85% of prey in a large sample of Oregon nests (Reynolds and Meslow 1984), and 11 of 18 species contributed 67% of prey in Arizona (Boal and Mannan 1994). Also, rarely does a single prey species contribute more than 30% of total numbers of prey in a diet; in fact, most prey species contributes less than 5% of the total. If a threshold for identifying a suite of important prey was chosen to include all species contributing more than 2% of individuals in a goshawk diet, then the suite would include eight prey species (57% of total species) in Schnell's (1958) California study, 18 species (49%) in Reynolds and Meslow's (1984) Oregon study, and 11 species (61%) in Boal and Mannan's (1994) Arizona study.

However, because larger prey contribute more food biomass to the energy budget of goshawks, they can be more important than small prey even when small prey are eaten more often. Using the above 2% threshold in Table 1 excludes three large species— Belding's ground squirrel (*Citellus beldingi*), mountain cottontail (*Sylvilagus nuttalli*), Ruffed Grouse (*Bonasa umbellus*)—that perhaps should be included in a suite of important prey because of their body mass. In Table 1, thresholds lower than two individuals per species may include too many incidental prey. Alternatively, including too

TABLE 1. AN EXAMPLE FOR IDENTIFYING A SUITE OF IMPORTANT GOSHAWK PREY, INCLUDING THE NUMBERS AND PERCENT FREQUENCY OF INDIVIDUALS BY SPECIES, AND A FREQUENCY AND BIOMASS RANKING OF EACH SPECIES IN DIETS OF BREEDING GOSHAWKS IN OREGON (29 SPECIES, 227 INDIVIDUALS; REYNOLDS AND MESLOW 1984).

Species	Number[a]	Percent	Frequency rank	Biomass[b] rank
Steller's Jay (*Cyanocitta stelleri*)	29	12.8	1	4
Snowshoe hare (*Lepus americanus*)	24	10.6	2	1
American Robin (*Turdus migratorius*)	20	8.8	3	12
Golden-mantled ground squirrel (*Citellus lateralis*)	17	7.4	4	5
Northern flying squirrel (*Glaucomys sabrinus*)	15	6.6	5	7
Northern Flicker (*Colaptes auratus*)	15	6.6	5	10
Douglas' squirrel (*Tamiasciurus douglasi*)	13	5.7	7	6
Mountain Quail (*Oreortyx pictus*)	10	4.4	8	8
Mourning Dove (*Zenaida macroura*)	7	3.1	9	16
Chipmunk spp. (*Eutamias* spp.*)	7	3.1	9	17
Blue Grouse (*Dendragapus obscurus*)	5	2.2	11	2
Gray squirrel (*Sciurus grisesus*)	5	2.2	11	3
Gray Jay (*Perisoreus canadensis*)	5	2.2	11	19
-----------------------Greater than four individuals/species threshold[c]-----------------------				
Belding's ground squirrel (*Citellus beldingi*)	4	1.8	14	15
Varied Thrush (*Ixoreus naevius*)	4	1.8	14	20
---------------------Greater than three individuals/species threshold[c]-----------------------				
Mountain cottontail rabbit (*Sylvilagus nuttalli*)	3	1.3	16	11
Townsend's chipmunk (*Eutamias townsendii*)	3	1.3	16	23
-----------------------Greater than two individuals/species threshold[c]-----------------------				
Mallard (*Anas platyrhynchos*)	2	0.9	18	9
Ruffed Grouse (*Bonasa umbellus*)	2	0.9	18	14
Townsend's ground squirrel (*Citellus townsendii*)	2	0.9	18	24
European Starling (*Sturnus vulgaris*)	2	0.9	18	27
Hairy Woodpecker (*Picoides villosus*)	2	0.9	18	30
Williamson's Sapsucker (*Sphyrapicus thyroideus*)	2	0.9	18	32
Western Tanager (*Piranga ludoviciana*)	2	0.9	18	34
Finch spp. (*Carpodacus* spp.)	2	0.9	18	36
Dark-eyed Junco (*Junco hyemalis*)	2	0.9	18	39
Great horned Owl (*Bubo virginianus*)	1	0.4	27	13
Cooper's Hawk (*Accipiter cooperi*)	1	0.4	27	18
Bushy-tailed woodrat (*Neotoma cinerea*)	1	0.4	27	21
Pileated Woodpecker (*Dryocopus pileatus*)	1	0.4	27	22
Woodrat spp. (*Neotoma* spp.)	1	0.4	27	25
Dusty-footed woodrat (*Neotoma fuscipes*)	1	0.4	27	26
Black-billed Magpie (*Pica pica*)	1	0.4	27	28
Western Screech-Owl (*Otus kennicottii*)	1	0.4	27	29
Lewis' Woodpecker (*Melanerpes lewis*)	1	0.4	27	31
Red-winged Blackbird (*Agelaius phoeniceus*)	1	0.4	27	33
Red-naped Sapsucker (*Sphyrapicus nuchalis*)	1	0.4	27	35
Black-headed Grosbeak (*Pheucticus melanocephalus*)	1	0.4	27	37
Least chipmunk (*Eutamias minimus*)	1	0.4	27	38

[a] After Reynolds and Meslow (1984).

[b] Biomass = number of individuals of a species in diet x mass of the species determined from the literature and museum collections (Baldwin and Kendeigh 1938, Hartman 1955, Collins and Bradley 1971, Dunning 1984, Reynolds and Meslow 1984, Bosakowski and Smith 1992) .

[c] Thresholds define three possible suites of important prey, with minimums of 4, 3, and 2 individuals per species. If the threshold of 4 individuals per species were used, the suite would contain 15 important prey, with some contributing as little as 1.8 % of items.

few species may result in an insufficiently diverse and abundant food resource to sustain goshawks through poor food years. Other information, such as a comparison of the abundance of a marginally important prey species in unmanaged forests to its abundance and frequency in goshawk diets in managed forests, may help decide on whether or not to include marginal species in the suite of important prey. Finally, we pointed out that the diversity of habitats provided for the suite of 14 prey species in southwestern forests also provided habitats for many incidental prey species as well as non-prey species (Reynolds et al. 1992).

PREY HABITATS

After identifying a suite of important prey, the distributions, life histories, abundances, and habitats of the prey can be assessed in the literature and by expert opinion (Reynolds et al. 1992). Much information on the ecology and habitats of a variety of goshawk prey is available in Reynolds et al. (1992) and Drennan et al. (*this volume*). Often, information on the ecologies, habitat relations, and foods of prey species within a certain forest type is limited. In these cases, information from the same or a similar forest type in adjacent regions could be used. Limitations of these kinds of data include: (1) incomplete information on a species' life histories, population ecologies, and how these vary among forest types, (2) uncertainty about relationships between a species' demography and habitat conditions, (3) difficulties distinguishing a species' habitat use from its habitat preference, and (4) the appropriateness of using studies designed to investigate other questions (Morin 1981, VanHorne 1983, White and Garrott 1990).

FOREST HABITAT ELEMENTS OF PREY

Once the life histories, habitats, and foods of important prey are assessed, a list of forest habitat elements (FHE), including items such as vegetation structural stages, size of openings, edges, understory and overstory compositions and structures, woody debris, snags, nesting and feeding substrates, and interspersion of forest age classes, for each prey species can be developed. This process can be facilitated with matrices that display the frequencies of the relative importance of FHEs for each prey species (Table 6 in Reynolds et al. 1992). An overall relative importance of FHEs for the suite of prey can be estimated by summing the levels of importance of each FHE across species (Table 6 in Reynolds et al. 1992).

Such assessments for the suite of goshawk prey in southwestern forests resulted in an understanding of the importance of sustaining large amounts of mid-aged to old forests dispersed at a fine scale within landscapes (Reynolds et al. 1992, Long and Smith 2000).

FOREST ECOLOGY

Forests, and by extension forest habitats, are dynamic ecosystems that undergo change through plant growth and succession and periodic natural and anthropogenic disturbances such as wind, fire, insects, and vegetation management. Each of these factors changes the composition, structure, and pattern of plant communities, which in turn have short- and long-term effects on wildlife habitats. Thus, describing and managing forest habitats for plants and animals in the goshawk food web requires an understanding of forest dynamics as well as the habitat relationships of the plants and animals. Here we identify sources of essential information on how to develop and sustain desired forest conditions through management, how to identify limits or constraints on such variables as maximum tree sizes and longevity, sizes of plant aggregations and tree densities, and the species composition, structure, and landscape pattern of desired landscapes. Some important processes that occur during forest development include plant establishment, development, senescence, competitive exclusion, biomass accumulation, canopy gap initiation, understory re-initiation, maturation, decadence development, and mortality (Franklin et al. 2002). Each of these processes, which typically vary among forest types, is often integrated into potential vegetation classifications. Moreover, these classifications provide estimates of forest productivity, vegetation development rates, plant occurrence and position (e.g., canopy layer), life form (e.g., grass, forb, or shrub), their roles in plant succession (e.g., early, mid-, or late seral), and include physical and biological components such as climate, soil, geology, and vegetation (Daubenmire and Daubenmire 1968, Cooper et al. 1991, Hann et al. 1997). These classification systems can also be integrated with known fire relations (Bradley et al. 1992, Agee 1993, Hann et al. 1997, Graham et al. 1999b, Kaufmann et al. 2000) and are compatible with efforts for defining and mapping fire regime condition classes for forests (Schmidt et al. 2002). Sources of data on current forest conditions include Forest Inventory and Analysis and Geospatial Analysis Processes (USGS National Gap Analysis Program 1995, O'Brien 2002).

SYNTHESIS OF COMPONENTS

Once information on goshawks, their prey, and forest ecology is assembled, it is synthesized into desired habitat that benefits the goshawk and all its important prey (Fig. 1). The SWGS used a vegetation structural stage (VSS) classification to describe forest development. VSS is an integrative approach that combines vegetation growth and maturation into generalized descriptions of forest conditions from young to old vegetation complexes (Thomas et al. 1979, Verner and Boss 1980, Oliver and Larson 1990, Reynolds et al. 1992, Franklin et al. 2002). The FHEs were incorporated with VSS into generalized landscapes that included abundant and dispersed large tree components (large live trees, large snags, and large logs), groups (<0.2 ha in ponderosa pine) of trees with interlocking crowns, small openings around tree groups with a well developed grass/forb/shrub vegetation (Fig. 2), and a high level of interspersion (intermixing) of all VSS, each a small group of trees (Reynolds et al. 1992, Long and Smith 2000; Fig. 2).

In ponderosa pine, groups of trees with interlocking crowns allow the tassel-eared squirrel (*Sciurus aberti*) and red squirrel (*Tamiasciurus hudsonicus*) to move among tree crowns, a critical habitat element especially around their nests (Reynolds et al. 1992, Dodd et al. 2003). Because mycorrhizal fungi are an important food for squirrels, and because the fungi are more abundant in mid-aged forests, an interspersion of mature and old VSS groups with mid-aged VSS groups benefits squirrels. Small (Fig. 1) openings containing grasses, forbs, and shrubs around tree groups are habitat for prey such as rabbits, ground squirrels, and grouse that require openings for feeding or brood rearing. These openings should remain treeless because they are often occupied by roots of the grouped trees (Pearson 1950), facilitating nutrient uptake and vigorous tree growth. Openings, because they are occupied by important prey, offer hunting opportunities for goshawks (Reynolds et al. 1992). For southwestern forests, the three older VSS were the most important habitats for the suite of prey, followed by openings.

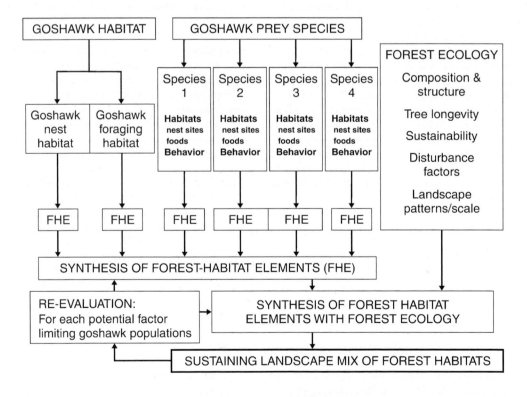

FIGURE 1. Essential components and two levels of synthesis of goshawk habitats, prey habitats, and the composition, structure, and pattern of forests used to identify mixes of desired habitats in the southwestern goshawk conservation strategy (Reynolds et al. 1992).

FIGURE 2. The desired groups of trees with interlocking crowns surrounded by openings in southwestern ponderosa pine forests.

FOREST SETTING

An integration of information on the autecology and synecology of forest vegetation is essential for developing and sustaining goshawk and prey habitats (Fig. 1). A wealth of information on forest development can provide guidance for the development of the desired habitats. This information includes, but is not limited to, vegetation classifications, forest vegetation simulations, fire histories, natural-area descriptions, and wild-land, fuel-management strategies (Haig et al. 1941, Pearson 1950, Daubenmire and Daubenmire 1968, White 1985, Fulé et al. 1997, Reinhardt and Crookston 2003, Graham et al. 2004). Such information is used to fine tune the desired goshawk and prey habitats in a particular forest type to increase the likelihood that both can be attained and sustained.

Sustaining the desired landscape mix of goshawk and prey habitats requires the incorporation of the spatial and temporal dynamics of forest vegetation. Vegetation dynamics, including the establishment, development, senescence, and its composition, structure, and pattern, can be estimated and modeled (Oliver and Larson 1990, Reynolds et al. 1992, Franklin et al. 2002, Reinhardt and Crookston 2003). For example, sustaining the maximum amount of mature and old VSS in southwestern forests for goshawks and their prey was best achieved with about 10% of landscape in VSS 1 (grass-forb-shrub), 10% in VSS 2 (seedling-sapling), 20% in VSS 3 (young forest), 20% in VSS 4 (mid-aged forest), 20% in VSS 5 (mature forest), and 20% in VSS 6 (old forest) (Reynolds et al. 1992). These proportions reflect forest development from cohort establishment through canopy closure to old forests. However, classification systems that depict forest development over 1,000 yr tend to display greater proportions of a forest in the mature and old classes than classification systems depicting forest development through periods <300 yr. For example, Franklin et al. (2002) showed over 70% of the forest occurring in structural stages greater than 800 yr, as did Spies and Franklin (1996). Integrating a VSS distribution with goshawk habitats (nest area, PFA, foraging area) and tree-group metrics favoring the suite of southwestern prey, resulted in desired landscapes comprised of shifting mosaics of VSS through time and space (Reynolds et al. 1992, Long and Smith 2000).

Probably because of plant and animal adaptations to the natural compositions, structures, and patterns, the desired conditions developed in the SWGS approximated the composition, structure, and landscape pattern existing in southwestern forests before fundamental changes in natural disturbance regimes (Pearson 1950, White 1985, Fulé et al. 1997, Long and Smith 2000) (Fig. 2). Of course, it is important that the plant and animal habitat relations used to develop ecosystem-based conservation strategies be internally consistent as well as consistent with current knowledge (Guldin et al. 2003).

IMPLEMENTATION OF THE GOSHAWK STRATEGY

Once the desired compositions, structures, and mixes of goshawk and prey habitats are described, management actions can be developed and implemented through appropriate planning processes. The SWGS recommended that goshawk breeding habitat be partitioned into nest areas, PFAs, and foraging areas, and because the movements of breeding goshawks are energetically limited to some finite space around their nests, that these home range components be approximately centered on the nest. Goshawk conservation strategies can be implemented at a variety of spatial scales depending on management objectives. For example, implementation at the goshawk home range scale is appropriate for developing and protecting habitats in known territories. If the intent is to provide habitat for undiscovered goshawks or for an expansion of a goshawk population, the scale must be larger, e.g., a national forest or ecoregion (Reynolds et al. 1992, Graham et al. 1999b). Implementing the strategy in entire landscapes accommodates seasonal, annual, and geographic variation in goshawk home range sizes (Hargis et al. 1994, Boal et al. 2003), and eliminates the need to specify the number, their juxtaposition, and connectivity of breeding territories to sustain goshawk populations.

Specific management actions and the intensity that they are applied should be contingent on the differences between the existing conditions and the desired conditions. If differences are great (e.g., no old-forest structure), centuries may be needed to develop the desired conditions. For example, >200 yr are required to develop old-forest structure in southwestern ponderosa pine forests (Reynolds et al. 1992), and >1,200 yr are required to develop all of the structural stages found in northwestern Douglas-fir forests (Franklin et al. 2002). The capability of forests to produce the desired conditions can vary among sites depending on factors such as soils, slope, exposure, elevation (Daubenmire and Daubenmire 1968, Wykoff and Monserud 1988, Basset et al.

1994). Thus, differing growth potentials require that site-specific desired conditions be matched to a site's capabilities. Not all sites within a landscape can, nor should they have, the same exact conditions.

The Kaibab National Forest in Arizona began implementing the SWGS in ponderosa pine forests in 1993. Figure 3 displays one such implementation (right portion of photo) adjacent to 12–16 ha seed-tree cuts (center, lower left), a forest treatment in which a few trees are retained as seed sources, and a natural area (top center) that had recent low-intensity surface fires and little tree cutting. Note the similarities in the aggregation of ponderosa pine trees and surrounding openings in the implementation area and the natural area. A lesson learned from multiple implementations is to avoid removing trees from within groups (especially in mid-aged, mature, and old VSS). Thinning groups often eliminates the interlocking of tree crowns, critical habitat for tree squirrels (Dodd et al. 2003). Rather, when tree cutting is needed to create or sustain the desired conditions, an entire group of trees should be regenerated as opposed to thinning within a group. The desired within-group structures in both mature and old VSS could be developed with appropriate forest treatments (e.g., thinning or prescribed fire) in the younger age classes (e.g., seedling-sapling, young forests, and mid-aged forests; Reynolds et al. 1992).

EVALUATION OF IMPLEMENTATION

Squires et al. (1998) suggested that the SWGS be tested before large scale implementation. Testing is needed to determine if management actions successfully moved existing forest conditions toward the desired conditions and if the actions had the desired effects on goshawks and their prey. One such test is to compare goshawk reproduction and survival in forests that are in or near the desired conditions to those in contrasting forests (paired-landscape approach). Such comparisons, however, could be confounded by ecological differences (e.g., soil types) in the areas being compared. Another approach is to monitor the effects of implementation on the same sample of goshawk territories before and after treatment design. However, depending on the degree of difference between existing and desired forest conditions, and because annual forest treatments are typically small relative to goshawk home ranges, achieving the desired conditions on a study sample of goshawk home ranges could take decades. Of course, interim monitoring and evaluating the effectiveness of implementation on moving the existing forest conditions toward the desired conditions

FIGURE 3. Aerial photo showing a 1994 implementation of the southwestern goshawk conservation strategy (Reynolds et al. 1992) adjacent to seed tree harvests and a natural area in ponderosa pine forest in Arizona.

and on increasing the abundance of goshawk prey species should be undertaken. Such monitoring (versus a testing program focused on goshawks) could be achieved at greatly reduced costs because much smaller areas would be needed. Whatever approach is taken, a sound experimental design is required to evaluate implementation. Some potential problems in assessing the effectiveness of implementation are the needs for replications, risks of incorrectly assigning causal inferences due to ecological complexity and interactions within an ecosystem framework, and risks of spatial and temporal autocorrelations within the data (Mellina and Hinch 1995). Considerable economic costs would also be associated with testing the SWGS in sufficiently large landscapes. Because of these difficulties, combined with the improved likelihood that the broad-based ecosystem approach of the SWGS will successfully sustain goshawks, and because implementation initiates the restoration of management-altered forest habitats and ecosystems, we suggest that immediate implementation in broad landscapes is a better option than the long wait for experimental tests of the SWGS's effectiveness. During implementation, however, we advocate monitoring programs that track the habitats and

populations of goshawk and their prey, not necessarily within a testing framework, but as integral parts of an adaptive management program (McDonnell et al. 1997, Murry and Marmorek 2003). The SWGS was based on the habitat relationships of many plants and animals, an understanding of the autecology and synecology of the forest vegetation, and on knowledge of vegetation treatments to create the desired forest conditions. Do we know that this approach is appropriate or that the desired conditions are correct and sustainable (Long and Smith 2000)? Some degree of uncertainty exists regarding these questions; however, we do know that past management fundamentally altered forest ecosystems and that active management in many cases is needed to restore the ecosystems.

ADDED BENEFITS OF IMPLEMENTATION

Reynolds et al. (1992) identified a number of added benefits from implementing the SWGS. A main benefit is restoration of forest ecosystems. Implementing of the SWGS benefits many plants and animals of southwestern forests by restoring tree densities, structures, and patterns similar to

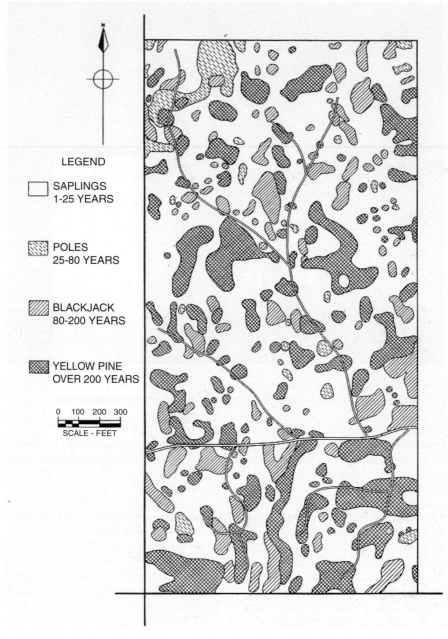

FIGURE 4. Historical mix of groups of different aged ponderosa pine trees on the Fort Valley Experimental Forest, Flagstaff, Arizona (from Pearson 1950, White 1985). This and other information (see text) provided references for supporting the desired sizes and mix of vegetation structural stages that could likely be sustained in southwestern ponderosa pine forests (Reynolds et al. 1992).

those occurring pre-settlement (circa 1850; Fig. 4). Throughout much of interior of western North America, tree densities in dry conifer forests have greatly increased since the initiation of fire exclusion in the early 1900s (Cooper 1960, Weaver 1961, Covington and Moore 1994b, Graham et al. 2004). In pre-settlement times, frequent surface fires maintained open forest conditions by cleaning the forest floor and killing small trees (Weaver 1943, Graham et al. 2004). In addition, timber harvests and associated treatments tended to homogenize forest composition, structure, and pattern (Nyland 2002).

Thus, forests have become increasingly dense and less diverse. These changes increased inter-plant competition for moisture and nutrients, resulting in decreased tree vigor, increased tree disease and insect epidemics, and increased frequency of lethal wildfires (Weaver 1943, Fellin 1979, Williams and Marsden 1982, Anderson et al. 1987, Swetnam and Lynch 1989, Covington and Moore 1994b, Graham 2003, Graham et al. 2004).

The desired forest conditions described in the SWGS resembled the historical conditions of southwestern ponderosa pine forests described by Pearson (1950) and White (1985). These similarities suggest that implementing the SWGS would move forests towards restoration of pre-settlement conditions (Long and Smith 2000). For example, the SWGS restores old structures—large live trees, snags and logs—maintains groups of trees with interlocking crowns, promotes the grass-forb-shrub layer, and minimizes the risk of lethal wildfires by reducing surface and ladder fuels (Reynolds et al. 1992, Graham 2003, Graham et al. 2004). In addition, by favoring lower stand densities, the strategy reduces the likelihood of disease and insect epidemics (Schmid and Mata 1992, Harvey et al. 1999). These conditions also are similar to those suggested as being desirable in the Healthy Forests Initiative and Healthy Forests Restoration Act (USDA Forest Service 2004).

The SWGS has been described as single-species management (Beier and Maschinski 2003). However, the SWGS is a multi-species strategy because it included the habitats and ecological relationships of many plant and animals in the goshawk food web (Reynolds et al. 1992, Long and Smith 2000). Thus, the SWGS shifts the focus from single-species and stand-level management to vegetation management for food webs in large landscapes (Reynolds et al. 1992, Long and Smith 2000). The SWGS utilized the concept of desired forest conditions. Advantages of this concept include the recognition that long time periods may be required to attain the desired conditions, allows variable management actions depending on existing conditions, calls attention to native disturbance regimes and how these operated at multiple temporal and spatial scales, and focuses on resources that are left after treatment rather than on what resources are removed (Reynolds et al. 1992, Haynes et al. 1996, Graham et al. 1999b, Franklin et al. 2002).

SUMMARY

The strategy for conserving goshawks in the southwestern US described desired forest landscapes intended to sustain the habitats of both goshawks and their prey (Reynolds et al. 1992). The approach and procedures developed in this conservation strategy are readily adapted to other locations and forests. However, the specific desired conditions for other forests are likely to be different because the kinds of prey available as well as the composition, structure, pattern, and dynamics of the vegetation often differs among forests. The approach we present identifies goshawk nest and feeding habitats and nest and feeding habitats of important goshawk prey in particular forest types (Fig. 1). Goshawk habitats were summarized in the SWGS, as were the habitats and life histories of 14 important goshawk prey species. Moreover, we described a procedure for reducing a full list of species eaten by goshawks to a manageable suite of important prey. The information assembled for the goshawk and its prey should be integrated with the ecological dynamics of the vegetation in a focal forest type and we provided suggestions as to how this integration can be accomplished (Fig. 1). Depending on the current forest conditions—we provide suggestions on how they can be determined—management actions may be as simple as doing nothing to actively managing forests to develop and maintain goshawk and prey habitats. While we believe that the approach used in the SWGS for identifying and developing desired habitats for goshawks is sound, economically feasible, and, due to its diversity of components, robust to failure to sustain goshawks, we also realize that forest management is fraught with uncertainties and that managing goshawk and prey habitats is a long-term proposition. What is needed is an in-depth analysis of implementation projects as they come on line to make preliminary judgments about what works, what does not, and how success should be measured.

ACKNOWLEDGMENTS

We wish to thank our original coauthors who were instrumental in developing the SWGS. We also thank the many forest managers, scientists, and stakeholders who interacted with us over the past 15 yr. Their many challenges caused us to frequently reexamine of our approach and desired forest conditions in the SWGS. In our minds, these re-examinations re-affirmed the appropriateness and value of our approach and its consequence. We thank T. Jain, K. Graham, D. Lund, and two anonymous reviewers of various drafts of the manuscript, and C. Erickson for help formatting the manuscript.

Studies in Avian Biology No. 31:312–325

GOSHAWK STATUS AND MANAGEMENT: WHAT DO WE KNOW, WHAT HAVE WE DONE, WHERE ARE WE GOING?

Douglas A. Boyce, Jr., Richard T. Reynolds, and Russell T. Graham

Abstract. Although the Northern Goshawk (*Accipiter gentilis*) is not listed as a threatened or endangered species in the US, five of nine regions of the USDA Forest Service have designated the goshawk as a sensitive species. The Nature Conservancy (TNC) believes goshawks are secure but some TNC state offices believe the species to be rare. A recent literature review found no strong evidence for a range-wide population decline (Kennedy 1997). The vastness of the North American forests and the elusiveness of goshawks prevent a reliable estimate of the number of breeding goshawks. In Alaska alone, the size of the boreal forest exceeds the size of the states of Oregon and Washington combined. In the continental US, the number of known breeding areas breeding documented at least once has been tallied for years and is estimated to exceed 3,000. However, habitat change is believed to have reduced the number of breeding goshawks by degrading the structural character of forests used for nesting and foraging. Forest fragmentation is known to have caused goshawk declines in Europe, and extensive forest cutting in the 18th and 19th centuries probably caused goshawk declines in the northeastern US. Habitat quality and availability are also important for supporting the diverse array of goshawk prey species. Goshawks nest and hunt in many forest types. However, in the western US, 78% of the known nesting areas are in ponderosa pine forests (*Pinus ponderosa*) and Douglas-fir forests (*Pseudotsuga menziessi*). Awareness of the potential effects of habitat change on goshawks has increased among land managers responsible for these and other forest types. Important changes in management have taken place since the 1970s as a result of increased understanding of essential goshawk resources and the extent of spatial and temporal scales that require simultaneous consideration for long-term management of goshawks. A conservation strategy that restores and sustains forest ecosystems to support goshawks has been implemented throughout the southwestern US. The concepts in the southwestern goshawk conservation strategy are used extensively to manage goshawks, and they are complementary to regional management strategies such as the Northwest Forest Plan and the Sierra Nevada Forest Plan Amendment.

Key Words: *Accipiter gentilis*, habitat management, habitats, management, Northern Goshawk, status.

ESTADO Y MANEJO DEL GAVILÁN: QUÉ SABEMOS, QUÉ HEMOS HECHO, A DÓNDE VAMOS?

Resumen. A pesar de que el Gavilán Azor (*Accipiter gentilis*) no está enlistado como una especie amenazada o en peligro en los Estados Unidos, cinco de nueve regiones del USDA Servicio Forestal han designado al gavilán como una especie sensible. De The Nature Conservancy (TNC) cree que los gavilanes están seguros, pero algunas oficinas de TNC estatales, consideran a la especie como rara. Una reciente revisión bibliográfica mostró evidencia poco fuerte en la declinación de la población de amplio rango (Kennedy 1997). La inmensidad de los bosques de Norte América y lo esquivo de los gavilanes, impiden un estimado confiable de los gavilanes reproductores. Solamente en Alaska, el tamaño del bosque boreal excede el tamaño de los estados de Oregon y Washington combinados. En EU continental, el número de áreas de reproducción (reproducción documentada al menos una vez) ha sido cuantificado por años, y se estima que excede 3,000. Sin embargo, se cree que el cambio del hábitat ha reducido el número de gavilanes reproductores, al degradar las características estructurales de los bosques utilizados para la anidación y forrajeo. Se sabe que la fragmentación del bosque ha causado decaimientos del gavilán en Europa, mientras el corte excesivo del bosque durante los siglos 18 y 19, causó probablemente el decaimiento en el noreste de EU. La calidad y la disponibilidad del hábitat son también importantes para soportar el diverso acomodo de las especies presa del gavilán. Los gavilanes anidan y cazan en varios tipos de bosque. Sin embargo, en el oeste de EU, 78% de las áreas de anidación se encuentran en bosques de pinos ponderosa (*Pinus ponderosa*) y bosques de abeto douglas (*Pseudotsuga menziessi*). La conciencia sobre los efectos potenciales en el cambio de hábitat ha incrementado entre los administradores de la tierra, responsables de estos tipos de bosque. Cambios importantes en el manejo han tenido lugar desde los finales de la década de los setenta (1979), como resultado del incremento en el entendimiento de los recursos esenciales del gavilán, y la magnitud de las escalas temporales y espaciales que requieren consideración simultánea para el manejo de los gavilanes a largo plazo. Una estrategia de conservación, la cual restaura y sustenta los ecosistemas forestales para soportar al gavilán, ha sido implementada por todo el suroeste de EU. Los conceptos en la estrategia de conservación del suroeste, son utilizados extensivamente para manejar a los gavilanes, y son complementarios a estrategias regionales de manejo, tales como el Plan Forestal del Noroeste y el Plan Enmienda Forestal de Sierra Nevada.

Extensive harvesting of mature and old trees during the 1960s and 1970s created concern for the welfare of species inhabiting older forests. The issue continued to grow through the 1980s and early 1990s as old forests disappeared or became highly fragmented. Numerous administrative appeals and lawsuits were filed in whole or in part over concern for the welfare of the Northern Goshawk (*Accipiter gentilis*). During the past decade, managers began to turn their focus away from individual species needs to address emerging concerns about managing ecosystems, and more recently to concerns about forest health. One catalyst for change was the increased number, size and devastation of wildfires that have destroyed much of the remaining old forests (Graham et. al. 2004). More than 80 yr of fire exclusion resulted in a population explosion of small trees, creating fuel ladders for surface fires to ignite forest canopies. The increased frequency and devastation of catastrophic wildfires focused the nation's attention on forest health problems as indicated by the emphasis and funding placed on it by the U.S. Congress. Increases in tree density and warming weather have allowed forest destruction by insects. For example, the spruce beetle (*Dendroctonus rufipennis*) killed 80% of all standing spruce trees on the Kenai Peninsula in Alaska (USDA Forest Service 2000b). A principle management tool to improve forest health is tree-thinning (Graham et al. 1999a). However, as forests are thinned, managers have become concerned about forest-dependent species that may be affected by these treatments, including the Northern Goshawk. The loss of old-forest structure, regardless of the cause, is a major concern.

We begin with a discussion of goshawk population status from the perspective of a federal regulatory agency, the USDI Fish and Wildlife Service (USFWS), a federal land management agency, the USDA Forest Service (USFS), a non-profit environmental organization, The Nature Conservancy (TNC), and two published reviews of existing information on goshawk ecology and populations (Kennedy 1997; Andersen et. al. 2004, 2005). We then discuss the distribution and abundance of breeding goshawks followed by a brief description of their use of habitat. From this we move into a description of goshawk management prior to 1990 followed by post-1990 forest management. Trends in habitat management are described followed by a concluding section on what we think the future holds. We describe several landscape-scale management plans in the western US, one of which was developed for goshawks specifically and others that were developed

for other species which may affect goshawks. We focus, however, on the conceptual strength of a management plan developed specifically for southwestern forests which addresses goshawk nest and foraging habitats and the habitats of plants and animals in the goshawk food web.

STATUS

A species status is determined in a review of available information on trends in the populations, reproduction, survival, threats to populations, and trends in its habitats. For the USFWS, status is a formal designation with legal consequences. For non-profit organizations such as TNC, a species' status helps prioritize the importance, i.e., for funding, of the species relative to others. For state wildlife management agencies, the status of a species helps prioritize the agency's management attention.

USDI Fish and Wildlife Service

In July 1991, believing goshawk populations were declining due to forest cutting and habitat loss, a petition was filed with the USFWS (USDI Fish and Wildlife Service 1992a) to have the goshawk protected as endangered in Arizona, Colorado, New Mexico, and Utah under provisions of the Endangered Species Act (1973). In a review of the petition, the USFWS determined that the species in the four-state area was not a distinct population and therefore could not be listed. The USFWS noted that evidence existed to suggest the species may be declining and placed the goshawk, including the Queen Charlotte subspecies (*Accipiter gentilis laingi*), on its category II species list (USDI Fish and Wildlife Service 1991). Category II species were those that the USFWS determined required protection under the Endangered Species Act (ESA), but for which conclusive data regarding its population status and threats to its habitat were insufficient to support a proposed rule. By placing the goshawk on the category II list, the USFWS by-passed the petitioner's request for listing until more data were gathered. An amendment to the petition was submitted shortly thereafter (26 September 1991) asking for protection of the goshawk west of the 100th meridian. The USFWS considered the amended request a separate petition.

In January 1992, the USFWS began a status review of the goshawk, a process to acquire and analyze information about a species in an attempt to determine its current status and threats. Since the goshawk breeds across the continent, one issue turned on the term species. Species, as defined in the ESA (16 U.S.C 1532(16)), includes subspecies and any distinct population segment that interbreeds when mature. On 16 June 1992, the USFWS found that the new petition was not warranted because the petitioner failed to demonstrate that goshawks in the petitioned region may be a population segment distinct from other populations in its North American range. The USDI Fish and Wildlife Service (1992b) turned down the listing request stating that, "Our present knowledge of goshawk movements, and potential gene flow, suggest that although movement of goshawks may be limited, there is opportunity for genetic interchange. Goshawk habitat and populations are virtually continuous from the petitioned region into Canada and Mexico, and across Canada to the goshawk population in the eastern US." The USFWS based its decision, in part, on the lack of genetic evidence that demonstrated the petitioned population was distinct from adjacent populations. Following this ruling, the petitioner filed a lawsuit in U.S. District Court arguing that the USFWS was arbitrary and capricious in its determination. The district court agreed with the petitioner, finding that the USFWS made several post-1978 listing decisions using several contradictory policies. The district court required the USFWS to use its most recent evaluation policy and revisit the petition to list the goshawk as endangered. In 1994, the USFWS vacated its 1992 finding replacing it with a new finding with the same determination, listing not warranted (USDI Fish and Wildlife Service 1994).

Using the new distinct population segment policy (USDI Fish and Wildlife Service 1996), the USFWS reasoned that organisms in a population are members of a single species or lesser taxon, and that taxons were equivalent to subspecies (USDI Fish and Wildlife Service 1996). Since the petition requested protection for goshawks west of the 100th meridian, an area that included three goshawk subspecies (*A. g. atricapillus, A. g. laingi, A. g. apache*), the USFWS found that the goshawk was not a listable entity. The petitioner filed another lawsuit challenging the ruling and the court ruled once more that the USFWS acted arbitrarily and capriciously. In a re-evaluation of the petition, the USFWS determined that a status review was needed.

During attempts to list goshawks in the continental US, a separate petition to list the Queen Charlotte subspecies as endangered in southeast Alaska was received by the USFWS on 9 May 1994. On 26 August 1994, the USFWS announced that the petitioner presented information suggesting

the petition may be warranted. On 29 June 1995, after reviewing the best commercial and scientific information available, the USDI Fish and Wildlife Service (1995a) published their finding that listing the Queen Charlotte Goshawk was not warranted. Continuing legal challenges and a court order required the USFWS to reconsider their listing decision which is underway (USDI Fish and Wildlife Service 2005).

In late 1997, the USFWS determined in a 90-d finding that enough information existed to suggest that listing goshawks west of the 100th meridian may be warranted (USDI Fish and Wildlife Service 1997). In 1998, the USFWS completed their status review of the goshawk west of the 100th meridian and determined that its distribution did not appear to have changed from its historical range and that the available information did not show a decline in goshawk populations. The USFWS also determined that 78% of goshawk habitat was on federal forest lands and that many regional management strategies focused on retention or restoration of older forest. Therefore, the goshawk did not require protection under the ESA (USDI Fish and Wildlife Service 1998b). The Center for Biological Diversity and 18 other organizations filed a federal lawsuit claiming the USFWS was arbitrary and capricious in its finding. The U.S. District Court ruled on 28 June 2001 affirming the USFWS decision. The goshawk, therefore, has not been protected under provisions of the ESA. However, it is protected under provisions of the Migratory Bird Treaty Act (1918).

USDA FOREST SERVICE

Sensitive species

The USFS is responsible for managing the nation's national forests, plants, and wildlife habitat. The National Forest Management Act (NFMA 1973, NFMA 1982 implementing regulations at 36 CFR 219.19) provides for maintenance of vertebrate species viability in the planning area. To help meet this responsibility, the USFS has a threatened, endangered, and sensitive species management program. Sensitive species are those whose populations are sensitive to habitat-altering management activities. The USFS (USDA Forest Service 1988b) requires that every sensitive species in a management area undergo a biological evaluation (BE) documenting the probable effects of the proposed management on the species.

During the 1980s and early 1990s, the goshawk was added to regional sensitive species' lists in the Pacific

Southwest Region (California, 1981), Southwestern Region (Arizona, New Mexico, 1982), Intermountain Region (southern Idaho, Nevada, Utah, and western Wyoming, 1992), Rocky Mountain Region (Colorado, South Dakota, eastern Wyoming, 1993), and the Alaska Region (1994). The Pacific Northwest Region (Oregon, Washington) and the Northern Region (northern Idaho, North Dakota, Montana) do not list the goshawk as sensitive, and only some national forests within the Eastern Region list the goshawk as a sensitive species, while others designate the goshawk as a management indicator species.

Management indicator species

The management indicator species (MIS) concept assumes that certain species are not only sensitive to habitat change but are indicators of population changes of other species in a community. Theoretically, monitoring a few MIS reduces the difficulty of managing ecosystems by focusing limited funding on species that are representative of others. Thirty-seven of 104 national forests designated the goshawk as a MIS. The USFWS status review (USDI Fish and Wildlife Service 1998b) concluded that the goshawk was not a good MIS because it is difficult to locate and its habitat use is too general.

THE NATURE CONSERVANCY

The Nature Conservancy maintains a national biotic database in collaboration with state governments known as the Natural Heritage Program (NHP). One function of the NHP is to describe the status of plant and animal species at several spatial scales—global, national, and state. The NHP developed a ranking system to describe how secure a species is on a scale of one–five; one being species at high risk, such as those listed under the ESA, and five being species of little concern. The ranking criteria are based on the number of documented populations and number of individuals in those populations. TNC currently ranks the goshawk as globally secure (G4). The New Mexico NHP, for example, ranks the goshawk as relatively rare either as a breeder or non-breeder within the state (S2; Table 1). Because the goshawk is considered either abundant, a non-resident species, a non-breeder, or it does not occur at high enough numbers in the winter to be of concern, many states do not rank the goshawk, or if they do, they rank it as S3 or higher (Table 1).

In Canada, *A. g. atricapillus* it is not considered to be at risk in the boreal forest, but *A. g. laingi* is considered threatened in western British Columbia

by the Canadian government (Cooper and Stevens 2000, Cooper and Chytyk 2000, COSEWIC 2000, SARA 2002). The USFWS is currently reviewing the need to protect *A. g. laingi* (USDI Fish and Wildlife Service 2005). In Mexico, *A. g. apache* is informally considered threatened (Squires and Reynolds 1997). The Apache subspecies is not recognized by the American Ornithologists' Union (1998) because it is not distinctly different from *A. g. atricapillus*, but others believe it is a distinct subspecies (van Rossem 1938, Phillips et al. 1964, Wattel 1973, Hubbard 1992, Whaley and White 1994).

PUBLISHED REVIEWS OF GOSHAWK STATUS

Kennedy (1997) reviewed the literature regarding the status of goshawk populations in North America and evaluated the available evidence supporting or refuting population declines including contraction in geographic range, decreases in numbers of goshawks, and trends in their reproduction and survival. Kennedy (1997) found no strong evidence supporting a population decline but noted that studies she reviewed had not been designed to detect population change making her review problematic. Kennedy was subsequently criticized for not using the information provided to the USFWS by the petitioner in her evaluation (Peck 2000).

In 1999, The Raptor Research Foundation and The Wildlife Society established a technical committee to review the status of the goshawk. They determined that existing data were inadequate to assess population trends or to genetically differentiate among recognized subspecies using DNA analytical techniques and, that basing the status of goshawks solely on the distribution of late-successional forests is not appropriate (Andersen et al. 2004).

BREEDING LOCATIONS IN THE UNITED STATES

When estimating the status of goshawk populations, it is important to understand their breeding distribution. To appreciate the nuances of determining goshawk distribution requires knowledge of the components and sizes of goshawk home ranges. Goshawk home range has been estimated to be about 2,000–3,000 ha (Eng and Gullion 1962, Reynolds 1983, Reynolds et al. 1992, Kennedy 1990, Boal et al. 2003). For the purpose of managing goshawk breeding habitat, breeding home ranges have been partitioned into foraging area (FA), post-fledging family area (PFA), and nest area(s) (NA) (Reynolds et al. 1992). Each home range may include one or

TABLE 1. THE 2003 STATUS OF NORTHERN GOSHAWKS (*ACCIPITER GENTILIS ATRICAPILLUS*) AS REPORTED BY THE NATURE CONSERVANCY (NATURAL HERITAGE PROGRAM [NHP] STATE RANKINGS FROM THEIR BIOLOGICAL CONSERVATION DATABASE) AND THE STATE GAME AND FISH AGENCIES (STATE ENDANGERED [E] OR THREATENED [T]).

State	NHP-ranking[a]	State classification T or E?[b]	Falconry permitted?	Comments
Alabama	S3B, S4N	No	Yes	Accidental in state.
Alaska[c]	S4	No	Yes	Abundant in state.
Arizona	S3	No	Yes	Harvest being considered.
Arkansas	SA	No	Yes	Accidental in state.
California	S3	No	Yes	Review underway.
Colorado	S3B, SZN	No	Yes	1–6/yr. resident only.
Connecticut	S4B, SZN	No	No	Possession permit only.
Delaware	SZN	No	Yes	Winter visitant only.
District of Columbia	SA	No	Yes	No regulations.
Florida	S?	No	Yes	Extremely rare in winter.
Georgia	SA	No	Yes	Very rare transient in state.
Hawaii	Not tracked	No	No	Exotic species not allowed.
Idaho	S4	No	Yes	No out of state permits issued.
Illinois	SZN	No	Yes	Accidental in state.
Indiana	SZN	No	Yes	Rare winter visitor.
Iowa	SZN	No	Yes	Rare winter visitor.
Kansas	SZN	No	Yes	Non-breeding.
Kentucky	SZN	No	Yes	Follow federal regulations.
Louisiana	SA	No	Yes	Accidental in state,
Maine	S3?B, S3?N	No	Yes	few taken.
Maryland	S1B, SZN	Endangered	No	Conflicting laws.
Massachusetts	S3	No	No	Uncommon.
Michigan	S3		Yes	No take allowed.
Minnesota	SU		Yes	Sensitive species.
Mississippi	SA	No	Yes	Accidental in state.
Missouri	Not tracked	No	Yes	
Montana	S3S4	No	Yes	
Nebraska	S?N	No	Yes	No take allowed.
Nevada	S3	No	Yes	Take allowed (10).
New Hampshire	S4	No		On watch list.
New Jersey	S1B, S4N	Threatened	Yes	Take passage birds only.
New Mexico	S2B, S2N	No	Yes	Take allowed (6).
New York	S4B, S3N	No	Yes	Take allowed.
North Carolina	SUB, SZN	No	Yes	Follow federal regulations.
North Dakota	S?	No	Yes	Follow federal regulations.
Ohio	S?	No	Yes	None breeding.
Oklahoma	S2N	No	Yes	Infrequent visitor.
Oregon	S3	No	Yes	Take allowed (12).
Pennsylvania	S2, S3B, S3N	No	Yes	Take allowed (7).
Rhode Island	S1B, S1N	No	Yes	No take allowed.
South Carolina	S?	No	Yes	Accidental—one record in 50 yr.
South Dakota	S3B, S2N	No	Yes	Take allowed.
Tennessee	SPB, S2N	No	Yes	No breeding.
Texas	Not tracked	No	Yes	Accidental.
Utah	S3	No	Yes	Take allowed.
Vermont	S3, S4B, SZN	No	Yes	Take allowed.
Washington	S3B, S3N	No	Yes	Take allowed.
West Virginia	S1B, S1N	No	Yes	No state ESA.

TABLE 1. CONTINUED.

State	NHP-ranking[a]	State classification T or E?[b]	Falconry permitted?	Comments
Wisconsin	S2N, S2B	No	Yes	Take allowed.
Wyoming	S2, S3B, S4N	No	Yes	Take allowed.

[a] S1 = 1–5 occurrences; S2 = 6–20 occurrences; S3 = 21–100 occurrences; S4 = 100 or more occurrences, taxa is widespread, abundant and apparently secure, but cause for long-term concern; S5 = demonstrably widespread, abundant, and secure; B = breeding, N = non-breeding; A = abundant; U = uncommon; Z = zero occurrences in state.

[b] The goshawk is officially designated by the state as threatened or endangered.

[c] In Alaska, *Accipiter gentilis laingi* is ranked as S2B (NatureServe 2005).

more NAs (about 12 ha) generally located within the PFA (Reynolds et al. 1992). Prior to 1985, <500 nesting sites were known in the US, but no systematic effort had been made to find or monitor nest sites (USDI Fish and Wildlife Service 1998). Until 1992, no coordinated west-wide attempt by the USFS to monitor nests existed except in the Southwest Region (Arizona and New Mexico). Searching for nests consisted of visiting suitable nest habitat within or adjacent to planned tree cutting units. In 1990, a protocol for systematically surveying large areas for breeding goshawks was developed (Kennedy and Stahlecker 1993) and later refined (Joy et al. 1994). This technique which used sampling stations at fixed distances on transects from which goshawk vocalizations are broadcast with tape recorders, increased the efficiency of searching for goshawks in large areas. During the 1990s, many national forests began inventorying project areas for nesting goshawks using this technique.

Since the early 1980s, the number of documented goshawk nest sites on USFS lands has steadily increased (Fletcher and Sheppard 1994). In response to a 1992 questionnaire sent by one of us (DAB) to all USFS regions with breeding goshawks, a total of 1,871 nest sites (1,722 nest sites for western US) on public lands were documented (Table 2). Because the eastern US contains little USFS land, and about three-quarters of America's private forests are in the eastern US (Stein et al. 2005), the number of nest sites on USFS lands in the eastern US was <10% of the known USFS nest sites (Table 2). It is unknown how many of these nest sites were visited in 1992, but 700 were reported as occupied (one or more goshawks present). It is difficult to estimate the total number of breeding goshawks in the US because of the wide variation among the USFS regions in the intensity of surveying and monitoring goshawk nests.

In 1998, the USFWS goshawk status review contained information on >2,900 occupied territories (breeding activity in ≥1 yr) in the western US. (excluding Alaska) on private, state, and federal lands (95% of territories were on USFS land [USDI Fish and Wildlife Service 1998b]). The USDI report (USDI Fish and Wildlife Service 1998b) defined territory as a location where no other occupied nests were found within a 1.6 km radius from the previous nest site. If we assume a similar increase in known territories for the eastern US, then a conservative estimate in 2004 of the number of territories in the US would be about 3,200. If each territory was occupied in a given year (very dubious assumption), about 6,400 goshawks would be breeding in the continental US.

Goshawks also nest in Alaska, Canada, and northern Mexico. Numbers of breeding goshawks in Canada and Alaska fluctuate dramatically over years in response to large fluctuations in prey (McGowan 1975, Mueller et al. 1977, Doyle and Smith 1994, Squires and Reynolds 1997). Considering this, and the fact that the expansive boreal forest has the potential to contain many goshawks, it is difficult to describe the total population size for North America.

National forests generally do not have the budgets to apply the Kennedy and Stahlecker (1993) protocol to all forested lands. Thus, knowledge of goshawk breeding locations comes mainly from lands designated for commercial use and not from lands such as wilderness, national recreation areas, wild and scenic river corridors, experimental forests, and national parks. No formal monitoring protocol for goshawk populations has been established for national forests. However, Hargis and Woodbridge (*this volume*) have developed such a monitoring protocol. Limited funding typically results in biologists visiting historical nest sites on an opportunistic basis. Intensive monitoring of goshawk populations, such as documenting the re-occupancy rate of nest areas, nest success and productivity has been limited to a few research sites.

Although goshawks typically exhibit strong fidelity to territories (Detrich and Woodbridge 1994, Reynolds et al. 1994), a problem that confounds monitoring breeding goshawks is that a high

TABLE 2. NUMBER OF GOSHAWK NESTING AREAS LOCATED ON USDA FOREST SERVICE LANDS THROUGH 1992, DISPLAYED BY REGION AND FOREST COVER TYPE.

Forest type	USDA Forest Service regions[a]								Total
	R1	R2	R3	R4	R5	R6	R9	R10	
Northern hardwoods[b]	0	0	0	0	0	0	92	0	92
Red pine	0	0	0	0	0	0	16	0	16
Oak-pine	0	0	0	0	0	0	10	0	10
Mixed conifer	30	3	71	25	309	123[c]	0	0	561
Yellow pine	11	43	215	35	80	9	0	0	393
True fir	0	0	2	0	75	2	0	0	79
Douglas-fir	25	0	4	51	53	77[c]	0	0	210
Spruce-fir	0	5	0	15	0	0	0	0	20
Lodgepole pine	10	33	0	42	13	8	0	0	106
Aspen	3	45	2	125	1	0	13	0	189
Aspen-lodgepole	0	18	0	8	0	0	0	0	26
Mixed aspen-conifer-spruce-fir	1	15	0	15	0	0	0	0	31
Sitka spruce-hemlock	0	0	0	0	0	0	0	10	10
Misc. types[d]	9	0	2	1	2	0	0	0	14
Unrecorded	30	13	46	10	13	0		0	112
Total	119	175	342	321	546	219	131	4	1,857

[a] R1 = northern (ID, MT); R2 = Rocky Mountain (CO, SD, WY); R3 = southwestern (AZ, NM); R4 = intermountain (ID, NV, UT, WY); R5 = Pacific Southwest (CA); R6 = Pacific Northwest (OR, WA); R9 = eastern (IL, IN, MI, MN, NH, PA, VT, WV, WI); R10 (AK).

[b] Includes Allegheny hardwood forest type (N = 9) that contain 50% or more cherry trees (*Prunus* spp.). Includes northern hardwood-mixed conifer forest cover types (N = 9).

[c] Region six reported 136 nest areas located in Douglas-fir or mixed-conifer forest. We did not know the correct classification so we split them evenly between forest types (Gene Silovsky, pers. comm.).

[d] Miscellaneous types includes cottonwood (R1,1; R4, 1), pinyon-juniper (R3,2), subalpine fir (R5,2), western red cedar-hemlock (*Thuja plicata-Psuga heterophylla*) (R1,8).

percentage of pairs (up to 75%) change nest locations yearly and these nests can be as far as 2.4 km from a previously used nest (Reynolds et al. 2005). Because of shifting nest use, monitoring goshawks typically requires repeated searches over large areas to determine if the goshawks are breeding (Reynolds et al. 2005). A potential problem then is that many territories may be mislabelled as unoccupied because of insufficient sampling effort. If only a single annual visit is made to a nest site, roughly 35% of occupied goshawk nests can be misclassified as unoccupied by searchers who were testing three common search techniques (Boyce et al. 2005). Failure to search sufficiently regardless of the number of re-visits often leads to mislabelling territories as unoccupied (Reynolds et al. 2005). Watson et al. (1999) studied goshawk detection rates with the broadcast technique at three distances from known active nests (100, 250, and 400 m), and reported that five visits were needed at 100 m to attain 90% or higher detection rate, eight visits at 250 m from the nest, and 10 visits at 400 m. Boyce et al. (2005) provide guidance on the estimated number of re-visits needed to have confidence in verifying a nest area as occupied.

Because of annual movement among alternate nests within territories, Reynolds et al. (2005) suggest

that the appropriate scale for reporting occupancy is the territory, and that due to the difficulty of proving that territories are not occupied, territories should be classed as active if goshawks laid eggs, occupied if adult(s) are present in a nest area but no eggs are laid, and unknown if there is no (or insufficient) evidence of activity or occupancy. Habitat alternating management decisions are made daily based on varying degrees of uncertainty; having complete knowledge is almost never the case.

The extent of annual variation in the proportion of goshawk territories occupied by egg-laying pairs is known only in a few study areas (Doyle and Smith 1994, Reynolds et al. 2005; Keane and Morrison, *this volume*; Reynolds and Joy, *this volume*). Even in areas where nests are intensively monitored, estimates of population size or trend are difficult to attain because: (1) the proportion of territories with egg-laying adults (hence, their probability of detection) can be extremely variable year to year (7–87%; Reynolds et al., pers. obs.), (2) reproductive failure and nest abandonment may occur before breeding pairs can be detected, and (3) the high frequency of movement among alternate nests lowers their probability of detection (Reynolds et al. 2005; Reynolds and Joy, *this volume*). Reynolds et al. (*this volume*) showed that about 60–80 territories require monitoring in good breeding years and >100 territories are required in poor breeding years for reliable estimates of nesting success. Mark-recapture of goshawks is the best method for estimating vital rates and population trends (Cormack 1964, Jolly 1965, Seber 1965). However, cost is prohibitive because a large number of goshawks must be marked and recaptured over many years before reliable estimates can be obtained (DeStefano et al. 1994b, Kennedy 1997, Reynolds et al. 2004; Reynolds and Joy, *this volume*). We believe that monitoring goshawks is valuable, but understanding the habitat needs of goshawks and their prey are also important. Habitat management can only improve if we have a clear understanding of goshawk habitat and the habitat of species in their food web.

GOSHAWK HABITAT

The Effect of Habitat Change

The extent of habitat change matters. Mid-aged to old forests are fundamentally important to goshawks and many of their prey (Reynolds et al. 1992), but they are also a valued timber resource for society. In the northeastern US, the number of nesting goshawks may have declined because of timber harvesting and severe wildfires over the past 200 yr (Speiser and Bosakowski 1984). However, goshawk populations appear to be expanding as those forests are recovering (Bull 1974, Speiser and Bosakowski 1984, DeStefano 2005). In Europe, it is believed that goshawk populations declined in areas where forests were clear cut (Ivanovsky 1995, Widén 1997). Today those boreal forests are highly fragmented and breeding goshawks there underwent a 50–60% decline in densities (Ivanovsky 1995, Widén 1997). Railroad logging at the turn of the century removed extensive areas of mature trees in much of the western US, but the effect of this on goshawks is unknown.

With the arrival of European settlers in the western US, the pace and extent of habitat modification was extensive. Human activities that altered goshawk habitat included tree harvesting (Crocker-Bedford 1990), fire exclusion (McCune 1983), livestock grazing (Lucas and Oakleaf 1975, Mueggler 1989), and road building (Speiser and Bosakowski 1987, Grubb et al. 1998). Fire exclusion across the western US allowed young trees to become established. In ponderosa pine forest, for example, the understory structure of open forest has been converted to a

closed understory of dense trees beneath old pine trees (Covington and Moore 1994b).

In some areas, goshawk nest habitat is vulnerable to livestock grazing. In northern Nevada, for example, goshawks frequently nest in stands of quaking aspen (*Populus tremuloides*) in otherwise treeless landscapes (Lucas and Oakleaf 1975, Younk and Bechard 1994a). Aspen is a relatively short-lived tree ($\approx$ 120 yr) and browsing by elk (*Cervus elaphus*), deer (*Odocoileus* spp.), and cattle (*Bos* spp.), retards its regeneration eventually leading to the loss of stands (Lucas and Oakleaf 1975). Grazing can also reduce herbaceous fuels that can stimulate aspen regeneration. Grazing can be particularly destructive because aspen stands often grow on level benches in swales and next to creeks where ungulates tend to concentrate.

In areas where extensive railroad logging did not occur, such as on the Kaibab Plateau in northern Arizona, a combination of light forest cutting (single-tree selection began in the 1920s) and intensive shelter-wood seed-cut harvests (between 1985–1991), was believed to have resulted in a goshawk decline from 260 pairs prior to tree harvests to 60 pairs by 1988 (Crocker-Bedford 1990). However, long-term research on the Kaibab Plateau goshawk population has shown that the Kaibab Plateau currently has the highest density of nesting territories reported for the species in a large area (Reynolds et al. 2005; Reynolds and Joy, *this volume*). Nonetheless, Crocker-Bedford (1990) findings resulted in a renewed focus on the effects of forest management on goshawks.

Most discussions of threats to goshawk populations suggest that forest management, especially tree harvesting, may be causing declines in goshawks (Reynolds et al. 1982, Moore and Henny 1983, Reynolds 1983, Crocker-Bedford 1990, Woodbridge and Detrich 1994). These arguments rest on the goshawk's affinity for mature and old forest and the effects of human and natural disturbance on that forest's structure. Although it is believed that extensive habitat modifications are detrimental, it remains unclear exactly how goshawk populations are responding to habitat modification because of inadequate study of the effects across a gradient of tree-harvesting intensities. Research is needed to examine how goshawks respond to light to intermediate tree harvesting and how their prey species respond to these harvests.

Goshawk Use of Habitat

An important conservation issue still argued is the relationship between goshawks and their habitat, and the importance of mature to old-forest composition, structure, and pattern. Is the goshawk an old-growth obligate? The literature shows that goshawks prefer to place their nests in mature to old-forest settings (Reynolds et al., *this volume*). However, if mature to old-forest habitat is not available, goshawks will nest in younger forest (Reich et al. 2004). As the scale of consideration increases, the diversity of habitat used by goshawks provides a broader understanding of the adaptability of goshawks at regional and continental scales. Goshawks can adjust to environmental conditions and occasionally nest in essentially treeless areas (Swem and Adams 1992) or in areas with small patches of trees and hunt in open shrub-steppe habitats (Younk and Bechard 1994a).

Whether considered at the home-range, population, or the regional scale, goshawks are not restricted to one forest environment. The literature does not support the notion that the goshawk is an old-growth obligate (Reynolds et al., *this volume*). However, though they do not depend on a single forest age class for nesting, they often prefer mature and older forests for nest sites (Reynolds et al. 1982, Crocker-Bedford and Chaney 1988, Hayward and Escano 1989). McGrath et al. (2003) found that plots within nest areas contained more mature to old trees then plots within random sites 83 ha in size; a similar finding noted by others (Bartlet 1974, Reynolds et al. 1982, Saunders 1982, Hall 1984, Lang 1994, Siders and Kennedy 1994, Desimone 1997, Patla 1997, Daw et al. 1998). Goshawk home ranges during the breeding season are variable, but typically large (about 26 km²; Reynolds et al. 1992, Boal et al. 2003). Radio-telemetry studies indicate that, while foraging goshawks prefer mature forest, they also use younger forests as well as edges and openings (Fisher 1986, Hargis et al. 1994, Bright-Smith and Mannan 1994; Reynolds et al., *this volume*).

PREY HABITAT

A key to raptor survival and reproduction is an adequate supply of food (Newton 1979a, 1986). Goshawk foraging areas need to provide abundant and accessible prey. Widén (1997) concluded that forest management may degrade hunting habitat and prey populations and was the prime factor behind the goshawk decline in Fennoscandia. Goshawk habitat use may in part reflect the habitat of the prey. This was supported in an analysis of habitat use of major goshawk prey species in southwestern US forests (Reynolds et al. 1992). Reynolds et al. (1992) also observed that although the entire range of forest vegetative structural stages was used by goshawk prey, the older vegetative structural stages and small openings were of higher value to the greatest number of prey species. This resulted in a recommendation to have the maximum sustainable amount of old forest with interspersed small openings in a southwestern goshawk landscape.

Kenward and Widén (1987), Reynolds et al. (1992), and Beier and Drennan (1997) suggested that accessibility of prey to goshawks is influenced by forest structure. In pre-settlement (circa 1900) ponderosa pine forests, historical photographs and accounts describe the forest as park-like with forest floors being open (Cooper 1960), a condition where prey are easier to detect and pursue by hunting goshawks. Now, due mostly to fire exclusion, livestock grazing, and road building, forest structure and pattern has been altered with forests being much denser in many areas of the western US (Covington and Moore 1994b, Graham et al. 2004). This population of small trees has filled in the sub-canopy space where goshawks do much of their hunting. Management practices that improve goshawk hunting by reducing the density of young trees should improve the quality of hunting habitat. How goshawk and prey habitat are changed by forest management is a critical issue for the long-term welfare of goshawks.

THE DIVERSITY OF FORESTS USED

In 1994, we surveyed each national forest nationwide to determine the forest types used by goshawks and the known number of goshawk nests in each (Table 2). Two forest types, Douglas-fir and ponderosa pine, contained 78% of the known nest areas in the western US. The trend in forest structure and pattern of these two forest types is important for predicting the status of goshawk populations. In the East, hardwood forest was used extensively for nesting and to the north, use of boreal forests have been well documented.

The winter ecology of goshawks is poorly known, but habitats used during winter show a wider variation than during the breeding season as adults and juveniles move down in elevation from spruce-fir (*Picea engelmannii-Abies lasiocarpa*) forests, mixed conifer forests, or ponderosa pine forests to pinyon-juniper (*Pinus edulis-Juniperous* spp.) forests to woodland and shrub communities (Reynolds et al. 1994, Squires and Ruggiero 1995, Stephens 2001, Sonsthagen 2002). Movement from boreal forests south is well known. In a Wyoming population, goshawks migrated over 160 km from breeding territories during winter months (Squires

TABLE 3. GOSHAWK NEST AREAS BY FOREST COVER TYPE IN THE WESTERN US THAT CONTAIN 99% OF THE KNOWN GOSHAWK NESTING AREAS WEST OF THE 100TH MERIDIAN (HECTARES × 1,000; DATA FROM USDI FISH AND WILDLIFE SERVICE 1998B).

Forest cover type	Number of goshawk nest areas (%)	Hectares of forest cover type (%)
Douglas-fir	2,771 (55.4)	15,474 (24.3)
Spruce-fir	363 (7.3)	7,678 (12.1)
Lodgepole pine[a]	356 (7.1)	11,744 (18.5)
Ponderosa pine	1,130 (22.6)	22,089 (34.7)
Western hardwoods	67 (1.3)	5,302 (8.3)
Aspen-birch[b]	318 (6.4)	1,295 (2.0)
Totals	5,005 (100)	63,583 (100)

[a] *Pinus contorta.*
[b] *Betula* spp.

and Ruggiero 1995). Movement away from breeding areas during winter increases the scale of management consideration. Information is needed on habitat use of goshawks and their prey during the non-breeding season to improve our understanding of forest management options that might increase the likelihood of sustaining goshawks (Graham et al. 1999b).

MANAGEMENT

Numerous human-related activities potentially threaten goshawks population viability including shooting, poisons, and falconry (Reynolds 1989), but the primary threat appears to be modification of forest habitat caused by management and natural disturbance (Reynolds 1989, Crocker-Bedford 1990, Squires and Reynolds 1997). Natural factors such as disease, parasites, exposure, and predation affect individuals more than populations (Squires and Reynolds 1997; Reynolds et al., *this volume*).

MANAGEMENT PRIOR TO 1990

The effect of tree harvests in nest areas on goshawk reproduction has been a concern since the early 1970s (Reynolds 1971, Bartelt 1977, Hennessy 1978, Reynolds et al. 1982, Crocker-Bedford 1990). As a result, goshawk nest trees were the first component of goshawk habitat to be protected (Reynolds 1971). By the mid- to late 1970s, most national forests in the western US protected goshawk nest trees in management areas. Forest managers gradually began incorporating nest area management guidelines into their project designs. But from the early 1970s through the 1980s, most national forests did not have formal goshawk nest area management standards or guidelines.

As cutting of forests in the US accelerated, public concern escalated over the effects that timber harvesting was having on wildlife. Managers started to protect small areas around goshawk nests. However, because management guidelines for federal lands were unavailable, the size of the protected nest areas varied from 1–10 ha. By 1985, the USFS in California required 20-ha buffers around goshawk nests in all national forests, and in 1986 the state of California Department of Fish and Game recommended a 50.6 ha buffer around goshawk nests; a recommendation adopted by only a few national forests in California (B. Woodbridge, pers. comm.). During the late 1980s and early 1990s, concerns arose about the effects of tree cutting beyond protected nest areas (Reynolds 1989, Crocker-Bedford 1990, Reynolds et al. 1992, Bright-Smith and Mannan 1994, Hargis et al. 1994) where goshawks foraged. In particular, there were concerns about how tree harvesting was changing goshawk and prey habitat (Kenward and Widén 1989, Reynolds et al. 1992, Widén 1997).

MANAGEMENT SINCE 1990

Concerns about the effects of tree harvesting on goshawk reproduction and population viability continued into the 1990s (Crocker-Bedford 1990, Bright-Smith and Mannan 1994, Beier and Drennan 1997). Crocker-Bedford (1990) and Woodbridge and Detrich (1994) noted that the rate of re-occupancy of nest stands by goshawks was related to the size of the forest stand containing nests. Bühler and Oggier (1987) reported that goshawk nest density increased as the proportion of woodland in a landscape increased. Telemetry research on adult female and goshawk fledging movements (Kennedy 1989, 1990; Kennedy et al. 1994), made it clear that an area larger than the NA was also important and researchers turned their attention to developing recommendations for larger areas around goshawk nests. Reynolds et al. (1992) recommended that three 10–12 ha nest areas and three 10–12 ha replacement nest areas be managed per goshawk breeding territory, and that a PFA about 170 ha in size (excluding the nest areas) be managed based on the estimated size of the adult female core area that contained the goshawk nest (Kennedy 1990). The collective recommendation was that the nest areas, replacement nest areas, and PFA total 243 ha per breeding home range. By 1994, the USFS in Oregon and Washington began protecting PFA habitat (DeStefano et al. 1994a).

Reynolds et al. (1992) developed habitat management recommendations for the Northern Goshawk (MRNG) that included available knowledge on goshawk nesting, fledging, and foraging habitats, and the foods and habitats of their important prey. The MRNG described sets of desired forest compositions, structures, and landscape patterns for three southwestern forest types (ponderosa pine, mixed conifer, and spruce-fir). Furthermore, the MRNG states that certain habitat elements—downed logs, woody debris, and snags—be present in landscapes, and suggested management prescriptions to attain the desired conditions (Reynolds et al. 1992). The focus of habitat management expanded from nest areas to PFAs, then foraging areas to landscapes, and finally to ecological function.

The MRNG were implemented on all national forests in the southwestern US on an interim basis in June 1991 (USDA Forest Service 1991b; amended [USDA Forest Service 1991c] to clarify public issues, 1992b; extended 1993a) and formally adopted on a permanent basis in June 1996 through an amendment of all forest plans. In addition, six national forests in Utah (USDA Forest Service 2000a), the Black Hills National Forest in South Dakota (USDA Forest Service 2001a), and the Tongass National Forest in Alaska changed their forest plans to incorporate the approach and concepts developed in Reynolds et al. (1992).

Management scale

Reynolds et al. (1992) recommended creating and sustaining goshawk and prey habitats at multiple landscape scales. Because of the overall importance of mid-aged, mature, and old vegetative structural stages to the goshawk and its suite of prey, the recommended goshawk landscape would have as much mid-aged-to-old structural stages as could be sustained. Because of vegetation growth, sustaining mid-aged to old structural stages required that all vegetative structural stages be present in the landscape. Vegetative structural stages were to be distributed in a fine-scale mosaic (Reynolds et al. 1992). In ponderosa pine forest, for example, the sustainable distribution approximated 10% of the area occupied by grasses, forbs, or shrubs, 10% by seedling-saplings, 20% by young trees, 20% by mid-aged trees, 20% by mature trees, and 20% by older trees (Reynolds et al. 1992, Bassett et al. 1994). Unlike many other wildlife habitat management plans, the MRNG is not a habitat-reserve approach where management within reserves is restricted or not allowed. Instead, active management is encouraged to develop or maintain the desired forest conditions (Reynolds et al. 1992). The pace and direction of change needed to attain the desired forest conditions is determined by the existing conditions.

Long-distance movement of goshawks away from their breeding areas during winter increases the scale of management consideration (Graham et al. 1999b). Habitat management recommendations for goshawk habitats have not been developed for non-breeding areas, but the desired breeding habitats identified in the MRNG were intended to provide for sufficient prey during winter to minimize the needs for goshawks to leave their breeding home ranges in search of food.

TRENDS IN HABITAT MANAGEMENT

Prior to 1900, tree harvests occurred first in valley bottoms near population centers. Once this source of trees was exhausted, harvesting activities moved upslope and away from populated areas. As the amount of old forests declined, conservationists began to oppose forest management practices that threatened the remaining old forests. A forest survey of the Southwest Region of the USFS in 1992, for example, found an abundance of young to mid-aged trees and a deficit in mature and old trees (Johnson 1994). The USFS Pacific Southwest and Pacific Northwest regions also reported decreasing trends in the amount of mature forest (Thomas et al. 1990). As a result, many believed that goshawk habitat had been degraded or destroyed. USDI Fish and Wildlife Service (1998b) concluded that considerable forest habitat modification had occurred which likely affected goshawks, but the effects had not been measured. However, in the northeastern US, the number of mature and old trees has increased from the time of early settlement (Nyland 2002).

WHERE ARE WE GOING?

MANAGING FOR THE FUTURE

In the western US, 78% of the habitat occupied by nesting goshawks is federally managed lands (USDI Fish and Wildlife Service 1998b). Therefore, the federal government alone can maintain well-distributed breeding goshawks throughout the western US. In their review (USDI Fish and Wildlife Service 1998b) the USFWS concluded that the MRNG model for the southwestern US (Reynolds et al. 1992) would likely sustain goshawks. Since forests in the eastern US forests are largely privately owned, sustaining goshawk's there depends on the development of conservation strategies, prevailing attitudes about management of private forests, and ultimately a pre-cautionary approach to management (O'Riordan and Cameron 1994). Prospects for improved future man-agement depend on validating goshawk subspecies designations, determining the level and importance of dispersal in maintaining viable populations of goshawks, modelling climate change to understand how forests may change as temperatures increase in North America, continuing demographic inves-tigations into factors limiting goshawk populations (habitat, food, predators, competitors, disease, and weather) and how these are affected by forest man-agement, identifying suites of important goshawk prey by forest types, identifying habitats of prey and synthesizing these with forest ecology to develop forest type-specific desired forest conditions, and testing the effectiveness of food web and/or eco-system-based conservation strategies for sustaining goshawks. Testing should include economic factors associated with implementation.

Northwest Forest Plan

An important question is what existing conserva-tion strategy should managers implement? Several conservation plans that might benefit goshawks are available, but several of these were created for reasons other than to directly protect goshawks. The President's Northwest Forest Plan (NWFP) established a network of habitat conservation areas (HCA) to protect Spotted Owls (*Strix occidentalis*) in northern California, Oregon, and Washington. The NWFP is essentially a system of old-forest reserves; each large enough to accommodate 20 pairs of Spotted Owls and presumed to be large enough to provide self-sufficient habitat to sustain other organ-isms (Johnson et al. 1991, USDA Forest Service 1992a, Thomas et al. 1993). Low-elevation areas were not as well represented as higher-elevation reserves due to patterns of private and public land ownership. Connectivity among reserves is provided by a matrix of habitat, considered to be permeable by species, between reserves. Managed riparian cor-ridors also offer connectivity.

Forest management is restricted in the NWFP Spotted Owl reserves but is permitted in the matrix between the reserves. The idea is to provide enough reserves well-distributed in the landscape to sustain the owl and other species that are old-growth depen-dent. It remains uncertain if the NWFP strategy can

sustain goshawks, in particular whether the number and sizes of the reserves, as well as the composition and structure of the matrix, are sufficient to support viable populations of goshawks. A similar forest habi-tat reserve plan is being used in Alaska to accomodate other species such as the marten (*Martes americana*). Conservation strategies dependent on reserves may not recognize the dynamics of forests and the needs of species that are dependent on those dynamics for survival. Sustaining goshawk's in managed forests depends on management plans that incorporate the ecological dynamics of each forest type.

Sierra Nevada Forest Plan and 2004 amendment

The California Sierra Nevada Forest Plan (SNFP; USDA Forest Service 2001b) as amended (USDA Forest Service 2004) provides protection for goshawk activity centers (PAC), surrounding all known goshawk nests in national forests located in the Sierra Nevada Mountains. The PACs are defined as the largest contiguous patch of at least 81 ha of forested habitat near known or suspected goshawk nests. Surveys are required prior to management activities to establish nest or activity centers when management is planned in or adjacent to a PAC. PACs are to be maintained regardless of goshawk occupancy status unless the habitat is rendered unsuitable by stand-replacing events.

The SNFP clearly addressed the nest-area require-ments of goshawks, but was silent on goshawk PFAs, foraging habitats, and prey habitats. The NWFP has no explicit direction for the goshawk and we could not find a clear discussion in either the NWFP or the SNFP of the habitat of goshawk prey. Nonetheless, both the SNFP and NWFP incorporated information on species that comprise the goshawk food web as well as extensive analyses of other plant and animal species. Lacking a specific goshawk and prey analy-sis, the capability of the SNFP and NWFP to sustain goshawks remains unknown. However, the manage-ment approaches in the SNFP and NWFP provide a suitable framework for applying other conservation plans, such as the MRNG (Reynolds et al. 1992); the MNRG, which describes forest stand and landscape attributes that are suitable for the goshawk and its prey species, could be implemented in the matrix between Spotted Owl reserves and goshawk PACs.

Goshawk management in southwestern forests

The MRNG (Reynolds et al. 1992) has been the focus of numerous critical reviews. USDI Fish and Wildlife Service (1998b) identified the MRNG as a management plan that would likely sustain goshawks. In their review, the Committee of Scientists (U.S. Department of Agriculture 1999) highlighted the process used to develop the MRNG as the first example of a food-web based bioregional assessment for a large-scale conservation strategy. The Wildlife Society and the American Ornithologists' Union concluded that the scientific basis of the MRNG was sound and that management of a food web is an important step towards keeping goshawks from becoming threatened or endangered, and provides the basis for adaptive management that strives for a naturally functioning ecosystem (Braun et al. 1996). One review focused on whether the desired conditions in the MRNG were sustainable in southwestern forests (Long and Smith 2000). Long and Smith (2000) wrote that "With the adoption of the goshawk guidelines in 1996, the FS embarked on a truly ambitious restoration effort. The guidelines mandate nothing short of fundamentally restructuring southwestern ponderosa pine forests at a regional scale. The underlying management strategy, while superficially another example of a narrow, single-species focus, is in fact a coarse filter approach that includes a mosaic of age and structural classes intended to provide habitats and food chains for a broad spectrum of wildlife species, including goshawk prey species. This landscape-scale mosaic will be created and maintained under an uneven-aged silvicultural system intended to approximate the composition, structure, and landscape patterns existing in southwestern ponderosa pine forests before fundamental changes in natural disturbance regimes and forest structure."

Other reviews of the MRNG were negative. These include a FWS review (USDA Forest Service 1992a), a State of Arizona review (Arizona Game and Fish Department 1993), and a petition filed to correct the MRNG under Public Law 106-554 §515 (Federal Data Quality Act 2001) by Olsen et al. (2003a, b). In 1992, the Regional Director of the USFWS in New Mexico listed the agency's concerns as: (1) the MRNG would fragment forests which is deleterious to goshawks, because goshawks need large tracts of mature closed-canopy forests for foraging, (2) goshawks are adapted to closed physical environments and opening forests allows competitors and predators to invade, (3) goshawks are limited by habitat structure not food, (4) prey abundance is a function of forest structure, (5) important prey species in the Southwest are not known, (6) goshawks are prey generalists, and specific information on habitat of prey is not known or presented, (7) using minimum values for nest areas, PFAs, and foraging areas is not recommended, and (8) no data exist to support managing PFA habitat as a transition between nest area and foraging habitat.

Similarly, the State of Arizona (Arizona Game and Fish Department 1993) was concerned about: (1) the degree to which forest structure in goshawk foraging habitat would be opened and fragmented, (2) implementing the MRNG in lands allocated as old growth or unsuitable for timber production, (3) the cumulative effects of past and future timber harvest activities, (4) existing forest conditions are already below minimum thresholds identified in the MRNG, (5) a replacement of existing land and resource management plan standards and guidelines by the MRNG, and (6) implementation of the MRNG at the landscape scale.

Olsen et al. (2003a) used the FDQA to petition the USFS to remove the MRNG publication from circulation and set-aside management decisions based on the MRNG throughout the western US. In response to the Olsen et al. (2003a) petition, the USFS (USDA Forest Service 2003) conducted an in depth review of the petition and found it to be without merit. The USFS also contracted with the Ecological Society of America to provide three blind reviews of the Olsen et al. (2003a) petition. The Ecological Society of America concluded that MRNG meets the requirements of federal information quality guidelines and is accurate, clear, transparent, and unbiased. Olson et al. (2003b), disagreeing with the USFS finding, requested reconsideration from the USDA. In response, a specially convened USDA panel reviewed the case and denied the petitioner's request for further reconsideration.

The MRNG was published in 1992 and it has withstood over 13 yr of reviews and criticisms. During these years managers have learned through adaptive implementation how to create the desired goshawk habitats. The desired forest conditions are within the range of natural variability (i.e., forest composition, structure, and pattern); therefore, confidence in the strategy's ability to sustain the desired conditions is increased. Thus, the MRNG is a cautious and conservative approach for managing southwestern forests (Long and Smith 2000). An added value of the MRNG is a reduction of unnaturally high tree densities and the return of naturally frequent, low-intensity surface fires. Implementing the MRNG provides forest managers with the opportunity to simultaneously recreate healthy forests, restore diversity, sustain food webs and ecological processes, and allows managers to reduce fire fuel loads that lead to the destruction of homes and loss of life. The MRNG remains a compelling forest management strategy.

Barriers to implementing ecosystem-based conservation plans include: (1) difficulties associated with increasing management complexities as spatial and temporal scales increase, (2) integration of management knowledge across disciplines and collaboration among professionals representing the disciplines, (3) not carefully reading and understanding complex documents, (4) competition among conservation plans slows the acceptance, implementation, and testing of the strategies, (5) pressures to accept locally developed solutions first, regionally developed solutions second, and nationally developed solutions last, (6) emerging issues, such as healthy forests, turn the focus of policymakers away from existing management plans, and (7) inadequate funding.

ACKNOWLEDGMENTS

We thank P. Hardy, W. Smith, R. Szaro, and B. Woodbridge for their thoughtful review of the manuscript.

LITERATURE CITED

AGEE, J. K. 1993. Fire ecology of Pacific Northwest forests. Island Press, Washington, DC.

AGEE, J. K. 2000. Disturbance ecology of North American boreal forests and associated northern mixed/subalpine forests. Pp. 39–82 in L. F. Ruggiero, K. B. Aubry, S. W. Buskirk, G. M. Koehler, C. J. Krebs, K. S. McKelvey, and R. Squires (editors). Ecology conservation of lynx in the United States. University Press of Colorado, Boulder, CO.

AGUILAR, R. F., D. P. SHAW, J. P. DUBEY, AND P. REDIG. 1991. Sarcocystis-associated encephalitis in an immature Northern Goshawk (Accipiter gentilis atricapillus). Journal of Zoo and Wildlife Medicine 22:466–469.

AKAIKE, H. 1973. Information theory as an extension of the maximum likelihood principle. Pp. 267–281 in B. N. Petrov, and F. Csaki (editors). Second international symposium on information theory. Akademiai Kiado, Budapest, Hungary.

AKAIKE, H. 1974. A new look at the statistical model identification. IEEE Transactions on Automatic Control 19: 716–723.

ALASKA DEPARTMENT OF FISH AND GAME DIVISION OF WILDLIFE CONSERVATION. 1993. Ketchikan forest raptor study final report: a summary of survey, radio-telemetry, and other results regarding Goshawk field studies in southeast Alaska. Contract No. 43-0109-0323. USDA Forest Service, Ketchikan Area Wildlife, Fish, and Subsistence Management, Juneau, AK.

ALBIG, A., AND A. SCHREIBER. 1996. Bestandsentwicklung von Habicht, Sperber und Mäusebussard auf einer Fläche in der Stader Geest (Nord-West-Niedersachsen). Seevögel 17:15–19.

ALERSTAM, T. 1987. Radar observations of the stoop of the Peregrine Falcon Falco peregrinus and the Goshawk Accipiter gentilis. Ibis 129:267–273.

ALLEN, A. W. 1984. Habitat suitability index models: eastern cottontail. USDI Fish and Wildlife Service. FWS/OBS-82/10.66. Washington, DC.

ALLEN, B. A. 1978. Nesting ecology of the Goshawk in the Adirondacks. M.S. thesis, State University of New York, Syracuse, NY.

ALLEN, C. D., M. SAVAGE, D. A. FALK, K. F. SUCKLING, T. W. SWETNAM, T. SCHULKE, P. B. STACEY, P. MORGAN, M. HOFFMAN, AND J. T. KLINGEL. 2002. Ecological restoration of southwestern ponderosa pine ecosystems: a broad perspective. Ecological Applications 12: 1418–1433.

ALLISON, B. 1996. A landscape characterization of nesting Goshawk habitat in northern California using remote sensing and GIS. M.S. thesis, Southern Illinois University, Edwardsville, IL.

ALLISON, P. D. 1999. Logistic regression using the SAS® system: theory and application. SAS Institute Inc., Cary, NC.

ALTENKAMP, R. 1997. Forum: Anmerkungen zur Arbeit von O. Krüger & U. Stefener 1996: Vogelwelt 117:1–8. Vogelwelt 118:339–341.

ALTENKAMP, R. 2002. Bestandsentwicklung, Reproduktion und Brutbiologie einer urbanen Population des Habichts Accipiter gentilis (Linné 1758). Diploma thesis, University of Berlin, Berlin, Germany.

ALTENKAMP, R., AND S. HEROLD. 2001. Habicht (Accipiter gentilis). Pp. 175–179 in ABBO. Die Vogelwelt von Brandenburg und Berlin. Verlag Natur & Text, Rangsdorf, Germany.

ALVERSON, D. R., AND R. NOBLET. 1977. Spring relapse of Leucocytozoon smithi (Sporozoa: Leucocytozoidae) in turkeys. Journal of Medical Entomology 14:132–133.

AMERICAN ORNITHOLOGISTS' UNION. 1998. Check-list of North American birds, 7th edition. American Ornithologists' Union, Washington, DC.

ANDERSEN, D. E., S. DeSTEFANO, M. I. GOLDSTEIN, K. TITUS, D. C. CROCKER-BEDFORD, J. J. KEANE, R. G. ANTHONY, AND R. N. ROSENFIELD. 2004. The status of Northern Goshawks in the western United States. Technical Review 04-1, The Wildlife Society, Bethesda, MD.

ANDERSEN, D. E., S. DeSTEFANO, M. I. GOLDSTEIN, K. TITUS, C. CROCKER-BEDFORD, J. J. KEANE, R. G. ANTHONY, AND R. N. ROSENFIELD. 2005. Technical review of the status of Northern Goshawks in the western United States. Journal of Raptor Research 39:192–209.

ANDERSON, D. R., K. P. BURNHAM, AND G. C. WHITE. 1985. Problems in estimating age-specific survival rates from recovery data of birds ringed as young. Journal of Animal Ecology 54:89–98.

ANDERSON, D. W., AND J. J. HICKEY. 1974. Eggshell changes in raptors from the Baltic region. Oikos 25:395–401.

ANDERSON, L., C. E. CARLSON, AND R. H. WAKIMOTO. 1987. Forest fire frequency and western spruce budworm outbreaks in western Montana. Forest Ecology and Management 22:251–260.

ANDERSSON, M., AND R. Å. NORBERG. 1981. Evolution of reversed sexual size dimorphism and role partitioning among predatory birds, with a size scaling of flight performance. Biological Journal of the Linnean Society 15:105–130.

ANDREN, H. 1994. Effects of habitat fragmentation on birds and mammals in landscapes with different proportion of suitable habitat: review. Oikos 71:355–366.

ANDREWARTHA, H. G., AND L. C. BIRCH. 1954. The distribution and abundance of animals. University Chicago Press, Chicago, IL.

ANDREWARTHA, H. G., AND L. C. BIRCH. 1984. The ecological web: more on the distribution and abundance of animals. University of Chicago Press, Chicago, IL.

ANDRLE, R. F., AND J. R. CARROLL (EDITORS). 1988. The atlas of breeding birds in New York State. Cornell University Press, Ithaca, NY.

ANGELSTAM, P. 1984. Sexual and seasonal differences in mortality of the Black Grouse *Tetrao tetrix* in boreal Sweden. Ornis Scandinavica 15:123–134.

ANGELSTAM, P., E. LINDSTRÖM, AND P. WIDÉN. 1984. Role of predation in short-term population fluctuations of some birds and mammals in Fennoscandia. Oecologia 62:199–208.

ANONYMOUS. 1989. Goshawk breeding habitat in lowland Britain. British Birds 82:56–67.

ANONYMOUS 1990 Breeding biology of Goshawks in lowland Britain. British Birds 83:527–540.

ANONYMOUS. 1991a. Birds of the Coconino National Forest: a checklist. U.S. Department of Agriculture. Flagstaff, AZ.

ANONYMOUS. 1991b. Mammals of the Coconino National Forest: a checklist. U.S. Department of Agriculture. Flagstaff, AZ.

APAROVA, I. 2003. Nesting of Goshawk in urban forest park. Pp.13–15 *in* V. P. Belik (editor). Goshawk: position in ecosystems of Russia. Materials of the 4th North-Eurasian Conference on Raptors, Penza, Russia. (in Russian).

APFELBAUM, S. I., AND A. HANEY. 1984. Note on foraging and nesting habitats of Goshawks. Loon 56:132–133.

APFELBAUM, S. I., AND P. SEELBACH. 1983. Nest tree, habitat selection, and productivity of seven North American raptor species based on the Cornell University nest record card program. Journal of Raptor Research 17: 97–113.

ARBEITSGRUPPE GREIFVÖGEL NWO. 2002. Ergebnisse einer 30-jährigen Erfassung der Bestandsentwicklung und des Bruterfolgs beim Habicht (*Accipiter gentilis*) in Nordrhein-Westfalen von 1972–2001 (Fortschreibung 1986–2001). Charadrius 38:139–154.

ARCESE, P. 1989. Intrasexual competition, mating system and natal dispersal in Song Sparrows. Animal Behaviour 38:958–979.

ARIZONA GAME AND FISH DEPARTMENT. 1993. Review of US Forest Service strategy for managing Northern Goshawk habitat in the southwestern United States. Arizona Game and Fish Department, Phoenix, AZ.

ARNTZ, W. 1998. Voedselkeuze van de Havik in het natuurreservaat Salmorth. De Mourik 24:22–24.

AUSTIN, K. K. 1993. Habitat use and home range size of breeding Northern Goshawks in the southern Cascades. M.S. thesis, Oregon State University, Corvallis, OR.

BAGG, A. C., AND S. A. ELIOT, JR. 1937. Birds of the Connecticut Valley in Massachusetts. Hampshire Bookshop, Northhampton, MA.

BAILEY, A. M., AND R. J. NIEDRACH. 1965. Birds of Colorado. Denver Museum of Natural History, Denver, CO.

BAILEY, R. G. 1980. Description of the ecoregions of the United States. U.S. Department of Agriculture Miscellaneous Publication 1391, Washington, DC.

BAKER, J. A., AND R. J. BROOKS. 1981. Distribution patterns of raptors in relation to density of meadow voles. Condor 83:42–47.

BAKER, W. L., and D. EHLE. 2001. Uncertainty in surface-fire history: the case of ponderosa pine forests in the western United States. Canadian Journal of Forest Research 31:1205–1226.

BAKKER, T. 1996. Haviken in de regio Bergen op Zoom. Veerkracht 6:15–17.

BALBONTÍN, J., V. PENTERIANI, AND M. FERRER. 2003. Variations in the age of mates as an early warning signal of changes in population trends? The case of Bonnelli's Eagle in Andalusia. Biological Conservation 109:417–423.

BALDWIN, S. P., AND S. C. KENDEIGH. 1938. Variations in weights of birds. Auk 55:416–467.

BARBOUR, M. G., AND W. D. BILLINGS. 1988. North American terrestrial vegetation. Cambridge University Press, New York, NY.

BARTELT, P. E. 1977. Management of the American Goshawk in the Black Hills National Forest. M.S. thesis, University of South Dakota, Vermillion, SD.

BASSETT, R. L., D. A. BOYCE, JR., M. H. REISER, R. T. GRAHAM, AND R. T. REYNOLDS. 1994. Influence of site quality and stand density on goshawk habitat in southwestern forests. Studies in Avian Biology 16:41–45.

BAYARD DE VOLO, S., R. T. REYNOLDS, J. R. TOPINKA, B. MAY, AND M. F. ANTOLIN. 2005. Population genetics and genotyping for mark–recapture studies of Northern Goshawks (*Accipiter gentilis*) on the Kaibab Plateau, Arizona. Journal of Raptor Research 39:286–295.

BECHARD, M. J. 1982. Effect of vegetative cover on foraging site selection by Swainson's Hawk. Condor 84: 153–159.

BECKER, T. E. 2000. Habitat selection and ecology of Northern Goshawk in Connecticut. M.S. thesis, Southern Connecticut State University, New Haven, CT.

BECKER, T. E., AND D. G. SMITH. 2000. Northern Goshawk nesting ecology in Connecticut. Connecticut Warbler 20:149–156.

BEDNAREK, W. 1975. Vergleichende Untersuchungen zur Populationsökologie des Habichts (*Accipiter gentilis*): Habitatbesetzung und Bestandsregulation. Jahrbuch des Deutschen Falkenordens 1975:47–53.

BEDNAREK, W., W. HAUSDORF, U. JÖRISSEN, E. SCHULTE, AND H. WEGENER. 1975. Über die Auswirkungen der chemischen Umweltbelastung auf Greifvögel in zwei Probeflächen Westfalens. Journal für Ornithologie 116: 181–194.

BEDNARZ, J. C., AND T. J. HAYDEN. 1991. Skewed brood sex ratio and sex-biased hatching sequence in Harris's Hawks. American Naturalist 137:116–132.

BEDNARZ, J. C., D. KLEM JR., L. J. GOODRICH, AND S. E. SENNER. 1990. Migration counts of raptors at Hawk Mountain, Pennsylvania, as indicators of population trends, 1934–1986. Auk 107:96–109.

BEEBE, F. L. 1974. Goshawk. Pp. 54–63 *in* F. L. Beebe (editor). Field studies of the Falconiformes of British Columbia. Occasional Paper No. 17. British Columbia Provincial Museum, Victoria, BC, Canada.

BEEBE, F. L. 1976. The Goshawk. Pp. 185–195 *in* F. L. Beebe, and H. M. Webster (editors). North American falconry and hunting hawks, 4th edition. North American Falconry and Hunting Hawks, Denver, CO.

BEEDY, E. C., AND S. L. GRANHOLM. 1985. Discovering Sierra birds. Yosemite Natural History Association, Yosemite National Park, CA.

BEERS, T. W., P. E. DRESS, AND L. C. WENSEL. 1966. Aspect transformation in site productivity research. Journal of Forestry 64:691–692.

BEGON, M., J. L. HARPER, AND C. R. TOWNSEND. 1996: Individuals populations and communities. Blackwell Scientific Publications, Boston, MA.

BEHLE, W. H. 1942. Distribution and variation of the Horned Larks (*Otocoris alpertris*) of western North America. University of California Publications in Zoology 46:205–316.

BEIER, P., AND J. E. DRENNAN. 1997. Forest structure and prey abundance in foraging areas of Northern Goshawks. Ecological Applications 7:564–571.

BEIER, P., AND J. MASCHINSKI. 2003. Threatened, endangered, and sensitive species. Pp. 306–327 *in* P. Friedrici (editor). Ecological restoration of southwestern ponderosa pine forests. Island Press, Inc., Washington, DC.

BEISSINGER, S. R. 1995. Modeling extinction in periodic environments: Everglades water levels and Snail Kite population viability. Ecological Applications 5: 618–631.

BELOVSKY, G. E. 1987. Extinction models and mammalian persistence. Pp. 35–57 *in* M. E. Soulé (editor). Variable populations for conservation. Cambridge University Press, Cambridge, UK.

BENDOCK, T. 1975. Appendix III *in* J. D. McGowan. Distribution, density and productivity of Goshawks in interior Alaska. Alaska Department of Fish and Game, Juneau, AK.

BENKMAN, C. W. 1993. Logging, conifers, and the conservation of crossbills. Conservation Biology 7:473–479.

BENNETTS, R. E., AND B. R. McCLELLAND. 1997. Influence of age and prey availability on Bald Eagle foraging behavior in Glacier National Park, Montana. Wilson Bulletin 109:393–409.

BENT, A. C. 1937. Life histories of North American birds of prey. Part 1. U.S. National Museum Bulletin 167. Washington, DC.

BENT, A. C. 1938. Life histories of North American birds of prey, Part 2. U.S. National Museum Bulletin 168. Washington, DC.

BENT, A. C. 1939. Life histories of North American woodpeckers. U.S. National Museum, Bulletin 174. Washington, DC.

BENT, A. C. 1946. Life histories of North American jays, crows and titmice. U.S. National Museum, Bulletin 191. Washington, DC.

BENZINGER, J. B. 1994. Hemlock decline and breeding birds. I. hemlock ecology. Records of New Jersey Birds 20: 2–12, addendum 1–8.

BERNDT, R. K., B. KOOP, AND B. STRUWE-JUHL. 2002. Vogelwelt Schleswig-Holsteins, Band 5, Brutvogelatlas. Wachholtz Verlag, Neumünster, Germany.

BERTHOLD, P. 1993. Bird migration: a general survey. Oxford University Press, New York, NY.

BESSIE, W. C., AND E. A. JOHNSON. 1995. The relative importance of fuels and weather on fire behavior in subalpine forests. Ecology 76:747–762.

BEVIER, L. R. (EDITOR). 1994. The atlas of breeding birds of Connecticut. State Geological and Natural History Survey of Connecticut Bulletin No. 113, Hartford, CT.

BEZZEL, E., R. RUST, AND W. KECHELE. 1997a. Revierbesetzung, Reproduktion und menschliche Verfolgung in einer Population des Habichts *Accipiter gentilis*. Journal für Ornithologie 138:413–441.

BEZZEL, E., R. RUST, AND W. KECHELE. 1997b. Nahrungswahl südbayerischer Habichte *Accipiter gentilis* während der Brutzeit. Ornithologischer Anzeiger 36:19–30.

BIELEFELDT, J., R. N. ROSENFIELD, AND J. M. PAPP. 1992. Unfounded assumptions about diet of the Cooper's Hawk. Condor 94:427–436.

BIJLEVELD, M. 1974. Birds of Prey in Europe. Macmillan, London, UK.

BIJLSMA, R. G. 1989. Goshawk *Accipiter gentilis* and Sparrowhawk *A. nisus* in the Netherlands during the 20th century: Population trend, distribution and breeding performance. Pp. 67–89 *in* J. T. Lumeij, W. P. F. Huijskens, and N. Croin Michielsen (editors). Valkerij in perspectief. Nederlands Valkeniersverbond "Adriaan Mollen"/Stichting Behoud Valkerij, Monnickendam, The Netherlands.

BIJLSMA, R. G. 1991a. Trends in European Goshawks *Accipiter gentilis*: an overview. Bird Census News 4:3–47.

BIJLSMA, R. G. 1991b. Replacement of mates in a persecuted population of Goshawks *Accipiter gentilis*. Birds of Prey Bulletin 4:155–158.

BIJLSMA, R. G. 1993. Ecologische atlas van de Nederlandse roofvogels. Schuyt & Co., Haarlem, The Netherlands.

BIJLSMA, R. G. 1997. Handleiding veldonderzoek roofvogels. KNNV Uitgeverij, Utrecht, The Netherlands

BIJLSMA, R. G. 1998. Hoe selectief bejagen Haviken *Accipiter gentilis* en Buizerds *Buteo buteo* de hongerige hordes? Limosa 71:121–123.

BIJLSMA, R. G. 1998–2003. Trends en broedresultaten van roofvogels in Nederland in 1997–2002. De Takkeling 6:4–53, 7:6–51, 8:6–51, 9:12–52, 10:7–48, 11:6–54.

BIJLSMA, R. G. 1999a. Stelselmatige vernietiging van bezette roofvogelnesten door Staatsbosbeheer. De Takkeling 7:59–64.

BIJLSMA, R. G. 1999b. Zomervellingen desastreus voor broedvogels. Nederlands Bosbouw Tijdschrift 71:42–46.

BIJLSMA, R. G. 2003. Havik *Accipiter gentilis* legt superdwergei, of: leven en dood in een 30-jarig territorium op het voedselarme Planken Wambuis (Veluwe). De Takkeling 11:133–142.

BIJLSMA, R. G. 2004a. Long-term trends of rabbits *Oryctolagus cuniculus* on Pleistocene sands in the central and northern Netherlands. Lutra 47:3–20.

BIJLSMA, R. G. 2004b. Wat is het predatierisico voor Wespendieven *Pernis apivorus* in de Nederlandse bossen bij een afnemend voedselaanbod voor Haviken *Accipiter gentilis*. De Takkeling 12:185–197.

BIJLSMA R. G., F. HUSTINGS, AND C. J. CAMPHUYSEN. 2001. Algemene en schaarse vogels van Nederland (Avifauna van Nederland 2). GMB Uitgeverij/KNNV Uitgeverij, Haarlem/Utrecht, The Netherlands.

BIJLSMA, R. G., AND S. SULKAVA. 1997. *Accipiter gentilis* Goshawk. Pp. 154–155 *in* E. J. M. Hagemeijer, and M. J. Blair (editors). The EBCC atlas of European breeding birds: their distribution and abundance. T. & A.D. Poyser Ltd., London, UK.

BILDSTEIN, K. L. 1998. Long-term counts of migrating raptors: a role for volunteers in wildlife research. Journal of Wildlife Management 62:435–445.

BIRCH, L. C. 1957. The meanings of competition. American Naturalist 91:5–18.

BJÖRKLUND, H., SAUROLA, P., AND J. HAAPALA. 2002. Breeding and population trends of common raptors and owls in Finland in 2002—many new records saw the daylight. Pp. 28–40 *in* K. Ruokolainen. (editor). Linnut-vuosikirja 2002. BirdLife, Helsinki, Finland.

BLOCK, W. M. 1989. Spatial and temporal patterns of resource use by birds in California oak woodlands. Ph.D. dissertation, University of California, Berkeley, CA.

BLOCK, W. M., M. L. MORRISON, AND M. H. REISER (EDITORS). 1994. The Northern Goshawk: ecology and management. Studies in Avian Biology 16:1–136.

BLOOM, P. H. 1987. Capturing and handling raptors. Pp. 99–123 *in* B. A. Giron Pendleton, B. A. Millsap, K. W. Cline, and D. M. Bird (editors). Raptor management techniques manual. National Wildlife Federation Science Technical Series No. 10, Washington, DC.

BLOOM, P. H., G. R. STEWART, AND B. J. WALTON. 1986. The status of the Northern Goshawk in California, 1981–1983. California Department of Fish and Game, Wildlife Management Branch Administrative Report 85-1, Sacramento, CA.

BLOXTON, T. D. JR. 2002. Prey abundance, space use, demography and foraging habitat of Northern Goshawks in western Washington. M.S thesis, University of Washington, Seattle, WA.

BLOXTON, T. D., A. S. ROGERS, M. F. INGRALDI, S. ROSENSTOCK, J. M. MARZLUFF, AND S. P. FINN. 2002. Possible choking mortalities of adult Northern Goshawks. Journal of Raptor Research 36:141–143.

BOAL, C. W. 1993. Northern Goshawk diets in ponderosa pine forests in northern Arizona. M.S. thesis, University of Arizona, Tucson, AZ.

BOAL, C. W. 1994. A photographic and behavioral guide to aging nestling Northern Goshawks. Studies in Avian Biology 16:32–40

BOAL, C. W., AND J. E. BACORN. 1994. Siblicide and cannibalism in Northern Goshawk nests. Auk 111:748–750.

BOAL, C. W., AND R. W. MANNAN. 1994. Northern Goshawk diets in ponderosa pine forests on the Kaibab Plateau. Studies in Avian Biology 16:97–102.

BOAL, C. W., AND R. W. MANNAN. 1999. Comparative breeding ecology of Cooper's Hawks in urban and exurban areas of southeastern Arizona. Journal Wildlife Management 63:77–84.

BOAL, C. W., AND R. W. MANNAN. 2000. Cooper's Hawks in urban and exurban areas: a reply. Journal Wildlife Management 64:601–604.

BOAL, C. W., D. E. ANDERSEN, AND P. L. KENNEDY. 2001. Home range and habitat use of northern goshawks in Minnesota: final report. Unpublished Report. Minnesota Cooperative Research Unit, University of Minnesota, St. Paul, MN.

BOAL, C. W., D. E. ANDERSEN, AND P. L. KENNEDY. 2002. Home range and habitat use of Northern Goshawks (*Accipiter gentilis*) in Minnesota. Forest systems of the upper Midwest: research review. Cloquet Forestry Center, University of Minnesota, USDA Forest Service and Minnesota Forest Resources Council, Cloquet, MN.

BOAL, C. W., D. E. ANDERSEN, AND P. L. KENNEDY. 2003. Home range and residency status of Northern Goshawks breeding in Minnesota. Condor 105: 811–816.

BOAL, C. W., D. E. ANDERSEN AND P. L. KENNEDY. 2005a. Productivity and mortality of Northern Goshawks in Minnesota. Journal of Raptor Research 39:222–228.

BOAL, C. W., D. E. ANDERSEN, AND P. L. KENNEDY. 2005b. Foraging and nesting habitat of Northern Goshawks breeding in the Laurentian mixed forest province, Minnesota. Journal of Wildlife Management 69: 1516–1527.

BOAL, C. W., E. L. BIBLES, AND R. E. BROWN. 1994. Unusual parental behaviors by male Northern Goshawks. Journal of Raptor Research 28:120–121.

BOAL, C. W., R. W. MANNAN, AND K. S. HUDELSON. 1998. Trichomoniasis in Cooper's Hawks from Arizona. Journal of Wildlife Diseases 34:590–593.

BOCK, C. E., AND L. W. LEPTHIEN. 1976. Synchronous eruptions of boreal seed-eating birds. American Naturalist 11:559–571.

BOND, R. M. 1940. A Goshawk nest in the upper sonoran life-zone. Condor 42:100–103.

BOND, R. M. 1942. Development of young Goshawks. Wilson Bulletin 54:81–88.

BOND, R. M., AND R. M. STABLER. 1941. Second-year plumage of the Goshawk. Auk 58:346–349.

BOSAKOWSKI, T. 1993. Erratum. Ecography 16:189.

BOSAKOWSKI, T. 1999. The Northern Goshawk: ecology, behavior, and management in North America. Hancock House, Blaine, WA.

BOSAKOWSKI, T., AND D. G. SMITH. 1992. Comparative diets of sympatric nesting raptors in the eastern deciduous forest biome. Canadian Journal of Zoology 70:984–992.

BOSAKOWSKI, T., AND D. G. SMITH. 1997. Distribution and species richness of a forest raptor community in relation to urbanization. Journal of Raptor Research 31: 26–33.

BOSAKOWSKI, T., AND D. G. SMITH. 2002. Status and distribution of *Accipiter* Hawks in New Jersey. Records of New Jersey Birds 28:6–8.

BOSAKOWSKI, T., AND R. SPEISER. 1994. Macrohabitat selection by nesting Northern Goshawks: implications for managing eastern forests. Studies in Avian Biology 16:46–49.

BOSAKOWSKI, T., B. MCCULLOUGH, F. J. LAPSANSKY, AND M. E. VAUGHN. 1999. Northern Goshawks nesting on a private industrial forest in western Washington. Journal of Raptor Research 33:240–244.

BOSAKOWSKI, T., D. G. SMITH, AND R. SPEISER. 1992. Niche overlap of two sympatric nesting hawks, *Accipiter* spp. in the New Jersey-New York Highlands. Ecography 15:358–372.

BOUTIN, S. 1990. Food supplementation experiments with terrestrial vertebrates: patterns, problems and the future. Canadian Journal of Zoology 68:203–220.

BOWERMAN, W. W., S. R. CHRISTIANSEN, AND W. L. ROBINSON. 1998. Current management and research on woodland raptors in Michigan. Pp. 11–12 *in* J. Noll West (editor). Status of the Northern Goshawk in the Midwest: workshop proceedings USDI Fish and Wildlife Service, Fort Snelling, MN.

BOYCE, D. A., JR., P. L. KENNEDY, P. BEIER, M. F. INGRALDI, S. R. MACVEAN, M. S. SIDERS, J. R. SQUIRES, AND B. WOODBRIDGE. 2005. When are goshawks not there? Is a single visit enough to infer absence at occupied nesting areas? Journal of Raptor Research. 39:285–291.

BOYCE, M. S. 1994. Population viability analysis exemplified by models for the Northern Spotted Owl. Pp. 3–18 *in* D. J. Fletcher, and B. F. J. Manly (editors). Statistics in ecology and environmental monitoring. University of Otago Press, Dunedin, New Zealand.

BOYCE, M. S., AND L. L. MCDONALD. 1999. Relating populations to habitats using resource selection functions. Trends in Ecology and Evolution 14:268–272.

BRAAKSMA, S., W. H. TH. KNIPPENBERG, AND V. LANGENHOFF. 1959. Enige broedvogels in Noord-Brabant. Limosa 32:206–212.

BRADLEY, A. F., N. V. NOSTE, AND W. C. FISCHER. 1992. Fire ecology of forests and woodlands in Utah. USDA Forest Service General Technical Report INT-287. USDA Forest Service, Intermountain Research Station, Ogden, UT.

BRAUN, C. E., J. H. ENDERSON, M. R. FULLER, Y. B. LINHART, AND C. D. MARTI. 1996. Northern Goshawk and forest management in the southwestern United States. Technical Review 96-2. The Wildlife Society, Bethesda, MD.

BRAUN, L. 1950. Deciduous forests of eastern North America. Blakiston Co., New York, NY.

BRAUNING, D. W. (EDITOR). 1992. Atlas of breeding birds in Pennsylvania. University of Pittsburgh Press, Pittsburgh, PA.

BREWER, R., G. A. MCPEEK, AND R. J. ADAMS, JR. 1991. The atlas of breeding birds of Michigan. Michigan State University Press, East Lansing, MI.

BRIGHT-SMITH, D. J., AND R. W. MANNAN. 1994. Habitat use by breeding male Northern Goshawks in northern Arizona. Studies in Avian Biology 16:58–65.

BRINK, C. H., AND F. C. DEAN. 1966. Spruce seed as a food of red squirrels and flying squirrels in interior Alaska. Journal of Wildlife Management 30:503–512.

BRITTEN, M. W., P. L. KENNEDY, AND S. AMBROSE. 1999. Performance and accuracy evaluation of small satellite transmitters. Journal of Wildlife Management 63:1349–1358.

BRODEUR, S., R. DÉCARIE, D. M. BIRD, AND M. FULLER. 1996. Complete migration cycle of Golden Eagles breeding in Northern Quebec. Condor 98:293–299.

BROHN, A. 1986. Report of the subcommittee on falconry rules. International Association of Fish and Wildlife Agencies, Washington, DC.

BRONSON, M. T. 1979. Altitudinal variation in the life history of the golden-mantled ground squirrel (*Spermophilus lateralis*). Ecology 60:272–279.

BROOKS, R. T. 1989. Status and trends of raptor habitat in the Northeast. Pp. 123–132 *in* B. Giron Pendleton (editor). Northeast raptor management symposium and workshop. National Wildlife Federation Scientific and Technical Series No. 13, Washington, DC.

BROWN, D. E. (EDITOR) 1982. Biotic communities of the American Southwest—United States and Mexico. Desert Plants 4:1–341.

BROWN, J. H. 1971. Mechanisms of competitive exclusion between two species of chipmunks. Ecology 52:305–311.

BROWN, J. K. 2000. Introduction and fire regimes. Pp. 1–7 *in* J. K. Brown, and J. K. Smith (editors). Wildland fire in ecosystems: effects of fire on flora. USDA Forest Service General Technical Report RMRS-GTR 42 Vol. 2. USDA Forest Service, Rocky Mountain Research Station, Fort Collins, CO.

BROWN, J. L. 1963. Aggressiveness, dominance and social organization in the Steller Jay. Condor 65:460–484.

BROWN, L., AND D. AMADON. 1968. Eagles, hawks, and falcons of the world. McGraw-Hill, New York, NY.

BRÜLL, H. 1964. Das Leben deutscher Greifvögel. Fischer Verlag, Stuttgart, Germany.

BRÜLL, H. 1984. Das Leben europäischer Greifvögel. 4th ed. Gustav Fischer Verlag, Stuttgart, Germany.

BRYAN, T., AND E. D. FORSMAN. 1987. Distribution, abundance, and habitat of Great Gray Owls in southcentral Oregon. Murrelet 68:45–49.

BRYANT, A. A. 1986. Influence of selective logging on Red-shouldered Hawks, *Buteo lineatus*, in Waterloo Region, Ontario, 1953–78. Canadian Field-Naturalist 100:520–525.

BUCHANAN, J. B. 1996. A comparison of behavior and success rates of Merlins and Peregrine Falcons when hunting dunlins in two coastal habitats. Journal of Raptor Research 30:93–98.

BUCHANAN, J. B., L. L. IRWIN, AND E. L. MCCUTCHEN. 1993. Characteristics of Spotted Owl nest trees in the Wenatchee National Forest. Journal of Raptor Research 27:1–7.

BUCHANAN, J. B., R. W. LUNDQUIST, AND K. B. AUBRY. 1990. Winter populations of Douglas squirrels in different-aged Douglas-fir forests. Journal of Wildlife Management 54:577–581.

BUCKLAND, S. T., D. R. ANDERSON, K. P. BURNHAM, J. L. LAAKE, D. L. BORCHERS, AND L. THOMAS. 2001. Introduction to distance sampling: estimating abundance of biological populations. Oxford Press, Oxford, UK.

BUELL, M.F., A. LANGFORM, D. DAVIDSON, AND L. OHMANN. 1966. The upland forest continuum in northern New Jersey. Ecology 47:416–432.

BÜHLER, U., AND R. KLAUS. 1987. Resultate von Habichtberingungen *Accipiter gentilis* in der Schweiz. Der Ornithologische Beobachter 84:111–121.

BÜHLER, U., R. KLAUS, AND W. SCHLOSSER. 1987. Brutbestand und Jungenproduktion des Habichts *Accipiter gentilis* in der Nordostschweiz 1979–1984. Der Ornithologische Beobachter 84:95–110.

BÜHLER, U., AND P.-A. OGGIER. 1987. Bestand und Bestandsentwicklung des Habichts *Accipiter gentilis* in der Schweiz. Der Ornithologische Beobachter 84: 71–94.

BULL, E. L., AND J. H. HOHMANN. 1994. Breeding biology of Northern Goshawks in northeastern Oregon. Studies in Avian Biology 16:103–105.

BULL, J. 1974. Birds of New York state. Doubleday Natural History Press, Garden City, NY.

BURKE, D. M., AND E. NOL. 1998. Influence of food abundance, nest-site habitat, and forest fragmentation on breeding Ovenbirds. Auk 115:96–104.

BURNETT, F. L., AND R. W. DICKERMAN. 1956. Type locality of the Mogollon red squirrel, *Tamiasciurus hudsonicus mogollonensis*. Journal of Mammalogy 37:292–294.

BURNETT, H. 1991. Green island in the sky. American Forests 97:44–47, 62.

BURNHAM, K. P., AND D. R. ANDERSON. 1992. Data-based selection of an appropriate biological model: the key to modern data analysis. Pp. 16–30 *in* D. R. McCullough, and R. H. Barrett (editors). Wildlife 2001: populations. Elsevier applied Science, London, UK.

BURNHAM, K. P., AND D. R. ANDERSON. 2002. Model selection and multimodel inference: a practical information-theoretic approach. 2nd ed. Springer-Verlag, New York, NY.

BURNHAM, K. P., D. R. ANDERSON, G. C. WHITE, C. BROWNIE, AND K. H. POLLOCK. 1987. Design and analysis methods for fish survival experiments based on release-recapture. American Fisheries Society Monograph 5: 1–412.

BURNS, B. S., AND H. TRAIL, JR. 2000. Recovery of hemlock in Vermont from defoliation by the spring hemlock looper, *Lambdina athasaria* (Walker). Pp. 177–180 *in* Proceedings of a symposium on sustainable management of hemlock ecosystems in eastern North America. USDA Forest Service General Technical Report NE-267. USDA Forest Service, Northeastern Research Station, Newtown Square, PA.

BURNS, R. M., AND B. H. HONKALA. 1990. Silvics of North America. Vol. 1, conifers. Agricultural Handbook 654. USDA Forest Service. Washington, DC.

BURT, W. H., AND R. P. GROSSENHEIDER. 1980. A field guide to the mammals. Houghton Mifflin Company, Boston, MA.

BUSCHE, G., AND V. LOOFT. 2003. Zur Lage der Greifvögel im Westen Schleswig Holsteins im Zeitraum 1980 2000. Vogelwelt 124:63–81.

BUSCHE, G., H.-J. RADDATZ, AND A. KOSTRZEWA. 2004. Nistplatz-Konkurrenz und Prädation zwischen Uhu (*Bubo bubo*) und Habicht (*Accipiter gentilis*): erste Ergebnisse aus Norddeutschland. Vogelwarte 42:169–177.

BYHOLM, P. 2003. Reproduction and dispersal of Goshawks in a variable environment. Ph.D. dissertation, University of Helsinki, Helsinki, Finland.

BYHOLM, P. 2005. Partial brood-loss and offspring sex ratio in Goshawks. Annales Zoologici Fennici 42:81–90.

BYHOLM, P., J. E. BROMMER, AND P. SAUROLA. 2002a. Scale and seasonal sex-ratio trends in Northern Goshawk *Accipiter gentilis* broods. Journal of Avian Biology 33:399–406.

BYHOLM, P., E. RANTA, V. KAITALA, H. LINDÉN, P. SAUROLA, AND M. WIKMAN. 2002b. Resource availability and Goshawk offspring sex ratio variation: a large-scale ecological phenomenon. Journal of Animal Ecology 71:994–1001.

BYHOLM, P., P. SAUROLA, H. LINDÉN, AND M. WIKMAN. 2003. Causes of dispersal in Northern Goshawks (*Accipiter gentilis*) banded in Finland. Auk 120:706–716.

CAFFREY, C., AND C. C. PETERSON. 2003. West Nile virus may be a conservation issue in the northeastern United States. American Birds 57:14–21.

CANNING, R., AND S. CANNING 1996. British Columbia. A natural history. Greystone Books, Vancouver, BC, Canada

CAREY, A. B. 1995. Sciurids in Pacific Northwest managed and old-growth forests. Ecological Applications 5: 648–661.

CAREY, A. B., S. P. HORTON, AND B. L. BISWELL. 1992. Northern Spotted Owls: influence of prey base and landscape character. Ecological Monographs 62: 223–250.

CARLTON, W. M. 1966. Food habits of two sympatric Colorado sciurids. Journal of Mammalogy 47: 91–103.

CARREL, W. K., R. A. OCKENFELS, J. A. WENNERLUND, AND J. C. DEVOS, JR. 1997. Topographic mapping, LORANC, and GPS accuracy for aerial telemetry locations. Journal of Wildlife Management 61:1406–1412.

CARROLL, C. 1999. Regional-scale predictive models of the distribution of the California Spotted Owl: an exploratory analysis. USDA Forest Service, Pacific Southwest Research Station, Arcata, CA.

CARROLL, C., R. F. NOSS, AND P. C. PAQUET. 2001. Carnivores as focal species for conservation planning in the Rocky Mountain region. Ecological Applications 11: 961–980.

CARROLL, C., R. F. NOSS, P. C. PAQUET, AND N. H. SCHUMAKER. 2003a. Use of population viability analysis and reserve selection algorithms in regional conservation plans. Ecological Applications 13:1773–1789.

CARROLL, C., M. K. PHILLIPS, C. A. LOPEZ-GONZALEZ, AND N. H. SCHUMAKER. 2006. Defining recovery goals and strategies for endangered species using spatially-explicit population models: the wolf as a case study. BioScience. 56:25 37.

CARROLL, C., M. K. PHILLIPS, N. H. SCHUMAKER, AND D. W. SMITH. 2003b. Impacts of landscape change on wolf restoration success: planning a reintroduction program based on static and dynamic spatial models. Conservation Biology 17:536–548.

CARROLL, C., W. J. ZIELINSKI, AND R. F. NOSS. 1999. Using presence-absence data to build and test spatial habitat models for the fisher in the Klamath region, U.S.A. Conservation Biology 13:1344–1359.

CARTWRIGHT, C. W., JR. 1996. Record of decision for amendment of forest plans. Arizona and New Mexico. USDA Forest Service, Southwestern Region, Albuquerque, NM.

CAVÉ, A. J. 1968. The breeding of the Kestrel, *Falco tinnunculus* L., in the reclaimed area Oostelijk Flevoland. Netherlands Journal of Zoology 18:313–407.

CAYOT, L. J. 1978. Habitat preferences of the mountain cottontail. M.S. thesis, Colorado State University. Fort Collins, CO.

CHAPMAN, J. A., AND J. E. FLUX. 1990. Rabbits, hares and pikas. ICUN, Gland, Switzerland.

CHAPMAN, J. A., AND D. E. TRETHEWEY. 1972. Movements within a population of introduced eastern cottontail rabbits. Journal of Wildlife Management 36:155–158.

CHAVEZ-RAMIREZ, F., G. P. VOSE, AND A. TENNANT. 1994. Spring and fall migration of Peregrine Falcons from Padre Island, Texas. Wilson Bulletin 106:138–145.

CLARK, W. S. 1981. A modified dho-gaza trap for use at a raptor banding station. Journal of Wildlife Management 45:1043–1044.

CLARK, W. S. 1999. A field guide to the raptors of Europe, the Middle East, and North Africa. Oxford University Press, Oxford, UK.

CLINE, K. W. 1985. Habitat protection for raptors on private lands. Eyas 8:3, 23.

CLOTHIER, R. R. 1969. Reproduction in the gray-necked chipmunk, *Eutamias cinereicollis*. Journal of Mammalogy 50:642.

CLOUGH, L. T. 2000. Nesting habitat selection and productivity of Northern Goshawks in west-central Montana. M.S. thesis, University of Montana, Missoula, MT.

COCHRAN, W. W., AND R. D. APPLEGATE. 1986. Speed of flapping flight of Merlins and Peregrine Falcons. Condor 88:397–398.

COCKRUM, E. L., AND Y. PETRYSZYN. 1992. Mammals of the southwestern United States and northwestern Mexico. Treasure Chest Publications, Tucson, AZ.

COHEN, W. B., T. A. SPIES, AND M. FIORELLA. 1995. Estimating the age and structure of forests in a multiownership landscape of western Oregon, U.S.A. International Journal of Remote Sensing 16:721–746.

COLLINS, C. T., AND R. A. BRADLEY. 1971. Analysis of body weights of spring migrants in southern California: part II. Western Bird Bander 46:48–51.

COLLINS, S. L., F. C. JAMES, AND P. G. RISSER. 1982. Habitat relationships of wood warblers (Parulidae) in northern central Minnesota. Oikos 39:50–58.

COLLOPY, M. W. 1983. A comparison of direct observations and collections of prey remains in determining the diet of Golden Eagles. Journal of Wildlife Management 47:360–368.

CONAWAY, C. H., H. M. WIGHT, AND K. C. SADLER. 1963. Annual production by a cottontail population. Journal of Wildlife Management 27:171–175.

CONNELL, J. H. 1980. Diversity and the coevolution of competition, or the ghost of competition past. Oikos 35:131-138.

CONRAD, B. 1977. Die Giftbelastung der Vogelwelt Deutschlands. Kilda Verlag, Greven, Germany.

CONRAD, B. 1978. Korrelation zwischen Embryonen-Sterblichkeit und DDE-Kontamination beim Sperber (*Accipiter nisus*). Journal für Ornithologie 119:109–110.

CONRAD, B. 1981. Zur Situation der Pestizidbelastung bei Greifvögeln und Eulen in der Bundesrepublik Deutschland. Ökologie der Vögel 3:161–167.

COONS, J. S. 1984. Elevational zonations and monthly changes in the bird community on San Francisco Mountain, Arizona. M.S. thesis, Northern Arizona University, Flagstaff, AZ.

COOPER, C. F. 1960. Changes in vegetation, structure, and growth of southwestern pine forest since white settlement. Ecological Monographs 30:129–164.

COOPER, J. E. 1981. A historical review of Goshawk training and disease. Pp. 175–184 *in* R. E. Kenward, and I. M. Lindsay (editors). Understanding the Goshawk. International Association for Falconry and Conservation of Birds of Prey. Oxford, UK.

COOPER, J. E., AND S. J. PETTY. 1988. Trichomoniasis in free-living Goshawks (*Accipiter gentilis gentilis*) from Great Britain. Journal of Wildlife Diseases 24:80–87.

COOPER, J. M., AND P. A. CHYTYK. 2000. Update COSEWIC status report on the Northern Goshawk *Laingi* subspecies *Accipiter gentilis laingi* in Canada, *in* COSEWIC assessment and update status status report on the Northern Goshawk *Laingi* subspecies *Accipiter gentilis laingi* in Canada. Committee on the Status of Endangered Wildlife in Canada. Ottawa, ON, Canada.

COOPER, J. M., AND V. STEVENS. 2000. A review of the ecology, management and conservation of the Northern Goshawk in British Columbia. Wildlife Bulletin No. B-101. British Columbia Ministry of Environment, Lands, and Parks, Victoria, BC, Canada.

COOPER, S. V., K. E. NEIMAN, AND D. W. ROBERTS. 1991. Forest habitat types of northern Idaho: a second approximation. USDA Forest Service. General Technical Report INT 236. USDA Forest Service, Intermountain Research Station, Ogden, UT.

CORMACK, R. M. 1964. Estimates of survival from the sighting of marked animals. Biometrika 51:429–438.

COSEWIC. 2000. COSEWIC assessment and update status report on the Northern Goshawk *Laingi* subspecies *Accipiter gentilis laingi* in Canada. Committee on the Status of Endangered Wildlife in Canada. Ottawa, ON, Canada. <http://www.sararegistry.gc.ca/virtual_sara/files/cosewic/sr%5Fnorthern%5Fgoshawk%5Fe%2Epdf> (11 January 2006).

COSTELLO, C. M., D. E. JONES, K. A. G. HAMMOND, R. M. INMAN, K. H. INMAN, B. C. THOMPSON, R. A. DEITNER, AND H. B. QUIGLEY. 2001. A study of black bear ecology in New Mexico with models for population dynamics and habitat suitability. New Mexico Game and Fish, Albuquerque. NM.

COUGHLIN, L. E. 1938. The case against the tuft-eared squirrel. USDA Forest Service, Rocky Mountain Region. Bulletin 21:10–12.

COVINGTON, W. W., AND M. M. MOORE. 1994a. Southwestern ponderosa forest structure: changes since Euro-American settlement. Journal of Forestry 92:39–47.

COVINGTON, W. W., AND M. M. MOORE. 1994b. Postsettlement changes in natural fire regimes and forest structure: ecological restoration of old-growth ponderosa pine forests. Pp. 153–181 in R. N. Sampson, and D. L. Adams (editors). Assessing forest ecosystem health in the inland West. The Haworth Press Inc, Binghamton, NY.

CRAIGHEAD, D., AND R. SMITH. 2003. The implications of PTT location accuracy on the study of Red-tailed Hawks. Argos Animal Tracking Symposium. Available on a CD from Service Argos, Inc., 1801 McCormick Drive, Suite 10, Largo, MD.

CRAIGHEAD, J. J., AND F. C. CRAIGHEAD. 1956. Hawks, owls and wildlife. Stackpole Co., Harrisburg, PA.

CRAMP, S., AND K. E. L. SIMMONS (EDITOR). 1980. Handbook of the birds of Europe, the Middle East, and North Africa. The Birds of the Western Palearctic Vol. 2. Oxford University Press, Oxford, UK.

CRAWLEY, M. J. 1993. GLIM for ecologists. Blackwell Scientific Publications, London, UK.

CRESSIE, N. 1991. Statistics for spatial data. John Wiley and Sons, Inc., New York, NY.

CRIST, E. P., AND R. C. CICONE. 1984. Application of the tasseled cap concept to simulated thematic mapper data. Photogrammetric Engineering and Remote Sensing 50: 343–352.

CROCKER-BEDFORD, D. C. 1990. Goshawk reproduction and forest management. Wildlife Society Bulletin 18: 262–269.

CROCKER-BEDFORD, D. C. 1998. The value of demographic and habitat studies in determining the status of Northern Goshawk (Accipiter gentilis atricapillus) with special reference to Crocker-Bedford (1990) and Kennedy (1997). Journal of Raptor Research 32:329–336.

CROCKER-BEDFORD, D. C., AND B. CHANEY. 1988. Characteristics of Goshawk nesting stands. Pp. 210–217 in R. L. Glinski, B. Giron Pendleton, M. B. Moss, M. N. LeFranc Jr., B. A. Millsap, and S. W. Hoffman (editors). Proceedings of the southwest raptor management symposium and workshop. National Wildlife Federation Scientific and Technical Series No. 11. National Wildlife Federation, Washington, DC.

CZUCHNOWSKI, R. 1993. Ptaki drapieżne Puszczy Niepołomickiej w latach 1987–1990. Notatki Ornitologiczne 34:313–318.

DALBECK, L. 2003. Der Uhu Bubo bubo (L.) in Deutschland—autökologische Analysen an einer wieder angesiedelten Population—Resümee eines Artenschutzprojekts. Ph.D. dissertation, University of Bonn, Shaker Verlag, Aachen, Germany.

DALE, V. H., L.A. JOYCE, S. MCNULTY, R. P. NEILSON, M. P. AYRES, M. D. FLANNIGAN, P. J. HANSON, L. C. IRLAND, A. E. LUGO, C. J. PETERSON, D. SIMBERLOFF, F. J. SWANSON, B. J. STOCKS, AND B. M. WOTTON. 2001. Climate change and forest disturbances. BioScience 51:723–34.

DALY, C., R. P. NEILSON, AND D. L. PHILLIPS. 1994. A statistical-topographic model for mapping climatological precipitation over mountainous terrain. Journal of Applied Meteorology 33:140–158.

DANKO, Š., A. DARALOVÁ, AND A. KRIŠTÍN. 2002. Rozšírenie vtákov na Slovensku. VEDA, Bratislava, Slovakia.

DANKO, Š., T. DIVIŠ, J. DVORSKÁ, M. DVORSKÝ, J. CHAVKO, D. KARASKA, B. KLOUBEC, P. KURKA, H. MATUŠIK, L. PEŠKE, L. SCHRÖPFER, AND R. VACÍK. 1994. Stav potnatkov o početnosto hniezdnych populácií dravcov (Falconiformes) a sov (Strigiformes) v Českej a Slovenskej republike k roku 1990 a ich populačný trend v rokoch 1970–1990. Buteo 6:1–89.

DARK, S. J., R. J. GUTIERREZ, AND G. I. GOULD. 1998. The Barred Owl (Strix varia) invasion in California. Auk 115:50–56.

DARVEAU, M., L. BELANGER, J. HUOT, E. MELANCON, AND S. DEBELLEFEUILLE. 1997. Forestry practices and the risk of bird nest predation in a boreal coniferous forest. Ecological Applications 7:572–580.

DASZAK, P., A. A. CUNNINGHAM, AND A. D. HYATT. 2000. Emerging infectious diseases of wildlife—threats to biodiversity and human health. Science 287:443–449.

DAUBENMIRE, R. 1952. A canopy-coverage method of vegetative analysis. Northwest Science 33:43–64.

DAUBENMIRE, R., AND R. B. DAUBENMIRE. 1968. Forest vegetation of eastern Washington and northern Idaho. Washington Agriculture Experiment Station Technical Bulletin 60. Washington State University, Pullman, WA.

DAVIS, T. 1979. Telemetry study of a family of Goshawks. M.S. thesis, University of Minnesota, Duluth, MN.

DAW, S. K. 1997. Northern Goshawk nest site selection and habitat associations at the post-fledging family area scale in Oregon. M.S. thesis, Oregon State University, Corvallis, OR.

DAW, S. K., AND S. DESTEFANO. 2001. Forest characteristics of Northern Goshawk nest stands and post-fledging areas in Oregon. Journal of Wildlife Management 65: 59–65.

DAW, S. K., S. DESTEFANO, AND R. J. STEIDL. 1998. Does survey method bias the description of Northern Goshawk nest-site structure? Journal of Wildlife Management 62:1379–1384.

DE FRAINE, R., AND, R. VERBOVEN. 1997. Doorbraak van de Havik Accipiter gentilis als broedvogel in de Zuiderkempen (Vlaanderen, België). Oriolus 63: 46–48.

DEKKER, A. L., A. HUT, AND R. G. BIJLSMA. 2004. De opkomst van de Havik Accipiter gentilis in de stad Groningen. De Takkeling 12:205–218.

DEL HOYO, J., A. ELLIOTT, AND J. SARGATAL (EDITORS). 1994. Handbook of the birds of the world, Vol. 2. Lynx Edicions, Barcelona, Spain.

DELANNOY, C. A., AND A. CRUZ. 1991. Philornis parasitism and nestling survival of the Puerto Rican Sharp-shinned Hawk. Pp. 93–103 in J. E. Loye, and M. Zuk (editors).

Bird-parasite interactions: ecology, evolution, and behaviour. Oxford University Press, New York, NY.

DELBEKE, K., JOIRIS, C., AND G. DECADT. 1984. Mercury contamination of the Belgian avifauna 1970–81. Environmental Pollution (Series B) 7:205–221.

DELLASALA, D. A., J. R. STRITTHOLT, R. F. NOSS, AND D. M. OLSON. 1996. A critical role for core reserves in managing inland northwest landscapes for natural resources and biodiversity. Wildlife Society Bulletin 24:209–221.

DEMENT'EV, G. P., N. A. GLADKOV, E. S. PTUSHENKO, E. P. SPANGENBERG, AND A. M. SUDILOVSKAYA. 1966. Birds of the Soviet Union. Volume 1. Israel Program for Scientific Translations. Jerusalem, Israel.

DEPPE, H.-J. 1976. Ernährungsbiologische Beobachtungen beim Habicht (Accipiter gentilis) in einem großstadtnahen Revier. Ornithologische Berichte für Berlin (West) 1:317–325.

DERRICKSON, S. R., S. R. BEISSINGER, AND N. F. R. SNYDER. 1998. Directions in endangered species research. Pp. 111–123 in J. M. Marzluff, and R. Sallabanks (editors). Avian conservation: research and management. Island Press, Washington, DC.

DESIMONE, S. M. 1997. Occupancy rates and habitat relationships of Northern Goshawks in historic nesting areas in Oregon. M.S. thesis, Oregon State University, Corvallis, OR.

DESTEFANO, S. 1998. Determining the status of Northern Goshawks in the West: is our conceptual model correct? Journal of Raptor Research 32:342–348.

DESTEFANO, S. 2005. A review of the status and distribution of Northern Goshawks in New England. Journal of Raptor Research. 39:342–250.

DESTEFANO, S., AND T. L. CUTLER. 1998. Diets of Northern Goshawks in eastern Oregon. USGS, Arizona Cooperative Fish and Wildlife Research Unit, Tucson, AZ.

DESTEFANO, S., S. K. DAW, S. M. DESIMONE, AND E. C. MESLOW. 1994a. Density and productivity of Northern Goshawks: implications for monitoring and management. Studies in Avian Biology 16:88–91.

DESTEFANO, S., AND J. MCCLOSKEY. 1997. Does vegetation structure limit the distribution of Northern Goshawks in the Oregon coast ranges? Journal of Raptor Research 31:34–39.

DESTEFANO, S., J. A. THRAILKILL, K. A. SWINDLE, G. S. MILLER, B. WOODBRIDGE, AND E. C. MESLOW. 1995. Analysis of habitat quality and relative survival using capture-recapture data. Pp. 466–469 in P. R. Krausman, and J. A. Bissonette (editors). Integrating people and wildlife for a sustainable future. Proceedings of the First International Wildlife Management Congress, The Wildlife Society, Bethesda, MD.

DESTEFANO, S., B. WOODBRIDGE, AND P. J. DETRICH. 1994b. Survival of Northern Goshawks in the southern Cascades of California. Studies in Avian Biology 16: 133–136.

DETRICH, P. J., AND B. WOODBRIDGE. 1994. Territory fidelity, mate fidelity and movements of color-marked Northern Goshawks in the southern Cascades of California. Studies in Avian Biology 16:130–132.

DEUBEL, V., L. FIETTE, P. GOUNON, M. T. SROUET, H. KUHN, M. HUERRE, C. BONET, M. MALKINSON, AND P. DESPERES. 2001. Variations in biological features of West Nile viruses. Annals of the New York Academy of Sciences 951:49–58.

DEVAULT, T. L., STEPHENS, W. L., REINHART, B. D., RHODES, O. E., AND I. L. BRISBIN, JR. 2003. Aerial telemetry accuracy in a forested landscape. Journal of Raptor Research 37:147–151.

DEVILLERS, P., W. ROGGEMAN, J. TRICOT, P. DEL MARMOL, C. KERWIJN, J.-J. JACOB, AND A. ANSELIN. 1988. Atlas des oiseaux nicheurs de Belgique. Institut Royal des Sciences Naturelles de Belgique, Bruxelles, Belgium.

DEVINE, A., AND D. G. SMITH. 1996. Connecticut birding guide. Thompson-Shore Publishing Company, East Lansing, MI.

DEWEY, S. R., AND P. L. KENNEDY. 2001. Effects of supplemental food on parental care strategies and juvenile survival of Northern Goshawks. Auk 118:353–365.

DEWEY, S. R., P. L. KENNEDY, AND R. M. STEPHENS. 2003. Are dawn vocalization surveys effective for monitoring goshawk territory occupancy? Journal of Wildlife Management 67:390–397.

DICK, T., AND D. PLUMPTON. 1998. Review of information on the status of the Northern Goshawk (Accipiter gentilis atricapillus) in the western Great Lakes Region. Unpublished Report. USDI Fish and Wildlife Service, Fort Snelling, MN.

DICK, T. D., AND A. STRONACH. 1999. The use, abuse and misuse of crow cage traps in Scotland. Scottish Birds 20:6–13.

DIETRICH, J. 1982. Zur Ökologie des Habichts—Accipiter gentilis—im Stadtverband Saarbrücken. Diploma thesis, University of the Saarland, Saarbrücken, Germany.

DIETRICH, J., AND H. ELLENBERG. 1981. Aspects of Goshawk urban ecology. Pp. 163–175 in R. E. Kenward, and I. M. Lindsay (editors). Understanding the Goshawk. International Association for Falconry and Conservation of Birds of Prey, Oxford, UK.

DIETZEN, W. 1978. Der Brutbiotop des Habichts Accipiter gentilis in drei Gebieten Bayerns. Anzeiger der Ornithologischen Gesellschaft in Bayern 17:141–159.

DIGGLE, P. J. 1983. Statistical analysis of spatial point patterns. Academic Press, London, UK.

DINGLE, H. 1996. Migration. The biology of life on the move. Oxford University Press, New York, NY.

DIVIŠ, T. 1990. Evolution of the populations of some species of birds of prey in the Náchod district (Czechoslovakia) in 1978–1988. Pp. 329–331 in K. Šťastný, and V. Bejček (editors). Bird Census and Atlas Studies. Proceedings XIth International Conference on Bird Census and Atlas Work, Prague, Czech Republic.

DIVIŠ, T. 2003. Z biologie a ekologie jestřába lesniho (Accipiter gentilis). Panurus 13:3–32.

DIXON, J. B., AND R. E. DIXON. 1938. Nesting of the Western Goshawk in California. Condor 40:3–11.

DOAK, D. 1995. Source-sink models and the problem of habitat degradation: general models and applications to the Yellowstone grizzly. Conservation Biology 9: 1370–1379.

DOBLER, G. 1990. Brutbiotop und Territorialität bei Habicht (*Accipiter gentilis*) und Rotmilan (*Milvus milvus*). Journal für Ornithologie 131:85–93.

DOBLER, G. 1991. Klimatische Einflüsse auf Dichte, Brutzeit und Bruterfolg von Habicht *Accipiter gentilis* und Rotmilan *Milvus milvus*. Vogelwelt 112:152–162.

DOBLER, G., AND K. SIEDLE. 1993. Fänge von Habichten (*Accipiter gentilis*) im Wurzacher Ried: Kritische Fragen zu einem behördlich genehmigten Wiederein-bürgerungsprojekt. Journal für Ornithologie 134: 165–171.

DOBLER, G., AND K. SIEDLE. 1994. Wurzacher Ried: Habichte illegal gefangen und getötet. Berichte zum Vogelschutz 32:61–74.

DODD, N. L., J. S. STATES, AND S. S. ROSENSTOCK. 2003. Tassel-eared squirrel population, habitat condition, and dietary relationships in north-central Arizona. Journal of Wildlife Management 67:622–633.

DOERR, P. D., AND J. H. ENDERSON. 1965. An index of abun-dance of the Goshawk in Colorado in the winter. Auk 82:284–285.

DOLBEER, R. A. 1973. Reproduction in the red squirrel (*Tamiasciurus hudsonicus*) in Colorado. Journal of Mammalogy 54:536–540.

DOMASHEVSKIY, S. V. 2003. Ecology of Goshawk in the north of Ukraine. Strepet 1:72–85.

DONALD, P. F., R. E. GREEN, AND M. F. HEATH. 2001. Agricultural intensification and the collapse of Europe's farmland bird populations. Proceedings of the Royal Society of London, Series B 268:25–29.

DOOLITTLE, T. 1998. Goshawk winter movement study in northern Wisconsin. P. 6 *in* J. Noll West (editor). Status of the Northern Goshawk in the Midwest: workshop proceedings. USDI Fish and Wildlife Service, Fort Snelling, MN.

DOUCET, J. 1987. Aspects de la prédation de l'Autour (*Accipiter gentilis*) cn période de nidification. Aves 1987, numéro spécial: 62–65.

DOUCET, J. 1989a. Réapparition de la nidification du Hibou grand-duc (*Bubo bubo*) en Wallonie: Sa réintroduction en Europe occidentale. Aves 26:137–158.

DOUCET J. 1989b. Statut évolutif d'une population d'Autour des palombes (*Accipiter gentilis*) et remarques sur les dénombrement d'animaux. Aves 1989, numéro spécial: 103–112.

DOYLE, F. I. 1995. Bald Eagle (*Haliaeetus leucocephalus*) and Northern Goshawk (*Accipiter gentilis*), nests ap-parently preyed upon by a wolverine(s), (*Gulo gulo*), in the southwestern Yukon Territory. Canadian Field Naturalist 109:115–116.

DOYLE, F. I. 2000. Timing of reproduction by Red-tailed Hawks, Northern Goshawks and Great Horned Owls in the Kluane boreal forest of southwestern Yukon. M.S. thesis, University of British Columbia, Vancouver, BC, Canada.

DOYLE, F. I. 2003. Biological review and recommended interim strategy direction for Northern Goshawks on Haida Gwaii/Queen Charlotte Islands. BC Ministry of Environment, Lands and Parks. Smithers, BC, Canada.

DOYLE, F. I., AND J. M. N. SMITH. 1994. Population re-sponses of Northern Goshawks to the 10-year cycle in numbers of snowshoe hares. Studies in Avian Biology 16:122–129.

DOYLE, F. I., AND T. MAHON. 2001. Inventory of the Northern Goshawk in the Kispiox Forest District Annual Report 2000. BC Ministry of Environment, Lands and Parks. Smithers, BC, Canada.

DRACHMANN, J., AND J. T. NIELSEN. 2002. Danske duehøges populationsøkologi og forvaltning. Faglig rapport fra DMU, nr. 398. Danmarks Miljøundersøgelser. Århus, Denmark.

DRAULANS, D. 1984. Dagroofvogels te Mol-Postel en om-geving. De Wielewaal, Turnhout, The Netherlands.

DRAULANS, D. 1988. Timing of breeding and nesting suc-cess of raptors in a newly colonized area in north-east Belgium. Gerfaut 78:415–420.

DRAZNY, T., AND A. ADAMSKI. 1996. The number, repro-duction and food of the Goshawk *Accipiter gentilis* in central Silesia (SW Poland). Populationsökologie Greifvogel- und Eulenarten 3:207–219.

DREITZ, V. J., R. E. BENNETTS, B. TOLAND, W. M. KITCHENS, AND M. W. COLLOPY. 2001. Spatial and temporal vari-ability in nest success of Snail Kites in Florida: a meta-analysis. Condor 103:502–509.

DRENNAN, J. E., AND P. BEIER 2003. Forest structure and prey abundance in winter habitat of Northern Goshawks. Journal of Wildlife Management 67:177–185.

DRONNEAU, C., AND B. WASSMER. 2004. Autour des palombes *Accipiter gentilis*. Pp. 85–89 *in* J.-M. Thiollay, and V. Bertagnolle (editors). Rapaces nicheurs en France. Distribution, effectifs et conservation. Delachau et Niestlé, Paris, France.

DUFFY, D. C., AND S. JACKSON. 1986. Diet studies of sea-birds: a review of methods. Colonial Waterbirds. 9: 1–17.

DUFTY, A. M., JR., AND J. R. BELTHOFF. 2001. Proximate mechanisms of natal dispersal: the role of body con-dition and hormones. Pp. 217–229 *in* J. Clobert, E. Danchin, A. A. Dhondt, and J. D. Nichols (editors). Dispersal. Oxford University Press, Oxford, UK.

DUNCAN, P., AND D. A. KIRK. 1995. Status report on the Northern Goshawk *Accipiter gentilis* in Canada. Committee on the status of endangered wildlife in Canada. Manitoba Conservation Data Centre, Winnipeg, MB, Canada.

DUNNING, J. B., JR. 1984. Body weights of 686 species of North American birds. Monograph number 1. Western Bird Banding Association. Cave Creek, AZ.

DUNNING, J. B. (EDITOR). 1993. CRC Handbook of avian body masses. CRC Press Inc., Boca Raton, FL.

DVORAK, M., A. RANNER, AND H.-M. BERG (EDITORS). 1993. Atlas der Brutvögel Österreichs: 120–121. Bundesministerium für Umwelt und Familie, Wien, Austria.

EDWARDS, T. C., JR., C. G. HOMER, S. D. BASSETT, A. FALCONER, R. D. RAMSEY, AND D. W. WIGHT. 1995. Utah gap analysis: an environmental information system. Final project report 95-1, Utah Cooperative Fish and Wildlife Research Unit, Utah State University, Logan, UT.

EHRING, R. 2004. Bestands- und Reproduktionskontrollen am Habicht (Accipiter gentilis) 1970–2002 in Nordwestsachsen. Mitteilungen des Vereins Sächsischer Ornithologen 9:397–405.

ELKINS, N. 1983. Weather and bird behaviour. T. & A.D. Poyser Ltd., Staffordshire, UK.

ELLENBERG, H. (EDITOR). 1981. Greifvögel und Pestizide. Versuch einer Bilanz für Mitteleuropa. Ökologie der Vögel 3, Sonderheft:1–420.

ELLENBERG, H., AND J. DIETRICH. 1981. The Goshawk as a bioindicator. Pp. 69–88 in R. E. Kenward, and I. M. Lindsay (editors). Understanding the Goshawk. International Association for Falconry and Conservation of Birds of Prey, Oxford, UK.

EMLEN, J. M. 1973. Ecology: an evolutionary approach. Addison-Wesley Publishing Company, Reading, MA.

ENDANGERED SPECIES ACT of 1973. Public Law 16 U.S.C. §§ 1531-1544, December 28, 1973, as amended.

ENG, R. L., AND G. W. GULLION. 1962. The predation of Goshawks upon Ruffed Grouse on the Cloquet Forest Research Center, Minnesota. Wilson Bulletin 74: 227–242.

ENNIS, K. R., J. BLUM, J. KELLY, C. SCHUMACHER, E. PADLEY, AND T. SCHUETZ. 1993. Management recommendations for the Northern Goshawk on the Huron-Manistee National Forests. Huron-Manistee National Forest, USDA Forest Service, Cadillac, MI.

ERDMAN, T. C., D. F. BRINKER, J. P. JACOBS, J. WILDE, AND T. O. MEYER. 1998. Productivity, population trend, and status of Northern Goshawks, Accipiter gentilis atricapillus, in northeastern Wisconsin. Canadian Field Naturalist 112:17–27.

ERICKSON, M. G. 1987. Nest site habitat selection of the Goshawk (Accipiter gentilis) in the Black Hills National Forest of South Dakota. M.S. thesis, University of South Dakota, Vermillion, SD.

ERKENS, J., AND F. HENDRIX. 1984. Prooidieren van buizerd en havik. De Nederlandse Jager 89:328–329.

ERLICH, P. R., D. S. DOBKIN, AND D. WHEYE. 1988. The birder's handbook: a field guide to the natural history of North American birds. Simon and Schuster, New York, NY.

ERLINGE, S., G. GÖRANSSON, G. HÖGSTEDT, G. JANSSON, O. LIBERG, J. LOMAN, I. N. NILSSON, T. VON SCHANTZ, AND M. SYLVÉN. 1984. Can vertebrate predators regulate their prey? American Naturalist 123:125–133.

ERLINGE, S., G. GORANSSON, G. HOGSTEDT, O. LIBERG, I. N. NILSSON, T. NILSSON, T. VON SCHANTZ, AND M. SYLVEN. 1982. Factors limiting numbers of vertebrate predators in a predator prey community. Transactions of the International Congress of Game Biologists 14:261–268.

ERRINGTON, P. L. 1930. The pellet analysis method of raptor food habits study. Condor 32:292–296.

ERRINGTON, P. L. 1932. Technique of raptor food habits study. Condor 34:75–86.

ERZEPKY, R. 1977. Zur Art des Nahrungserwerbs beim Habicht (Accipiter gentilis). Ornithologische Mitteilungen 29:229–231.

ESCH, G. W. 1975. An analysis of the relationship between stress and parasitism. American Midland Naturalist 93: 339–353.

ESRI. 1996. Using Arc View GIS. ESRI, Redlands, CA

ESRI. 1998. ArcView® 3.1. Environmental Research Institute, Inc., Redlands, CA.

ESTES, W. A., S. R. DEWEY, AND P. L. KENNEDY. 1999. Siblicide at Northern Goshawk nests: does food play a role? Wilson Bulletin 111:432–436.

ETHIER, T. J. 1999. Breeding ecology and habitat of Northern Goshawks (Accipiter gentilis laingi) on Vancouver Island: a hierarchical approach. M.S. thesis, University of Victoria, Victoria, BC, Canada.

EVANS, B. I., AND W. J. O'BRIEN. 1988. A re-analysis of the search cycle of a planktivorous salmonid. Canadian Journal of Fisheries and Aquatic Sciences 45:187–192.

EVANS, D. L. 1981. Banding recoveries from Hawk Ridge. Prairie Naturalist 32:18.

EVANS, D. L. 1983. Hawk Ridge Research Station, 1982. P. 12 in Hawk Ridge Annual Report. Duluth Audubon Society, Duluth, MN.

EVANS, D. L., AND C. R. SINDELAR. 1974. First record of the Goshawk for Louisiana—a collected, banded bird. Bird-Banding 45:270.

EVERETT, R., P. HESSBURG, M. JENSEN, AND B. BORMAN (EDITORS). 1993. Eastside forest ecosystem health assessment. Volume I: Executive summary. USDA Forest Service General Technical Report GTR-317. USDA Forest Service, Pacific Northwest Research Station, Portland, OR.

EVERETT, R. L., AND J. F. LEHMKUHL. 1996. An emphasis-use approach to conserving biodiversity. Wildlife Society Bulletin 24:192–199.

EVERETT, R. L., AND J. F. LEHMKUHL. 1997. A forum for presenting alternative viewpoints on the role of reserves in conservation biology? A reply to Noss (1996). Wildlife Society Bulletin 25:575–577.

EYRE, F. H. 1980. Forest cover types of the United States and Canada. Society of American Foresters, Washington, DC.

FAIRHURST, G. D. 2004. Northern Goshawk (Accipiter gentilis) population analysis and food habits in the Independence and Bull Run mountains, Nevada. M.S. thesis, Boise State University, Boise, ID.

FAIRHURST, G. D., AND M. J. BECHARD. 2005. Relationships between winter and spring weather and Northern Goshawk (Accipiter gentilis) reproduction in northern Nevada. Journal of Raptor Research 39:229–236.

FARENTINOS, R. C. 1972. Observations on the ecology of the tassel-eared squirrel. Journal of Wildlife Management 36:1234–1239.

FEDERAL DATA QUALITY ACT of 2001. Public Law 106–554 §515; H.R. 5658. Also known as the treasury and general government appropriations act for fiscal year 2001 [See also Federal Register September 28, 2001 66:49718–49725].

FELLIN, D. G. 1979. A review of some interactions between harvesting, residue management, fire, and forest insects and diseases. Pp. 335–415 *in* Environmental consequences of timber harvesting in Rocky Mountain coniferous forests. USDA Forest Service General Technical Report INT-90. USDA Forest Service, Intermountain Forest and Range Experiment Station, Ogden, UT.

FINDLEY, J. S., A. H. HARRIS, D. E. WILSON, AND C. JONES. 1975. Mammals of New Mexico. University of New Mexico Press. Albuquerque, NM.

FINN, S. P., J. M. MARZLUFF, AND D. E. VARLAND. 2002a. Effects of landscape and local habitat attributes on Northern Goshawk site occupancy in western Washington. Forest Science 48:427–436.

FINN, S. P., D. E. VARLAND, AND J. M. MARZLUFF. 2002b. Does Northern Goshawk breeding occupancy vary with nest-stand characteristics on the Olympic Peninsula, Washington? Journal of Raptor Research 36:265–279.

FISCHER, D. L. 1986. Daily activity patterns and habitat use of coexisting *Accipiter* hawks in Utah. Ph.D. dissertation, Brigham Young University, Provo, UT.

FISCHER, W. 1980. Die Habichte. Die Neue Brehm-Bücherei, Magdeburg, Germany.

FISCHER, W. 1995. Die Habichte. Die Neue Brehm-Bücherei, Bd. 158, 3rd ed. Westarp Wissenschaften, Magdeburg, Germany.

FITCH, J. S., B. GLADING, AND V. HOUSE. 1946. Observations on Cooper's Hawk nesting and predation. California Fish and Game 32:144–154.

FITZGERALD, J. P., C. A. MEANEY, AND D. M. ARMSTRONG. 1994. Mammals of Colorado. University Press of Colorado, Niwot, CO.

FLATTEN, C., K. TITUS, AND R. LOWELL. 2001. Northern Goshawk monitoring, population, ecology and diet on the Tongass National Forest. Research Final Performance Report 1 April 1991–30 September 2001, Alaska Department of Fish and Game, Division of Wildlife Conservation, Juneau, AK.

FLEMING, T. L. 1987. Northern Goshawk status and habitat associations in western Washington with special emphasis on the Olympic Peninsula. Unpublished report. USDA Pacific Northwest Forest and Range Experiment Station, Old-Growth Research Laboratory, Olympia, WA.

FLETCHER, N., AND G. SHEPPARD. 1994. The Northern Goshawk in the southwestern region 1992 status report. USDA Forest Service, Southwestern Region, Albuquerque, NM.

FLOUSEK, J., K. HUDEC, AND U. N. GLUTZ VON BLOTZHEIM. 1993. Immissionsbedingte Waldschäden und ihr Einfluß auf die Vogelwelt Mitteleuropas. Pp. 11–30 *in* U. N. Glutz von Blotzheim, and K. M. Bauer (editors). Handbuch der Vögel Mitteleuropas, Band 13/I. AULA-Verlag, Wiesbaden, Germany.

FORBUSH, E. H. 1925. Birds of Massachusetts and other New England states. Massachusetts Department of Agriculture, Boston, MA.

FOREST ECOSYSTEM MANAGEMENT ASSESSMENT TEAM. 1993. Forest ecosystem managements: and ecological, economic, and social assessment. Report of the Forest Ecosystem Management Assessment Team. USDA Forest Service, USDC National Oceanographic and Atmospheric Administration and National Marine Fisheries Services, USDI Bureau of Land Management, USDI Fish and Wildlife Service, National Park Service, and the U.S. Environmental Protection Agency, Washington, DC.

FORMAN, R. T. T., AND M. GORDON. 1981. Patches and structural components for a landscape ecology. BioScience 31:733–740.

FORSMAN, E. D., E. C. MESLOW, AND H. M. WIGHT. 1984. Distribution and biology of the Spotted Owl in Oregon. Wildlife Monographs 87:1–64.

FORSMAN, D., AND T. SOLONEN. 1984. Censusing breeding raptors in southern Finland: methods and results. Annales Zoologici Fennici 21:317–320.

FOWELLS, H. A., AND G. H. SCHUBERT. 1956. Seed crops of forest trees in the pine region of California. USDA Forest Service Technical Bulletin No. 1150. USDA Forest Service, Pacific Southwest Research Station, Redding, CA.

FOX, N. 1981. The hunting behaviour of trained Northern Goshawks. Pp. 121–133 *in* R. E. Kenward, and I. M. Lindsay (editors). Understanding the Goshawk. International Association for Falconry and Conservation of Birds of Prey, Oxford, UK.

FRANKLIN, A. B., D. R. ANDERSON, E. D. FORSMAN, K. P. BURNHAM, AND F. W. WAGNER. 1996. Methods for collecting and analyzing demographic data on the Northern Spotted Owl. Studies in Avian Biology 17: 12–20.

FRANKLIN, A. B., D. R. ANDERSON, R. J. GUTIÉRREZ, AND K. P. BURNHAM. 2000. Climate, habitat quality, and fitness in Northern Spotted Owl populations in northwestern California. Ecology Monograph 70:539–590.

FRANKLIN, J. F. 1993. Preserving biodiversity: species, ecosystems, or landscapes? Ecological Applications 3:202–205.

FRANKLIN, J. F., AND C. T. DYRNESS. 1973. Natural vegetation of Oregon and Washington. USDA Forest Service General Technical Report PNW-8. USDA Forest Service, Pacific Northwest Forest and Range Experiment Station, Portland, OR.

FRANKLIN, J. F., AND J. A. FITES-KAUFMANN. 1996. Assessment of late-successional forests of the Sierra Nevada. Pp. 627–669 *in* Sierra Nevada ecosystem project, final report to Congress, Vol. 2, assessments and scientific basis for management options. Centers for Water and Wildland Resources, University of California, Davis, CA.

FRANKLIN, J. F., T. A. SPIES, R. VAN PELT, A. B. CAREY, D. A. THORNBURGH, D. RAE BERG, D. B. LINDENMAYER, M. E. HARMON, W. S. KEETON, D. C. SHAW, K. BIBLE, AND J.

CHEN. 2002. Disturbances and structural development of natural forest ecosystems with silvicultural implications, using Douglas-fir forests as an example. Forest Ecology and Management 155:399–423.

FRETWELL, S. D., AND H. L. LUCAS. 1970. On territorial behavior and other factors influencing habitat distribution in birds. Acta Biotheoretica 19:16–36.

FRØSLIE, A., G. HOLT, AND G. NORHEIM. 1986. Mercury and persistent chlorinated hydrocarbons in owls Strigiformes and birds of prey Falconiformes collected in Norway during the period 1965–1983. Environmental Pollution (Series B) 11:91–108.

FULÉ, P. Z., W. W. COVINGTON, AND M. M. MOORE. 1997. Determining reference conditions for ecosystem management of southwestern ponderosa pine forests. Ecological Applications 7:895–908.

FULLER, M. R. 1996. Forest raptor population trends in North America. Pp. 167–208 in R. M. DeGraaf, and R. I. Miller (editors). Conservation of faunal diversity in forested landscapes. Chapman & Hall, London, UK.

FULLER, M. R., AND J. A. MOSHER. 1987. Raptor survey techniques. Pp. 37–65 in B. A. Giron Pendleton, B. A. Millsap, K. W. Cline, and D. M. Bird (editors). Raptor management techniques manual. National Wildlife Federation Scientific and Technical Series 10, Washington, DC.

FULLER, M. R., W. S. SEEGAR, AND L. S. SCHUECK. 1998. Routes and travel rates of migrating Peregrine Falcons (Falco Peregrinus) and Swainson's Hawks (Buteo swainsoni) in the western hemisphere. Journal of Avian Biology 29:433–440.

GABRIËLS, J. 2004. Havik (Accipiter gentilis). Pp. 166–167 in G. Vermeersch, A. Anselin, K. Devos, M. Herremans, J. Stevens, and B. Van Der Krieken (editors). Atlas van de Vlaamse broedvogels 2000–2002. Mededelingen van het Instituut voor Natuurbehoud, Brussels, Belgium.

GALBRAITH, C. A., D. A. STROUD, AND D. B. A. THOMPSON. 2003. Towards resolving raptor-human conflicts. Pp. 527–535 in D. B. A. Thompson, S. M. Redpath, A. H. Fielding, M. Marquiss, and C. A. Galbraith (editors). Birds of prey in a changing environment. Scottish Natural Heritage/The Stationary Office, Edinburgh, UK.

GAINES, D. 1988. Birds of Yosemite and the east slope. Artemisia Press. Lee Vining, CA.

GALLI, A. E., C. F. LECK, AND R. T. T. FORMAN. 1976. Avian distribution patterns in forest islands of different sizes in central New Jersey. Auk 93:356–364.

GALUSHIN, V. M. 1974. Synchronous fluctuations in populations of some raptors and their prey. Ibis 116:127–134.

GAMAUF, A. 1988a. Hierarchische Ordnung in der Wahl der Nistplatz- und Jagdhabitate dreier sympatrischer Greifvogelarten (Buteo buteo, Pernis apivorus, Accipiter gentilis). Ph.D. dissertation, University of Vienna, Vienna, Austria.

GAMAUF, A. 1988b. Der Einfluß des Waldsterbens auf die Horstbaumwahl einiger Greifvogelarten (Accipitridae). Ökologie der Vögel 10:79–83.

GAMAUF, A. 1991. Greifvögel in Österreich: Bestand-Bedrohung-Gesetz. Monographien Bd. 29. Bundesministerium für Umwelt, Jugend und Familie, Vienna, Austria.

GARSHELIS, D. L. 2000. Delusions in habitat evaluation: measuring use, selection, and importance. Pp. 111–164 in L. Boitani, and T. K. Fuller (editors). Research techniques in animal ecology: controversies and consequences. Columbia University Press, New York, NY.

GATTO, A. E., T. G. GRUBB, AND C. L. CHAMBERS. 2005. Red-tailed Hawk dietary overlap with Northern Goshawks on the Kaibab Plateau, Arizona. Journal of Raptor Research 39:439–444.

GAVIN, T. A., R. T. REYNOLDS, S. M. JOY, D. LESLIE, AND B. MAY. 1998. Genetic evidence for low frequency of extra-pair fertilizations in Northern Goshawks. Condor 100:556–560.

GEDEON K. 1984. Daten zur Brutbiologie des Habichts, Accipiter gentilis (L.), im Bezirk Karl-Marx-Stadt. Faunistische Abhandlungen Staatliches Museum für Tierkunde in Dresden 11:157–160.

GEDEON, K. 1994. Monitoring Greifvögel und Eulen. Grundlagen und Möglichkeiten einer langfristigen Überwachung von Bestandsgrößen und Reproduktionsdaten. Ph.D. dissertation, University of Halle, Halle, Germany.

GEUENS, A. 1994. Havik Accipiter gentilis. Pp. 82–83 in J. Gabriëls, J. Stevens, and P. Van Sanden (editors). Broedvogelatlas van Limburg: Veranderingen in aantallen en verspreiding na 1985. Provincie Limburg, Genk, The Netherlands.

GILES, R. H., JR. 1978. Wildlife management. W. H. Freeman and Co., San Francisco, CA.

GILMER, D. S., P. M. KONRAD, AND R. E. STEWART. 1983. Nesting ecology of Red-tailed Hawks and Great Horned Owls in central North Dakota and their interactions with other large raptors. Prairie Naturalist 15:133–143.

GILPIN, M. 1991. The genetic effective size of a metapopulation. Biological Journal of the Linnean Society 42:165–175.

GLUTZ VON BLOTZHEIM, U. N., K. M. BAUER, AND E. BEZZEL (EDITORS). 1971. Handbuch der Vögel Mitteleuropas. Bd. 4. Akademische Verlagsgesellschaft, Frankfurt am Main, Germany.

GONZÁLEZ-SOLÍS, J., D. ORO, V. PEDROCCHI, L. JOVER, AND X. RUIZ. 1997. Bias associated with diet samples in Audouins Gulls. Condor 99:773–779.

GOOD, R. E. 1998. Factors affecting the relative use of Northern Goshawk (Accipiter gentilis) kill areas in southcentral Wyoming. M.S. thesis, University of Wyoming, Laramie, WY.

GOOD, R. E., S. H. ANDERSON, J. R. SQUIRES, AND G. MCDANIEL. 2001. Observations of Northern Goshawk prey delivery behavior in southcentral Wyoming. Intermountain Journal of Science 7:34–40.

GOODWIN, J. G., JR., AND R. C. HUNGERFORD. 1979. Rodent population densities and food habits in Arizona ponderosa pine forests. USDA Forest Service Research

Paper RM-214. USDA Forest Service, Rocky Mountain Forest and Range Experiment Station. Fort Collins, CO.

GOSZCZYŃSKI, J. 1997. Density and productivity of Common Buzzard *Buteo buteo* and Goshawk *Accipiter gentilis* populations in Rogów, Central Poland. Acta ornithologica 32:149–155.

GOSZCZYŃSKI, J. 2001. The breeding performance of the Common Buzzard *Buteo buteo* and Goshawk *Accipiter gentilis* in Central Poland. Acta ornithologica 36: 105–110.

GOSZCZYŃSKI, J. A., AND T. PIŁATOWSKI. 1986. Diet of Common Buzzard (*Buteo buteo* L.) and Goshawk (*Accipiter gentilis* L.) in the nesting period. Ekologia Polska 34:655–667.

GÖTMARK, F., AND P. POST. 1996. Prey selection by Sparrowhawks *Accipiter nisus*—relative predation risk for breeding passerine birds in relation to their size, ecology and behaviour. Philosophical Transactions of the Royal Society of London B 351:1559–1577.

GRAFEN, A., AND R. HAILS. 2002. Modern statistics for the life sciences. Oxford University Press, Oxford, UK.

GRAHAM, R. T, R. T. REYNOLDS, M. H. REISER, R. L. BASSETT, AND D. A. BOYCE, JR. 1994. Sustaining forest habitat for the Northern Goshawk: a question of scale. Studies in Avian Biology 16:12–17.

GRAHAM, R. T. (TECHNICAL EDITOR). 2003. Hayman fire case study. USDA Forest Service General Technical Report RMRS-GTR-114. USDA Forest Service, Rocky Mountain Research Station, Ogden, UT.

GRAHAM, R. T., A. E. HARVEY, T. B JAIN, AND J. R TONN. 1999a. The effects of thinning and similar stand treatments on fire behavior in western forests. USDA Forest Service General Technical Report PNW-GTR-463. USDA Forest Service, Pacific Northwest Research Station. Portland, OR.

GRAHAM, R. T., R. L. RODRIGUEZ, K. M. PAULIN, R. L. PLAYER, A. P. HEAP, AND R. WILLIAMS. 1999b. The Northern Goshawk in Utah: habitat assessment and management recommendations. USDA Forest Service General Technical Report RMRS-GTR-22. USDA Forest Service, Dixie National Forest, Cedar City, UT.

GRAHAM, R. T., S. MCCAFFREY, AND T. B. JAIN (TECHNICAL EDITORS). 2004. Science basis for changing forest structure to modify wildfire behavior and severity. USDA Forest Service General Technical Report RMRS-GTR-120. USDA Forest Service, Rocky Mountain Research Station, Ogden, UT.

GREENWALD, D. N., D. C. CROCKER-BEDFORD, L. BROBERG, K. F. SUCKLING, AND T. TIBBITTS. 2005. A review of Northern Goshawk habitat selection in the home range and implications for forest management in the western United States. Wildlife Society Bulletin 33:120–129.

GREENWOOD, P. J. 1980. Mating systems, philopatry, and dispersal in birds and mammals. Animal Behaviour 28:1140–1162.

GREENWOOD, P. J., AND J. H. HARVEY. 1982. The natal and breeding dispersal in birds. Annual Review of Ecology and Systematics 13:1–21.

GRELL, M. B. 1998. Fuglenes Danmark. Gads Forlag, Copenhagen, Denmark.

GRINNELL, J., AND A. H. MILLER. 1944. The distribution of the birds of California. Cooper Ornithological Club, Pacific Coast Avifauna Number 27.

GROMME, O. J. 1935. The Goshawk (*Astur atricapillus atricapillus*) nesting in Wisconsin. Auk 52:15–20.

GRØNNESBY, S., AND T. NYGÅRD. 2000. Using time-lapse video monitoring to study prey selection by breeding Goshawks *Accipiter gentilis* in central Norway. Ornis Fennica 77:117–129.

GROVES, C. R., M. W. BECK, J. V. HIGGINS, E. C. SAXON, AND M. L. HUNTER. 2003. Drafting a conservation blueprint: a practitioner's guide to planning for biodiversity. Island Press, Covelo, CA.

GRUBAČ, B. 1988. Contributions to the ecology and ethology of the Goshawk (*Accipiter gentilis*) in south-eastern Yugoslavia. Larus 40:97–110.

GRUBB, T. G., L. L. PATER, AND D. K. DELANEY. 1998. Logging truck noise near nesting Northern Goshawks. USDA Forest Service Research Note RMRS-RN-3. USDA Forest Service, Rocky Mountain Research Station, Ft. Collins, CO.

GRÜNHAGEN, H. 1981. Zur Jagd des Habichts (*Accipiter gentilis*) aus dem hohen Kreisen. Charadrius 17: 68–70.

GRÜNHAGEN, H. 1983. Regionale Unterschiede im Alter brütender Habichtweibchen (*Accipiter gentilis*). Vogelwelt 104:208–214.

GRÜNKORN, T. 2000. Untersuchungen zum Einfluß des Uhus (*Bubo bubo*) auf Verbreitung und Bruterfolg einiger Großvogelarten im Wald. Gutachten für den Landesverband für Eulenschutz e.V. Schleswig-Holstein. Schleswig, Germany.

GRZYBOWSKI, J. A., AND S. W. EATON. 1976. Prey items of Goshawks in southwestern New York. Wilson Bulletin 88:669–670.

GULDIN, J. M., D. CAWRSE, R. GRAHAM, M. HEMSTROM, L. JOYCE, S. KESSLER, R. MCNAIR, G. PETERSON, C. SHAW, P. STINE, M. TWERY, AND J. WALTER. 2003. Science consistency reviews: a primer for application. USDA Forest Service FS-771. USDA Forest Service, Washington, DC.

GULLION, G. W. 1981a. A quarter century of Goshawk nesting at Cloquet. Loon 53:3–5.

GULLION, G. W. 1981b. The impact of Goshawk predation upon Ruffed Grouse. Loon 53:82–84.

GULLION, G. W., AND A. A. ALM. 1983. Forest management and Ruffed Grouse populations in a Minnesota coniferous forest. Journal of Forestry 81:529–532, 536.

GURNELL, J. 1984. Home range, territoriality, caching behavior and food supply of the red squirrel (*Tamiasciurus hudsonicus fremonti*) in a subalpine lodgepole pine forest. Animal Behavior 32:1119–1131.

HAGEN, Y. 1942. Totalgewichts-Studien bei norwegischen Vogelarten: 63. *Accipiter g. gentilis* (L.) Habicht. Archiv für Naturgeschichte 11:50–63.

HAGEN, Y. 1952. Rovfuglene og viltpleien. Gyldendal Norsk forlag, Oslo, Norway.

HAHN, E., K, HAHN, AND M. STOEPPLER. 1989. Schwermetalle in Federn von Habichten (*Accipiter gentilis*) aus unterschiedlich belasteten Gebieten. Journal für Ornithologie 130:303–309.

HAIG, I. T., K. P. DAVIS, AND R. H. WEIDMAN. 1941. Natural regeneration in the western white pine type. USDA Technical Bullletin No. 767. Washington, DC.

HAILA, Y., AND O. JÄRVINEN. 1990. Northern forests and their bird species assemblages. Pp. 61–85 *in* A. Keast (editor). Biogeography and ecology of forest bird communities. SPB Academic Publishing bv, The Hague, The Netherlands.

HAKKARAINEN, H., S. MYKRÄ, S. KURKI, R. TORNBERG, S. JUNGELL, AND A. NIKULA. 2004. Long-term change in territory occupancy pattern of Goshawks (*Accipiter gentilis*). Ecoscience 11:399–403.

HALDEMAN, J. R. 1968. Breeding birds of a ponderosa pine forest in the San Francisco Mountains, Arizona. M.S. thesis, Northern Arizona University, Flagstaff, AZ.

HALL, E. R. 1981. The mammals of North America. John Wiley and Sons, New York, NY.

HALL, J. G. 1981. A field study of the Kaibab squirrel in Grand Canyon National Park. Wildlife Monographs 75:6–54.

HALL, L. S., P. R. KRAUSMAN, AND M. L. MORRISON. 1997. The habitat concept and a plea for standard terminology. Wildlife Society Bulletin 25:173–182.

HALL, P. A. 1984. Characterization of nesting habitat of Goshawks (*Accipiter gentilis*) in northwestern California. M.S. thesis, Humboldt State University, Arcata, CA.

HALLEY, D. J. 1996. Movements and mortality of Norwegian Goshawks *Accipiter gentilis*: an analysis of ringing data. Fauna Norvegica Ser C Cinclus 19:55–67.

HALLEY, D. J., T. NYGARD, AND B. WISETH. 2000. Winter home range and summer movements of a male Goshawk *Accipiter gentilis* from fledging to first breeding. Ornis Norvegica 23:31–37.

HAMMERSTROM, F., AND R. N. HAMMERSTROM. 1973. Nest boxes: an effective management tool for Kestrels. Journal of Wildlife Management 37:400–403.

HANAUSKA-BROWN, L. A., M. J. BECHARD, AND G. J. ROLOFF. 2003. Northern Goshawk breeding ecology and nestling growth in mixed coniferous forests of west-central Idaho. Northwest Science 77:331–339.

HANN, W. J., J. L. JONES, M. G. KARL, P. F. HESSBURG, R. E. KEANE, D. G. LONG, J. P. MENAKIS, C. H. MCNICOLL, S. G. LEONARD, R. A. GRAVENMIER, AND B. G. SMITH. 1997. Landscape dynamics of the Basin. Pp. 338–1055 *in* T. M. Quigley, and S. J. Arbelbide (technical editors). An assessment of ecosystem components in the interior Columbia Basin and portions of the Klamath and Great Basins: Volume II. USDA Forest Service General Technical Report PNW-405. USDA Forest Service, Pacific Northwest Research Station, Portland, OR.

HANSKI, I. 1982. Dynamics of regional distribution: the core and satellite species hypothesis. Oikos 38:210–221.

HANTGE, E. 1980. Untersuchungen über den Jagderfolg mehrerer europäischer Greifvögel. Journal für Ornithologie 121:200–207.

HARGIS, C. D., C. MCCARTHY, AND R. D. PERLOFF. 1994. Home ranges and habitats of Northern Goshawks in eastern California. Studies in Avian Biology 16:66–74.

HARMATA, A. R., AND D. W. STAHLECKER. 1993. Fidelity of Bald Eagles to wintering grounds in southern Colorado and northern New Mexico. Journal of Field Ornithology. 64:1–9.

HARRADINE, J., N. REYNOLDS, AND T. LAWS. 1997. Raptors and gamebirds—a survey of game managers affected by raptors. British Association for Shooting and Conservation. Marford Mill, UK.

HARRIS, L. D., T. S. HOCTOR, AND S. E. GERGEL. 1996. Landscape processes and their significance to biodiversity conservation. Pp. 319–345 *in* O. E. Rhodes, R. K. Chesser, and M. H. Smith. (editors). Population dynamics in ecological time and space. University of Chicago Press. Chicago, IL.

HART, E. B. 1976. Life history notes on the cliff chipmunk, *Eutamias dorsalis*, in Utah. Southwestern Naturalist 21:243–246.

HARTMAN, F. A. 1955. Heart weight in birds. Condor 57: 221–238.

HARVEY, A. E., R. T. GRAHAM, AND G. I. MCDONALD. 1999. Tree species composition change forest soil organism interaction: potential affects on nutrient cycling and conservation processes in interior forests. Pp.137–145 *in* R. Meurisse, W. G. Ypsllantis, and C. Seybold (technical editors). USDA Forest Service General Technical Report PNW-461. USDA Forest Service, Pacific Northwest Research Station, Portland, OR.

HATT, R. T. 1943. The pine squirrel in Colorado. Journal of Mammalogy 24:311–345.

HAUKIOJA, E., AND M. HAUKIOJA. 1970. Mortality rates of Finnish and Swedish Goshawks (*Accipiter gentilis*). Finnish Game Research 31:13–20.

HAUSCH, I. 1997. Habicht *Accipiter gentilis* (Linné 1758). Chapter 8.1.11.1 *in* K.-H. Berck, R. Burkhardt, O. Diehl, W. Heimer, M. Korn, and W. Schindler (editors). Avifauna von Hessen, 3. Lieferung. Hessische Gesellschaft für Ornithologie und Naturschutz e.V., Echzell, Germany.

HAVERA, S. P., AND R. E. DUZAN. 1986. Organochlorine and PCB residues in tissues of raptors from Illinois, 1966–1981. Bulletin of Environmental Contamination and Toxicology 36:23–32.

HAWK MOUNTAIN NEWS. 1979. The migration: Hawk Mountain 1978. Hawk Mountain News 51:30–35.

HAYNES, R. W., R. T. GRAHAM, AND T. M. QUIGLEY. 1996. A framework for ecosystem management in the interior Columbia Basin and portions of the Klamath and Great Basins. USDA Forest Service and USDI Bureau of Land Management General Technical Report PNW-374. USDA Forest Service, Pacific Northwest Research Station, Portland, OR.

HAYWARD, G. D., AND R. E. ESCANO. 1989. Goshawk nest-site characteristics in western Montana and northern Idaho. Condor 91:476–479.

HEATH, M., C. BORGGREVE, AND N. PEET. 2000. European bird populations: estimates and trends. BirdLife International, Cambridge, UK.

HEIJ, G. J., AND T. SCHNEIDER (EDITORS). 1991. Acidification research in The Netherlands. Studies in Environmental Science 46. Elsevier, Amsterdam, The Netherlands.

HEINTZELMAN, D. S. 1976. A guide to eastern hawk watching. Keystone Books, Pennsylvania State University Press, University Park, PA.

HEISE, G. 1986. Siedlungsdichte und Bruterfolg des Habichts (Accipiter gentilis) im Kreis Prenzlau, Uckermark. Beiträge zur Vogelkunde 32:113–120.

HENJUM, M. G. 1996. Maintaining ecological integrity of inland forest ecosystems in Oregon and Washington. Wildlife Society Bulletin 24:227–232.

HENNESSY, S. P. 1978. Ecological relationships of accipiters in northern Utah with special emphasis on the effects of human disturbance. M.S. thesis, Utah State University, Logan, UT.

HENNY, C. J., R. A. OLSEN, AND T. L. FLEMING. 1985. Breeding chronology, molt, and measurements of Accipiter Hawks in northeastern Oregon. Journal of Field Ornithology 56:97–112.

HENSLER, G. L., AND J. D. NICHOLS. 1981. Mayfield method of estimating nesting success: model, estimators and simulation results. Wilson Bulletin 93:42–53.

HENTTONEN, H. 1989. Metsien rakenteen vaikutuksesta myyräkantoihin ja sitä kautta pikkupetoihin-hypoteesi. Suomen Riista 35:83–90.

HERRON, G. B., C. A. MORTIMORE, AND M. S. RAWLINGS. 1985. Nevada raptors: their biology and management. Biological Bulletin No. 8, Nevada Department of Wildlife, Reno, NV.

HERZKE, D., R. KALLENBORN, AND T. NYGÅRD. 2002. Organochlorines in egg samples from Norwegian birds of prey: congener-isomer- and enantiometer specific considerations. Science of the total environment 291:59–71.

HEUVELINK, G. B. M. 1998. Error propagation in environmental modelling with GIS. Taylor & Francis, London, UK.

HICKEY, J. J. (EDITOR). 1969. Peregrine Falcon populations: their biology and decline. University of Wisconsin Press, Madison, WI.

HILLERICH, K. 1978. Ergebnisse aus20–jähriger Planberingung von Greifvögeln der Beringungsgemeinschaft Rothmann. Luscinia 43:187–205.

HIRONS, G. J. M. 1985. The importance of body reserves for successful reproduction in the Tawny Owl (Strix aluco). Journal of Zoology, London (B) 1:1–20.

HOFFMAN, S, W,, J P SMITH, AND T. D. MEEHAN. 2002. Breeding grounds, winter ranges, and migratory routes of raptors in the mountain west. Journal of Raptor Research 36:97–110.

HOFFMEISTER, D. F. 1971. Mammals of Grand Canyon. University Illinois Press. Urbana, IL.

HOFFMEISTER, D. F. 1986. Mammals of Arizona. University of Arizona Press, Tucson, AZ, and Arizona Game and Fish Department, Phoenix, AZ.

HOFSLUND, P. B. 1973. An invasion of Goshawks. Raptor Research 7:107–108.

HÖGLUND, N. 1964a. Der Habicht (Accipiter gentilis L.) in Fennoskandia. Viltrevy 2:195–269.

HÖGLUND, N. 1964b. Über die Ernährung des Habichts (Accipiter gentilis L.) in Schweden. Viltrevy 2:271–328.

HOLLING, C. S. 1959. Some characteristics of simple types of predation and parasitism. Canadian Entomologist 91:385–398.

HOLSTEIN, V. 1942. Duehøgen. Hirschsprung, Copenhagen, Denmark.

HOLZAPFEL, C., O. HÜPPOP, AND R. MULSOW. 1984. Die Vogelwelt von Hamburg und Umgebung, Band 2. Wachholtz Verlag, Neumünster, Germany.

HÖLZINGER, J. 1987. Forstwirtschaft. Pp. 92–115 in J. Hölzinger (editor). Die Vögel Baden-Württembergs, Band 1.1. Eugen Ulmer Verlag, Stuttgart, Germany.

HOOGE, P. N., W. EICHENLAUB, AND E. SOLOMON. 1999. The animal movement program. USGS, Alaska Biological Science Center, Anchorage, AK.

HORTON, S. P., AND R. W. MANNAN. 1988. Effects of prescribed fire on snags and cavity-nesting birds in southeastern Arizona pine forests. Wildlife Society Bulletin 16: 37–44.

HOSMER, D. W., AND S. LEMESHOW. 1989. Applied logistic regression. John Wiley and Sons, New York, NY.

HOUSTON, C. S. 1975. Close proximity of Red-tailed Hawk and Great Horned Owl nests. Auk 92:612–614.

HOUSTON, C. S., D. G. SMITH, AND C. ROHNER. 1998. Great Horned Owl (Bubo virginianus). In A. Poole, and F. Gill (editors). The birds of North America, No. 372. The Academy of Natural Sciences, Philadelphia, PA and The American Ornithologists' Union, Washington, DC.

HOUSTON, D. C. 1975. Ecological isolation of African scavenging birds. Ardea 63:55–64.

HOWE, R. W., G. J. NIEMI, S. J. LEWIS, AND D. A. WELSH. 1997. A standard method of monitoring songbird populations in the Great Lakes Region. Passenger Pigeon 59:183–194.

HOWELL, J., B. SMITH, J. B. HOLT, JR., AND D. R. OSBORNE. 1978. Habitat structure and productivity in Red-tailed Hawks. Bird Banding 49:162–171.

HUBBARD, J. P. 1992. A taxonomic assessment of the Northern Goshawk in southwestern North America. New Mexico Department of Game and Fish, Santa Fe, NM.

HUHTALA, K. 1976. Kanahaukan ravinnosta. Suomen Luonto 35:305–309.

HUHTALA, K., AND S. SULKAVA. 1976. Kanahaukan pesimäbiologiasta. Suomen Luonto 35:299–303.

HUHTALA, K., AND S. SULKAVA. 1981. Environmental influences on Goshawk breeding in Finland. Pp. 89–104 in R. E. Kenward, and I. M. Lindsay (editors). Understanding the Goshawk. International Association for Falconry and Conservation of Birds of Prey, Oxford, UK.

HUNT, W. G. 1998. Raptor floaters at Moffat's equilibrium. Oikos 82:191–197.

HUNTER, M. D., T OHGUSHI, AND P. W. PRICE (editors). Effects of resource distribution on animal-plant interactions. Academic Press. San Diego, CA.

HUTTO, R. L. 1990. Measuring the availability of food resources. Studies in Avian Biology 13:20–29.

HUTTO, R. L., AND J. S. YOUNG. 2002. Regional landbird monitoring: perspectives from the northern Rocky Mountains. Wildlife Society Bulletin 30:738–750.

HYSLOP, C. 1995. A report on results of national and regional ornithological surveys in Canada. Canadian Wildlife Service, Bird Trends. 4:1–32.

INGLES, L. G. 1965. Mammals of the Pacific states. Stanford University Press. Stanford, CA.

INGRALDI, M. F. 1998. Population biology of Northern Goshawks in east-central Arizona. Arizona Game and Fish Department Technical Report 133. Phoenix, AZ.

INGRALDI, M. F. 1999. Population biology of Northern Goshawks (Accipiter gentilis) in east-central Arizona. Ph.D. dissertation, Northern Arizona University, Flagstaff, AZ.

INGRALDI, M. F., AND S. R. MacVEAN. 1994. Nest-site selection by Northern Goshawks in a ponderosa pine forest in east-central Arizona. Technical Report 47. Nongame and Endangered Wildlife Program, Arizona Game and Fish Department, Phoenix, AZ.

INSIGHTFUL CORP. 2001. S-plus for Windows v. 6.0. Insightful Corporation, Seattle, WA.

IVANOVSKY, V. V. 1998. Current status and breeding ecology of the Goshawk Accipiter gentilis in northern Belarus. Pp. 111–115 in R. D. Chancellor, B. -U. Meyburg, and J. J. Ferrero (editors). Holarctic Birds of Prey, ADENEX-WWGBP, Calamonte, Spain.

IVERSON, G. C, G. D. HAYWARD, K. TITUS, E. DeGAYNER, R. E. LOWELL, D. C. CROCKER-BEDFORD, P. F. SCHEMPF, AND J. LINDELL. 1996. Conservation assessment of the Northern Goshawk in southeast Alaska. USDA Forest Service General Technical Report PNW-GTR 387. USDA Forest Service, Pacific Northwest Research Station, Portland, OR.

JACOB, M., AND K. WITT. 1986. Beutetiere des Habichts (Accipiter gentilis) zur Brutzeit in Berlin 1982–1986. Ornithologische Berichte für Berlin (West) 11:187–195.

JAKSIC, F. M. 1983. The trophic structure of sympatric assemblages of diurnal and nocturnal birds of prey. American Midland Naturalist 109:152–162.

JÄLEFORS, K. 1981. A Goshawk with severe throat injury. Var Fagelvarld 40:218–219.

JAMES, D. A., AND J. C. NEAL. 1986. Arkansas birds: their distribution and abundance. University of Arkansas Press, Fayetteville, AR.

JAMES, F. C., C. A. HESS, AND D. KUFRIN. 1997. Species-centered environmental analysis: indirect effects of fire history on Red-cockaded Woodpeckers. Ecological Applications 7:118–129.

JAMES, F. C., AND H. H. SHUGART, JR. 1970. A quantitative method of habitat description. Audubon Field Notes 24:727–736.

JAMESON, E. W., JR., AND H. PEETERS. 1988. California mammals. University of California Press. Berkeley, CA.

JANES, S. W. 1984. Influences of territory composition and interspecific competition on Red-tailed Hawk reproductive success. Ecology 65:862–870.

JANES, S. W. 1985a. Habitat selection in grassland and open-country birds. Pp. 191–226 in M. L. Cody (editor). Habitat selection in birds. Academic Press, Inc., San Diego, CA.

JANES, S. W. 1985b. Habitat selection in raptorial birds. Pp. 159–188 in M. L. Cody (editor). Habitat selection in birds. Academic Press, Inc., San Diego, CA.

JANSSEN, R. B. 1987. Birds in Minnesota. University of Minnesota Press, Minneapolis, MN.

JĘDRZEJEWSKA, B., AND W. JĘDRZEJEWSKI. 1998. Predation in vertebrate communities. The Białowieża Forest as a case study. Springer Verlag, Berlin, Germany.

JOHANSSON, C., P. J. HARDIN, AND C. M. WHITE. 1994. Large-area habitat modeling in Dixie National Forest using vegetation and elevation data. Studies in Avian Biology 16:50–57.

JOHNSGARD, P. A. 1990. Hawks, eagles, and falcons of North America. Smithsonian Institution Press, Washington, DC.

JOHNSON, D. H. 1979. Estimating nest success: the Mayfield method and an alternative. Auk 96:651–661.

JOHNSON, D. H. 1992. Spotted Owls, Great Horned Owls, and forest fragmentation in the central Oregon Cascades. M.S. thesis, Oregon State University, Corvallis, OR.

JOHNSON, D. R. 1989. Body size of Northern Goshawks on coastal islands of British Columbia. Wilson Bulletin 101:637–639.

JOHNSON, K. N., J. F. FRANKLIN, J. W.THOMAS, AND J. GORDON. 1991. Alternatives for management of late-successional forests of the Pacific Northwest. A report to the Agriculture Committee and the Merchant Marine and Fisheries Committee of the U.S. House of Representatives, Washington, DC.

JOHNSON, M. A. 1994. Changes in southwestern forests: stewardship implications. Journal of Forestry. 12:16–19.

JOHNSON, M. L., AND M. S. GAINES. 1990. Evolution of dispersal: theoretical models and empirical tests using birds and mammals. Annual Review of Ecology and Systematics 21:449–480.

JOIRIS, C., AND K. DELBEKE. 1985. Contamination by PCBs and organochlorine pesticides of Belgian birds of prey, their eggs and their food, 1969–1982. Pp. 403–414 in H. W. Nurnberg (editor). Pollutants and their Ecotoxicological Significance. John Wiley & Sons Ltd., London, UK.

JOLLY, G. M. 1965. Explicit estimates from capture-recapture data with both death and immigration—stochastic model. Biometrika 52:225–247.

JØRGENSEN, H. E. 1989. Danmarks Rovfugle—en statusoversigt. Frederikshus, Øster Ulslev, Denmark.

JØRGENSEN, H. E. 1998. Status for de danske rovfuglebestande. Dansk Ornitologisk Forenings Tidsskrift 92:299–306.

JOUBERT, B. 1994. Autour des palombes. Pp. 190–191 in D. Yeatman-Berthelot (editor). Nouvel atlas des oiseaux nicheurs de France 1985–1989. Société Ornithologique de France, Paris, France.

JOUBERT, B., AND T. MARGERIT. 1986. Aspects du comportement de l'Autour, *Accipiter gentilis*, en Haute-Loire. Nos Oiseaux 38:209–228.

JOY, S. M. 1990. Feeding ecology of Sharp-shinned Hawks and nest-site characteristics of accipiters in Colorado. M.S. thesis, Colorado State University, Ft. Collins, CO.

JOY, S. M. 2002. Northern Goshawk habitat on the Kaibab National Forest in Arizona: factors affecting nest locations and territory quality. Ph.D. disseration, Colorado State University, Ft. Collins, CO.

JOY, S. M., R. T. REYNOLDS, AND D. G. LESLIE. 1994. Northern Goshawk broadcast surveys: hawk response variables and survey cost. Studies in Avian Biology 16:24–30.

KALABÉR, L. 1984. Notes on the biology and the post-embryonic development of the Goshawk *Accipiter gentilis* in Romania. Rivista Italiana di Ornitologia 54: 179–190. (in Italian).

KAPLAN, E. L., AND P. MEIER. 1958. Nonparametric estimation from incomplete observations. Journal of the American Statistical Association 53:457–481.

KARR, J. R., I. J. SCHLOSSER, AND M. DIONNE. 1992. Bottom-up versus top-down regulation of vertebrate populations: lessons from birds and fish. Pp, 243–286 *in* M. D. Hunter, T. Ohgushi, and P. W. Price (editors). Effects of resource distribution on animal-plant Interactions. Academic Press, San Diego, CA.

KAUFMANN, M. R., C. M. REGAN, AND P. M. BROWN. 2000. Heterogeneity in ponderosa pine/Douglas-fir forests: age and size structure in unlogged and logged landscapes of central Colorado. Canadian Journal of Forest Research 30:698–711.

KAUHALA, K., P. HELLE, AND E. HELLE. 2000. Predator control and the density and reproductive success of grouse populations in Finland. Ecography 23:161–168.

KAYSER, Y. 1993. Le régime alimentaire de l'Autour des palombes, *Accipiter gentilis* (L.), en Alsace. Ciconia 17:143–166.

KAZAKOV, V. P. 2003. Goshawk in the Balatov forest park of city Perm. Pp. 82–83 *in* V. P. Belik (editor). Goshawk: position in ecosystems of Russia. Materials of the 4th North-Eurasian Conference on Raptors, Penza, Russia. (in Russian).

KEANE, J. J. 1999. Ecology of the Northern Goshawk in the Sierra Nevada, California. Ph.D. dissertation, University of California, Davis, CA

KEANE, J. J., AND M. L. MORRISON. 1994. Northern Goshawk ecology: effects of scale and levels of biological organization. Studies in Avian Biology 6:3–11.

KEHL, G., AND M. ZERNING. 1993. Der Greifvogelbestand und seine Reproduktion auf einer Kontrollfläche bei Potsdam. Naturschutz und Landschaftspflege Brandenburg 2 (Special issue 2):10–18.

KEITH, J. O. 1965. The Abert squirrel and its dependence on ponderosa pine. Ecology 46:150–165.

KEITH, L. B., AND D. H. RUSCH. 1989. Predation's role in the cyclic fluctuations of Ruffed Grouse. Proceedings of the International Ornithological Congress 14: 699–732.

KEITH, L. B., A. W. TODD, C. J. BRAND, R. S. ADAMCIK, AND D. H. RUSCH. 1977. An analysis of predation during a cyclic fluctuation on snowshoe hares. Proceedings International Congress of Game Biologists 13:163–174.

KELLY, E. G., E. D. FORSMAN, AND R. G. ANTHONY. 2003. Are Barred Owls displacing Spotted Owls? Condor 105:45–53.

KEMP, G. A., AND L. B. KEITH. 1970. Dynamics and regulation of red squirrel (*Tamiasciurus hudsonicus*) populations. Ecology 51:763–779.

KENNEDY, J. 2003. A report on results of national ornithological surveys in Canada. Canadian Wildlife Service, Bird Trends 9:1–68.

KENNEDY, P. L. 1988. Habitat characteristics of Cooper's Hawks and Northern Goshawks nesting in New Mexico. Pp. 218–227 *in* R. L. Glinski, B. Giron Pendleton, M. B. Moss, M. N. LeFranc Jr., B. A. Millsap, and S. W. Hoffman (editors). National Wildlife Federation Scientific and Technical Series No. 11, Washington, DC.

KENNEDY, P. L. 1989. The nesting ecology of Cooper's Hawks and Northern Goshawks in the Jemez Mountains, NM. Final Report 35. USDA Forest Service, Santa Fe National Forest. Santa Fe, NM

KENNEDY, P. L. 1990. Home ranges of Northern Goshawks nesting in north central New Mexico. P. 259 *in* P. R. Klausmen, and N. S. Smith (editors). Managing wildlife in the Southwest symposium. Arizona Chapter of the Wildlife Society, Phoenix, AZ.

KENNEDY, P. L. 1991. Reproductive strategies of Northern Goshawks and Cooper's Hawks in north-central New Mexico. Ph.D. dissertation, Utah State University, Logan, UT.

KENNEDY, P. L. 1997. The Northern Goshawk (*Accipiter gentilis atricapillus*): is there evidence of a population decline? Journal of Raptor Research 31:95–106.

KENNEDY, P. L. 1998. Evaluating Northern Goshawk (*Accipiter gentilis atricapillus*) population trends: a reply to Smallwood and Crocker-Bedford. Journal of Raptor Research 32:336–342.

KENNEDY, P. L. 2003. Northern Goshawk conservation assessment for Region 2, USDA Forest Service. <http://www.fs.fed.us/r2/projects/scp/assessments/ northerngoshawk.pdf> (27 September 2005).

KENNEDY, P. L., AND D. E. ANDERSEN. 1999. Research and monitoring plan for Northern Goshawks in the western Great Lakes region, Final Report. Minnesota Cooperative Fish and Wildlife Research Unit, University of Minnesota, St. Paul, MN.

KENNEDY, P. L., AND D. W. STAHLECKER. 1993. Responsiveness of nesting Northern Goshawks to taped broadcasts of 3 conspecific calls. Journal of Wildlife Management 57:249–257.

KENNEDY, P. L., AND J. M. WARD. 2003. Effects of experimental food supplementation on movements of juvenile Northern Goshawks (*Accipiter gentilis atricapillus*). Oecologia 134:284–291.

KENNEDY, P. L., J. M. WARD, G. A. RINKER, AND J. A. GESSAMAN. 1994. Post-fledging areas in Northern

Goshawk home ranges. Studies in Avian Biology 16: 75–82.

KENNTNER, N., O. KRONE, R. ALTENKAMP, AND F. TATARUCH. 2003. Environmental contaminants in liver and kidney of free-ranging Northern Goshawks (*Accipiter gentilis*) from three regions of Germany. Archives of Environmental Contamination and Toxicology 45: 128–135.

KENWARD, R. E. 1976. The effect of predation by Goshawks, *Accipiter gentilis*, on Woodpigeon, *Columba palumbus*, populations. Ph.D. dissertation, University of Oxford., Oxford, UK.

KENWARD, R. E. 1977. Predation on released pheasants (*Phasianus colchicus*) by Goshawks (*Accipiter gentilis*) in central Sweden. Viltrevy 10:79–109.

KENWARD, R. E. 1978a. Hawks and doves: factors affecting success and selection in Goshawk attacks on Woodpigeons. Journal of Animal Ecology 47:449–460.

KENWARD, R. E. 1978b. The influence of human and Goshawk *Accipiter gentilis* activity on Woodpigeons *Columba palumbus* at brassica feeding sites. Annals of Applied Biology 89:277–286.

KENWARD, R. E. 1979. Winter predation by Goshawks in lowland Britain. British Birds 72:64–73.

KENWARD, R. E. 1982. Goshawk hunting behaviour and range size as a function of food and habitat availability. Journal of Animal Ecology 51:69–80.

KENWARD, R. E. 1986. Problems of Goshawk predation on pigeons and some other game. Proceedings of the International Ornithological Congress 18:666–678.

KENWARD, R. E. 1996. Goshawk adaptation to deforestation: does Europe differ from North America? Pp. 233–243 *in* D. M. Bird, D. E. Varland, and J. J. Negro (editors). Raptors in human landscapes. Academic Press. New York, NY.

KENWARD, R. E. 2000. Socio-economic problems and solutions in raptor predation. Pp. 565–570 *in* R. D. Chancellor, and B.-U. Meyburg (editors). Raptors at risk. WWGBP/Hancock House, Berlin, Germany.

KENWARD, R. E. 2002. Identifying the real threats to raptor populations. Pp. 15–21 *in* R. Yosef, M. L. Miller, and D. Pepler (editors). Raptors in the new millenium. International Birding and Research Center in Eilat, Eilat, Israel.

KENWARD, R. E. 2004. Management tools for raptors. Pp. 329–339 *in* R. D. Chancellor, and B.-U. Meyburg (editors). Raptors worldwide. World Working Group on Birds of Prey and Owls, Berlin, Germany.

KENWARD, R. E., HALL, D. G., WALLS, S. S., AND K. H. HODDER. 2001. Factors affecting predation by Buzzards (*Buteo buteo*) on released pheasants (*Phasianus colchicus*). Journal of Applied Ecology 38:813–822.

KENWARD, R. E., M. KARLBOM, AND V. MARCSTRÖM. 1983. The price of success in Goshawk trapping. Raptor Research 17:84–91.

KENWARD, R. E., AND I. M. LINDSAY (EDITORS). 1981. Understanding the Goshawk. International Association for Falconry and Conservation of Birds of Prey, Oxford, UK.

KENWARD, R. E., AND V. MARCSTRÖM. 1981. Goshawk predation on game and poultry: some problems and solutions. Pp. 152–162 *in* R. E. Kenward, and I. M. Lindsay (editors). Understanding the Goshawk. International Association for Falconry and Conservation of Birds of Prey, Oxford, UK.

KENWARD, R. E., AND V. MARCSTRÖM. 1988. How differential competence could sustain suppressive predation on birds. Proceedings of the International Ornithological Congress 14:733–742.

KENWARD, R. E., V. MARCSTRÖM, AND M. KARLBOM. 1981a. Goshawk winter ecology in Swedish pheasant habitats. Journal of Wildlife Management 45:397–408.

KENWARD, R. E., V. MARCSTRÖM, AND M. KARLBOM. 1990. The impact of man and other mortality on radio-tagged Goshawks. Transactions of the International Union of Game Biologists 19:116.

KENWARD, R. E., V. MARCSTRÖM, AND M. KARLBOM. 1991. The Goshawk (*Accipiter gentilis*) as predator and renewable resource. Gibier et Faune Sauvage 8: 367–378.

KENWARD, R. E., V. MARCSTRÖM, AND M. KARLBOM. 1993a. Post-nestling behaviour in Goshawks, *Accipiter gentilis*: I. The causes of dispersal. Animal Behaviour 46: 365–370.

KENWARD, R. E., V. MARCSTRÖM, AND M. KARLBOM. 1993b. Post-nestling behaviour in Goshawks, *Accipiter gentilis*: II. Sex differences in sociality and nest-switching. Animal Behaviour 46:371–378.

KENWARD, R. E., V. MARCSTRÖM, AND M. KARLBOM. 1993c. Causes of death in radio-tagged Northern Goshawks. Pp. 57–61 *in* P. Redig, J. Cooper, D. Remple, D. Hunter, and T. Hahn (editors). Raptor biomedicine. University of Minnesota Press, Minneapolis, MN.

KENWARD, R. E., V. MARCSTRÖM, AND M. KARLBOM. 1999. Demographic estimates from radio-tagging: models of age-specific survival and breeding in the Goshawk. Journal of Animal Ecology 68:1020–1033.

KENWARD, R. E., M. MARQUISS, AND I. NEWTON. 1981b. What happens to Goshawks trained for falconry? Journal of Wildlife Management 45:803–806.

KENWARD, R. E., AND S. S. WALLS. 1994. The systematic study of radio-tagged raptors: I. survival, home-range and habitat-use. Pp. 303–315 *in* B.-U. Meyburg, and R. D. Chancellor (editors). Raptor conservation today. WWGBP/The Pica Press, East Sussex, UK.

KENWARD, R. E., S. S. WALLS, K. H. HODDER, M. PAHKALA, S. N. FREEMAN, AND V. R. SIMPSON. 2000. The prevalence of non-breeders in raptor populations: evidence from rings, radio-tags and transect surveys. Oikos 91: 271–279.

KENWARD, R. E., AND P. WIDÉN. 1989. Do Goshawks *Accipiter gentilis* need forests? Some conservation lessons from radio tracking. Pp. 561–567 *in* B.-U. Meyburg, and R. D. Chancellor (editors). Raptors in the modern world. World Working Group on Birds of Prey, Berlin, Germany.

KERAN, D. 1981. The incidence of man-caused and natural mortalities to raptors. Raptor Research 15:108–112.

KEYMER, I. F. 1972. Diseases of birds of prey. Veterinary Record 90:579–594.

KEYMER, I. F., M. R. FLETCHER, AND P. I. STANLEY. 1981. Causes of mortality on British Kestrels (*Falco tinnunculus*). Pp. 143–151 *in* J. E. Cooper, and A. G. Greenwood (editors). Recent advances in the study of raptor diseases. Chiron Publications, Ltd., Keighley, West Yorkshire, UK.

KIIL, A. D., AND J. E. GRIGEL. 1969. The May 1968 forest conflagrations in central Alberta. Information Report A-X-24. Forest Research Laboratory, Edmonton, AB, Canada.

KIMMEL, J. T. 1995. Spatial hierarchy of habitat use by Northern Goshawks in two forest regions of Pennsylvania. Ph.D. dissertation, The Pennsylvania State University, University Park, PA.

KIMMEL, J. T., AND R. H. YAHNER. 1994. The Northern Goshawk in Pennsylvania: habitat use, survey protocols, and status Final Report. School of Forestry Resources, The Pennsylvania State University, University Park, PA.

KIRK, D. A., AND C. HYSLOP. 1998. Population status and recent trends in Canadian raptors: a review. Biological Conservation 83:91–118.

KLENNER, W., AND C. J. KREBS. 1991. Red squirrel population dynamics. I. The effect of supplemental food on demography. Journal of Animal Ecology 60:961–978.

KLUTH, S. 1984. Untersuchung zur Beutewahl des Habichts (*Accipiter gentilis* L.): Test der Telemetrie und Kritik bisher angewandter Methoden. Diploma thesis, University of Munich (Ludwig-Maximilian), Munich, Germany.

KNÜWER, H. 1981. Ergebnisse einer fünfjährigen Greifvogelbestandsaufnahme im Münsterland. Charadrius 17: 131–143.

KOCHERT, M. N., B. A. MILLSAP, AND K. STEENHOF. 1987. Pp. 325–334 *in* B. Giron Pendleton (editor). Effects of livestock grazing on raptors with emphasis on the southwestern United States. Proceedings of the western management symposium and workshop. National Wildlife Federation Scientific and Technical Series 12. Washington, DC.

KOEMAN, J. H., AND H. VAN GENDEREN. 1965. Some preliminary notes on residues of chlorinated hydrocarbon insecticides in birds and mammals in the Netherlands. Mededelingen Landbouwhogeschool Gent 30: 1879–1887.

KOENIG, W. D., D. VAN VUREN, AND P. N. HOOGE. 1996. Detectability, philopatry, and the distribution of dispersal distances in vertebrates. Trends in Ecology and Evolution 11:514–517.

KOLLINGER, D. 1974. Erkenntnisse über den Habicht (*Accipiter gentilis*) und seinen heutigen Stand. Jahrbuch des Deutschen Falkenordens 1974:9–18.

KONING, F. J., AND G. BAEYENS. 1990. Uilen in de duinen. Stichting Uitgeverij Koninklijke Nederlandse Natuurhistorische Vereniging, Utrecht, The Netherlands.

KORPIMÄKI, E. 1985. Rapid tracking of microtine populations by their avian predators: possible evidence for stabilizing predation. Oikos 45:281–284.

KORPIMÄKI, E. 1993. Does nest-hole quality, poor breeding success or food depletion drive the breeding dispersal of Tengmalm's Owls? Journal of Animal Ecology 62: 606–613.

KORPIMÄKI, E. 1994. Rapid or delayed tracking of multiannual vole cycles by avian predators? Journal of Animal Ecology 63:619–628.

KORPIMÄKI, E., H. HAKKARAINEN, AND G. F. BENNETT. 1993. Blood parasites and reproductive success of Tengmalm's Owls: detrimental effects of females but not males. Functional Ecology 7:420–426.

KORPIMÄKI, E., AND C. J. KREBS. 1996. Predation and population cycles of small mammals: a reassessment of the predation hypothesis. BioScience 46:754–764.

KORPIMÄKI, E., K. LAGERSTRÖM, AND P. SAUROLA. 1987. Field evidence for nomadism in Tengmalm's Owl *Aegolius funereus*. Ornis Scandinavica 18:1–4.

KORPIMÄKI, E., AND K. NORRDAHL. 1989. Predation of Tengmalm's Owls: numerical responses, functional responses and dampening impact on population fluctuations of microtines. Oikos 54:154–164.

KORPIMÄKI, E., AND K. NORRDAHL. 1991. Do breeding nomadic avian predators dampen population fluctuations of small mammals? Oikos 62:195–208.

KORPIMÄKI, E., AND K. NORRDAHL. 1997. Can the alternative prey hypothesis explain the occurrence of short-term population cycles of small game in Finland? Suomen Riista 43:72–84.

KOS, R. 1980. Der Habicht in der Bundesrepublik Deutschland. Vogelwelt 101:161–175.

KOSTRZEWA, A. 1986. Quantitative Untersuchungen zur Ökologie, Habitatstruktur und Habitattrennung von Mäusebussard (*Buteo buteo*), Habicht (*Accipiter gentilis*) und Wespenbussard (*Pernis apivorus*) unter Berücksichtigung von Naturschutzmanagement und Landschaftsplanung. Ph.D. dissertation, University of Cologne, Cologne, Germany.

KOSTRZEWA, A. 1987a. Quantitative Untersuchungen zur Habitattrennung von Mäusebussard (*Buteo buteo*), Habicht (*Accipiter gentilis*) und Wespenbussard (*Pernis apivorus*). Journal für Ornithologie 128: 209–229.

KOSTRZEWA, A. 1987b. Territorialität, Konkurrenz und Horstnutzung dreier baumbrütender Greifvogelarten (Accipitres). Journal für Ornithologie 128:495–496.

KOSTRZEWA, A. 1991. Interspecific interference competition in three European raptor species. Ethology, Ecology and Evolution 3:127–143.

KOSTRZEWA, A. 1996. A comparative study of nest-site occupancy and breeding performance as indicators for nesting-habitat quality in three European raptor species. Ethology, Ecology and Evolution 8:1–18.

KOSTRZEWA, A., AND R. KOSTRZEWA. 1990. The relationship of spring and summer weather with density and breeding performance of the Buzzard *Buteo buteo*, Goshawk *Accipiter gentilis* and Kestrel *Falco tinnunculus*. Ibis 132:550–559.

KOSTRZEWA, A., AND G. SPEER (EDITORS). 2001. Greifvögel in Deutschland: Bestand, Situation, Schutz. 2., vollst. neu bearb. und erw. Auflage. AULA-Verlag, Wiebelsheim, Germany.

KOSTRZEWA, A., R. SPEER, W. VON DEWITZ, AND H. WEISER. 2000. Zur Populationsökologie des Habichts (*Accipiter gentilis*) in der Niederrheinischen Bucht (1981–1998). Charadrius 36:80–93.

KOSTRZEWA, R., AND A. KOSTRZEWA. 1991. Winter weather, spring and summer density, and subsequent breeding success of Eurasian Kestrels, Common Buzzards, and Northern Goshawks. Auk 108:342–347.

KRAMER, V. 1972. Habicht und Sperber. Die Neue Brehm-Bücherei, Bd. 158 (2nd ed.). Ziemsen Verlag, Wittenberg Lutherstadt, Germany.

KREBS, C. J. 1996. Population cycles revisited. Journal of Mammalogy 77:8–24.

KREBS, C. J., S. BOUTIN, AND R. BOONSTRA. 2001. Ecosystem dynamics of the boreal forest: the Kluane Project. Oxford University Press, Oxford, UK.

KREBS, J. R., M. I. AVERY, AND A. I. HOUSTON. 1987. Delivering food to a central place: three studies of Bee-eaters *Merops apiaster*. Pp. 173–192 *in* A. C. Kamil, J. R. Krebs, and H. R. Pulliam (editors). Foraging behavior. Plenum Press, New York, NY.

KREBS, J. R., J. D. WILSON, R. B. BRADBURY, AND G. M. SIRIWARDENA. 1999. The second silent spring? Nature 400:611–612.

KREN, J. 2000. Birds of the Czech Republic. Helm, London, UK.

KRÓL, W. 1985. Breeding density of diurnal raptors in the neighbourhood of Susz (Iława Lakeland, Poland) in the years 1977–79. Acta Ornithologica 21:95–114.

KRONE, O. 1998. Endoparasiten (Faunistik, Epizootiologie, Pathogenität) bei wildlebenden Greifvögeln aus drei verschiedenen Gebieten Deutschlands. Ph.D. dissertation, University of Berlin (Freie), Berlin, Germany.

KRONE, O., R. ALTENKAMP, AND N. KENNTNER. 2005. Prevalence of *Trichomonas gallinae* in Northern Goshawks from the Berlin area of northeastern Germany. Journal of Wildlife Diseases 41:304–309.

KRONE, O., J. PRIEMER, J. STREICH, P. SÖMMER, T. LANGGEMACH, AND O. LESSOW. 2001. Haemosporida of birds of prey and owls from Germany. Acta Protozoologica 40:281–289.

KRÜGER, O. 1996. Besonderheiten der Revierstruktur des Habichts (*Accipiter gentilis*) im Teutoburger Wald. Charadrius 32:110–112.

KRÜGER, O. 2002a. Analysis of nest occupancy and nest reproduction in two sympatric raptors: Common Buzzard *Buteo buteo* and Goshawk *Accipiter gentilis*. Ecography 25:523–532.

KRÜGER, O. 2002b. Interactions between Common Buzzard *Buteo buteo* and Goshawk *Accipiter gentilis*: trade-offs revealed by a field experiment. Oikos 96:441–452.

KRÜGER, O., AND J. LINDSTRÖM. 2001. Habitat heterogeneity affects population growth in Goshawk *Accipiter gentilis*. Journal of Animal Ecology 70:173–181.

KRÜGER, O., AND U. STEFENER. 1996. Nahrungsökologie und Populationsdynamik des Habichts *Accipiter gentilis* im östlichen Westfalen. Vogelwelt 117:1–8.

KRÜGER, O., AND U. STEFENER. 2000. Populationsfluktuation und die Rolle der Reproduktion in einer Population des Habichts *Accipiter gentilis*. Populationsökologie Greifvogel- und Eulenarten 4:263–271.

KÜHNAPFEL, O., AND J. BRUNE. 1995. Die Mauserfeder als Hilfsmittel zur Altersbestimmung und Individualerkennung von Habichten (*Accipiter gentilis*). Charadrius 31:120–125.

KURKI, S., P. HELLE, H. LINDÉN, H., AND A. NIKULA. 1997. Breeding success of Black Grouse and Capercaillie in relation to mammalian predator densities on two spatial scales. Oikos 79:301–310.

LA SORTE, F. A., R. W. MANNAN, R. T. REYNOLDS, AND T. G. GRUBB. 2004. Habitat associations of sympatric Red-tailed Hawks and Northern Goshawks on the Kaibab Plateau. Journal of Wildlife Management 68:307–317.

LACK, D. 1966. Population studies of birds. Oxford University Press, Oxford, UK.

LAHAYE, W. S., G. S. ZIMMERMAN, AND R. J. GUTIÉRREZ. 2004. Temporal variation in the vital rates of an insular population of Spotted Owls (*Strix occidentalis occidentalis*): contrasting effects of weather. Auk 121:1056–1069.

LAMBECK, R.J. 1997. Focal species: a multi-species umbrella for nature conservation. Conservation Biology 11:849–856.

LANDE, R. 1987. Extinction thresholds in demographic models of territorial populations. American Naturalist 130:624–635.

LANDE, R., S. ENGEN, AND B. E. SÆTHER. 2003. Stochastic population dynamics in ecology and conservation. Oxford University Press, Oxford, UK.

LANDRES, P. B., J. VERNER, AND J. W. THOMAS. 1988. Ecological uses of vertebrate indicator species: a critique. Conservation Biology 2:316–328.

LANG, P. A. 1994. Spatial analyses of Northern Goshawk ponderosa pine nest site habitat in east-central Arizona. M.S. thesis, Northern Arizona University Flagstaff, AZ.

LAPINSKI, N. W. 2000. Habitat use and productivity of the Northern Goshawk in the upper peninsula of Michigan. M.S. thesis, Northern Michigan University, Marquette, MI.

LAPINSKI, N., W. BOWERMAN, AND S. SJOGREN. 2000. Factors affecting the Northern Goshawk in the Upper Peninsula of Michigan. Pp. 182–191 *in* R. Yosef, M. L. Miller, and D. Pepler (editors). Raptors in the new millenium. International Birding and Research Center, Eilat, Israel.

LARSEN, K. W., AND S. BOUTIN. 1995. Exploring territory quality in the North American red squirrel through removal experiments. Canadian Journal of Zoology 73:1115–1122.

LAWRENCE, L. DE K. 1967. A comparative life-history study of four species of woodpeckers. Ornithological Monographs No. 5.

LAYNE, J. N. 1954. The biology of the red squirrel *Tamiasciurus hudsonicus loquax* (Bangs), in central New York. Ecological Monographs 24:227–267.

LEBRETON, J. D., AND J. CLOBERT. 1991. Bird population dynamics, management, and conservation: the role of mathematical modeling. Pp. 105–125 *in* C. M. Perrins, J. D. Lebreton, and G. J. Hirons (editors). Bird population studies: relevance to conservation and management. Oxford University Press, Oxford, UK.

LECHNER, B. S. 2003. Home Ranges urbaner und ruraler Habichte (*Accipiter gentilis*): Fallbeispiele aus Hamburg und Schleswig-Holstein. Diploma thesis, University of Vienna, Vienna, Austria.

LEE, J. A. 1981a. Comparative breeding behavior of the Goshawk and the Cooper's Hawk. M.S. thesis, Brigham Young University, Provo, UT.

LEE, J. A. 1981b. Habituation to human disturbance in nesting accipiters. Raptor Research 15:48–52.

LEHMAN, R. N., AND J. W. ALLENDORF. 1987. Pp. 236–244 *in* B. Giron Pendleton (editor).The effects of fire, fire exclusion, and fire management on raptor habitats in the western United States. Proceedings of the western management symposium and workshop. National Wildlife Federation Scientific and Technical Series 12. Washington, DC.

LEHMKUHL, J. F., AND M. G. RAPHAEL. 1998. Habitat pattern around Northern Spotted Owl locations on the Olympic Peninsula. Journal of Wildlife Management 57:302–315.

LELOV, E. 1991. Breeding raptors and owls at Halinga, SW Estonia, in 1978–1989. Ornis Fennica 68:119–122.

LENSINK, R. 1997. Range expansion of raptors in Britain and the Netherlands since the 1960s: testing an individual-based diffusion model. Journal of Animal Ecology 66: 811–826.

LENSINK, R. 2002. Nijlgans *Alopochen aegyptiacus*. Pp. 108–109 *in* SOVON. Atlas van de Nederlandse Broedvogels 1998–2000, Nederlandse Fauna 5. Nationaal Natuurhistorisch Museum Naturalis, KNNV Uitgeverij and European Invertebrate Survey-Nederland, Leiden, The Netherlands.

LESSOW, O. 2001. Photograph in "Monthly Marathon" (plate 108). British Birds 94:214–215.

LEVINS, R. 1969. The effects of random variations of different types on population growth. Proceedings of the National Academy of Sciences 62:1061–1065.

LEVINS, R. 1970. Extinction. Lectures on Mathematics in the Life Sciences 2:75–107.

LEVY, P. S., AND S. LEMESHOW. 1999. Sampling of populations: methods and applications, 3rd edition, John Wiley and Sons New York, NY.

LEWIS, S. B. 2001. Breeding season diet of Northern Goshawks in southeast Alaska with a comparison of techniques used to examine raptor diet. M.S. thesis, Boise State University, Boise, ID.

LEWIS, S. B. 2003. Delivery and consumption of a Pigeon Guillemot by nesting Northern Goshawks in southeast Alaska. Wilson Bulletin 115:483–485.

LEWIS, S. B., M. R. FULLER, AND K. TITUS. 2004. A comparison of 3 methods for assessing raptor diet during the breeding season. Wildlife Society Bulletin 32:373–385.

LI, P AND, T. E. MARTIN. 1991. Nest-site selection and nesting success of cavity-nesting birds in high elevation forest drainages. Auk 108:405–418.

LIERZ, M., T. GÖBEL, AND E. F. KALETA. 2002a. Investigations on the prevalence of *Chlamydophila psittaci*, falcon herpesvirus and paramyxovirus 1 in birds of prey and owls found injured or debilitated Tierärztliche Praxis Ausgabe Kleintiere Heimtiere 30:139–144.

LIERZ, M., T. GÖBEL, AND R. SCHUSTER. 2002b. Review and investigations on parasites in birds of prey and owls found injured or debilitated. Berliner und Munchener Tierarztliche Wochenschrift 115:43–52.

LILIEHOLM, R. J., W. B. KESSLER, AND K. MERRILL. 1993. Stand density index applied to timber and goshawk habitat objectives in Douglas-fir. Environmental Management 17:773–779.

LILIEHOLM, R. J., J. N. LONG, AND S. PATLA. 1994. Assessment of Goshawk nest area habitat using stand density index. Studies in Avian Biology 16:18–23.

LINDÉN, H., I. P. DANILOV, A. N. GROMTSEV, P. HELLE, E. N. IVANTER, AND J. KURHINEN. 2000. Large-scale forest corridors to connect the taiga fauna to Fennoscandia. Wildlife Biology 6:179–188.

LINDÉN, H., AND P. RAJALA. 1981. Fluctuations and long-term trends in the relative densities of tetraonid populations in Finland 1964–1977. Finnish Game Research 39:13–34.

LINDÉN, H., AND M. WIKMAN, 1980. Kanahaukan poikuekoon vaihtelusta suhteessa metsäkanalintujen runsauteen. Suomen Riista 27:63–69.

LINDÉN, H., AND M. WIKMAN. 1983. Goshawk predation on tetraonids: availability of prey and diet of the predator in the breeding season. Journal of Animal Ecology 52: 953–968.

LINDSTRÖM, E. R., H. ANDREN, P. ANGELSTAM, G. CEDERLUND, B. HÖRNFELDT, L. JÄDERBERG, P. LEMNELL, B. MARTINSSON, K. SKÖLDT, AND J. E. SWENSON. 1994. Disease reveals the predator: sarcoptic mange, red fox predation, and prey populations. Ecology 75: 1042–1049.

LINK, H. 1981. Goshawk status in Bavaria. Pp. 57–68 *in* R. E. Kenward, and I. M. Lindsay (editors). Understanding the Goshawk. International Association for Falconry and Conservation of Birds of Prey, Oxford, UK.

LINK, H. 1986. Untersuchungen am Habicht (*Accipiter gentilis*): Habitatwahl, Ethologie, Populationsökologie. DFO Schriftenreihe, Heft 2. Ph.D. dissertation, University of Erlangen-Nürnberg, Nürnberg, Germany.

LINKOLA, P. 1957. Kanahaukkakannan romahdus vuonna 1956. Luonnon tutkija 61:49–58.

LINT, J., B. NOON, R. ANTHONY, E. FORSMAN, M. RAPHAEL, M. COLLOPY, AND E. STARKEY. 1999. Northern Spotted Owl effectiveness monitoring plan for the Northwest Forest Plan. USDA Forest Service General Technical Report PNW-GTR-440. USDA Forest Service, Pacific Northwest Research Station, Portland, OR.

LÕHMUS, A. 1993. Kanakulli (*Accipiter gentilis*) toitumisest Eestis aastatel 1987–92. Hirundo 2:3–14.

LÕHMUS, A. 2001. Selection of foraging habitats by birds of prey in northwestern Tartumaa. Hirundo 14:39–42.

LÕHMUS, A. 2004. Röövlinnuseire 1999–2003: kanakulli kadu ja hiiretsüklite kellavärk. Hirundo 17:3–18.

LONG, J. N., AND F. W. SMITH. 2000. Restructuring the forest, goshawks and the restoration of southwestern ponderosa pine. Journal of Forestry 98:25–30.

LOOFT, V. 1981. Habicht—*Accipiter gentilis*. Pp. 101–115 *in* V. Looft, and G. Busche (editors). Vogelwelt Schleswig-Holsteins, Band 2: Greifvögel. Karl Wachholtz Verlag, Neumünster, Germany.

LOOFT, V. 1984. Die Entwicklung des Habichtbestandes (*Accipiter gentilis*) in Schleswig-Holstein 1968–1984. Corax 10:395–400.

LOOFT, V. 2000. The ups and downs of a Northern Goshawk *Accipiter gentilis* population over a 30 year period—natural dynamics or an artefact? Pp. 499–506 *in* R. D. Chancellor, and B.-U. Meyburg (editors). Raptors at risk. World Working Group on Birds of Prey and Owls, Berlin, Germany.

LOOPE, L. L. 1969. Subalpine and alpine vegetation of northeastern Nevada. Ph.D. dissertation, Duke University, Durham, NC.

LOWE, P. O. 1975. Effects of wildfire on wildlife populations in Arizona ponderosa pine. M.S. thesis, University of Arizona, Tucson, AZ.

LUCAS, P., AND R. J. OAKLEAF. 1975. Population surveys, species distribution, and key habitats of selected non-game species. Federal Aid Wildlife Restoration Project. W-53-R, Study 1, Nevada Department of Fish and Game, Reno, NV.

LUMEIJ, J. T., G. M. DORRESTEIN, AND J. W. E. STAM. 1981. Observations on tuberculosis in raptors. Pp. 137–141 *in* J. E. Cooper, and A. G. Greenwood (editors). Advances in the study of raptor diseases: proceedings of the international symposium on diseases of birds of prey. Chiron Publishers, West Yorkshire, UK.

LUTTICH, S. N., L. B. KEITH, AND J. D. STEPHENSON. 1971. Population dynamics of the Red-tailed Hawk (*Buteo jamaicensis*) at Rochester, Alberta. Auk 88:73–87.

LUTTICH, S., D. H. RUSCH, E. C. MESLOW, AND L. B. KEITH. 1970. Ecology of Red-tailed Hawk predation in Alberta. Ecology 51:190–203.

MACCRACKEN, J. G. 1996. Forest health in the inland Northwest: maintaining the focus. Wildlife Society Bulletin 24:325–329.

MACE, R. D., J. S. WALLER, T. L. MANLEY, K. AKE, AND W. T. WITTINGER. 1999. Landscape evaluation of grizzly bear habitat in western Montana. Conservation Biology 13:367–377.

MACKENZIE, D. I., J. D. NICHOLS, J. E. HINES, M. G. KNUTSON, AND A. B. FRANKLIN. 2003. Estimating site occupancy, colonization, and local extinction when a species is detected imperfectly. Ecology 84:2200–2207.

MACKENZIE, D. I., J. D. NICHOLS, G. B. LACHMAN, S. DROEGE, J. A. ROYLE, AND C. A. LANGTIMM. 2002. Estimating site occupancy rates when detection probabilities are less than one. Ecology 83:2248–2255.

MÄDLOW, W., AND C. MAYR. 1996. Die Bestandsentwicklung ausgewählter gefährdeter Vogelarten in Deutschland 1990–1994. Vogelwelt 117:249–260.

MADSEN, S., D. EVANS, T. HAMER, P. HENSON, S. MILLER, S. NELSON, D. ROBY, AND M. STAPANIAN. 1999. Marbled Murrelet effectiveness monitoring plan for the Northwest Forest Plan. USDA Forest Service General Technical Report PNW-GTR-439. USDA Forest Service, Pacific Northwest Research Station, Portland, OR.

MAHON, T. F., AND F. I. DOYLE. 2003a. The Northern Goshawk in the Lakes and Morice Forest Districts: 5-year project summary and management recommendations. Babine Forest Products Ltd., Burns Lakes, BC and Houston Forest Products Ltd., Houston, BC, Canada.

MAHON, T., F., AND F. I. DOYLE. 2003b. Foraging habitat selection, prey availability, and reproductive success of Northern Goshawks in northwest British Columbia. Forest Innovative Investment Project. Houston Forest Products Ltd., Houston, BC, Canada.

MAHON, T., F. I. DOYLE, AND M. NELLIGAN. 2003. Effect of forest development on the reproductive success of Northern Goshawks (*Accipiter gentilis*) in the Prince Rupert Forest Region. Houston Forest Products Ltd., Houston, BC, Canada.

MAMMEN, U. 1999. Monitoring von Greifvogel- und Eulenarten: Anspruch und Wirklichkeit. Egretta 42:4–16.

MANEL, S., H. C. WILLIAMS, AND S. J. ORMEROD. 2001. Evaluating presence-absence models in ecology. Journal of Applied Ecology 38:921–931.

MANLY, B. F. J., L. L. MCDONALD, AND D. A. THOMAS. 1993. Resource selection by animals. Chapman and Hall, London, UK.

MANNAN, R. W., R. N. CONNER, B. MARCOT, AND J. M. PEEK. 1994. Managing forestlands for wildlife. Pp. 689–721 *in* T. A. Bookhout (editor). Research and management techniques for wildlife and habitats, 5th ed. The Wildlife Society, Bethesda, MD.

MANOLIS, J. C., D. E. ANDERSEN, AND F. J. CUTHBERT. 2000. Patterns in clearcut edge and fragmentation effect studies in northern hardwood-conifer landscapes: retrospective power analysis and Minnesota results. Wildlife Society Bulletin 28:1088–1101.

MAÑOSA, S. 1991. Biologia trofica, us de l'habitat I biologia de la reproduccio de l'Astor *Accipiter gentilis* (Linnaeus 1758) a la Segarra. Ph.D. dissertation, University of Barcelona, Spain.

MAÑOSA, S. 1993. Selección de hábitat de nidificación en el Azor (*Accipiter gentilis*): recomendaciónes para su gestión. Alytes 6:125–136.

MAÑOSA, S. 1994. Goshawk diet in a Mediterranean area of northeastern Spain. Journal of Raptor Research 28:84–92.

MAÑOSA, S., R. MATEO, C. FREIXA, AND R. GUITART. 2003. Persistent organochlorine contaminants in eggs of Northern Goshawk and Eurasian Buzzard from northeastern Spain: temporal trends related to changes in the diet. Environmental Pollution 122:351–359.

MAÑOSA, S., J. REAL, AND E. SANCHEZ. 1990. Comparació de l'ecologia de dues poblacions d'astor *Accipiter gentilis* a Catalunya: el Vallès-Moianès I la Segarra. El Medi Natural del Vallès 2:204–212.

MARCSTRÖM, V., AND R. E. KENWARD. 1981a. Sexual and seasonal variation in condition and survival of Swedish Goshawks *Accipiter gentilis*. Ibis 123:311–327.

MARCSTRÖM, V., AND R. E, KENWARD. 1981b. Movements of wintering Goshawks in Sweden. Swedish. Wildlife Research 12:1–36.

MARCSTRÖM, V., R. E. KENWARD, AND E. ENGREN. 1988. The impact of predation on boreal tetraonids during vole cycles: an experimental study. Journal of Animal Ecology 57:859–872.

MARCUM, C. L., AND D. O. LOFTSGAARDEN. 1980. A non-mapping technique for studying habitat preferences. Journal of Wildlife Management 44:963-968.

MARQUISS, M. 1981. The Goshawk in Britain—its provenance and current status. Pp. 43–55 *in* R. E. Kenward, and I. M. Lindsay (editors). Understanding the Goshawk. International Association for Falconry and Conservation of Birds of Prey, Oxford, UK.

MARQUISS, M. 1993. Goshawk *Accipiter gentilis*. Pp. 108–109 *in* D. W. Gibbons, J. B. Reid, and R. A. Chapman (editors). The new atlas of breeding birds in Britain and Ireland: 1988–1991. T. & A.D. Poyser Ltd., London, UK.

MARQUISS, M. AND I. NEWTON. 1982. The Goshawk in Britain. British Birds 75:243–260.

MARQUISS, M., S. J. PETTY, D. I. K. ANDERSON, AND G. LEGGE. 2003. Contrasting population trends of the Northern Goshawk (*Accipiter gentilis*) in the Scottish / English Borders and north-east Scotland. Pp. 143–148 *in* D. B. A. Thompson, S. M. Redpath, A. H. Fielding, M. Marquiss, and C. A. Galbraith (editors). Birds of Prey in a changing environment. Scottish Natural Heritage/The Stationary Office, Edinburgh, UK.

MARSDEN, H. M., AND C. H. CONAWAY. 1963. Behavior and the reproductive cycle in the cottontail. Journal of Wildlife Management 27:161–170.

MARSHALL, D. B. 1992. Status of the Northern Goshawk in Oregon and Washington. Audubon Society of Portland, Portland, OR.

MARSHALL, J. T. 1957. Birds of pine-oak woodland in southern Arizona and adjacent Mexico. Pacific Coast Avifauna 32:125.

MARTELL, M., AND T. DICK. 1996. Nesting habitat characteristics of the Northern Goshawk (*Accipiter gentilis*) in Minnesota. Minnesota Department of Natural Resources, Nongame Wildlife Program. Final Report Project No. 9407382. St. Paul, MN.

MARTI, C. D. 1987. Raptor food habitat studies. Pp. 67–80 *in* B. Giron Pendleton, B. A. Millsap, K. W. Cline, and D. M. Bird (editors) Raptor management techniques manual. National Wildlife Federation, Scientific Technical Series No. 10. Washington, DC.

MARTI, C. D., E. KORPIMÄKI, AND F. M. JAKSIC. 1993. Trophic structure of raptor communities: a three continent comparison and synthesis. Pp. 47–137 *in* D. M. Power (editor). Current Ornithology, Volume 10. Plenum Press, New York, NY.

MARTIN, C. 1998. Notice of a 12-month finding on a petition to list the Northern Goshawk in the contiguous United States west of the 100th meridian. Federal Register 63:35183–35184.

MARTIN, T. E. 1987. Food as a limit on breeding birds: a life-history perspective. Annual Review of Ecology and Systematics 18:453–487.

MARZLUFF, J. M., M. G. RAPHAEL, AND R. SALLABANKS. 2000. Understanding the effects of forest management on avian species. Wildlife Society Bulletin 28:1132–1143.

MARZLUFF, J. M., M. S. VEKASY, AND C. COODY. 1994. Comparative accuracy or aerial and ground telemetry locations of foraging raptors. Condor 96:447–454.

MASMAN, D., S. DAAN, AND H. J. A. BELDHUIS. 1988. Ecological energetics of the Kestrel: daily energy expenditure throughout the year based on time-energy budget, food intake and doubly labeled water methods. Ardea 76:64–81.

MATTSON, D. J., B B. BLANCHARD, AND R. R. KNIGHT. 1992. Yellowstone grizzly bear mortality, human habituation, and whitebark pine seed crops. Journal of Wildlife Management 56:432–442.

MAURER, J. R. 2000. Nesting habitat and prey relations of the Northern Goshawk in Yosemite National Park, California. M.S. thesis, University of California, Davis, CA.

MAYFIELD, H. 1961. Nesting success calculated from exposure. Wilson Bulletin 73:255–261.

MCCLAREN, E. 2003. Northern Goshawk *Accipiter gentilis laingi* population inventory summary for Vancouver Island, British Columbia. 1994–2002. BC Ministry of Environment, Lands and Parks. Nanimo, BC, Canada.

MCCLAREN, E. L., AND C. L. PENDERGAST. 2003. Relationship between forest age class distribution around Northern Goshawk nests and occupancy and nest productivity patterns at three spatial scales. BC Ministry of Environment, Lands and Parks. Nanimo, BC, Canada.

MCCLAREN, E. L., P. L. KENNEDY, AND S. R. DEWEY. 2002. Do some Northern Goshawk nest areas fledge more young than others? Condor 104:343–352.

MCCLAREN, E. L., P. L. KENNEDY, AND D. D. DOYLE. 2005. Northern Goshawk (*Accipiter gentilis laingi*) post-fledging area size on Vancouver Island, British Columbia. Journal of Raptor Research. 39:253–263.

MCCLOSKEY, J. T., AND S. R. DEWEY. 1999. Improving the success of a mounted Great Horned Owl lure for trapping Northern Goshawks. Journal of Raptor Research 33:168–169.

MCCOY, R. H. 1999. Effects of prey delivery on fledging success of the Northern Goshawk. M.S. thesis, Humboldt State University, Arcata, CA.

MCCUNE, B. 1983. Fire frequency reduced two orders of magnitude in the Bitterroot Canyons, Montana. Canadian Journal Forestry Research 13:212–218.

MCCUNE, B., J. B. GRACE, AND D. L. URBAN. 2002. Analysis of ecological communities. MjM Software, Gleneden Beach, OR.

MCDONNELL, M. J., S. T. A. PICKETT, P. GROFFMAN, P. BOHLEN, R. V. POUYAT, W. C. ZIPPERER, R. W. PARMELEE, M. M. CARREIRO, AND K. MEDLEY. 1997.

Ecosystem processes along an urban-to-rural gradient. Urban Ecosystems 1:21–36.

McGowan, J. D. 1975. Distribution, density, and productivity of Goshawks in interior Alaska. Final Report, Federal Aid in Wildlife Restoration Projects W-17-3, W-17-4, W-17-5 and W-17-6, Job 10.6R, Alaska Department of Fish and Game, Juneau, AK.

McGrady, M. J., T. L. Maechtle, L. S. Schueck, J. J. Vargas, W. S. Seegar, and M. Catalina Porras Peña. 2002. Migration and ranging of Peregrine Falcons wintering on the Gulf of Mexico Coast, Tamaulipas, Mexico. Condor 104:39–48.

McGrady, M. J., M. Ueta, E. Potapov, I. Utekhina, V. B. Masterov, M. Fuller, W. S. Seegar, A. Ladyguin, E. G. Lobkov, and V. B. Zykov. 2000. Migration and wintering of juvenile and immature Steller's Sea Eagles. Pp. 83–90 in First Symposium on Steller's and White-tailed Sea Eagles in East Asia. Wild Bird Society of Japan, Tokyo, Japan.

McGrath, M. T. 1997. Northern Goshawk habitat analysis in managed forest landscapes. M.S. thesis, Oregon State University, Corvallis, OR.

McGrath, M. T., S. DeStefano, R. A. Riggs, L. L. Irwin, and G. J. Roloff. 2003. Spatially explicit influences on Northern Goshawk nesting habitat in the interior Pacific Northwest. Wildlife Monographs 154:1–63.

McInvaille, W. B., and L. B. Keith. 1974. Predator-prey relations and breeding biology of the Great Horned Owl and Red-tailed Hawk in central Alberta. Canadian Field Naturalist 88:1–20.

McKay, D. O., and B. J. Verts. 1978. Estimates of some attributes of Nuttall's cottontail. Journal of Wildlife Management 42:59–168.

McKee, E. D. 1941. Distribution of the tassel-eared squirrels. Plateau 14:12–20.

McKeever, S. 1964. The biology of the golden-mantled ground squirrel, Citellus lateralis. Ecological Monographs 34:383–401.

McKelvey, K. S., and J. D. Johnston. 1992. Historical perspectives on the forests of the Sierra Nevada and the Transverse Ranges of southern California: forest conditions at the turn of the century. Pp. 225–246 in J. Verner, K. S. McKelvey, B. R. Noon, R. J. Gutierrez, G. I. Gould Jr., and T. W. Beck (technical coordinators). The California Spotted Owl: a technical assessment of its current status. USDA Forest Service General Technical Report PSW-GTR-133. USDA Forest Service, Pacific Southwest Research Station, Albany, CA.

McLeod, M. A., and D. E. Andersen. 1998. Red-shouldered Hawk broadcast surveys: affecting detection of responses and population tends: Journal of Wildlife Management 62:1385–1397.

McNab, W. H., and P. E. Avers. 1994. Ecological subregions of the United States: section descriptions. USDA Forest Service Ecosystem Management WO-WSA-5. Washington, DC.

Mebs, T. 2002. Greifvögel Europas: Biologie, Bestandsverhältnisse, Bestandsgefährdung. 3. Auflage. Franckh-Kosmos, Stuttgart, Germany.

Mebs, T., and W. Scherzinger. 2000. Die Eulen Europas. Biologie, Kennzeichen, Bestände. Franckh-Kosmos, Stuttgart, Germany.

Meier, T. 2002. Vergleichende Analyse der Habitatnutzung des Habichts—Accipiter gentilis—im urbanen und ruralen Lebensraum. Diploma thesis, University of Hamburg, Hamburg, Germany.

Meijer, T. 1988. Reproductive decisions in the Kestrel Falco tinnunculus. A study in physiological ecology. Ph.D. dissertation, University of Groningen, The Netherlands.

Meinertzhagen, R. 1950. The Goshawk in Great Britain. Bulletin of the British Ornithologists' Club 70:46–49.

Melchior, E., E. Mentgen, R. Peltzer, R. Schmitt, and J. Weiss (editors). 1987. Atlas der Brutvögel Luxemburgs. Lëtzebuerger Natur- a Vulleschutzliga, Luxembourg, Germany.

Melián, C. J., and J. Bascompte. 2002. Food web structure and habitat loss. Ecology Letters 5:37–46.

Mellina, E., and S. G. Hinch. 1995. Overview of large-scale ecological experimental designs and recommendations for the British Columbia watershed restoration program. Watershed Restoration Project Report No. 1, Watershed Restoration Program, Ministry of Environment, Lands, and Parks, BC, Canada.

Mendall, H. L. 1944. Food of hawks and owls in Maine. Journal of Wildlife Management 8:198–208.

Meng, H. 1959. Food habits of nesting Cooper's Hawks and Goshawks in New York and Pennsylvania. Wilson Bulletin 71:169–174.

Meslow, C. E., R. S. Holthausen, and D. A. Cleaves. 1994. Assessment of terrestrial species and ecosystems. Journal of Forestry 92:24–27.

Michaels, J. A., L. R. Neville, D. Edelman, T. Sullivan, and L. A. DiCola. 1992. New York-New Jersey Highlands Regional Study. USDA Forest Service, Radnor, PA.

Migratory Bird Treaty Act of 1918. Public Law 16 U.S.C. §§ 703-712, July 3, 1918, as amended.

Mikkelsen, J. D. 1986. Rovfugle og fasanudsædninger i Danmark. Danske Vildtundersøgelser 40:1–32.

Mikkola, H. 1983. Owls of Europe. T. & A.D. Poyser Ltd., Calton, UK.

Miller, H. W., and D. H. Johnson. 1978. Interpreting the results of nesting studies. Journal of Wildlife Management 42:471–476.

Minitab. 2000. MINITAB Release 13.20. Minitab, State College, PA.

Minnesota Forest Resources Council. 2000. Minnesota north central landscape current conditions and trends assessment. Minnesota Forest Resources Council Document LT-0500. St. Paul, MN.

Mitschke, A., and S. Baumung. 2001. Brutvogel-Atlas Hamburg. Hamburger avifaunistische Beiträge 31:1–344.

Möckel, R., and D. Günther. 1987. Die Reproduktion des Habichts Accipiter gentilis (L.) im Westerzgebirge in den Jahren 1974–1983. Populationsökologie Greifvogel- und Eulenarten 1:217–232.

Moilanen, P. 1976. Kanahaukkatapot ja fasaani. Suomen Luonto 6:315–318.

Moir, W. H., and J. B. Deteriech. 1988. Old-growth ponderosa pine from succession in pine-bunchgrass forests in Arizona and New Mexico. Natural Areas Journal 8: 17–24.

Møller, A. P. 1987. Copulatory behaviour in the Goshawk, *Accipiter gentilis*. Animal Behaviour 35:755–763.

Mönkkönen, M., Huhta, E., Mäkelä, J., and Rajasärkkä, A. 1999. Pohjois-Suomen vanhojen metsien linnusto ja metsämaiseman muutos. Pp. 39–46 *in* E. Lammi. (editor). Linnut-vuosikirja 1999. BirdLife, Helsinki, Finland.

Moore, K. R., and C. J. Henny. 1983. Nest site characteristics of three coexisting accipiter hawks in northeastern Oregon. Journal of Raptor Research 17:65–76.

Moore, W. S. 1995. Northern Flicker (*Colaptes auratus*). *In* A. Poole and F. Gill (editors). The Birds of North America, No. 166. The Academy of Natural Sciences, Philadelphia, PA, and The American Ornithologists' Union, Washington, DC.

Morillo, C., and J. Lalanda. 1972. Primeros datos sobre la ecologiá de las Falconiformes en llos montes de Toledo. Boletin de la Estacion Central de Ecologia 2:57–70.

Morin, P. J. 1981. Predatory salamanders reverse the outcome of competition among three species of anuran tadpoles. Science 212:1284–1286.

Mosher, J. A. 1989. Accipiters. Pp. 47–52 *in* B. Giron Pendleton (editor). Northeast raptor management symposium and workshop. National Wildlife Federation Scientific and Technical Series No. 13. Washington, DC.

Mosher, J. A. 1997. Falconry harvest in the United States. Journal of Raptor Research 31:294–295.

Mrlík, V., and P. Koubek. 1992. Relation of birds of prey to the place of release of artificially-bred pheasant chicks. Folia Zoologica 41:233–252.

Mueggler, W. F. 1989. Status of aspen woodlands in the West. Pp. 32–37 *in* B. Giron Pendleton, C. E. Ruibal, D. L. Krahe, K. Steenhof, M. N. Kochert, and M. L. LeFranc, Jr. (editors). Proceedings of the Western Raptor Management Symposium and Workshop. National Wildlife Federation Scientific Technical Series. No.12. Washington, DC.

Mueller, H. C., and D. D. Berger. 1968. Sex ratios and measurements of migrant Goshawks. Auk 85: 431–436.

Mueller, H. C., D. D. Berger, and G. Allez. 1977. The periodic invasions of Goshawks. Auk 94:652–663.

Mullally, D. P. 1953. Hibernation in the golden-mantled ground squirrel, *Citellus lateralis bernardinus*. Journal of Mammalogy 34:65–73.

Murphy, D. D., and B. R. Noon. 1991. Coping with uncertainty in wildlife biology. Journal of Wildlife Management 55:773–782.

Murphy, D. D., and B. R. Noon. 1992. Integrating scientific methods with habitat planning: reserve design for Northern Spotted Owls. Ecological Applications 2:3–17.

Murray, C., and D. Marmorek. 2003. Adaptive management and ecological restoration. Pp. 417–428

in P. Friederici (editor). Ecological restoration of southwestern ponderosa pine forests. Island Press, Washington, DC.

Müskens, G. 2002. Havik *Accipiter gentilis*. Pp. 160–161 *in* SOVON. Atlas van de Nederlandse Broedvogels 1998–2000, Nederlandse Fauna 5. Nationaal Natuurhistorisch Museum Naturalis, KNNV Uitgeverij and European Invertebrate Survey-Nederland, Leiden, The Netherlands.

Myrberget, S. 1989. Diet of goshawks during the breeding season in northern coastal Norway. Fauna Norvegica. Series C. Cinclus 12:100–102.

Nagy, A. C. 1977. Population trend indices based on 40 years of autumn counts at Hawk Mountain Sanctuary in north-eastern Pennsylvania. Pp. 243–253. *in* R. D. Chancellor (editor). Proceedings of the ICBP world conference on birds of prey, Vienna, Austria.

National Forest Management Act (NFMA). 1976. 16 U.S.C. §§ 1600-14.

National Forest Management Act. 1982. Implementing Regulations. 36 CFR 219.19.

NatureServe. 2005. NatureServe explorer: an online encyclopedia of life. Version 4.5. NatureServe, Arlington, VA. <http://www.natureserve.org/explorer> (9 August 2005)

Neideman. C., and E. Schönbeck. 1990. Erfarenheter från 10 års ringmärkning av fångade duvhökar. Anser 29: 245–260.

Nelson, B. B., and K. Titus. 1989. Silviculture practices and raptor habitat associations in the Northeast. Pp. 171–179 *in* B. Giron Pendleton (editor). Northeast raptor management symposium and workshop. National Wildlife Federation Scientific and Technical Series No. 13. Washington, DC.

Newton, I. 1979a. Population ecology of raptors. T. & A.D. Poyser, Berkhamsted, UK and Buteo Books, Vermillion, SD.

Newton, I. 1979b. Effects of human persecution on European raptors. Raptor Research 13:65–78.

Newton, I. 1986. The Sparrowhawk. T. & A.D. Poyser Ltd., Calton, UK.

Newton, I. 1988a. Commentary—Population regulation in Peregrines: an overview. Pp. 761–770 *in* T. J. Cade, J. H. Enderson, C. G. Thelander, and C. M. White (editors). Peregrine Falcon populations: their management and recovery. The Peregrine Fund Inc., Boise, ID.

Newton, I. 1988b. Determination of critical pollutant levels in wild populations, with examples from organochlorine insecticides in birds of prey. Environmental Pollution 55:29–40.

Newton, I. 1989. The control of Sparrowhawk *Accipiter nisus* nesting densities. Pp. 1969–1980 *in* B.-U. Meyburg, and R. D. Chancellor (editors). Raptors in the modern world. WWGBP, Berlin, Germany.

Newton, I. 1991. Population limitation in birds of prey: a comparative approach. Pp. 3–21 *in* C. M. Perrins, J.-D. Lebreton, and G. J. M. Hirons (editors). Bird population studies. Oxford University Press, Oxford, UK.

NEWTON, I. 1993. Causes of breeding failures in wild raptors: a review. Pp. 62–71 *in* P. T. Redig, J. E. Cooper, J. D. Remple, D. B. Bruce, and T. Hahn (editors). Raptor biomedicine. University of Minnesota Press, Minneapolis, MN.

NEWTON, I. 1998. Population limitation in birds. Academic Press, San Diego, CA.

NEWTON, I. 2003a. The role of natural factors in the limitation of bird of prey numbers: a brief review of the evidence. Pp. 5–23 *in* D. B. A. Thompson, S. M. Redpath, A. H. Fielding, M. Marquiss, and C. A. Galbraith (editors). Birds of prey in a changing environment. Scottish Natural Heritage/The Stationary Office, Edinburgh, UK.

NEWTON, I. 2003b. The contribution of Peregrine research and restoration to a better understanding of Peregrines and other raptors. Pp. 335–347 *in* T. J. Cade, and W. Burnham (editors). Return of the Peregrine: a North American saga of tenacity and teamwork. The Peregrine Fund Inc., Boise, ID.

NEWTON, I. 2003c. The speciation and biogeography of birds. Academic Press, London, UK.

NEWTON, I., AND M. MARQUISS. 1983. Dispersal of Sparrowhawks between birthplace and breeding place. Journal Animal Ecology 52:462–477.

NEWTON, I., AND M. MARQUISS. 1986. Population regulation in Sparrowhawks. Journal of Animal Ecology 55: 463–480.

NEWTON, I., AND M. MARQUISS. 1991. Removal experiments and the limitation of breeding density in Sparrowhawks. Journal of Animal Ecology 60:535–544.

NEWTON, I., M. MARQUISS, D. N. WEIR, AND D. MOSS. 1977. Spacing of Sparrowhawk nesting territories. Journal of Animal Ecology 46:425–441.

NEWTON, I., AND I. WYLLIE. 1996. Monogamy in the Sparrowhawk. Pp. 249–267 *in* J. M. Black (editor). Partnerships in birds: the study of monogamy. Oxford University Press, Oxford, UK.

NEWTON, I., I. WYLLIE, AND R. MEARNS. 1986. Spacing of Sparrowhawks in relation to food supply. Journal of Animal Ecology 55:361–370.

NEYMAN, J., AND E. SCOTT. 1957. On a mathematical theory of populations conceived as a conglomeration of clusters. Cold Spring Harbor Symposia on Quantitative Biology 22:109–120.

NIELSEN, J. T. 1998. Duehøgens prædation på Brevduer i Vendsyssel. Dansk Ornitologisk Forenings Tidsskrift 92:327–332.

NIELSEN, J. T. 2003. Lav duehøgebestand en følge af ulovlig bekæmpelse ved fasanudsætninger. Dansk Ornitologisk Forenings Tidsskrift 97:173–174.

NIELSEN J. T., AND J. DRACHMANN. 1999a. Development and productivity in a Danish Goshawk *Accipiter gentilis* population. Dansk Ornitologisk Forenings Tidsskrift 93:153–161.

NIELSEN, J. T., AND J. DRACHMANN. 1999b. Prey selection of Goshawks *Accipiter gentilis* during the breeding season in Vendsyssel, Denmark. Dansk Ornitologisk Forenings Tidsskrift 93:235–240.

NIELSEN, J. T., AND J. DRACHMANN. 1999c. Dispersal of Danish Goshawks *Accipiter gentilis* as revealed by ringing recoveries. Dansk Ornitologisk Forenings Tidsskrift 93:85–90.

NIELSEN, J. T., AND J. DRACHMANN. 2003. Age-dependent reproductive performance in Northern Goshawks *Accipiter gentilis*. Ibis 145:1–8.

NIELSEN, O. 1999. Gyrfalcon predation on ptarmigan: numerical and functional responses. Journal of Animal Ecology 68:034–1050.

NIELSEN, O. K., AND T. J. CADE. 1990. Seasonal changes in food habits of Gyrfalcons in NE-Iceland. Ornis Scandinavica 21:202–211.

NOAA. 2003a. Storm events <http://www4.ncdc.noaa.gov/cgi-win/wwcgi.dll?wwevent~storms> (11 August 2005).

NOAA. 2003b. State climatological observations <http://cdo.ncdc.noaa.gov/dly/DLY> (11 August 2005).

NOER, H., AND H. SECHER. 1990. Effects of legislative protection on survival rates and status improvements of birds of prey in Denmark. Danish Review of Game Biology 14:1–63.

NOLL WEST, J. (EDITOR). 1998. Status of the Northern Goshawk in the Midwest: workshop proceedings. Midwest regional raptor management and peregrine symposium. USDI Fish and Wildlife Service, Fort Snelling, MN.

NOON, B. R., AND C. M. BILES. 1990. Mathematical demography of Spotted Owls in the Pacific Northwest. Journal of Wildlife Management 54:18–27.

NORE, T. 1979. Rapaces diurnes communs en Limousin pendant la période de nidification. II: autour, épervier et faucon crécerelle. Alauda 47:259–269.

NORGALL, A. 1988. Beobachtungen zum Balzverhalten des Habichts (*Accipiter gentilis*) im Freiland. Diploma thesis, University of Göttingen, Göttingen, Germany.

NOSS, R. F. 1990. Indicators for monitoring biodiversity: a hierarchical approach. Conservation Biology 4: 355–364.

NOSS, R. F. 1996. On attacking a caricature of reserves: response to Everett and Lehmkuhl. Wildlife Society Bulletin 24:777–779.

NOSS, R. F., C. CARROLL, K. VANCE-BORLAND, AND G. WUERTHNER. 2002. A multicriteria assessment of the irreplaceability and vulnerability of sites in the greater Yellowstone ecosystem. Conservation Biology 16: 895–908.

NOSS, R. F., AND A. COOPERRIDER. 1994. Saving nature's legacy. Island Press, Washington, DC.

NOSS, R. F., M. A. O'CONNELL, AND D. D. MURPHY. 1997. The science of conservation planning: habitat conservation under the Endangered Species Act. Island Press, Washington, DC.

NUDDS, T. D., AND M. L. MORRISON. 1991. Ten years after "reliable knowledge:" Are we gaining? Journal of Wildlife Management 55:757–760.

NYGÅRD, T. 1991. Rovfugl som indikatorer på forurensning i Norge. NINA Utredning 21:1–34.

NYGÅRD, T., D. J. HALLEY, B. WISETH, S. GRØNNESBY, AND P. M. GRØNLIEN. 1998. Hva skjer med hønshauken?-

Foreløpige resultater fra et forskningsprosjekt om hønsehaukens arealkrav, naring, dødsarsaker og vandringer. Vår Fuglefauna. 21:5–10.

NYLAND, R. D. 2002. Silviculture: concepts and applications, 2nd edition. McGraw-Hill, New York, NY.

O'BRIEN, R. A. 2002. Arizona's forest resources, 1999. USDA Forest Service Resource Bulletin RMRS-RB-2. USDA Forest Service, Rocky Mountain Research Station, Ogden, UT.

O'BRIEN, W. J., H. I. BROWMAN, AND B. I. EVANS. 1990. Search strategies of foraging animals. American Scientist 78:152–160.

O'BRIEN, W. J., B. I. EVANS, AND H. I. BROWMAN. 1989. Flexible search tactics and efficient foraging in saltatory searching animals. Oecologia 80:100–110.

O'RIORDAN, T., AND J. CAMERON. 1994. The history and contemporary significance of the precautionary principle. Pp. 12–30, in T. O'Riordan, and J. Cameron (editors). Interpreting the precautionary principle. Earthscan Publications Ltd, London. UK.

OAKLEAF, R. J. 1975. Population surveys, species distribution and key habitats of selected nongame species. Federal Aid in Wildlife Restoration Project W-53-R. Nevada Department of Fish and Game, Reno, NV.

OBERHOLSER, H. C. 1974. The bird life of Texas. University of Texas Press, Austin, TX.

OELKE, H. 1981. Greifvogel-Monitoruntersuchung 1977–1980 im Landkreis Peine (Hannover-Braunschweig, Niedersachsen). Beiträge zur Naturkunde Niedersachsens 34:12–50.

OGGIER, P.-A. 1980. Habicht. Pp. 96–97 in A. Schifferli, P. Géroudet, and R. Winkler (editors). Verbreitungsatlas der Brutvögel der Schweiz. Schweizerische Vogelwarte, Sempach, Switzerland.

OGGIER, P.-A., AND U. BÜHLER. 1998. Habicht. Pp. 196–197 in H. Schmid, R. Luder, B. Naef-Daenzer, R. Graf, and N. Zbinden (editors). Schweizer Brutvogelatlas. Verbreitung der Brutvögel in der Schweiz und im Fürstentum Liechtenstein 1993–1996. Schweizerische Vogelwarte, Sempach, Switzerland.

OHMANN, L. F., AND M. F. BUELL. 1968. Forest vegetation of the New Jersey Highlands. Bulletin of the Torrey Botanical Club 95:287–298.

OLECH, B. 1997. Diet of the Goshawk Accipiter gentilis in Kampinoski National Park (central Poland) in 1982–1993. Acta ornithologica 32:191–200.

OLECH, B. 1998. Population dynamics and breeding performance of the Goshawk Accipiter gentilis in central Poland in 1982–1994. Pp. 101–110 in R. D. Chancellor, B.-U. Meyburg, and J. J. Ferrero (editors). Holarctic birds of prey. World Working Group on Birds of Prey and Owls, Berlin, Germany.

OLIVER, C. D., AND B. C. LARSON. 1996. Forest stand dynamics. McGraw-Hill, New York, NY.

OLSEN, W. K., H. HUTCHINSON, W. PICKELL, AND A. RIBELIN. 2003a. Petition to correct information disseminated by the USDA Forest Service (GTR-RM-217). On file, Rocky Mountain Research Station, Ft. Collins, CO.

OLSEN, W. K., H. HUTCHINSON, W. PICKELL, AND A. RIBELIN. 2003b. Petition to correct information disseminated by the USDA Forest Service (GTR-RM-217), request for reconsideration. Letter on file, Rocky Mountain Research Station, Ft. Collins, CO.

OPDAM, P. 1975. Inter- and intraspecific differentiation with respect to feeding ecology in two sympatric species of the genus Accipiter. Ardea 63:30–54.

OPDAM, P. 1978. De Havik. Het Spectrum, Utrecht and Antwerpen, The Netherlands.

OPDAM, P., AND G. MÜSKENS. 1976. Use of shed feathers in population studies of Accipiter hawks (Aves, Accipitriformes, Accipitridae). Beaufortia 24:55–62.

OPDAM, P., J. THISSEN, P. VERSCHUREN, AND G. MÜSKENS. 1977. Feeding ecology of a population of Goshawk Accipiter gentilis. Journal für Ornithologie 118:35–51.

ORIANS, G. H., AND N. E. PEARSON. 1979. On the theory of central place foraging. Pp. 155–177 in D. J. Horn, G. R. Stairs, and R. D. Mitchell (editors). Analysis of ecological systems. Ohio State University Press, Columbus, OH.

ORIANS, G., AND F. KUHLMAN. 1956. Red-tailed Hawk and Great Horned Owl populations in Wisconsin. Condor 58:371–385.

ORTLIEB, R. 1990. Horstwechsel, Nahrungsanalysen und Jagdweise des Habichts im Südostharz. Der Falke 37:151–155, 199–204.

ORWIG, D. A., AND D. R. FOSTER. 2000. Stand, landscape, and ecosystem analyses of hemlock wolly adelgid outbreaks in southern New England. Pp. 123–125 in Proceedings of a symposium on sustainable management of hemlock ecosystems in eastern North America. USDA Forest Service General Technical Report NE-267. USDA Forest Service, Northeastern Research Station, Newtown Square, PA.

OSTFELD, R. S., C. G. JONES, AND J. O. WOLFF. 1996. Of mice and mast. BioScience 46:323–330.

OTVOS, I. S., AND R. W. STARK. 1985. Arthropod food of some forest-inhabiting birds. Canadian Entomologist 117:971 990.

OVERSKAUG, K., P. SUNDE, AND G. STUVE. 2000. Intersexual differences in the diet composition of Norwegian raptors. Ornis Norvegica 23:24–30.

PADIAL, J. M., J. M. BAREA, F. J. CONTRERAS, F. AVILA, AND J. PÉREZ. 1998. Dieta del Azor Común (Accipiter gentilis) en las Sierras Béticas de Granada durante el periodo de reproducción. Ardeola 45:55–62.

PAIN, D. J., AND M. W. PIENKOWSKI (EDITORS). 1997. Farming and birds in Europe. Academic Press, London, UK.

PALMER, R. S. 1988. Handbook of North American birds. Vol. 4, Diurnal Raptors. Yale University Press. New Haven, CT.

PARAGI, T. F., AND G. M. WHOLECHEESE. 1994. Marten, Martes americana, predation on a Northern Goshawk, Accipiter gentilis. Canadian Field Naturalist 108:81–82.

PATLA, S. M. 1997. Nesting ecology and habitat of the Northern Goshawk in undisturbed and timber harvest areas on the Targhee National Forest, greater Yellowstone ecosystem. M.S. thesis, Idaho State University, Pocatello, ID.

PATTON, D. R. 1975a. Nest use and home range of three Abert squirrels as determined by radio-tracking. USDA Forest Service Research Note 281. USDA Forest Service, Rocky Mountain Forest and Range Experiment Station. Fort Collins, CO.

PATTON, D. R. 1975b. Abert squirrel cover requirements in southwestern ponderosa pine. Research Note 272. USDA Forest Service, Rocky Mountain Forest and Range Experiment Station, Fort Collins, CO.

PATTON, D. R. 1984. A model to evaluate Abert squirrel habitat in uneven-aged ponderosa pine. Wildlife Society Bulletin 12:408–404.

PATTON, D. R., AND W. GREEN.1970. Abert's squirrels prefer mature ponderosa pine. USDA Forest Service Research Note RM-169. USDA Forest Service, Rocky Mountain Forest and Range Experiment station. Fort Collins CO.

PEARSON, G. A. 1950. Management of ponderosa pine in the southwest. USDA Forest Service Agricultural Monograph No. 6. U.S. Government Printing Office, Washington, DC.

PECK, G. K., AND R. D. JAMES. 1983. Breeding birds of Ontario: nidology and distribution. Vol.1, Non-passerines. Miscellaneous Publications, Royal Ontario Museum of Life Sciences, Toronto, ON, Canada.

PECK, J. 2000. Seeing the forest through the eyes of a hawk: an evaluation of recent efforts to protect Northern Goshawk populations in southwestern forests. Natural Resources Journal 40:125–156.

PEDERSON, J. C., R. N. HASENYAGER, AND A. W. HEGGEN. 1976. Habitat requirements of the Abert squirrel (Sciurus aberti navajo) on the Monticello district, Manti-La Sal National Forest of Utah. Utah State Division of Wildlife Resources. Publication No. 76-9. Salt Lake City, UT.

PEIRCE, M. A., AND J. E. COOPER. 1977. Haematozoa of birds of prey in Great Britain. Veterinary Record 100:493.

PENTERIANI, V. 1996. Il gufo reale. Edagricole—Edizioni Agricole, Bologna, Italy.

PENTERIANI, V. 1997. Long-term study of a Goshawk breeding population on a Mediterranean mountain (Abruzzo Apennines, central Italy): density, breeding performance, and diet. Journal of Raptor Research 31:308–312.

PENTERIANI, V. 2001. The annual and diel cycles of Goshawk vocalizations at nest sites. Journal of Raptor Research 35:24–30.

PENTERIANI, V. 2002. Goshawk nesting habitat in Europe and North America: a review. Ornis Fennica 79: 149–163.

PENTERIANI, V., AND B. FAIVRE. 1997. Breeding density and nest site selection in a Goshawk Accipiter gentilis population of the central Apennines (Abruzzo, Italy). Bird Study 44:136–145.

PENTERIANI, V., AND B. FAIVRE. 2001. Effects of harvesting timber stands on Goshawk nesting in two European areas. Biological Conservation 101:211–216.

PENTERIANI, V., B. FAIVRE, AND B. FROCHOT. 2001. An approach to identify factors and levels of nesting habitat selection: a cross-scale analysis of Goshawk preferences. Ornis Fennica 78:159–167.

PENTERIANI, V., B. FAIVRE, J. MAZUC, AND F. CEZILLY. 2002a. Pre-laying vocal activity as a signal of male and nest stand quality in Goshawks. Ethology, Ecology and Evolution 14:9–17.

PENTERIANI, V., M. MATHIAUT, AND G. BOISSON. 2002b. Immediate species responses to catastrophic natural disturbances: windthrow effects on density, productivity, nesting stand choice, and fidelity in Northern Goshawks (Accipiter gentilis). Auk 119:1132–1137.

PERCO, F., AND E. BENUSSI. 1981. Nidificazione e distribuzione territoriale dell' Astore (Accipiter gentilis gentilis L.) sul Carso Triestino. Atti Primo Convegno Ecologia Territori Carsici, La Grafica, Gradisca d'Isonzo: 207–216.

PETERSEN, L. R., AND J. T. ROEHRIG. 2001. West Nile virus: a reemerging global pathogen. Emerging Infectious Diseases 7:611–614.

PETRONILHO, J. M. S., AND J. V. VINGADA. 2002. First data on feeding ecology of Goshawk Accipiter gentilis during the breeding season in the Natura 2000 site Dunas de Mira, Gândara e Gafanhas (Beira Litoral, Portugal). Airo 12:11–16.

PETTY, S. J. 1996a. History of the Northern Goshawk Accipiter gentilis in Britain. Pp. 95–102 in J. S. Holmes, and J. R. Simons (editors). The introduction and naturalisation of birds. HMSO, London, UK.

PETTY, S. J. 1996b. Adaptations of raptors to man-made spruce forests in the Uplands of Britain. Pp. 201–214 in D. M. Bird, D. E. Varland, and J. J. Negro (editors). Raptors in human landscapes: adaptations to built and cultivated environments. Academic Press, London, UK.

PETTY, S. J. 2002. Northern Goshawk. Pp. 232–234 in C. Wernham, M. Toms, J. Marchant, J. Clark, G. Siriwardena, and S. Baillie (editors). The migration atlas: movements of the birds of Britain and Ireland. T. & A.D. Poyser Ltd., London, UK.

PETTY, S. J., D. I. K. ANDERSON, M. DAVIDSON, B. LITTLE, T. N. SHERRATT, C. J. THOMAS, AND X. LAMBIN. 2003a. The decline of Common Kestrels Falco tinnunculus in a forested area of northern England: the role of predation by Northern Goshawks Accipiter gentilis. Ibis 145:472–483.

PETTY, S. J., P. W. W. LURZ, AND S. P. RUSHTON. 2003b. Predation of red squirrels by Northern Goshawks in a conifer forest in northern England: can this limit squirrel numbers and create a conservation dilemma? Biological Conservation 111:105–114.

PETTY, S. J., I. J. PATTERSON, D. I. K. ANDERSON, B. LITTLE, AND M. DAVISON. 1995. Numbers, breeding performance, and diet of the Sparrowhawk Accipiter nisus and Merlin Falco columbarius in relation to cone crops and seed-eating finches. Forest Ecology and Management 79:133–146.

PHALEN, D. N., C. TAYLOR, S. W. PHALEN, AND G. F. BENNETT. 1995. Hemograms and hematozoa of Sharp-shinned

(*Accipiter striatus*) and Cooper's Hawks (*Accipiter cooperii*) captured during spring migration in northern New York. Journal of Wildlife Diseases 31:216–222.

PHILLIPS, A., J. MARSHALL, AND G. MONSON. 1964. The birds of Arizona. University of Arizona Press, Tucson, AZ.

PIANKA, E. R. 1983. Evolutionary ecology, 3rd edition. Harper and Row Publishers, Inc. New York, NY.

PIELOU, E. C. 1960. A single mechanism to account for regular, random and aggregated populations. Journal of Ecology 48:575–584.

PIELOWSKI, Z. 1961. Über den Unifikationseinfluss der selektiven Nahrungswahl des Habichts, *Accipiter gentilis* L., auf Haustauben. Ekologia Polska A 9: 183–194.

PIELOWSKI, Z. 1968. Studien über die Bestandsverhältnisse einer Habichtspopulation in Zentralpolen. Beiträge zur angewandten Vogelkunde 5:125–136.

POLLOCK, K. H., J. D. NICHOLS, C. BROWNIE, AND J. E. HINES. 1990. Statistical inference for capture-recapture experiments. Wildlife Monographs 107:1–97.

POLLOCK, K. H., J. E. HINES, AND J. D. NICHOLS. 1985. Goodness-of-fit tests for open capture-recapture models. Biometrics 41: 399–410.

POLLOCK, K. H., S. R. WINTERSTEIN, C. M. BUNCK, AND P. D. CURTIS. 1989. Survival analysis in telemetry studies: the staggered entry design. Journal of Wildlife Management 53:7–15.

PORTER, T. W., AND H. H. WILCOX, JR. 1941. Goshawk nesting in Michigan. Wilson Bulletin 53:43–44.

POSTUPALSKY, S. 1974. Raptor reproductive success: some problems with methods, criteria, and terminology. Pp. 21–31 *in* F. N. Hamerstrom, Jr., B. E. Harrell, and R. R. Olendorf (editors). Management of raptors. Raptor Research Report No. 2, Raptor Research Foundation, Vermillion, SD.

POSTUPALSKY, S. 1993. Goshawks in Michigan. Pp. 31 *in* Proceedings of the Northern Goshawk management workshop. USDA Forest Service and Wisconsin Department of Natural Resources, Madison, WI.

POWERS, R. A., AND B. J. VERTS. 1971. Reproduction in the mountain cottontail rabbit in Oregon. Journal of Wildlife Management 35:605–612.

PRESTON, F. W., AND R. T. NORRIS. 1947. Nesting heights of breeding birds. Ecology 28:241–273.

PUCEK, Z., W. JEDRZEJEWSKI, B. JEDRZEJEWSKA, AND M. PUCEK. 1993. Rodent population dynamics in a primeval deciduous forest (Bialowieza National Park) in relation to weather, seed crop, and predation. Acta Theriologica 38:199–232.

PUGACEWICZ, E. 1996. Lęgowe ptaki drapieżne Polskiej części puszczy Białowieskiej. Notatki Ornitologiczne 37.173 224.

PULLIAM, H. R., AND B. J. DANIELSON. 1991. Sources, sinks, and habitat selection: a landscape perspective on population dynamics. American Naturalist 137:50–66.

RADDATZ, H.-J. 1997. Greifvogelbestände im Kreis Pinneberg (Schleswig-Holstein) von 1985 bis 1997. Hamburger avifaunistische Beiträge 29:137–158.

RAFAEL, M. G., AND M. WHITE. 1984. Use of snags by cavity-nesting birds in the Sierra Nevada. Wildlife Monograph 86:1–66.

RANTA, E., P. BYHOLM, V. KAITALA, P. SAUROLA, AND H. LINDÉN. 2003. Spatial dynamics in breeding performance of a predator: the connection to prey availability. Oikos 102:391–396.

RASSMUSSEN, D. I. 1941. Biotic communities of the Kaibab plateau, Arizona. Ecological Monographs 11: 229–275.

RASSMUSSEN, L.U., AND K. STORGÅRD. 1989. Ynglende rovfugle i Sydøstjylland 1973–1987. Dansk Ornitologisk Forenings Tidsskrift 83:23–34.

RATCLIFF, T.D., D. R. PATTON, AND P. F. FFOLLIOT. 1975. Ponderosa pine basal area and the Kaibab squirrel. Journal of Forestry 73:284–286.

RATTI, J. T., AND E. O. GARTON. 1994. Research and experimental design. Pp. 1–23. *in* T. A. Bookhout (editor). Research and management techniques for wildlife and habitats. The Wildlife Society, Bethesda, MD.

REAL, L. A. 1996. Sustainability and the ecology of infectious disease. BioScience 46:88–97.

REDIG, P. T., M. R. FULLER, AND D. L. EVANS. 1980. Prevalence of *Aspergillus fumigatus* in free-living Goshawks (*Accipiter gentilis atricapillus*). Journal of Wildlife Diseases 16:169–174.

REDPATH, S. M., AND S. J. THIRGOOD. 1999. Numerical and functional responses in generalist predators: Hen Harrier and Peregrines on Scottish grouse moors. Journal of Animal Ecology 68:879–892.

REDPATH, S. M., R. CLARKE, M. MADDERS, AND S. J. THIRGOOD. 2001. Assessing raptor diet comparing pellets, prey remains, and observational data at Hen Harrier nests. Condor 103:184–188.

REDROBE, S. 1997. Pathological conditions and cause of death relating to age and sex in Eurasian Buzzards (*Buteo buteo*) in Scotland. Proceedings Conference European Committee Association Avian Veterinarians London:181–187.

REESE, J. G. 1970. Reproduction in a Chesapeake Bay Osprey population. Auk 87:747–759.

REGHAB. 2002. Reconciling gamebird hunting and biodiversity (REGHAB). Workpackage reports 1–6. <www.uclm.es/irec/Reghab/inicio.html> (3 November 2005).

REICH, P. B., AND P. BAKKEN, D. CARLSON, L. E. FRELICH, S. K. FRIEDMAN, AND D. F. GRIGAL. 2001. Influence of logging, fire, and forest type on biodiversity and productivity in southern boreal forests. Ecology 82: 2731–2748.

REICH, R. M., AND R.A. DAVIS. 2002. Spatial library for the S-PLUS© statistical software package. Department of Forest, Rangeland, and Watershed Stewardship, Colorado State University, Fort Collins, CO <http://www.cnr.colostate.edu/~robin/>. (25 April 2005)

REICH, R. M., S. M. JOY, AND R. T. REYNOLDS. 2004. Predicting the location of Northern Goshawk nests: modeling the spatial dependency between nest locations and forest structure. Ecological Modeling 176: 109–133.

REINHARDT, E., AND N. L. CROOKSTON (TECHNICAL EDITORS). 2003. The fire and fuels extension to the forest vegetation simulator. USDA Forest Service General Technical Report RMRS-GTR-116. USDA Forest Service, Rocky Mountain Research Station, Ogden, UT.

REITSMA, L. R., R. T. HOLMES, AND T. W SHERRY. 1990. Effects of removal of red squirrels, *Tamiasciurus hudsonicus*, and eastern chipmunks, *Tamias striatus*, on nest predation in a northern hardwood forest: an artificial nest experiment. Oikos 57:375–380.

RENKIN, R. A., AND D. G. DESPAIN. 1992. Fuel moisture, forest type, and lightning-caused fire in Yellowstone National Park. Canadian Journal of Forest Research 22:37–45.

REYNOLDS, H. G. 1966. Abert's squirrel feeding on pinyon pine. Journal of Mammalogy 47:550–551.

REYNOLDS, R. T. 1971. Nest-Site selection of the three species of *Accipiter* hawks in Oregon. Pp. 51–53 *in* Proceedings Fish and Wildlife Habitat Management Training Conference., USDA Forest Service, Eugene, OR.

REYNOLDS, R. T. 1972. Sexual dimorphism in accipiter hawks: a new hypothesis. Condor 74:191–197.

REYNOLDS, R. T. 1975. Distribution, density, and productivity of three species of accipiter hawks in Oregon. M.S. thesis, Oregon State University, Corvallis, OR.

REYNOLDS, R. T. 1978. Food and habitat partitioning in two groups of coexisting *Accipiters*. Ph.D. dissertation, Oregon State University, Corvallis, OR.

REYNOLDS, R. T. 1982. American *Accipiter* hawks. Pp. 288–289 *in* D. E. Davis (editor). CRC handbook of census methods for terrestrial vertebrates. CRC Press, Boca Raton, FL.

REYNOLDS, R. T. 1983. Management of western coniferous forest habitat for nesting *Accipiter* hawks. USDA Forest Service General Technical Report RM-102. USDA Forest Service, Rocky Mountain Research Station, Ft. Collins, CO.

REYNOLDS, R. T. 1989. *Accipiters*. Pp. 92–101 *in*: B. Giron Pendleton, C. E. Ruibal, D. L. Krahe, K. Steenhof, M. N. Kochert, and M. L. LeFranc, Jr. (editors). Proceedings of the Western Raptor Management Symposium and Workshop. National Wildlife Federation Scientific Technical Series No.12. Washington, DC.

REYNOLDS, R. T., W. M. BLOCK, AND D. A. BOYCE. 1996. Using ecological relationships of wildlife as templates for restoring southwestern forests. Pp. 35–43 *in* W. Covington, and P. K. Wagner (technical coordinators). Conference on adaptive ecosystem restoration and management: restoration of cordilleran conifer landscapes of North America, USDA Forest Service General Technical Report RM-GTR-278, USDA Forest Service, Rocky Mountain Research Station, Ft. Collins, CO.

REYNOLDS, R. T., R. T. GRAHAM, M. H. REISER, R. L. BASSETT, P. L. KENNEDY, D. A. BOYCE, JR., G. GOODWIN, R. SMITH, AND E. L. FISHER. 1992. Management recommendations for the Northern Goshawk in the southwestern United States. USDA Forest Service General Technical Report

RM-217. USDA Forest Service, Rocky Mountain Forest and Range Experiment Station. Fort Collins, CO.

REYNOLDS, R. T., AND S. M. JOY. 1998. Distribution, territory occupancy, dispersal, and demography of Northern Goshawks on the Kaibab Plateau, Arizona. Final Report for the Arizona Game and Fish Heritage Project No. 194045. USDA Forest Service, Rocky Mountain Research Station, Ft. Collins, CO.

REYNOLDS, R. T., S. M. JOY, AND D. G. LESLIE. 1994. Nest productivity, fidelity, and spacing of Northern Goshawks in northern Arizona. Studies in Avian Biology 16:106–113.

REYNOLDS, R. T., AND E. C. MESLOW. 1984. Partitioning of food and niche characteristics of coexisting *Accipiter* during breeding. Auk 101:761–779.

REYNOLDS, R. T., E. C. MESLOW, AND H. M. WIGHT. 1982. Nesting habitat of coexisting *Accipiter* in Oregon. Journal of Wildlife Management 46:124–138.

REYNOLDS, R. T., G. C. WHITE, S. M. JOY, AND R. W. MANNAN. 2004. Effects of radiotransmitters on Northern Goshawks: do tailmounts lower survival of breeding males? Journal of Wildlife Management 68:25–32.

REYNOLDS, R. T., D. J. WIENS, S. M. JOY, AND S. R. SALAFSKY. 2005. Sampling considerations for demographic and habitat studies of Northern Goshawks. Journal of Raptor Research 39:274–285.

REYNOLDS, R. T., AND H. M. WIGHT. 1978. Distribution, density, and productivity of *Accipiter* hawks breeding in Oregon. Wilson Bulletin 90:182–196.

RHODES, L. I. 1972. Success of Osprey nest structures at Martin National Wildlife Refuge. Journal of Wildlife Management 36:1296–1299.

RICE, W. R. 1989. Analyzing tables of statistical tests. Evolution 43:223–225.

RICHMOND, W. K. 1959. British Birds of Prey. Lutterworth Press, London, UK.

RICHTER, M. 1994. Beobachtungen an stadtnahen Greif- und Rabenvogel-Revieren in Wuppertal-Ost. Falke 41:60.

RIPLEY, B. D. 1981. Spatial statistics. John Riley and Sons, New York, NY.

RISCH, M., A. DWENGER, AND H. WIRTH. 1996. Der Sperber (*Accipiter nisus*) als Brutvogel in Hamburg: Bestandsentwicklung und Bruterfolg 1982–1996. Hamburger avifaunistische Beiträge 28:43–57.

RISCH, M., V. LOOFT, AND F. ZIESEMER. 2004. Alter und Reproduktion weiblicher Habichte (*Accipiter gentilis*) in Schleswig-Holstein—ist Seneszenz nachweisbar? Corax 19:323–329.

RISSLER, L. J. 1995. Habitat structure analysis of Northern Goshawk, *Accipiter gentilis atricapillus*, and Northern Spotted Owl, *Strix occidentalis caurina*, nesting stands in the eastern Cascades. M.S. thesis, Utah State University, Logan, UT.

ROBBINS, C. S. 1979. Effects of forest fragmentation on bird populations. Pp. 198–212 *in* Management of northcentral and northeastern forests for nongame birds. USDA Forest Service General Technical Report NC-51. USDA Forest Service, Northcentral Forest Experiment Station, Minneapolis, MN.

ROBBINS, C. S., D. BYSTRAK, AND P. H. GEISSLER. 1986. The breeding bird survey: its first fifteen years, 1965–1979. USDI Fish and Wildlife Service Resource Publication 157:1–196. Washington, DC.

ROBBINS, M. B., AND D. A. EASTERLA. 1992. Birds of Missouri: their distribution and abundance. University of Missouri Press, Columbia, MO.

ROBERSON, A. M. 2001. Evaluating and developing survey techniques using broadcast conspecific calls for Northern Goshawks in Minnesota. M.S. thesis, University of Minnesota, St. Paul, MN.

ROBERSON, A. M., D. E. ANDERSEN, AND P. L. KENNEDY. 2003. The Northern Goshawk (*Accipiter gentilis atricapillus*) in the western Great Lakes Region: a technical conservation assessment. Minnesota Cooperative Fish and Wildlife Research Unit, University of Minnesota, St. Paul, MN.

ROBICHAUD, B., AND M. F. BUELL. 1973. Vegetation of New Jersey: a study in landscape diversity. Rutgers University Press, New Brunswick, NJ.

ROBINSON, J. C. 1990. An annotated checklist of the birds of Tennessee. University of Tennessee Press, Knoxville, TN.

ROBINSON, S. K., AND R. T. HOLMES. 1982. Foraging behavior of forest birds: the relationships among search tactics, diet, and habitat structure. Ecology 63:1918–1931.

RODENHOUSE, N. L., T. W. SHERRY, AND R. T. HOLMES. 1997. Site-dependent regulation of population size: a new synthesis. Ecology 78:2025–2042.

ROGERS, A. S. 2001. Use of remote cameras to assess diet of Northern Goshawks (*Accipiter gentilis*) on the Apache-Sitgreaves National Forest, Arizona. M.S. thesis, University of Arizona, Tucson, AZ.

ROHNER, C. 1996. The numerical response of Great Horned Owls to the snowshoe hare cycle: consequences of non-territorial 'floaters' on demography. Journal of Animal Ecology 65:359–370.

ROHNER, C., AND F. I. DOYLE. 1992. Food-stressed Great Horned Owl kills adult Goshawk: exceptional observation or community process? Journal of Raptor Research 26:261–263.

ROLOFF, G.J., AND J. B. HAUFLER. 1997. Establishing population viability planning objectives based on habitat potentials. Wildlife Society Bulletin 25:895–904.

ROMESBURG, H. C. 1981. Wildlife science: gaining reliable knowledge. Journal of Wildlife Management 45:293–313.

ROMME, W. H., M. G. TURNER, D. B. TINKER, AND D. H. KNIGHT. 2004. Emulating natural forest disturbances in the wildland-urban interface of the Greater Yellowstone Ecosystem. Pp. 243–250 in A H. Perera, L. J. Buse, and M. G. Weber (editors). Emulating natural forest landscape disturbances: concepts and applications. Columbia University Press, New York, NY.

ROOT, M., AND B. ROOT. 1978. A nesting census of the uncommon raptors in northwest Connecticut '77. Hawk Mountain News Annual Report 35:5–13.

ROOT, T. 1988. Atlas of wintering North American birds. An analysis of Christmas bird count data. University of Chicago Press, Chicago, IL.

ROSENBERG, D. K., AND K. S. MCKELVEY. 1999. Estimation of habitat selection for central-place foraging animals. Journal of Wildlife Management 63:1028–1038.

ROSENBERG, K. V., AND R. J. COOPER. 1990. Approaches to avian diet analysis. Studies in Avian Biology 13:80–90.

ROSENBERG, K. V., R. D. OHMART, W. C. HUNTER, AND B. W. ANDERSON. 1991. Birds of the lower Colorado River Valley. University of Arizona Press, Tucson, AZ.

ROSENDAAL, C.W.C. 1990. Haviken in Zuid-Twente I: voedselonderzoek 1984–1988. Vogeljaar 38:198–207.

ROSENFIELD, R. N., AND J. BIELEFELDT. 1993. Trapping techniques for breeding Cooper's Hawks. Journal of Raptor Research 27:171–172.

ROSENFIELD, R. N., J. BIELEFELDT, AND S. M. VOS. 1996. Skewed sex ratios in Cooper's Hawk offspring. Auk 113:957–960.

ROSENFIELD, R. N., J. BIELEFELDT, R. K. ANDERSON, AND J. M. PAPP. 1991. Raptor status reports: *Accipiters*. Pp. 42–49 in B. Giron Pendleton, D. L. Krahe, M. N. LeFranc, Jr., K. Titus, J. C. Bednarz, D. E. Andersen, and B. A. Millsap (editors). Proceedings of the midwest raptor management symposium and workshop. National Wildlife Federation Science Technical Series 15, Washington, DC.

ROSENFIELD, R. N., J. BIELEFELDT, D. R. TREXEL, AND T. C. J. DOOLITTLE. 1998. Breeding distribution and nest-site habitat of Northern Goshawks in Wisconsin. Journal of Raptor Research 32:189–194.

ROSENFIELD, R. N., T. C. J. DOOLITTLE, AND J. BIELEFELDT. 1996. Status of forest-dependent raptors on the Northern Highland/American Legion State Forest and the Bois Brule River State Forest: a preliminary study. University of Wisconsin-Stevens Point, Stevens Point, WI.

ROTENBERRY, J. T., AND J. A. WIENS. 1991. Weather and reproductive variation in shrubsteppe sparrows: a hierarchical analysis. Ecology 72:1325–1335.

RUDEBECK, G. 1950–51. The choice of prey and modes of hunting of predatory birds with special reference to their selective effect. Oikos 2:67–88, 3:200–231.

RUGGIERO, L. F., K. B. AUBRY, S. W. BUSKIRK, G. M. KOEHLER, C. J. KREBS, K. S. MCKELVEY, AND J. R. SQUIRES. 2000. Ecology and conservation of lynx in the United States. University Press of Colorado, Boulder, CO.

RUGGIERO, L. F., AND K. S. MCKELVEY. 2000. Toward a defensible lynx conservation strategy: a framework for planning in the face of uncertainty. Pp. 5–19. in L. F. Ruggiero, K. B. Aubry, S. W. Buskirk, G. M. Koehler, C. J. Krebs, K. S. McKelvey, and J. R. Squires (editors). Ecology and conservation of lynx in the United States. University Press of Colorado, Boulder, CO.

RUGGERIO, L. F., D. E. PEARSON, AND S. E. HENRY. 1998. Characteristics of American marten den sites in Wyoming. Journal of Wildlife Management 62:663–673.

Rusch, D. A., and W. G. Reeder. 1978. Population ecology of Alberta red squirrels. Ecology 59:400–420.

Russell, E. W. B. 1981. Vegetation of Northern New Jersey before European settlement. American Midland Naturalist 105:1–12.

Rust, R., and T. Mischler. 2001. Auswirkungen legaler und illegaler Verfolgung auf Habichtpopulationen in Südbayern. Ornithologischer Anzeiger 40:113–136.

Rust, R., and W. Kechele. 1996. Altersbestimmung von Habichten Accipiter gentilis: Langfristige Vergleiche gemauserter Handschwingen. Ornithologischer Anzeiger 35:75–83.

Rutz, C. 2001. Raum-zeitliche Habitatnutzung des Habichts—Accipiter gentilis—in einem urbanen Lebensraum. Diploma thesis, University of Hamburg, Hamburg, Germany.

Rutz, C. 2003a. Assessing the breeding season diet of Goshawks Accipiter gentilis: biases of plucking analysis quantified by means of continuous radio-monitoring. Journal of Zoology, London 259:209–217.

Rutz, C. 2003b. Post-fledging dispersal of Northern Goshawks Accipiter gentilis in an urban environment. Vogelwelt 124:93–101.

Rutz, C. 2004. Breeding season diet of Northern Goshawks Accipiter gentilis in the city of Hamburg, Germany. Corax 19:311–322.

Rutz, C. 2005a. Extra-pair copulation and intraspecific nest intrusions in the Northern Goshawk Accipiter gentilis. Ibis 147:831–835.

Rutz, C. 2005b. The Northern Goshawk: Population dynamics and behavioural ecology. D.Phil. dissertation, University of Oxford, Oxford, UK.

Rutz, C., and R. G. Bijlsma. In press. Food limitation in a generalist predator. Proceedings of the Royal Society of London, Series B.

Rutz, C., M. J. Whittingham, and I. Newton. 2006. Age-dependent diet choice in an avian top predator. Proceedings of the Royal Society of London, Series B 273:579–586.

Rutz, C., A. Zinke, T. Bartels, and P. Wohlsein. 2004. Congenital neuropathy and dilution of feather melanin in nestlings of urban-breeding Northern Goshawks (Accipiter gentilis). Journal of Zoo and Wildlife Medicine 35:97–103.

Ryttman, H. 2001. Offspring sex ratio and male quality in Goshawk Accipiter gentilis. Ornis Svecica 11:79–82.

Sæther, B. E., and Ø. Bakke. 2000. Avian life history variation and contributions of demographic traits to the population growth rate. Ecology 81:642–653.

Sage, J. H., L. B. Bishop, and W. P. Bliss. 1913. The birds of Connecticut. Connecticut Geological and Natural History Survey Bulletin No. 20, Hartford, CT.

Salafsky, S. R. 2004. Covariation between prey abundance and Northern Goshawk reproduction on the Kaibab Plateau, Arizona. M.S. thesis, Colorado State University, Ft. Collins, CO.

Salafsky, S., R, T. Reynolds, and B. R. Noon. 2005. Patterns of temporal variation in Goshawk reproduction and prey resources. Journal of Raptor Research 39:237–246.

Sallabanks, R., E. B. Arnett, and J. M. Marzluff. 2000. An evaluation of research on the effects of timber harvest on bird populations. Wildlife Society Bulletin 28: 1144–1155.

Sallabanks, R., R. A. Riggs, and L. E. Cobb. 2001. Bird use of forest structural classes in grand fir forests of the Blue Mountains, Oregon. Forest Science 48:311–321.

Samoilov, B. L., and G. V. Morozova. 2001. The Goshawk. Pp. 115–117 in The red data book of Moscow City. ABF Press. Moscow, Russia. (in Russian).

Samuel, M. D., and M. R. Fuller. 1996. Wildlife radio telemetry. Pp. 370–418 in T. A. Bookhout (editor), Research and management techniques for wildlife and habitats. 5th ed. The Wildlife Society, Bethesda, MD.

SARA. 2002. Species at risk act. Schedule 1, Part 3. Canada. <http://www.speciesatrisk.gc.ca/default_e.cfm>   (11 January 2006).

SAS Institute Inc. 1988. SAS/STAT user's guide: statistics. SAS Institute, Inc., Cary, NC.

SAS Institute, Inc. 2001. SAS/STAT user's guide, release 8.2. SAS Institute, Inc, Cary, NC.

SAS Institute Inc. 2004. SAS/STAT® 9.1 user's guide. SAS Institute Inc., Cary, NC.

Saunders, L. B. 1982. Essential nesting habitat of the Goshawk (Accipiter gentilis) on the Shasta-Trinity National Forest, McCloud District. M.S. thesis, California State University, Chico, CA.

Saurola, P. 1976. Kanahaukan kuolevuus ja kuolinsyyt. Suomen Luonto 35:310–314

Schaeffer, W. W. 1998. Northern Goshawk (Accipiter gentilis) habitat characterization in central Alberta. M.S. thesis, University of Alberta, Edmonton, AB, Canada.

Scharenberg, W., and V. Looft. 2004. Reduction of organochlorine residues in Goshawk eggs (Accipiter gentilis) from Northern Germany (1971–2002) and increasing eggshell index. Ambio 33:495–498.

Schipper, W. J. A., L. S. Buurma, and P. H. Bossenbroek. 1975. Comparative study of hunting behaviour of wintering Hen Harriers Circus cyaneus and Marsh Harriers Circus aeruginosus. Ardea 63:1–29.

Schlosser, W. 2000. Sturmschäden an Brutplätzen des Habichts Accipiter gentilis: Auswirkungen des Orkans "Lothar". Der Ornithologische Beobachter 97: 335–337.

Schmid, J. M., and S. A. Mata. 1992. Stand density and mountain pine beetle-caused tree mortality in ponderosa stands. USDA Forest Service General Technical Report RM-GTR-275. USDA Forest Service, Rocky Mountain Research Station, Ft. Collins, CO.

Schmidt, K. M., J. P. Menakis, C. C. Hardy, W. J. Hann, and D. L. Bunnell. 2002. Development of coarse-scale spatial data for wildland fire and fuel management. USDA Forest Service General Technical Report RM-GTR-87. USDA Forest Service, Rocky Mountain Research Station, Ft. Collins, CO.

Schneider, H.-G., A. Gottmann, and M. Wilke. 1986. Ergebnisse langjähriger Untersuchungen zur Bestandsentwicklung, Siedlungsdichte, Siedlungsweise und Brutbiologie des Habichts (Accipiter gentilis) auf

3 Probeflächen in Nordhessen. Vogelkundliche Hefte Edertal 12:15–28.

SCHNELL, J. H. 1958. Nesting behavior and food habits of Goshawks in the Sierra Nevada of California. Condor 60: 377–403.

SCHOENER, T. W. 1968. Sizes of feeding territories among birds. Ecology 49:123–141.

SCHOENER, T. W. 1971. Theory of feeding strategies. Annual Review of Ecology and Systematics 2:369–404.

SCHOENER, T. W. 1984. Size differences among sympatric bird-eating hawks: a worldwide survey. Pp. 254–281 in D. R. Strong, Jr., D. Simberloff, L. G. Abele, and A. B. Thistle (editors). Ecological communities. Conceptual issues and evidence. Princeton University Press, Princeton, NJ.

SCHOENHERR, A. A. 1992. A natural history of California. University of California Press, Berkeley, CA.

SCHOENNAGEL, T., T. T. VEBLEN, and W. H. ROMME. 2004. The interaction of fire, fuels, and climate across Rocky Mountain forests. BioScience 54:661–676.

SCHÖNBRODT, R., AND H. TAUCHNITZ. 1991. Greifvogel-horstkontrollen der Jahre 1986 bis 1990 bei Halle. Populationsökologie Greifvogel- und Eulenarten 2: 61–74.

SCHRÖDER, H. D. 1981. Diseases of birds of prey with special reference to infectious diseases. Pp. 37–39 in J. E. Cooper, and A. G. Greenwood (editors). Recent advances in the study of raptor diseases. Chiron Publications Ltd., Keighley, West Yorkshire, UK.

SCHULLERY, P. 1989. The fires and fire policy. BioScience 39:686–694.

SCHWAB, F. E., AND A. R. E. SINCLAIR. 1994. Biodiversity of diurnal breeding bird communities related to succession in the dry Douglas-fir forests of southeastern British Columbia. Canadian Journal of Forestry Research 24:2034–2040.

SCHWARZ, G. 1978. Estimating the dimension of a model. Annals of Statistics 6:461–464.

SCOTT, V. E., AND G. L. CROUCH. 1988. Summer birds and mammals of aspen-conifer forests in west-central Colorado. USDA Forest Service Research Paper RM-280. USDA Forest Service, Rocky Mountain Forest and Range Experiment Station. Fort Collins, CO.

SCOTT, V. E., AND D. R. PATTON. 1975. Cavity-nesting birds of Arizona and New Mexico Forests. USDA Forest Service General Technical Report RM-10. USDA Forest Service, Rocky Mountain Forest and Range Experiment Station. Fort Collins, CO.

SCOTT, V. E., K. E. EVANS, D. R. PATTON, AND P. L. STONE. 1977. Cavity-nesting birds of North American forests. USDA Forest Service, Agricultural handbook. Washington, DC.

SCRIBNER, K. T., AND R. J. WARREN. 1990. Seasonal movements of cottontail rabbits on isolated playas. Journal of Wildlife Management 54:403–409.

SEAMANS, M. E., R. J. GUTIÉRREZ, AND C. A. MAY M. 2002. Mexican Spotted Owl (Strix occidentalis) population dynamics: influence of climatic variation on survival and reproduction. Auk 119:321–334.

SEBER, G. A. G. 1965. A note on the multiple-recapture census. Biometrika 52:249–259.

SELÅS, V. 1989. Prey selection in the Goshawk during the breeding season. Fauna Norvegica Ser C, Cinclus 42: 104–110.

SELÅS, V. 1997a. Influence of prey availability on re-establishment of Goshawk Accipiter gentilis nesting territories. Ornis Fennica 74:113–120.

SELÅS, V. 1997b. Nest-site selection by four sympatric forest raptors in southern Norway. Journal of Raptor Research 31:16–25.

SELÅS, V. 1998a. Does food competition from red fox (Vulpes vulpes) influence the breeding density of Goshawk (Accipiter gentilis)? Evidence from a natural experiment. Journal of Zoology, London 246:325–335.

SELÅS, V. 1998b. Hønsehaukbestanden I tilbakegang—også I Aust-Agder. Vår fuglefauna 21:149–154.

SELÅS, V., AND C. STEEL. 1998. Large brood sizes of Pied Flycatcher, Sparrowhawk and Goshawk in peak microtine years: support for the mast depression hypothesis. Oecologia 116:449–455.

SERGIO, F., L. MARCHESI, AND P. PEDRINI. 2003. Spatial refugia and the coexistence of a diurnal raptor with its intraguild owl predator. Journal of Animal Ecology 72:232–245.

SERGIO, F., AND I. NEWTON. 2003. Occupancy as a measure of territory quality. Journal of Animal Ecology 72: 857–865.

SERRANO, D. 2000. Relationship between raptors and rabbits in the diet of Eagle Owls in southwestern Europe: competition removal or food stress? Journal of Raptor Research 34:305–310.

SESNIE, S., AND J. BAILEY. 2003. Using history to plan the future of old-growth ponderosa pine. Journal of Forestry 101:40–47.

SHAFFER, M. L. 1981. Minimum population sizes for species conservation. BioScience 31:131–134.

SHAWYER, C., R. CLARKE, AND N. DIXON. 2000. A study into the raptor predation of domestic pigeons. Department of the Environment, Transport and the Regions, London, UK.

SHELFORD, V. E. 1963. The ecology of North America. University of Illinois Press, Urbana, IL.

SHIGESADA, N., AND K. KAWASAKI. 1997. Biological invasions: theory and practice. Oxford University Press, Oxford, UK.

SHUSTER, W. C. 1980. Northern Goshawk nest site requirements in the Colorado Rockies. Western Birds 11: 89–96.

SIDERS, M. S., AND P. L. KENNEDY. 1994. Nesting habitat of Accipiter hawks: is body size a consistent predictor of nest habitat characteristics? Studies in Avian Biology 16:92–96.

SIDERS, M. S., and P. L. KENNEDY. 1996. Forest structural characteristics of accipiter nesting habitat: is there an allometric relationship? Condor 98:123–132.

SILVER, R. D., A. MACFARLANE, M. SAUBER, C. I. SANDELL, S. M. HITT, P. GALVIN, T. SCHULKE, S. W. HOFFMAN, S. WOTKYNS, S. HIRSCH, AND G. WARDWELL. 1991. Northern

Goshawk listing petition to Secretary of the Interior, U.S. Department of Interior, Washington, DC.

SILVERMAN, B. W. 1986. Density estimation for statistics and data analysis. Chapman and Hall, London, UK.

SIMMONS, R. E., D. M. AVERY, AND G. AVERY. 1991. Biases in diets determined from pellets and remains: correction factors for a mammal and a bird-eating raptor. Journal of Raptor Research 25:63–67.

SINCLAIR, A. R. E. 1989. Population regulation in animals. Pp. 197–241 in J. M. Cherrett (editor). Ecological concepts, Blackwell, Oxford, UK.

SMALL, A. 1994. California birds: their status and distribution. Ibis Publishing, Vista, CA.

SMALLWOOD, K. S. 1998. On the evidence needed for listing Northern Goshawks (*Accipiter gentilis*) under the Endangered Species Act: a reply to Kennedy. Journal of Raptor Research 32:323–329.

SMALLWOOD, K. S., J. BEYEA, AND M. L. MORRISON. 1999. Using the best scientific data for endangered species conservation. Environmental Management 24: 421–435.

SMITH, C. C. 1968. The adaptive nature and social organization of tree squirrels *Tamiasciurus*. Ecological Monographs 38:31–63.

SMITH, C. C. 1970. The coevolution of pine squirrels (*Tamiasciurus*) and conifers. Ecological Monographs 40:349–371.

SMITH, C. C., AND R. P. BALDA. 1979. Competition among insects, birds, and mammals for conifer seeds. American Zoologist 19:1065–1083.

SMITH, D. G., AND A. DEVINE. 1994. Northern Goshawk. Pp. 98–99 in L. R. Bevier (editor). Breeding bird atlas of Connecticut. State Geological and Natural History Survey. Bulletin No. 113. Hartford, CT.

SMITH, D. G., AND J. R. MURPHY. 1973. Breeding ecology of raptors in the eastern Great Basin of Utah. Brigham Young University Science Bulletin, Biological Series 18, Provo, UT.

SMITH, D. M. 1986. The practice of silviculture. John Wiley and Sons, Inc., New York, NY.

SMITH, J. P., S. W. HOFFMANN, AND J. A. GESSAMAN. 1990. Regional size differences among fall-migrant *Accipiters* in North America. Journal of Field Ornithology 61:192–200.

SMITH, M. C. 1968. Red squirrel response to spruce cone failure in interior Alaska. Journal of Wildlife Management 32:305–317.

SMITHERS, B. L. 2003. Northern Goshawk food habits in Minnesota: an analysis using time-lapse video recording systems. M.S. thesis, Texas Technical University, Lubbock, TX.

SMITHERS, B. L., C. W. BOAL, AND D. E. ANDERSEN. 2005. Northern Goshawk diet in Minnesota: an analysis using video recording systems. Journal of Raptor Research 39:264–273.

SNYDER, H. A. 1995. Apache Goshawk conservation biology in southeast Arizona. Arizona Game and Fish Department, Final Report. Heritage Project No. I92065, Phoenix, AZ.

SNYDER, M. A. 1993. Interactions between Abert's squirrel and ponderosa pine: the relationship between selective herbivory and host plant fitness. American Naturalist 141:866–879.

SNYDER, N. F. R., AND H. A. SNYDER. 1991. Birds of prey. Natural history and conservation of North American raptors. Voyageur Press, Inc., Stillwater, MN.

SNYDER, N. F. R., AND J. W. WILEY. 1976. Sexual size dimorphism in hawks and owls of North America. Ornithological Monographs 20:1–96.

SNYDER, N. F. R., S. R. BEISSINGER, AND M. R. FULLER. 1989. Solar radio-transmitters on Snail Kites in Florida. Journal of Field Ornithology 60:171–177.

SNYDER, N. F. R., H. A. SNYDER, J. L. LINCER, AND R. T. REYNOLDS. 1973. Organochlorines, heavy metals, and the biology of North American accipiters. BioScience 23:300–305.

SOKAL, R. R., AND F. J. ROHLF. 1981. Biometry. W.H. Freeman and Company, New York, NY.

SOLLIEN, A. 1979. Bestandsutviklingen hos hønsehauk *Accipiter gentilis,* i Norge de siste 100 år. Vår Fuglefauna 2:95–106.

SONSTHAGEN, S. A. 2002. Year-round habitat, movement, and gene flow of Northern Goshawks breeding in Utah. M.S. thesis, Brigham Young University, Provo, UT.

SONSTHAGEN, S. A., S. L. TALBOT, AND C. M. WHITE. 2004. Gene flow and genetic characterization of Northern Goshawks breeding in Utah. Condor 106:826–836.

ŠOTNÁR, K. 2000. Prípevol k hniezdnej biológii a potravnej ekológii jastraba veľkého (*Accipiter gentilis*) na hornom Ponitrí. Buteo 11:43–50.

SOUTHERN, H. N. 1970. The natural control of a population of Tawny Owls (*Strix aluco*). Journal of Zoology, London 162:197–285.

SOUTO, D. R., AND K. S. SHIELDS. 2000. Overview of hemlock health. Pp. 76–80 in Proceedings of a symposium on sustainable management of hemlock ecosystems in eastern North America. USDA Forest Service General Technical Report NE-267. USDA Forest Service, Northeastern Research Station, Newtown Square, PA.

SPEAR, M. J. 1993. Comments on the US Forest Service management recommendations for the Northern Goshawk in the southwestern United States. Pp. 91–102 in Arizona Game and Fish Department Review of U.S. Forest Service strategy for managing the Northern Goshawk in the southwestern United States. Arizona Game and Fish Department, Phoenix, AZ.

SPEISER, R. 1981. Breeding birds of the Ramapo-Hudson Highlands, New Jersey and New York. M.S. thesis, Marshall University, Huntington,WV.

SPEISER, R. 1992. Notes on the natural history of the Northern Goshawk. Kingbird 42:133–137.

SPEISER, R., AND T. BOSAKOWSKI. 1984. History, status, and future management of Goshawk nesting in New Jersey. Records of New Jersey Birds 10:29–33.

SPEISER, R., AND T. BOSAKOWSKI. 1987. Nest site selection by Northern Goshawks in northern New Jersey and southeastern New York. Condor 89:387–394.

SPEISER, R., AND T. BOSAKOWSKI. 1988. Nest site preferences of Red-tailed Hawks in the highlands of southeastern New York and northern New Jersey. Journal Field Ornithology 59:361–368.

SPEISER, R., AND T. BOSAKOWSKI. 1989. Nest trees selected by Northern Goshawks along the New York-New Jersey border. Kingbird 39:132–141.

SPEISER, R., AND T. BOSAKOWSKI. 1991. Nesting phenology, site fidelity, and defense behavior of Northern Goshawks in New York and New Jersey. Journal of Raptor Research 25:132–135.

SPENCER, W. D. 1987. Seasonal rest-site preferences of pine martens in the northern Sierra Nevada. Journal of Wildlife Management 51:616–621.

SPERBER, G. 1970. Brutergebnisse und Verlustursachen beim Habicht (Accipiter gentilis). Berichte der Deutschen Sektion des Internationalen Rates für Vogelschutz 10:51–56.

SPIES, T. A., AND J. F. FRANKLIN. 1996. The diversity and maintenance of old-growth forests. Pp. 296–314 in R. C. Szaro, and D. W. Johnson (editors). Biodiversity in managed landscapes: theory and practice. Oxford Press, New York, NY.

S-PLUS. 1995. Statistical software package for personal computers. StatSci Division, MathSoft, Inc., Seattle, WA.

SQUIRES, J. R. 1995. Carrion use by Northern Goshawks. Journal of Raptor Research 29:283.

SQUIRES, J. R. 2000. Food habits of Northern Goshawks nesting in south central Wyoming. Wilson Bulletin 112:536–539.

SQUIRES, J. R., G. D. HAYWARD, AND J. F. GORE. 1998. The role of sensitive species in avian conservation management. Pp.155–176 in J. M. Marzluff, and R. Sallabanks (editors). Avian conservation research and management. Island Press, Washington, DC.

SQUIRES, J. R., AND R. T. REYNOLDS. 1997. Northern Goshawk (Accipiter gentilis). In A. Poole, and F. Gill (editors). The Birds of North America, No. 298. The Academy of Natural Sciences, Philadelphia, PA, and The American Ornithologists' Union, Washington, DC.

SQUIRES, J. R., AND L. F. RUGGIERO. 1995. Winter movements of adult Northern Goshawks that nested in southcentral Wyoming. Journal of Raptor Research 29:5–9.

SQUIRES, J. R., AND L. F. RUGGIERO. 1996. Nest-site preference of Northern Goshawks in southcentral Wyoming. Journal of Wildlife Management 60:170–177.

ŠŤASTNÝ, K., A. RANDÍK, AND K. HUDEC. 1987. The atlas of breeding birds in Czechoslovakia 1973/77). Academia Praha, Praha, Czech Republic.

ŠŤASTNÝ, K., V. BEJČEK, AND K. HUDEC. 1996. Atlas hnízdního rozšíření ptáků v České republice 1985–1989. Nakladatelství a vydavatelství H&H, Praha, Czech Republic.

STATE OF UTAH. 2000. Automated geographic reference center. <http://agrc.its.state.ut.us/> (4 November 2005).

STATE OF UTAH. 2001. Automated geographic reference center. <http://agrc.utah.gov/> (11 August 2005).

STATES, J. S. W. S. GAUD, W. S. ALLRED, AND W. J. AUSTIN. 1988. Foraging patterns of tassel-eared squirrels in selected ponderosa pine stands. In R. Szaro, K. Severson,

D. Patton (editors). Management of amphibians, reptiles and small mammals in North America. USDA Forest Service General Technical Report RM-166. USDA Forest Service, Rocky Mountain Forest and Range Experiment Station, Fort Collins, CO.

STAUDE J. 1987. Ergebnisse mehrjähriger Brutbestandsaufnahmen von Greifvögeln im Weserbergerland. Vogelkundliche Berichte aus Niedersachsen 19:37–45.

STEEN, O. F. 2004. Hønsehauken i Buskerud–tetthet, bestand och hekkesuksess. Vår Fuglefauna 27:18–24.

STEENHOF, K. 1987. Assessing raptor reproductive success and productivity. Pp. 157–170 in B. Giron Pendleton, B.A., Millisap, K. W. Cline, and D. M. Bird (editors), Raptor management techniques manual. National Wildlife Federation, Washington, DC.

STEENHOF, K., AND M. N. KOCHERT. 1982. An evaluation of methods used to estimate raptor nesting success. Journal of Wildlife Management 46:885–893.

STEENHOF, K., M. N. KOCHERT, L. B. CARPENTER, AND R. N. LEHMAN. 1999. Long-term Prairie Falcon population changes in relation to prey abundance, weather, land uses, and habitat conditions. Condor 101:28–41.

STEIN, S. M., R. E. MCROBERTS, R. J. ALIG, M. D. NELSON, D. M. THEOBALD, M. ELEY, M. DECHTER, AND M. CARR. 2005. Forests on the edge: housing development on America's private forests. USDA Forest Service General Technical Report PNW-GTR-636. USDA Forest Service, Pacific Northwest Research Station, Portland, OR.

STEINER, H. 1998. Wald und Greifvögel. Lebensraumqualität im fragmentierten Wald, Räuber-Beute-Beziehung und Grundlagen für ein Naturschutzmanagement. Ph.D. dissertation, University of Salzburg, Salzburg, Austria.

STEINER, H. 1999. Der Mäusebussard (Buteo buteo) als Indikator für Struktur und Bodennutzung des ländlichen Raumes: Produktivität im heterogenen Habitat, Einfluß von Nahrung und Witterung und Vergleiche zum Habicht (Accipiter gentilis). Stapfia 62:1–74.

STENSETH, N. C., AND W. Z. LIDICKER (EDITORS). 1992. Animal dispersal. Small mammals as a model. Chapman and Hall, London, UK.

STEPHENS, D. W., AND J. R. KREBS. 1986. Foraging theory. Princeton University Press, Princeton, NJ.

STEPHENS, R. M. 2001. Migration, habitat use, and diet of Northern Goshawks (Accipiter gentilis) that winter in the Uinta Mountains, Utah. M.S. thesis, University of Wyoming, Laramie, WY.

STEPHENSON, R. L. 1974. Seasonal food habits of the Abert's squirrel, Sciurus aberti. Journal of the Arizona Academy of Science 9. Proceedings Supplement, Tucson, AZ.

STOHLGREN, T., D. T. BARNETT, AND J. T. KARTESZ. 2003. The rich get richer: patterns of plant invasions in the United States. Frontiers in Ecology and the Environment 1: 11–14.

STORER, R. W. 1966. Sexual dimorphism and food habits in three North American Accipiters. Auk 83:423–436.

STORGÅRD, K., AND F. BIRKHOLM-CLAUSEN. 1983. En status over Duehøgen i Sydjylland. Proceedings of the Third Nordic Congress of Ornithology 1981:59–64.

STRAUSS, D. J. 1975. A model for clustering. Biometrika 62:467–475.

STRAAß, V. 1984. Telemetrische Untersuchungen über die Raumnutzung des Habichts (Accipiter gentilis L.) im Landkreis Freising/Oberbayern. Diploma thesis, University of Munich (Tech.), Munich, Germany.

STUBBE, M., H. ZÖRNER, H. MATTHES, AND W. BÖHM. 1991. Reproduktionsrate und gegenwärtiges Nahrungsspektrum einiger Greifvogel arten im nördlichen Harzvorland. Populationsökologie Greifvogel- und Eulenarten 2:39–60.

SULKAVA, S. 1964. Zur Nahrungsbiologie des Habichts, Accipiter gentilis L. Aquilo Seria Zoologica 3:1–103.

SULKAVA, S. 1999. Luita, sulkia, karvoja - rengastajien keräämät saalislähteet kertovat petolintujen ravinnosta. Pp. 148–151 in E. Lammi (editor). Linnut-vuosikirja 1999. BirdLife, Helsinki, Finland.

SULKAVA, S., K. HUHTALA, AND R. TORNBERG. 1994. Regulation of Goshawk Accipiter gentilis breeding in western Finland over the last 30 years. Pp.67–76 in B.-U. Meyburg, and R. D. Chancellor (editors). Raptor conservation today. World Working Group on Birds of Prey and Owls, Pica Press, East Sussex, UK.

SULLIVAN, T. P. 1990. Responses of red squirrel (Tamiasciurus hudsonicus) populations to supplemental food. Journal of Mammalogy 71:579–590.

SULLIVAN, T. P., B. JONES, AND D. S. SULLIVAN. 1989. Population ecology and conservation of the mountain cottontail, Sylvilagus nuttalli, in southern British Columbia. Canadian Field-Naturalist 103:335–342.

SULLIVAN, T. P., AND R. A. MOSES. 1986. Red squirrel populations in natural and managed stands of lodgepole pine. Journal of Wildlife Management 50:595–601.

SULLIVAN, T. P., AND D. S. SULLIVAN. 1982. Population dynamics and regulation of the Douglas squirrel (Tamiasciurus douglasii) with supplemental food. Oecologia 53:264–270.

SUNDE, P. 2002. Starvation mortality and body condition of Goshawks Accipiter gentilis along a latitudinal gradient in Norway. Ibis 144:301–310.

SUTHERLAND, W. 1996. Predicting the consequences of habitat loss for migratory populations. Proceedings of the Royal Society, Series B 263:1325–1327.

SUTTON, G. M. 1925. Notes on the nesting of the Goshawk in Potter County, Pennsylvania. Wilson Bulletin 37:193–199.

SUTTON, G. M. 1931. The status of the Goshawk in Pennsylvania. Wilson Bulletin 43:108–113.

SUZUKI, D. 2003. A look at world parks. Science 301:1289.

SVENSSON, S. 2002. Development of the Goshawk Accipiter gentilis population in Sweden since 1975. Ornis Svecica. 12:147–156.

SWEENEY, S. J., P. T. REDIG, AND H. B. TORDOFF. 1997. Morbidity, survival and productivity of rehabilitated Peregrine Falcons in upper midwestern U.S. Journal of Raptor Research 31:347–352.

SWEM, T., AND M. ADAMS. 1992. A Northern Goshawk nest in the tundra biome. Journal of Raptor Research 26:102.

SWENSON, S. 1991. Social organization of Hazel Grouse and ecological factors influencing it. Ph.D. dissertation, University of Alberta, Edmonton, AB, Canada.

SWETNAM, T. W., AND A. M. LYNCH. 1989. A tree-ring reconstruction of western spruce budworm history in the southern Rocky Mountains. Forest Science 35:962–986.

SWETS, J. A. 1988. Measuring the accuracy of diagnostic systems. Science 240:1285–1293.

SZARO, R. C., AND R. BALDA. 1979. Bird community dynamics in a ponderosa pine forest. Studies in Avian Biology 3:1–66.

TAPPER, S. 1992. Game heritage: an ecological review from shooting and gamekeeping records. Game Conservancy, Fordingbridge, UK.

TAUCHNITZ, H. 1991. Zur Aktivität des Habichts. Populationsökologie Greifvogel- und Eulenarten 2:313–315.

TAVERNER, P.A. 1940. Variation in the American Goshawk. Condor 42:157–160.

TELLA, J. L., AND S. MAÑOSA. 1993. Eagle Owl predation on Egyptian Vulture and Northern Goshawk: possible effect of a decrease in European rabbit availability. Journal of Raptor Research 27:111–112.

TELLUS INSTITUTE. 2003. The most influential Supreme Court ruling you've never heard of. <www.Defending Science.org/SKAPP-daubert-report-abstract.cfm>. (27 September 2005).

TEMELES, E. J. 1985. Sexual size dimorphism of bird-eating hawks: the effect of prey vulnerability. American Naturalist 125:485–499.

TERRASSE, J.-F. 1969. Breeding populations of birds of prey in France. Pp. 353–355 in J. J. Hickey (editor). Peregrine Falcon populations: their biology and decline. University of Wisconsin Press, Madison, Milwaukee, WI.

TERRES, J. K. 1991. The Audubon Society encyclopedia of North American birds. Wings Books, New York, NY

TESTER, J. R. 1995. Minnesota's natural heritage: an ecological perspective. University of Minnesota, Minneapolis, MN.

TEVIS, L. JR. 1952. Autumn foods of chipmunks and golden-mantled ground squirrels in the northern Sierra Nevada. Journal of Mammalogy 33:198–205.

TEVIS, L. JR. 1953. Stomach contents of chipmunks and mantled ground squirrels in northeastern California. Journal of Mammalogy 34:316–324.

TEVIS, L. JR. 1955. Observations on chipmunks and mantled squirrels in northeastern California. American Midland Naturalist 53:71–78.

TEVIS, L. JR. 1956. Invasion of a logged area by golden-mantled ground squirrel. Journal of Mammalogy 37:291–292.

THIOLLAY, J.-M. 1967. Ecologie d'une population de rapaces diurnes en Lorraine. La Terre et la Vie—Revue D'Écologie Appliquée 21:116–183.

THIOLLAY, J.-M., AND J.-F. TERRASSE (EDITORS). 1984. Estimation des effectifs de rapaces nicheurs diurnes et non rupestres en France. Fonds d'Intervention pour les Rapaces, Paris, France.

THIRGOOD, S. J., S. M. REDPATH, P. ROTHERY, AND N. J. AEBISCHER. 2000. Raptor predation and population limitation in Red Grouse. Journal of Animal Ecology 69:504–516.

THISSEN, J., G. MÜSKENS, AND P. OPDAM. 1981. Trends in the Dutch Goshawk *Accipiter gentilis* population and their causes. Pp. 28–43 *in* R. E. Kenward, and I. M. Lindsay (editors). Understanding the Goshawk. International Association for Falconry and Conservation of Birds of Prey, Oxford, UK.

THOMAS, J. W. 1979. Wildlife habitats in managed forests: the Blue Mountains of Oregon and Washington. U.S. Department of Agriculture. Handbook 553. U.S. Government Printing Office, Washington, DC.

THOMAS, J. W. 1999. Learning from the past and moving to the future. Pp. 11–25 *in* K. N. Johnson, F. Swanson, M. Herring, and S. Greene (editors). Bioregional assessments: science at the crossroads of management policy. Island Press, Covelo, CA.

THOMAS, J. W., R. G. ANDERSON, C. MASER, AND E. L. BULL. 1979. Snags. Pp. 60–77 *in* J. W. Thomas (editor). Wildlife habitats in managed forest: the Blue Mountains of Oregon and Washington. USDA Forest Service Agricultural Handbook No. 553. U.S. Government Printing Office, Washington, DC.

THOMAS, J. W., E. D. FORSMAN, J. B LINT, C. E. MESLOW, B. R. NOON, AND J. VERNER. 1990. A conservation strategy for the Northern Spotted Owl. A report by the Interagency Scientific Committee to address the conservation of the Northern Spotted Owl. USDA Forest Service, USDI Bureau of Land Management, Fish and Wildlife Service, and National Park Service, Portland, OR.

THOMAS, J. W., M. G. RAPHAEL, R. G. ANTHONY, E. D. FORSMAN, A. G. GUNDERSON, R. S. HOLTHAUSEN, B. G. MARCOT, G. H. REEVES, J. R. SEDELL, AND D. M. SOLIS. 1993. Viability assessments and management considerations for species associated with late-successional and old-growth forests of the Pacific Northwest. USDA Forest Service, Portland, OR.

THOMPSON, I. D., I J. DAVIDSON, S. O'DONNELL, AND F. BRAZEAU. 1989. Use of track transects to measure the relative occurrence of some boreal mammals in uncut forest and regeneration stands. Canadian Journal of Zoology 67:1816–1823.

THRAILKILL, J. A., L. S. ANDREWS, AND R. M. CLAREMONT. 2000. Diet of breeding Northern Goshawks in the coast Range of Oregon. Journal of Raptor Research 34:339 340.

TINBERGEN, L. 1936. Gegevens over het voedsel van Nederlandse Haviken (*Accipiter gentilis gallinarum* (Brehm)). Ardea 25:195–200.

TITUS, K., AND J. A. MOSHER. 1981. Nest-site habitat selected by woodland hawks in the central Appalachians. Auk 98:270–281.

TITUS, K., C. FLATTEN, AND R. LOWELL. 1994. Goshawk ecology and habitat relationships on the Tongass National Forest. Alaska Department of Fish and Game, Douglas, AK.

TITUS, K., C. FLATTEN, AND R. LOWELL. 1996. Goshawk ecology and habitat relationships on the Tongass National Forest: selected analyses and 1995 field season progress report. Federal Aid in Wildlife Restoration Research Progress Report, Grant SE-4-2. Alaska Department of Fish and Game, Douglas, AK.

TITUS, K., C. FLATTEN, AND R. LOWELL. 1997. Goshawk ecology and habitat relationships on the Tongass National Forest. Field progress report and preliminary stable isotope analysis 1996. Alaska Department of Fish and Game, Division of Wildlife Conservation, Juneau, AK.

TITUS, K., AND M. R. FULLER. 1990. Recent trends in counts of migrant hawks from northeastern North America. Journal of Wildlife Management 54:463–470.

TODD, C. R., AND M. A. BURGMAN 1998. Assessment of threat and conservation priorities under realistic levels of uncertainty and reliability. Conservation Biology 12:966–974.

TOMIAŁOJĆ, L. 1980. The combined version of the mapping method. Pp. 92–106 *in* H. Oelke (editor). Bird census work and nature conservation. Proceedings VI International Conference Bird Census Work and IV Meeting European Ornithological Atlas Committee. Dachverband Deutscher Avifaunisten, Lengede, Germany.

TOMIAŁOJĆ, L., AND T. STAWARCZYK. 2003. Awifauna Polski. Rosmieszczenie, liczebność i zmiany. PTPP "pro Natura", Wrocław, Poland.

TORNBERG, R. 1997: Prey selection of the Goshawk *Accipiter gentilis* during the breeding season: The role of prey profitability and vulnerability. Ornis Fennica 74:15–28.

TORNBERG, R. 2000. Effect of changing landscape structure on the predator-prey interaction between Goshawk and grouse. Ph.D. dissertation, Acta Universitatis Ouluensis, Oulu, Finland.

TORNBERG, R. 2001. Pattern of Goshawk *Accipiter gentilis* predation on four forest grouse species in northern Finland. Wildlife Biology 7:245–256.

TORNBERG, R., AND A. COLPAERT. 2001. Survival, ranging, habitat choice and diet of the Northern Goshawk *Accipiter gentilis* during winter in northern Finland. Ibis 143:41–50.

TORNBERG, R., E. KORPIMÄKI, S. JUNGELL, AND V. REIF 2005. Delayed numerical response of Goshawks to population fluctuations of forest grouse. Oikos 111:408–415.

TORNBERG, R., M. MÖNKKÖNEN, AND M. PAHKALA. 1999. Changes in diet and morphology of Finnish Goshawks from 1960s to 1990s. Oecologia 121:369–376.

TORNBERG, R., AND S. SULKAVA. 1990. Kanalintujen kannanvaihtelun vaikutus kanahaukan ravinnonkäyttöön ja pesimistulokseen Oulun alueela vuosina 1965–88. Suomen Riista 36:53–61.

TORNBERG, R., AND S. SULKAVA. 1991. The effect of changing tetraonid populations on the nutrition and breeding success of the Goshawk (*Accipiter gentilis* L.) in northern Finland. Aquilo Seria Zoologica 28:23–33.

TORNBERG, R., AND V. VIRTANEN. 1997. Milloin ja miksi kanahaukat kuolevat? Linnut 32:10–13.

TOYNE, E. P. 1994. Studies on the ecology of the Northern Goshawk *Accipiter gentilis* in Britain. Ph.D. dissertation, Imperial College of Science, Technology and Medicine, London, UK.

TOYNE, E. P. 1997. Nesting chronology of Northern Goshawks (*Accipiter gentilis*) in Wales: implications for forest management. Forestry 70:121–127.

TOYNE, E. P. 1998. Breeding season diet of the Goshawk *Acipiter gentilis* in Wales. Ibis 140:569–579.

TOYNE, E. P., AND R. W. ASHFORD. 1997. Blood parasites of nestling Goshawks. Journal of Raptor Research 31: 81–83.

TRENT, T. T., AND O. J. RONGSTAD. 1974. Home range and survival of cottontail rabbits in southwestern Wisconsin. Journal of Wildlife Management 38:459–472.

TRIMBLE NAVIGATION LTD. 1992. Trimble PFINDER™ software user's guide. Sunnyvale, CA.

TRIMBLE NAVIGATION LTD. 1994. Mapping systems general reference for Trimble global positioning system (GPS) products. Sunnyvale, CA.

TROMMER, G. 1964. Trichomoniasis bei Habichtsnestlingen in freier Wildbahn. Jahrbuch des Deutschen Falkenordens 1964:69–70.

TUCKER, G. M., AND M. F. HEATH. 1994. Birds in Europe: their conservation status. BirdLife International, Cambridge, UK.

TUFTS, R. W. 1961. Birds of Nova Scotia. Nova Scotia Museum, Halifax, NS, Canada.

TUHY, J.S., C. CARROLL, P. COMER, G. GREEN, G. LAMPMAN, M.L. KHOURY, C. MCCARTHY, B. NEELY, AND M. TUFFLY. 2004. A conservation assessment of the Utah high plateaus ecoregion. The Nature Conservancy, Moab Project Office, Moab UT.

TURCHIN, P. 2003. Complex population dynamics. A theoretical/empirical synthesis. Monographs in Population Biology 35. Princeton University Press, Princeton, NJ.

TURNER, M. G., AND W. H. ROMME. 1994. Landscape dynamics in crown fire ecosystems. Landscape Ecology 9:59–77.

TURNER, M. G., W. H. ROMME, AND D. B. TINKER. 2003. Surprises and lessons from the 1988 Yellowstone fires. Frontiers in Ecology and the Environment 1:351–358.

U.S. DEPARTMENT OF AGRICULTURE. 1999. Sustaining the people's lands: recommendations for stewardship of the national forests and grasslands into the next century. Committee of Scientists Report, Washington Office, Washington, DC.

U.S. NAVAL OBSERVATORY NAUTICAL ALMANAC OFFICE. 1999. The astronomical almanac for the year 1999. U.S. Government Printing Office, Washington, DC.

UETA, M., F. SATO, E. G. LOBKOV, AND N. MITA. 1998. Migration route of White-tailed Sea Eagles (*Haliaeetus albicilla*) in northeastern Asia. Ibis 140:684–686.

UETA, M., F. SATO, H. NAKAGAWA, AND N. MITA. 2000.

Migration routes and differences of migration schedule between adult and young Steller's Sea Eagles. Ibis 142:35–39.

UNGER, W. 1971. Habicht, *Accipiter gentilis*, und Sperber, *Accipiter nisus*, im Spiegel der Beringung. Beiträge zur Vogelkunde 17:135–154.

URQUHART, N. S., AND T. M. KINCAID. 1999. Trend detection in repeated surveys of ecological responses. Journal of Agricultural, Biological and Environmental Statistics 4:404–414.

USDA AND USDI. 1994. Final supplemental environmental impact statement on management of habitat for late-successional and old-growth forest related species within the range of the Northern Spotted Owl. Portland, OR.

USDA FOREST SERVICE. 1980. Cassia timber environmental assessment. USDA Forest Service, Sawtooth National Forest, Twin Falls, ID.

USDA FOREST SERVICE. 1987. Land and resource management plan for the Sawtooth National Forest. USDA Forest Service, Sawtooth National Forest, Twin Falls, ID.

USDA FOREST SERVICE. 1988a. Forest inventory and analysis database. On file at Interior West Resources Inventory, Monitoring and Evaluation. USDA Forest Service, Intermountain Region, Ogden, UT.

USDA FOREST SERVICE. 1988b. Wildlife, fish, and sensitive plant habitat management. Forest Service Handbook. Amendment 2600-95-6. Washington, DC.

USDA FOREST SERVICE. 1991a. Threatened, endangered, and sensitive species of plants and animals. Manual 2600, USDA Forest Service, Sawtooth National Forest, Twin Falls, ID.

USDA FOREST SERVICE. 1991b. Management guidelines for the Northern Goshawk in the southwestern region. Federal Register 56:28853–28859.

USDA FOREST SERVICE. 1992a. Final environmental impact statement on management for the Northern Spotted Owl in the national forests. USDA Forest Service, Pacific Northwest Region, Portland, OR.

USDA FOREST SERVICE. 1992b. Management guidelines for the Northern Goshawk in the southwestern region. Federal Register 57:27424–27435.

USDA FOREST SERVICE. 1993a. Northern Goshawk management, southwestern region. Federal Register 58: 63910–63911.

USDA FOREST SERVICE. 1993b. Viability assessments and management considerations for species associated with late-successional and old-growth forests of the Pacific Northwest. Scientific Analysis Team, Portland, OR.

USDA FOREST SERVICE. 1994a. Revised decision notice for the continuation of interim management direction establishing riparian, ecosystem and wildlife standards for timber sales. Regional Forester's Plan Amendment #1, USDA Forest Service, Region 6, Portland, OR.

USDA FOREST SERVICE. 1994b. Record of decision for amendments to Forest Service and Bureau of Land Management planning documents within the range of the Northern Spotted Owl. USDA Forest Service, Pacific Northwest Region, Portland, OR.

USDA FOREST SERVICE. 1995. Final environmental impact statement for amendment of forest plans. USDA Forest Service, Southwestern Region, Albuquerque, NM.

USDA FOREST SERVICE. 1996. Record of decision for amending forest plans for Arizona and New Mexico. USDA Forest Service, Southwestern Region Albuquerque, NM.

USDA FOREST SERVICE. 1997. Tongass land management plan revision. R10-MB-338b, Ketchikan, AK.

USDA FOREST SERVICE. 2000a. Survey methodology for Northern Goshawks in the Pacific Southwest Region. USDA Forest Service Pacific Southwest Region. Vallejo, CA.

USDA FOREST SERVICE. 2000b. Spruce bark beetle in Alaska. Alaska Region Briefing Paper, Juneau, AK.

USDA FOREST SERVICE. 2004. The healthy forests initiative and healthy forests restoration act: interim field guide. USDA Forest Service and USDI Bureau of Land Management FS-799. Washington, DC.

USDA FOREST SERVICE. 2001a. Black Hills National Forest phase I amendment. Black Hills National Forest, Custer, SD.

USDA FOREST SERVICE. 2001b. Sierra Nevada forest plan amendment final environmental impact statement and record of decision. Pacific Southwest Region, Vallejo, CA.

USDA FOREST SERVICE. 2003. Review of the request to correct information disseminated by USDA Forest Service "In management recommendations for the Northern Goshawk in the southwestern United States." USDA Forest Service, Rocky Mountain Research Station, Ft. Collins, CO.

USDA. FOREST SERVICE. 2004. The Sierra Nevada forest plan amendment final supplemental environmental impact statement and record of decision. R5-MB-046. USDA Forest Service, Pacific Southwest Region, Vallejo, CA.

USDI FISH AND WILDLIFE SERVICE. 1988. Final environmental assessment: falconry and raptor propagation regulations. Washington, DC.

USDI FISH AND WILDLIFE SERVICE. 1991. Endangered and threatened wildlife and plants; animal candidate review for listing as endangered or threatened species, proposed rule. Federal Register 56:58804–58836.

USDI FISH AND WILDLIFE SERVICE. 1992a. Endangered and threatened wildlife and plants; initiation of status review and request for information on the northern goshawk. Federal Register 57:544–548.

USDI FISH AND WILDLIFE SERVICE. 1992b. Endangered and threatened wildlife and plants; notice of 90-day finding on petition to list the northern goshawk as endangered or threatened in the southwestern United States. Federal Register 57:28474–28476.

USDI FISH AND WILDLIFE SERVICE. 1994. August 26, 1994. Endangered and threatened wildlife and plants; 90-day finding for a petition to list the Queen Charlotte goshawk and request for additional information. Federal Register 59:44124.

USDI FISH AND WILDLIFE SERVICE. 1995a. June 29, 1995. Endangered and threatened wildlife and plants; 12-month finding for a petition to list the Queen Charlotte goshawk as endangered. Federal Register 60:33784–33786.

USDI FISH AND WILDLIFE SERVICE. 1995b. Recovery plan for the Mexican Spotted Owl. Vol. 1. USDI Fish and Wildlife Service, Albuquerque, NM.

USDI FISH AND WILDLIFE SERVICE. 1996. Policy regarding the recognition of distinct vertebrate population segments under the Endangered Species Act. Federal Register 61:4722–4725.

USDI FISH AND WILDLIFE SERVICE. 1997. Endangered and threatened wildlife and plants; 90-day finding for a petition to list the Northern Goshawk in the contiguous United States west of the 100th meridian. Federal Register 62:50892–50896.

USDI FISH AND WILDLIFE SERVICE. 1998a. Status review of the Northern Goshawk in the forested West. Office of Technical Support, Forest Resources, Portland, OR. <http://pacific.fws.gov/news/pdf/gh_sr.pdf> (23 September 2005).

USDI FISH AND WILDLIFE SERVICE. 1998b. Endangered and threatened wildlife and plants; notice of 12-month finding on a petition to list the Northern Goshawk in the contiguous United States west of the 100th meridian. Federal Register 63:35183–35184.

USDI FISH AND WILDLIFE SERVICE. 2005. 12-Month finding on a petition to list the Queen Charlotte goshawk as threatened or endangered. Federal Register 70: 74284–74285.

USGS GAP ANALYSIS PROGRAM. 1995. State gap analysis data. Utah Cooperative Fish and Wildlife Research Unit. Utah State University, Logan, UT.

USGS GAP ANALYSIS PROGRAM. 2000. A handbook for conducting gap analysis <www.gap.uidaho.edu/handbook> (4 November 2005).

USGS SURVEY. 1997. Digital elevation model (90 m) for Wyoming. Spatial Data and Visualization Center, Laramie, Wyoming <www.sdvc.uwyo.edu/clearinghouse/All.html> (4 November 2005).

USGS SURVEY. 2000. Arizona national biological information infrastructure. <usgsbrd.srnr.arizona.edu> (4 November 2005).

UTAH DIVISION OF WILDLIFE RESOURCES. 2000. Utah black bear management plan. Publication No. 00-23. Utah Division of Wildlife Resources. Salt Lake City, UT.

UTAH DIVISION OF WILDLIFE RESOURCES. 2005. Utah wolf management plan. Publication No. 05-17. Utah Division of Wildlife Resources. Salt Lake City, UT.

UTTENDÖRFER, O. 1952. Neue Ergebnisse über die Ernährung der Greifvögel und Eulen. Eugen Ulmer Verlag, Stuttgart, Germany.

VAHLE, J. R. 1978. Red squirrel use of southwestern mixed coniferous habitat. M.S. thesis, Arizona State University, Tempe, AZ.

VAHLE, J. R., AND D. R. PATTON. 1983. Red squirrel cover requirements in Arizona mixed conifer forests. Journal of Forestry 81:14–15.

Väisänen, R. A., Järvinen, O. and P. rauhala. 1986. How are extensive human-caused habitat alterations expressed on the scale of local bird populations in boreal forest? Ornis Scandinavica 17:282–292.

Väisänen, R.A, Koskimies, P., and E. Lammi. 1998. Muuttuva pesimälinnusto. Otava, Keuruu, Finland.

Valkama, J., and J. Haapala. 2002. Rengastusvuosi 2002. Pp. 109–117 in K. Ruokolainen. (editor). Linnut-vuosikirja 2002. BirdLife, Helsinki, Finland.

Valkeajärvi, P., and L. Ijäs. 1994. Comparison of breeding success between fed and unfed Black Grouse in central Finland. Suomen Riista 40:98–109.

van Beusekom, C. F. 1972. Ecological isolation with respect to food between Sparrowhawk and Goshawk. Ardea 60:72–94.

Van Horne, B. 1983. Density as a misleading indicator of habitat quality. Journal of Wildlife Management 47: 893–901.

Van Horne, B., G. S. Olson, R. L. Schooley, J. G. Corn, and K. P. Burnham. 1997. Effects of drought and prolonged winter on Townsend's ground squirrel demography in shrub steppe habitats. Ecological Monographs. 67:295–315.

van Lent, T. 2004. De Havik Accipiter gentilis op de Utrechtse Heuvelrug van 1965–1970: broedresultaten, prooiresten en ruiveren. De Takkeling 12:118–144.

van Manen, W. 2004. Waarom kiest de Havik Accipiter gentilis in Białowieża (Oost-Polen) voor naaldbos? De Takkeling 12:76–80.

van Rossem, A. J. 1938. A Mexican race of the Goshawk (Accipiter gentilis [Linnaeus]). Proceedings Biological Society Washington 51:99–100.

Vander Wall, S., and R. P. Balda. 1981. Ecology and evolution of food-storing behavior in conifer-seed caching corvids. Zeitschrift fuer Teirpsychologic und Futtermittelkunde 56:217–242.

Vander Wall, S. and R. P. Balda. 1983. Remembrance of seeds stashed. Natural History 92:60–65.

Varga, Z., Á. Bezeczky, and L. Darányi. 2000. Survey on the population changes and breeding success of birds of prey and the Raven (Corvus corax) in the Börzsöny hills (Hungary) between 1983–1994. Aquila 105–106: 56–69.

Veiga, J. P. 1982. Ecologia de las rapaces de un ecosistema de montaña. Aproximación a su estructura comunitaria. Ph.D. dissertation, University of Madrid, Madrid, Spain.

Veit, R. R., and W. R. Petersen. 1993. Birds of Massachusetts. Massachusetts Audubon Society, Lincoln, MA.

Verdejo, J. 1994. Datos sobre la reproducción y alimentación del Azor (Accipiter gentilis) en un área mediterranea. Ardeola 41:37–43.

Verner, J. 1985. Assessment of counting techniques. Current Ornithology 2:247–302.

Verner, J., and A. S. Boss. 1980. California wildlife and their habitats: western Sierra Nevada. USDA Forest Service General Technical Report PSW-37. USDA Forest Service, Pacific Southwest Forest and Range Experiment Station, Berkley, CA.

Verts, B. J., and L. N. Carraway. 1984. Keys to the mammals of Oregon, 3rd ed. Oregon State University, Corvallis, OR.

Village, A. 1983. The role of nest-site availability and territorial behaviour in limiting the breeding density of Kestrels. Journal of Animal Ecology 52:635–645.

Village, A. 1990. The Kestrel. T. & A.D. Poyser Ltd., Calton, UK.

Voipio, P. 1946. Zur rassenfrage der Finnischen Huhnerhabichte. Ornis Fennica 1:3–18.

Waardenburg, P. A. 1976. Die Auswirkungen einiger menschlicher Störungsfaktoren auf die Siedlungsdichte des Habichts (Accipiter gentilis). Jahrbuch des Deutschen Falkenordens 1976/77:46–49.

Walls, S. S., and R. E. Kenward. 1995. Movements of radio-tagged Common Buzzards Buteo buteo in their first year. Ibis 137:177–182.

Walls, S. S., and R. E. Kenward. 1998. Movements of radio-tagged Buzzards Buteo buteo in early life. Ibis 140:561–568.

Walsh, J., V. Elia, R. Kane, and T. Halliwell. 1999. Birds of New Jersey. New Jersey Audubon Society, Bernardsville, NJ.

Walters, C. J., and C. S. Holling. 1990. Large-scale management experiments and learning by doing. Ecology 71:2060–2068.

Ward, J. M., and P. L. Kennedy. 1994. Approaches to investigating food limitation hypotheses in raptor populations: an example using the Northern Goshawk. Studies in Avian Biology 16:114–118.

Ward, J. M., and P. L. Kennedy. 1996. Effects of supplemental food on size and survival of juvenile Northern Goshawks. Auk 113:200–208.

Ward, J. P., Jr. 2001. Ecological responses by Mexican Spotted Owls to environmental variation in the Sacramento Mountains, New Mexico. Ph.D. dissertation, Colorado State University, Fort Collins, CO.

Wassink, G. 2003. Eerste broedgeval van Oehoe Bubo bubo in de Achterhoek. Limosa 76:1–10.

Watson, J. 1997. The Golden Eagle. T. & A.D. Poyser Ltd., London, UK.

Watson, J. W., D. W. Hayes, S. P. Finn, and P. Meehan-Martin. 1998. Prey of breeding Northern Goshawks in Washington. Journal of Raptor Research 32:297–305.

Watson, J. W., D. W. Hays, and D. J. Pierce. 1999. Efficacy of Northern Goshawk broadcast surveys in Washington State. Journal of Wildlife Management 63:98–106.

Wattel, J. 1973. Geographical differentiation in the genus Accipiter. Publications of the Nuttall Ornithology Club No. 13.

Weathers, W. W., and K. A. Sullivan. 1993. Seasonal patterns of time and energy allocation by birds. Physiological Zoology 66:511–536.

Weaver, H. 1943. Fire as an ecological and silvicultural factor in the ponderosa pine region of the Pacific slope. Journal of Forestry 41:7–14.

Weaver, H. 1961. Ecological changes in the ponderosa pine forest of Cedar Valley in southern Washington. Ecology 42:416–420.

WEBER, M. 2001. Untersuchungen zu Greifvogelbestand, Habitatstruktur und Habitatveränderung in ausgewählten Gebieten von Sachsen-Anhalt und Mecklenburg-Vorpommern. Ph.D. dissertation, University of Halle, Halle, Germany.

WEBSTER, J. D. 1988. Some bird specimens from Sitka, Alaska. Murrelet 69:46–48.

WEGGE, P., I. GJERDE, J. ROLSTAD, L. KASTALEN, AND S. STORAAS. 1990. Does forest fragmentation increase the mortality rate of Capercaillie? Transactions of the International Union of Game Biologists 19:448–453.

WESOŁOWSKI, T., D. CZESZCZEWIK, C. MITRUS, AND P. ROWIŃSKI. 2003. Ptaki Białowieskiego Parku Narodowego. Notatki Ornitologiczne 44:1–31.

WHALEY, W. H., AND C. M. WHITE. 1994. Trends in geographic variation of Cooper's Hawks and Northern Goshawk in North America: a multivariate analysis. Proceedings of the Western Foundation of Vertebrate Zoology 5:161–209.

WHARTON, S. W., AND M. F. MYERS. 1997. MTPE EOS data products handbook. Vol. 1. Publication 902, NASA Goddard Space Flight Center, Greenbelt, MD.

WHEELER, B. K. 2003. Raptors of western North America. Princeton University Press, Princeton, NJ.

WHEELER, B. K., AND W. S. CLARK. 1995. A photographic guide to North American raptors. Academic Press, San Diego, CA.

WHITCOMB, R. F., C. S. ROBBINS, J. F. LYNCH, B. L. WHITCOMB, M. K. KLIMKIEWICZ, AND D. BYSTRAK. 1981. Effects of forest fragmentation on avifauna of the eastern deciduous forests. Pp. 125–205 in R. L. Burgess, and D. M. Sharp (editors). Forest island dynamics in man-dominated landscapes. Springer-Verlag, New York, NY.

WHITE, A. S. 1985. Presettlement regeneration patterns in a southwestern ponderosa pine stand. Ecology 66: 589–594.

WHITE, C., AND L. KIFF. 1998. Language use and misapplied selective science; their roles in swaying public opinion and policy as shown with two North American raptors. Proceedings of the Holarctic Birds of Prey Conference. Badajoz, Spain.

WHITE, C. M., G. D. LLOYD, AND G. L. RICHARDS. 1965. Goshawk nesting in the upper Sonoran in Colorado and Utah. Condor 67:269.

WHITE, G. C., AND GARROTT, R. A. 1990. Analysis of wildlife radio-tracking data. Academic Press, San Diego, CA.

WHITE, M. A., AND J. L. VANKAT. 1993. Middle and high elevation coniferous forest communities of the north rim region of Grand Canyon National Park, Arizona, USA. Vegetatio 109:161–174.

WHITNEY, S. 1979. A Sierra Club naturalists guide: the Sierra Nevada. Sierra Nevada Books. San Francisco, CA.

WIDÉN, P. 1981. Activity pattern of goshawks in Swedish boreal forests. Pp. 114–120 in R. E. Kenward, and I. M. Lindsay (editors). Understanding the Goshawk. International Association for Falconry and Conservation of Birds of Prey, Oxford, UK.

WIDÉN, P. 1984. Activity patterns and time-budget in the Goshawk Accipiter gentilis in a boreal forest area in Sweden. Ornis Fennica 61:109–112.

WIDÉN, P. 1985a. Population ecology of the Goshawk (Accipiter gentilis L.) in the boreal forest. Ph.D. dissertation, Acta Universitatis Upsaliensis, Upsala, Sweden.

WIDÉN, P. 1985b. Breeding and movements of Goshawks in boreal forests in Sweden. Holarctic Ecology 8: 273–279.

WIDÉN, P. 1987. Goshawk predation during winter, spring and summer in a boreal forest area of central Sweden. Holarctic Ecology 10:104–109.

WIDÉN, P. 1989. The hunting habitats of Goshawks Accipiter gentilis in boreal forests of central Sweden. Ibis 131:205–213.

WIDÉN, P. 1994. Habitat quality for raptors: a field experiment. Journal of Avian Biology 25:219–223.

WIDÉN, P. 1997. How and why is the Goshawk (Accipiter gentilis) affected by modern forest management in Fennoscandia? Journal of Raptor Research 31:107–113.

WIDÉN, P., P. ANGELSTAM, AND E. LINDSTRÖM. 1987. The effect of prey vulnerability: Goshawk predation and population fluctuations of small game. Oikos 49:233–235.

WIELICZKO, A., T. PIASECKI, G. M. DORRESTEIN, A. ADAMSKI, AND M. MAZURKIEWICZ. 2003. Evaluation of the health status of Goshawk chicks (Accipiter gentilis) nesting in Wrocław vicinity. Bulletin of the Veterinary Institute of Pulawy 47:247–257.

WIENS, J. 1996. Wildlife in patchy environments: metapopulations, mosaics, and management. Pp. 53–84 in D. R. McCullough (editor). Metapopulations and wildlife conservation. Island Press, Washington, DC.

WIENS, J. A. 1989. The ecology of bird communities. Vol. 2. Processes and variations. University Press, Cambridge, UK.

WIENS, J. A. 2001. The landscape context of dispersal. Pp. 96–109 in J. Clobert, E. Danchin, A. A. Dhondt, and J. D. Nichols (editors). Dispersal. Oxford University Press, Oxford, UK.

WIENS, J. D. 2004. Post-fledging survival and natal dispersal of juvenile Northern Goshawks in Arizona. M.S. thesis, Colorado State University, Fort Collins, CO.

WIENS, J. D., B. R. NOON, AND R. T. REYNOLDS. 2006a. Post-fledging survival of Northern Goshawks: the importance of prey abundance, weather, and dispersal. Ecological Applications 16:406–418.

WIENS, J. D., AND R. T. REYNOLDS. 2005. Is fledging success a reliable index of fitness in Northern Goshawks? Journal of Raptor Research 39:210–221.

WIENS, J. D., R. T. REYNOLDS, AND B. R. NOON. 2006b. Juvenile fidelity and natal dispersal in an isolated population of Northern Goshawks. Condor 108:253–269.

WIESMÜLLER, T., P. SÖMMER, M. VOLLAND, AND B. SCHLATTERER. 2002. PCDDs/PSDFs, PCBs, and organochlorine pesticides in eggs of Eurasian Sparrowhawks (Accipiter nisus), hobbies (Falco subbuteo), and Northern Goshawks (Accipiter gentilis) collected in the area of Berlin-Brandenburg, Germany. Archives of Environmental Contamination and Toxicology 42: 486–496.

WIJANDTS, H. 1984. Ecological energetics of the Long-eared Owl (*Asio otus*). Ardea 72:1–92.

WIKMAN, M., AND H. LINDÉN. 1981. The influence of food supply on Goshawk population size. Pp. 105–113 *in* R. E. Kenward, and I. M. Lindsay (editors). Understanding the Goshawk. International Association for Falconry and Conservation of Birds of Prey, Oxford, UK.

WIKMAN, M., AND V. TARSA. 1980. Kanahaukan pesimäaikaisesta ravinnosta Länsi-Uudellamaalla 1969–77. Suomen Riista 28:86–96.

WILLIAMS, B. K., J. D. NICHOLS, AND M. J. CONROY. 2002. Analysis and management of animal populations. Academic Press, San Diego, CA.

WILLIAMS, D. L. 1986. Mammalian species of special concern in California. Wildlife Management Division Administrative Report 86-1. California Department of Fish and Game. Sacramento, CA.

WILLIAMS, R. E., AND M. A. MARSDEN. 1982. Modeling probability of root disease center occurrence in northern Idaho forests. Canadian Journal of Forest Research 12:876–882.

WILSON D. E., AND S. RUFF (EDITORS). 1999. The Smithsonian book of North American mammals. Smithsonian Institution Press, Washington, DC.

WINKLER, R. 1999. Avifauna der Schweiz. Zweite, neu bearbeitete Auflage. Der Ornithologische Beobachter, Beiheft 10.

WITTENBERG, J. 1985. Habicht *Accipiter gentilis* jagt zu Fuß in der Stadt. Anzeiger der Ornithologischen Gesellschaft in Bayern 24:180.

WOETS, D. 1998. De Havik *Accipiter gentilis* als broedvogel in De Weerribben: 1980–1997 (deel I). De Noordwesthoek 25: 51–58.

WOLFF, J. O. 1996. Population fluctuations of mast-eating rodents are correlated with production of acorns. Journal of Mammalogy 77:85–856.

WOOD, T. J. 1967. Ecology and population dynamics of the red squirrel (*Tamiasciurus hudsonicus*) in Wood Buffalo National park. M.S. thesis, University of Saskatchewan, SK, Canada.

WOODBRIDGE, B., AND P. J. DETRICH. 1994. Territory occupancy and habitat patch size of Northern Goshawks in the southern Cascades of California. Studies in Avian Biology 16:83–87.

WOODBRIDGE, B., P. DETRICH, AND P. H. BLOOM. 1988. Territory fidelity and habitat use by nesting Northern Goshawks: implications for management. Unpublished report. USDA Forest Service, Klamath National Forest, Macdoel, CA.

WOOLFINDEN, G. E., AND J. W. FITZPATRICK. 1991. Florida Scrub Jay ecology and conservation. Pp. 542–565 *in* C. M. Perrins, J. D. Lebreton, and G. J. M. Hirons (editors). Bird population studies: relevance to conservation and management. Oxford University Press, New York, NY.

WÜRFELS, M. 1994. Entwicklung einer städtischen Population des Habichts (*Accipiter gentilis*) und die Rolle der Elster (*Pica pica*) im Nahrungsspektrum des Habichts—Ergebnisse vierjähriger Beobachtungen im Stadtgebiet von Köln. Charadrius 30:82–93.

WÜRFELS, M. 1999. Ergebnisse weiterer Beobachtungen zur Populationsentwicklung des Habichts (*Accipiter gentilis*) im Stadtgebiet von Köln 1993–1998 und zur Rolle der Elster (*Pica pica*) im Nahrungsspektrum des Habichts. Charadrius 35:20–32.

WYKOFF, W. R., AND R. A. MONSERUD. 1988. Representing site quality in increment models: a comparison of methods. Pp.. 184–191 *in* A. R. Ek, S. R. Shifley, and T. E. Burk (editors). Forest growth modeling and prediction. USDA Forest Service General Technical Report NC-120. USDA Forest Service, North Central Research Station, St. Paul, MN.

YEATMAN, L. 1976. Atlas des oiseaux nicheurs de France. Société Ornithologique de France, Paris, France.

YOUNK, J. V. 1996. Breeding ecology of the Northern Goshawk in relation to surface gold mining in naturally-fragmented aspen forests of northern Nevada. M.S. thesis, Boise State University, Boise, ID.

YOUNK, J. V., AND M. J. BECHARD. 1994a. Breeding ecology of the Northern Goshawk in high-elevation aspen forests of northern Nevada. Studies in Avian Biology 16:119–121.

YOUNK, J. V., AND M. J. BECHARD. 1994b. Effect of gold mining activity on Northern Goshawks breeding in Nevada's Independence and Bull Run Mountains. Final Report, Raptor Research Center, Boise State University, Boise, ID.

ZACHEL, C. R. 1985. Food habits, hunting activity, and post-fledging behavior of Northern Goshawks (*Accipiter gentilis*) in interior Alaska. M.S. thesis, University of Alaska, Fairbanks, AK.

ZAMMUTO R. M., E. C. FRANKS, AND C. R. PRESTON. 1981. Factors associated with the interval between feeding visits in brood rearing Chimney Swifts. Journal of Field Ornithology 52:134–139.

ZANETTE, L., P. DOYLE, AND S. M. TREMONT. 2000. Food shortage in small fragments: evidence from an area-sensitive passerine. Ecology 81:1654–1666.

ZANETTE, L., AND B. JENKINS. 2000. Nesting success and nest predators in forest fragments: a study using real and artificial nests. Auk 117:445–454.

ZANETTE, L., J. N. M. SMITH, H. VAN OORT, AND M. CLINCHY. 2003. Synergistic effects of food and predators on annual reproductive success in Song Sparrows. Proceedings of the Royal Society of London, Biological Sciences 270:799–803.

ZANG, H. 1989. Habicht. Pp. 118–134 *in* H. Zang, H. Heckenroth, and F. Knolle (editors). Die Vögel Niedersachsens und des Landes Bremens—Greifvögel-Naturschutz und Landschaftspflege in Niedersachsen, Sonderreihe B, Heft 2.3.

ZANGHELLINI, S., AND M. FASOLA. 1991. Breeding habitats of the Sparrowhawk and the Goshawk at three spatial scales in the southern Alps. Atti V Convegno Italiano di Ornitologia 17:329–332.

ZAR, J. H. 1996. Biostatistical analysis. 3rd ed. Prentice-Hall, Upper Saddle River, NJ.

ZARET, T. M., AND A. S. RAND 1971. Competition in tropical stream fishes: support for the competitive exclusion principle. Ecology 52:336–342.

ZAWADZKA, D., AND J. ZAWADZKI. 1998. The Goshawk *Accipiter gentilis* in Wigry National Park (NE Poland)—numbers, breeding results, diet composition and prey selection. Acta Ornithologica 33:182–190.

ZEINER, D. C., W. F. LAUDENSLAYER, JR., K. E. MAYER, AND M. WHITE. 1990. California's wildlife. Vol. 2, birds. California Department of Fish and Game, Sacramento, CA.

ZIELINSKI, W. J., W. D. SPENCER, AND R. D. BARRETT. 1983. Relationship between food habits and activity patterns of pine martens. Journal of Mammalogy 64:387–396.

ZIESEMER, F. 1981. Methods of assessing Goshawk predation. Pp. 144–150 *in* R. E. Kenward, and I. M. Lindsay (editors). Understanding the Goshawk. International Association for Falconry and Conservation of Birds of Prey, Oxford, UK.

ZIESEMER, F. 1983. Unterschungen zum Einfluss des Habichts (*Accipiter gentilis*) auf Populationen seiner Beutetiere. Beiträge zur Wildbiologie Heft 2. Ph.D. dissertation, University of Kiel, Kiel, Germany.

ZIESEMER, F. 1999. Habicht (*Accipiter gentilis*) und Wespenbussard (*Pernis apivorus*)—zwei Jäger im Verborgenen: Was hat die Telemetrie Neues gebracht? Egretta 42:40–56.

ZIGLIO, E. 1996. The Delphi method and its contribution to decision-making. Pp. 4–33 *in* M. Adler, and E. Ziglio (editors). Gazing into the Oracle: the Delphi method and its application to social policy and public health. Jessica Kingsley Publishers, Bristol, PA.

ZIJLMANS, N. 1995. De Havik *Accipiter gentilis* in en om Amsterdam. De Takkeling 3:36–39.

ZINN, L. J., AND T. J. TIBBITTS. 1990. Goshawk nesting survey, 1990. North Kaibab Ranger District, Kaibab National Forest, Arizona. CCSA # 07-90-02, Nongame and Endangered Wildlife Program. Arizona Game and Fish Department, Phoenix, AZ.

ZIRRER, F. 1947. The Goshawk. Passenger Pigeon 9:79–94.

ZWICKLE, F. C. 1992. Blue Grouse. The Birds of North America, No. 15. *In* A. Poole, P. Stettenheim, and F. Gill (editors). The Academy of Natural Sciences, Philadelphia, PA and The American Ornithologists' Union, Washington, DC.